Boogie Man

Boogie

Charles Shaar Murray

Man

The Adventures of John Lee Hooker

in the American Twentieth Century

St. Martin's Press ≉ New York

www.stmartins.com

Library of Congress Cataloging-in-Publication Data

Murray, Charles Shaar.
    Boogie Man : the adventures of John Lee Hooker in the American twentieth
century / Charles Shaar Murray.
        p. cm.
    Includes index.
    ISBN 0-312-26563-8
    1. Hooker, John Lee. 2. Blues musicians—United States—Biography. I. Title.

ML420.H635 M87 2000
781.643'092—dc21
[B]

                                                                    00-031720

First Edition: October 2000

10 9 8 7 6 5 4 3 2 1

Dedicated to the memories of
Kathy Acker (1947–1997) and
Agnes Schaar Murray (1912–1997)

and to **Anna Chen**
—here's looking at you, comrade . . .
for ever, schweetheart

Contents

Intro

I got a history long as from here to London, England, and back, and back again. I got so much to tell, and so much to write about. Everything you read on the album covers is not true, and every album cover reads different. People using their own ideas; they didn't come to me, to get it from me. John Lee did this, he did that. I'm gonna tell you, as far as I know, the truth about my life. I got nothin' to hold back. Some things I have forgotten. Some things you ask me, I know but I done forgotten. I just about know what I did, but some people may say . . . tell you some things I didn't do. Nobody know John Lee Hooker. They know as much about my cat as they know about me. It was a hard road.

Sometimes I don't enjoy talkin' about it, but it's true. Some of it you hate to think about, you just want to throw it out your mind. You don't even want to think about what you come through, because sometimes it brings you down thinking about the hard times, the rough times, what happened to you over the years. There's a lot of misery, hatred, disappointment . . . all that. I hate to talk about it . . . but it's there. A lot of them were rough years. You just want to think about the good things, the happy things. There's so many things I regret, I can't put my hand on it. I made my decisions early in life, to be a musician. Before that, I was a hard-working person. I didn't like handouts. I'd get out there and work, earn a living and stuff like that, but that wasn't what I was going to do the rest of my life. I knew that.

That was a hard road, right up to now. It was a *hard* road.

Boogie Man

1. They Don't Give This Old Boy Nothin'

High noon in the lobby of a generic airport hotel on the outskirts of Newark, New Jersey. John Lee Hooker, the blues singer, is leaning on the reception desk methodically charming the pants off the receptionist. He is an elderly, dark-skinned man of slightly below medium height, lean and wiry except for a neat, globular pot-belly, and dressed like a Japanese banker, albeit a Japanese banker fond of augmenting his immaculate pin-striped three-piece suit with menacing wraparound sunglasses, a rakish Homburg hat decorated with a guitar-shaped brooch, and socks emblazoned with big white stars.

He turns from his banter to greet a recent acquaintance. "Huh-huh-how you doin', young man?" he says in a deep, resonant voice, as grainily resilient as fine leather. Electronics companies make fortunes by manu-facturing reverberation and equalization devices which make voices sound like that. Hooker sounds as if he has $100,000 worth of sophisticated digital goodies built into his chest and throat. Yet his voice is quiet and muted, its tonal richness offset by a residual stammer and blurred by the deepest alluvial accents of the Mississippi Delta. He extends a hand as softly leathery as his voice, a hand like a small cushion, but he leaves it bonelessly limp in his acquaintance's grasp. The top joint of his right thumb joins the root at an angle of almost ninety degrees, the legacy of more than six decades of plucking blues guitar bass runs. Were the acquaintance sufficiently injudicious to give Hooker's hand an overly enthusiastic squeeze, the response would have been a warning glance from behind the wraparounds, and a mock-agonized wince and flap of the offended paw. No one crushes John Lee Hooker's hand, just as no one allows cigarette smoke to drift into his breathing space. That hand, and its opposite number, create a blues guitar sound which nobody, no matter how gifted, has ever been able to duplicate effectively; that voice is one of the world's cultural treasures. You endanger either at your own peril.

It's August of 1991 and Hooker, a rhythm and blues veteran whose first million-selling record, "Boogie Chillen," had been released over forty years earlier but whose career had been in effective hibernation for more than fifteen years, is surfing a renewed wave of popularity without any real precedent in the history of the turbulent relationship between blues, rock and the mass market. His last major record contract, with the once-mighty ABC label, had been allowed to expire in 1974, by mutual consent, after the last of an increasingly dismal series of rock-oriented albums, which reflected little credit on either company or artist, had died an ignominious death in the stores. Subsequent recordings, for small independent outfits, had been few and far between; often of indifferent quality, and generating only mediocre sales. In the mid-'80s, management of Hooker's career had devolved onto the shoulders of Mike Kappus, an ambitious young music-business entrepreneur. A California-based transplant from the Midwest, Kappus came up with the idea of an album project to make a real, proper John Lee Hooker record and facilitate "a paying of tribute by friends." To this end, he had assembled a bevy of Hooker's famous admirers—including stars like Carlos Santana and Bonnie Raitt, plus his own other clients like George Thorogood, the fast-rising young blues star Robert Cray, and the East Los Angeles Chicano roots-rockers Los Lobos—to co-star on a new record which would restate the fundamental values of Hooker's music, untainted by undignified concessions to transitory pop-rock fashion, and reintroduce the frail titan to the pop mainstream. Shopping the resulting album, *The Healer*, to the major record companies, he had found no serious takers. It saw eventual release in the winter of 1989 via two decidedly minor independent companies: Chameleon Records in the U.S. and Silvertone in the U.K. To the surprise of just about everyone, it was a hit. First in the U.K. and then in the U.S., the album climbed the pop charts. One week, Hooker was even outselling Madonna.

By the New Year, the illiterate septuagenarian from the Mississippi Delta had become the world's oldest and unlikeliest pop star. During the summer of 1990, Hooker and his band, their fee now jacked into the stratosphere, hit every major blues, folk and jazz festival in the Northern hemisphere. By autumn, the tour had grossed a figure not unadjacent to three million dollars.

In the summer of 1991, a sequel, *Mr. Lucky*, stood ready for release. This time, the co-stars included Keith Richards of The Rolling Stones, Ry Cooder, Albert Collins, Johnny Winter and Van Morrison; and once again, Hooker was on the road, prised from his suburban California hideaway to perform three concerts on the East Coast in locations ranging from grimy New Jersey to genteel New England. In the baking heat of the hotel parking lot, Hooker's car is ready: a rented white Buick Park Avenue with Georgia plates. His driver is a young emissary from Mike Kappus's Rosebud Agency. Like all the Rosebuddies, he combines brisk efficiency with laid-back San Francisco cool, and an absolute devotion to Hooker's comfort. The baggage—including Hooker's all-important Gibson guitars—is slung into the trunk, and Hooker creakily installs himself in the back seat with his traveling companion, the diminutive singer Vala Cupp, who serves as warm-up act with Hooker's group, The Coast To Coast Blues Band. Chameleon have just released her solo album, nominally produced by Hooker and featuring him on the duet version of his venerable "Crawlin' King Snake" which they perform together at every show. Can the acquaintance think of any U.K. labels which might be interested in releasing it?

The duet has become one of the major theatrical set-pieces of Hooker's show. The song itself, learned on the front porch of his childhood home from his earliest blues mentor Tony Hollins, is among the oldest in Hooker's repertoire, first recorded by him in 1949 and—rerecorded in tandem with Keith Richards—one of *Mr. Lucky*'s showpieces. Performed with Cupp, it becomes a sensual epic: she hovers around Hooker's chair like a butterfly, trading lines with him in a progressively more fevered exchange which culminates in a reassuringly daughterly peck on the cheek. Not surprisingly, there is a certain amount of speculation concerning the exact nature of Hooker's relationship with Cupp, generally among white male rockers of what we might call "a certain age," to whom the great man's predilection for surrounding himself with attractive young women is something of an inspiration; cause for an optimistic vision of their own rapidly approaching twilight years. "Hooker," wrote Dennis Hopper in the notes to the soundtrack (by Hooker and Miles Davis) for his movie *The Hot Spot*, "proves you can still make a steady diet of fried chicken well into your seventies and still try to get all of those pretty young things into a hot tub." The nudge-nudge-wink-wink response generally received by Hooker's own denials—"they ain't my girlfriends, we just *friends*"—obscures the fact that, most of the time, he's telling the truth. There are exceptions, though. A friend of the acquaintance is fond of recounting the tale of when, attending the New Orleans Jazz and Heritage Festival, he and a buddy found that the hotel room that they were sharing was kitty-corner from Hooker's. The buddy, an obsessive Hooker fan, insisted on knocking at the great man's door so that he could press the flesh and testify to his devotion. So he did. After a long delay, Hooker came to the door in his shirtsleeves. Visible behind him, in the bed, was this fabulous blonde; you know, *really* fabulous. After a brief exchange of pleasantries, Hooker announced, "Well-uh-uh-uh, it certainly has been a pleasure meetin' you, young man, but right now I got me some business to 'tend to.'" And then he closed the door.

The reality of Cupp's situation, though, is simply that he enjoys her company. When they check into hotels, her room adjoins his; she keeps track of his possessions and talks to room service for him. Plus her presence—neat figure, ready smile, cascading brown hair—fuels his legend.

Once ensconced, Hooker removes his hat and shades, and wriggles into the most comfortable position. His hair, apart from a bald spot on his crown and the widow's peak which runs in his family, is still thick and healthy: it is dyed a rich reddish black and left nappy and uncombed beneath the trademark Homburg. Silver stubble gleams against his mahogany cheeks and jaw. His left eyelid droops slightly, leaving one eye wide and guileless, the other hooded and watchful. Without the dentures which he wears for video shoots and major photo sessions, his remaining upper and lower teeth are an almost exact mirror-image, requiring him to sling his jaw to one side in order to chew his food. As the Buick noses out to the freeway, the one-time Detroit auto-factory worker disapprovingly notes the number of Japanese cars on the road. The Chevrolet, now that was a *fine* car. Made of U.S. steel, *real* steel. You get into an accident in one of them, you can get out and walk a-way. Mm-*hm*. Not like now. You get in an accident in one of them Japanese cars, you get *hurt*.

For most of the journey to the first show, Hooker is asleep. He can sleep just about anywhere, just doze right off like an old tomcat in front of a warm fire. The night's concert is to be held at a 7,000-seater auditorium set in the grounds of a lush, wooded park; he is to share the bill with fellow Rosebud stars Los Lobos and Robert Cray. When on tour, Hooker rarely headlines a show if he can avoid it. He prefers the middle spot on the bill: this facilitates the quick getaways he favors whenever there's a long drive between his show and his bed. As Hooker's Buick pulls in, Los Lobos are in the home stretch of their set. By the time Hooker has found the most comfortable sofa in his dressing room, popped a can of lite beer and issued instructions for the precise constitution of his plateful of cold cuts from the buffet, Los Lobos's vocalists David Hidalgo and Cesar Rosas are in the dressing room to pay their respects. "Hello, John," they say, their voices soft and their eyes shining. Hooker extends a regal flipper. "Huh-huh-how you doin', young man?" he replies.

The Coast To Coast Blues Band have already arrived in the rather less luxurious circumstances of a collective van, and have established themselves next door in a welter of guitar and saxophone cases. There is a minor crisis within their ranks: one of the band's mainstays, organist and master of ceremonies Deacon Jones, has opted to stay home in San Francisco to play a series of shows with his own band for rather more money than a Coast To Coast sideman's wage. His replacement is pianist Lizz Fischer, a sinewy pixie with a Rapunzelesque blond braid, formidable jazz chops and one of Coast To Coast's only two clean driving licenses. Her other qualification is that she looks absolutely stunning in stiletto heels and a little black dress; Hooker, murmurs one of the male Coast To Coasters, would be happy to have an entire band of attractive female musicians.

As the band gather sidestage, quiet comments are passed concerning the forest of guitars awaiting the attentions of The Robert Cray Band. Hooker carries two (one in standard tuning, one in the open "Spanish" tuning in which he plays his show's boogie finale) and the rest of the band's guitarists—stocky, snub-nosed Mike Osborn on lead; gaunt, hirsute Rich Kirch on rhythm; spiky, *nuevo-wavo* Jim Guyett on bass—make do with one each. They have, after all, flown in from California, traveling light: the drums, amplifiers and piano are rented. They hit the stage with a slow blues: "Cold Cold Feeling," originated by T-Bone Walker, who more or less invented modern blues guitar and who, back in the Detroit of the late '40s, gave Hooker his first electric instrument. It's sparked by a rich, resonant vocal by Cupp—whose voice sounds like it should emanate from someone at least three times her size—and Osborn's plangent, sinuous lead guitar. Then the band settle into a rocking boogaloo as Cupp, head held high, strides into the wings and Guyett, depping as M.C. for the absent Jones, takes the microphone to announce John Lee Hooker.

The man from Mississippi ambles into the spotlight, adjusting his shades and waving to the audience, as the man from Rosebud moves a folding wooden chair into position and adjusts a microphone stand. The band's only black member, the large, melancholy-looking saxophonist Kenny Baker,[1] whose *nom de blues* is "Dr. Funkenstein," hands Hooker his guitar, painstakingly tuned by Osborn a few minutes earlier, and the maestro regally seats himself before thumbing off a fusillade of jangling notes that hang in the air like an unruly swarm of splintered neon-blue razor-blades.

Essentially, it's the same set he always plays, last overhauled to include songs from *The Healer*. Hooker doesn't so much dislike rehearsals as disdainfully refuse to recognize even the simple fact of their existence. In 1979, Mike Osborn played his first show with Hooker entirely unrehearsed, and the only subsequent ones have been called by Osborn himself: to rehearse the band in Hooker's absence. The maestro simply can't be bothered: anyone who lacks the instincts to play his music spontaneously shouldn't be playing it at all. Once upon a time—as thrillingly documented on any number of his records—John Lee Hooker used to rock any house with just his relentless boogie guitar, his inexorably stomping feet and his tireless, incantatory singing. Dance 'til you drop? Those records could make you feel tired just *listening* to them. However, that was then. John Lee can't put out like that anymore: the solo boogie is a young man's art, an energy-draining ritual which requires the painstaking cultivation and maintenance of Olympic stamina and endurance. Energy is the most precious commodity Hooker possesses: he tires very easily, and his every move is finely calibrated for maximum economy. So now The Coast To Coast Blues Band—two guitars, bass, drums, keyboard and tenor sax—supply the muscle and the momentum. They unfurl the carpet beneath his chair, they build the pedestal for his monument. They are a literal workhorse of a band: big and powerful and tireless, but also disciplined and reliable and self-effacing. They are sensitive to their boss's every nuance; in collective person-years they have invested almost half a

---

1 Sadly, Kenny Baker passed away in January 1999.

century into interpreting Hooker's wants and delivering what he needs when he needs it without so much as a second's hesitation.

Nevertheless, there are songs he rarely entrusts to them. The title tune from *The Healer* is one such: for Hooker, it is his credo, and it is inextricably linked to its co-composer and featured soloist, Carlos Santana. Even though it is one of the most popular pieces in his repertoire, Hooker hardly ever performs it unless Santana himself is there alongside him. As for the songs from the imminently available *Mr. Lucky*, which could use some promotional exposure . . . forget it. They ain't in the set. Not tonight, anyway.

Though the band's repertoire is large enough to permit song shifts from show to show, the structure invariably remains the same. Slouched in his chair and protected by his shades, Hooker works through his tales of lust and anger, sorrow and loneliness, regret and despair. They call certain kinds of blues "low down," and sometimes what is meant by that is a social judgment on certain sorts of people and certain sorts of lifestyle. In Hooker's case, "low down" is a barometer reading of the emotional depths. This is as bad as it gets. Oh, the details may vary. He ain't got no money. He ain't got no place to go. He wants her. She don't want him. She wants him. He don't want her. But into each scenario, the grain of his voice breathes verisimilitude—*I been there*—and compassion—it hurts, I *know* it—and the sheer fact of his presence seemingly guarantees that, just as he survived it all, so will we. The inevitable climax is the joyful catharsis of his trademark boogie. It is for this moment that he goes to such extreme lengths to conserve his energy: that electrifying instant when he casts his guitar aside, tears off his shades, leaps to his feet and prowls the stage, all frailty or fatigue forgotten, exhorting both band and audience to greater effort. From the bluesman, arm-wrestling his pain and the world's on a Delta front porch or in a rat-infested ghetto apartment, he is transformed into the preacher, who cajoles and bullies us toward salvation.

Like the preacher, he speaks in tongues. This closing boogie does little more than allude to his signature tune "Boogie Chillen"; it certainly doesn't include any of that song's celebrated monologues. All it is is a riff and a string of solos over which Hooker drops his nigh-wordless exhortations and incantations: "Hey-hey," "l-l-l" and the like. Transcribed, it would be not so much meaningless as languageless: the words, such as they are, are nothing, but the sound of his voice is everything. It is utterly primal; it reaches us on a level far deeper than any which can be accessed by words, or meaning, or language. It is a direct link from soul to soul. "You know what?" asks Hooker's son Robert, once his on-the-road keyboard player, now himself a preacher. "If you ever listen to him in that son 'Boogie With The Hook' at his closing act, do it to you kinda sound like he's preachin' in there?"

This is what Hooker calls "preachin' the blues," though his storefront pulpit is the neighborhood bar—or, more recently, the recording studio and the concert hall. Over that single hammering riff that he learned from his stepfather some six or so decades before, he orchestrates the celebration of this fact: that all present have triumphed over current adversities simply by finding this one moment—*here, now*—of solidarity and joy. If anything can truly be said to be the philosophical core of the blues, it is this: when you suffer, you can at least boogie, and when you boogiein', you ain't sufferin'. But, first, you got to face the fact that you're sufferin'. Once you've acknowledged your pain, you can get to dealing with it.

The problem that a lot of people—not so much white people, but many younger blacks—have with the blues is that their perception of it never reaches that second stage. All they ever hear is that pain: that raw, naked pain. And they complain about "wailing self-pity"; they are more comfortable with the soul man's sophistication or the rapper's rage. The blues makes them feel bad, and they can't get past that. They never reach the realization common not only to every blues singer but to every participant in blues culture, which is that the blues is not about feeling bad, but about feeling good despite every factor in the world which conspires to make you feel bad.

And this is why the blues is the Devil's music: because the church tells it one way and the blues tells it the other. If you boogie, says the church, you will suffer, because joy which does not come from God is not relief from sin but a sin in itself. Hooker turns that dictum on its head: he shows us first that he understands just how much pain there is in the world, and also that—even if only temporarily—it can be vanquished; exorcized in an ecstatic explosion of clapping and singing and chanting.

And this is his art: the art of the Healer. This is what a blues singer actually does. Behind all of the idiosyncrasies of taste and style, behind all the stagecraft and devices which any long-term performer develops, behind the songs and the riffs and the schtick and the musicianship, is the bluesman's true role: that of our confidant. The bluesman hasn't heard our personal, individual story—not unless he's a close personal friend, that is—but he should make us feel that he knows it anyway, that he has heard us and understands us. By telling his story—or a variation of his story, or several variations of his story, or even an outright embroidery of his story—John Lee Hooker enables us to face our own. In this sense, the bluesman is our confessor, our shrink; it is his job to forgive us and comfort us, shoulder our burdens as he invites us to help him shoulder his own. Against the forces of wickedness, the preacher is our leader; the general who marshals our forces; the conductor who orchestrates our instruments. But when the preacher's mantle passes to the bluesman, it is so that he can enlist us in an epic battle against despair. When the blues-man hollers *"Good mornin', Mr. Blues"* or tells us of blues walkin' just like a man, he's talking about what Winston Churchill called his "black dog": the personification of despair. If he were a doctor, he would inject us with a small, controllable dose of that despair, an inoculation to pro-tect us from ultimately succumbing to it. And it doesn't matter who you are. I haven't lived like John Lee Hooker. Neither have you. Nor has anyone who didn't come up in the racist apartheid South between the wars. But his pain—recollected in tranquillity as it may be, but evoked with the immediacy of a fresh bruise—sounds as if it feels like mine. When Hooker sings, in "Dark Room," *"and the tears roll down my face"* I remember how my own tears feel, rolling down my own face. I remember what it is to feel so flat-out, rock-bottom bad that you simply, involun-tarily, apropos of nothing in particular, begin to weep. And I know that, eventually, the weeping stops. And then the boogie begins.

And this is why John Lee Hooker is not simply some funny old geezer in a hat who's mastered the art of Zen showmanship to the point where he can enrapture an audience by doing virtually nothing at all. His music has, even if only temporarily, inoculated us against despair; and that tri-umphal, climactic boogie is where we testify that the cure, for the time being, proved successful. Once again, the Healer has done his work. Rob-ert Cray is still in full cry as Hooker's limo speeds away through the night.

Another night, another hotel. Muzzy with fatigue and still faintly dys-peptic from a Mac Attack sustained *en route* some time during the wee small hours, the assembled company awakens the following morning to discover that it is somewhere in Connecticut. To be precise, in a town called New London, which bears precious little resemblance to the old London a few thousand miles away. Presumably due to lack of demand, the hotel disdains to offer any kind of news-stand facility to its clientele:

enquiries as to the location of the nearest bookshop produce only puzzled stares and—eventually—directions to an establishment which does indeed stock books, but only of a Christian nature. Around mid-morning, Hooker rises regally from his slumbers to proceed to his next port of call: the Newport Jazz Festival.

Some thirty-one years earlier, this self-same occasion had provided the springboard for the second phase of Hooker's professional career. In 1960, the festival had presented an afternoon showcase for an assortment of blues performers, headlined by Muddy Waters' Chicago Blues Band and featuring Hooker as one of the most prominent guests, alongside the likes of Louisiana's old-timey guitar/fiddle duo Butch Cage & Willie Thomas, the urbane Count Basie veteran Jimmy "Mr. Five By Five" Rushing, and the cabaret-blues stylist Betty Jeanette. At the time, this was a mildly controversial move, since contemporary blues of the amplified ensemble variety was disdained by purists as a degenerate music only fractionally less despicable than that damned rock and roll; though the likes of Waters and Hooker had considerably more to do with jazz than, say, Eartha Kitt or The Kingston Trio, both of whom had appeared in previous years as part of the organizers' misguided attempt to broaden the festival's appeal. However, as controversies went, the blues afternoon paled into utter insignificance compared to the moral panic—concerning the critical mass achieved by that year's combination of teenagers, beer and rhythmic music—which virtually capsized the festival's future as an institution. The final two days' concerts were hurriedly cancelled, and for a while it was feared that the blues afternoon would represent the institution's swansong. Indeed, the climax of the afternoon was the performance, by Waters' pianist half-brother Otis Spann, of the impromptu "Goodbye Newport Blues," the lyrics of which had been hurriedly scribbled on the back of a telegram form by the poet Langston Hughes. It was sung by Spann, rather than Waters himself, because Waters—like Hooker and many other Southerners of their generation—didn't read too fluently; and Spann, fifteen years younger and considerably better educated, was far better equipped to sing lyrics which had just been placed in front of him.

Newport survived, and both Waters and Hooker did considerably better than that. (Incidentally, history repeated itself less than a decade later when, in the wake of the late-'60s flirtation between jazz and progressive rock, the 1968 festival included a rock night headlined by Jethro Tull, The Mothers Of Invention and The Jeff Beck Group, and all those bad kids—or rather, their younger brothers and sisters—went wild again. Tsk tsk tsk. However, this time there was no moral panic: they simply stopped booking rock acts.) Seeming simultaneously shy and feral, Hooker stood up in his slick sharkskin suit with Muddy Waters' band behind him, and performed deep, brooding versions of classics like "Maudie," a surprisingly mordant song dedicated to his then wife, and "It's My Own Fault," later to become a cornerstone of B. B. King's repertoire. He climaxed a rocking finale of "Come Back Baby" by walking offstage, still playing, and leaving the band to finish the tune; a marked contrast to the downhome demeanor of Cage & Thomas, wearing their best church suits and broad-brimmed hats and busily playing away while seated in their folding chairs.

More than three decades later, it is Hooker, Mr. Natty Urbanite of 1960, who performs from a chair and sports the broadcloth-three-piece-and-Homburg-hat which is the traditional formal dress of rural black Southerners. Nevertheless, the wooden Newport stage still looks the same, and the tranquil bay is still crowded with the yachts of the opulent. However, in this, the golden age of corporate sponsorship, the Newport Jazz Festival is now the J.V.C Jazz Festival and is spread over a variety of sites, including the original setting in Newport, Rhode Island, itself. You reach the grounds via immaculately maintained roads of neat bungalows where the weekend yard sale is a way of life, a sobering contrast to the potholed death-traps of New Jersey. Hooker is received like royalty. He barely has time to disembark from his limo before he is surrounded by well-wishers. Nevertheless, he heads for shelter at the first opportunity, unlike B. B. King, who tours the backstage area, greeting one and all with the ambassadorial graciousness which is his trademark. Once he's ensconced in his trailer, Hooker's co-stars queue up to pay their respects. Virtually his first visitors are a lean Englishman in his late fifties with a majestically pony-tailed silver mane, and a bulbous, bearded, bereted gent leaning on a Louisiana conjure stick. They are, in fact, John Mayall, "the father of British blues," and the New Orleans piano maestro Mac "Dr. John" Rebennack, and they're almost knocking each other over in their eagerness to be the first to receive the passive handshake and the ritual greeting, "Huh-huh-how you doin,' young man?" Excitable young women in shorts and halter tops vie with each other to be photographed sitting on his lap. Taking care not to dislodge his Homburg, they feed him chocolate and ice-cream. The fearsome Boogie Man, the soulful, compassionate bluesman, the galvanic preacher: all are now replaced with the genial, guffawing, sleepy-eyed teddy bear.

As three o'clock approaches, The Coast To Coast Blues Band mount the stage, inspect the rented amplifiers, keyboards and drums, and declare them adequate. Cupp and Fischer have squeezed themselves into the drop-dead dresses normally reserved for after dark, and some of the male band members have gone so far as to change their shirts and comb their hair. The venerable sage's only concession to the heat is to remove his jacket and unbutton his waistcoat. Soon he settles into his folding chair, unleashes fusillades of deep blue notes from his much-travelled Gibson guitar, and chants his Mississippi soliloquies into incongruously blazing sunshine. He is rapturously received by a thoroughly broiled audience, many of whom should be discouraged from ever appearing in public in swimwear, and a tiny proportion of whom should never appear in anything else. Halfway through the show, Hooker sends the group down from the stage and brings on his longtime friend John Hammond, a tall, patrician singer/guitarist who is the son and namesake of the great talent scout who recorded everybody from Bessie Smith and Billie Holiday to Bob Dylan and Bruce Springsteen. Armed with an old steel-bodied guitar and a harmonica, Hammond accompanies Hooker as he sings "Highway 13" from the new record: *"And it rained, it rained so hard,"* sings Hooker, *"I couldn't hardly see the road."* Even without the sympathetic brushed drums—soothingly shushing like windscreen wipers—which anchor the song on record, it requires a positive effort of will to remember that we're sitting in ninety-plus temperatures under a burnished, cloudless sky, rather than huddled in a car, locked in a tiny, scudding bubble of dry warmth as a storm pounds on windows and roof. But Hooker is only nominally here with us under the Newport sun; his heart and mind are somewhere else, where things are very different, muscling an automobile through punishing rain. And such is the strength of his spell that he can carry us with him: to overpower our experience with his.

As it turns out, the devastation he's evoking is not so much to somewhere else as to some*when* else. Hurricane Bob was still a day away when Hooker hit Newport, and twenty-four hours later, New England would be practically underwater. The fine weather is still holding as Hooker heads back to New London, but come morning the pressure begins to build, as the limo noses through Long Island under gunmetal skies, en route to the Wantagh resort of Jones Beach. The ensemble is decanted into a courtyard ringed with small, cell-like dressing rooms: Hooker and his crew here, Etta James and her team next door, The Robert Cray Band across the way, and B. B. King's posse somewhere over *there*. Hooker's has a puddly shower as its annex: Cupp and Fischer, who use it as their changing room, must be grateful for their high-heeled shoes. The bands and crew, preparations more or less complete, lounge around the court-yard, chomping their way through the backstage catering, and beginning to shiver in their summer clothes. Outside, Hurricane Bob is closing in on the New York area, and the blues lovers of Wantagh, Long Island, huddle damply and resentfully in their rainwear, awaiting performances by Hooker, King, Cray and the gargantuan James, and slapping irritably at the clouds of mosquitoes which boil around them, intoxicated by the scent of fresh prey. The air is thick and humming with the sense that something is about to happen. "They don't give this old boy *nothin'*," complains Hooker, reclining mock-mournfully on his dressing room sofa. "No radio, no TV, can't watch no baseball . . ."

The show is the standard set which Hooker and his gentlemen and ladies performed the day before, and the day before that, but this time it's different. The Newport show, apart from that stunning performance of "Highway 13," was *sunny*, in every sense of the word; this one is stormy, ominous, full of foreboding. Cupp's curtain-raising "Cold Cold Feeling" is as appropriate a prologue as any novelist or movie director could have chosen, and she rises to the occasion: singing her heart out before striding back to the wings through the mosquitoes, chest heaving, as Hooker emerges to commence the main event. This time, he rides the building storm to the final explosive boogie climax. Afterward, the team dissolves into its component parts: Cupp is commencing a new day job the following Monday and thus will travel back to San Francisco with the band, but since Hooker has a few days' business in New York City, Lizz Fischer has been asked to stay on in order to keep him company. New to the organization and unfamiliar with its ways, she is a trifle con-cerned. Naturally, she is thrilled, but nevertheless she worries about ex-actly what such companionship will entail and what she might be expected to . . . *umm* . . . Just a few minutes ahead of the relentless down-pour which will, the following day, have the flood warnings out on every radio station, John Lee Hooker rolls into Manhattan in a long black limousine. He will give a handful of interviews and, in a week of hurri-canes, celebrate what he will claim to be his seventy-first birthday.

"When I die, they'll bury the blues with me," he states proudly to a well-wisher at the exit. "But the *blues* will never die."

2. Bluebird, Bluebird, Take a Letter Down South for Me

In my mind, music is made by those whom music saves.
Jimi Hendrix could not have done anything else with himself.
John Lee Hooker, what else is he going to do? Work at McDonalds?
—Henry Rollins, interviewed in *Rolling Stone*

Alabama's got me so upset
Tennessee made me lose my rest
And everybody knows about Mississippi . . .
Goddam!
—Nina Simone, from *Mississippi Goddam*

I know why the best blues artists come from Mississippi.
Because it's the worst state. You have the blues all right
if you're down in Mississippi.
—John Lee Hooker, interviewed in *Melody Maker*, October 1964

So how you gonna keep 'em down on the farm once they've seen the big city? Some people just can't wait to get out of the country, feel some pavement under their feet, scrape the mud off their boots and morph, as smoothly as possible, into urban slickers ready to parade their new-found sophistication at the expense of the rubes fresh off the latest bus from down home. Every big city is full of people from the sticks or the 'burbs who've taken on urban coloration like so many concrete chameleons, shedding their country skins, going native on Broadway or in Hollywood, pumped and cranked all the way up, and primed to mud-wrestle the locals for that big-town pay-check. For others, the basic fact of who they are changes not one iota no matter where they may find themselves.

John Lee Hooker left the Mississippi Delta while still in the turbulence of adolescence. Nevertheless, Mississippi never left him. Though he's lived in major conurbations—first Cincinnati, then Detroit, then Oakland, California, and finally the suburbs of the San Francisco Bay Area—ever since reaching his late teens, he remains a quintessential man of the Delta. His slow, deliberate drawl has never revved itself up to city speed. His manners are still country-courtly. His fondness for traditional Southern food remains unaffected by the temptations of any exotic delicacies from Europe, Asia or, come to that, anywhere else you could name. He's seen it all and he's not terribly impressed, but he's far too much the country gentleman to give offense.

The Delta formed his voice, and he in turn became the voice of the Delta: the very incarnation of the traditional culture of its African diaspora; a king in voluntary exile. However, the suggestion that "Mississippi made him" would be an outrageous oversimplification. There is only so much for which purely sociological heredity-and-environment hypotheses will account; there is no process, no set of circumstances, which can truly be said to "explain" John Lee Hooker. We can certainly state without fear of significant contradiction that the "environment" of the Mississippi Delta not only produced considerably more than its fair share of blues singers, but was most probably the spawning ground of the primal blues from which all the different varieties of blues-as-we-know-it ultimately derived. The blues of the Delta is the oldest, deepest blues there is; it therefore creates no major rupture of the laws of probability to propose that the Mississippi Delta (as opposed to, say, Surrey, England) would produce the artist with the most profound ability to tap into that primal blues, and the chromatic range of human emotions it explores. Even within the small community in which Hooker spent his formative years, two of his former playmates became blues singers and good ones at that: but not great ones. We can also discard immediate heredity: even considering the complex interaction between the two primary factors of heredity and environment fails to take us significantly further forward. John Lee Hooker came from a large family, but none of his many brothers and sisters became professionally successful blues singers, though his younger cousin Earl did. "I was different from any of my family, as night and day," he says today, "I never know why I was so different from the rest of 'em."

This is, of course, the big question. Why was Hooker "so different from the rest of 'em"? Of course, almost every person who becomes successful and famous and admired grows up among "normal" people (read: people who don't). Statistically it could hardly be otherwise, even if—in the cable and satellite era—it now seems impossible that anybody at all will be able to live through an entire lifetime without being seen, at least once, on television. It also seems as if every successful person elects to strive for that success from a very young age. Yet John Lee Hooker came up at a time when the majority (read: white) culture had decided that the sons and daughters of black Southern sharecroppers were not supposed even to entertain the possibility that they could escape their fate and take control of their own lives. Their culture was so "primitive" that, by the standards of the times into which Hooker was born, it barely qualified as culture at all. The "leaders" of the black communities, in their turn, decided that blacks not only could but most definitely would "make progress" despite white opposition, but they would do so by self-improvement, by proving their worth to a society which treated them as though they were worthless. By dint of sobriety and study, they would haul themselves, hand over hand, up an American ladder from which most of the rungs had been cut away. Hooker steered precisely the opposite course: that of taking a fierce, incandescent pride in the identity he already had, and exploring the implications of that identity no matter what the consequences.

The story of John Lee Hooker's life is, essentially, the story of his resistance to any and all attempts to change him, to dilute an intrinsic sense of self which has successfully withstood all pressures, including those of institutionalized racism, family, church and the music business. That resistance has been, at times, virtually a passive one: throughout his life, Hooker has remained polite, deferential, quiet-spoken and accommodating. Despite the occasional peevish or impatient outburst, he doesn't argue, he doesn't bluster, he doesn't bully. And then finally, when absolutely no alternative remains, he quits. By which I mean: he leaves, he splits, he dusts, he's outta there, he's nothin' but a cool breeze. It doesn't matter if it's a marriage, a record contract, a family, a home: once Hooker decides he's had enough, that is *it*. No discussion, no recrimination, nothing. Just *gone*. And the reason he does it is to protect himself. Not because he's callous, or cowardly. He is neither. But himself—or rather, *his self*—is that which makes the music, and that will be protected at all costs; yea, e'en to the ends of the earth.

So Mississippi, after all, made many people, but only one John Lee Hooker. Rather, Mississippi provided the wherewithal for John Lee Hooker to make himself. During his first fifteen or so years, Hooker took three key decisions which set him on a collision course with all the prevailing values of his family and community; he stood by those decisions and received validation beyond his wildest dreams. At a time when most people are still struggling to discover who they are, Hooker knew not only who he was, but who he wanted to be. Like all great bluesmen, Hooker is his own greatest creation, and the creation without which none of his other creations would have been possible. The "self-made man" can be found somewhere near the front of The Great Book Of Facile Truisms (right next to the notion that "you can take the boy out of the country but you can't take the country out of the boy," in fact), but Hooker fulfills it to the *n*th degree. The self he chose to make is that of a man supremely fitted to sing and play the blues, and virtually little else. After all—as Henry Rollins asks—what would John Lee Hooker be doing if he wasn't singing the blues?

If he had decided to play the game through strictly on the hand he was dealt, he would have lived and died a Delta sharecropper and nobody outside his community would ever have heard of him. What would he have had if, even without his music as the spur, he had still headed for the city? A lifetime of the kind of dead-end jobs he plied in the various cities before his artistic breakthrough: janitor, usher and so forth. The kind of jobs a man does when he has neither the physique nor inclination for hard manual labor, nor the education for anything else. He could conceivably have sung gospel—which would, at least, have pleased his preacher father—but his extreme distaste for what he came to perceive as the narrow-mindedness and bigotry of the ostentatiously devout would surely have precluded that. John Lee Hooker would not be John Lee Hooker if he wasn't singing the blues. And the blues he sings is the blues that only he can sing.

When his first hit record "Boogie Chillen" was released in late 1948, it fitted easily into a burgeoning market for downhome blues. Two years earlier, the Texan bluesman Lightnin' Hopkins had bucked the existing trends by enjoying a surprise "race" hit with "Short Haired Woman"; one year after that Muddy Waters—a Delta-raised, Chicago-based near-contemporary of Hooker's—had done likewise with "I Can't Be Satisfied." Both records were deep-country blues with only the faintest discernible urban gloss but, by comparison with "Boogie Chillen," they were downright conventional. Both used a standard twelve-bar blues structure (though Muddy, characteristically, dropped one bar in each verse) and each boasted the cleanest and clearest recorded sound that the impecunious independent record companies of the time could manage.

"Boogie Chillen," however, definitely proved that there was something new under the sun. Its insistent, droning one-chord vamp, driven by an obsessive, impatient foot-tapped beat as impossible to resist as a flu bug, harked back to the rural prehistory of the blues, a style so archaic that it seems to predate even the earliest blues recordings that can be found today. At the same time, it was contemporary and urban in a way that the Hopkins and Waters records weren't: it seemed to crackle with electricity. Hooker's guitar and voice were recorded with a rough, distorted electric edge, his pounding feet reverberated with the hard slap of city pavements. This was back-porch, fish-fry, house-party country blues adapted to the accelerated pace and claustrophobic ambience of the big city. The lyrics told two linked stories: one of a youth defying his parents in order to live the rockin' life; the other of a country boy hitting the big town and deciding that it was good. Both stories were Hooker's own: the song was an empowering parable of the experience of the thousands upon thousands of Southern migrants who had established their foothold in the big Northern cities, but the record provided the sonic metaphor for that experience. Even if you didn't listen to the words, the record itself told you that the people of the Delta had come to the big industrial cities and become part of them without compromising the fundamentals of who they were.

On one level "Boogie Chillen" was an extraordinarily simple record: a one-man show with zero chord changes, repetitive lyrics and little melody. On another, it was a work of sheer genius in which one man's personal story deftly encapsulated the collective experience of a community in the throes of profound and far-reaching social change. Plus—in the finest traditions of what was, a little later, to become rock and roll—it had a great beat and you could dance to it. To call "Boogie Chillen" a "hit" is actually an understatement. Hopkins' and Waters' records were "hits" by the standards of the time: "Short Haired Woman" sold somewhere between 60,000 and 70,000 records, and "I Can't Be Satisfied" did slightly better than that. "Boogie Chillen" was a *smash*: it sold around a million copies. It was the record that John Lee Hooker, thirty-one years old at the time it was recorded, had spent more than two-thirds of his life preparing to make. Or rather, he had spent more than two-thirds of his life becoming the only man who *could* have made it.

To choose one single mission in life and methodically unfit yourself for all else is a demonstration of the deepest, most profound faith in oneself and the promptings of one's inner voice. To stay with that course when it seems like it's getting you nowhere is either folly of near-suicidal proportions, or the sign of the truly dedicated. The point here is that John Lee Hooker didn't choose to sing the blues because it was a cool career move or because he had a prophetic vision of having his music featured in TV commercials, but because singing the blues completes him, realizes him, soothes him, arouses him . . . the blues is John Lee Hooker's key not only to the highway, but to the universe. It is his means of satisfying that most powerful of all human urges: to find a means of comprehending the world around him and interpreting it to others. He does so in his own terms, through his own vision. That vision was formed in Mississippi, and has never really changed. Hooker's own inner Mississippi traveled with him wherever he went, his own unique personal property: a Mississippi of the mind which sustained and forever defined the man whom he chose to become; a Mississippi in which the weeping scars of both the childhood Mississippi he left behind and the real, contemporary Mississippi which exists in his, and our, present have healed.

If this book could be boiled down to one sentence . . . I'd be a fool to admit it. But if, and only if, it could, that sentence would run: John Lee do not do, he be. In fact, he do as little as possible; but he be all that an artist in the twentieth century can be. His gift to us is not so much his music—monumental though that music is—but the sensibility that created that music, a sensibility which gives us the ultimate gift: a new way to see ourselves, and to experience ourselves. A new way to understand and, finally, to live with ourselves.

Chris Blackwell, the Anglo-Jamaican entrepreneur who founded Island Records and forever changed the course of popular music by promoting Bob Marley & The Wailers to an international audience, used to be fond of saying that "there are no facts in Jamaica." In impeccably Jamaican style, this remark is capable of sustaining a considerable variety of interpretations. It could mean, for example, that in a society which places little value on the lives of the majority of its people, much of their existence and experience takes place away from official scrutiny, unrecorded as formalized data, but preserved as folklore and collective memory. It can also mean that the region's ostensible political culture, and its accompanying rhetoric, bear little relation to the daily lives of its citizens, much less their inner lives. Or that, in a community which sustains a hidden world of mystical and spiritual experience behind, below and beside its orthodox religious life, anything can happen. Or even simply that only the initiated know what's really going on, and that even if outsiders are capable of asking the right questions—that is, questions that make sense to those questioned—the answers cannot be guaranteed to make sense to the outsider. The hidden (African) world which shares Mississippi's 40,000-odd square miles with the mundane, statistical world of factuality is, to shoplift an aphorism from Carlos Castenada, a "separate reality."

All of which adds up to this: that of course there are "facts," but these facts explain comparatively little of what actually goes on in a culture which is, despite increasingly widespread literacy, primarily an oral one. Mississippians of African descent have little faith in so-called "objective" reality: "facts" tend to be part of outside descriptions of their lives; accounts of who they are into which their input has rarely been sought, and rarely accepted when proffered. So they replace these imposed facts with their own, and the distinctions between "truth" and "folklore" tend to blur until the distinction becomes all but meaningless. At best, it is irrelevant. This is as true of Mississippi as it is of Jamaica: Mississippi is old country, secret country, deep country. In whitebread terms, popular American mythology demands that the nation's moral center should coincide with its geographical center: amidst fields of waving Midwestern corn, where adorable tow-headed children with freckles, accompanied by appropriately cute pets, forever chase baseballs and fish in the creek. This is, after all, where Jerry Siegel and Joe Shuster, two introverted Jewish kids from the decidedly unlovely conurbation of Cleveland, Ohio, chose to place the adoptive home of Superman, the American savior from the stars. Nevertheless, the secret heart of America is located in the South: for the descendants of those who involuntarily became African-Americans, it's where the unhappy story of their lives on this continent began, and the Mississippi Delta is the wounded heart of that South. Mississippi was the hardest of hardcore Jim Crow.

African slaves were first imported en masse into Mississippi in the 1830s, around the time that the Native American Chickasaw and Choctaw tribes were finally dispossessed. The slaves' first task was the clearance of massive tracts of forest in order to render the land arable; their second to pick the cotton which briefly made Mississippi, in the period immediately prior to the Civil War, the wealthiest state in the Union. After the war, it became the poorest, and it shares with Alabama the dubious distinction of emerging from the Civil War as the most racist states in the Union. The worst thing that could happen to a slave would be to be "sold down the river" from Virginia or Maryland, comparatively less brutal only insofar as the condition of slavery is at all quantifiable, to Mississippi or Alabama, whose plantations have been comparable only to "prisons run by sadists." It had the richest soil and the poorest people in the nation, and it still does today. The most famous by-product of the Civil War was the end of legal slavery and its eventual replacement by the various bits of segregationist legislation which came to be known as the "Jim Crow" laws, specifically designed to reproduce slavery as closely as possible despite its technical abolition. It may seem surprising that Mississippi was rarely the first state to opt for formal adoption of each new chunk of Jim Crow; this was no indication of any comparative liberalism, but the exact reverse. In Mississippi, the substance of those laws was already common practice and there was no immediate or pressing need for their formal enshrinement in law. The etiquette of oppression crystallized into an obscene and elaborate dance: blacks and whites walked the same streets, but in different worlds. Equality under the law—or, indeed, anywhere else—wasn't even a theory. In any case, "law" was pretty much for whites only: the black experience of it was the receiving end. They had to make do with the informal protection of the local plantation boss, who would look after his workers—provided that they were in conflict with other blacks rather than with whites—simply because he needed their labor. The lives of blacks were not considered to hold any intrinsic value whatsoever. Lynching remained legal there until 1938.

"People would get killed, beat up, shot, out in the country," John Lee Hooker remembers. "It wasn't such a thing as the *po*-lice could be right there. The *po*-lice would get shot and killed. Your boss who owned all the land would take care of all his people. He would come out with the sheriffs, and they'd be a day gettin' out there. It ain't like it is now, police there in a moment or a flash if something go wrong and someone get hurt or beat up, get killed. Police right here. You way out in the country, the closest thing be the sheriff in one of those towns, and you couldn't get to a phone, somebody had to get him. It was just olden days, you know. Nothin' happen in a flash. Black people, Chinese people, Spanish: they wasn't important at all. They didn't count Spanish people as white, they counted 'em right along with us and Chinamen. There was just a very few Chinamen was there, but a *lotta* Spanish people. We all lived in the same area, in the same houses, shared the same things. So they had to live under the same gun that the blacks lived under. That's the way it was."

There was no way, says Hooker, to work around the system. "It was just that way, and we never thought it *would* change. But people had faith that one day it would change, and it did, but we never thought it would change so soon. It was a long, long time." By the time he or she was five or six, any black child living in the South would have already learned how he or she was supposed to act around white people. "They taught you that when you had the ability to talk. Your parents taught you what you had to do and what you couldn't do. They [whites] taught they kids not to fool with us, and they taught our kids not to fool with them, so we knowed. We stayed on our own territory. My dad, we had enough land so we didn't have to fool with them. We couldn't mix, you know. It was pretty rough and pretty hard. I was fortunate enough to get out of it when I was that age. I was very aware of what it was, what it was like. We had no contact at all, but I knew stuff was going on. I knew some black people did get into lots of trouble, but we knew what to do and not to do; my daddy would tell us. He told me a million things. I can't repeat just what they said, but roughly: *you just got to stay in your place*. You can't do *that*, you can't do *that*. I can't tell you just what he said—this word and that word—but he said, 'You can *not* mess with those people.' He kept pounding it into our heads. We knew that, we see'd that. Everybody would be in they own place."

Except that John Lee Hooker decided that he wasn't going to stay in his.

A certain amount of confusion exists around the precise place and date of John Lee Hooker's birth; much of it created by Hooker himself. He's always cited his birthday as 22 August, but the year has been variously reported as 1915, 1917, 1920 and 1923. For a while, Hooker was insistent that he was born in 1920, rather than the more commonly cited (and probably accurate) 1917. "We all was born with a midwife, which was not in a hospital. We had our records in a big old bible, our parents did, they might not have put it in a courthouse." Even if they had done so, it would make no difference: almost all records were destroyed in a fire which consumed the county courthouse in 1927. As it is, surviving state records contain no mention of anyone by the name of John Lee Hooker.

Hooker has always given his place of birth as Clarksdale, Mississippi, the nearest urban center of any significant size. "That was my town that we would go to," as he puts it. "We would say, 'Well, we from Clarksdale,' because that's where [Reverend Hooker] did all his business, buy the groceries. Every weekend we would get supplies from Clarksdale, and we would go there. We run out to the candy store, get back on the wagon and go back to the country." In fact he was born out in the country on his father's farm, approximately ten miles south of the city. "It was close to Highway 49. It went to Tutwiler and Clarksdale and Memphis," Hooker remembers. "There were many songs wrote about that Highway 49. We didn't stray too far from that." "Clarksdale," blues singer Bukka

White used to say, "is just a little old small town, but a lotta good boys bin there." Bessie Smith, the diva of the "classic" blues of the '20s and '30s and according to Hooker and not a few others "one of the greatest blues singers ever been alive," died there; John Lee's younger cousin Earl Hooker, generally acknowledged as one of the finest Chicago guitarists ever to pick up a slide, claimed it as his home town, as did Ike Turner and harmonicist/vocalist Junior Parker. The unofficial capital of the Delta, it's the third largest city in the state and even today, after successive waves of northward migration have carried away its best, brightest and most ambitious youth, it boasts a population of over 20,000.

Glendora is a tiny hamlet some twenty-five miles along Highway 49 from Clarksdale. It earns its place in the blues history books as the birthplace of Alex "Rice" Miller, best known as the second of the two major singer/harmonicists who used the name Sonny Boy Williamson. John Lee's mother, the former Minnie Ramsey, was born there in 1875; his father, William Hooker, a decade or so earlier. The Civil War wasn't "history" yet—in some parts of the South, it still isn't—and the shadow of slavery lay heavy across both their births.

Hooker recalls being one of ten children, but as his nephew Archie gleans from his own studies of the family history, "I always thought there was thirteen of 'em, but some died. See, what happened was . . . stillbirth you don't count." John Lee's older brothers were William, Sam and Archie; the younger boys were Dan, Jesse and Isaac; and John Lee's sisters were Sis, Alice, Sarah and Doll Baby.

"Doll Baby's name was Mary," opines Archie. "One of them's supposed to have been blind. I think it was Aunt Mary. I think she was the last sister that died. She was the oldest child. They wouldn't use names. They would use nicknames. Sis might be Mary." Minnie kept on having children until she was nearly fifty; this, according to Archie, was not uncommon. "Womens were different [then]. They could have kids and two days later be back in the fields. More kids you had, the more crops you could produce. Simple. And every one of *them* had big families."

The family lived and worked on what Hooker remembers as "a big farm, close to a hundred acres," which would put the Hookers into whatever passed for the middle classes of the Delta. Slightly more than half of the farms in the region were 80 acres or smaller, while 30 percent were over 300 acres, and the very largest spread to as much as 2,000 acres. "It was an old wooden house with a tin-top roof, but we was comfortable, you know, we had a lot to eat. I never been hungry a day in my life. We had cattle, horses, pigs, chickens, farmland . . . he had people working for him. Down South there was merchant people who saw him as being in the same category. He had a few Spanish people working for him, not many, maybe a couple. Two Spanish, Mexican, my older brothers, four or five more black people. He was a sharecropper, you know."

The practice of sharecropping meant that the larger plantations managed to keep the majority of the black workers on the land, substituting economic ties for forced labor. A tenant farmer would take responsibility for a certain area of land and would work it, together with his family and any sub-tenants and day laborers, with equipment and cash advances supplied by the "boss." When each year's crop was harvested, the farmer and the landlord split the proceeds, and if the farmer and his team had worked especially conscientiously, there would indeed be a profit after the boss deducted his advances. If the crop failed, or if, for any other reason, sufficient profits did not materialize, the tenants began the following year in debt. Given a few bad years, a sharecropper could easily fall so far in debt that it was impossible ever to break even again. Once that happened, the 'cropper would virtually be enslaved all over again, and entirely legally. William Hooker must indeed have been a skilled and conscientious farmer: the records of the S. N. Fewell Company, based on the Fewell plantation close to nearby Vance (where the Hookers moved a few years after John was born) show that in 1928 "Will Hooker Sr. and Jr." made a profit of twenty-eight dollars. By the standards of the time, this was a more than respectable sum.

The work was back-breakingly hard, and getting it done was entirely down to the muscle-power of humans and animals. In the rural Mississippi of the '20s and '30s, the twentieth century hadn't quite arrived. Since cars and tractors were still comparatively rare, horses and mules did double duty as agricultural implements and personal transport. Country backwaters like the Mississippi Delta weren't yet wired up for electricity; Hooker remembers that it wasn't until his mid-teens, when he first traveled to sophisticated, progressive Memphis, that he saw his first electric light. (For the record, Buddy Guy—nineteen years Hooker's junior and raised in rural Louisiana—tells substantially the same story: he, too, had to go to Memphis as a teenager to see a lightbulb for the first time.) "When I was there [in the Delta]," Hooker says of electricity, "it wasn't there." The telephone was another piece of hi-tech exotica: something that folks had in the city and which you could occasionally see at the movies. The phonograph in the family parlor was "the Victrola, the kind you wind up," where the energy of a weighted pulley drives the turntable and the sound is amplified acoustically through a large horn. There was also an old crystal radio, on which they would listen to *Amos And Andy*, and "music from a radio station in Helena, Arkansas."

"Sacred" music only, though. William Hooker was a part-time preacher, a pastor at a local Macedonian church, and family life revolved around farm, church and school. "We had," says John Lee, "to work." They also had to sing in church, as Hooker's nephew Archie, son and namesake of John Lee's immediate elder brother, explains: "He'd been singin' for, like, years. If you's ever been a minister's son, you gonna have to *participate* in church. They *made* him go to church, and if you go to church, you gonna learn how to sing basic hymns, so it stuck. It stuck to him, and when he be workin' he would always try to sing." As Hooker himself proudly recalls, "I used to sing in the church when I was nine or ten. I was a *great* gospel singer. Macedonian, where my father was a pastor. It was in the country. I was a very talented young man, and everybody around in the county looked up to me and said, 'Oh, that kid is somethin' else, he can sing better than anybody I ever seen.' When I come into the church everybody look round, and when I started singin', people start shoutin' and hollerin'. I had such a tremendous voice. I was nine, ten years old."

And there was farm-work, though John Lee was neither physically nor mentally suited to the toil of agricultural labor. He just flat-out didn't like working in the fields, and down there working in the fields was all there was. "My daddy," says Archie Hooker, "was more a mechanical type. He worked with his hands, and Uncle John didn't." However, there was also play. In the rural South, you either made your own entertainment, or else you got very, very bored. "There was this old mule we had, an old mare mule, and she was *very stubborn*, but she was a gentle old mule and she know us kids. She was a very wise old mule. She wouldn't hurt us, and she really cared about us. We'd ride her back and she'd let us ride 'til she get tired, and then she rub up against a barbed-wire fence. You know what a barbed-wire fence is? She'd just swing you right into the barbed-wire fence and scratch you and you'd have to jump right off her back! You'd get so mad with her you'd start bitin' her lip and be cussin' her. 'You bitch! You . . . !' There'd be one behind kickin' her, *bam!* Right up against the barbed-wire fence! *Whoo! Whoo!* Old Kate, that was her name. She'd drag you right into a barbed-wire fence! You had to hop right off her or get stuck with the wire! Yeah! She'd see us comin' and if she didn't want to be bother, she just lay down, get on her knees and lay down. Old Kate. Hell of an old mule. She knew when twelve o'clock come and we'd been workin' in the fields, when time to eat she started hollerin' *Whoo! Whoo!* and she wouldn't go no further. She lay down in the middle of the field 'til she knew that you were gonna take her and get her somethin' to eat. A lot of memories in that old mule."

Chicago drummer S. P. Leary, a veteran of The Muddy Waters Band who worked with Hooker on the 1966 sessions for *The Real Folk Blues*, would certainly agree on that: "Everyone I worked [with] taught me something but John Lee Hooker. Me and him fell out. You have to watch your p's and q's with John Lee; he'd tear a house up, he'd tear the top off a house. If you make him mad, you talk about a mule . . . ha ha. I think a mule showed John Lee a hard time."

And then there was the usual kid stuff.

"I met a midget once. Did I tell you about the midget? There was some pretty little girls around, and I was the big bully of the town. I was a *bully*. There was a little midget, 'bout *this* high. There was about four or five little girls around, and he was peekin' on one girl, and I said 'Leave him to *me*.' I was showin' off for the girls. I was nine years old, and I thought I was gonna walk all *over* him. They said,"—Hooker shifts his voice into a taunting, little-girl falsetto—" 'We gon' make John whup your ass. John, will you hold him for us?' I said,"—roughening to a stylized "tough" voice—" 'Yeah, I'll take care of it.' And I slap him, *pow!* And he said, 'Don't hit me no more.' I say,"—toughly again—" '*What you say?' Bop!* He say, 'I said don't hit me no more.' I say, 'You little short thing, I'm gonna whup the piss outcha.' He said, 'Y'all don't hit me no more.' I hit him again, and, boy, he grabbed me. He was a tough 'un. He whupped me and he tore off all my clothes, and the girls was there: 'Get up, John! John, get up! Get him! Don't let him getcha! John, get up! Get up! Get up! Get him off the ground! John, he on top of you!' We get up and he say, 'Now, I don't wanna hurt you, so don't slap me no more.' I said, 'I'm gonna see you again, and the next time I see you I'm gonna be ready.' And Loreen—the girl—said,"—in falsetto—" 'John wasn't ready then!' But I never jumped on another midget. Yeah, he showed me!"

The idea of John Lee Hooker as "the bully of the town" seems somewhat unlikely. He was small for his age and tormented by a chronic stutter; his only known attempt at a macho act was to slap a midget, and that particular exercise in boyish swaggering ended rather less than gloriously. Singer/guitarist Jimmy Rogers, a veteran of the great Muddy Waters bands of the '50s and a Chess Records hitmaker in his own right during that time, grew up around the Vance area and counted Hooker and harmonicist Snooky Pryor among his playmates. Rogers paints a slightly different picture: "Oh, he was just a youngster just like me and Snooky [Pryor] was, just a young country boy . . . we would play marbles together, play ball . . . there weren't nothin' special goin' on in his life at all, nothin' different from any other youngster back then. We was kids then, and he was just a regular guy. There weren't nothin' special about him that I know of. We just met up, and Snooky knew him before I did. He didn't mean nothin' to me; he was just another boy. It's been so long since I been in Vance; I was a kid then and I'm sixty-eight now. I know he's a good four, five, six years older than me, at least five." It's hard to imagine "the bully of the town" spending much time playing marbles and ball with kids half a decade his junior without standing out from the crowd. Hooker and Rogers were reunited in Chicago during the '50s; curiously, while they remained friendly right up until Rogers's death in 1998 and occasionally spoke on the phone, and Hooker has clear and affectionate memories of their childhood encounters—"I knowed him from my little childhood days down there. We'd shoot marbles together"—Hooker remains adamant that he has no such recollection of Snooky Pryor, who Rogers claims introduced them.

The "bully of the town" notion definitely doesn't stand up. If anyone was the family desperado, it was Hooker's brother Dan, who later killed his wife, and then walked ten miles to turn himself in. "I met Uncle Dan," recalls Archie. "The first time I met him, he was in prison. Doin' ten years for killin' his wife. Straight ten years: no parole. I was about five, six. My dad took me down. He was at Parchman, Mississippi. Short, heavy-set man. Cookin', made trustee. But his violence had to be provoked, because in the process of makin' trustee, he carried a gun. If a guy was escapin', he wouldn't shoot. So that mean for him to really get mad, to hurt somebody, someone had to push him. That mean a woman had to push him. John always said he didn't have to fight, they always took care'a him. My dad said John was always fragile, never was one to want to be a fighter. He was always kindhearted, and I'm thinkin', basically, that's what it is now. John's not a fighter. That ain't the way he was raised. He don't believe in it. My dad didn't. Unless you pushed him. That's why his brothers took care of him. They didn't want him to turn the other cheek. They was tough, they would fight . . . deep down inside, he was more of a minister's son [than the others]. He might've sung the blues for relief, or for money, because you can't make a lot of money singing spirituals, but deep down inside he always had God in his heart. John may have ran away, true, but he ran away from poverty."

According to Archie, there were other pastimes, too: "Things like stealin' a neighbor's chickens. [John Lee] said, 'We couldn't steal grandad's chickens, 'cause he *counted* 'em, but you'd go out and get a neighbor's chickens.' He didn't want to do the fields, and him and all the boys, they had nothin' else to do, so that was they entertainment. They started like . . . his music really was his turnaround."

John Lee could conceivably have stayed down on the farm, working in the fields, singing in church and perhaps following his father into the ministry, acquiring some schooling—the year before he was born, the state of Mississippi had finally gotten around to instituting a public education policy—and raising a family of his own to work the land in their turn. Instead, a chance encounter was to change his life. An itinerant bluesman named Tony Hollins took a powerful shine to John's sister Alice, and soon he was coming around to court her. He ended up making a bigger impression on his adored one's little brother than he did on Alice herself.

"Oh, I loved him so much, couldn't he play guitar! I was hangin' around him like a hungry dog hang around a bone. I was just a little kid, seven, eight. He recorded, but I can't think of *what* he recorded. Last I heard of him, he was a barber in Chicago. Whether he's still around or gone, I don't know, but anyway he got rid of the first guitar he had, an old Silvertone. It wasn't no heck of a guitar, but it *was* a guitar, and that was heaven to me because I had never had no guitar. It could have had three strings, but it was a guitar. I never know what happened to that guitar that Tony give me, but anyway we used to sit on the porch, on the pasture by the woods, with the cows and stuff like that with my sister, and he would play for us. One day he said, 'Hey kid, I got a guitar for you.' I said okay, and that was my first guitar."

It's not hard to second-guess Hollins's reasoning. Giving an old, worn-out guitar to John meant that he could send the youngster off on his own to practice, and—once the young gooseberry was safely distracted and out of the way—enjoy some precious time alone with the loved one. The acquisition of the guitar created an immediate problem with the loving but stern Reverend William Hooker. "Finally, you know, I went to play guitar," Hooker reminisces. "Had an old piece of guitar and be bangin' on it." The main reason that Tony Hollins had to lurk by the front porch when he came by to see Alice was because of Rev. Hooker's disapproval of his reckless, hard-traveling, blues-singing ways. Reluctantly, William Hooker allowed John to keep the guitar, as long it never crossed the threshold of the family home. "I couldn't play it in the house, because . . . I had to keep it out in the barn. All the time I was pluckin' on it, and my daddy called it the Devil. He said, 'You can't bring the Devil in this house.' They all feel like it Devil music back then. They call blues and guitar and things the Devil's music. That was just the way they thought. Not only my father, *everybody* thought that. The white and the black ministers, they thought it was the Devil's music."

To the Reverend Hooker, it must indeed have seemed like that. Tony Hollins didn't stick around very long, but his beat-up old guitar did. The second young John Lee got his hands on the discarded instrument, whatever interest he may have had in his schooling went right out of the window. "When I was a kid comin' up, I would pretend I was goin' to school and hide out in the woods with my old guitar. When the other kids come out of school, I come back along with them like I'd been to school. I hadn't been to school for a long time, and then they caught me and used to whup me and beat me." For John Lee, the choice was absolutely clear-cut. "You never knew this, I'm a very, very wise person. I'm a very good songwriter in the blues, but I never got education because I had two choices. Stay, go to school and get a good education, stay down in Mississippi and be a farmer the rest of my life and never be a musician; and I took the choice of leavin', comin' North and being a musician. In my mind, I was very smart. I wouldn't have been a musician, living in Mississippi, farming, sharecropping. I had two choices: going to school, and become a well-known whatever—I never would have been known just working the rest of my life in Mississippi or wherever—or take off and get famous, which is what happened."

Around this time his musical ambitions received some encouragement from an unlikely source. "I never will forget this lady . . . I was a young man then. I went to this big carnival they had. I didn't know her and she walked up to me. I had *never* made not a record, and she walked up to me and said, 'Young man, come here.' She was a gypsy woman or somethin'. She said, 'You gonna be famous *aaaaall* over the world. You gonna become very rich, you gonna become very famous.' We were all just a bunch of kids; we just kinda laughed. I just wondered *how.* I was just plunkin' on an old guitar, and it come true. I usually don't believe in things like that, but she come pick me out and it come true. I never believe in that shit, but I'm just sayin' what she told me. She might have been just guessin'. She was a fortune-teller and people would give her a little somethin', but I didn't have nothin' to give her. She said, 'You ain't got no money,' and I didn't. She said, 'Kid, you ain't got no money, but you gonna be famous one of these days.' We was just a bunch of kids; we kinda laughed when she left." He shifts into a taunting schoolyard falsetto: " 'John Lee Hooker gonna be *faaaaa*-mous! Gonna be *faaaaa*-mous!' All ridin' me and ribbin' me . . ."

The Hooker boys were growing up. Archie Hooker remembers the boyhood tales told him by his father. "My daddy told me about how when they was growin' up they would swim in the creek, and my daddy was a moonshine maker, they would make corn whiskey. 'I made John drunk once—he was just a little boy—from white lightnin'.' Down in the woods, they would go down to the still and let him sample. 'That's how you could tell how good it was. If it made him drunk, it was good.' My dad was a little bit older than Uncle John, just a couple of years. Not a whole lot, but they was real close." John Lee, too, remembers his elder brother's homebrew experiments. "He was making homebrew in a little cabin, and the stuff was good, too. We'd cap it, bag it and take it to a party one night, and I had it on my back and the thing goes to bustin', beer got warm, explodin'. He made the corn liquor too, same thing as whiskey, made outta corn . . ."

Needless to say, this too contravened Rev. Hooker's house rules; it's as well that he never found out what his sons were up to in the little cabin out the back. "Oh yeah! Ooohh! *Never* be caught with a bottle. The *Devil* in the bottle! It's funny, but it's true. The Devil in the bottle. Anything with alcohol, the Devil puts it there."

In many ways, the Reverend's hard-nosed attitude to his son's musical ambitions backfired. If he had allowed John to play his guitar in the house, John might well have stayed in Mississippi. On the other hand, he might not. "I could have stayed home and played, but there wasn't no producers, radio stations and record companies. Weren't none of that in Mississippi. I could have stayed down there and played and gotten real good, like so many down there right now are real good, but they never come to be a star because there's nothin' there. I could have stayed there like you say. You right. If they ever let me stay there and play, I could've become a grown-up musician, a real good musician, but there's nothing down there like producers, managers, record companies, booking agencies could've heard me and discovered me. The country people could've discovered me, but . . . I was very wise. I was different from any of my family, as night and day. I was just . . . I never know why I was so different from the rest of 'em. The rest of 'em grew up, got educations, stayed down there . . . they all gone now. But from twelve or fourteen I wanted to be a city boy, a musician. I wanted to explore my music. I were very humble, very mellow, very nice; I were raised very good, to be a Christian and respect everybody, love people. But it wasn't what I wanted in Mississippi. I said I'd never reach my goal livin' there, goin' to school, sharecroppin', come home from the fields . . ."

Hooker takes considerable pride in his lack of schooling. In a sense, he's absolutely right to do so—after all, how many illiterate millionaires are there, anyway?—but in the short term, it certainly made his life harder. He won't concede the point without an argument, nor—for that matter—even *with* an argument. To Hooker, his illiteracy is what provides him with the sensitivity to sonic detail and emotional nuance which he needs to make his music, and he defends it fiercely. "I see people right today got college educations, all kinds of different degrees, can't even get a job. Back then too, they couldn't get a job. It wouldn't have made, I feel, too many difference. I had to work my way up, do little jobs, until I got to the big man who could open the door for me because I *know* I had the music. I *know* I had the talent. I *know* I was good. I knew it, but I knew I had to work up to find someone to open that door for me to come in. I was knockin' on the door, but wasn't nobody there to *say*, 'Come in.' No matter how much education I didn't have, that book education didn't have what was in *here*"—he taps his chest—"and in *here*"—he taps his head. "I could've been a professor, but I repeat myself to you and to whoever read this book after I'm gone: you can*not* get what I got, out of a book. You got to have a talent.

"I never change, and I won't change. When I did 'The Healer,' the first take was it. Live with the band. The first take was the best one. We did two, but we played it over and over and decided that the first take was it. I can train my voice directly to whatever they play. I can fit my voice into anything, directly like a lock and key, come out with the right words and bars, just lock right in there, automatic. No schoolin', no readin', because I don't have that. But I have the talent. Let me put it this way. Ray Charles, for instance, and Stevie Wonder, they don't read and write 'cause they can't see, right? But both of them are genius." Against such rock-solid conviction, though, it cuts very little ice to point out that both Charles and Wonder taught themselves to read and write fluent Braille. "Yeah, right," Hooker grudgingly concedes. "Ye-e-e-e-s. But they can't see. I can see, but . . . I don't believe in no *paper*. Take your paper, stick a match to it. My paper's right in *here*, and in *here*. I lay down at night, and a song will come to me. I can be talkin' to you, and you can say things, and I can make a song out of it."

As John Lee was reaching his adolescence, serendipity struck again, this time in fairly baleful disguise: Rev. Hooker and the former Minnie Ramsey decided to split up. John never learned why, and he knew better than to ask. "They weren't *involved*; kids can tell that. We'd know when they was arguin', we'd see it, but we couldn't get in and say, 'You stop it.' But we knew what was goin' on, that they weren't getting along. I repeat, we didn't get into they business. We knew that they was arguin' about something that wasn't right, but we didn't know who was right and who was wrong. They were very strict on kids in them days. We was raised better: my sisters wasn't even allowed to date until they was nineteen, twenty, twenty-one."

In her mid-fifties, Minnie Hooker found herself a new man. He was a local sharecropper named Will Moore, originally from Shreveport, Louisiana, and—like Rev. Hooker—some ten or twelve years Minnie's senior. As might be expected in the days before "family meetings" and "quality time," John Lee remains unclear about exactly when and where Moore and Minnie first met, or the precise circumstances under which their relationship began. "Kids at that time didn't have their nose into the old people's business, like it is now. Kids in them days, if they put they nose into they parents' business, they was told that they get a whuppin' like they never had in they life, you know. They didn't allow them to sneak around finding what old people was doin' and what they was up to, stuff like that. They was more stricter on kids; they were raised better. We was raised to be obedient to old people, say *yes-ma'am* and *no-sir*. Not yes and no, but yes-*ma'am* and no-*sir*. And mind our business and stay out of theirs. That's why I don't know how they met."

The break-up of his parents' marriage led to the second key decision of John Lee's life. In many ways, it was the most important choice he ever made. He had come to his first crossroad when he opted to pursue the guitar rather than school and church; and the second appeared before him when William and Minnie separated. Whereas all his brothers and sisters elected to stay with their father, John chose to leave with his mother and take Will Moore to be his stepfather. The main reason was that Will Moore played guitar, and he was a bluesman through and through. He was a popular entertainer at local dances and parties, and would appear alongside the likes of Charley Patton or Blind Lemon Jefferson whenever they were performing in the area. "I was fourteen. My real father, he didn't want the guitar in the house. He called it Devil music. My stepfather Will Moore, he played guitar what I'm playing now. I learned from what he played: that's what he played, what I'm playing right now, identical to his style. I went to play my guitar. I didn't go because I wasn't treated right; I was treated pretty good. I left because I couldn't play my guitar in the house, and he didn't mind me going to my mother's. I told him, 'Dad, I wanna stay with my mom.' "

The Reverend considered the departure of his son to be a sign of failure on his part, but on one thing at least, he and John Lee were in complete agreement. If John insisted on living where he was allowed to play his guitar indoors, he had to go. "Well, you know how church people are. He loved the heck outta us, he would give his right arm for us. They believed in the church, in God, in the Lord, and he didn't want his son . . . he felt that I was givin' myself to the Devil. He didn't want me to do that, and that's they way of thinkin'. He felt like he wasn't doin' nothin' wrong, he felt that he could guide me the right way. That was the way he lived, and he wanted all his children to be churchgoing people. But my mother had as much authority over me as he did, and he said, 'You go live with your mom and her husband, if that's the way you wanna go. You welcome to stay here, but you just cannot do this in the house.' " Mrs. Hooker felt differently. "Well, my mother was open-hearted, very open. She wanted me to do what I wanted to do best, because she felt that if I was forced to go to church, it wouldn't be for real. So she said, 'I'm not gonna force you. If this is what you wanna do, you and Will go ahead and I won't object.' "

Will Moore gave his new stepson his next guitar: an old mail-order Stella to replace Tony Hollins's battered gift. Moore became John Lee Hooker's spiritual and artistic father-figure: the father who approved, the father who encouraged, the father who supported, the father who empowered. William Hooker had loved John dearly and raised him according to the best and finest principles he knew, but an unbridgeable abyss lay between them. With all his heart, the Reverend hated, feared and despised that which John Lee wanted, above all else, to become. Inevitably, a battle would have been fought for the erring son's immortal soul, and whatever the outcome, both father and son would have been irreparably damaged by the conflict. Will Moore appeared when he was needed, and he gave John more than a beat-up guitar and a home with a room of his own in which to play it: he gave him the means to become the man he wanted to be.

He gave him the boogie.

Master bluesmen have traditionally adopted "sons" to be schooled in the craft, ethos and lore of the blues. "You like my *son*," Muddy Waters famously told a young Buddy Guy one chilly '50s night in Chicago. Guy, scarcely out of his teens, was fresh up from Louisiana, green as swamp moss, with little more to his name than the Stratocaster with which he was looking to carve up the Southside bars. This particular night, Buddy hadn't eaten for almost three days. A cutting contest with Otis Rush and Magic Sam was scheduled for that night, and Buddy was so hungry he could hardly stand up. Then Muddy Waters appears out of nowhere. He sends out for bread and salami. With his own hands, he makes a sandwich. He offers it to the ravenous Buddy. Buddy says no. That's when Muddy slaps him in the face. That's when Muddy tells him, "You like my *son*." That's when Buddy eats the sandwich.

That's when Buddy wins the contest.

Throughout the story of the blues, there are countless examples of such "adoptions." Son House "fathered" both Robert Johnson and Muddy Waters. Sonny Boy Williamson II and Howlin' Wolf both, at different times, "adopted" James Cotton. Little Walter took Junior Wells as his "son." Later on, Albert King "adopted" Stevie Ray Vaughan; and Albert Collins, Robert Cray. These relationships involve more than simply tuition, though tuition is indeed the formal basis, the foundation upon which they rest. Above all, they are spiritual lessons in life, and in living. Yet John Lee Hooker's connection to Will Moore was deeper still than that: Moore became John's father in every sense other than the strictly biological. Let's say this: Rev. William Hooker was the father of Johnny the child, but Will Moore was the father of John Lee Hooker the artist, and—because it is impossible to separate the two in any meaningful terms—of John Lee Hooker the man. Hooker remembers Moore as "a nice-lookin' man, about my complexion, maybe a little lighter, kinda medium tall. Very pleasant." Evidently, Moore took his new-found parental responsibilities very seriously. "Will Moore object to me drinkin', but he did [drink]. Back then, they thought kids that young . . . they never did taught me to drink, my stepdad and mom. He would take a drink, but he wouldn't drink it around me. Was Will Moore strict? Not on what I wanted to do. He was married to my mother and so he wasn't . . . he was strict enough for me to know not to get outta line. He would tell me what's right and what's wrong, and if he would tell me I wouldn't do it, because back in them days if you did something wrong that you shouldn't'a didn't'a did, you get a good whuppin'. An' he was allowed to do that because I wasn't real pampered. My mother would tell him that if I got outta line, whup us. But he never had to do that because I never did get outta line."

Where Will Moore, *in loco parentis*, drew the paternal line was over whether to carry John with him when he went out to play with Patton, Son House and other wandering players of the time. In the Delta, a boy of sixteen was generally considered to be practically a full-grown man, but Moore felt that John was too young, and because those Delta dances could get pretty rough, Moore "wouldn't take a chance on taking me to one of those places." Clearly, John Lee was considered more vulnerable than many another youth his age; more urgently in need of shelter and protection. It's fascinating to contemplate the spectacle of the adolescent John Lee Hooker sat at the feet of such towering blues patriarchs amidst the smoke, crush and clamor of a Delta house party, but the evidence suggests that he learned all he needed to know at home. If the feats of the student are anything to go by, the teacher did his job well. "He wanted me to do what I wanted to do best, long as it was right. He guided me and helped me to do that. He is *my roots* because he is the man that caused me who I am today. I understudied under him, Will Moore. He made me what I am with his style. He give it to me, like you got a piece of bread and I ain't got none, and he said, 'Here's a piece of my bread.' He gave me a piece of his music. What I'm doin' today, that's him. Identical, the same thing that he taught me by watchin' him. I wanted to play just like him, and I did, but he was *so bluesy*. The first thing I learned, the first tune I learned from him, I never forgot. It wasn't one of his tunes, but he played it all the time. Called 'The Peavine Special,' by Charley Patton. '*I thought I heard that Peavine when she blows.*' I would'na thought that song goes back so far. '*I ain't got no special rider now.*' That was the first thing I learned."

Not necessarily the first but without doubt the most important of the musical lessons John Lee learned from Will Moore was the boogie. This was Moore's personal beat, his distinctive rhythmic pattern, his signature, his mark, his call. It is the most profound gift that a master bluesman can give to his apprentice, and just as it had been Will Moore's trademark around the Clarksdale area, it eventually became John's, recognized as such all around the world. His first hit, "Boogie Chillen," cut in Detroit at the tail end of 1948, a decade and a half after he finally shook the Delta dust off his feet, was the piece that established him at the forefront of the "downhome revival" which was one of the dominant trends of postwar blues. Its galvanic, hypnotic boogie groove was pure, unreconstructed Will Moore. "I got that from my stepdad," Hooker acknowledges, not only freely, but with palpable pride. "That was his tune, that was his beat. I never thought I would make nothin' out of it, and he didn't either. But I come out with it and it just happened."

But there was rather more to "Boogie Chillen" than a beat, no matter how funkily irresistible. It also told part of the story of John Lee Hooker's early life.

Well, my mama didn't 'low me
Not to stay out all night long
Oh lord . . .
Well, I didn't care what mama didn't' 'low
Went on boogyin' anyhow . . .

One night I was layin' down,
I heard mama, papa talkin'.
I heard papa tell mama
"Let that boy boogie-woogie

Because it's in him
And it got to come out"
And I felt so good
Went on boogyin' just the same . . .
Boogie, chillen!

So who were the protagonists of the real-life conversation which provided the seed of the song? "It could have been between my father and my mother, or my mother and her last husband. The song was *'mama and papa,'* but it would relate more to my real father, because mama said, *'Let that boy boogie-woogie.'* It could've been either one, but I didn't do it upon that basis, though. It's so true, when you're a kid and you wanna get out there and boogie and your parents don't want you to do it, and one of them will give in and say, 'Let him go 'head. *It's in him, and it got to come out.*' You can relate to that, because what's in you has got to come out, and it was in me from the day I was born. It was a great talent I had, and so I come from . . . not a very poor family, wasn't *rich*, but wealthy in food. I was brought up—not *all* the way up—religious, and to this day some of that is in me. Lovin' people, helpin' people. I was taught that by my parents, to do that, and I come up some rough roads since."

One of the great tragedies of Hooker's life, and one of his few genuinely profound regrets, is that Will Moore never lived to hear what John Lee achieved with his legacy. "Oohh, he woulda bin so proud. It would have made him feel like a big champ, knowin' that he was responsible for this. It's too bad that that's the way it was. I think about that a lotta times, wishin' that he could've been around just a little while to know that I was doin' this."

Will Moore forever redefined John Lee's relationship with the music for which he was prepared to sacrifice anything, and anybody, with whom he was born and raised. He also redefined John's relationship with his blood father's primal resource: the church. For the Rev. Hooker's bleak fundamentalist world of fiery retribution and divine punishment, John Lee substituted Moore's vision of a nondenominational, nonjudgmental world of compassion and trust. "He [Will Moore] was a religious man, but he didn't believe in running to church and so forth. He was like me. I'm a religious person, but I don't believe in going to church. The way I look at it, your heaven is here, and your hell is here. [Right now] I feel like I'm in my heaven. A lotta people love me, I got a few dollars, a place to live . . . that's my heaven. And lovin' people, that's heaven to me. But people that's sufferin', hungry, sleepin' in the streets, don't know where they next meal is comin' from, out in the cold . . . they livin' in hell. For a long time, my parents had me believin' that there was a burnin' hell and there was a heaven, but it has come to me in myself, as I grew older and knowledge grew in me, that if there was a God, then he was an unjust God for burnin' you forever an' ever, stickin' fire to you. If the God was a heavenly father, a *good* God, then he wouldn't torture you and burn you. He wouldn't do that, he wouldn't see you burn. But he tortures you, in a way, if you got nothin' to eat and hungry, don't know where you gonna get your next meal, don't know where you gonna sleep at, half sick, can't work, driftin' from door to door . . . that's your hell. But you're not bein' tortured with fire, where you get down in this hole being tortured with flames, with fire forever. *No.* So you not gonna fly outta there with wings in the sky like an angel, milk and honey, as I was taught, if you go to heaven. You not gonna do that. There's nothin' up there but sky. The only heaven is up there in the big jets and airplanes, with the beautiful ladies walkin' in the aisles. *That's* your heaven."

Only if you're in first class, John.

The present-day Hooker, resplendent in his living room, laughs. "Yeah, first class. That's your heaven. You'll never get it through to people, because the church has got 'em brainwashed to *death*, the ministers, the preachers. I believe in a Supreme Being, don't get me wrong, but I don't believe that there's a hell that you're gonna be tortured in. I believed in all of that, then I grew up and realized, and I wrote the song: *'Ain't no heaven, ain't no burnin' hell/where you go when you die, nobody can tell.'* Nobody knows. Nobody come back and tell you, 'Hey, it's all right, c'mon down.' " He laughs again, louder this time. "It ain't all right. I could be wrong, but I don't think I'm wrong."

"Burnin' Hell" was a song Hooker first recorded in 1949, at the very outset of his career. Set to the remorseless, foot-stomping beat of Will Moore's primal boogie, it takes as its point of departure the line quoted above, which first cropped up on record as the second verse of Son House's "My Black Mama (Part 1)," which House originally recorded in 1930. Its folk origins are undisguised, but both its form and its agenda are uniquely Hooker's. Accompanied only by the piercing harmonica of Eddie Burns—originally from the neighboring community of Dublin, Mississippi—Hooker chants his credo of defiance to the church and its philosophy of endurance on earth to earn rewards in heaven. But the song is no simple hymn to secular values, no straightforward rejection of the spiritual life: in its own way, it is an affirmation. In its central section, Hooker goes down to the church, and falls down on his knees. He asks the preacher—"Deacon Jones," the folkloric archetype of the black divine—to pray for him. He prays all night long, and having thus paid his respects, in the morning he goes on his way freed from the constraints of belief, but a believer nonetheless. "Ain't *no hell*! Ain't *no hell*!" he shouts triumphantly; even if there is a hell for others, it can no longer claim him. He has traded the promise of salvation for freedom from damnation; thus liberated, he can make his own way in the world. It is one of the most powerful works in his extensive catalog and—revisionist though the notion may be—I'd argue that the 1970 remake (recorded with the late Alan Wilson, of the blues-rock band Canned Heat, replacing Burns on harp)—

is more powerful still: if only because, during the two decades which separate the recordings, the original version's slight tentativeness has been burned away by Hooker's increased confidence in both his hard-earned artistic powers, and in the validity of his philosophy. In purely musical terms, it is a perfect example of Hooker's ability to link the deeply traditional with the startlingly radical; while its content demonstrates how, time and time again, he can dig deep into his personal history to produce a universal metaphor for the contradictions of belief. It is where the adult John Lee replies to his father, restating both his challenge and his love. Finally, it is yet another variation on a perennial Hooker theme: the need to respect one's past while still reserving the right to define one's own values, write one's own future, and find one's own way in the world.

So Moore's notion of a loving and compassionate Supreme Being displaced, in John's vision, Rev. Hooker's vengeful Old Testament deity; just as the Rev. Hooker himself was replaced in John's life by Will Moore. In other words, having visualized God in Rev. Hooker's image, John remade him in Will Moore's. And it is Will Moore's Supreme Being in whom John Lee continues, to this very day, to believe. "As years go by, I learned more and more about the world. The world growed, and I growed with the world and learned more about the world. When I was in Mississippi, I was strictly in a spiritual world. When I was with Will Moore and my mother, my mother was spiritual, but she didn't object to me playing the blues. I was restricted to a lot of things I couldn't do there, but when I was eighteen, nineteen, twenty, I filled up with all these things. I could do what I wanted to do."

And thus, armed with everything which Will Moore could teach him, John Lee Hooker was ready to take his third key decision, which was to leave. As we've seen, he had already figured out that there was nothing in Mississippi that could further his ambitions and desires. He knew full well that all of the great Mississippi blues singers had had to go elsewhere in order to make their names and to do what John most wanted to do: to make records. Mississippi had no record companies, no recording studios, no booking agents. All it had was an abundance of talent, the kind of talent he had, and the kind that Will Moore had. However, Moore had stuck with his farming and rarely left the Delta, and had thus been denied the opportunity to have his music heard across the Southland, let alone across the nation, and—most especially—across the world. So around 1933, probably still only fifteen or sixteen, and just a year or so after he first began to learn his future trade at the knee of his mentor,

John Lee Hooker made his third life-changing decision. He grabbed his guitar and some clothes, and upped and split for the bright electric lights of Memphis, Tennessee.

"Yeah, I left home then. I went to Memphis because it was the closest, about ninety miles from Clarksdale. That was the closest I could go with no money, by the direct route." For someone in the Delta who has a mind to travel anywhere else (other than further south, of course), Memphis was—and is—the only place to go. That holds true metaphorically as well as literally; Memphis was a cultural as well as a geographical cross-roads; the unofficial capital of the black South, a place where hix-from-the-stix could rub shoulders with their more sophisticated cousins from the Southwest Territories, the gateway to the big Northern cities like Chicago or Detroit. It was also a wide-open town which at one time enjoyed the dubious honor of having the highest per-capita murder rate in America. Its epicenter was Beale Street ("The Home Of The Blues") but it was still fundamentally a racist Southern town despite its relative enlightenment and sophistication. It was different, but not *that* different. "Oh yeah, a little different. Not a lot, but a little looser. You could spread a little bit more, but then you weren't allowed to ride on the bus and trains with 'em [whites], but then we had our places we could go and them *not* go. All the towns down there was like that. Oh, it was rough for years and years. I didn't go back down there too much after I grew up until all that was over. I *played* down there after I got famous and it was like that, we had to play in certain places. There was certain places you couldn't. You couldn't be flirtin' with the white; you stay *here* and they stay *there*. You could go out with Chinese, with the Spanish, but I never seen what difference that it made. We was the same color they was."

Many wonderful and intriguing stories have arisen surrounding John Lee's sojourn in Memphis. Some—including Hooker's own autobiographical lyric to the title song of his 1960 album *That's My Story*—place him there for as long as two years. Others depict him as leading a gospel quartet, or attending house parties with the young likes of B. B. King and Bobby Bland. The latter tale, unfortunately, collapses as soon as you consider that B. B. didn't relocate from the Delta to Memphis until 1947—by which time John Lee was a fullgrown adult husband and father living and working in Detroit—and that even if Riley B. King had been in Memphis in 1933, when John Lee hitched his way into town, he would have been barely eight years old, and Bland still a mere toddler. The truth is somewhat more mundane.

"I had an aunt named Emma Lou—I forget her last name, just Emma Lou—on my mother's side in Memphis, and she had this big boarding house on a backstreet. The boarding house is long gone now, and she gone too. I worked there [in Memphis] as an usher, you know, seatin' people in the New Daisy Theater for about two, three dollars a week. You could live on that: a nickel would get you almost two loaves of bread. You could just about get along on that, it was *good*. You had five bucks, you had a lotta money. There was two of them: New Daisy and Old Daisy on Beale Street. I would sing and play in my room, and once in a while I would sit outside and do it. She let me stay there about two weeks, and then she called my mother and told her. They could have got the mail, and they never did tell me how she know. I was two weeks there, so she must have wrote. After so long, they came and got me and I went back to Mississippi." This enforced return to hearth and home was most definitely not to John's liking. He took it for as long as he could, and then he legged it once more. This time he headed for somewhere where the support of his extended family couldn't be used as a net with which to drag him home.

"I didn't like working in the fields. I stayed there maybe another two or three weeks, I ran off again. I didn't go to my auntie because I knew she'd tell on me again." After a year-long stay in Memphis, he moved on to Cincinnati.

When I first started hoboin'
Started hoboin'
I took a freight train to be my friend
Oh Lord . . .
—John Lee Hooker, *"Hobo Blues"*

Like the Memphis sojourn, the period between John Lee's departure from the South and his arrival in Detroit has become the stuff of legend, conjecture and romantic embroidery. The liner notes to some of the albums he cut during the late '50s and early '60s for the Chicago-based Vee Jay label are full of such myth-making. The text accompanying 1961's *The Folklore Of John Lee Hooker* refers to "a life of drifting and restless traveling" and goes on to claim "The itinerant's life lasted for sixteen years—during which time John Lee had spent relatively long stays in Memphis . . ." while *I'm John Lee Hooker* goes further still: "He is an itinerant soul, a body who strayed from the Gulf of Mexico, from Corpus

Christi to Brownsville, to the Blue Ridge Mountains of Virginia—and plenty of area in between."

Now, hype is the raw material of which the music business, in all its forms, is built and, as hypes go, this is all good stuff; the kind of rhetorical flourish that's perfectly suited and highly appropriate for cementing the public image and professional status of the artist whom Vee Jay was successfully marketing as the king of electric downhome blues. The problem is that it's bullshit. Hooker's present account is radically different.

"Between Memphis and Cincinnati I was in a little town, I don't know what you call . . . Knoxville? Stayed there a little while. Me and a guy called Jerry went there. He was older than I was. I followed him there. I got no stories to tell you about it. It was about like Memphis. I was about seventeen, maybe eighteen. We left there and come to Cincinnati, and when we crossed the Mason-Dixon line, it was a big difference, you know. *Ooh! Much* different! You could go wherever you wanted there. You could ride with 'em [whites] on the same buses, go to the same places they go. That felt good. I stayed in Cincinnati a good long time, two–three years, two and a half years. I worked at the Philip Tank & Pump Company up on Walnut Hill. I was working in the plant making rings for cars. I was a helper for one of the people run the machines, and that was way out in the hills. Redd and Rose, this main street that had nothin' but used cars, new cars, and it was way out there, so we had to take a bus out there every day. I finally got an old car, an old Ford, and I thought I had somethin'. An old '37 Ford! But it run good; I thought I was livin' in heaven. I had an old guitar I played, and I stayed in a little restaurant called Mom's place, was workin' as a janitor, dishwasher before I got a job sweepin' and janitor at the old Philip Tank & Pump Company plant. I was always smart. I never did like to sit around. I always had me a job to pay my little rent, any kind of little handy job I would do. I would make about ten bucks a week. Oh, that was big money then. The Depression never did bother me. I never did feel it. My daddy always had a lot of food; it never did bother any'us."

In Cincinnati, the once-sheltered boy began taking his first serious steps into adulthood. He began to mingle at the kind of house parties and blues dances of which Rev. Hooker had disapproved, and from which Will Moore had excluded him. And, for the first time, he began to play his guitar to others. Nothing ambitious at first—"Aww, it was routine stuff, just songs in general. Nothin' that I wrote too much. Oh yeah, I was playing 'King Snake,' stuff that I'm playing right today, stuff that I come up on"—but his social life was beginning to pick up. "Mom, she had a daughter called Coon." You're kidding, John. "No!" Hooker laughs uproariously at the memory. "Daughter named Coon! They called her Coon, and they had this big house where she would give house party on the weekends in Cincinnati, and I started playing at the party for her. Boy, I wasn't quite into women then because I was younger, not quite twenty, but she was so good to me. Everybody would love me and like me because I was a malleable kid. I was very intelligent, I had class, and I knew how to treat older people and young people, so everybody would take a liking to me. I would play there for her on a Saturday night and weekends, and do janitor work, you know. And I would work in theaters, seating people. Wasn't making much money, but it was good money."

Nevertheless, John wasn't quite ready to shoot for the big time. "Cincinnati was a good town. There was more happenin' in Cincinnati than in Memphis or Mississippi, that was for sure, but as far as record companies . . . there was a big record company there [King Records, a small but hard-working label dealing in both R&B and country music, later became best-known in the '50s and '60s as the musical home of James Brown, the Godfather Of Soul], but I wasn't known, wasn't even thinkin' about it. I didn't have a chance then."

As far as John's family—or, to be more precise, his families—back in Vance, Mississippi, were concerned, their boy had simply disappeared back in 1933. John Lee Hooker had "just vanished out of the world." As far as John himself seems to have been concerned, so had they. There was a desultory exchange of correspondence over the years, mainly to reassure them that he was alive and well, but John Lee never saw William Hooker, Will Moore or Minnie Ramsey Hooker Moore ever again.

"I never met grandmother when I was little," says Archie. "I only knew what my mom and dad told me. They said she had long pretty hair. Said she was on a bed of affliction when I was born. That meant she only lived eight, nine months after I was born, and I was born in '49. That meant grandmama had to die in '50. That meant she was dead when [John Lee] came back [to Mississippi]. I seen John when I was four years old. He had made it."

"I wrote to [the family] a coupla times," says John Lee, "wrote 'em a letter an' we got a good response back. They were glad to hear from me, glad that I was doin' all right. Very glad to hear from me before she died. She died when I was livin' in Detroit, thirty-five or forty years ago. I forgot what time it was at. He died before she did. He was way up in age, about ten, twelve years older than my mother. She was seventy-five when she died. My father lived to be a hundred and two. A very strong man."

Allowing for John Lee's shaky maths—neither Rev. Hooker nor Will Moore survived into their eighties—one can only concur that he'd have had to be.

Today Vance, Mississippi, just about qualifies as a one-horse town. To reach it, you follow Highway 49 south out of Clarksdale, through Matson, and through Dublin. When you reach Tutwiler, turn onto Highway 3 and pretty soon you're in Vance, on the Quitman/Tallahatchie county line. The post office and the general store are on your left, and the mansion which was once the headquarters of the old Fewell plantation on your right. Then you pass a few shacks and trailers on each side of the road, and the graveyard adjoining St. Mark's Baptist Church, containing those few remaining graves which haven't yet been plowed over. A couple of seconds later, you're out the other side, en route to Lambert, Marks and the junction with Highway 6. John Lee Hooker sighs heavily when he thinks of Vance. "Yeah. Zoom-zoom, right through. There's nothin' there. It'll never grow into nothin'."

Vance is a town waiting to die, except that it can't quite summon the energy. The only thing that really qualifies it as a town at all is the fact that it still has its own post office. The official state map—brightly festooned with attractive touristy images of riverboats, Elvis and the Civil War—lists the populations of most of the various towns and cities in Mississippi, ranging from Jackson, the state capital, which can boast over 200,000 souls and actually has its own airport, down to the likes of Learned, in Hinds County, with its registered population of 113. Places with a head count below three figures don't carry a listing at all. Vance is one of those.

In blues parlance, Delta landscapes like those surrounding Vance are dubbed "the lowlands." That's because they're about as perfectly flat as a landscape can possibly get, and the long straight highways scythe through them to the horizon, decisive gray slashes designed to take you somewhere else as fast as possible. Around those parts, a "thousand-yard stare" implies chronic short-sightedness. Every place you go in the deep country, you see fields: cotton, soya, pecans, all growing green or gold wherever the red earth is not puddled and paddied with water. Your line of vision ends only when you sight the light woodlands far in the distance.

Away from the comparative bustle of Clarksdale—where any building over three stories high dominates its immediate vicinity like some Delta equivalent of the World Trade Centre, like the building which houses radio station WROX, where blues and gospel DJ Early Wright spins Little Milton and Bobby Bland records and thunders out community news and commercials for local businesses—everything is quiet, blanketed in a silence so deep it seems to have remained unbroken forever. This is a place with few distractions; a place where people have no option but to face themselves head-on; to come to some kind of accommodation with their thoughts, with their feelings, and their circumstances. Anyone failing to reach such an accommodation has no options other than to go crazy or else to get out.

This is where you find the richest soil and the poorest people in the U.S.A. The richest soil: a rusty loam sufficiently fertile and welcoming to nourish just about anything you care to put into it. When it's been raining for a while, the terrain can look as if all the blood spilt there has started bubbling back up. The poorest people: everything in Mississippi is cheap. A shirt, a guitar, a meal, a bottle of beer, a packet of cigarettes, a motel room: they'll all cost you less than you'd have to pay just about anywhere else in the U.S. That's because people around here have proportionately less money than elsewhere in the U.S. The horses and mules have disappeared, replaced by tractors and BluesMobiles: battered cars with mismatched doors, eczema-scabbed with rust, kept running by faith and ingenuity alone. The shacks which appear so "picturesque" and "authentic" in old photos and on the covers of reissue blues albums look quite different up close on a wet afternoon in Vance. And the spectacle of ten members of one family—three generations ranging from squalling babe-in-arms to wheezing grandmother—crammed into a three-room trailer hoisted up on cinder blocks off to the side of a dirt road makes a complete and utter mockery of the American Dream. These people haven't failed: they've been betrayed.

John Lee Hooker is easily the most famous person ever to come out of Vance. Indeed, he's the *only* famous person—'nuff respect both to Snooky Pryor, a fine musician if not exactly a household name, and to Andrew "Sunnyland Slim" Luandrew, a founding father of Chicago blues piano—the poor burg ever produced. As such, the locals are keen to claim him as one of their own, even though their reminiscences—such as they are, having been filtered through half a century of local folklore—are vague to the point of utter insubstantiality. The church where Rev. Wil-

liam Hooker used to preach has long burned down. Some of those as yet
undesecrated graves near St. Mark's carry the names of members of the
families whom Hooker recalls as his childhood neighbors: Cage, Hard-
man and Johnson, plus one or two Pryors from Snooky's clan; but
"Hooker Hill," where John Lee's family was buried, has long since vanished into Mississippi limbo; dumped into the bayou during the late '60s.
If we could magically materialize John Lee Hooker at our sides, there's
nothing here, other than the imposing English-style mansion that dominates the virtually empty landscape, which he would recognize.

Slavery was replaced by Jim Crow, Jim Crow displaced in its turn by
a statutory equality which nowadays means little more than the right to
share an endemic poverty side by side. The old South has gone, taking
with it both the institutionalized racism of old, and the warm, yeasty sense
of family and community which enabled the descendants of kidnapped
Africans to withstand the depredations of a society explicitly constructed
not only to keep them under but to discourage them from ever looking
up. The new South which was supposed to replace it may have manifested
elsewhere in the region—in the proud metropolis of Atlanta, for example—but it never arrived in Mississippi. It wasn't until 1995 that the state
finally got around to passing the anti-slavery laws into the statute books.

"John Lee's from Mississippi," says Archie, in case anyone should
need reminding. "Most people that came from Mississippi want to forget
it . . . or escape. It's like a bad nightmare, and most of 'em want to try
and sleep it off, sleep it away."

"Leaving a place when you're fourteen [*sic*], it's pretty hard at my
age to say, 'It were right there,' " confesses Hooker. "Things change so.
Back then, the big white man had all the land, acres and acres and hundreds of acres and stuff like that. Now it's all cut up and sold, and all
them farmers ain't there no more. It's farming, but everybody got they
own thing. Everything is equal down there now. It is equal, so it's cut up,
the land is taken. If I went to Detroit now, I'd get so turned around with
all these buildings tore down . . . Mississippi probably worse, because
they done took all the land from all the big old rich people, and the
government took it and made everybody equal, cut it up and said, 'This
is yours, build on this.' The mules, they gone. They got tractors, they got
different things. It's so turned around down there. It's a different world.
All that's tore down. There's apartment buildings where them old houses
used to be. People done say, 'Mr. Hooker, you wouldn't know where
nothin' at, you went down there now.' I was down in Greenville, Missis-

sippi, and everything was so *different*. I played down there: Greenville, Dublin, Drew-Mississippi, Jackson . . . it's built up, and there ain't no big fields, no cotton belts down there. It's fields, but everybody got they own little patch, sharecroppers got they own land. So all them old houses are gone. Them old houses? Shoot, man, they *gone*. It's *history*."

Vance remains helplessly suspended between a painful past and a threatening future. If it was my hometown, I wouldn't want to go back there, either. Neither would you. Maybe this goes some way toward explaining why, whenever a movie about the Deep South—be it *Gone With The Wind*, *The Color Purple* or *Mississippi Burning*—shows up on television, John Lee Hooker reaches for the remote control, and switches channels.

3. The Real Folk Blues?

The Mississippi Delta is land both created and shaped by its
river. Ambiguous union of fluid and firm, the delta is a liquid
land where life responds to both tidal and freshwater urgings.
The processes of creation have been going on for a
long time here . . . there is about the delta something
original, primeval. We look to the delta for many of
the oldest continuing life forms . . .
—Barbara Cannon, from *Mississippi River:*
A Photographic Journey

[The blues is] the only thing after all these years that
still sounds fresh to me. The serious old blues guys
get it from somewhere else, it seems to me, and
that's what I want to know about.
—Eric Clapton, interviewed in the *Guardian*

I guess all songs is folk songs—I never heard
no horse sing 'em.
—Big Bill Broonzy, possibly apocryphal

In 1966, during a brief hiatus between lengthy stints with the Chicago
independent label Vee Jay Records and the New York-based major ABC,
John Lee Hooker allowed himself a brief dalliance with Chess Records,
to whom some of his Detroit sides had been leased a dozen or so years
earlier. The sole product of this union was one album: *The Real Folk
Blues*, a title loaded with ambiguities. For a start, Chess released it as a
companion volume to a series of albums by three stalwarts of its 1950s
electric-downhome roster: Howlin' Wolf, Muddy Waters and Sonny Boy
Williamson. However, the Williamson, Wolf and Waters *Real Folk Blues*
entries were all compilations of previously uncollected singles, whereas
Hooker's album was derived from sessions recorded specifically for album release. Moreover, the use of the *Real Folk Blues* title was little
more than a marketing device, since the music on the album consisted
entirely of the kind of rocking small-band electric blues which Hooker
had recorded between 1955 and 1964 for Vee Jay, Chess's principal Chicago rival, providing them with hits like "Dimples" and "Boom Boom"

during the late '50s and early '60s. The Waters, Wolf and Williamson collections had assembled 45s recorded for Chess's traditional core clientele—working-class Southern-born blacks, either relocated to the great metropolitan centers or still resident "down home"—and repackaged them for a newly developing audience: white teenagers whose interest in blues had been piqued by the success of The Rolling Stones and other long-haired, blues-based white acts. Some of these new-found customers perceived and experienced blues as a revered ancestor of rock and others as a subset of "folk music," but both factions were linked, above all else, by a shared craving for "authenticity," for a more profound set of human values and a higher degree of emotional truth than were available from either the white or black pop mainstreams of the time. And since this new audience was considerably more affluent than the blue-collar blacks who were the traditional supporters of the blues economy, what they wanted they got.

Their desire for authenticity was partially rooted in a rejection of the conformist social norms of the '50s. Spearheaded by the ubiquity of television, the explosive expansion of commodified mass culture had threatened the survival of unique ethnic and regional cultures and identities which youthful cultural dissidents deemed valuable and deserving of preservation. This resistance to the seeming homogenization and blanding-out of once-vital forms of popular expression often manifested itself as a fear of pop; or rather, a fear of the implications of a new form of linkage between pop's two central ideas: the people's voice and the people's choice. Broadly speaking, folkies attempted to preserve and protect the former against the remorseless incursions of the latter. They infinitely preferred the art which people made for themselves to the art which they chose to buy once someone else had created it. By the same token, their combination of nostalgic tastes and progressive politics represented no implicit contradiction; both were cut from the self-same cloth. Their notion of a "popular" idiom was one of and by the people; by contrast, the commodity culture defined it as that which was most obviously and demonstrably *for* the people: that is, the one chosen by the largest possible audience and voted for with the largest number of dollars. The two cultures had spectacularly collided in 1950, when The Weavers had scored a huge hit with a sentimental version of Leadbelly's "Goodnight Irene"; unfortunately, Leadbelly himself didn't live to enjoy either the success and the money, or the manifold ironies of their spectacularly belated arrival. However, since The Weavers' overtly leftist cultural and political stance was considered unacceptable in the Eisenhower '50s, their speedy exile to the blacklists left a vacuum deftly filled by the depoliticized, anodyne Kingston Trio. Their clean-cut collegiate version of the hootenanny defined the mass perception of "folk music" until the liberal but wholesome Peter, Paul & Mary enabled Bob Dylan to infiltrate the pop mainstream via the side entrance by peeling the husk and bark off Dylan songs like "Blowin' In The Wind" and "Don't Think Twice, It's All Right," rendering them AM-radio-friendly in a way that their composer never could. The next thing you knew, there was an entire sub-industry called "folk-rock." Purism never stood a chance.

"Folk-rock" of the white variety essentially consisted of two wings and a center. On its nominal left, there was an attachment to traditional instrumentation (acoustic guitar, particularly the exotic and resonant twelve-string beloved of Leadbelly and Blind Willie McTell, banjo and mandolin) and melodies as settings for radical new lyrics; on its new right, a blend of actual traditional and original neo-trad material performed with the instrumentation of the post-Beatles rock band. Byrds founder Jim (later Roger) McGuinn virtually invented that new center by flitting from one wing to the other. Armed with an impeccably traditional twelve-string acoustic guitar, he initially livened up his folk-club appearances by injecting Beatles songs into the standard hootenanny repertoire; later, he and his Byrds colleagues, including David Crosby, sweetened the new electric Dylan just as Peter, Paul & Mary had softened his earlier, acoustic incarnation. In other words, folk-rock was a juggling act involving new wine (post-Dylan singer-songwriterisms) in old bottles (trad instrumentation and melodies) and old wine (folkloric materials) in new bottles (electric guitars, drum kits, serious amplification). By contrast, The Rolling Stones—the matchmaking middlemen who made by far the most profound contributions to the *rapprochement* between electric blues and '60s rock—were themselves self-identified blues purists. As far as they were concerned, they weren't softening the music at all: they were playing it just as authentically and sincerely as they knew how to do. However, since they happened to be ugly-cute lower-middle-class English boys who sounded exactly like who they were despite their best efforts to the contrary, they ended up sweetening it anyway.

The Stones' eclectic repertoire included material borrowed from soul contemporaries like Otis Redding, Wilson Pickett and Marvin Gaye, which was displayed alongside their trademarked blues items gleaned from Slim Harpo, Jimmy Reed or Muddy Waters. However, even their more modern songs were performed in a style derived from their primary source: Chess records from the '50s, complete with harmonica and slide-guitar riffs assiduously learned from Muddy Waters' records; prominent maracas and judderingly reverbed rhythm guitar on loan (metaphorically, at least) from Bo Diddley; plus, of course, the Chuck Berry guitar licks that inspired Keith Richards to take the first steps on the path which ultimately led him to formulate one of the most idiosyncratic guitar stylings in all of rock. In this context, the application of the "folk" tag to Chicago blues provided an index of the extent to which perception of the music had shifted since its commercial heyday in the 1950s. To academics and purists who considered acoustic rural blues the only acceptably authentic form of the music, the likes of Waters, Wolf and Hooker were apostates selling a noisy, commercialized dilution of the pure milk (or maybe that should be "a watering-down of the pure whiskey") of the blues. The notion that "Chicago blues"—the rumbustious, clamorous soundtrack of the urban world of Delta migrants transplanted to the big cities—had cultural value equivalent to that of the downhome rural forms was an entirely new one, and not entirely unfree from controversy. In Britain, harmonicist Cyril Davies and guitarist Alexis Korner were sufficiently inspired by a live album cut by the Waters band at the 1960 Newport Folk Festival to form a band of their own which was, quite possibly, the first white electric blues band in the world. After one of their earliest attempts to perform in public resulted in their expulsion from a London jazz club for the heinous crime of bringing in amplifiers, Davies and Korner started their own club; and it was that club which gave the Stones their first real platform.

The standard dogma had stoutly maintained that the genuine folk artist remains, by definition, unaffected by the demands of either High Art or the vulgar mass market. The innate fallacy of this argument is that the majority of the pre-war rural bluesmen (and women) of the '20s and '30s had been hustling the vulgar market—or, indeed, any market they could find—virtually as soon as they had gained sufficient mastery over their instruments to be able to perform in public without being pelted with rotten fruit. Many got their start on street corners, singing what passers-by wanted to hear, be it blues, popular ballads, vaudeville songs, hillbilly songs or gospel. They were recorded not by idealistic philanthropists seeking to preserve and protect the People's Art, but by grasping small businessmen who knew that there was money to be made by issuing records of rural blues artists, and they wanted to release and sell as many records as possible while spending as little money as possible. In other words, they were in the pop business, and—as far as they were concerned—they were making pop records.

Nevertheless, these artists' music qualified as "folk" because it was rural in origin and archaic in form. It had also by this time long ceased to be pop, or even popular; long supplanted first by commercial, ensemble rhythm and blues, and subsequently by the gospel-inflected dance music and balladry which, by the mid-'60s, would be universally known as "soul." In its turn, the "electric downhome" sound of the Chicago bluesmen (and the equivalent music which Hooker had been making in Detroit, on the other side of Lake Michigan) also succumbed, a casualty of the evolution of the self-image of their ghetto constituents as they began to perceive themselves as city-dwellers rather than Delta migrants. Typically, John Lee Hooker's last appearance in the R&B singles charts was in 1962. Inevitably, he and his fellow titans of '50s city blues needed to develop a fresh, new audience in order to survive: they sought, and they did indeed find. The pivot point had been that very same 1960 Newport Folk Festival, when Muddy Waters, backed by his full Chicago Blues Band including James Cotton on harmonica and the great pianist Otis Spann, had headlined a blues afternoon co-starring Hooker himself. It simultaneously marked the music's formal acceptance by the (mainly white) jazz and folk establishments, and its passing as the indigenous voice of the ghetto. Orphaned, city blues was now up for adoption, first into the "folk" family and then into the community of what was about to become "rock."

The most crucial, as well as the most frequently overlooked, point about "folk music" is that the constituency whom it most truly represents doesn't consider it to be "folk music," but simply their music. "Folk music" is, invariably, a term applied from outside the cultures and communities to which it refers. In terms of theory, "folk" music—the traditional set of forms, styles and songs indigenous to a people, a culture or a locale—is radically distinguishable from "art" music, of both the classical and avant-garde varieties, and from "popular" music, mass-produced for and mass-marketed to a mass audience. In practice, it's getting harder and harder to tell them apart.[1] Before the advent of re-

---

1 One example—taken from the current pop charts as this section is written—is the rap hit "Come Baby Come" by K7. Its call-and-response chorus is virtually an unalloyed field holler (which qualifies it as "folk"); it's selling in the hundreds of thousands (which makes it "pop"); and its hi-tech mode of creation deploys techniques which, only a short while ago, were considered avant-garde (which, I guess, makes it art).

cording, these distinctions were not so much a critical device as a precise description of the class system: which is not surprising, since these are essentially European definitions, and reflect prevailing European social structures. European classical music operates according to a strict hierarchical structure, with the composer (the monarch, so to speak) at the top. The composer's wishes are interpreted and enforced by the conductor (the general) and carried out by the orchestra (the troops). During their lifetimes, the great composers often also functioned as the featured soloists, but after their deaths their music became fixed and formalized, those who succeeded them rarely inherited their license to improvise.

The classic model of "folk" is—as David Evans points out in his invaluable *Big Road Blues: Tradition & Creativity In The Folk Blues*[2]—the similarly formal tradition of the Anglo-American ballads, with their fixed musical structures and set narrative lines. To perform one of these ballads, a singer is by definition required to preserve intact both its storyline and its musical setting. The Anglo-American use of the term "folk" music implies that such music exists, simply and solely, to fulfil the needs of a particular community. They create it by and for themselves over a period of centuries as part of a single collective process, only slightly more personal to any given individual than the shaping of a rock by water. Through oral transmission, it filters down through the generations, serving both as a touchstone of the community's history and values, and as an index of how its communal life has changed. It is this latter attribute which many traditionalists find alarming or repugnant. For them, the key element is the preservation of a piece's pure and unsullied essence, and the imposition of an alien style onto a traditional piece is deemed an act of presumption verging on outright heresy: at the very least, it effectively amputates the piece from its native roots. For this precise reason, Bob Dylan was regarded with some suspicion by serious folkies long before he swapped his Martin acoustic for a Fender Stratocaster. Everything he sang, whatever its origin, was thoroughly Dylanized; by the same token, this was exactly why rockers loved him. If the term "post-modern" had existed when Dylan was starting out, it might well have been applied to him. Dylan came to folk music with attitudes formed by teenage experiences of pop (specifically, the rock and R&B of the '50s), a tradition which is overwhelmingly individualist. Pop is personality-driven; it's about stars, icons and the Great Man Theory, and, until "Good Old Rock

2 Da Capo Books, 1982.

And Roll" was nostalgically revisited in the late '60s, remained a defiantly forward-looking idiom which refused to admit that it had a tradition at all.

In the blues world, over on the African side of the African-American hyphen, the picture is far more complex. In Africa itself, songs, ballads and poems have traditionally served as vessels by which the community transmits its history and its values to its youth, but for those particular Africans who found themselves involuntarily transformed into Americans (of a sort), that history and those values had been forcibly stripped away. As a result, blues obeys a correspondingly different set of imperatives— one radically distinguishable from both its African and Anglo-Celtic ancestors—and simultaneously holds the following truths to be self-evident: yes, there is a strong and very clearly defined tradition, and yes, its practitioners are expected to improvise freely within it, re-creating it anew to meet the immediate needs of both performer and audience. There are set themes, and there are specified functions: dance songs, work songs, celebrations, laments, love songs, hate songs, and so forth. The tradition is unfixed; indeed, it demands to be freshly reinvented with each performance, re-created anew to reflect the changing needs and circumstances of its time and place. Blues artists both ancient and modern have worked from a "common stock" of folk materials: instrumental motifs and vocal tics, melodies, lyrical tags, chord progressions and even complete songs are derived directly from the tradition, and some of them, as we have already seen, long predate the era of recording, let alone the conventional mechanics of publishing and copyright law. What counts above all in the blues is individuality: the development of a unique and unmistakable voice, the ability to place an ineradicable personal stamp on those "common stock" materials freely available to all. While instrumental dexterity, vocal facility and stylistic versatility are heartily respected within the blues community, what distinguishes the truly great from the merely professional is the fully realized man (or woman)'s communicated essence of self; the ability to serve as a conduit for the full gamut of human emotion, to feel those emotions with sufficient depth and intensity to reach out and touch listeners in places that those listeners might not even have known that they had. Without exception, every blues singer who has managed to pull ahead of the pack or haul himself (or herself) from the hordes of hopefuls chasing the blues-lovers' dollar has this quality. Any competent blues artist should have the ability to entertain—those who don't should simply bacdafucup and find another line of work before they starve to death—but the measure of true mastery, from '20s pioneers like Blind Lemon Jefferson or Charley Patton to contemporary brand leaders like Robert Cray or Ben Harper—is the scale on which performers are capable of being themselves in public. And, by extension, the depth and complexity of that self. To serve as a neutral transmitter simply don't cut it here.

Naturally, real life is never quite as cut-and-dried as the above might suggest. The boundaries between these two traditions are of necessity blurred—with considerable movement of repertoire and instrumentation—and examples of each approach can be found in each camp. Nevertheless, they share this belief, both in theory and in practice: that "folk" music—like folk tales, folkways and folklore in general—is the collective property of a community. Everybody uses it, and nobody owns it: a musician can draw on the common stock and use the tools of that heritage to create and express, and those creations can then be added to the common stock, becoming freely available to a fresh generation. Songs and ideas traveled as and when people did; "oral transmission"—an oddly medical term more appropriate these days to viruses than art, unless one considers that art is a virus—was the only way that a song or an idiom could boldly go where none of its siblings had gone before. And since music exists to be played rather than read, a written lyric or notated piece of music is to a song as a recipe is to a meal: a series of instructions as to how a thing is prepared, rather than the thing itself. No two chefs will prepare a dish in exactly the same way even if they're working from the same recipe and using similar ingredients; and therefore no two performances of a written (or memorized) piece will be exactly the same. The definitive performances of the music of Mozart or Liszt would, in theory, have been those of Mozart or Liszt themselves, but since those gents were sufficiently inconsiderate to have lived, worked and died before the development of recording technology, we are denied their improvisations and must make do with their notes. This means that there are no definitive performances of Mozart or Liszt; only good ones and less good ones. It also means that you can't eat a recipe. A skilled chef can read a recipe, form an instant impression of how the meal described would taste, and apply his or her accumulated knowledge and experience to the task of creating a customized personal variation, but this is of only theoretical interest to someone who happens to be hungry.

Essentially, recording did to oral transmission what photography did to painting; in other words, relieved it of the burden of simple representation. It was no longer the painter's primary responsibility to produce a permanent visual account of what people and things looked like, but rather to provide some insight into what things meant and, simply, to create objects and images which were beautiful or intriguing in their own right. Similarly, recording meant that songs and pieces of music did not need to be written down—or even memorized—in order to be preserved for posterity. A recorded performance is, literally, recorded: short of the destruction of the master tape and all known copies, it will survive, exactly as it was originally performed, long beyond the lifespan of the musician(s) who played it. Another artist, approaching those same materials afresh, has no need to reproduce what went before except insofar as (s)he wishes to demonstrate the contrast between the basic themes and the fresh elements with which they are replenished and renewed. Nowhere is this principle better illustrated than in be-bop, where a standard melody—the "head"—is stated at the beginning of a piece as the springboard for the improvisations which follow. The standard melody and chord changes provide the bread, but the improvisation puts the meat into the sandwich: it's what everybody has actually come to hear. And when those improvisations are flowing thick and fast, it would take a fiendishly accelerated hand and ear to transcribe them in sufficient detail for another musician to be able to come along the following morning to sight-read and play them precisely as they were improvised. In a sense, this is what makes improvisation so special: it occurs in the here-and-now, to be imagined, played and heard as part of a single process; and once played, it's gone—unless, of course, someone recorded it.

Recording was the first of a series of linked phenomena which forever altered the folk process. Via recording, songs and styles could travel wherever the physical object—that is, the cylinder or disc—went, and radio removed even that limitation, permitting the music to transform itself into a phantom of the airwaves, solidified and realized by the presence of an appropriately tuned radio receiver. And, via copyright, what was once common intellectual property was effectively privatized. A classic example: during the early '60s, the British folk singer/guitarist Martin Carthy made the acquaintance of several visiting Americans, two of whom happened to be named Bob Dylan and Paul Simon. During club sessions and late-night jams, Carthy introduced his new friends to his arrangements of a number of Anglo-Celtic traditional pieces. Dylan set a lyric of his own, later recorded as "Bob Dylan's Dream," to the melody and guitar arrangement of "Lord Franklin," a technique literally as old as the folk process itself. Indeed, one of his most famous early songs,

"With God On Our Side," uses the same traditional Irish melody as Dominic Behan's "The Patriot Game;" and, while the combination of that melody with Dylan's lyric is copyrighted, the melody itself—one of several known as "The Fiddling Soldier," or "The Soldier And The Lady"—is still "out there." Simon, on the other hand, was particularly intrigued by a tune called "Scarborough Fair," which he and his partner Art Garfunkel subsequently recorded more or less intact. However, Simon and Garfunkel copyrighted the arrangement, which—after its use in Mike Nichols's enormously popular 1968 movie *The Graduate*—eventually went on to become a Muzak and AOR radio staple and to generate serious amounts of money. The issue of whether or not Simon's action appropriated Martin Carthy's creativity and violated his intellectual property is one best left to m'learned friends in the legal profession (or rather, to those who can afford to hire their services), but the end result was the removal of an ancient song from the public domain and its transformation into a copyrighted item for the use of which Simon & Garfunkel must receive payment. There was indeed a financial settlement—the details of which remain relevant only to the participants—but Carthy was more upset by this heisting of what he had considered to be a communally-owned cultural asset than by any possible financial loss to himself.

To reverse the argument, the copyrighting of a traditional blues piece has often proved to be the salvation of blues singers who have fallen victim to creative accounting, or—as was often the case with the storefront independent labels who pioneered blues recording—no accounting at all. Big Joe Williams almost certainly wasn't the author of that beloved old chestnut "Baby Please Don't Go"—a Delta staple memorably recorded by Muddy Waters as well as by John Lee Hooker—but the royalties generated by the Waters and Hooker versions (not to mention subsequent covers of the song by assorted blues-rock bands, most prominently the young Van Morrison's Belfast rude-boy posse Them) provided Williams with some form of compensation for all the songs which he undoubtedly did write, but for which he was never paid. Skip James's funeral expenses were met by the royalties generated by Cream's cover of his "I'm So Glad"; a version which, incidentally, James despised. Still, it says something for Cream's integrity that they credited him at all (especially considering that they had rearranged the song so drastically that they could probably have gotten away with claiming it as an entirely new composition), let alone made sure that the money reached him. In the blues world, the person who copyrighted a song might not necessarily be the person who wrote it, and—by the same token—the person in whose name a song was copyrighted wasn't necessarily the one who collected the money. Case in point: Willie Dixon, who found that, while the library of classic songs he composed for Muddy Waters, Howlin' Wolf and other Chess stars was indeed copyrighted in his name, extracting the resulting moolah from Arc Music, Chess's music-publishing subsidiary, was another matter entirely.

The conventional notion of song copyright resides in a song's lyrics, melody and chord changes: register those, and the piece is yours. If someone cops your song—in other words, borrows your melody or lyrics-you can, given sufficient funding to hire heavy-duty lawyers, take them to court and hose them down, big time. (Just ask George Harrison about the "My Sweet Lord" court case, but be prepared to duck.) You can't copyright a rhythm or a bass line, let alone a "groove;" if you could, Bo Diddley would be a seriously wealthy man and James Brown would be infinitely richer than he already is. You can, of course, copyright a recorded performance, and if someone samples a snatch of one of Mr. Brown's records and recycles it without authorization or payment, they'll soon be hearing from legal eagles representing Mr. Brown and/or Polydor Records. "I know they say that they're only taking a little bit of the record," says Brown of the sampler-happy hip-hoppers who've squeezed so much juice from his inimitable grooves, "[but] how would you like it if I cut the buttons off *your* suit?" But if somebody wants to assemble a bunch of musicians to play your beat themselves, they've got it; and if this wasn't the case, then most of the history of the blues would consist of lawsuits rather than records. Imagine if someone had successfully copyrighted the twelve-bar blues structure, or the shuffle beat, or the "Dust My Broom" slide-guitar motif (from Elmore James out of Robert Johnson, Son House, Charley Patton and beyond), or even the line "Woke up this mornin'." Then imagine how many bluesmen would have been able to function freely under the resulting restrictions.

So let's take stock. On the one hand we have a tradition based on a relatively free-flowing interaction of musical ideas and motifs; on the other a copyright system which tends to reward the cunning and well connected as well as (in some cases, read "rather than") the creative and imaginative. In its own post-hi-tech way, the sampling technology which drives rap and dance music would seem to be a way of reviving that free-flowing oral tradition (by "quoting" existing works with all the digital fidelity of a 44,100-Mhz [slices-per-second] sampling rate), but said oral tradition developed in a time when there weren't millions of dollars' worth of royalties at stake. There are powerful arguments on both sides: on the "oral" wing, we have the flow of ideas, the collective development of fresh variations of time-honored traditions, the entire notion of folk and community culture. On the other side of the fence, we have the basic fiscal facts of the entertainment industry, the concept of inviolable intellectual property, and the impregnable right of the individual to receive and, wherever possible, enjoy the rewards of his or her creative labors. And in between, we have an artist like John Lee Hooker, whose work is uncompromisingly based in a deep and rich tradition and which draws freely on the resources of that tradition, but whose indisputable individuality rests on the uniqueness of his relationship with that tradition. The central issues that his *œuvre* raises are these: how an artist can simultaneously be an utterly unique creative personage whose achievement, identity and agenda are totally and completely personal, while remaining inextricably linked, in the deepest roots of his creative being, to the cultural tradition of the community in which he was raised; and how that artist, born in 1917 and first recorded at the tail end of the '40s, could achieve spectacular sales with music which seemed "older" than the earliest country blues records, cut almost a quarter of a century before. The solution to such seeming paradoxes lies in the nature of the relationship between an individual and a tradition; and the innate flexibility of a tradition that not only permits, but specifically demands, that each individual who works within it should make it completely his or her own.

When John Lee Hooker says that he was "born with the blues," he speaks naught but the literal truth: for all practical purposes, he and his chosen art-form are exact contemporaries. Hooker is not *actually* as old as the blues—no living performer could be—but he is almost exactly the same age as *recorded* blues. It's a shame that we have to abandon the 1920 birthdate, because it implies a lovely symmetry; it would have meant that he was born the year that the first blues record—"Crazy Love," a vaguely bluesy urban ballad sung by the otherwise unremarkable Mamie Smith—was released; a mere three years before the first rural blues records were made (by the little-known Sylvester Weaver), and an even less significant five before the Texan street-singer Blind Lemon Jefferson became the music's first superstar. Hooker's childhood and early adolescence coincided with the first great boom in blues recording: in strict chronological terms, this places him squarely in the center of the generation of musicians who dominated the first wave of postwar blues. Again, that 1920 birthdate would have made him five years younger than Muddy Waters or Willie Dixon and five years older than B. B. King; ten years younger than T-Bone Walker and Howlin' Wolf and ten years older than Otis Spann and Bobby Bland; twenty or more years younger than Leadbelly or Blind Jefferson or Alex "Rice" Miller, the man best known as the second Sonny Boy Williamson . . . but here the analogy begins to break down, because the generation of bluesmen born between the mid-'30s and the mid-'40s is the one which begins with Buddy Guy and Junior Wells and takes in the likes of Jimi Hendrix, Eric Clapton and The Rolling Stones. Let's leave it with this: had he *really* been born in 1920, Hooker would have been thirty-five years younger than Leadbelly, and thirty-five years older than Stevie Ray Vaughan.

As Hooker himself would put it, "At that time there wasn't no songwriters, there wasn't no publishers, nothin'. They just made songs up in the cotton fields and stuff like this." Needless to say, there wasn't no recording studios, neither, so information about what the blues sounded like before it was first recorded is, by definition, anecdotal. We know who first copyrighted the basic blues themes, but that doesn't tell us an awful lot about who might have originally created them. Staples like "Catfish Blues," "Crawlin' King Snake," "Walkin' Blues" or "Rollin' And Tumblin'" certainly long predate their earliest recorded manifestations, and each exists in numerous variations, none of which could with any certainty be described as "earlier" or "more authentic" than the others. Virtually every Delta singer had his (only very rarely "her") distinctive personal version of the standard fistful of guitar or piano riffs and lyrical motifs. Generally, blues tyros learned from an older singer in their neighborhood, who may well have learned it either from one of the many itinerant bluesmen who would pass through the saloons, levee camps or plantations, or from a city-based performer taking a swing through the South with a tent show.

Hooker's earliest musical experiences came through the oral tradition: from direct contact with Tony Hollins, who taught him his first chords and songs, and from Will Moore, who gave him the boogie. Hollins was a professional bluesman, though not a particularly successful one, who traveled the highways and by-ways of the South and eventually wound up in Chicago; Will Moore was a popular and respected player among his local community, but was never recorded. Hollins's only direct legacy is a fistful of songs cut in Chicago between 1941 and 1951 which, at the time of writing, mostly remain unreissued—including some which, like

"Crawlin' King Snake" and "Crosscut Saw," became "standards" only through other artists' recorded versions. Moore, as previously noted, never recorded at all. Hooker was their only direct inheritor. He eagerly imbibed songs and ideas from whatever early blues recordings came his way, but his most profoundly formative influences came from direct, face-to-face encounters with musicians who had themselves learned their stuff the hard way, the old way, the traditional way: from their elders, the elders who were themselves the first generation of bluesmen.

They were his folk. According to the online thesaurus thoughtfully provided by Microsoft as part of my word-processing software, "folk" is not only synonymous with "clan," "kith" and "family," but also with "house," "kindred," "lineage" and "race." The *Concise Oxford Dictionary* goes a little further: its primary definition of "folk" cites "a people" and "a nation."

> The music [blues] is not indigenous to a time or place, it's indigenous to the people.
> —Taj Mahal, quoted in Tom Nolan's liner note to Taj's first album, 1968

> That stuff [the blues] transcends music and gets into realms of language. It goes beyond good taste into religion.
> —Frank Zappa, interviewed in *Musician*

> Maybe our forefathers couldn't keep their language together when they were taken away, but this—the blues—was a language we invented to let people know that we had something to say. And we've been saying it pretty strongly ever since.
> —B. B. King speaking at Lagos University, 1973; quoted in Valerie Wilmer's *Mama Said There'd Be Days Like This*

Listen to the blues, and it will tell you its own story. It will tell you who it is, what it is, and how it came to be: who made it, and why. The details of the precise circumstances of how this music came to exist are present in its every nuance, just as DNA, the basic source code of life itself, is present in each and every molecule of each and every organic entity.

It is the story of millions of people—men, women and children—who are forcibly abducted from their native lands. As an integral part of this process, they are separated not only from their families and friends, but from anybody else who speaks the particular language of their tribe and region. They are crammed like cargo into rotting, leaky ships headed for a variety of destinations; chained in the dark for weeks, fed on scraps, sluiced with unclean water, left to wallow in their own excrement. Invariably, over half of the captives imprisoned in each vessel die of disease, malnutrition and maltreatment during each long journey to their new homes. Many of them are forced to lie chained to the decaying dead for days on end. Periodically the sick, the dead and the dying are simply pitched overboard to take their chances with the sharks. Once docked in the particular one of these new "homes" with which we are specifically concerned here, they are not only sold into servitude, but subjected to a process designed to strip them systematically of everything they own and everything they are, leaving them with nothing other than their capacity for physical labor and their ability to reproduce. Denied the use of their own languages, they are taught only enough of their captors' language to enable them to comprehend and obey simple commands. As with their languages, their own spiritual beliefs are withheld from them. They are taught only as much of their captors' religion as is judged necessary to convince them to accept their new status: somewhere just below the lowest rung of humanity.

Their new masters are often, in their own terms, highly religious and deeply spiritual men. As such, they will encounter severely distressing ethical and moral dilemmas if they enslave those whom they consider to be their fellow humans and spiritual equals. On the other hand, in order to found the new society—indeed, the New World—which they believe is theirs by divine right and manifest destiny, they desperately need the labor which slavery will provide. So, in order to salve their consciences, they justify this "peculiar institution" with a cunning and sophisticated variety of arguments. Since there are minor physiological differences between captors and slaves—the enslaved peoples have darker skin, more crisply textured hair, thicker lips and broader noses—it is suggested that they are not actually human beings, but some sort of humanoid animal, or great ape, entitled to no better treatment than any other beast of the field or jungle. Others regard this view as overly cynical. They prefer to believe that these unfortunate creatures are indeed humans; albeit of some degenerate variety, so dreadfully backward and savage that enslavement-of their minds as well as their bodies—provides the best possible way to wean them from their primitive ways, and lead them by the hand into the civilized world. To achieve this laudable end requires nothing less than the enforced induction of a kind of collective amnesia. They are Adam and Eve reborn, the juices of the forbidden fruit still dripping from their chops. Its seductive flavor must be cleansed from their palates; its tainted knowledge erased from their minds. The masters have a similar attitude to the native peoples of the land which they have colonized; the majority of these are exterminated, the remainder herded onto reservations often far from their home territories, and their lands confiscated to serve the needs of those better qualified to inhabit and cultivate them.

Naturally, the slaves pay a price for the unsolicited gift of the civilizing process. They are denied their languages, and the right to language; denied their beliefs, and the right to those beliefs; denied family, and the right to family; denied culture, and the right to culture; denied their history, and the right to that history; denied expression, and the right to expression; denied mobility, and the right to mobility; denied pride in themselves or their traditions, and the right to that pride. To their bodies they do indeed retain limited rights, available to them whenever exercise of those rights does not conflict with the needs of their masters. They are encouraged to reproduce, but not to form permanent attachments to mates or children, since one or more family members might, at any time, be sold or traded away. They are taught that their physical differences are proof that they are intrinsically evil, as is their belief that the power that drives the universe is manifested among many different gods and spirits. Their own ancestral deities, they are repeatedly told, are in fact demons in the service of the Great Adversary and fit only to be destroyed by the One True God: that of the masters. Furthermore, they learn that this single (albeit tripartite) Supreme Being, despite His love for them, is punishing them for their unbelief in Him, and that He will continue to do so until they have earned His approval by passively accepting and enduring their fate. They are taught that their masters are good and that they are evil; that their masters are intelligent and that they are stupid ; that their masters are beautiful and that they are ugly. Most crucially, they learn that their masters have won, and that they have lost.

The slaves survive as captive peoples always survive under circumstances where escape is virtually impossible, and where the only possible consequence of insurrection would inevitably be to provoke the extinction which only compliance, or the illusion of compliance, can keep at bay. Their first act of survival is the creation of a space within which they can share some small degree of intellectual and emotional privacy. Within this space, they develop methods of using any and every resource at their command to make some sense of their condition; and of preserving their humanity against what eventually turns out to be centuries of captivity or near captivity. In other words, they set out—each separate grouping in their own way, in isolation or near-isolation from their peers both near and far, working with whatever they have—to transform a group of victims snatched at random from a variety of peoples, each with its own language and customs, into a People; one People with a common means of expression, a common awareness of their condition, and a set of common goals.

The first tool which comes to hand is the masters' language. This is rapidly reinvented and modified into something entirely new, spoken and understood by the People but rendered impenetrable to the masters. From the captors' tongue evolves a new one, deceptively similar to the old, but one in which the meanings of each word, each phrase, each sentence are radically affected by microtonal shifts of pitch and infinitely subtle shades of intonation. The new language is restricted in vocabulary, by comparison with its predecessor, but it is infinitely richer in nuance. First and foremost, it is a secret, private language that has emerged: words from the People's various native languages—handed down, despite their formally proscribed nature, from generation to generation—are incorporated into the new *lingua franca*. Their work songs and "field hollers" become means of conversing freely even in the presence of an overseer; the songs of the masters are subversively transformed to serve as the basis for new songs lampooning the masters, commenting on recent events, bemoaning their fate, and praising the new heroes: the rebels and runaways who defy the masters. Those whom the masters call "bad" are the most thoroughly respected and the most fulsomely praised; in the new language, "bad" becomes the highest accolade there is. Every member of the People grows up effectively bilingual, speaking one language in the inner world, another in the outer: the single language which they were forced to share, both with each other and with the master race, becomes two. With each language comes a face: the face they show to their masters, and the face they wear among themselves.

The masters' musical instruments, especially, are approached in new ways; they begin to make sounds never intended by their manufacturers, sounds reminiscent of the by-now near-mythical homeland whence the slaves had been wrenched all those years before. The part of the process incorporating elements of music and dance is an integral one, since the

People came from cultures where music and dance were an integral aspect of everyday community life, and literally everybody sang, danced and played some sort of instrument. (Their musical traditions involved plucked stringed instruments, wind instruments and percussion; the latter pair also serving as means of communication. The People are therefore forbidden access to the drum and the fife in case they are used to send wordless, but articulately phrased and pitched, messages which contain or transmit any whiff of sedition.) To the more devout among the masters, to whom all dance is anathema and for whom music is only acceptable if it is religious in nature, this is in itself evidence of innate primitivism, and all the more reason to replace their indigenous music with the hymns and ballads which the masters, and their ancestors before them, have brought from their own homelands.

The second tool is the masters' religion, which was supposed to justify their oppression. One particular text of this religion yields up a central metaphor which becomes the linchpin of a powerful liberation theology: the tale of a captive People held in slavery in a foreign land until, eventually, they win their freedom and triumphantly return home. Almost as crucial as its content is the manner in which this religion is adapted to the spiritual needs of the captives: where the masters' worship is staid and complacent, in the hands of the captives the same worship becomes visceral, becomes transcendental, becomes a rite of transformation, of possession, of joyous surrender to the spirit of the divine.

Time passes: the slave trade is finally banned, by which time the number of slaves has vastly increased. Because new arrivals are no longer forthcoming, the masters feel obliged to treat their existing slaves marginally better; since there is no longer a theoretically infinite supply of them; they now represent an asset which must be conserved rather than wasted. For the first time, the skills and knowledge of a slave are perceived as assets comparable in value to his or her strength and fertility. As a consequence, the masters find newer uses for their slaves. Some receive a broader education than their peers and become household servants, or even skilled personal assistants. Some of the enslaved women become sexual playthings for the male masters; their offspring never acknowledged as members of the owning families, but nevertheless highly prized as more valuable slaves. A convention arises that the visible evidence of even one slave ancestor among eight could outweigh any amount of the masters' genetic inheritance in identifying someone as a slave. The proudest of the People take this to mean that their bloodline is measurably and demonstrably more potent than that of their masters; the most thoroughly intimidated take it as a sign that the shame of their origins is utterly ineradicable.

Toward the end of their second century of captivity, there is a war among the masters. Though the freeing of the slaves is not the specific objective of the side who eventually prove victorious, it is nevertheless part of their agenda, if only as a means of weakening the losers' economic base. As such, it is successful. Unfortunately, what the People actually receive is a nominal liberation only; a legalistic simulacrum of freedom which reproduces slavery in all but name. It keeps the bulk of the People in economic bondage to the former owners, hems in the better-educated and more ambitious by blocking their progress with a comprehensive net of laws and codes, and denies them the legal and civil rights granted to any citizen who looks as though his or her genetic inheritance from the stock of the masters is untainted by any visible ancestors from among the People. The People's exclusion from the public life of the nation continues to be justified on the grounds that they are intrinsically inferior beings who are nonetheless extremely dangerous. Those who had been forced to breed as if they were stud cattle are, as a consequence, considered overly sexual; those who have faithfully and lovingly nursed their masters' children are deemed profligate and cruel; those who had been routinely subjected to corporal punishment nigh unto the point of death for the slightest infraction of an unfulfillable code are deemed uncontrollably violent. And what remains unarguably true is that their skin is still a different color. For the fruits of their liberation, they have genuine freedom of movement and association in very few places indeed. They are not entitled to vote, and any attempt to apply for the right to do so is, informally but invariably, cause for spontaneous corporal punishment. Their word can be freely contradicted in a court of law by any member of the master race. They may be physically attacked with impunity. They are subject to the full penalties of the law, whether or not they have committed an actual offense, but not entitled to its protection against a member of the master race.

There is more. They are forbidden to travel in the same rail carriages and streetcars as descendants of the former masters, to eat in the same restaurants, to drink from the same fountains, and relieve themselves in the same toilets. Even when they gain the right to serve in the armed forces, they may not serve in the same units. They receive rare and minimal promotion, and are discouraged from learning to operate more complex equipment, generally on the grounds that their intelligence is unequal to the complexity of such tasks. They are given the most menial tasks away from the battlefield and the most dangerous duties upon it. They are required to fight and die in the nation's wars, ostensibly to protect the basic principles of freedom and democracy at home and abroad, but they see precious little of either in the nation which is nominally theirs. In their nation's cities (with very rare exceptions), even those few who could afford to do so are barred from living in the same areas as the master race. In the areas designated for them, they are charged higher rents for worse accommodation. Even when they are permitted access to the same jobs as members of the master race, they receive lower wages and infrequent promotion. It is considered just about permissible for a male of the master race to have sexual relations with a female of the People, provided that he pays for the privilege in cash and does nothing so foolish or self-incriminating as to form any kind of emotional attachment to her. Sexual relationships between males of the People and females of the master race are unacceptable under any circumstances. Even the unsupported allegation that a male of the People has made a sexual approach to a female of the master race is a capital offense: formally in some parts of the country, informally in those regions which are considered to be more enlightened. In this context, eye contact, however brief, is considered adequate evidence of a sexual approach. Any attempt by any former slave, or descendant thereof, to advance his or her circumstances is mocked or blocked. Any expression of anger, discontent or dissatisfaction with their lot is blamed on the activities of "outside agitators"; the descendants of the slaves are deemed insufficiently sensitive or intelligent to realize when they are being ill-treated without some form of external prompting.

Nevertheless, many succeed even against such concerted opposition. Former slaves and the children of former slaves enter the arts and the professions. They migrate from the rural regions, the scene of their centuries-long humiliation, to the bigger cities where discrimination needs to be enforced by law rather than simply occurring as custom. They are mocked and caricatured in the masters' theaters, in which they are not permitted to perform, and the masters' newspapers, for which they are never employed to write; they thus have no means of redress and no forum in which to state the case for their defense. Against all the odds, authors and poets, musicians and athletes, philosophers and scientists, dentists and accountants, soldiers and entrepreneurs, activists and leaders all begin to emerge. And all of the People have learned, with their mothers' milk, how to survive in two worlds. One is the world of the master race, which controls the laws and the money; the homes and the jobs; the frames of reference and the rules of the game. The other is their own world, which they themselves have created, and re-create daily, from scraps: the scraps which they managed to retain from their original, faraway homelands, and the scraps tossed them by the master race. The world of the former owners is the one in which they are compelled to exist; their own world is the one in which they actually *live*. They apply their creative skills, the only bequest from their ancestors which they have ever been allowed to keep, to the task of reinvention. Stripped of their traditional resources, they generate new ones; force-fed another's culture, they transform it to meet their own needs. Barred from the institutions of the master race, they institute their own. And from the materials and implements of the master race's music, they create their own. In one place—a comparatively sophisticated and cosmopolitan urban center— the discarded military-band instruments of one of the now-departed minor occupying powers stimulates the creation of one kind of new music. In another area—harsher, more rural and vastly less tolerant—something else emerges.

Somewhere around the beginning of the twentieth century, what we now call the blues began to be heard in the Southern part of mainland America. It was a scion of a whole extended family of musics: the field holler and the ballad, the hymn and the rag, the vaudeville showpiece and the work song and the chain-gang shanty. In the blues, we hear the raw materials of the master race's music filtered through the tonalities, textures, rhythms, intonations and agenda which centuries of brainwashing and intimidation had failed to eradicate from the collective consciousness of a People inadvertently brought into being by abduction and slavery. It was sung on back porches and in taverns, in work camps and in urban theaters, in tents and jails. It was played on whatever instruments were available: here on pianos and trumpets, there on drums and mandolins, elsewhere on fiddles and saxophones and, in the South, most of all on the guitar, an instrument which—in a singular and felicitous example of cultural synchronicity—was ready for the blues around the time that the blues was ready for the guitar. Slowly evolving from a series of families of stringed instruments, the guitar had eventually divorced itself from the mandolin family by abandoning the notion of a variable number of "courses" (sets of paired strings) in favor of six single strings, tuned (from low strings to high) E-A-D-G-B-E. This instrument emerged in France and Italy during the last years of the eighteenth century, but revealed its full potential most dramatically in Spain, where gifted luthiers refined and strengthened its structure and, through the medium of flamenco, gypsy musicians began to explore its expressive range.

By contrast, its earliest years in America recalled the courtly tradition of the instruments which were the guitar's immediate predecessors, rather than the flamboyant *duende* of the flamenco guitarists. The typical American guitar of the nineteenth century was a small-bodied, short-necked, gut-stringed instrument: fragile of construction, low in volume, easy on the fingers and essentially delicate in nature. It was therefore considered to be a ladies' instrument, ideally suited for boudoir and parlor; a very different beast from the "special rider," an itinerant Southern bluesman's powerful, resilient traveling companion. The transformation of the genteel "parlour guitar" into something that could travel unscathed in a boxcar and still holler like a bird the next night came at the hands of a couple of innovators and a host of popularizers. In the early 1890s, Orville Gibson applied principles derived from violin-building—principally a carved, arched top and specially tooled steel strings—to his guitars; by 1900, the C. F. Martin company (founded in the 1830s by C. F. Martin himself, a recent immigrant from Germany) had combined Gibson's steel strings with the reinforced necks and bodies which they had been developing for their gut-string models since the 1830s. The result was a flat-top guitar sturdy enough to take steel strings: a template for the majority of acoustic guitars constructed since. Other major luthiers followed, and so did a host of mass-production houses who flooded the nation with cheap but highly serviceable guitars. Thousands of customers who weren't fortunate enough to live in a town which could support its own music store ordered guitars made by Stella and Harmony from the mail-order catalogues of Sears Roebuck and Montgomery Ward: in 1908, you could pay anything between $1.89 and $28.15, and have yourself an instrument. To be precise, a new instrument: fundamentally related to an older one, but essentially an instrument which had never before existed; exactly what was required in order to conjure into existence a music which had never before existed.

Were it at all possible to rob a human being of absolutely everything that makes someone human, to transform a human being into nothing more than a dumb beast of burden, the aforementioned treatment would have done it. What the blues tells us is that humanity is indestructible. When everything that can possibly be taken away is indeed taken away, the blues is what's left: the raw, irreducible core of the human soul.

The first known account of the music we now call Delta blues is a description, by the pianist, composer and entrepreneur W. C. Handy, of a guitarist whom he encountered while waiting for a train in a Mississippi railroad station in 1903. It has been frequently quoted, and quite rightfully so: it is perhaps the first truly significant American cultural signpost of the new century, so—with your indulgence—here it is again.

> *A lean, loose-jointed Negro had commenced plunking a guitar beside me while I slept. His clothes were rags, his feet peeped out of his shoes. His face had on it some of the sadness of the ages. As he played, he pressed a knife on the strings of the guitar in a manner popularized by Hawaiian guitarists who used steel bars. The effect was unforgettable. His song too, struck me instantly. "Goin' to where the Southern cross the Dog." The singer repeated the line three times, accompanying himself on the guitar with the weirdest music I had ever heard.*

Virtually everything Handy tells us has a specific significance. First of all, he notes the guitarist's obvious signs of destitution. The traveling bluesman was the poet and entertainer of an underclass within the underclass. Delta people were considered hicks and peasants by the more educated and sophisticated blacks who had established themselves in the cities; and within those rural communities the bluesman was, in turn, frowned upon by the upwardly mobile. Specifically, he was hated and despised by the black churches, who believed his trade to be the Devil's music, a living reminder of all that evil African stuff they were supposed to have left behind as part of their painful induction into the social mainstream. With his work-shy ways, his never-ending perambulations, his bawdy, earthy songs and his fatal attraction to normally respectable women, he was an outlaw, a virtual pariah. Even when a bluesman was popular and successful, with a smart suit on his back, rings on his fingers and a fistful of money to buy a round of drinks, rather than poverty-stricken and ragged like Handy's avatar, he was still a virtual outlaw among the devout and respectable. Maybe our faceless, nameless vagrant was a professional musician down on his luck, waiting for transport to somewhere offering richer pickings to an itinerant entertainer; or maybe he was just a working man on his way to where the work was—to a levee camp, a construction project, or simply day labor on a plantation or farm—whiling away the time with a meditation on his circumstances.

Then Handy describes the guitarist playing slide, fretting his instrument with a knife. Since he cites the "Hawaiian guitarists who used steel bars," we can presume that in this particular case the guitar was played flat on the lap, rather than in the conventional guitarists' position used by those who played with a glass bottleneck, or a short length of metal tube, on one left-hand finger. Nevertheless, while the technique of slide or bottleneck guitar may owe something to the touring Hawaiian ensembles so popular in the late 1880s and '90s, the substance and content was an unmistakable African retention. One traditional practice which predated the cheap mass-produced mail-order guitar—and in fact survived well into the mid-twentieth century among those for whom even an instrument costing a buck eighty-nine was an inaccessible extravagance—was the trick of nailing a length of wire to a barn wall and using a piece of glass or metal to change the pitch. Known as a "diddley-bow," such contrivances provided a first experience of plucked-string instruments for many a wannabe guitarist, including the young John Lee Hooker and B. B. King. Under the influence of the slide or the hand-bent string, the rigid, tempered European scale melted to reveal all the hidden places between the notes: the precise, chiming instrument giving forth a liquid African cry.

If we were doing this as a TV movie, or if we had any other motive to milk this event for spuriously augmented dramatic irony, we could cheat by replacing that nameless guitarist by someone with mythic resonance of his own: Charley Patton, The Father Of Delta Blues his own self, for instance; or a still more enigmatic figure, like the mysterious, unrecorded Henry Sloan, the bard of Dockery's Plantation, from whom Patton had learned; or even the sinister Ike Zinneman, who taught Robert Johnson and who, according to Robert Palmer, claimed to have learned to play the blues by visiting graveyards at midnight. If we wanted to be *really* portentous in a Movie-Of-The-Week sort of way, we could go the whole hog and speculate that it might have been Hooker's stepfather, Will Moore himself.

Or maybe it was just some ordinary guy who happened to play a bit of guitar, some working stiff eking out his survival on the road, someone completely unknown outside of his own community, one forgotten drifter among many. Whoever he was, whatever he happened to be doing in that particular station on that particular night, wherever he was going, whatever his story had been, whatever fate finally overtook him along those highways and railroads on those dark spectral Mississippi nights, he stumbled into history that night and never knew it. What Handy heard him playing, right there in the station, was undoubtedly among the first Delta blues, a music that anyone who traveled extensively through the black Delta would end up hearing sooner or later. This was the earliest stirring of one of the most profoundly influential movements in all of the popular culture of the twentieth century, but at that time the sound was still sufficiently localized for Handy to find it strange and unfamiliar. And if this music sounded weird to W. C. Handy, an urban black man and an experienced, gifted professional musician, just imagine what the average turn-of-the-century white person would have made of it.

Handy's observation that the singer repeated his one line—*"Goin' to where the Southern cross the Dog"*—three times without variation, slides yet another piece of the jigsaw into place. The "classic" three-line blues-verse template, the norm from the mid-'20s to the present day, has an A-A-B structure: statement, restatement, and rhymed response. The verse quoted here, which simply goes A-A-A, exemplifies a contemporary form which coexisted with the A-A-B pattern as the music was teething; but by the mid-'20s, when the first rural blues records were made, it was already an archaism which grew progressively rarer with each passing year. The content of the line was a specific local reference to the intersection between two railroad lines: the Southern, and the Yazoo and Mississippi Valley (the latter popularly known as "the Yellow Dog") which met at Moorehead, in Sunflower County. Maybe our man was headed in that direction to work, maybe to play music, maybe to visit family, maybe to see a woman, maybe just to be on the move. Or possibly he was simply whiling away the time, thinking back to some other time that he'd traveled there, reminiscing to himself about what he'd found or possibly about what had found him.

Crucially, Handy locates this encounter in Tutwiler, just over the Coahoma county line, in the north-eastern corner of Tallahatchee County. Tutwiler is where Highway 49, ten or so miles southwest of Clarksdale, intersects with Highway 3. It's roughly five miles southeast of Vance.

Let me propose a working definition of the term "folk artist." Though it applies equally to artists working in any medium you care to name, I'm primarily concerned with the "folk singer": one who draws upon the traditional arts of their community, and uses their mastery of those arts in order to tell the story of their "clan," "kith" and "family;" their "house," "kindred," "lineage" and their "race"; ultimately, the tale of their "people," and their "nation." In contrast, the bluesman's vision is, almost by definition, personal. His value to his community—and to the world—is directly contained in his ability to reflect, in a manner uniquely and distinctively and unmistakably his own, his life in particular and, through that personal story, the life of the community in general. The bluesman makes himself the focus of his work; by placing himself at the center of his art, he is taking possession of his life. He is asserting his right to interpret his own existence, to create his own definition of his own identity; first in his own eyes, then in the eyes of his community, in those of the world at large and, finally, in the eyes of God.

And whether that life is easy or hard, happy or sad, comic or tragic, what the bluesman tells us is, first and foremost, that his life is *his*, and that his self is intact. If the folk singer tells us "this is how we lived," and the bluesman's message is "this is how it is for me," then what could John Lee Hooker's music possibly be, other than "the real folk blues"?

4. Frisco Blues

"Whuh-whuh-whuh-where the car at?"

Anybody who tells you an anecdote about John Lee Hooker as a young man—and Buddy Guy is the current champ, by a very short head indeed, of the Hooker Impressionists' League—will inevitably end up mimicking his characteristic stutter. Bernard Besman, who recorded Hooker's early hits in Detroit during the late '40s and early '50s, claims to this day that his primary reason for deciding to record the young bluesman in the first place was that he was intrigued by the notion of a man who stuttered when he spoke, but not when he sang. In a puckish spirit of self-parody, Hooker himself employs an exaggerated version of it when telling stories against himself. In 1953, recording a bunch of tunes in Cincinnati for producer/entrepreneur Henry Stone, he improvised "Stuttering Blues," a classic monologue on that very subject wherein he appears, against the background of one of his primal riffs, in the role of a stammering seducer making a determined play for a hot babe even though his passion renders him so shivery that he can barely speak. "*Oh, when I fuh-fuh-first saw you,*" he murmurs, "*you almost nuh-nuh-knocked me off my feet. I couldn't hah-hah-hardly play, I was lookin' at you.*" Mock-artlessly, he piles up the compliments, pretends that he's trying to conceal the effect that she's having on him, slips a request for her address and phone number (*"s-s-s-so I can c-c-c-c-c-caw-caw-call you up"*) into the conversation so casually that she's giving up the info before she even realizes he'd asked. And then comes the pay-off. "Ah, excuse me baby . . . *I can't g-g-g-g-geh-geh-get my words out just like I want to de-de-de-zi-zi-zide to get 'em out . . . but I can get my lovin' like I want it."* The guitar stops. A moment's silence. *"I'll call you tomorrow."* Against all the odds, he's scored, and he hits one last triumphant chord on his guitar—*yesss!*—to celebrate his victory.

One of his old Detroit buddies recalls a real-life incident which tells pretty much the same story: "I know one day we was talkin' and some ladies was here, and the lady kinda crackin' on John a little bit. He was bangin' about goin' out with him and so she would never give him the okay, but she say, 'You know, you can't talk at all,' just like that. He say, 'Ma-ma-ma-ma-ma-man, I can't talk but I can get my point across.' She says, 'Yeah, okay.' " Hooker's vulnerability is a vital ingredient of his strength: what may superficially resemble weakness is actually the secret of his success.

Relaxed and self-confident as he is, John Lee Hooker rarely stutters these days. When he does, it's the equivalent of an Early Warning System: the first giveaway sign of incipient confusion or distress. Like right now: John Lee is growing steadily more and more agitated. It's a warm early December afternoon in San Francisco, and Hooker is standing on a downtown street corner, sucking fresh-squeezed orange juice through a straw and waiting for his ride home. He's just completed a radio interview in a small, cramped studio high above the city, promoting a couple of shows he'll be doing in the city later that week even though they're both foregone sell-outs. The station staff had practically abandoned their work when he arrived, downing tools as soon as he walked through the door, blocking corridors, queueing up to meet him and shake his hand . . . *gently* though, of course. The interview itself was no problem at all. Hooker hardly stutters once, and his formidable charm and spontaneity carry him through even though radio chat isn't really his forte. Unlike his old pal B. B. King, who actually put in a few years as a DJ on WDIA in Memphis before his records got huge and the road swallowed him up, Hooker never cultivated the particular skills and mannerisms necessary to give good radio. The art of radio-friendliness demands that pitch and pacing and volume are all smooth and even, that syntactical structure is coherent, diction is clear and that the interviewee never ceases to be aware that the host and his microphone merely represent a bridge to those wonderful folks out there in radioland. Hooker doesn't deign to address himself to a radio microphone; rather, he talks to the person behind it as if the two of them were sitting together in his living room, chatting intimately. He shifts in his chair in mid-sentence, he drops his voice into a murmur occasionally, he allows lengthy moments of silence to elapse while he considers his answers, he emphasizes his points with gesture and eye contact, and he never modifies his accent to suit anybody else's convenience.

So anyway, the interview is completed, everybody shakes hands all over again, and Hooker and a recent acquaintance wander down to street level to wait until Hooker's nephew Archie—Hooker's live-in chauffeur, chef and butler—retrieves the cream Lincoln Town Car with the DOC HOOK vanity plate from the multi-story car park across the street. Unfortunately, there is some sort of inexplicable delay, and for nearly five minutes now, Hooker has just been left there, hanging on the corner. At first, this was no hardship: his public arrived. First one, then a couple more, then finally whole knots of people have begun to recognize him; their jaws dropping with awe as if some creature out of legend, like a centaur or unicorn, had suddenly appeared right before their eyes, casually lounging against a wall, sluicing from a carton of fresh-squeezed OJ. "Are you John Lee Hooker?" they ask reverently. Hooker smiles seraphically. He presses the flesh—*gently* though, of course—he murmurs greetings but, nevertheless, the stress begins to look like it's getting to him. Something unpredictable and unforeseen has happened. A situation has developed over which he seems to have no control. He is powerless. In real terms, of course, he is in no danger whatsoever. Even if Archie and the Lincoln had been somehow sucked into a black hole and vanished completely off the face of San Francisco only to reappear somewhere near Betelgeuse in the late twenty-fourth century, all Hooker would have to do would be to drop a dime and call The Rosebud Agency, and in ten minutes or thereabouts, someone would have arrived to attend to his every need. He turns to his bemused companion, some English guy he barely knows who's a stranger to San Francisco, and pulls him by the sleeve, pointing into the car park's exit, right into the gaping maw from which the cars emerge back onto the street.

"G-go up there look for Archie," he orders, "fuh-find out where he at."

Obediently, the Brit shambles off to locate the errant Lincoln and, not surprisingly, achieves little more than a few hair's-breadth escapes from sudden death as an assortment of cars—none of them the Hook-mobile—zoom within inches of him. Fortunately, Archie reappears, Lincoln intact, before there's any permanent damage to safety or sanity, and Hooker clambers thankfully back into the comfortable, familiar environment of his car. Hooker loves cars, even though he hasn't driven one himself for years, and he'll buy a new one at the drop of a Homburg. The stereo is playing a tape of one of John's own albums. John likes to listen to his own music—*oh yeah*—and through just about any conversation he'll keep an ear cocked to the tape, ready to repeat and emphasize any lyrical sally of which he is particularly fond or proud, either echoing the intonation of his recorded voice or responding to it. Normally, to say that someone loves the sound of their own voice is tantamount to an accusation of being the kind of raving egomaniac or rampant solipsist that Hooker so patently isn't. He literally *does* love the sound of his own voice; he'd love it just as much if it were somebody else's, and he considers his proprietorship of that voice a "blessing" from the Supreme Being; a blessing to be celebrated with all due humility. This album playing now isn't one of the ones which blues buffs or Hooker aficionados consider to be one of his classics; far from it. *Free Beer And Chicken* is a gooey psychedelic-soul confection dating from the artistic nadir of the early '70s, when he was signed to a major corporate record label whose pursuit of the rock-fan's dollar gracelessly shoe-horned him into a succession of ever more contrived and inappropriate progressive-rock studio formats. However, even though Hooker himself has little good to say of this particular phase of his recorded career, he picks this album for in-car listening over and above his recognized masterpieces. For over a week, this has been the tape that has kicked in whenever John Lee has set loafer-shod foot past his own front door.

When he's making one of his rare forays into downtown San Francisco, or paying a quick visit to the bank—Archie claims John Lee has opened an account at every local bank where he's ever spotted a good-looking female cashier—or picking up a visitor from the airport, or traveling to a concert, this music is what wafts him there and brings him back. For in-car entertainment, at least, he prefers it to both the reverberant, itchy-foot Detroit recordings which form the foundation-stones of his legend, and the triple-distilled, oak-barrelled mellowness of his contemporary hits. A considerable part of *Free Beer*'s appeal is that it features the virtuoso Fender electric piano of John's second son Robert, once the youngest member of John Lee's touring band and now a minister back in

Detroit, out of "the world" and the blues life for good. The same album plays again when John heads out to visit his tailor. It's been a long time— a decade and a half, easily—since anybody's seen Hooker in anything other than those smart pinstripe suits: so where does he get 'em? If he so desired, he could easily become a valued customer of Giorgio Armani, Gianni Versace, Paul Smith or even—if he was feeling exceptionally adventurous and fancied the built-in nipple-clamps—Jean-Paul Gaultier. He could shop at Saks Fifth Avenue in New York, or any number of fine establishments in London's Savile Row or Rome's Via Veneto. He can certainly afford it, and if there's one thing that a celebrity designer truly loves, it's a celebrity customer. Nevertheless, John Lee prefers to shop at H. Jon's, a Jewish tailor based at a shopping mall from hell in Oakland, California; an hour or so's drive from his home in a cozy San Francisco Bay Area dormitory town named Redwood City.

Oakland is where John Lee first settled when he relocated from Detroit to Northern California almost three decades ago, and it's where several members of his family still live. The accusation that black celebrities "lose touch with the ghetto" when they make enough money to move out is a common accusation, but a short-sighted one. Unless, like Bob Marley or Ice-T, they simply "move the ghetto uptown" with them, or unless they make so much money that they can afford to move their entire communities with them—or unless they do literally turn their backs on everyone they used to know—the black celeb remains keenly aware of how the less fortunate live. They have relatives and friends still out there where, with each passing day, the jobs grow scarcer and the crack houses more plentiful. John Lee still shops in Oakland, because H. Jon provides friendly personal service, and at least has the merit of being local and therefore easily accessible. The mall is eerily reminiscent of similar establishments in Warsaw under Communism; there, even those visitors who were, by bourgeois Western standards, not overburdened with liquid capital could afford most of what was on display, except that they wouldn't want the stuff even—as they say—at any price. This is where poor people shop, and by prevailing community standards, H. Jon's *is* Armani, Versace and Savile Row.

Jon's range includes just about everything the well-dressed blues singer could desire. If you crave eyeball-threatening big-collared polyester shirts in acidic lime green or vintage Bridget Riley–style op-art, you got it. If you need a double-knit cream-colored leisure suit with mildly flared pants, seek ye no further. If there's an acute shortage of patent-leather tasselled loafers in your life, consider your problem solved. For younger patrons, there's a selection of "X" baseball caps and T-shirts, red-green-and-gold leather pendants in the shape of the African continent, and thinly gold-plated chains which might just fool a hardcore gangbanger at fifty paces if he happened to be on the pipe at the time. For John Lee Hooker, there are rich soft bolts of the pinstriped broadcloths and slate-blue mohairs he favors, and H. Jon himself ready and waiting to cut suits to John's measure, or to alter an off-the-peg item until it's guaranteed to fit to perfection. Plus there are unlimited supplies of star-spangled socks, Hooker's most distinctive sartorial fetish. Apart from anything else, H. Jon has the merit of familiarity and reliability. Such dependability represents one of the most important aspects of Hooker's life: comfort, continuity, stability and, above all, trustworthiness. Familiar objects, familiar people, familiar foods, familiar clothes: they all serve to anchor and orient him. They're the signposts by which he navigates.

By way of contrast, he displays little more permanent attachment to his homes than he does to his cars. He never seems to have less than two houses at a time; one principal dwelling place which serves as a permanent open house to family, friends and acquaintances alike, and one bolt-hole elsewhere to which he retreats when he's had enough of the pressure and clamor inevitably generated by his legions of invited, semi-invited and downright *un*invited guests. Right now, the pleasant bungalow in white-bread suburban Redwood City is his main place of residence, supplanting a six-bedroom ranch-style spread in Vallejo, the other side of the Bay, which had become a virtual bunkhouse for band members and assorted friends and hangers-on. The Redwood City location was originally chosen for its close, easy proximity to San Francisco airport, a mere twenty-minute drive away, and to the city of San Francisco itself, just a few additional miles further down the freeway. Hooker's home is in a comfortable little close, at the far end of a long hilly avenue. There's nothing distinctive about the outside of the house, other than the cars—the cream Lincoln, a black Cadillac Brougham (vanity plate: LES BOGY), and Archie's roadworn Cadillac De Ville—but inside it's a different story. There's lush cream carpet in which you can practically lose your shoes, comfortable matching sofas and easy chairs, a great big fat cat called—inevitably—Fluffy, and cream-papered walls covered in plaques and awards, citations and honors, framed original prints of portraits of the distinguished occupant.

"Look on my wall," commands Hooker. "What do you see? You see the awards and the gold records, trophies . . . all them years brought me that. That hard road. You heard the song say *'I ain't goin' down that big road by myself"*? I went down by myself. That brought me all of this, but I don't let that, you know, go to my head. It just something that I achieve, that I want people to look at when they come into my home."

There are gold discs and silver discs from a half-dozen different territories, commemorating the substantial sales of *The Healer* and *Mr. Lucky*: 50,000 here, and 100,000 there. Over in the corner, behind the dining table, is a rack of award statuettes: W. C. Handy awards, Bay Area Music awards, and—of course—John's 1990 Grammy, the one he and Bonnie Raitt shared for their "I'm In The Mood For Love" duet from *The Healer*. Here's a huge framed photo of John Lee and Bonnie on their night of triumph, clutching their Grammies. There's a reproduction of John's ad for Remy Martin cognac. John, of course, no longer drinks cognac, and even back in his drinking days he was a Courvoisier man. Nearby there's a gold disc and matching gold cassette awarded for sales of George Thorogood's *Bad To The Bone* album, which included a version of John Lee's "Boogie Chillen." And everywhere are photos of John Lee with his peer group. With B. B. King, with Albert King, with Albert Collins, with Carlos Santana and Bill Graham, with Robert Cray and Stevie Ray Vaughan; and, more recently, Hooker and Mike Kappus with Bill Clinton. On the mantelpiece is a framed clipping of a lead story from *Rolling Stone*'s "Random Notes" section, reporting John Lee's Atlantic City guest appearance with The Rolling Stones during their 1989 "Steel Wheels" tour. The page features two principal photographs, each depicting one of the head Stones cavorting with their most suitably matched star guest. In one shot, John Lee is shown grooving with Keith Richards, standing up for a change as he leads the ensemble, which on this occasion also includes Eric Clapton, through a hectic "Boogie Chillen." In the other, Mick Jagger appears buddying up to the microphone with Guns N' Roses' "troubled" lead singer, Axl Rose.

Then there's some serious hi-fi and a matching TV, video, cable and satellite system; not one of those ostentatious projection jobs, but nevertheless boasting more than respectable screen acreage. It gets more use than the hi-fi, which occasionally pumps out some of Hooker's vintage recordings, or tapes or recent recordings by various members of his inner circle, but mainly it remains silent while the TV blasts movies or sport. Lately, John Lee's grown fond of screening a recently assembled stash of his own videos, and visitors are likely to be regaled with the promo clips for his own recent singles from *The Healer* or *Mr. Lucky*, or that in-concert "Boogie Chillen" workout with Clapton and the Stones, or—delving back into the archives—Hooker's celebrated spot from the 1960 Newport Jazz Festival with The Muddy Waters Band rocking right behind him. Rarer still is a flickering, washed-out late-'60s clip from some local Detroit TV show featuring Hooker, in dashiki and black leather pillbox hat, perched on a stool performing "Never Get Out Of These Blues Alive" with his teenage son Robert comping, hunched studiously over the keyboard of the Wurlitzer organ his dad bought him.

Off to one side is a narrow corridor, also lined with plaques, posters and awards, from which the bedrooms and bathroom branch off. The first one you pass is a small one, all bed, closets and framed photos, which is occupied by Archie; at the end are two facing doors. The left-hand guest bedroom is currently occupied by John's son, John Lee Hooker, Junior; the other is the master bedroom, which is the ultimate refuge for John himself. It has its own luxury-size TV and video, permanently tuned to a satellite sports channel, its own toilet and water cooler, capacious closets for all his suits, and for his small but impressive collection of Gibson and Epiphone guitars. Hooker owns a couple of tobacco-sunburst Gibson ES-335s, one the workhorse instrument he has used since the early '70s and the other a newer model presented to him by Carlos Santana; the cherry-red mid-'60s Epiphone Sheraton with which he poses on the cover of *Mr. Lucky*; and a spanking-new cherry-red Gibson B. B. King "Lucille" signature model which he used when sitting in with The Rolling Stones in Los Angeles. And, of course, there's Old Blondie. Old Blondie is the only one of his guitars about which Hooker is sentimental: she's the big-bodied, single-cutaway Epiphone Broadway which Hooker acquired in the late '50s and carried with him everywhere for the next decade and a half. Blondie doesn't travel anymore; the 335s are the working guitars. The old one, in standard tuning, is the one Hooker uses for the bulk of each performance; the Santana guitar, tuned up to open A, is reserved for the closing boogies. But unless there's work to be done, or unless a visitor requests a guided tour of the guitar collection, the closet is where they stay. Hooker doesn't sit around the house playing the guitar, let alone strumming in a rocking chair on his back porch.

Meanwhile, there's nearly always something cooking in Archie's tiled, open-plan kitchen. Only on particular ceremonial occasions are meals consumed at any particular set time; sometimes it seems as if the entire day consists of people wandering in and out helping themselves to microwaved leftovers from the previous evening's feast, or improvised snacks from the fridge, or to the freshly prepared delicacies *du jour*. The cuisine is the kind of Southern soul food that you don't get in restaurants, the kind of stuff you only ever get to taste if you're fortunate enough to get your knees under the table of someone who learned their culinary chops down home. There's cornbread to die for. Fish, baked in foil, fresh from the Bay. Ribs from heaven. Chicken from hell. A colander of turnip greens sprinkled with chunks of fatback done . . . just . . . right. Peach or pun'kin pie. *Mmmmwah!* Sometimes Archie, in affectionate exasperation, wishes out loud that he could plan his menus far enough ahead to allow him to do a week's worth of shopping at one time, but John Lee only decides what he wants to eat about two or three hours before he's fixing to be ready to eat it. Sometimes even then he changes his mind, and a raiding party gets dispatched to "The Colonel's"—that's Kentucky Fried Chicken, to folks not born and raised in the South—for buckets of chicken and fries and mashed potato and biscuits and gravy.

And it's warm. Somewhere along the line, Hooker developed a marked aversion to being cold, and—as someone raised in the heat of the South—he defines "cold" very differently from those accustomed to cooler climes. Sometimes the temperature in the Hooker home reaches the eighties. "Well, I lived in Detroit so long in the winter that when I come out here I was used to the heat," he explains. "Back in Detroit it didn't bother me at all, cold weather. I used to shovel my car out, take my kids to school. Got out here, I just . . . I guess my blood got thin. Don't like cool weather no more."

Everything's *laid back* at John's house. It's *mellow*. Everything's cool. Everything's easy, just the way John likes it. There's no hustle, no hurry-up. Everything happens when it's supposed to: not earlier, not later. The only surprises are pleasant ones. No one shouts at anybody else. No one quarrels with anybody else. No one gets angry or uptight or loud. There are comparatively few house rules, and as long as those rules are obeyed, everybody has a good time, all the time. Anyone can take a drink—they can help themselves to a little nip from John's well-stocked liquor cabinet, or if they so desire they can fetch in a case of beer or a bottle of wine from one of the nearby stores—but noticeable intoxication is frowned upon, and regular display of its symptoms constitutes grounds for withdrawal of visiting privileges. Ever since John Lee himself abandoned tobacco, under no circumstances does anybody smoke in the house. John Lee's health in general (and his increasingly delicate throat in particular) is the household's most precious asset, and therefore a total-exclusion smoke-free zone is rigorously maintained within the four walls. However, if you should happen to crave a cigarette, all you got to do is step over the threshold, and then you can smoke to your heart's content. Similarly, it's not a major problem if a visitor feels like enhancing the joys of a warm summer evening by blowing a little weed in the back yard, but anybody foolish enough to bring serious drugs anywhere near the premises will find themselves under extremely heavy manners. That shit has done too much damage to too many of John's nearest and dearest for it to be anything but *banned*. Above all, Hooker's Law states that anybody who steps into the house is required to display courtesy and respect to everybody else on the set.

"I'm a crawlin' king snake," sings Hooker in one of his signature songs, *"and I rules my den."* How does he rule his real-life den? Like a benevolent patriarch who issues few direct orders anymore, because his wants and needs are so clearly established that they no longer need to be stated. The only thing he lacks is privacy: his door is *literally* always open. Like this one time, a few months later: John was sitting on the sofa chatting to an acquaintance, laughing over some of the misconceptions surrounding him and his career, and the degree of attachment which many people bring to pet misconceptions, based on an over-literal assumption that all Hooker's lyrics are directly autobiographical. The one about the freight train, for example, from "Hobo Blues." That's one of Hooker's most affecting performances, the one that begins *"When I first started hoboin', I took a freight train to be my friend, oh lord . . ."* And ever since he cut it, it's been trotted out as an article of faith that Hooker spent years as a hobo, riding the blinds on the Southern freights. "I never rode a freight train!" he insists, laughing.

"Oh John, it's such a great story," replies the acquaintance. "How can you spoil it for everyone?"

"I would never spoil it," ripostes Hooker, laughing all the harder. "Go right ahead and say it! That'll ruin they ego, they illusions. Tell 'em I rode all over the world, freight trains here, there . . . got *shot* on freight trains, broke my *leg* on freight trains . . . tell 'em all that! They likes all that!"

"Tell 'em you *robbed* a freight train," interposes Martin Thompson, lounging in a nearby armchair. Martin is a big, iron-pumped guy with a droopy mustache, a lazy grin and a deadpan sense of humor. He started out as a handyman, doing some work on one of John's houses, and the two men hit it off to the extent that Martin graduated to being John's deputy driver and occasional bodyguard. He and Archie are taking a beer-cooled break from the arduous task of varnishing the hardwood floor of the living room's lower level, when suddenly a truck door slams outside.

"Oh God," breathes Hooker. "*Jeff.*"

We're calling this particular guy Jeff because it's not his real name. He's one of those people Hooker just *meets*, and he seems to have become semi-permanent. It could have been at the vet's surgery while getting some essential maintenance work done on Fluffy, because Jeff's dog had been run over by a careless driver and needed considerable veterinary work, and Hooker—who likes to think of himself as being tough and hard-headed about money but in fact seems to end up putting his hand in his newly capacious pocket for the benefit of at least half the people he knows—wound up footing the pooch's bills. Bearded, plaid-clad, long-haired, baseball-capped Jeff is hugely amiable and essentially harmless, but undeniably a touch on the weird side. For example, he has this story that he regularly insists on telling: apparently before they got famous The Beatles flew John Lee to London *for a whole year* so that he could teach them guitar, and it was only after John Lee thought they were ready that they made their first records. So why hasn't this story ever been told before? Easy; it was *hushed up*. And they paid John a lot of money not to tell anybody.

So here's Jeff tramping up the front garden path and before you know it, there's a whole family of complete strangers standing over John in his sofa, and a thick-set blind guy is shaking hands with John, telling him that he's been a big, big fan since forever and it's a *real thrill*. Seems Jeff met these people somewhere, mentioned that he knew John, asked if they felt like meeting him, and here they are. So they all shake hands, and then John tells Jeff that he's busy—which he's not, particularly—and that they'll all get together soon. And so Jeff leads them all out again.

"This kid Jeff, he's a nice kid but he's a *pest*," sighs Hooker once the coast is clear, mopping his brow with a handkerchief. "You know me, I'm a very easy-going, quiet person. I'm just a softie. I don't tell 'em to go to hell or get out or nothin'; I don't do that. A lotta stars, they couldn't even get in the house, but I'm not like that. That blind guy, he really nice. A lot of 'em nice. This Jeff kid nice. They *all* be nice. But . . ."

Exactly. *But.* John Lee—as he never tires of repeating—loves people. All people. All kinds of people. People in general, and people in particular. *But* . . . that doesn't necessarily mean that he wants all of them in his house, all the time. However, sometimes that's what he gets. So, while we're briefly looking ahead to spring, imagine a quiet Saturday night in Redwood City. Tell you the truth, it's moderately difficult to imagine any *other* kind of Saturday night in Redwood City, but on this particular Saturday evening, the only real option seems to be to call up a mutual friend to hustle a lift over to John Lee's house. It'll be *mellow*. It'll be so nice and *laid back*. Just sit around, watch a movie or a game, pop a couple of lite beers, chit-chat a little and *kick back*.

To start with, that's just exactly how it goes down. There's something fairly inconsequential like a *Karate Kid* movie on TV, and John is recounting Albert King's riposte to a female fan who asked if she could take his picture—"*Buy my album, there's a picture of me on the cover!*"—when there's a crunch of miscellaneous footsteps outside, and craziness walks in. First of all, there's a hard-bodied bleach-blond woman in an elaborate black leather and PVC ensemble, waving a bottle of tequila and screaming in an ersatz Southern accent. By comparison, Madonna comes across like a morbidly prim Victorian schoolgirl. Because it's not her name, let's call her Cathy. It later turns out that, during the week, Cathy is a seriously high-powered business whiz in San Francisco, holding down an extremely responsible and grueling job involving eleven-hour days, seven-figure budgets and entire floorsful of people reporting to her. During the week, she works out conscientiously, she touches not one drop of alcohol, she is the precise, rigorous, disciplined, supremely organized Ms. Jekyll. Guess who emerges at the weekend. Following in her wake is a bemused-looking, guffawing, denim-clad high-school kid with a blond shag-cut and a wispy mustache; two quiet and extremely obese women in stretch slacks, cardigans and training shoes; and assorted others whose best bet for weekend fun is to hang out at the home of the world's most accessible superstar. Instant party. In fact, Cathy is a party all by herself: laughing and screaming like a jam session between a hyena and an air-raid siren, strutting and stomping in her stilettos, teasing everybody in the room in enthusiastic parodies of their own accents, she steals the show from *The Karate Kid*. Soon the TV is silenced, replaced by a rocking Albert Collins tape. She even starts flirting with Hooker's Brit acquaintance, despite the fact that he is the kind of pallid-skinned muscle-free zone not generally considered attractive in California.

Hooker delivers polite, cordial greetings and encourages everybody to make themselves at home, but within moments he's disappeared, barricading himself in his bedroom at the back of the house with his TV and his telephone. An hour or so passes, the noise level mounts and suddenly—*brrriiinnnnggg!*—there's an insistent ring on Archie's private telephone line. It's John Lee, calling from the back room, demanding that the noise be held down. Fortunately, a natural break in the proceedings soon occurs as the booze runs out. Cathy threatens to drive out and pick up fresh supplies of beer and tequila and come right back to continue the festivities, but she's eventually persuaded to gather up her entourage and seek her next round of wild delights elsewhere, preferably somewhere a long way out of John Lee's earshot. The following morning, Archie and Martin ruefully assess the damage to the still-soft varnish of the hardwood floor. The varnished surface they'd so painstakingly applied, coat by coat, only two or three days before is now scarred with hundreds of tiny, shallow bullet-pocks, each one the approximate size of a stiletto heel. "No more fat broads," they announce, but it's another couple of days before anyone remembers that the "fat broads" had been not only trainer-clad but as quiet as a pair of admittedly generously-sized mice. The "fat broads" probably won't be back. But Cathy will. After all, she's a friend.

The regular cast of characters *chez* John is a fascinating one, and we may well meet more of them later on. However, right now we've got a show to go to, and we don't want to be late.

Christmas is coming, and John Lee is playing his major hometown showcase of the season. As its name might suggest, the 600-capacity Great American Music Hall is tricked out in velvet-plush Victorian kitsch. Archie rolls the Lincoln in with one hand on the wheel, the other holding a walkie-talkie into which he's talking quietly and urgently, making sure that the pavement is clear, the parking space is free, and the side door is open so that John Lee can disembark as smoothly and easily as possible. Inside, the band is assembled at rather more than full strength. The elusive Deacon Jones is back, there being no other activities with a prior claim on his attention, and so is his wife's T-shirt stall. Deacon Jones is a screwdriver-jiver and a half: slick, loud, impossible to ignore on or off stage. In contrast to the laid-back hippie demeanor of his colleagues, Jones is dressed out to the nines and beyond; a vision of elegance in his crisp pinstripes, snowy French cuffs with gold cufflinks, tie pierced with a diamond stickpin, and an immaculate black Homburg hat easily the match of Hooker's perched on his head. He seems to have some friends with him: the basement dressing room designated for the band is full of moustachioed guys in major hats, commandeering the table, pulling tricksy one-hand riverboat-gambler shuffles with their decks of cards, and saying things like "My name is Jake and your money I'll take." Even with Jones back in the band, his replacement Lizz Fischer is still around, celebrating the season by topping off her Little Black Dress with a jauntily drooping red Father Christmas cap. As it turned out, her fears concerning the precise nature of her role as Hooker's companion during that summer's New York sojourn had been entirely unfounded. She'd occupied the hotel room next to John Lee, all that had been required of her was her company, and she'd had a hugely enjoyable time.

Yep, 'tis the season of good will; yep, John Lee is headlining a major San Francisco venue of the kind that he works during his increasingly infrequent road trips, as opposed to the unadvertised small-club gigs he normally plays in the Bay Area, both to stay in shape and help out the friends who run his favorite bars. But there's something else that's very special about the show tonight: if you caught sight of the Music Hall's marquee on the way in you'll have noticed the other name on the bill. It's a family affair: tonight's opening act is Zakiya Hooker.

Zakiya is John Lee's Number Two daughter. Originally christened "Vera," she subsequently changed her name to something she felt suited her better. She's a tiny little woman with a slick cap of hair that looks as if it had been painted across her head with a single stroke, and if you saw her only from a distance you might be tempted to describe her as "doll-like." Close-up, though, the warmth and mobility of her mouth and the humor and pain in her eyes would wither the word on your lips. She is in her early forties, though most people would find it hard to reconcile her hip, youthful appearance with her chronological age unless they were shown a birth certificate first. Tonight she's making her major-league debut, fronting a band led and directed by her partner Ollan Christopher, formerly a member of The Natural Four, a vocal group who used to record for Curtis Mayfield's Chicago-based soul set-up, Curtom Records. However, this is more than a simple coming-out party for a late-blooming "new artist," even one who happens to be related to the headliner. Just a few weeks previous, Zakiya had lost her youngest son, John Sylvester, in a road accident. By all accounts, he'd been a lovable, sparky teenage kid; for his entire life a favorite of all who knew him. His doting grandad's friends adored him, too.

"His grandson must've been about five years old, and John used to bring him over to see me," recalled B. B. King. "For some reason, his little grandson, named John, like his grandfather, *liked* me. I don't know why, but he took up with me, seemed to like me, and John knew it. So every time he would come or I'm near him, he'd always bring little John. And when little John got old enough and big enough, he would ask [John Lee] to take him to see me. And then, about a year or so ago, I had a call from John telling me that his grandson had been killed in an automobile accident." The Coast To Coast Blues Band have their own memories of that awful night. John Lee was playing a low-key show at his favorite club, The Sweetwater in Marin County, and he was given the terrible news of young John's death only seconds before show-time. His face just closed up like a fist before, as Rich Kirch remembers, "he hit that stage . . . rockin'."

By all accounts, it was one of the most powerful shows anyone could recall him playing. When Hooker found himself tumbling into a moment of deep, intense personal sorrow and agony, his music was there to catch him, to bind the wound, to enable the Healer to begin the painful, wrenching process of healing himself. And tonight it is Zakiya's turn to face the world from her father's stage, to assert her position as her father's daughter and her son's mother, and to dedicate herself, slowly and haltingly, to the new future toward which those relationships steer her as she begins her life afresh. Her show is more significant this particular night for what it represents than for what it is; a few harsh words are exchanged after the band comes offstage, and the line-up is radically reshaped shortly afterwards. Reminded of this occasion some two years later, after Zakiya has her first solo album under her belt and her second one halfway to completion, Ollan Christopher is happy to dismiss it. "Different artist," he says, with crunching finality, but the artist Zakiya is now could not exist without standing on the shoulders of the artist she was then.

To someone who had never seen him before, John Lee's show would be a revelation. To someone more familiar with his set, it's a better-than-okay night which definitely has its moments. Vala Cupp flutters around him like a thirsty butterfly hovering over a succulent plant when they duet a feverish "Crawlin' King Snake"; a puffy-eyed Gregg Allman sits in—on guitar, as it happens—to perform what he evidently expects to be a marathon version of T-Bone Walker's "Stormy Monday Blues," only to find John Lee bringing the song to a close, somewhat irritably, after a single verse and a couple of solos. A stalwart young woman with a baritone sax flanks Kenny Baker on tenor, providing the band with the rich thickness of an actual brass section. The textures created by the blend of Lizz Fischer's deep-rolling piano and Deacon Jones's exuberant Hammond organ are almost obscenely luxurious, and the climactic boogie—Jones launching great washes of Hammond that threaten to drown the audience in funk—induces a joyful, sweat-slick meltdown that blows the last remaining particles of dust off the mock-Victorian velvet seats in the balcony.

A good job well done, in other words. Backstage again, Hooker greets his final flock of visitors as regally as ever, before settling back into the Lincoln for his forty-minute ride home. Before the car clears the city limits, his eyelids begin to droop. He is fast asleep well before the headlights lick on the street-sign reading "Hastings Avenue."

5. When I First Come to Town, People

When I first come to town, people,
I was walkin' down Hastings Street,
Everybody talkin' 'bout Henry's Swing Club,
I decided to drop in there that night.
When I got there,
I said "Yes, people, yes,"
They were really havin' a ball.
Yes, I know . . .
Boogie, chillen!
—John Lee Hooker, "Boogie Chillen," 1948

The late thirties: halfway around the world, thousands of miles away, the Nazis were on the march and Europe was heading toward war. Closer to home, John Lee Hooker was desperate to join the U.S. army. These two facts were, however, entirely unconnected. Like the vast majority of Americans at that time, Hooker was sublimely unconcerned with the geopolitical implications of an imminent distant foreign war. His desire to enter the armed forces had rather more to do with the strangely aphrodisiac effect that military uniforms seemed to exert on the local girls.

Hooker had now moved to Detroit from Cincinnati: he had a little money in his pocket and, for the first time, he hadn't had to hitch-hike. "I'd heard about all these big things in Detroit. The Motor City it was then, with the factories and everything, and the money was flowing. You could get a job paying money in any city in the United States, but this was the Motor City. All the cars were being built there. I said, 'I'm going there,' and I went. Took me the Greyhound and I went straight to Detroit. Detroit was *the city* then. Work, work, work, work. Plenty work, good wages, good money at that time." He soon settled in, finding himself lodgings with a rather friendlier landlady than the one he subsequently immortalized in "House Rent Boogie." "She would give parties too, and

I would work in the theater and come down play on the weekend, Saturday night parties. It was nothin' but work goin' on there." Unfortunately, Hooker's cozy Detroit applecart was soon upset. "When I come to town I had a girlfriend and I lost her. The army was a big thing; the soldiers became heroes and when they come into town all the girls was flocking up to them. She just flocked up to those soldiers, and I said, 'I'm going to go to the army.' I went in on account of girls. They wanted a uniform. Guys come to the army, come out on a break with the uniform on, girls'd eat 'em up. Now uniforms don't mean nothin', but back then, uniforms was a big, big thing. I loved army life because that was the thing: the women would go crazy over an army suit. You get on a suit, you could get any woman, any chick you wanted."

So Hooker, led by his libido, enlisted in the U.S. army. Stationed just outside Detroit, he spent the next few months a mere spitting distance from the Ford Motor Company's famous River Rouge plant. Half a century later, he still has fond memories of what turned out to be an extremely brief taste of military life. "I didn't get too far with basic training; I mostly stayed around the camp. We would come into town every weekend. I would play on the barracks, go out, work in the kitchen. I never would even go out on the shootin' range. I never would do that, just work 'round the barracks. They liked'ed me in there. I would play in there, and they all crazy 'bout me in there." Hooker's sunny disposition enables him to enjoy, at five or so decades' remove, a rose-colored view of race relations within the U.S. army of the '30s which is entirely uncorroborated by mainstream contemporary accounts. Ask him if he experienced the army of that time as segregated and he answers in a firm negative. "No. Not in Detroit. If they did I didn't know it. They loved'ed me in there, white, black and everybody. They didn't allow that stuff [segregation] in the army. They maybe do it on the sly, but all I can tell you that I didn't feel it. We all was together."

This would have come as something of a shock to President Roosevelt and to his Assistant Secretary of War, Robert Patterson. In 1940, in answer to repeated urgings from black community leaders, Patterson published a position paper which amounted to a formal statement defining government policy on racial matters within the military. Six of its seven clauses were, broadly speaking, positive: they established the rights of "Negroes" to receive training in areas, like aviation, from which they had hitherto been barred, and—radical step, this—to assume ranks and positions for which they had actually qualified. The seventh, however, was the cruncher: it stated that "the policy of the War Department is not to intermingle colored and white enlisted personnel in the same regimental organizations." A clarifying statement from the office of the Adjutant General insisted that the army would not be maneuverd into taking "a stand with respect to Negroes which is not compatible with the position attained by the Negro in civilian life." In other words, the army would remain officially segregated until further notice: until 1950, in fact, when President Truman signed a military desegregation order as America entered the Korean War. Pandering to populist prejudice rather than biological fact, even blood supplies were segregated during World War II.

Sadly, Hooker's military idyll didn't last long. In his enthusiasm to don the khaki and get his leg over, he had blithely ignored the then-current proviso that enlisted men under twenty-one required the consent of a parent or guardian. Finding himself a little shy of his formal majority, John Lee managed to find a way to revise his birth date somewhat—thereby creating a miasma of ambiguity and confusion concerning his age which persists to this day. "I went into the army on false pretense, and they found it out real quick. I was in there four-five-six months. When they found out I lied, they kicked me out . . . The army is strict, you know, they got to go by the rules no matter what they think of you. They called me into the office and said, 'You know you lied about your age. You lied, kid.' And I said, 'What can I say? I wanted to serve my country and I wanted to be part of it.' And that kind of got to him when I said that. They didn't know what I *really* wanted. 'Yeah,' he said, 'I'm gonna have to let you go on a discharge, but everybody around here really love little Hooker. Everyone around here love you, they love your music, kid.' They let me went . . . but they let me keep the uniform.

"And that's the story. I said, 'Can I keep the uniform?' The guy says yeah. I wore it around town a bit, and the girls were thinkin' I was in the army until they found out I was kicked out and I wasn't a soldier anymore." Which was probably just as well. As a result of his discharge from the service, Hooker was ineligible for the draft introduced later when, in the immediate wake of Pearl Harbor, America finally entered the war. This meant that he could spend the war years safe in Detroit, working on his music and enjoying his pick of home-front factory jobs instead of being sent overseas to be shot at by foreigners. "Yeah, and I'm glad I got out, because if I'd stayed in I probably wouldn't have been famous. When you that age, you don't think. You not scared of nothin'. You don't even think about that, because you thinkin' of the glory and the fun, what you gonna do then, right then, how these army suits gonna bring you fun and joy with the women. You don't think they're gonna send you over there and kill you. I just settled in Detroit, right. No, I didn't go anywhere from the army but back to Detroit, where I didn't leave anymore. Just stayed right there. When I come out, that's when I started my research on trying to get on record, on a label, playing around, stuff like that."

From this distance it's impossible to know how many of these details are true, or even whether this took place in Detroit or earlier in Cincinnati. All we can say with any certainty is that Hooker, despite being a healthy man in his twenties with no dependants, didn't go to war; and that by the '40s he was living and working in Detroit. Only John Lee Hooker himself knows the full story and, for whatever reason, he's not telling.

Detroit was hardly the most obvious base for an ambitious young bluesman looking to launch a career. Though the bulk of its black population originated in the southeastern states—from Alabama or Georgia— it had a small pool of the homesick Delta migrants essential to support the career of any transplanted Mississippi bluesman. However, there was a serious lack of the necessary infrastructure: record labels, booking agents, talent scouts and the like. In sharp contrast, over on the other side of Lake Michigan was Chicago, aka Chi-Town or the Windy City, a primary urban focus for black migrants from the Deep South. The city's South and West Sides were packed with Delta expatriates, and during the '40s their numbers were swelling literally by the day. The white blues-harpist Charlie Musselwhite, a close friend of Hooker's, whose own journey from Mississippi to Memphis to Chicago to California unwittingly reenacted the twentieth-century odyssey of the blues, explains it this way. "If you look at the map," he says, "a lot of people in California came out from Texas or Oklahoma. Philadelphia and New York get the Carolinas. Chicago gets people from the Deep South, from Tennessee, Mississippi, Alabama, Arkansas. Highway 51 and Highway 61 both go straight up there."

Even before the genesis of the distinctive postwar strain of Windy City amplified ensemble blues most frequently associated with Chess Records, Chicago had been a major regional recording center for about as long as the recording industry had been in existence, a status it owed, indirectly, to the New Orleans authorities' decision to close down the red-light district of Storyville in 1917, which in turn prompted an exodus of the city's musicians to Chicago. Many of the great rural blues artists had also traveled there to make their records and, inevitably, some of them decided to settle in Chicago. Equally inevitably, a distinctive local sound began to emerge. Georgia transplant Hudson "Tampa Red" Whittaker soon became one of the kingpins of the prewar South Side scene, and Big Bill Broonzy was its primary figurehead, but the Godfather of pre-war Chicago blues recording was entrepreneur Lester Melrose: imagine a combination of Leonard Chess and Willie Dixon, who didn't actually compose or perform, but simply decided who got to record and who didn't, and who pocketed the resulting income, and you've got it. For Chess, Chicago's leading postwar blues independent label, read Bluebird, the Chicago-based "race records" subsidiary of the formidable Victor label.

Melrose ran Bluebird as a personal fiefdom: it was he, not the artists, who had the contract with Victor. At various times the Melrose stable of Chicago-based blues stars included Broonzy, Tampa Red, Memphis Minnie, Memphis Slim, Big Joe Williams, Arthur "Big Boy" Crudup, Jazz Gillum, John Lee—the original "Sonny Boy"—Williamson and Washboard Sam. Hooker's original mentor Tony Hollins was there (albeit running a barber shop), and so was Tommy McClennan, one of the very few blues artists whose recorded work had any audible effect on Hooker's music. Hooker's Vance homeboys Snooky Pryor and Jimmy Rogers were there, too. Rogers had been in and around Chicago since 1939, working the Maxwell Street market for tips; a decade or so later, he would eventually join forces with one McKinley Morganfield, a burly extrovert from Rolling Fork, Mississippi, soon to be better known as Muddy Waters, to form the blues band which would end up defining the city's indigenous postwar blues idiom. "A lot of them came up from Mississippi," says Hooker today, "and most of them upped into Chicago. They were all interested because Chicago was the big blues scene. I didn't want to go to Chicago because, at that time, I had a lot of competition. At that time there were some heavies there, so I didn't have no idea for going there and living there. Detroit . . . it was my town when I got bigger."

The Detroit John Lee found when he emerged from the army was a roughneck, blue-collar town dominated by the auto industry and the aftermath of Prohibition. Unions were deemed un-American, the local chapter of the FBI was virtually a wholly owned subsidiary of the Ford Motor Company, and it was not considered totally unreasonable for white workers to refuse to man the production lines alongside blacks. Thanks to its close proximity to the Canadian border, the city became such a reliable source of fine imported whiskey that bootlegging was considered second only to cars among the linchpins of the city's economy. The end result was a city with a thriving gang culture and an eminently bribable police force. It was also a deeply racist town with an extremely active Ku Klux Klan, not to mention a chapter of the Klan's elite group, the Black Legion. Admittedly Detroit was something of an improvement over Mississippi, but then that's not saying very much. Cops were recruited not only from the Irish and Italian communities, but from among white Southern migrants with necks of deepest red; these latter, often not unsympathetic to the Klan, were then sent in to "police" the black community. The city authorities required a minimum IQ of 100 from potential recruits to the Fire Department, but a rating of 65 was considered sufficient qualification for candidates for the police force.

As the city's heavy industry ramped up, housing became progressively more and more scarce, particularly for black defense workers. It was this issue which ripped Detroit apart during John Lee's early years in the city. A housing project—named, ironically enough, after Sojourner Truth, the nineteenth-century heroine of the fight against slavery—had been designated specifically for black workers until somebody noticed that the resulting homes, in an area generally considered "white," were actually going to be quite nice. The project was then reassigned for white occupancy, with the promise that some new homes for blacks would be constructed . . . at some unspecified point in the future, and outside the city. Blacks attempted to occupy the building anyway. Whites, led by the Klan, picketed City Hall. FBI agents "detected" pro-Axis agitators among the white opponents of black occupancy. Liberal whites lined up alongside the blacks, and the reassignment of Sojourner Truth to white occupancy was overturned. On February 27, 1942, the Klan burned a cross outside the project. The first black families arrived to move in the following morning, but were barred from doing so by approximately 1,200 picketing whites, some of whom were armed. The result was a pitched battle in the streets which required 200 police to quell. Of 104 people arrested, 102 were black. It was the first of a series of riots, not as celebrated as the legendary "Burn Baby Burn" conflagrations of 1967 but no less significant. Three months later, the building was finally occupied and—surprise, surprise—the black occupants and their new white neighbors ended up getting along just fine.

When America entered the war, Detroit underwent a magical transformation: all of a sudden it became the Arsenal of Democracy. Henry Ford refused to deliver airplane engines directly to the British on the grounds that it was against his principles to supply military equipment to active belligerents, despite the fact that both his British and German subsidiaries were already busy cranking out war material on behalf of their respective host countries as fast as was physically possible. John Lee contributed to the war effort in his own inimitable way: "All the men went off to the war, and the women did the work. Worked in the steel mills, drove the buses, streetcars . . . I was working in plants: Ford, General Motors, CopCo Steel, making stuff for the war. Somebody had to do it. I was on the lines, or I was the janitor. I did that mostly. I was a common laborer, but a janitor more. They used to catch me asleep, fire me and then rehire me when they needed people, and they needed people *bad* then. They fire you: you could walk across the street and get you another job. I'd be up all night playing my guitar, I'd sweep and then go in the corners and fall asleep, and they'd catch me a few times before they fired me. Captain'd wake me up and I'd go back to work."

With so many of the city's able-bodied men away in the armed forces, John Lee found that his soldier suit was no longer a necessary prerequisite for success with the opposite sex. "You can get married, you can have about five or six wives inside of five years if you really want to. Like the big movie-star woman, Elizabeth Taylor, have about nine husbands. The first time I got married it didn't last long, about two–three months. I was too young. My first wife's name was Alma Hopes. She was half Indian. I was young and she was young . . . we met at house parties and stuff, at her mom's house. I used to hang out there, started courting her daughter. She from Dublin, Mississippi. A lot of people in Detroit from Mississippi, but I left there so young I didn't know none of 'em. She said, 'Oh, you from Mississippi!' like that, and we got talkin' about different towns. I said, 'Oh, that's my home town.' It wasn't my home town, but [Dublin and Clarksdale] wasn't too far apart. We got to datin' together, and we got married. Stayed together a few months, then we broke up." Alma Hopes relocated to Chicago, where she raised Frances, the daughter who was her only souvenir of her brief marriage. John Lee stayed in touch and visited them whenever his blues career took him to Chicago. Fifty or so years later, he invited Frances to California, first to visit and then to live in his five-bedroom house in Vallejo, which he had vacated but not sold. "She was my first kid ever. She was my first child. She come up from Chicago and she had no place to go. She was stayin' there, and I said,

'Hey, I never did nothin' for you. I never gave you nothin'. This house is yours, this house.' "

Most of the time, John Lee claims a total of three marriages. Most of the time. "I been married three times. No, four times! I keep forgettin'! I done left one out there. I keep sayin' three times, but it was four times. Didn't stay with Sarah Jones long, about a year. We didn't have no kids and so I hardly ever thinks about her." The wife he thinks about most often is the one he generally refers to either as his "second" or "main" wife, the former Maude Mathis, "who I got all the kids with. I stayed with Maude longer'n any of 'em. Stayed with Maude about twenty-five years and we grew old together."

When Maude Mathis met John Lee Hooker, she was even newer to Detroit than he was. The youngest-but-one of Frank and Addie Mathis's seven children, she and her family had relocated to Detroit's Fourth Street from Augusta, Arkansas—"a little town in northeast Arkansas, sittin' on the White River," according to her younger brother Paul—in 1942. The Mathis family made the acquaintance of John Lee Hooker some time in late 1944. "We were living in an area of Detroit called Black Bottom, which is no more," Paul Mathis remembers today. The exact boundaries of Black Bottom shifted by a street or two every so often, but it was broadly definable as the blocks enclosed by Russell and Chene Streets to the east and Van Dyke to the west. Eddie Burns, who was to become one of Hooker's key musical sidekicks during the late '40s and early '50s, places Black Bottom as "downtown. It's all built up now, but it used to be a whole area there. Now it ain't Black Bottom anymore, it's some of the most modern part of Detroit." Next door and extending as far east as Woodward Avenue, was Paradise Valley; its spine was the legendary Hastings Street, though the area at its base was generally considered part of the Bottom. Both the Valley and the Bottom were bounded to the north by the outskirts of suburban Hamtranck, and to the south by the Detroit River, the natural border with Canada. As Burns told blues historian Mike Rowe: "Hastings ran north and south and the bottom of Hastings, I would say, was part of the Black Bottom . . . the Valley was off Hastings. It was a neighborhood of its own, y'know. Something of everything was happening down there."

"They called it Black Bottom, on the east side of Detroit," continues Paul Mathis, "but it was a mixed neighborhood. It had Mexicans, Polish, Italian, but we all went to school together and got on like a house on fire. We had our little scraps, but wasn't no such thing as prejudice. We used to go to they house, have a sandwich, and they would come to mine, have a sandwich, you know. It was a good neighborhood, really. There were seven of us: four boys and three girls. My brother Frank got called to the army—he was the only one in the army at that time goin' to war—and the other brothers was workin' in the factories. I'm the youngest, and Maude. They used to do what they called keno games and house parties, and I can't really give you a true picture of how it all came about, but I do remember that this Saturday night the party be at my mom's house; the next Saturday night it would be at Lucinda's house; the next Saturday night it would be at Anna Lou's house . . . like a circuit. Gamblin' and sellin' beer and booze and hamburgers and fish sandwiches and things of that nature. After the gamblin' was over, they'd start the party. This particular night, John and a friend of his came by. It was Broomstick Charles. John had this little small guitar, and he was playing and Charles was beatin' on the floor with this broomstick, you know, keepin' time. It sounded quite nice, really." He laughs at the memory. "Then John . . . I don't know where he was livin' at the time, but he moved on the same street that I lived on, Fourth Street. A lady called Miz Simms had a small rooming house, and John just got friendly with my family. I don't know how this came about, but he did get friendly with my family. And then he got even more friendly with my sister Maude."

Today Maude Hooker is a formidably stolid church lady of imposing mien and impassive reserve, but the positively impish grin which occasionally breaks through suggests a very different younger self, and she still giggles when she thinks back to her early encounters with John Lee Hooker. "I was sixteen when I met Johnny. You know, he used to play music, play his guitar in different places, houses. I don't know exactly how we met, but anyway he'd be playing at different houses and he met my parents and then he started coming to the house, you know, back and forth. He was living just down the street from us at the time when we met." So what specifically attracted the lively sixteen-year-old Maude to the quiet twenty-seven-year-old John Lee? "Oh God!" she laughs. "He used to just, you know, buy me nice little things. He was a very nice person and he would buy me nice little gifts, and so that's the way we met. Didn't anything happen like we fell in love with each other, it was just one of those things that happened. A girl and a man, that's all there was. That's the way it was. A young girl and a man, so that's what happened."

Paul Mathis is rather less coy. "And, you know, they carried on car-ryin' on, and Diane was born. He was just part of the family, really, and mom would always fix him some black-eyed peas and cornbread cooked whenever he came by, because that was his thing, black-eyed peas and cornbread. Miz Addie, you know. She used to jump on his case, because being as young as I was, I was having it off with an older woman . . . she used to jump on his case, man, she used to give him a bollocking, you know. I'm always being called the baby, you know. 'You know what my baby's doin'!' 'I-I-I-I don't know, Miz Addie.' He used to stutter pro-fusely, you know. Oh, he get kinda little excited, he couldn't say a word. Every time he come by . . . 'Is Addie home?' 'Yes, she is.' 'Well, I be back.' 'No, c'mon in here.' That was my mom, God rest her soul. As it hap-pened, John just became a part of the Mathis family, and he's been a part of the Mathis family from that until this."

John and Maude's first child, Diane, was born on November 24, 1946. The couple set up their first home in a rooming house on Madison Street. By this time, with the war long since ended, the boomtime was officially over. "Well, all the men come back home, most of them, and some of them didn't have jobs," remembers John Lee. "They come back and there was still work, but not enough work for everybody. After the war, things got rough." Maude recalls: "I remember my brother Frank was in the service, and he came out of the service and he couldn't get a job, so he went back in the air force. It was very hard to get a job there for a while."

Increasing competition in the job market provided a progressively greater incentive for Hooker to work harder and harder at his music. Giving up the day-to-day jobs altogether in favor of full-time music was less of an option than ever, though: after all, there were still bills to pay, each and every week. Paul Mathis's admiration for the tenacity and grit displayed by Hooker in those years remains wholly undiminished by the passing of time. "He didn't sit around and say, 'Well, it's gonna come along one day; I'm just gonna sit here and won't move, and all of a sudden a bag of gold'll drop into my lap.' The playing was strictly a weekend thing. Five days a week, he was punchin' a clock. Friday night, Saturday night, Sunday night, he was here, there and everywhere. He always had a job. Ushered movie houses, swept floors, pressed steel, helped assemble cars . . . the lot. He did it. It was hard graft. When I say 'hard graft' I mean the finger-bleedin' type'a hard graft. It was just a rough life. We never had a lotta money, but we always had plenty food. We always had a nice suit'a clothes to wear, but there never was a lot of money. But we always did eat good, and I'll sit here and testify that in those lean years, John never did falter. Determination kept him going. He was determined that he was gonna make it. He was workin' the steel mills. CopCo Steel. On Friday nights—which was payday—we'd have barbecue ribs. He stopped by the barbecue place, meet me at the barbecue place, we'd have barbecue ribs, which was a treat, you know, which was nice. I was throwin' papers, sellin' coal and ice, and doin' odd jobs. Anything anybody wanted to do, I would do it. Lookin' at John now, and I believe he will verify this, this is the day he thought he'd never see, where John Lee Hooker's name is universal. Everybody knows John Lee Hooker. But his success hasn't changed his train of thought, though he's grown a little less conservative than before his success. He used to hold onto that nickel, you know. But now he's a successful man and he's achieved his goals, and he don't mind givin' a stranger . . . 'Hey, take this twenty dollars and go get something to eat.' That sort of thing, you know. Before that, there was no money. It was very, very, very hard."

It was also very, very, very discouraging. "I was a hard-working person," John Lee insists. "I don't like handouts. I'd get out there and work, earn a living and stuff like that, but that wasn't what I was going to do the rest of my life. I knew that. That was a hard road, right up to now. It was a *hard* road. Many, many, many, many, *many* times I questioned [what I was doing]. Then my mind was saying, 'Don't go back. You done left there, you made a mistake.' One mind was sayin' I should have stayed, one mind said no. I was so strong into being a musician. All the rest of my sisters and brothers got good education but me. I could'a had, too. I could'a had number-one education, but I didn't want that. If I'd'a had that, I'd be down there right now. Maybe might'a been dead. Maybe got old just farmin' as a sharecropper, playin' an old guitar on the corner or in a roadhouse, but I was such a *strong* young man. Such *determination*. I would go out there, pretend I was goin' to school and wouldn't go, hide out in the woods with my old guitar and play. I was determined to be a musician, and my parents was determined that they wanted me to sit down and go to school. I had these two choices. I said, 'I'm not goin' to stay out here as a farmer,' and I didn't. I thought many a time, did I make the right decision? You know I thought about that! I thought that way, sure, but on the other hand, the other mind would say, 'You got to work to get up to this. You got to keep doin' this until you get what you want. You got to keep playin' here and there in little places 'til you find your goal.' And one mind would say, 'I ain't gonna make it. I didn't leave home for *this*.' Two minds: one sayin' 'Keep workin','; the other sayin', 'This ain't what you left for, to push a broom.' And the mind that said 'Keep on doin' it' paid off, but if I had been a little weak, and not strong, I'd'a said, 'Aw no, I give up, I'm goin' on back to Mississippi.' "

Instead, he got more and more serious about his music. Hooker had always played house parties whenever he had the chance, but now that he was beginning to think seriously about turning professional, he started to practice in earnest, refining the songs he'd brought with him from the Delta in the light of his new urban context. He and Maude had moved house again, this time to a shack behind a larger property on Monroe and Orleans which they shared with another couple, Jake and Bernethia Bullock, who had been fellow residents of the boarding house on Madison. As recent arrivals from Texas, the Bullocks were fairly unimpressed with the social climate of Detroit, not to mention the cramped conditions and squalid housing in the Black Bottom. "In 1946 my husband and I moved from Houston to Detroit under the impression that there was no segregation," says Mrs. Bullock. "In Texas we knew that it was segregated. We know that the blacks live on this side of the street and the whites live on that side of the street. We had as nice a home on this side of the street as they had on that side of the street. When we come here, when we moved in—it was nothing. The housing, to me, was horrible. They were needing painting, and most of them had no basements, they just had what you call cellars."

The shack was in a lamentable state of disrepair. Before the place could be certified as fit for human habitation, John Lee and Jake had to run water and power lines out from the main house, and exterminate the sizeable congregation of rats who'd taken up occupation. Worse! The shack was directly across the street from an exuberantly odoriferous stable. According to Bernethia Bullock: "Whenever we got ready to serve a meal, we had always to close the door if it was windy, because that dry manure would just blow right on into the house. My husband got busy and started working with the horse people, and what he would do on Saturday: he would help them clean the stable so that we wouldn't get the odor and what-not from it. Maude and I would always wash and wash the floors; we couldn't just mop, we had to actually put down water and soap and scrub and scrub the floors—the kitchen, bedrooms and everything—and then mop it up." Despite their best efforts, the place never quite developed that all-important patina of gentility. Jake Bullock's family never came to visit, and Maude's mother, aunt and brother were the only ones who would brave the inescapable *essence de cheval.* "Nobody else wanted to come over there, into that hoss-piss odor. They just didn't want to smell it.

"While they was living with us, Johnny decided that he was going to play the guitar, and he was going to start practicing. So he said to Jake, 'Would you mind if I do a little guitar practicing?' Jake said, 'No, I don't mind; just don't practice while I'm sleeping unless you're going to sit outside.' So one day Johnny was practicing, and he was just playing 'Step By Step,' and my husband was getting ready to go lay down and take a nap so that he could go to work at eleven o'clock, and he said to me, 'Lord, I'll be so happy when Johnny get up them steps.' Johnny would always practice out. If the weather was nice he would sit outside in the back. He worked days, and he'd come home in the evening and he'd sit out there and practice after he'd had his dinner. Sometimes he'd sit out there three or four hours, just picking different songs and different tunes or what-not, and then he'd come in and maybe get him a snack and he'd ask us, 'How did I sound?' I said, 'Well, you soundin' good, man. Keep up the good work.' I was a Baptist and I wasn't too much of a blues singer, but I figured that if there's something you love to do and you want to do it, right on with you for doing it. My husband sang with a [gospel] quartet, and they sang every Sunday morning. Sometimes he and Johnny would get out there and he'd be singing and Johnny would be playing . . . I said, 'You going to form a band or something of the kind?' He said, 'Me and Johnny might just do that. I'll do the singing and he'll do the playing.' I said, 'All Johnny's going to sing is the blues and you're not going to be making him sing no church songs, so shut up.' "

Jake Bullock turned out to be something of a soulmate to John Lee, acting as chauffeur and cheering section as Hooker made his first forays into graduating from the house-party circuit into the more demanding environment of the Detroit club scene. "My husband and Johnny would go to the nightclubs and I'd stay home. You see, Johnny didn't do a lot, didn't drive. I don't think he never did do very much driving. He would say, 'B-b-boy! Whatcha doin," Jake?' Jake would say, 'Well, I think maybe what I'm going to do tonight is go in early.' Johnny said, 'N-n-no, come on there, come on there. We gonna leave these gals at home and we're going out for a little while.' Maude went with them quite a bit. She was younger than I was and had a chance to get out, and they would go places. Johnny would play, just take his guitar, and while he was there, he'd probably ask if he could play a number, or if he could be on the show or what-not, and that's how he'd finally, you know, he got recognized. By doing things like that." Paul Mathis confirms: "We used to see John play at all the little bars around Detroit: the Caribbean Club, Apex Bar, Henry's Swing Club, which was in the Bottom, as we called it, Sensation . . . that was up north on Oakland. I can't really remember all those bars now, because it's been such a long time, but he played in every bar. He was playin' 'Boogie Chillen' and the 'Hobo Blues,' 'Sally Mae' and the 'Crawlin' King Snake,' those was some of the tunes that put him where he is. Blues was strugglin'. It was jitterbug and jivin' back in those days. The blues singers was playin' for a nickel over here, and the guy playin' the jitterbug, he's gettin' a quarter, that sort of thing."

"There wasn't too many clubs that you could play blues in during those days," confirms Eddie Burns. A sharp social division existed between the plusher, more sophisticated black nightclubs, catering to a more moneyed crowd and featuring jazzier, more urbane music, and the blue-collar, spit-and-sawdust taverns and bars which served as urban equivalents of the jook joints of the Delta, downhomes away from down home. It was to the latter which Hooker gravitated, partly because the plusher bars were far more likely to demand that a musician produce a union card than would the taverns, which were only one step away from the house parties. Inevitably, John Lee found himself drawn to Hastings Street. "It's a freeway now, the Chrysler Freeway. Oh, that was *the street, the street* in town. Everything you lookin' for on that street, *everything.* Anything you wanted was on that street. Anything you *didn't* want was on that street. Stores, pawnshops, clothing stores, winos, prostitutes. Like in 'Walkin' The Boogie' and 'Boogie Chillen' . . . *'when I first come to town, people, I was walkin' down Hastings Street.'* Everybody was talkin' about Hastings Street, and everybody was talking about Henry's Swing Club. That was a famous place. A famous street. Best street in all the world. Too bad they tore it down.'[1] Bernethia Bullock remembers the heyday of Hastings Street with rather less affection. "Oh, Hastings Street. There was a lot of guys on the street, a lot of hanging out. Hastings was one of the predominant places where most families wouldn't allow their children to go. Hastings was a rough street, that was the understood

---

1 Henry's Swing Club wasn't actually on Hastings Street itself, but on nearby Madison. Nevertheless, it was part of the Hastings Street milieu: here, as elsewhere, Hooker was flexing justifiable poetic license and adhering to the general usage of the community.

thing. If my husband and Johnny went to Hastings, I didn't have a knowledge of it. Because that's what Hastings was like. If you had any type of respect, you stay off Hastings."

One of Hooker's first fans from those early club appearances was a tall thin electrical engineer from Pensacola, Florida, who called himself Famous Coachman. Improbably enough, it was his real name. "My daddy's name was John Coachman. When I was born, my mother told my daddy, 'John, I hope he'll be a famous man' and my daddy said, 'Why don't we name him Famous?' They named me Famous, so I'm catchin' hell tryin' to *be* famous." Coachman came to Detroit in 1947, and he happened across John Lee playing out on a club on Lafayette. "It was a very small club and he was playing there every night for small change, and I used to come out to see him play on the weekend, and we would all be around and about at different clubs and different places, and so we just had a good time together. He and I used to pal around a bit and go out and chase around and eat fish. When I first met John I thought he was just an old guy—well, he was a younger guy then—a guy from outta the South that has migrated to Detroit to get a job and he's just picked up a *git*-tar. I thought he was just tryin' to learn how to play." Coachman laughs. "I was fooled. That's what he's been playin' ever since; I guess he's still learnin', but that's his style. He's just doin' Johnny Lee, and that's all it is. You can't take him away from bein' himself. But he played around Detroit, and he played in many, many clubs and places. Johnny Lee haven't had it easy. He haven't had it easy, he had it pretty tight, raisin' a family and gettin' no money from gigs and what-not. I mean, he worked in some places for a small amount, but he hadn't worked that much, and he tried to make music, take care of him and his family. It was just small money, that's all."

By this time, Hooker had gained his first celebrity admirer: none other than the great Aaron "T-Bone" Walker, a Texas-born, Oklahoma-trained guitarist whose influence on postwar Western popular music is almost impossible to overestimate. At the time, according to Hooker, Walker was "the hottest thing out there." The first to adapt the single-string improvisatory flourishes of the progressive country blues guitarists to the electric instrument and juxtapose the resulting joyful noise with the brassy blare of a swing band, Walker created a style and a repertoire which has long outlived him: wherever electric blues guitar is played, you're still hearing what T-Bone Walker developed in the '30s and '40s. His "T-Bone Blues" was first recorded in 1940, and he cut "Mean Old World" and a few others for the then-tiny Los Angeles-based Capitol label in 1942, but it was the seminal sides recorded between 1946 and 1948 for Capitol's Black & White subsidiary which caused the revolution. In Memphis, the young B. B. King heard Walker's 1947 recording "Stormy Monday Blues" (aka "Call It Stormy Monday") and went straight out to buy himself an electric guitar. Others like Clarence "Gatemouth" Brown, Lowell Fulson and Albert King were right behind him, and the word soon spread to hundreds and thousands more. T-Bone's mellifluous crooning vocals, sly lyrics, dry woody guitar tone and jumping jazzy backdrops made him the role model for an entire generation of bluesmen. A former dancer, he was also a hugely extrovert performer, copyrighting many of the guitar-badman stunts (favorite: playing the guitar behind his head while sinking into a perfect splits) which subsequently provided such sterling service for athletic performers like Chuck Berry, Bo Diddley, Guitar Slim, Buddy Guy, Albert Collins, Johnny Guitar Watson, Jimi Hendrix and Stevie Ray Vaughan. "Stormy Monday" itself became part of the core repertoire of the blues. Hooker met him at what later became the Rainbow Bar off Hastings Street. At that time it was Sporty Reed's Show Bar; subsequently immortalized as "Sportree's" in some of Elmore Leonard's Detroit-set novels. "T-Bone was playin' there," remembers Eddie Burns, "because they used to bring a lotta out-of-town acts into that club. It was a real nice club with padded leather walls."

"He played there, and he used to take me there with him," says Hooker. "I'd sit up there and watch him. He put me on the bandstand after the first time I went there, and I like freaked out. Boy, it was a high-class place, y'know, women with evening gowns an' stuff on . . . and I was just a kid. He give me some liquor and I got on the bandstand . . . 'Drink this down, kid.' So I drink it down to build up my nerve, and I had the house a-*rockin'*. He liked to drink, and he was sittin' out there drinkin'. He was a stone ladies' man. He was a *ladies' man*. Always was sharp, all the time; stayed dressed up all the time. You never see him in jeans an' stuff, he always would wear nice suits an' slacks an' stuff like that, but he had the money to buy that with. He'd just had 'Stormy Monday' and the streets were filled with women, looking for romance. He were just a great man . . . the great T-Bone Walker." The great man presented his protégé with a gift that would change his life: his first electric guitar. "It was like a gift from God, just like a gift from God, the Supreme Being, handed down from heaven. I tell everybody, 'Ol' T-Bone Walker give me that guitar.' 'You's a *liar*!' 'Oh yes he did! He did too!'

'He too big, he's a big star, he ain't give you nothin' like this!' But he was my buddy. He was crazy about me. He liked to call me 'kid.' 'C'mere, kid. Go do this, kid. Do this for me, kid.' I jumped like a *frog* an' do anything he said. I was in love with that man, and followed him around like a little puppy."

Hooker was almost thirty years old at the time; he was a father and a three-time husband, yet in most of his anecdotes from this time, people seemed to persist in calling him "kid." "Yeah! They *were*, 'cause I was little and skinny. They called me the Iron Man at one time. The Kid. The Iron Man. 'Man, that kid can sing.' I didn't look old. Till I was forty, forty-five, almost fifty, I looked like twenty-one or -two."

Hooker worked hard at his day jobs and his music alike, and he played hard, too. "He and my husband were both big drinkers," says Bernethia Bullock. "My husband and Johnny and the gang that they were with would come home some nights and I didn't want the kids to know that my husband had been drinking, so I would sit up and wait for him to come in, and steer him to the bedroom. Sunday morning when they'd wake up, we'd get up, take the kids to church and they didn't know he'd even had a drink. Sometimes five o'clock in the morning, I didn't want the neighbors to see 'em coming in. I said, 'God, what you going to say about y'all struggling in here at five o'clock in the morning?' He said, 'Ain't nothing they can say, we just been out of town, just getting back in.' It didn't make Maude no difference, she said some of the time she'd be one place and Johnny would be another and it didn't make any difference, because she was a nightlifer herself. Me not being a nightlifer, you know, it kind of worried me . . . it was just a little embarrassing to see them coming in that time of morning."

Initially, Maude Hooker claims, she didn't make too much of a fuss about her husband's new project. "Not at the beginning, because I knew that he would have to be workin' here and there and be out half the night. I understood that and I went along with that, you know. As my kids were born, I stayed home and tried to raise them to the best of my knowledge, that I could. Afterwards it got kinda hard, after the rest of the kids was born." Her brother Paul recalls that she wasn't always quite that sanguine. "I recollect a little party, just before he started making records, at this lady's house—the one that I was friendly with, Lucinda— John was playin' and we was havin' a good time. Oh, we was really havin' a good time. And Maude came in and said, 'C'mon John, let's go.' Well, John was havin' a good time, and John wasn't ready to go, so Maude promptly yanked the guitar out of his hands and hit it 'cross the amplifier and broke it into smithereens. She tore it into splinters. I don't think it was so much that she disapproved of his *playing*. The disapproval was that there was *women* there. There was women there, you know what I mean, and they *shakin'* it, you know what I mean, and he's playin', and that was the disapproval."

By 1948, John Lee was beginning to make some real headway. This was just as well, since his and Maude's second child, Vera, was born on April 1 of that year. He'd also graduated to playing an occasional show at Lee's Sensation, a slightly more upmarket club than his usual Black Bottom venues. "It was a kind of a swinging, classy joint, not really a blues bar," according to Eddie Burns. "Lee" was the name of the owner and "Sensation" was the name of the club—as Burns remembers it, anyway—but over the years the names of bar and boss have fused to the point where most people, including Hooker, remember both simply as "Lee Sensation." " 'The Lee Sensation Bar.' That was a nightclub. *Nice nightclub*, oh yeah. I used to play there for Lee Sensation. That was a high-class club. I played there, I thought I was in heaven. I thought I'd *never* get to play there. That was on Oakland, on the north end of Detroit. Lee Sensation, he named his club after his name. That was before I recorded . . . that was a long time ago. I wasn't too famous then. I'd been wanting to play in that bar for a long time, but nothin' but big people played there, big names and stuff like that. T-Bone Walker and Ivory Joe Hunter, Jackie Wilson, people like that . . . big people. I was so famous around town that he booked me in there.

"It was just a matter of findin' the break. I got discovered out of a little bar by my manager Elmer Barbee. He was a very good person, very smart. He was mixed Indian and black; very nice, very honest person. He knew how to get 'em. He the one discovered me, playin' around nightclubs, little honkytonk bars, house parties. I had a little trio, I was playing electric guitar." Before Maude broke it, one assumes. The trio was filled out by pianist James Watkin and drummer Curtis Foster, two musicians who could adapt to Hooker's rough-hewn, rural approach. "I was playing a little bar called the Apex Bar on Monroe Street, and I was the talk of the town. Little John Lee Hooker, they would be callin' me. And he come in there. He made a special trip to come in that bar and see me. He had never seen me, but he had heard of me. He had a little record store on San Antoine and Lafayette, 609 Lafayette, which is long gone. The building was tore down years gone. He was livin' in the back with his wife and son, and he come down to that place and saw me and he said, 'Kid, come down to my record shop. I'm a manager, and you are the best I ever heard.' I said, 'Yeah?' and I did, I went down there, and I went on about six months to a year, just recordin' in the back of his place."

"There was this record store called Barbee's," says Paul Mathis, "with a little studio in the back, and he would go down and try to play, and then nothin' never would happen, and he'd go back and try to make another record and nothin' never would happen, and he'd go back and make another record and nothin' never would happen."

"Nobody knew John Lee Hooker 'cept playin' at little clubs, no record, nothin'," says Hooker. "The clubs were packed every night with people wantin' to see me, but I wasn't known in those days. I come down to [Barbee's] place one Wednesday, and we started recordin' and talkin' all night, drinkin' wine and goin' over these different tunes, 'Boogie Chillen,' 'Hobo Blues.' Finally, he taken me downtown on Woodward Avenue with all this material to a big place like Tower Records, and the guy had a little label called Sensation . . . Bernie Besman and Johnny Caplan. They was partners, both of them was big wheels, and they heard the stuff and they went wild and they recorded me."

"Do you want me to tell you how Hooker got into the picture?" asks Bernard Besman expansively. "I didn't look for him; he just happened to come in. One of the dealers that we had brought him in. His name was Barbee."

To John Lee Hooker, still a country boy at heart despite his years in the big city, Elmer Barbee—or "E" Barbee, as he was also known—was a person of some consequence. To the considerably more worldly Besman, whose business had a million-dollar annual turnover, Barbee was simply "a very small record dealer who had a store. These people would come in every day bringing in artists. Barbee said, 'Here, I have a terrific blues singer for you and I'd like you to hear him.' He brought John by in person, and he brought a record that John had made in one of those auto . . . those music-machine booths . . . a record made in this quarter machine. I think I got it somewhere, but I don't know where it is. I haven't lost it, because we keep everything. I listened to the record, and it was already practically worn out, and you could hardly hear anything on it. Anyway, he sang 'Sally Mae' on that thing, a blues number, and I'd never recorded a blues artist up to that time. Although we were selling the blues and I was familiar with the blues, he didn't sound like any of the blues artists we were selling. The blues we were selling at that time were like Johnny Moore's Three Blazers with Charles Brown, T-Bone Walker . . . twelve bars, you know. This was something altogether different that I frankly didn't understand.

"On top of that, when he sat talking to me, he stuttered. I figured, 'Jesus, how can this guy sing for stuttering?' I didn't believe it was him. I thought, 'This guy must be lying. He's not singing here. This must be a fake.' So I said to Elmer Barbee, 'Okay, next time I have a session, bring him over and I'll make a dub at the studio with him.' So that's what happened. The reason I recorded him was the fact that he could sing and not stutter. Otherwise I wouldn't have recorded him. He didn't mean anything to me."

Not surprisingly, Hooker remembers these events from a very different perspective. "Me, I brought [Besman] a long ways," he says. "A *long* ways. He had a little old label named Sensation Records, a *little* label right there in Detroit, on Woodward Avenue. Barbee brought me in the store there. I had never met Bernie, I didn't know him from Adam. Me and Barbee played all those tunes ['Sally Mae,' 'Boogie Chillen' et al.] for him and Caplan right there in the store. Barbee had come in and said, 'Man, I got a kid. Discover this kid.' [Besman] know Barbee real good, they was good friends. 'Sally Mae,' yeah. Me and Barbee did that in a studio on Lafayette and St. Antoine; he had a record store. We would sit there *all night* . . . we'd be playin' guitar all night, me'n him, his wife and so on. Then he told me, 'I got a friend, Bernie Besman and Johnny Caplan. I'm gonna take you down to they store; they got a record store and a distributing company there.' Me'n him went down there. They had blanks then: they didn't have tape recorders, they had wax discs. We recorded [an acetate] on that, we went down there and we played it for them. 'Sally Mae,' 'Boogie Chillen' . . . I was playin' that in little old nightclubs around then, all the stuff that I recorded I was playin' around. All the stuff I played for Barbee I was playin' in parties, nightclubs, the Apex Bar. Barbee would come around nights when I wasn't playin', and we would play these tunes: 'Boogie Chillen,' 'Sally Mae,' 'Hobo Blues,' 'When My First Wife Left Me.' "

By the end of World War II, just about every definable section of the American public was ravenously hungry for the new music of which they'd been starved for the previous couple of years. Two separate bans on recording had just ended. One was caused by a shortage of shellac— the basic material from which the ten-inch 78rpm biscuits current at the

time were made—for which the war machine's need had taken understandable precedence over that of the record business. The second was
the result of a fierce industrial dispute between the major record companies and the American Federation of Musicians; by the time it was
resolved, a thriving crop of independent operators had started up, un-
impeded by the battle between the union and the majors, and serving the
markets for hillbilly and "race" music in which the majors were no longer
so interested. Or, as Eddie Burns puts it, "One of the reasons John got
in and a lot of us got in, was that the musicians' union had a ban on the
studios. What happened was them Jews found a way to record blues
musicians and people like that, but your contract wasn't worth the paper
that it was written on. They had a way of settin' these dates when they
released the stuff, sayin' it was recorded back then [i.e. before the ban].
So a lotta blues people got in on the deal, which mean that you auto-
matically was gonna get a screwin', because it wasn't legal in the first
place."

Together, the bans created an artificial caesura which served only to
magnify and dramatize the already immense cultural and demographic
shifts in the patterns of both production and consumption of popular
music, caused directly by the war. The dominant postwar blues styles
were indeed still the post-Basie jumpin' jive exemplified by Louis Jordan
and subsequently customized by Roy Brown, Eddie "Cleanhead" Vinson,
Amos Milburn and Wynonie Harris alongside—as Besman indicates—the
smooth and sophisticated nightclub-blues crooning of Johnny Moore And
His Three Blazers, featuring the sublime Charles Brown on piano and
vocals, plus T-Bone Walker, ruling the roost as both guitar hero and
matinee idol alike. Nevertheless, a new set of realities, a new set of circumstances, a new set of ambitions: these all required a new vocabulary
of expression, a fresh language of style. Of joyful necessity, old idioms
were required to reinvent themselves, and new ones began to emerge. One
such was a Northern industrial-metropolitan transformation of the music
of the Mississippi Delta diaspora: downhome blues electrically heated into
an urgent, streamlined distillation of its rural ancestor, an aural reflection
of the new experiences of rural peoples relocated to the rough ends of the
big cities. Furthermore, the first completely black-oriented radio station,
WDIA, had just commenced broadcasting from Memphis. Audiences, musicians and record labels alike were ready to roll. And they did.

The first signpost hit from this particular New Wave was "Short

Haired Woman," a surprise 1947 hit by Sam "Lightnin'" Hopkins (from Texas: regional boundaries aren't infallible, after all), which racked up the surprising aggregate of 50,000 sales for a tiny Houston independent label called Gold Star (and, incidentally, annoyed the hell out of Aladdin, the larger, Los Angeles–based label to which Hopkins was contracted at the time, by outselling the version he'd cut for them). A year later came Stick McGhee's light-hearted "Drinking Wine Spo-Dee-O-Dee," a cleaned-up version of a much older, much rawer downhome blues—the nonsense syllables replace the Oedipal compound noun—which sold somewhere in the region of 400,000 copies and served as the foundation stone for the Atlantic Records empire. Then there was Muddy Waters' "I Can't Be Satisfied," cut for Aristocrat Records in Chicago and featuring the big, booming Delta voice and urgent, amplified slide-guitar of a war-time Mississippi migrant, accompanied only by a fidgety, funkily slapped acoustic bass. Electric downhome had found a standard-bearer; that record, and its maker, laid the foundation stone upon which Chess Records' Chicago operation would soon be built. In Detroit, Bernard Besman and his partner Johnny Caplan had taken over Pan American, a derelict record-distribution company, and in a mere three years, they had built it up to a more than respectable size. Besman was well aware that a distributor could sell significant numbers of copies of the right single by a good downhome bluesman, and since downhome music was ridiculously cheap to record, a small label could break even on as few as 5,000 sales. In his other identity as boss of Sensation Records, an archetypal fledgling independent label with a name borrowed from a popular local club, he was equally well aware that he didn't have such a downhome bluesman under contract. But, in Elmer Barbee, he knew a man who did.

John Lee Hooker and Bernard Besman worked actively together for less than four years. Any direct comparison of the two men's accounts of their collaboration leads to the inescapable conclusion that they spent much of their time together speaking entirely different, and mutually incomprehensible, musical and cultural languages. Nevertheless, those four years were among the most intensively productive years of Hooker's career. His two biggest early hits, "Boogie Chillen" and "I'm In The Mood For Love," were both Besman productions, and Besman is undeniably one of the pivotal figures in the entire John Lee Hooker saga. It was Tony Hollins who first set the young John Lee's feet on the path, and it was Will Moore whose support, tuition and inspiration gave him the keys to the kingdom. Nevertheless, it was Besman's decision to record the stuttering little guy in the long raincoat, a decision taken—as he claims—on a whim one damp Detroit afternoon, which opened the floodgates for everything which was to follow. The history of the blues is littered with brilliant talents who failed to receive the fame and acclaim to which their gifts rightfully entitled them because they had the misfortune never to be in the right place at the right time, but John Lee Hooker would still have made his professional breakthrough—somehow, some time—even without Besman's intervention. The only relevant questions are: how big would that breakthrough have been, and how much longer would Hooker have had to wait?

The Bernard Besman you might meet today is a canny, alert octogenarian with a fondness for biscuit-colored leisure suits, and a luxuriant silver pompadour which wouldn't disgrace a superannuated rockabilly singer. He moves somewhat carefully, following a stroke a few years ago, but there is no hint of vagueness about him: he evokes the events of half a century before in crisp and loquacious detail. The trouble is that, in matters both fundamental and trivial, his recollections differ so strongly from Hooker's that it requires a considerable effort of will to remember that both men are, in fact, telling the same story. For example, we've already heard Hooker tell us that Besman and his partner "went wild" when they heard the acetates that he'd cut in the back of Barbee's store; by contrast, Besman remembers being played a disc from a quarter-in-the-slot record-your-voice booth,[2] and simply yielding to the mild curiosity he felt about a downhome bluesman who stuttered when he spoke but found his clarity when he sang. Each of them contradicts the other at almost every turn; and each of them is at some considerable pains to minimize the importance of the other's contribution to the work they did together. It is as if they both feel that the resulting achievement wasn't big enough for both of them . . . which, of course, it is. And what's more: they plainly don't trust each other the proverbial inch.

The answer to the question "So who is Bernard Besman, anyway?" goes something like this. He was born in Kiev, the capital of the Ukraine: a city which had known very little peace during World War I, the October

---

2 Besman has previously been quoted as stating that the demos he heard featured Hooker's gigging sidemen James Watkin (piano) and Curtis Foster (drums). If these two differing accounts are in any way reconcilable, all I can say is that it must have been a very *large* record-your-voice booth.

Revolution and the uneasy period thereafter. In the last months of the war, the southern Ukraine was annexed by Germany, and the Polish army seized Kiev itself in May 1920. They were ejected the following month, but the resulting military adventure ended the Ukraine's brief and ill-fated struggle for independence from the new-born Soviet Union. It gained them little more than the personal attentions of young Joseph Stalin himself, first as Political Commissar and then as Ukranian Chairman of the Council of Labour Armies. Not surprisingly, Besman's family fled in 1921, after the suppression of the Kronstadt uprising ended any significant challenge to Bolshevik hegemony. However, it wasn't until 1926 that they finally arrived in Detroit, having had to cool their heels for a British sojourn in Whitechapel, at the heart of the East End of London.

"I went to school there, at 32 Leman Street, because the quota had closed down for the United States, and I had to wait five years before we could come out. I came from a very musical family, and from the age of three I was playing piano. When I finally got to Detroit I formed a band with another fella, called Milt, and we called our band Milt Bernard. That's how I went through college, making my money by playing piano. My style was like Eddie Duchin or Tommy Cavallero. That's dance music, society-type smooth dance music, ballroom dancing. We played hotels and resorts. We played jazz as part of the program, but mainly it was for dancing, because that's all there was. Later I became a booking agent for bands, and I did pretty well. I made records in 1936. I had a band, and I booked bands, and I made demonstration records because as a booking agent, people would come to get a band and I'd play them these records for them to see which band they liked. When the war came along I had to close up, and go into the service, but while I was in the service I was in Special Services, and I did shows. I was with 5th Air Force, and we'd put on shows, and I had a band. We took care of the dances, scheduled dancers, things like that. So actually, I pursued the music club through the service. About three days after I was discharged, I was waiting for a friend of mine that was in the service with me, and one of our other friends walked by where we were waiting in downtown Detroit. He was in the photographic business before he got in the service and he had some records under his arm and he said, 'Say, Bernie, I was just in California and somebody there gave me these records and they wanted me to get into the business, but I know nothing about this business.' "

Besman's buddy was carrying an armful of Latin American records he'd been given by a company named Pan American.[3] "I didn't know anything about the record business at first, and he didn't want the business anyway. I'd only been out of the service three days so I said, 'Well, let me check into it and see what happens.' I called those people and they said, 'Sure, you can be a distributor, but you have to pay immediately for the records.' I put the money in advance in the bank before I even got the records. So I had about six thousand dollars at that time; that was my whole fortune. This friend of mine that I met, I told him about this deal and said, 'I have six thousand dollars, I don't know how long it'll last, do you want to be a partner with me?' He says, 'You try it for about three weeks, see what happens,' and later he came up with six thousand dollars and we became partners. The point was that when I did get the records and went out to sell them, nobody wanted them because they were primarily made in a Spanish vein, or Mexican type of music. But the people I went to see told me that if I had *this* record or *that* record, they'd buy it from me. So that's how I got involved, selling records primarily by black artists, and I was the first independent record distributor using these off-brand labels. The twelve thousand dollars didn't last very long, buying records on credit, and after three months it got too big for the area I rented. I rented this basement in one of the houses to start with, and we'd get the records through the window off the sidewalk, so we moved into much larger quarters at 3747 Woodward Avenue, which was the main street in Detroit. Four thousand square feet, and the rent was up from thirty dollars a month to about four hundred dollars, and I wondered how the hell we were going to make that, because it was quite a jump. But we were very, very successful. By the time I sold my share of the business to my partner to come to California for some other ventures that I had, we did close to a million and a half dollars a year."

With Besman's background, it was a short and predictably inevitable step from distributing records to producing them himself. "I had enough experience of making records: by making records I mean use a studio. A fellow that I knew in college went into that business, and we'd get the Capitol Theater and use their stage to record the bands. You ask how I

---

3 E-mail from Colin Escott to the author, April 2000: If you want chapter & verse on Pan American, it was started by Caplan & Besman in April 1946, but only covered Michigan and Ohio. They were pretty successful by 1948. They'd sold 175,000 copies of the Harmonicats "Peg O'My Heart" (you'll never believe how bad) and distributed Modern, Savoy, Aladdin, Aristocrat,
• Specialty, etc.

got into the record business after being a distributor? Well, all of our repertoire was black music, and because there were a lot of black people around, there were a lot of musicians, and good musicians, too. And we'd visit the different clubs and hear all these bands, and there were many clubs in Detroit at that time. Detroit was jumping, there were a lot of clubs, but Lee's club Sensation was one of the best ones, one of the biggest ones. Some of our customers who were black called me about a band called Todd Rhodes. That was the first band that I recorded. I went to visit the Sensation Club to see Todd Rhodes . . . that's where Hooker always mentions Lee Sensation discovered him. That's a lotta crap. In fact, my label that I started was called Sensation, and I used the name of this club which was very very popular, and Todd Rhodes was the first artist I recorded."

Though most of the time Besman freely agrees that John Lee Hooker "wasn't my first artist, but he turned out to be the best . . . so far. And the most lucrative artist," he has a perverse fondness for sometimes claiming the long-forgotten pianist Todd Rhodes, rather than Hooker, as his "best and biggest artist ever." In fact, Rhodes was already something of a has-been by July 1947, when Besman took him to United Sound Studios, at 5820 Second Boulevarde, for the inaugural Sensation Records sessions. Rhodes—born in Hopkinsville, Kentucky, in 1900—had co-founded the Springfield, Ohio-based Synco Septette with drummer William McKinley in the early '20s. Following a change of name to McKinney's Cotton Pickers, they earned themselves sufficient popularity to become one of the first black bands to broadcast live on nationwide radio. (The most famous, of course, was Duke Ellington's band, who broadcast live, first locally and then nationally, from the legendary Cotton Club in Harlem.) Rhodes left the Cotton Pickers in 1934, performed with several less distinguished bands and ended up in Detroit, where he worked the assembly line in the Fisher Body Plant during World War II while playing occasional gigs to stay in practice. Returning to full-time music after the end of the war, he took a four-piece band into the Triangle Bar on Michigan Avenue. They soon expanded to a septet, playing occasional blocks of one-nighters around the Midwest and deftly serving up the jump stylings of the time to satisfied customers at Club Sensation, which is where Besman happened across Rhodes during an eight-month residency which had started as a mere four weeks. Remember Paul Mathis's observation about how "the blues singers was playin' for a nickel over here, and the guy playin' the jitterbug, he's gettin' a quarter, that sort of thing?" The band

Todd Rhodes led in the late '40s was the kind of "jitterbug" act he was talking about.[4]

As Besman tells it: "He was the one [with whom] I had one of my biggest records, 'Bell Boy Boogie,' which was named after a disc jockey, Jack The Bellboy, who was the biggest disc jockey in Detroit. This was about '46, and I was just amazed at the music and the crowd there—it was all black—and he'd get off the stage during a number like the 'Bell Boy Boogie' and he'd just parade from the stage all around. The people would just get up and get behind him and dance—they didn't have the jitterbug yet but whatever—and the place was jumping. So I recorded that, and he had a number called 'Dance Of The Redskins' which was a real jazzy rhythm-and-blues dance number. I thought, 'Boy, this'd be a terrific record,' but let me tell you something: what you hear in the club and what you hear on the record is not the same, which taught me quite a bit. So I recorded that, and it was the first number I released on Sensation, but that wasn't the number that became a hit. 'Bell Boy Boogie,' the reverse, was the hit. So you see, whatever you plan, it doesn't turn out that way. So I started with Todd Rhodes. He became very big and very famous in Detroit; but they knew him: the black people did, anyway. But the white people picked him up because he did music for white dances. I recorded close to twenty different artists before I recorded Hooker, and I think maybe eight or ten were released on the Sensation label."

The first four Sensation releases all featured Rhodes and his orchestra in some capacity or other. The first, second and fourth of them were credited to the band itself, while they appeared on the third as accompanists to one Louie Saunders, "the newest sensational song stylist of the year." "Dance Of The Redskins," a slow, sultry blues subsequently reissued as "Blues For The Red Boy," was actually the B-side of "Blue Sensation," whereas the aforementioned "Bell Boy Boogie," from the same session, had "Flying Disc" as its flipside and was the first Sensation release. Outside the Michigan and Ohio area where Pan American held distributive sway, all four titles from Sensation's Jam Session series appeared on the long-vanished VitAcoustic label.

"After Todd Rhodes," Besman continues, "I had other bands and

---

4 Todd Rhodes's greatest contribution to the rock and roll era was the use of one of his tunes, "Blues For Moondog," as the signature tune of Cleveland-based DJ Alan Freed's hugely influential rock and roll radio show *Moondog Matinee*.

artists . . . T. J. Fowler, who was also from the same type as Hooker, played good music. Among the most famous that I recorded—became pretty big, bigger than Hooker ever got—was Milt Jackson, and also Sonny Stitt: terrific sax player. I was one of the first ones to record them." In the '50s, vibraphonist Jackson became such an integral part of pianist John Lewis's hugely successful chamber-jazz ensemble, The Modern Jazz Quartet, that, as far as many listeners were concerned, the initials MJQ might as well have stood for "Milt Jackson Quartet." Altoist Sonny Stitt emerged from the rhythm-and-blues dance orchestra world, where he'd co-led a big band with tenorist Gene Ammons, to become Charlie Parker's anointed successor, a brilliant musician who never quite escaped from under Bird's colossal, looming shadow. "Sonny Stitt, who I loved, now there was a real schooled musician. Charlie Parker was sensational, but Stitt equals him. I bailed Sonny Stitt out of jail once in Detroit, he'd been smoking marijuana and he called me at three in the morning. That's when I did the session with him: I got him out of jail, and he did this and he sure played beautiful music. The recording I have now is out on Fantasy Records. He does 'Stardust' in bebop style, so beautiful. This was back in '48, '49." In addition, Besman recalls, "I had a vocal group called The Vocalaires, and some spiritual groups. I rounded out the label: just like any of the black labels that you had around then I had spirituals out, jazz, blues . . ."

For the sake of convenience, Besman scheduled Hooker's first studio date as an extension of a previously booked Todd Rhodes session at United Sound, with Joe Siracuse, the twenty-seven-year-old son of the studio's owner, Jimmy Siracuse, at the controls. As a dance-band musician of the old school, Besman felt comfortable with Rhodes and his band, all of whom were trained, versatile, musically literate players who responded easily and docilely to productorial direction. Where he was ahead of his time was in his recognition of the studio as a brush rather than simply a canvas, and of the role of the record producer as something other than simply a passive transcriber of an existing event. Come to that, he was also a pioneer of the megalomaniac notion that "on all the records, I don't care who does it, it's more the producer than the artist who makes the record. I don't care what you say. The producer makes the record. I'm not talking about myself or anybody, because what you sound like in a hall is not the way it comes out on a record. How's it done? It's the producer who comes up with some gimmick or song." However, he and

Phil Spector can fight out the copyright to that particular assumption if they ever happen to find themselves trapped in the same elevator.

Besman claims that "[Hooker] came to me about late 1946, and I think the first session was in about November of '47." However, since he'll also opine, in the same conversation, that " 'Boogie Chillen' must've come out in early 1947," and attribute his "Bell Boy Boogie" Todd Rhodes session to 1946 rather than 1947, it is not impossible that his steel-trap memory is capable of occasionally playing him false. In fact, "Boogie Chillen" was released in November 1948. The session at which it was recorded was generally assumed, for many years, to have taken place in October or early November of that year, but recently surfaced paperwork suggests that "Boogie Chillen" and its B-side "Sally Mae"— plus the other items cut at the same session—were already safely in the can by September. Still, the controversy over the date of that session is negligible by comparison with the still-smouldering arguments over exactly what took place, who did what at whose behest, and why.

Despite Hooker's popularity as an in-person attraction playing trio with pianist James Watkin and drummer Curtis Foster in Black Bottom bars, Besman opted to record him solo, placing the aural focus even more squarely on the featured singer/guitarist than the successful Hopkins and Waters records had done. The object of the exercise was to lay down four releasable tracks, enough for the A- and B-sides of two 78rpm singles, during the three-hour session which was then the basic, union-recognized unit of studio time. Evidently, Besman and Hooker had agreed that the featured release was to be a slow blues, because Hooker arrived ready to perform three different numbers in that style. Well, sort of ready. "When Hooker came into the studio," claims Besman, "all he had was this one guitar, a box [acoustic] guitar he'd just got out of the pawn-shop. He had no guitar, when I gave him an advance before the recording he went and got the guitar and he said that after the session, which I also paid him, that he would buy it. Anyway, the first session that John Lee Hooker did, and the fact that he stutters, and the fact that he didn't have any experience, and the fact that he drove me crazy because he repeated the same song . . . I only did three numbers in the three-hour session that I was allotted. And I wanted four."

According to Besman's session notes, those first three tunes that Hooker played for him were "Sally Mae," "Highway 51" and "Wednesday Evening." However, if we consult Les Fancourt's definitive Hooker discography,[5] we find a slightly more complex story. According to Fancourt, the session did indeed begin with two takes of "Sally Mae"; the other songs, also deep slow blues, remained unreleased until the early '70s, when Besman demonstrated that he'd learned at least one specific lesson from Hooker by leasing the two takes he'd cut of each piece under two different titles to two different record companies for two different retrospective anthologies. Neither song had fully matured: Hooker returned again and again over the years to "Wednesday Evening," a song which mourned his failed marriage to Alma Hopes; later versions of this free-form slow blues attained depths of cathartic emotion which "She Was In Chicago" and "Crazy 'Bout That Woman" (the titles which Besman later assigned to the discarded takes from this particular session) failed to plumb. "War Is Over (Goodbye California)" shared the same eerie modalities as "Sally Mae," but had only a passing lyrical reference in common with "Highway 51," a traditional Delta theme approached rather more conventionally at a subsequent session.

Hooker's approach to what must have originally seemed like fairly standard material turned out to be so idiosyncratic that Besman, to whom the very notion of a free-form slow blues was utterly oxymoronic, must have wondered just what the hell he'd let himself in for. In fact, the session represented a flying leap into the unknown for both artist and producer. Thanks to several years of hard experience, Hooker was fully confident of his ability to rock the house solo or with a band, acoustically or amplified, at a house party or a club, but though his demo sessions with Barbee had taught him to compress his lengthy free-form improvisations to accommodate the limited recording-time available on the wax discs, he was still first and foremost a live performer, geared to instant communication with the hearts and feet of an audience he could see in front of him. Besman, by contrast, was a hard-bitten record man who knew both that a single had to grab its listeners within the first few seconds, and also that what worked brilliantly in a club or at a dance might not necessarily have the same effect when stripped of its original context and laid bare in the cold light of the recording studio.

Microphone fright was one problem which Hooker certainly didn't have. Shy or not, from the first take of "Sally Mae," he chorded his open-tuned guitar with rock-solid confidence and absolute rhythmic authority, and the rich, brooding baritone in which he sang bore nary a trace of the

---

5 *Boogie Chillen: A Guide To John Lee Hooker On Disc* (Blues & Rhythm, 1992).

hushed, stuttering murmur in which he spoke. It was what he played and sang—rather than how—which baffled the producer. For a start, Hooker's approach to the blues was utterly unlike anything which Besman—to whom form was infinitely more important than content—had heard before. To Besman, accustomed to categorizing musical styles according to their underlying harmonic and rhythmic structures rather than their social context or emotional content, a song was a set piece with a basic shape and form which it retained no matter how often it was performed. By the same token, a "blues" was one such specific form; one which rarely departed from its basic formal structure of a three-line twelve-bar pattern with an AAB rhyme scheme, and then only into one of a few familiar basic variations. Clearly, Besman was sublimely unaware of the older, looser, less formularized rural blues traditions within which Hooker had received his earliest schooling. "The blues that you know of and that I know of up to this time: they're all twelve bars or twenty-four bars, the standard blues," Besman still insists. "The blues are blues. It's just twelve bars. It's not a chord sequence, it's just a pattern. It's a pattern because the words and the stops that they have where they sing certain things, the breaks—whatever you call 'em—are there. I don't care how you cook it or how you slice it, when they get through, there's a pattern. Whether they're playing twelve bars, or eighteen bars, or twenty-four bars . . . not in the blues. It's got to be regular. Whether it's twelve, eighteen, or twenty-four, that's *it*."

The kind of sophisticated "urbane" blues which Besman was used to selling from his Woodward Avenue headquarters did indeed play by those rules. So—most of the time—did the citified country blues which Muddy Waters and Lightnin' Hopkins, their big country feet stuffed into slick city shoes which had to be loosened before they fit, were hauling into the studios of Chicago and Houston.[6] Hooker's music, by contrast, played by rules so utterly different from the rhythm-and-blues norm that Besman didn't recognize them as rules at all. For Hooker, no "song" was ever actually completed, finished, engraved into marble, rendered definitive. Rather, it was different each time it was performed. Each piece was a platform for improvisation, a loose framework of lyrical and instrumental motifs into which he poured the emotions of the moment. Ask him to

---

6 Actually, Muddy's breakthrough hit "I Can't Be Satisfied" was an eleven-bar rather than a strict twelve-bar. The song loses one bar, the nominal sixth, halfway through the second A-line of its A A B structure, but it does this regularly—and, once you're aware of it, predictably—in each and every verse.

perform the same song a year later, a month later, a week later, a night later, an hour later, or even five minutes later, and the piece would have changed, sometimes beyond recognition. The basic pool of riffs and verses upon which the song drew remained more or less constant, but it would be reconstructed anew; cooked from the same cupboard of ingredients, but served up fresh each time, remade not according to any detailed recipe but based entirely on the spontaneous emotional reactions of the chef. Thus the slow-to-medium-paced blues "Sally Mae," for example, was performed in two quite distinct incarnations,[7] with different lyrics. In both takes Hooker maintains the structural integrity of the twelve-bar pattern with rather more fidelity than was customary in his solo performances, but he alludes rather than adheres to the conventional rhyme scheme of the AAB structure: it is acknowledged more in the breach than in the execution.

As if that wasn't enough, Besman had never before been required to deal with the specific problem of how to record one man with an acoustic guitar. It may have seemed as if Hooker had strayed onto Besman's turf and that it was the bluesman, rather than the producer, who was on unfamiliar territory, but the mesmeric unorthodoxy of Hooker's music placed Besman as much on the defensive as his studio-neophyte artist. It was thus Besman's turn to take a shot in the dark; to throw away his preconceived ideas about recording and start thinking on his feet. "When I started recording [Hooker] I thought, "Jesus, this is so empty, how the hell'm I gonna make this one guy sound like something?' I'd never recorded one man before: Todd Rhodes had a seven- or eight-piece band. I saw a pallet full of cardboard boxes at the other side of the room, so I said to bring that over and put it under his foot. I hadn't noticed that he stomped: I just wanted some rhythm in there. We put a mike down there also and started doing that, and on most of his records—of mine, anyway—you can hear that. But I wanted to amplify his sound and we had no echo chambers at that time, so we set up [another] microphone in a toilet bowl. We took the speaker from the studio and put it in a toilet bowl, which was about sixty or seventy feet from the studio. Then we

---

7   The familiar version of "Sally Mae" on most of the recent reissue compilations of Hooker's work with Bernard Besman is actually the second take, which is stronger and more measured than its immediate predecessor. However, it was the first take—which seems more spontaneous, has more vitality and boasts the wonderful line *"If I was the chief of police, baby, I would run you out of town"*—which Besman decided to pair with "Boogie Chillen" for Hooker's first single release. The second take which eventually supplanted it stayed in the can until it was released on album in 1960.

put a microphone in front of that speaker and brought the speaker from *that* microphone back into the studio. I didn't know what would happen, but I realized that we would have an echo chamber. I had the speaker right on his guitar. And that's why he sounds so big. This one guy sounds like a whole band when he plays on those recordings. I shocked myself because I'd never tried it before, the tapping of the feet on the pallet thing. It was a very good rhythm, a one-man band. I couldn't get over it, myself." (For the record, Hooker vehemently denies the toilet-bowl story, probably because, as the anecdote passed down the line, Chinese-whispers style, it has somehow mutated into the mythic notion that Besman recorded Hooker by placing the singer himself in a bathroom. So it goes.) "I experimented a lot with him," Besman remembers proudly. "So I recorded him most often with that set-up, and he sounds big. People were amazed at how we got that sound. That sound was really surprising to me. It was unique for just the one man playing the guitar. It sounded almost like a band."

That sound was an inspired improvisation. The experiment paid off *big* time: Hooker sounded huge. What might have started as a back-porch meditation, a sound which customarily dissipated and escaped into the vastness of the night sky, was now so big that it threatened to crack the studio walls. Hooker's blues may have traveled from the low, low lands and reached its destination *virgo intacta*; but now it had unquestionably arrived in the city. The music reverbed off concrete and tile; it positively crackled with electricity. Maude may have smashed Hooker's electric guitar, but the way that Besman and Joe Siracuse had close-miked the pawn-shop acoustic created a sound pressure level high enough to overload the valve-powered recording machine, driving the meters into the red zone. The result was so distorted and "hot" that just about everybody who ever heard the results of that session swears blind that the guitar they're hearing was heavily amplified. In fact, it wasn't the guitar that was electric—it was the guitarist.

So right there Besman had two takes each of Hooker's first three titles, but he wanted more. "I needed four numbers. I was teed off already that I wasn't going to get four records. So I said, 'Do you know how to play a boogie?' because boogie was big, twelve-bar boogie. I figured if we could make a boogie then we maybe have a chance. And he says, 'No, I don't know how to play a boogie.' "

"And finally," says Paul Mathis, "he made 'Boogie Chillen' . . . and that's history."

6. "Boogie Chillen" Came Out Burnin'

Let the children use it,
Let the children lose it,
Let all the children boogie
—David Bowie, "Starman," 1972

I didn't understand the music at the time I recorded it.
—Bernard Besman, interview with the author, 1994

Boogie-woogie: style of playing blues on piano, marked by persistent bass rhythm [20th c.; origin unknown].
—*Concise Oxford Dictionary*

We hold this truth to be self-evident: that one man's boogie is another man's woogie. Let me explain.

"A long time ago," Hooker says, "they used to call it boogie-woogie, on an old piano. But as the years went by, as the time went by into the modern day, they called it the boogie. It ain't the boogie-woogie anymore, it was the boogie. And I think I started all of that. I originated that. There was nobody else doing it like that and calling it the blues, and I just called it 'Boogie Chillen.' "

By way of contrast, the incorrigibly literal-minded Bernard Besman's notion of exactly what constitutes "boogie-woogie" is more or less the same as that of the compilers of the *Oxford Dictionary*: an up-tempo, eminently danceable eight-to-the-bar piano blues with a regular "walking" left-hand bass line. In fact, both the style and the term had been around for decades before pianist Clarence "Pinetop" Smith brought them together on his 1928 hit "Pinetop's Boogie Woogie."[1] Variously known

---

1   Pianist Joe Willie Perkins (b. 1913 in Belzona, Mississippi) mastered this piece so thoroughly in his youth that his admiring friends nicknamed him "Pinetop," after Clarence Smith. As Pinetop Perkins, he replaced Otis Spann in Muddy Waters' band in 1970, and as of the time of writing still plays the boogie as well as any man living.

as "barrelhouse," "honky-tonk" or, intriguingly, "Dudlow Joe," this rumbustious idiom emerged out of Southwestern saloons and lumber camps some time in the late nineteenth century. The expression "boogie" (or "boogie-woogie" or "booga-rooga") dates from roughly the same time: it simply means to dance, to party, to rock, to have any kind of physical good time you care to name, specifically including the obvious one for which "jazz" and "rock'n'roll" have, over the years, also served as euphemisms. Hey—*you* know what I'm talking about.

The etymological origins of the word "boogie" remain obscure. It would be nicely symmetrical if we were somehow able to prove that it was an African term, that it shared the Wolof-via-Gullah derivation of "juke" (or "jook"); unfortunately, we can't. First among its closest linguistic cousins would appear to be "bogy," a nineteenth-century term for an evil spirit or goblin, or even for the Devil himself. This is itself descended from "bogle," a sixteenth-century Scottish word for a goblin, phantom or scarecrow, which—significantly enough—was also used in the mid-'90s to describe the state-of-the-art obeah-derived dirty dancing which accompanied ragga and jungle music. (No wonder religious folk disapproved of the boogie: its very name must have seemed like Satan's calling card.) Because of the number of "train"-oriented titles and rhythms prominent during the recorded idiom's early days in the wake of Meade Lux Lewis's epochal "Honky Tonk Train Blues" (he recorded the first of many versions in 1927), we could also throw in the portion of a train's undercarriage known as the "bogie." Also—though we're on rather less solid ground here—we could cite the numerous musical and titular allusions to "bugle" calls in piano recordings of the '20s.

All this notwithstanding, barrelhouse piano and the word "boogie" achieved their critical mass when Smith combined them in a cascade of rollicking stop-time piano choruses punctuated with exhortations and instructions to the dancers in general—"When I say stop, I want you to stop. *Stop!* Now git it!"—and to a seriously rocking girl with a red dress on in particular.[2] "Now this," he announces cheerfully, "is Pinetop's boogie-woogie," as if it could be anything else; sadly, Smith didn't live long enough to see the first anniversary of his record's release, let alone any royalties. It was several years before ASCAP—the American Society of Composers, Authors and Publishers, the body which controlled and

---

2 Which makes this piece an ancestor of Jerry Lee Lewis's "Whole Lotta Shakin' Goin' On" and Ray Charles's "What'd I Say"—in both of which the archetypal Girl In The Red Dress reappears, still shaking her stuff—as well as various other things.

administered musical copyrights—would permit boogies, even best-selling ones like "Honky Tonk Train Blues" or "Yancey Special" to be recognized and registered as legitimate compositions, let alone acknowledge their composers as "authors."[3] "Pinetop's Boogie-Woogie" soon became an American archetype, and much of the genre which was built upon its foundation was created in its image.

Progressive white musicians like Benny Goodman had begun to take an interest in boogie-woogie by the mid-'30s, but what enabled the music to break the surface of American culture was the crucial "From Spirituals To Swing" concert promoted by the producer, critic and entrepreneur John Hammond at Carnegie Hall in 1938. As well as showcasing gospel music, rural blues (by harpist Sonny Terry and guitarist Big Bill Broonzy, the latter standing in for Hammond's first choice, the recently murdered Delta bard Robert Johnson), chamber swing from Count Basie and Benny Goodman, and an exhibition of African tribal music and dance performed by actual Africans, Hammond treated the crowd to a positive avalanche of boogie by wheeling three pianos onto the stage and teaming up Albert Ammons, Meade Lux Lewis and Kansas City boogie champ Pete Johnson, complete with Joe Turner's sonorously authoritative vocals. This show— and its successor a year or so later—transformed boogie-woogie into a national craze. After Goodman came Bob Crosby, and after Crosby came The Andrews Sisters and their "Boogie Woogie Bugle Boy (From Company B)," and from there it was a comparatively short step to such pop-novelty nonsenses as "Chopsticks Boogie." After that things got seriously silly, and for a while just about *every* damn thing called itself a boogie of some sort or another.

Boogie-woogie had exploded into a pop craze in the '40s and, as pop crazes often will, it eventually burned itself out. Authentic barrelhouse piano became the territory of dyed-in-the-wool jazz collectors and committed aficionados, while boogie's signature beat and bassline were absorbed by the popular jump combos as the foundation for a slew of rocking jukebox singles with novelty lyrics and honking, booting tenor-sax solos. In the meantime, there was the redneck offshoot known as "hillbilly boogie." In *Country*,[4] Nick Tosches cites Johnny Barfield's "Boo-

---

3 ASCAP also excluded what was then known as "hillbilly" music, which meant that the rival BMI organization—the initials stood for "Broadcast Music Incorporated"—was able to scoop up vast tracts of these burgeoning markets, much to ASCAP's fury.
4 *Country: Living Legends And Dying Metaphors In America's Biggest Music* (Secker & Warburg, 1988).

gie Woogie," recorded for Bluebird in 1939, as the first swallow of this particular subgeneric summer, while also mentioning in dispatches The Demore Brothers, Arthur Smith—specifically Smith's 1949 "Guitar Boogie"—and pianist Moon Mullican, plus several late-'40s and early-'50s hits by Tennessee Ernie Ford, including "Smokey Mountain Boogie" and "Shotgun Boogie." The term "boogie" thus returned once again to its original meaning—a sexy, rocking good time—which it retained right through the "boogaloo" of the '60s and the era of "Boogie Nights." "Boogie Wonderland," "Yes Sir, I Can Boogie," "Boogie Oogie Oogie," "Blame It On The Boogie" and so on into the present day.[5]

Interestingly enough, in 1928—the very same year that Pinetop Smith had formally launched the boogie-woogie movement with "Pinetop's Boogie-Woogie"—the great ragtime guitarist Blind Blake had gone into Paramount Records' Chicago studio with Detroit pianist Charlie Spand to cut a rollicking piano/guitar duet called "Hastings Street." Primarily instrumental, and more a lightly swinging uptempo blues than a standard boogie, it nevertheless contained spoken dialogue between Blake and Spand which suggests that the term "boogie" had more than a little special significance in the Motor City. "Spand, you never been to Detroit in your life," chaffs Blake. "Aw, on Hastings Street they do the boogie . . . they do it very woogie. You can drive, but when you been off from Dee-troit three weeks you think that's a long, long time . . . go back there tonight, you can sure get woogie . . . I know you wanna go back to 169 Brady . . . I can't hardly rest. All the mens tellin' me 'bout Brady Street . . . wonder what's on Brady? Must be somethin' that's very marvelous . . . *mm mm mmm!* Make me think, make me feel *I* wanna go to Detroit . . . let's go back, let's see about gettin' the woogie." What *can* they be talking about? The only clue is that Brady Street was a direct turning off Hastings. The plot thickens.

So anyway, according to Bernard Besman's version of events, he and John Lee Hooker and Joe Siracuse the engineer are in United Sound. The first three titles have taken over three hours to record, the clock's still ticking, the studio time is running out, and Besman still doesn't have what he

---

5   Comparatively recently, rapper KRS-1 used the name "Boogie Down Productions" for his group, originally a team-up with the late DJ Scott La Rock. This is as good a time as any to state that for much of the above information, I am indebted to Pete Silvester's *A Left Hand Like God: The Story Of Boogie-Woogie* (Quartet Books, 1988), about as useful a history of all things boogoid and pianistic as it's possible to buy, even for real money.

considers to be four usable sides. "The first three numbers took over three hours, you know. Usually I paid for three hours, and I had a heck of a time because he would never sing the same song twice. Here you have someone singing a song, and you want to correct it and you play it the second time and it's an altogether different version of the same song, different words and so on. Those were all supposedly blues, and I thought I'd better have something else."

So he asks Hooker to play a boogie. Hooker—who maybe thinks he's being asked to play the piano—says he can't, and Besman has a brain-wave. "So I go up to the piano and play a few bars of a boogie. Todd Rhodes was still there, and he was a pianist, so I said, 'Todd, why don't you play some boogie for him and see what happens?' So he played, and I said to John, 'Do you think you can do that, some of that?' And he said, 'Oh yeah, sure.' That's why the word 'boogie' is in there. Nothing to do with the song, you know. 'Boogie Chillen' 's not a boogie. That was just what he thought was a boogie, and so I called it 'Boogie Chillen.' As you can see, it doesn't compare to boogie as you know boogie, but he played a lot of numbers in a similar rhythm which was quite original. So that's where 'Boogie Chillen' came from, but it was nothing like what I intended. I was real disappointed."

Considering the way things turned out, it's safe to say that nobody else was. Hooker, needless to say, remembers things rather differently. "[Besman] had Todd Rhodes on his little label Sensation," he recalls. "I can't remember the studio, but I remember Todd Rhodes. Piano player. I can't remember [being] in the studio with him; I remember [playing] on a show with [Rhodes], at the Capitol Theater in Detroit." For that matter, he doesn't remember Besman playing any piano, either. "He told you he played piano: I never seen him play piano. I saw him play organ once, on one tune; I never heard him play piano in my life. A lotta stuff he said he did he didn't do. Said he played the piano . . . he didn't. Said he wrote songs . . . he didn't. He couldn't play no piano. He didn't write . . . he didn't know one note of the blues. He claims he did everything."

Anyway, Siracuse loads up another acetate blank. Hooker picks up his guitar . . . and he launches into a rocking dance piece with which he's been wrecking the house at parties and clubs for years. Its structure is utterly free-form, its basic beat is the jumping, polyrhythmic groove which he learned in the Delta at Will Moore's knee, and into this vessel he pours extemporized autobiographical vignettes: snapshots of his mother arguing with Will Moore, and of his own initiation into Detroit nightlife. "My stepfather and myself, when I was a kid fifteen years old, he taught me to do that beat and I did it. *'Mama don't 'low me to stay out all night long'*: at that time I couldn't go out and stay, I had to be home. So I put it to *'I don't care what you don't 'low, I'm gonna boogie anyway.'* I been playin' that—oh *Lord*—at house parties and clubs; we *rocked* the house, me and Broomstick Charlie." It was as overwhelmingly personal a piece as anything ever done in the blues, or—come to that—anywhere else in the popular arts of the twentieth century: sunk to the knees in the rich, loamy tradition of the Delta, borrowing the open-ended, infinitely adaptable vehicle of the dance-music-with-commentary form used by Pinetop Smith twenty years earlier, but drawing on a musical inheritance and an individual history unique to the man who performed it. What emerged, three takes later, as "Boogie Chillen" was not only Hooker's key to the kingdom, but his calling card, his badge of selfhood; the ultimate statement of his personality, his experience, his identity, his very existence. For a man of John Lee Hooker's background, in that particular place and time, making records was just about the only possible outlet through which he could express himself, could tell the world who he was, how he lived, and what the world looked like from where he was. With "Boogie Chillen," Hooker used both hands to seize that opportunity to—to paraphrase a famous Muddy Waters song—let the whole damn world know he was here. If Bernard Besman wishes to consider it merely the result of Hooker's misunderstanding of, or inability to reproduce, something which Todd Rhodes had demonstrated to him a few moments earlier, that's his privilege. If we prefer to see it as a supreme example of a man creating art from the raw materials of his own life and his own experience of the world, that's ours.

Before stereo, before multi-track recording and certainly way before the advent of sequencing software and computerized mixing, recording studios already offered radically different possibilities both to those musicians who were primarily improvisers, and those who were what Evan Eisenberg, in *The Recording Angel*, calls "master builders." To cite a '60s example of the "master builder" tendency, the outtakes of The Beatles' sessions—highly prized by scholars and collectors before their eventual overhyped release, but fairly unrewarding for casual listeners—are little more than sketches, cartoons, painstaking stages of work in progress, individual steps leading to a finished result. For the improviser of genius— for a Louis Armstrong, a Robert Johnson, a Charlie Parker, a John Coltrane, a Jimi Hendrix, and certainly a John Lee Hooker—every performance, every "take," is a unique entity in its own right. In Hooker's case, every take of a particular piece is, at worst, a look at the work in question from a radically different angle and, at best, an entirely separate and distinct work based on the same theme. The slow blues pieces from that first United Sound session are examples of the former, but the "Boogie Chillen" variations flawlessly illustrate the latter.

In the clubs and bars and parties, the song generally ran for about as long as the dancers could hold out, and as long as Hooker could keep his own stomping feet and whiplash right hand going. To cut the piece down to a single-friendly three minutes or so, Hooker had the equivalent of an entire library of variations on which to draw. The very first take—unissued until more than twenty years later, when it emerged as "Johnny Lee's Original Boogie"—finds that unmistakable groove firmly in place, and the now-familiar narrative segments concerning Hooker's arrival on Hastings Street, his mother's reluctance to allow him to go out and rock, and the drowsy boy on the threshold of sleep hearing his folks debating whether the boogie in him should be allowed to come out—are all there, but it all seems sketchy and tentative. The second take, recorded just before the familiar hit version, itself disinterred from Besman's vaults for a 1970 compilation under the title "Henry's Swing Club," is far more confident and expansive. Less "Boogie Chillen" 's twin brother, delivered from the womb shortly before its famous sibling, than its first cousin, "Henry's Swing Club" demonstrates Hooker's unique skills as a raconteur—with no audible trace of a stutter—as well as his extraordinary rhythmic gifts.

It begins with a few clamorous, ear-catching chords and then, with Hooker's steady foot-tap setting the tempo, launches into a variation on the standard boogie-woogie bass-line normally assigned to a pianist's left hand, but instead of aping the customary progression, Hooker gives us a sinuous, eerie variation in an undulating, close-interval mode more reminiscent of Moorish or North African scales than the bluff, open progression of the conventional "walking" blues or boogie-woogie bass. From there he moves into the classic riff before making his vocal entry. "*My mama didn't 'low me to boogie-woogie,*" he announces, "*and I knowed that.*" From there, switching effortlessly from speech to song and back again, he leads the piece off with the archetypal dialogue—"*Papa said 'Mama, let this child boogie-woogie. It's in him, and it's got to come outta him'* "—between his mother and his stepfather. Then he offers us a garrulous, evocative Motor City memoir.

One day I was walkin' down Hastings Street
That was when I first come to town
I didn't know nobody
I asked the man "What town is this?"
He said "This is Detroit. Boy, it really jumps here"
I met a little chick, she said "Hey there!"
I said "Hey there, baby, where you goin'?"
She said "I'm goin' to Henry's Swing Club, I can jump tonight"

Then the guitar, which had been vamping remorselessly on Will Moore's primal rift, at last changes chord, and Hooker breaks into song: *"She said 'Let's go, daddy, I can really have a ball.' "* And then the guitar starts to dance before returning to the Moorish-boogie run with which the piece began. When the guitar returns to the main riff, Hooker is ready to continue his tale:

When I got there that night, boy, the chick was in the groove
I left my coat, you know
I'd just come to town, I didn't know all about the racket
She said "Siddown, aw, siddown"
I said "No baby . . ."

And he changes chord again, breaking back into the sung melody: *"Let's boogie-woogie while, while the band is jumpin' on."* The guitar restates the intro—*wake up!*—and then slides into a trance-like repetition of a plangent blues lick. *"Boy, that chick can boogie-woogie too,"* Hooker announces proudly. *"She started boogyin', Suzy-Q-in', jitterbuggin' and everything!"*

I never been the kind of guy, you know, that didn't know how
I sat around, you know
After awhile I started jumpin'
Boy, I was jumpin'

Then he shifts chord and moves back into the song:

I started jumpin'
I been jumpin' ever since that day.

The Moorish-boogie riff returns for an instant, then there's a brief pause, lulling the listener into a sense of utterly false security . . . and then *blam!* one final chord. It's an astonishing, exquisite performance, but it wasn't the one Besman wanted: that indefinable, unquantifiable, undeniable entity that is a surefire, can't-miss, all-conquering, no-argument hit single. That was when Besman took the key decision on which everything that followed depends: he demanded that Hooker perform one more take.

And *that's* when Hooker cut "Boogie Chillen."

In its own terms, the last side to emerge from that near-impromptu, spur-of-the-moment session is just about as perfect as it could be.[6] The boogie-woogie bass-line has disappeared, and the essential Will Moore-derived guitar riff rules the tune from start to finish. This time Hooker opens the piece with the sung account, referring back to the ancient "Mama don't allow" line, of his desire to boogie-woogie despite his mother's wishes, and the twin monologues, shorn of extraneous detail however entertaining, now have the pared-down eloquence of a Delta haiku. Most crucial of all, the song now has its hookline: each section ends with a repeatedly pounded chord, a telling pause and the exhortation—"*Boogie, chillen!*"—from which the song derives its title. Besman had his hit, though it would be a few months before either he or Hooker had the chance to prove it. "I told him to come back," says Besman, "and we'd sign a contract."

John Lee Hooker signed on the line. His deal was a specific agreement with Besman, rather than with Sensation or any other particular designated label. It was Besman's responsibility as an independent producer to cut the records, negotiate the leasing deals with the record companies, and pass the royalties onto Hooker, who was now a genuine recording artist, even though he hadn't yet released any records. While he waited for his first effort to reach the marketplace, life went on very much as before. Occasionally Besman (and others) have suggested that "Boogie Chillen" was preceded by an earlier Hooker release on Sensation which failed to sell in significant quantities, but neither Fancourt's session logs

---

6 The author must confess a perverse fondness for a remake of "Boogie Chillen" which Hooker cut a decade later for Vee Jay Records: the performance is fractionally steadier and more assured and the guitar Hooker used for the session has an odd resonance which creates a sour, eerie, sitar-like twang. However, it's marred by a clumsy, seemingly premature fade ending, and there's no question that the historical significance of the original renders it the truly definitive John Lee Hooker song. It's the Vee Jay version, however featured in *The Blues Brothers* as the BBs are pulling up outside Bob's Country Bunker.

nor the authoritative Hooker discography by Michael J. Sweeney and Robert Pruter[7] contain any mention of such an item. On November 3, 1948, a single pairing "Sally Mae" and "Boogie Chillen" was released, but not by Sensation. Instead of issuing it on his own label, which would have involved him in all the problems of wholesaling it to his fellow distributors outside Pan American's home turf of Michigan and Ohio, Besman leased the masters to Modern Records, an established L.A.-based R&B indie with proven national clout. Modern had opened for business in 1945, and had recorded, among others, Johnny Moore's Three Blazers: it was a family firm, run by three brothers—Joe, Jules and Saul Bihari— who were generally assumed to be of Lebanese origin though they were in fact Hungarian, the Memphis-born sons of a traveling salesman and grandsons of a Budapest University lecturer. Later on, a fourth Bihari, Lester, was placed in charge of a branch office in Memphis.

As Joe Bihari told Colin Escott, "I was running the [Modern] New York office and Saul was in Detroit. Bernie Besman and John Caplan were our distributors in Detroit. Pan American Distributors. Bernie had a label called Sensation, but couldn't sell records. He gave Saul an acetate of 'Boogie Chillen,' and told him to take it to me in New York and ask me what I thought of it. I said, 'Saul, it's a smash. Leave it with me.' I took it to Nashville, played it for Gene Nobles on [50,000 watt superstation] WL.A.C, and he said, 'Oh, let me have that.' He played it twelve straight times. The next day I spoke to Jules and he said, 'What is this "Boogie Chillen"?' I told him about it. We were getting calls from all over. I flew the master out to him, and it was an overnight smash."[8]

"I didn't put out 'Boogie Chillen' on Sensation," says Besman, "because I had several of his records like 'Sally Mae' and 'Hoogie Boogie' and at the same time Modern wanted it, so we thought we'd give it to them and then buy the records from them. So we bought it from them; it was cheaper to buy from them than me pressing it alone. They got it going when they started playing it down South; that's where it really took off. In Detroit you couldn't sell Hooker. You couldn't give it away. Here's another point that's very interesting. Hooker's style was called 'dirty blues' or 'low-down blues' [for] people who lived down South, the lower class of people. The black people who lived in Detroit weren't particularly lower class: they did not

---

7 *Goldmine* magazine, March 20, 1992.
8 E-mail to the author, April 2000.

accept this music and they would not buy that type of record. I had a store with my brother-in-law in a partially black area, but it wasn't in the Hastings Street area. When they'd come in and ask for a Hooker record, they'd put it under their coat so nobody would see them buying it, and no disc jockey would play John Lee Hooker records. That's why I leased it to Modern: they had better distribution down South. Down South, after Modern took it up, that became a very very big hit."

That's something of an understatement. "Boogie Chillen" was a *smash*. By the time Besman got around to recording Hooker again—in February 1949—"Boogie Chillen" had already boogied its way to Number One in *Billboard*'s R&B charts. "The label was so little, they didn't have distribution all over the country. But 'Boogie Chillen' came out *burnin'*," Hooker says proudly. "It was so big that they couldn't support it theyself, and they went to this label called Modern Records out in Los Angeles, the Bihari brothers. And they picked it up nationwide, and that thing was Number One everywhere. When I had 'Boogie Chillen' it were ringin' all over the country. It was a real dancing thing; it was a big, big, big hit. Boy, everywhere you went it was all you could hear. Every jukebox, every department store. Everywhere you went—all the drugstores, in the markets—that was all they played. Something new, new, *new*: 'Boogie Chillen.' "

"It didn't surprise me when 'Boogie Chillen' got to be a hit," says Hooker's running buddy Famous Coachman, "because John had pretensions of making hits anyway. He would do a lot of songs at the time in the clubs and get standing ovations and what-not, but when he did 'Boogie Chillen' it was one of the great things that he could have done. That's why I said it wasn't really a surprise, because he'd been doing some of the same things [in the clubs], and somebody picked it up and made it be a hit. That's the thing. 'Boogie Chillen' started him bein' the Boogie Man, and he is the Boogie Man now."

"Boogie Chillen" struck the R&B industry like a bolt of lightning. B. B. King, a year or so away from his own first big hit and soon to join Hooker on the Modern label, was still deejaying on the Memphis-based radio station WDIA when it hit. "John and I go back . . . oh God, at least forty years almost," he recalls. "See, John was *playin'* when I was *ploughin'*. John was an artist long before I was. 'Boogie Chillen' was such a big, big record. I was on the radio and I did play 'Boogie Chillen' quite often on my show because it was such a very, very good boogie tune that you could boogie on. There was no crossover as you have today. It was mostly in the black areas, on the black radio that was playing 'Boogie Chillen,' but it was very, very big at that time and hardly anybody around who was playing at that time didn't play 'Boogie Chillen.' That's just how heavy it was. Generally, when there's a hit record out all the musicians will hop on whatever's ahead at that time, and for most of us—I, for one, and many others who would go out and play—if you didn't play 'Boogie Chillen' at that time, people probably look at you and wonder what was wrong with you. It was such a big record . . ."

For many younger musicians and wannabes, it was the wondrous simplicity of Hooker's "Boogie Chillen" riff that intrigued them. It sounded totally cool, plus it created the illusion that it was easy enough not to be intimidating: by the time you got past its deceptive crudeness and naïvety to the complexity and sophistication that lay beneath, you were already hooked. In that respect, it was the R&B equivalent of punk rock. At least, that was how it seemed in Chicago to Mississippi-born Elias McDaniel, not yet ready to mutate into the mighty Bo Diddley, and encountering "Boogie Chillen" a few months shy of his twelfth birthday. "I think the first record I paid attention to was John Lee Hooker's 'Boogie Chillen,' " he told Andy McKaie. "When I found John Lee Hooker on the radio, I said, 'If that guy can play, I know I can.' I mean, John Lee's got a hell of a style."

Way down in Letchworth, Louisiana, the record had a similar effect on thirteen-year-old George Guy, known to his friends and relations as "Buddy." "Actually, that's the first thing I learned how to play. I was half asleep, my brothers and sisters had ran me out of the house with an acoustic guitar. Don't know how to tune it, don't know how to finger it, and you know what I'm talkin' about if you in the house with somebody that can't play *nothin'*, so they say, 'Mama, get him *outta* here.' Down South in Louisiana this time of year, you can go out and lay in the sun and if the wind's not blowin' it's warm. So I was layin' out there on a wood pile just pickin' away, and I dozed off. And when I woke up I had a riff like 'Boogie Chillen' and I played it for six hours, because I thought if I moved my fingers I never would find it again. I went found all of my country friends, which is about four, and I said, 'I got it.' And that was the first thing I thought I learned how to play that I knew sounded right when someone would listen. And each time I got to one of 'em that followed me I'd say, 'I got it.' 'Yes, you got it, that's it.' I'd say, 'I got this John Lee Hooker,' and that's the first thing I learned how to play."

Over in Texas, in Houston's Third Ward, the revelatory "Boogie Chillen" effect was similarly experienced by a young man named Albert Collins. "He was my influence: between him and Lightnin' Hopkins was my influence," Collins told a British TV crew during a break in filming a tribute concert to Hooker.

> *And the first tune I learned to play on the guitar was "Boogie Chillen." He have been my idol all these years, and I'm so glad that he still here to carry me along with him. I was raised up with Lightnin' Hopkins, who was a cousin of mine, in the family, but I said, "John Lee Hooker, I always wanted to meet the man and one of these days I'm gonna play 'Boogie Chillen' with him." Because he's my influence. I learned how to play listening to his type of music.*

In taverns and pool halls, in barber shops and record stalls, down South, up North, in the Delta itself and throughout the Delta's urban diaspora, "Boogie Chillen" just kept blasting, hanging in there on the *Billboard* chart for three full months. Legend has it that the record sold a million copies, though Besman disputes that. "Well, that's probably a crock of shit, pardon my French. I'm glad people say that now, but we didn't get paid for a million copies. No blues or any race record at that time sold a million, no way, but it's good publicity. I never said anything about it, and when you're writing you can use it or not use it, but that's what they all claimed. I think it's great, but I sure never saw that money. I know we hardly sold what you'd sell today in Detroit on a black artist, and on this thing—which wasn't accepted—I doubt that we sold five hundred in Detroit maybe. I would say that Modern probably sold more than the other blues records: there's a possibility that it could have gone to a quarter of a million, because down South they bought a hell of a lot more records than they did in the North. But I'm proud that they're saying a million. It's a good feeling. Hooker never got paid for a million, because we paid him royalties on what we got from Modern. The Biharis were a charming, terrific family, but as far as money was concerned? No. But everybody in the record business was crooked."

And therein lies the rub. Imagine, if you will, what happens in today's music industry when a young African-American artist with a brand-new sound scores an R&B Number One within a few weeks of the release of his debut single. He's all over MTV. He's on the cover of dozens of magazines. The record stands a considerably-better-than-even chance of "crossing over" to the far more lucrative pop market and scoring big in the pop charts. The artist then hits the mainstream rock magazines and gets played on pop radio. The record maybe gets used in commercials and the artist knocks down some very useful, high-paying endorsement deals. Then the artist sells a few songs to Hollywood for the soundtrack of an upcoming action movie and, given sufficient charisma, is offered the chance to do some acting. On the back of the hit single, the subsequent album racks up enough advance orders to ship platinum. Most important of all, the artist, and everybody associated with the artist's career, makes a hell of a lot of money.

Well, that may be what happened to Tupac Shakur and Snoop Doggy Dogg,[9] but it's not what happened to John Lee Hooker. In one sense, his troubles had just begun.

> When you get in the record business, someone gonna rip you anyway, so that don't bother me. If *you* don't rip me, *she* gonna rip me, and *she* don't rip me *he* gonna rip me, so I'm gonna get ripped. So you don't be bothered by that, because people 'round you gonna rip you if they can.
> —Muddy Waters, interview with the author, 1970

> Everybody in the record business was crooked. Everybody. I don't care how big they are, or how small they are . . . I'm not talking about *me* I don't count.
> —Bernard Besman, interview with the author, 1994

Some time in 1949, during the early days of Atlantic Records, the company's founder Ahmet Ertegun had a highly significant encounter with a seasoned executive from one of the major record companies. The fledgling record man was quizzing his more experienced colleague on various aspects of music-biz lore and practice, and Ertegun asked the veteran about artists' royalties. "You mean you're giving these artists *royalties?*" the man from the major replied, aghast. "You're going to ruin the business for all of us!"

Based on a set of standard practices applied to black and poor-white music ever since the earliest days of the record industry, rhythm and blues

---

9 For an account of what *did* happen to Tupac and Snoop, consult Ronin Ro's devastating *Have Gun Will Travel: The Spectacular Rise And Violent Fall Of Death Row Records* (Quartet Books, 1999). It also demonstrates that the more the music biz changes, the more it remains the same.

recording was little more than a sweatshop. The artists didn't even qualify as sharecroppers: they were strictly day labor, paid cash-in-hand on a flat rate of so many (or, rather more appropriately, so few) dollars per side.

Artists were encouraged to record original material, because that way no money needed to be diverted to outside publishers. Furthermore, since the artists' original songs were handled by the record company's in-house publishing companies, the royalties on all but the biggest and most successful tunes could—through the magic of creative accountancy—simply disappear into the black hole of a company's notional losses. Even a substantial hit could net the artist virtually nothing. In 1930, when Columbia Records' race-music-and-hillbilly subsidiary O Keh opened its doors for business, its standard deal was to pay the artist a flat fee of twenty-five dollars per side and an utterly derisory publishing royalty of no more than 0.0005 of a cent per copy sold. The artist, therefore, literally didn't make *one single cent* until he or she had sold at least 2,000 copies, and couldn't make a dollar until 200,000 units moved out of the door. When you consider that recording costs were then "billed back" to the artist, it was virtually impossible for these performers to make any money whatsoever from record sales.

By 1949, the rates had improved, but not by much. It was therefore necessary for performers to make their entire living out on the road. In that market, at that time, a hit record didn't guarantee a recording artist any noticeable amount of bankable cash. What it did guarantee was a reputation, a "name" and a regional or national fan base which might drive their in-person concert fee up to the point where it was possible for them to make some sort of a living from playing live. The price of earning that living was to spend years of their lives living out of a suitcase away from home, family and friends; burning up the highways to get to the next club, the next bar, the next dollar. "I didn't get money," says Hooker, "but I did get a big, big name."

The manner in which Modern did business was the rule rather than the exception. Hooker makes little distinction between the way they and the other prominent R&B independents of the time operated, but he has a special bitterness toward Modern. "The worst? Modern was the worst. They was *the worst*. Then here come Chess. They was bad. Here come Vee Jay: they took the clothes off your back. They was *terrible*. And Modern was just *ridiculous*. Nobody got nothin' from Modern Records. You go to the office and they hide, they said they wouldn't be there. You call, and when they find out who's callin,' they say, 'He ain't here.' " Still, for a hungry young blues artist out to make a name and get off the farm or out of the factory, companies like these were the only game in town. "I would've *paid* someone—not wanna *get* paid, but would've *paid* someone—to record," says B. B. King, another Modern Records alumnus, who joined the Biharis' roster in the summer of 1949 via a deal with their subsidiary label RPM.

He elaborates: "When you don't know something, like I didn't—I didn't know how to make a deal, and I still don't. This happens to people all the time. By having a manager that looks through all of this, that makes a difference. In so many words, I'm not puttin' a halo around their [the Biharis'] heads, but I'm sayin' that they was sorta like bidness as usual. It's like today: people make deals. If you don't know and I can get you, I'll get you. That's generally the American way: not to the point of where you *bleed* a guy, but you say, 'Man, that was a *deal*! God, I *really* pulled off a *deal*!' Possibly they felt the same way. Me, I would have paid them to record me. Then later on when I got a manager, he started to tell me the many things that they didn't do that they should've done; things that they did that hurt me that they *shouldn't* have done. Then I was able to see it. Maybe John knew about it long before I did. But even out of all the bad things that have happened, I still like 'em today. There was some good things that came out of it. Okay, maybe I was owed maybe one hundred dollars. They may have given me twenty-five or fifty. But next week if my son was hurt or somebody broke in my car or something and I needed another twenty-five dollars, I could go to them direct."

Even if it was only what the artist was owed in the first place? "Well, you know that. They knew that. But I didn't. And, God, unless you're a person who just started to play in the '90s or the late '80s, most of 'em didn't know. Kids today, they've got their publishing . . ." As Sid Seidenberg, B. B.'s manager, adds, "You've got to remember one thing. When Mr. Edison invented the telephone and made his deal, he got so much . . . he couldn't visualize the amount of money he could've gotten at that point. But when he got older, he didn't say"—Seidenberg slips into a stylized whiny voice—" 'Well, you know, I got screwed and I hate them.' At that point, they were the only company that gave him the money to do what he had to do to develop whatever he had to develop. They may have shorted him, but as a business person you have to look at it two different ways. You can't be inhuman, of course. I mean, I'm on the side of the writer and the performer, generally, morally speaking. But you got to look at it both sides."

"Paternalism" was the name of the game. In 1964, The Rolling Stones, flushed with their first American success, made their pilgrimage to Chicago to record at the Chess studios which had produced so much of the music that inspired them. They were horrified to discover that the burly decorator in overalls, painting the outside of the studio, was Muddy Waters, who had written the song from which they had derived their name, and whom they worshipped as a god.[10] Musicians who complained—or who needed sweetening or a reward—would have their dental bills paid, or be bought Cadillacs and other "presents," rather than receiving straight-up accounting or the royalties which would enable them to buy their own Cadillacs and pay for their own dentistry. The artists were by no means stupid men, but they weren't the best-educated guys around and, more to the point, nobody had ever bothered to tell them the rules of the game they were playing. "Back in them days," says Hooker, "the record companies was cut-throats. I hate sayin' it, but it's the truth, and you supposed to tell the truth. They was cut-throats because most blues artists, they didn't know about the publishers, the writers; and they didn't tell you about the publishers. We didn't know what a publisher was. They made good money, the publisher, but we didn't get none because we didn't know. We thought we got a royalty and that was all. I got contracts, but record-deal contracts, like for two years, three years; one cent, cent-and-a-half, two cents. But it didn't say anything about publishing, they didn't put any of that in there. They were just a rip-off. I never got a royalty statement from any of those companies. I was on Modern, and I made them tons of money."

"To be honest with you," remembers Paul Mathis, "[the success of 'Boogie Chillen'] didn't really change [Hooker's] circumstances. It was just 'Hey, I got a little more money now. I got a number one now and I'm gonna go all out, non-stop.' And that's what he done. Let's face it: everything the guy's got, it wasn't handed to him. He didn't find it lyin' by the wayside. He went out there and built it, stone by stone." Maude Hooker remembers only that "those was good days, very good days," but they were also very hard days. Not hard in quite the same way as the years of grinding poverty, non-stop manual work and little acknowledgment which preceded them, but hard nonetheless.

---

10 The late Willie Dixon's autobiography—*I Am The Blues: The Willie Dixon Story*, co-written by Don Snowden (Quartet Books, 1989)—provides as authoritative an account as could be desired of the business methods and operational procedures of a typical front-rank blues indie of the '50s and '60s.

Fortunately, Hooker had some new allies. Around the time that "Boogie Chillen" was released, he ran into a stocky, Jamaican-born guitarist some years his junior. "Little Eddie" Kirkland was a former amateur boxer who'd grown up in Alabama, and traveled the South in a minstrel show, as well as performing both gospel and blues, before settling in Detroit in 1943. "I was working for the Ford Motor Company in the foundry at the Dearborn plant," says Kirkland. "Me and Eddie Burns used to play house parties together, and then I went out one night in 1948 after I got off work, at around eleven or eleven-thirty, and I went to a house party on the north end of Detroit and guess who was playing there? Hooker. He had one record out, 'Boogie Chillen' and on the other side was 'Sally Mae.' He was playing by hisself, no band, not at a house party. At that time Hooker was playing by hisself in the bars. People knew me, so they asked John Lee, 'Why don't you let him play somethin' witcha?' Hooker said, 'Okay, c'mon.' I went back out to the car, got my guitar, came back. We sat down, started playin', I'm backin' him up, and the people loved what I was doin' behind him. They said, 'You and him ought to play together, y'all ought to make some records together.' So that put the idea in John's head, too. John accepted me as an accompanist playin' behind him. The background I was puttin' behind him, even his record manager loved it. That was Bernie [Besman] at Pan American."

Eddie Burns, twenty years old at the time and working as a double act with his traveling companion, guitarist John T. Smith, was a recent arrival from Waterloo, Iowa. However, he'd been born in Belzoni, Mississippi, and raised in the same area—around Clarksdale, Dublin, Tutwiler—as Hooker himself. Not surprisingly when you consider that he'd played with and learned from Alex "Rice" Miller (best known as Sonny Boy Williamson II) and pianist Joe Willie "Pinetop" Perkins in Clarksdale, he blew a mean mouth-harp as well as playing serviceable guitar. He and Smith had come to Detroit looking for a start in the music business. "House parties was real great back in those days. We was playin' in this house party, John T. and me, and it was like Saturday night, and about three or four o'clock, John was on his way home. He lived in the back of this place—we didn't know him then—so he heard us playin' and he knocked on the door. He didn't know the people, but they let him in, so he met us and he told us he was John Lee Hooker. He had cut 'Boogie Chillen' but it wasn't out then. He liked'ed me on the harmonica, and I think that was what attracted him to comin' up there. So when he got there, he sat down and he played some after he had introduced himself and everything and he liked'ed the way I was blowin' the harmonica, so he thought he wanted to sit in if it was okay. And naturally it was, and I blew the harmonica and John T. Smith played the guitar, and John did. I think he had a guitar, or we had two guitars.

"So he liked the way I was blowing the harmonica and he had a session coming up on Tuesday the next week, and he asked me would I like to do the session with him. I told him yes, and when Tuesday came we went and did the session. That was stuff like 'Burnin' Hell,' 'Miss Eloise,' 'Black Cat' . . . stuff like that." The session which produced these particular songs, though, is listed by Les Fancourt as having taken place some time in '49, with Andrew Dunham rather than John T. Smith as the second guitarist. However, according to Fancourt, the first post-"Boogie Chillen" session cut under Bernard Besman's supervision took place at United Sound on February 19, 1949, and was designed to produce the official follow-up to "Boogie Chillen." It was certainly a productive evening: its fruits included two more R&B Top Ten hits for Modern, "Crawlin' King Snake" (based on a theme he'd learned in his youth from Tony Hollins) and "Hobo Blues." Unknown to Besman, though, Hooker had already recorded again—not once, but several times—at the behest of his closest co-conspirator, Elmer Barbee. "The record companies was so crooked back then," according to Eddie Kirkland, "that's why the artists like Johnny were just sayin', 'The hell wit' it.' Whoever put up some money, that's who he make the record for."

"I was supposed to be under contract with Modern," says Hooker, "but I wasn't getting any money from them anyway, so I'd say, 'Yeah, I don't care.' I got so popular, and this record company Modern weren't payin' no money on a Number One hit. I never got any money out of that tune. Modern supposed to pay me. I never get none, but Bernie, they probably paid him. I never get nothin' out of Modern; they supposed to send me a contract and pay me the royalty which I never did get, but I'm sure they paid Bernie. Other record companies wanted me so bad, small record companies would give good money just to get me to do something on their label. And Barbee would go out and come and get me at night and go record and pay me nice, nice money under three, four different names, all on different labels. And Barbee would say, 'Kid, I'm gonna give you this name, use so-and-so.' He give me those names. I was survivin'. I didn't want to do it. He said, 'Look, kid, they ain't payin' no money, Modern. You got a big hit on your hands and you ain't gettin' nothin'. You gettin' peanuts outta them.' I believe what he say. We'd do this at night. He'd come and get me. I be in the bed. He'd say, 'John, I got a deal for you. Get up, put your clothes on . . .' I say, 'Okay.' I get up outta bed and put on my clothes, go in some studio, spend a couple hours recording. He say, 'I have a name for you tomorrow, I can't think of no name right now.' I say, 'Okay.' He got the money right on the spot. He was a smart guy. Right on the spot. *Big* rolls of cash. Down through the years, people they thought it was me givin' those names. I try to explain that that's the way it was, which was good. The guy have the cash, I'd go home and go to bed. I'd jump to all those little labels, like King Records. I was kinda hot then, *the* hot blues singer then. For a thousand dollars I'd jump over the moon. But you just had to do it. No time to polish, or go by the book: the book is in my heart and in my head. They wanted something by John Lee Hooker: they didn't care if it was a dog-bark, long as it had the John Lee Hooker sound. The record companies was goin' wild about that when I came out with that 'Boogie Chillen' thing. Barbee came running: 'C'mon! Get your clothes on! C'mon! Let's *go*! Let's go, kid! We got four, five thousand dollars out here!' "

So by the time the original firm of Hooker and Besman reconvened at United Sound, John Lee had already cut four under-the-table, cash-in-hand sessions for ghetto entrepreneur Joe Von Battle. "He was a black guy, the slickest guy on earth," remembers Hooker, "very rich guy, had this big record store."[11]

"Joe Von Battle was kind of a big-shot guy," says Eddie Burns. "Mouth full'a gold, rode around in Lincolns. He was a hotshot and he was cuttin' just about everything that walked up and down Hastings Street because Joe's record shop was on Hastings Street. He'd just go out there and flag 'em in, because he had a studio at the back. Wasn't no studio, really; but he had a big nice reel-to-reel back there." These flagrant breaches of contract were disguised with the flimsiest of fig-leaf pseudonyms. Bernard Besman was furious when he eventually found out. "It's very disappointing to me because he really screwed me, you might say,

---

11   E-mail from Colin Escott to the author, April 2000: I've just finished [compiling] a CD of Hooker's 1948–1949 Savoy recordings. In the files we found correspondence between Joe Von Battle and Herman Lubinsky (owner of Savoy). JVB proves ownership of the titles by sending Lubinsky a cashed check from Elmer Barbee for $500. On the back, Barbee has warranted that he owns the right to the sides, which sidesteps the question of whether he had the right to be recording them. JVB sold the first batch to Lubinsky for $1,000. Lubinsky was bitching about the sound quality . . . and with good reason. So I guess Hooker got, maybe, one hundred, 250 dollars from Barbee; Barbee got 500 from JVB; and JVB got $1,000 from Savoy. There's the record industry food chain.

because he'd record for me and two hours later go off and record for somebody else, you know, in the basement of a store, for anybody who'd give him money. The worst part was that I didn't know this, and some of these records that came out, came out before I ever released them on the same titles. I had nothing but trouble with titles. I said, 'Jesus, the only beneficial part was that he couldn't do the record exactly like he did for me, because they weren't made in the same kind of facility, but also because he couldn't remember what the hell he did.' Fourteen different names . . . it wasn't right for me, who originally invested the money and then have him do the same things on top of that, and I didn't know it. He was recording for me and about four or five other people in Detroit. At that time, in order to record, you had to have a license from the musicians' union, so that all the money that I would pay Hooker had to go through the musicians' union. They have to pay the tax and record it so that it would be a legitimate deal. But when he recorded with all these other people it would just be under the table, so here I was paying all the dues, union scale, and he was doing all these things underhanded."

"Joe [Von] Battle used to feed Leonard Chess a lot of Detroit music," says Famous Coachman. "Joe used to get the guys together in his record shop in the back room and cut 'em on a tape, and next day he been an' sold it to Leonard Chess, and they didn't even know nothin' about it. Next day Leonard Chess got a record out on you. You say, 'Hey man, that sound like me,' and it *is* you. Some guy done changed the name and go 'head on with it.' "

Hooker remains utterly unrepentant. As far as he is concerned, Modern Records were not doing right by him and he felt no obligation to do right by them. "[Modern Records] didn't pay nobody . . . you had to fight with them to get a little money in advance. They didn't have grounds to stand on when they knew what I was doin'. I work for the money. Just gimme a name! Texas Slim, Johnny Williams . . . what name you wanna give me? Gimme the money, just gimme any damn name you wanna give me. Pull the name out the hat. [Modern] wasn't payin' no money. They knowed that was me."

Besman, however, didn't. What is surprising is how long it took him to catch on. He maintains that most of these "illicit" sessions only surfaced much later on, after Besman had packed up and quit Detroit in the early '50s. Nevertheless, Hooker worked just as hard at record-making as he'd worked, back in the early days, in the steel mills and auto factories. In 1949, the year of his breakthrough, Hooker released no less than thirteen singles. Under his own name he had three "legitimate" Besman-produced releases on Modern and one on Sensation. As "Texas Slim" he had four discs out on the Cincinnati-based King label. As "Birmingham Sam And His Magic Guitar" he had one out on Savoy Records. He was "The Boogie Man" for one on Acorn Records, "Delta John" for one on Regent, and "Johnny Williams" for another on the tiny Staff label run by one Idessa Malone.

King and Savoy were big-time, nationally distributed labels, but most of the others were peewees whose releases only ran to a few hundred copies, most of which wound up in local jukeboxes. Staff was a typical case. "Idessa Malone, Staff Records. Boy, that's way back. Just a little small company, didn't ever get nowhere. It was just a little local thing, around town and in Chicago and that was it. Then she went out of bidness." Most peculiarly of all, he was "Little Pork Chops" for the Danceland label, run by one Morry Kaplan (no relation to Besman's partner, Johnny of that ilk); the song in question, "Wayne County Ramblin' Blues," was composer-credited to "Emkay Barbee" and bore the additional legend "Direction—El. Barbee" beneath the artist credit. Not surprisingly, Hooker dislikes this particular pseudonym more than any of the others and, unmistakable aural evidence to the contrary, fiercely denies being, or ever having been, "Little Pork Chops." " 'Little Pork Chops'? I never *heard* of such a thing. You put that in your book and I'll sue you!"[12] The "Pork Chops" session, incidentally, was the first one which Hooker cut with pianist James Watkin and drummer Curtis Foster, his regular accompanists at that time. Like the Chess brothers in Chicago, who persisted in recording Muddy Waters solo or with minimal backing from bass or harmonica even when he was regularly tearing up the South Side taverns with the greatest electric blues combo in the world, Besman believed that the compromises necessary for Hooker to fit in with his back-up men diluted his individuality to an unacceptable extent. Still, if the sessions demonstrated one thing it was this: that even though Hooker needed the money he got from those bootleg sessions, he also needed to express himself without the restrictions imposed by his occasionally didactic producer.

Most of the songs for those impromptu cash-in-hand sessions were, Hooker claims, written in the car on the way to the studio. While Barbee drove, Hooker would hum to himself and pick his guitar in the back seat.

---

12 This threat has subsequently been rescinded.

When they arrived, he would lay down the tunes in one or two takes and be back in bed before dawn, with only the roll of bills on the bedside table to tell him whether he'd really been out to cut a session, or simply dreamed that he had. He still gets faintly ruffled at any mention of a "three-hour session." "Three hours? No, wouldn't be no three hours! I never was in the studio that long. I was in about an hour and a half, maybe two, then I'm out of there. Three hours was the limit, but I was never up to that limit. I went in there and did a whole five or six songs in an hour, two hours. I'm gone!" Did good days produce uptempo boogies and bad days deep brooding slow blues? Hooker laughs at the very idea. "No comment! They *all* was good days . . ."—he pauses for effect— ". . . when I go out there knowin' that I'm gonna get some money that night. That was a good night. A good day. Rest a couple of hours at night and come on by." For a man who claimed that he "didn't go much on writing songs until I wrote 'Boogie Chillen'," Hooker proved to be astonishingly prolific. Given the pressure to produce which the intensive recording efforts demanded by Barbee necessitated, he created an extraordinary body of work virtually overnight. After "Boogie Chillen," says Hooker, "I got a real interest in writing songs. I can sit down in a studio or a house and write songs"—he snaps his fingers—"just like *that*."

"He'd do it for a few bucks," says Besman, somewhat crossly, "and he'd do it for a few drinks. He'd record for me, let's say, and two or three hours later he'd be in some record shop with someone with whom he was friendly and they probably give him a few drinks or some food or some money and he'd do the same song, supposedly, but they weren't the same because he couldn't play the same. He didn't know what he'd recorded in the first place." If it was any consolation to Besman, his Hooker recordings—rather than any of those Barbee-sponsored backroom sessions for Joe Von Battle and the others—were the ones that sold. By early summer, both sides of the "Hobo Blues"/ "Hoogie Boogie" pairing had charted separately, peaking at Number 5 and Number 9 respectively, and "Crawlin' King Snake" hit in early December, eventually reaching Number 6. Apart from the raging "Burnin' Hell," a devastating repudiation of Christian notions of the afterlife, with Hooker backed by Eddie Burns's harp, which Besman—understandably worried by its incendiary subject-matter— released locally on Sensation, everything Hooker cut which Besman felt was worthy of release was sent to Modern. The records sold, but Modern paid late, light and grudgingly, and Hooker and Besman got more and more peeved: both with the Biharis and with each other. "Bernie didn't tell me; you know they ain't gonna tell on each other. 'We ain't got to give him nothin', give him a few dollars, that'll make him happy. Give him seven— eight hundred dollars, that'll *keep* his mouth shut.' And it did." He laughs, not altogether humorously. "So for a long time I did that." Meanwhile, even today, Besman is fairly cagey about the full extent of the discrepancies between what he was paid for his masters, and what he estimates Modern actually earned from their sales.

"Well, I finally got to sue them; so did Hooker. We have no facts to speak of. When I settled with them, I regained all my masters that I leased them, and all the copyrights they had that they had no right to, and I got some money. Hooker sued 'em separately, and he and his attorneys regained the masters and the copyrights. He settled and I settled, so it's settled, closed, period. They had the masters, my masters I'd leased 'em, plus the copyrights of 'Boogie Chillen,' 'I'm In The Mood For Love' and all those songs. I didn't know that. I didn't know any better at the time that I recorded 'em. When I recorded, I recorded the records but I didn't know too much about the publishing. That was in 1984. Whatever they made, they made. I settled with 'em, he settled with 'em. So that chapter's closed. Right? So who cares?"

Hooker still cares, for a start. The memory of his relationship with Modern still rankles: he had a young family to support and bills to pay, his records were charting, and the money that he considered rightfully his seemed to be everywhere other than in his own pocket. "He got beat out of a lot of . . . a *lot* of money," says Maude Hooker. "But he never stopped. He just kept on going."

If you is not a fighter, you won't make it in Detroit. See what I'm sayin'? You will not make it in Detroit, because Chicago has always gotten all of the recognition. You got some super good musicians here, but they trapped. They don't know how to get out.
—Eddie Burns, interview with the author, 1992

During 1950, it seemed as if the law of diminishing returns was setting in. No less than twenty-two Hooker records came out on various labels under various names, but the closest he got to a hit that year, "Huckle Up Baby" on Sensation, only reached Number 15 on the Billboard chart. Under his own name, he released four singles on Modern, four on Sensation, two on Regal and one on Blues Classics. In addition, "Texas Slim" had three discs out on King; "Johnny Williams" had three on Staff, two on Swing Time and one each on Gotham and Prize, while "John Lee Booker" made his debut for Gone. ("Little Pork Chops," on the other hand, remained inactive.) Certainly he needed money: Famous Coachman remembers him as being broke a lot of the time, even after his first few hits, and in 1950 it must have seemed as if the hits were already drying up. "He became successful," says Besman, "on the spur of the first record session, and it was only because of this original kind of beat. His other blues records weren't successful like 'Boogie Chillen.' It was just this beat he originated." The problem was that, hits or no hits, there were limited possibilities for live work around Detroit. The clubs that he'd packed before "Boogie Chillen" couldn't get any fuller than they already were, and the working-class, blue-collar home crowd that he drew couldn't afford to pay much more to get in than they were already paying.

"He had it pretty tight," Coachman says, "raisin' a family and gettin' no money from gigs and what-not. I mean, he worked in some places for a small amount, but he hasn't worked that much, and he tried to make music, take care of him and his family. It was just small money, that's all. [After 'Boogie Chillen'] he got more money for shows. He used to work in different clubs, and bars, places like that. He used to work with a guy named Little Sonny, with Bobo Jenkins, and [the late pianist] Boogie Woogie Red, Mr. Bo, all of 'em. Used to go up the strip to Oakland Avenue, up and down the strip to Apex, Champion Bar, Sugar Hill, many many places, you could just go up and down the strip and work. They didn't do the advertising then like they do now, you know, sometimes they have to have a sound system on a truck go around to let you know that a certain show is gonna be. They didn't let 'em put it on the radio; the radio weren't open to 'em like it is now, you see. You never got a chance to go on the radio and play music 'til the later years, because this wasn't the music they were playin'. They didn't like it. Most people didn't like it who were goin' on the radio. So he stayed here in Detroit and worked at things that got tightened up and tightened up and tightened up . . . You know what it is with Detroit: one guy get a gig, he just starts the night to pick up Johnny Lee Hooker, Eddie Burns, Little Sonny and somebody else and go and make a gig. All of 'em weren't in the same band, but that's the group he choose that night for that gig. Now maybe Eddie Burns got a gig for tomorrow night, so tomorrow night they drop Eddie Burns and pick up someone else, and go runnin' with the gig. If the man there, somebody playin' the music that he wanted, he satisfied.

Mr. Bo was here at the same time Johnny Lee was here, at the Apex and Champion Bar, the Caribbean and other places these guys used to play. Like I say, one get a gig, everybody would sub under the title of the man that get the gig. See, it wouldn't be John Lee Hooker And His Blues Band, it'd be Mr. Bo And His Blues Band. No matter how big you was, you had to sub under the man who got the gig."

Elmer Barbee was still nominally Hooker's manager, but while he may have been a whiz at setting up bootleg recording sessions, he didn't have much of a clue about keeping his client in regular work. "He was managing Johnny, so-called," snorts Eddie Burns. "The management wasn't too strong, but he was John's mouthpiece at that time. He would try to keep up with John, and tell him what to don't do, and what wasn't good for him."

"When [Hooker] signed with me, he didn't have any manager to book him or get him jobs," says Besman, "so I got Todd Rhodes' manager Stutz Henderson, who was a very big wheel in Detroit, to become his manager. [Hooker] wanted me to become his manager for a while, but I had no time. So Stutz Henderson booked him, but I got him some gigs to start with through contacts I had with people. He would go to the jobs, you know, and there would always be people who would invite him to gamble, like dice between sets, and sometimes I would come to collect the money and it would be already gambled away, the money that he earned. People would always take advantage of him. It didn't matter how much you gave him, he always needed the money because even if he worked he probably gambled some of it away." This allegation infuriates Hooker, and he is at some pains to deny it with all the vehemence at his command. "I ain't never been a gambler. I never gambled in my life for money. I can't see myself doin' that. I hate to lose. I work too hard for my money to lose it in a game. They say, 'Why don't you go downstairs and gamble?' I say, 'Oh no. I ain't no gamblin' man.' I don't go where they gamble too much. No way."

Besman was still recording Hooker regularly, but more and more of the resulting material was remaining in the can. "I can only tell you about the times that I would come up and he would play and say that he would need some bread. When he came to the sessions, he never came alone. He always had a gang of people with him. He was gregarious. That's where Eddie Burns came in, Andrew Dunham, Sylvester Cotton, and they'd sit in. That was all right by me because he had an audience, which was good for him. He was easy to work with; he was never angry. One thing I had to do was what he called 'taste.' I had to bring some 'taste' down, which meant a little liquor . . . and sandwiches. He'd say, 'Bernie, don't forget to bring the taste.' He'd never get drunk or anything like that . . . he used to cook his own food for many many years; he'd carry this little electric thing whenever he'd go and play someplace. Listen, many times I recorded him for nine hours straight just to get the money back. I'd bring in corned-beef sandwiches, work as long as I had to. He didn't care."

Eddie Burns has slightly different memories of some of those sessions. "Bernie Besman used to have money on the table," he recalls. "Money and whiskey was *it*. Bernie would always have plenty whiskey around. Shenley Black Label, that was a real rotgut drink. So hundred-dollar bills would be stacked here, tape-recorder be runnin' *here*, and the whiskey sittin' *everywhere*. He used to ask John, 'How many [sides] can I get today, John?' John look at the money and say, 'Wellll . . . how many you want?' And by John liking the money and everything, you know, he would give him what he want, that way. I don't know how much money, because he would never share that information. I could see money but . . . I didn't ever know what John was getting. All I know was Bernie was getting what he wanted, and John was getting what he wanted."

And what they both wanted most of all was another hit. In mid-August of 1951, Hooker went into the studio with Besman, bringing Eddie Kirkland along to play second guitar, and cut a tune which he still insists was inspired by Glenn Miller's "In The Mood," though the resemblance has never occurred to anyone else. A haunting, incantatory, devastatingly sensual blues with a lyric which includes the most deliberately overt non-rhyme in the entire Hooker canon, it had "hit" emblazoned all over it in glowing blue neon letters. And Besman, whose ears were still not only attached to his head but definitely connected to both his brain and his wallet, rose to the occasion with what was possibly the most inspired production of his entire association with Hooker. "I thought I was going to try something else, and I may have been one of the first to do this, so when the mike and the speaker came back on 'I'm In The Mood' and I was quite happy with it, I said, 'Sing it over.' I was probably the first guy to overdub something like that.[13] But I just experimented. So he sang it with two voices. Then I did it the third time so I had three

13 Guitarist/inventor Les Paul was not only creating far more sophisticated multi-track recordings with his singer wife Mary Ford by this time, but had already enjoyed the first of a string of eerie hits in this style with "How High The Moon." Nevertheless, the procedure was still far from standard practice and it would be churlish to quibble with Besman's achievement.

voices, then a fourth time with four voices, with him doing it. The first release of 'I'm In The Mood' was with two voices: that's why it was a hit, because it was so different. I experimented a lot; we had fun. Not him: me and Joe Siracuse. I had only one channel to record, compared to now, so I used a lotta mikes wherever I could. It was still one channel, but I'd get some effects. The mike might be further away, or the instrument might be ten feet away. I would say it was maybe equal to ['Boogie Chillen'], possibly bigger."

" 'In The Mood,' that was tearin' the country up," Kirkland says, reminiscing with Hooker during one of their rare reunions. "That was a standard, man. They played that record in every club. Back then they had what you call 'high-class black clubs' at that time . . ."

"Black and tan," prompts Hooker.

"That record played in all the places."

"Drugstores, markets, everywhere. You walk in, they have that on. I felt like a king."

"Tore Nashville, tore Tennessee up, man."

"Oh boy."

"That was a hell of a record."

"Didn't get no money for it 'cause of the damn Modern Records company. Them the *cheatin'est* damn company. Record companies, *whoo*! You could have a big hit, wouldn't be gettin' nothin'."

"A cent, half a cent."

"Wouldn't even give you that."

"That was somethin' else, back then."

"Maybe a little somethin'," says Hooker, closing the discussion, "just to keep your mouth shut."

If "Boogie Chillen' introduced Hooker as a major blues artist, "I'm In The Mood" cemented that status. It even gained him the supreme accolade of an "answer" record: "I Ain't In The Mood" by veteran blues chantoose Helen Humes. By October, it was Number One on *Billboard*'s R&B chart. It stayed on the list for fifteen weeks, and its success finally gave Hooker enough commercial clout to make it worth his while to call up Eddie Kirkland, pack his bags, and go on the road. He stayed out there, on and off but mostly on, for the next forty years.

7. Ghostses on the Highway

Some of the stuff we go through, man, people would never
believe. I've known places that have picketed me for playin',
said we came in and takin' the money out of town. Also many
times when we wasn't even allowed to play in some places.
Certain places we wasn't allowed to play. Other times it
wasn't a race thing. Some places we went the black people
wouldn't let you play, so I've gone through that too.
—B. B. King on touring in the '50s,
interview with the author, 1992

The road is where the bluesman's faith is put to the test.
Here, on the dusty, hostile line between two points—his place
of departure and his destination—his knowledge and
courage will be shown for what they are. This aspect of the
bluesman's initiation is particularly intimidating because,
fraught with unpredictability as it is, there is never an end to
its trials and hardships. As long as he is "on the road,"
he will be tested . . . The blueslife on the road is a lonely,
weary and trying experience, and demands a constant
rekindling of strength and faith.
—Julio Finn, from *The Bluesman*[1]

If George Miller and Mel Gibson ever decide to shoot another *Mad Max*
movie, they could do a hell of a lot worse than to hire Eddie Kirkland
for a cameo role. A thickset, powerful man in the waistcoat and pants of
a pinstripe suit; red shirt, medallion, shades and a black leather cap over
a bandana, his heavy leather overcoat slung over his arm, they wouldn't
even need to send him over to wardrobe and props to kit him out with
the right clothes and vehicle: he's already a Road Warrior *par excellence*.
Right now he's arrived in San Francisco to join John Lee Hooker in his
musical home from home, the Russian Hill studio on Pacific, to cut a
couple of tunes for Kirkland's forthcoming album, and hopefully come
up with something suitable for possible inclusion on Hooker's next al-

---

1 *The Bluesman: The Musical Heritage Of Black Men And Women In The Americas* (Quartet,
1989). This extraordinary work, currently—and unforgivably—out of print, is the most obscure
and underrated of the essential texts on the subject of the blues.

bum, *Boom Boom*. The contrast between the circumstances of these two old comrades could hardly be more spectacular.

After a leisurely twenty-five-minute ride down 101, Hooker arrives at the studio with his tobacco-sunburst Gibson 335 and his handmade Bedrock amplifier in the trunk of his white Lincoln Town Car, piloted as ever by Archie Hooker. Meanwhile, Eddie Kirkland has driven non-stop from Denver, Colorado, chewing an unlit cigar while wrestling with the wheel of a beat-up, rusted-out Dodge van seemingly held together with a combination of electrician's tape and sheer willpower. Anybody wishing to park their carcass in the front passenger seat is required to clamber in through the driver's door, since the passenger door no longer opens. When Kirkland needs to take a break and catch some en route Zs, he curls up in a sleeping bag in the back of the van right next to his instruments. He carries three amplifiers—a big Peavey, an Acoustic, and an old Fender Bassman—and half a dozen assorted guitars. These include the pair he will use on this session: an ancient '50s Silvertone encrusted with rhinestones and more pickups than it seems possible to fit on one guitar— well, five—plus a similarly twisted Peavey T30 with the word ENERGY emblazoned upon it in stick-on letters.

Russian Hill is a small but luxurious studio. Wood-paneled, warmly lit, and pile-carpeted, it suggests what the bridge of the Starship *Enterprise* might look like after Laura Ashley got through redecorating it. Most of the West Coast sessions for *The Healer* and Hooker's subsequent renaissance sessions have been cut here: Hooker knows the studio like he knows his own house, and he's almost as comfortable in it. In a break from the precedent set by those previous sessions, Bowen Brown and Jim Guyett, The Coast To Coast Blues Band's drummer and bassist, have been chosen for this particular job, and they're already set up, miked up and warmed up. Hooker's producer, Roy Rogers, a bearded elf with a face-splitting grin and an almost telepathic awareness of his client's needs and wishes, has already sound-checked everything in sight; all Hooker has to do is walk in, sit down, plug in, and play. He and Kirkland catch sight of each other, and warmly wring each other's hands. They have not seen each other for five or six years, nor played together for three and a half decades.

"Hey, how you doin'?"

"You lookin' good."

"Yeah, it's young girls keep you young."

"Mm, got to try some of that."

Rogers does a final check on Brown and Guyett's drum and bass sounds. Hooker and Kirkland sit opposite each other as a cassette of an earlier version of "Ain't No Big Thing," the first tune Hooker and Rogers have chosen for the session, plays through the speakers. Hooker first cut the song back in 1964, during his final studio session for the long-since defunct Chicago label Vee Jay. *"When I first got you, baby, you didn't have a change of clothes . . . You ain't no big thing, baby, I'll replace you right away."*

"Let me hear your rhythm," requests Kirkland.

"I ain't quite sure yet."

"You gonna stay right there on the one?"

They begin to work the tune over, Kirkland playing sliding ninth chords, John Lee jabbing away with mean, low-down bass-string runs. Kirkland isn't happy. "It's all that background noise," he complains, putting down his guitar and standing up.

"Can I turn you up a little bit, Eddie?" asks Rogers from behind the desk.

"Jesus Christ . . ."

"It's clean out *there*, but . . ."

They try it again. The old telepathy operates only intermittently: sometimes they sound like they're playing one big guitar; at others like they're playing two different tunes. "Let's do it over," says John, even before the hiss of Bowen's cymbal has died away. "If you was startin' it," he asks Kirkland, "how would you start it?" Kirkland tries his hand at a new intro. John and Eddie discuss certain chords: "If it fit, do it," says Hooker. "If it don't fit, don't force it." They're rolling: the song's already changed from the demo tape. *"Now you got a few rags on your back and a car to drive, you ain't no big thing, baby. You got a big head. Your two-timing friends try to tell you what to do. Send you back to the lowlands, where I brought you from."*

"Let's do it quick so we can pay the fellas cheap," says John, glancing over at the rhythm section. "Gimme two on the top," requests Kirkland. Hooker stops the take after six bars. Rogers aborts the next one: John has "a string acting funny." This time, the lyrics change yet again. On the one-chord ride-out, Hooker hits a powerful guitar/voice unison: *"No more, no more, no more."* The groove rolls until Hooker cuts short the proceedings with a grave "Thank you, fellas," his favorite cue for an ending.

"You like that, boss?" asks Roy.

"Let's do 'Dimples.' That's old."

They hunt for the cassette featuring "Dimples." They find "Boom, Boom" and "Boogie Chillen" but no "Dimples." Kirkland adjusts his BOSS effects pedal and rolls some heavy Bo Diddley–style vibrato onto his guitar; the band jam while the cassette hunt goes on. Eventually they just jam the tune. "Well, it feel good to me," says Hooker.

"Bowen knows where to come in and he's going to come in right with you," advises Rogers. "We're rolling right . . . now!" It's faster and rougher than the original. Roy holds up his fingers to indicate I, IV or V chords. Next time through it sounds like "Baby Lee." "John, I got to stop you."

He races through into the studio.

"When he starts singing, you should be on the one. When he does that last line, Eddie, go to the five." There are still a few collisions.

"That were a little fast too, wasn't it?" asks Hooker.

"He's into it," replies Rogers. "Let him do it again."

"Take four," Hooker announces. Is this a record, heh heh. Yes, it is: everyone declares themselves satisfied. Rogers retunes Hooker's guitar to open A for the next tune: one of Eddie's songs entitled. "There's Gonna Be Some Blues." He wanders back into the studio and whispers in Hooker's ear before returning behind the desk. He turns around to smile conspiratorially at the assembled company. "I just told John his guitar is sounding exceptionally funky today," he says. This particular number is seriously rockin', with Hooker supplying the backing vocals and Eddie tailing into falsetto on the title line.

"I don't think you can do no better," Hooker announces proudly at the end of the first take. Nevertheless, they run through it again. Rogers lopes back into the studio to retune Hooker's guitar, switching it back from open-tuned A to regular-tuned E. The song seems to have turned into something called "Big City Behind The Sun."

By now, Hooker seems to be getting a little restive. "Let's go," he says, "I wanna look at pretty girls. They get the girls in here yet?" He cackles. Sheila McFarland, the red-haired female engineer, doesn't. They cut it. "That's it!" Jim Guyett and Sam Lehmer, the other engineer, debate a few changes which indicate a certain degree of differences of musical opinion between Jim and Eddie as to whether overdubs are required. Apparently they are not. Eddie packs up his gear. Archie packs up John's. The session has lasted exactly one hour and fifty minutes. John rides back to Redwood City in the Lincoln to watch TV, chow down on some of

Archie's virtuoso downhome cuisine, and chat to his friends on the phone. Kirkland climbs back into the Dodge, but tonight Hooker is treating his guest to the luxury of a night's rest in a nearby motel. Tonight Eddie Kirkland doesn't have to sleep in the back of the van.

The following morning, getting ready to drive up to Hooker's house to hang out and chit-chat for a while before climbing back behind the wheel of the Dodge to catch up with his next door job, Kirkland is still euphoric, still flying, after the experience of playing with his old buddy again after all those years. "One thing I always learned comin' up in the music," he insists, "was you listen to a man, what's comin' from his heart. You don't change that, you just figure out a way to do it. I would always listen to him, whatever he was doin', and think in my mind what to do to put on top of that to make what he done better. That's what I did the way I played behind him in those days, the same way I did yesterday."

He had a few problems, though, playing with the Coast To Coast rhythm section. "Even the musicians, the bass player, that I heard yesterday behind him was not playin' . . . good bass player, but he was not playin' on top of Hooker. On 'Dimples' the bass player was playin' another beat . . . that's why I talked him into playin' a cajun beat, because that fitted. I'm not downin' the musicians, but they did not have the idea *what* to put behind him. They was puttin' behind him what they feels, but it's not right. Whatever he do with his hands, you got to fit it. You don't play somethin' else. That's why I was more sensitive playin' with him than anybody else."

Both "There's Gonna Be Some Blues' and "Big City Behind The Sun," the two tracks on which Hooker backed Kirkland, end up on Kirkland's next album, *All Around The World*, heralded by a prominent cover sticker on which Hooker's name looms large. However, several months later, when Hooker, Roy Rogers and Mike Kappus—the three partners in Blue Rose Productions, the production company which makes and licenses Hooker's current records—review the session tapes, it is decided that there are simply too many bloopers on the Hooker/Kirkland tunes, "Ain't No Big Thing" and "Dimples," to justify their inclusion on any future Hooker release. Indeed, that session was the first one undertaken by Blue Rose since the inauguration of *The Healer* which produced no useable material whatsoever. But by the time the decision was taken, Kirkland was long gone. Back to the Midwest, driving 1,500 miles non-stop through a blizzard, to play a forty-five-minute set with a borrowed band.

―――――

Music didn't interest me. Money is the thing that interested me.
—Bernard Besman, interview with the author, 1992

In 1952, in the wake of "I'm In The Mood" 's success, Eddie Kirkland accompanied Hooker on his first major road trip—in every sense of the word. Kirkland was the band, the musical arranger, the road manager, the business manager, the driver, the mechanic, the bodyguard and anything else Hooker needed. His original partner in crime, Elmer Barbee, was out of the picture by now. According to Eddie Burns, Barbee "just disappeared. [He] used to run a record shop and he also was a good TV repairman. Barbee divorced his first wife and got married to another young lady and started a family all over, and he weren't that young a man. Kids, kids, kids . . ." "After 'In The Mood' I didn't have a manager, he dropped out," says Hooker. "I was on my own and didn't use a manager at all. I just had only the booking agency; I pick up the money and the booking agency pick up the deposit. I run my own business, pick up the money, look after the business on the road. I didn't need roadies and stuff, I didn't use 'em. We set up our own 'quipment. I did good with 'Boogie Chillen,' but 'In The Mood' made more money."

After "I'm In The Mood," Hooker says, his career "changed tremendous. 'Boogie Chillen' was much, much bigger, but when 'I'm In The Mood' come out I made more money than with 'Boogie Chillen,' because at that time I got more popular. I was popular with 'Boogie Chillen,' but I felt that I couldn't afford a band. It was a big, big success. I'd go out with just me and Eddie Kirkland, use pick-up bands, you know? Whatever we needed, drums, bass, piano or whatever. Different towns had different people. We didn't carry the band, we'd use a drummer in that town and move onto the next town. They'd know we was comin' and they have a band there for us rehearsed in each town, good blues bands."

One such band, in Montgomery, Alabama, included a young blind guitarist named Clarence Carter, who surfaced on Atlantic Records fifteen or so years later, as a deep-fried Southern soul star in his own right.

I learned how to play guitar from those old blues records. [Carter explained to Gerri Hershey].[2] John Lee Hooker, Lightnin' Hopkins,

―――――

2 Quoted in Hershey's *Nowhere To Run: The Story Of Soul Music* (Times Books, 1984).

Jimmy Reed, I used to imitate them. John Lee used to come down to Montgomery, where I come up, and every time the club owner that was booking him would get the same thing. John would say, "What the hell you got to back me up? If you ain't got those blind boys, I ain't comin'."

"I couldn't afford to take a band all around the country, Detroit and everywhere," Hooker explains. "They'd have to have transportation, need a van. I hadn't reached the stage when I could do that. For years I would travel with just a guitar, amplifier and a big old Pontiac. The car wasn't too good. We would just carry our guitars and amplifiers, pile it in an old four-door car, blow out our tires, fix 'em up with old pieces of tire 'cause we couldn't afford no new tires. We would get used tires, put two or three of 'em in the car if one blow out.

"Eddie Kirkland worked on the car, he could fix anything. I met him in Detroit. He was playing around when I was. He was scufflin' too. I got a break before he got a break, so he came with me, and we started travelin' all over the country. I had this big hit out there, and everybody know John Lee Hooker. We traveled the South the most, Georgia, Tennessee, Alabama. I made Macon, Georgia, my headquarters. Set up there, get a hotel or a rooming house, and stay there, go into other states. Our bookin' agent was old Clint Brantley. He was a big man, and he booked us all over Georgia, Alabama, some parts of Mississippi once in a while, everywhere he could book us."

Macon, Georgia, used to bill itself as having the highest proportion of churches per head of the population of any town in the U.S. Its most celebrated musical alumni include Little Richard, James Brown, Otis Redding—all Brantley clients in the early days of their careers—and the Allman Brothers. Some of those early tours could get chaotic: one time John was sharing a bill with the Muddy Waters Band just as "Juke," an instrumental single with Muddy's virtuoso harpist Little Walter as the featured artist, was starting to break big. When the tour reached Shreveport, Louisiana, Walter cut and run: he headed back to Chicago to put his own band together, and—according to Mike Rowe in *Chicago Breakdowns*[3]—when Muddy & Co. returned to Chicago after struggling through the rest of the dates without their popular harp man, Walter was on the leader's doorstep asking for his money from the

---

3 Eddison Bluesbooks, 1973.

tour. With truly epic restraint, Muddy replied, "I thought you brought it wit'cha."

"Then it was big, big money," says Hooker. "We got two, three hundred dollars, that was a lot of money. We could survive, had money in the pocket, send money back to the family, whatever. Some places we got five hundred dollars, some places less. Some places we do two shows in the same city one night; do one here and then jump over to the next club and do one. Oh, it was fun back in those days. Sometime I wish that I could relive it. The prices of food and clothes was now like it was then. Honest truth, the money was equally the same thing now as it was then. I'll explain this to you: we make a lot of money, *lots* of money. But you pay a lot of rent, *food* way up there, *everything* way up there. And if you look at it, it about equal out the same way it was then. Wages was very cheap and food was very cheap. Rent was very cheap, almost dirt cheap. The money you made then balanced out. Now you make big money and you got to pay big rent, big everything. It balance out, you know what I'm sayin'?"

"At that time," says Kirkland, "I was interested in helpin' Hooker. I had a pretty good job, I was doin' all right, and the money didn't matter. I felt like I wanted to give him a helpin' hand, you know. I supported him every way I could. I drove. Time when I had to take care of a little business, I took care [of it]. Time when I had to keep peoples off us, bad people, I was there. Ready. We went quite a bit of ways, man, we traveled all over the South, me and him. Played, done well, in clubs, in houses. Band be behind us, and me and Hooker be sittin' out front. If the band mess up we just keep on wailin', man, and end up with the show. We had a really great time. I learned a lot, me and Hooker both. At that time, Hooker didn't know anything about no road. We didn't actually know too much about traveling the highways. We just had somewhere to go; we just got out there and *went*. Mostly in Detroit we did by ourself, just two guitars. When we went South we'd tour with a band. We toured with Clint Brantley out of Macon, Georgia, and they'd put a band with us, a whole show with us. Lotta times the musicians didn't know how to play what we were doin' or didn't want to play what we were doin'. It didn't stop us: we still went on and did what we did together. We took the house, because a lot of bands out there with us didn't like us because John had that fame. He was Hooker, he was John Lee Hooker, and he was popular, and you know how jealous some musicians is. On some occasions they'd try to mess us up, but see: what I did, I'd stay right behind him, push it, and everything worked out lovely. It wasn't a hard job: it was very easy. I would keep that rhythm goin' right behind him and we would tear the house up . . . I was with him from '48 to '55, '56, '53, '54, I was off and on with him. In '53 he got his first band in Detroit behind him. A lotta times he had enough people that he couldn't afford to use me. I understood, but most times, when he got ready to go South he always want me to go with him. In 1953, I spent time in Georgia by myself, then went again in '54. And I toured with him in Georgia in 1955. He had to come home because his wife was sick; I stayed."

Listen to 'em. They're reminiscing now, the morning after the session, anecdotes from half a decade of touring flowing freely. Not surprisingly, after all that time on the road, the years tend to meld together. "*Keep that rhythm,*" says Hooker. "We would go all across the country, just me and him. Cars be blowin' up, Eddie would get out and fix 'em . . ."

"That damn Chevrolet we had, that was a hard ol' car. That Chevrolet was somethin' else. You know what we did? We started out in Cincinnati, we went to Columbus, Dayton, Nashville, Knoxville, Atlanta, Montgomery, Birmingham, on down to Jackson, Mississippi. Left out of Jackson, Mississippi, had to go all the way down to Cleveland. We drove all the way. It was packed in the car: me, Johnny, Cookie Brown . . . we had another lady with us, one blowed the trombone with The Sweethearts Of Rhythm."

"The woman was goin' with all of us, the horn player. With the other woman, too. She was gay."

"We drove from Jackson to Cleveland in one day," says Kirkland, laughing. "I drove all night long, man, made that job. Johnny said, 'Kirk, we ain't gonna make this one.' I said, 'Bet we do.' Drivin' a '48 Chevrolet Coupe De Ville. That was a good runnin' car, man. One thing I can say about a Chevrolet, that car *run*. Took us all those trips . . . I mean, we was doin' some one night stands, man, I mean some hell of a drivin'. Remember that time we was comin' out of Knoxville and it was fog and we stopped by the side of the highway to sleep, woke up the next morning and it was right at the cliff?"

"Oooh-weee! I had forgot about that! Hangin' over the cliff and it was *waaaayyyy* down! Another time we was drivin' and the hood flew off . . ."

"That was on that Oldsmobile."

"We made some long trips, man. We'd make some trips down to Georgia, and nine out of ten, we had so many miles on it when we come back Johnny had to get a new car. That doggone eight-eight Olds you had . . . boy, that was a runnin' thing."

"Well, I did all the drivin'," says Kirkland. "A lotta nights I drove all night long in order to get a place. We'd leave Detroit and wouldn't stop 'til we get to Macon, Georgia. No sleep. The only times we'd stop would be to get a cup of coffee, stop in Nashville sometimes. We spent a lotta time in Nashville, too. We'd stop for a few hours because we made a lotta good friends in Nashville, but it wouldn't be no sleep involved. Most of the time Hooker would stay up all night with me and talk, sometimes he'd get tired and go to sleep. He'd always sit in the front seat, never lay down in the back. At that time we'd see ghostses on the highway . . ."

He's not kidding. And he says it wasn't simply the effects of lack of sleep, either.

"No, that's the way it were. That was for real. He'll tell you hisself. We saw a lotta ghostses on the highway, in different places in the South that we traveled to, and that was back in the '50s. Nowadays, you don't have too many people sayin' that they seen ghostses. Me'n him both seen 'em. We seen 'em, man, cross the highways, man, jam the brakes an' shit, get out and there be nobody there. We was down South, livin' in this house in Macon, Georgia, called Brown House. We come in one night and an old lady come to the door: 'Let me in! Let me in!' We turn round, walk to the door, turn around, walk back, lady disappear. He tell you that."

And he does, too.

Then there were the traditional perks of the traveling musician. Like women. "We used to cut 'em, boy," says Kirkland. "I used to get into town . . . we been drivin' all night long, he'd go to bed . . ."

"I never did no drivin'," grunts Hooker.

". . . but he would very seldom fall asleep. Sometimes he would take a nap, and then wake up. He had to keep his eyes on me, said I drive too fast."

"He could leave here and drive to Detroit quicker'n anybody I know, because he don't make that many stops. He might just stop and take a nap . . ."

"I'd drive all day to get to Atlanta or Macon, and he'd go to bed. When he didn't know anything, I'm shakin' it, got two girls in the room."

"He'd get the women."

"I'd go out and get the women. All I had to do: say I play with John Lee Hooker. They follow me. 'C'mon, let's go the hotel together.' 'Let's go.' "

"I wouldn't go out in the streets," Hooker explains later. "I never did like going out much. I'd go to the hotel, he'd bring these women . . . 'Why you bring these women?' 'They say they want to see you.' Boy, he could drive all 'cross the country, man."

And he still does.

"*Don't* he, man. How can he do that, sixty-seven years old? A lotta *young* people can't do that. *Young* folks can't do that, man. He's a man of *steel*. He leave here bound for Detroit, Kentucky . . . I drive to L.A., I'm burned out. That's *true*! He drive all 'cross the country: night, bad weather, rain, snow . . . he got a young wife, got a child 'bout five years old. Oh boy, he's tough. He's a man of many surprises. I been knowin' him about thirty-some years, and he slowed up a bit, but I slowed down a *lot*." Hooker sums up. "Yeah, we went through some things together, me and this man. We was young and we never had enough of *nothin'*."

The road may have been fun but, nevertheless, the road was hard. "A lot of places in the South," says Kirkland, "they were kind of rough on blacks, especially two black mans traveling through there at night. It was real funny to me the way Hooker would act. He would look at me and he'd say, 'Kirk, you better d-d-d-d-d-d you better hurry and get out this little town. They d-d-d-d-d-don't want us,' and he'd be looking all around . . . like when we messed around and went the wrong way and got caught up on a mountain in Kentucky and . . . I was young back then and every chance that I get I would pick my guitar, so while he was gettin' gas and the man checkin' our water and all that, I was playin' my guitar . . ."

Hooker chuckles at the memory. " 'Come heah, boah! Heh heh! Play that thang!' "

". . . and now we *got* to play. We was *yodellin*!" 'Oh, that sound good!' "

" 'Keep goin! Keep goin', boah!' "

". . . 'You gotta play before you leave here.' When I was going to school in Indiana," Kirkland explains, "I started playing with a country band, so I knew some country music. I know how to yodel too, so it weren't no sweat. We come on back and went inside and played country and western and Hooker, he started flammin' in right along with me. So anyway, we did well: he gave us a bag of cookies and sardines and stuff and left. 'Okay, boah, y'all can go,' and they was all happy. After that when we got down the road John said, 'D-d-d-d-d we d-d-d-d-did all right, didn't we?' "

Tell us another, Mr. Kirkland.

"What happened, Johnny wanted to stop and get him a little half-pint bottle of somethin' . . ."

"I was drinkin' Beefeater."

"And Johnny got to kinda feelin' good. 'Whatsamatter, you can't step on it?' "

"Oh yeah! I forgot about that! 'Step on it! Step on the gas!' "

"Let's get to Georgia. Went down there, this old cop pulled us over, tooked us over to the judge's house, woke the judge up . . ."

"Sure did."

"How much that cost us, John, fifteen dollars?"

"Fifteen, twenty dollars. Back then that was big money."

"Big money back then, man. Fifteen dollars in your pocket, you could do a lot with that."

"They had little places way out in the fields. Little jails . . ."

"Little towns with but two, three stores in it . . . they stop you . . ."

Racism on the road was one problem. Missing the folks back home was another. Hooker had a young, growing family—his first son, John Lee Hooker Jr., had been born on January 13, 1952—and he was caught in an archetypal double bind. The only effective way he could earn the money that he needed in order to feed, clothe and house his family was to travel, which meant leaving them at home for long periods of time. That hurt.

"You heard that song *'at the crossroads, don't know which way to go'?* I made up my mind to keep on up the road, and I reached the goal. But many times I wanted to turn back. I was all I had. At the same time, goin' down that hard road to reach my destination, I had to deal with the family. I had kids to raise. I had kids to feed. Had to make money for bills and houses. I had to be facin' all of that, and them lookin' to me for that. I was a hard, game person, wasn't gonna let my family suffer. They never suffered a day in they life for food, for money. So I think about that, and I wouldn't go back. I look back, and say, 'I wish I could go back there, I should quit and go back,' but no, I can't go back now, I got a family and kids to support, I got to keep pushin'. And I kept doin' that, bringin' the bacon home. Out on the road, night and day. Sometimes out there all night long, travelin'. Workin' the next night, the same. Thinkin' about home, but I couldn't *go* back home, 'cause I had nothin' to go back there *with*. I had to bring the *bacon* back. When I go home I had to bring that money back. You follow me? Had to go out there and *git* it.

"They were there, they was at home, I just know I had a family and that's about *it*. Come home to 'em, stay a while and get right back out. Wasn't because I wanted to, but because I had to do that. I was young, I could handle it then, you know. I wanted to be home with them; I wished I could've, but I couldn't. Hey, I got to put food on this table, I got to go. So they grew up knowin' when I come through, knowin' that I did the right thing. I'm glad they know that, knowin' that I did that for them, for the kids. They didn't ask to come here. I got 'em here, so I got to take care of 'em. So that's what I did."

Back in Detroit, his prolific recording habits were beginning to get him into trouble. That year he released four singles on Modern under his own name (one of which was billed as a joint effort between himself and "Little" Eddie Kirkland) as well as appearing "as himself" for two on Chess. As "John Lee Booker" and "John L. Booker," he cut three more for Chance, but what finally got Bernard Besman's goat was Joe Von Battle finally playing things too fast and loose for comfort. In April 1951, Battle had recorded an extended Hooker session for Chess (one of the artistic peaks of Hooker's early recording career, as it happened) but Besman hit the roof when Battle sold two of the sides from that session, "Louise" and "Ground Hog Blues," to Modern—to whom Besman was supplying his "official" releases—who released them in 1952 under the incredibly subtle credit of "John L'Hooker." "He recorded for Modern, to whom I was leasing records," fumes Besman, "and while I was making the records which I would lease to them for the rest of the country, he was making records for them. At least he wasn't making the same tunes! But when I found out Modern did that, I was really teed off. I said, 'You're finished.' I broke his contract. I said, 'You wanna go with Modern?' They were gonna pay him a hell of a lot more than I did, because I started him. They promised him the moon, I suppose, I dunno, compared to me and how much bigger the company was. I said, 'Okay, I'll let you out of the contract, but I'm not paying you anymore royalties, with the money that I advanced you on the artists' royalties. No more. That's it, because you'll never pay me back what I've invested.'"

Those records subsequently sold more than a few, though.

"Well, subsequently," Besman concedes reluctantly, "but at that time I was way in the hole on Hooker. And one of the reasons that I sold my business to my partner and went to L.A. was because I spent so much money recording not only him but other . . . I was so much in the hole with him that my partner didn't get along with me too well. Four or five years later he sold the company to Handelman Brothers, the biggest record distributors probably in the world. They were on the Stock Exchange at that time, so he became president of that company. The company that I started with six thousand dollars is now one of the biggest companies in the world. The point is that I had advanced all this money and he always needed the money . . . oh what the hell, I'll record him. But he got so far behind that my partner didn't like that too well, so that's what happened. So when Modern did this I was really teed off, because I didn't know about that. I didn't know about the others until much later. [Modern] were going to pay him much more, they got bigger distribution, so the deal was I signed the release of his contract. So the contract had to go through the union also, and I canceled that, and I filed why it was canceled. Then when he got signed up with Modern, they were in California, so I don't know what they did. At that time you had to be licensed by the union to be a record producer."

The terms of "the release of his contract" meant that Hooker ceded Besman all artists' rights in the existing master recordings. Besman emphasizes that Hooker only waived his rights "as an artist, not on the music, not on the songwriting, the publishing," but what it effectively meant was that all Hooker received—or would ever receive—from the proceeds of the 250 or so sides that he and Besman cut together between 1948 and 1952 would be one-half of the composition credit. That's "one-half" because Besman had decided, as a parting gesture, that he would register himself as the co-writer of everything that he and Hooker ever recorded together, even though the initial singles had come out with the compositions label-credited to Hooker alone.

One key exception to the latter generalization was "I'm In The Mood": the original Modern issue listed the composers as "(Hooker/Taub)." "Taub" was one of the "house names"—two others being "Ling" and "Josea"—which were habitually appended to the composer credits of Modern artists, like B. B. King, in order to divert half the publishing royalties from potential hits back to the company. In the history of the recorded African-American music of the twentieth century, this kind of scammery was the rule, rather than the exception. In fact, it was business as usual. To cite one famous example: when Chess released Chuck Berry's first single, "Maybellene" in 1954, two powerful disc jockeys of the time, Russ Fratto and Alan Freed, were each awarded a third of the composer's royalties as an incentive to give the record heavy airplay. They certainly followed through on their end of the bargain: the record was indeed a hit and formed the foundation stone of the Chuck Berry legend which persists to this day, but that still doesn't make it right. Similarly, many of the great Bobby "Blue" Bland's early hits, credited to "Deadric Malone," were in fact written by members of Bland's justifiably fabled band, notably trumpeter/arranger Joe Scott and guitarist Wayne Bennett. "Malone" was a pseudonym for Don Robey, boss of the Houston-based Duke and Peacock labels, for whom Bland recorded: Robey was a notorious "heavy" who once, reputedly, punched Little Richard hard enough to give him a hernia when the flamboyant young pianist had the temerity to use the word "royalties." Apparently Robey had little difficulty inducing Bland's men to sign away their copyrights in exchange for a few bucks in front. "*Ohhhh* boy, Don Robey . . . he robbed *everybody*," Hooker chortles.

In fact, Duke Ellington, despite coming from the opposite extreme of the African-American social spectrum from Hooker—he was the urbane, educated, musically-literate scion of a White House chef, as opposed to an unlettered manual worker from the Delta—had very similar experiences in the New York City of the 1920s, during the dawn of his fame. Ellington worked with publisher Irving Mills, later the Ellington band's booker, manager and publicist, who was in the habit of buying blues tunes outright from indigent songwriters for fifteen or twenty dollars apiece. (In his autobiography, *Music Is My Mistress*,[4] Ellington recalls how Mills "hit the ceiling" when trumpeter Cootie Williams went down to Mills's office to sell him a blues. "Oh, no," Mills yelled at the unsuspecting hornman, "I own *all* the blues!")

"Every song [Duke] wrote had Irving's name on it as the co-composer," explained Mercer Ellington, Duke's son, in an interview conducted for a TV film of his father's life. "So he got half of the composer's end, *and* Irving was the publisher, and he got *all* of the publisher's end. So Ellington got twenty-five percent of the tune, while Irving got seventy-five percent." According to songwriter Mitchell Parrish, interviewed for the same program, this was known as a "cut-in," and it was simply the accepted common practice of the time for influential people to add their names to a composer credit even when they didn't have anything to do with the actual composition of the piece in question. "If I hadn't raved about him when I heard him the first night," claimed Mills himself, "he might have just been a bandleader. I was very fortunate. *Duke* was very fortunate." In other words,

---

4 W. H. Allen, 1974.

both Mills and Besman were claiming the equivalent of a "finder's fee" from the proceeds of their clients' work, in accordance with the standard practice of the time: the difference was that Mills never denigrated his client's talents—indeed, it was his efforts as a publicist which were primarily responsible for Ellington's early acceptance as a composer of genius rather than simply a sophisticated entertainer—and he never seriously claimed a major creative part in Ellington's artistic achievement. In the case of Besman and Hooker, things were very different.

"All the records he made for me are published by me," Besman insists, "and I'm the co-writer on all those songs. *All* of them. All that he did for me. Don't forget, he couldn't read or write—number one—number two, if I let him record, all the numbers would be the same. Most of the time he never came rehearsed, so he didn't know what we were gonna do, which was a terrific deal, because he was a one-man band. I'd get together with him on a subject and say, 'What're we gonna sing about today?' He'd say something, I'd say something, that was it. It wasn't like getting together and writing a song for a month. Whatever came out, came out. It was impromptu. He's like an old troubadour, you might say. You give him subject matter, like the rail strike in Detroit. I'd say, 'Let's sing about the strike' and give him a few sentences, and there it is. There's a song.[5] The next time, it'd become something else. But all the songs I recorded I had to [talk him through them], because if you didn't you'd just get the same thing. The 'Boogie Chillen' theme, with different words, out of the 250 records that I did with him, there are at least twenty songs using the 'Boogie Chillen' theme. It's the same thing: all he'd do is change the words. If I let him, he'd do 'Boogie Chillen' or 'Sally Mae' over and over again. So I'd be playing the different rhythms for him, to get him to change it a little bit. He has the talent to do that; not many people could do that. But he wouldn't remember what he did on the first song [*laughs*] or the second song. I've also played bongos or drums or organ, anything to keep the thing moving along. Because if I didn't, all his tunes would be the same as far as the music goes."

If anything can truly be said to contradict Besman's claim to have been Hooker's artistic muse—apart from Hooker's own account, that is—it's the remarkably varied music which Hooker made for Joe Von Battle,

---

5   Besman refers here to "Strike Blues," recorded in April 1950, but unissued until the early '70s.

Elmer Barbee and others during the period that the two men worked together. Though that "other" Hooker music may lack the tight commercial focus which Besman brought to his sessions, this loss is, with a few decades of hindsight, clearly counterweighted by the freewheeling invention and giddy leaps of improvisational inspiration which Hooker was able to produce when liberated from Besman's constraints. In any case, the majority of contemporary record producers routinely do for their artists what Besman claims to have done for Hooker without claiming a share of the composer credits for their work. Besman was—in the musical sense—Hooker's producer; in cinematic terms he was Hooker's director (and sometimes set designer), and if we prefer a literary analogy, he was Hooker's editor.

"I know *exactly* how they got those sounds," insists Eddie Burns. "Johnny always was a feet-stomper. He stomped a lot when he played, you know. Both feet goin' up and down. Floppin', you know. He be sittin' in the chair, but they had these wooden chairs that folds, you know. They would put them under his feet to get the sound, you know what I mean, because when he used to play he used to get happy, and them feet be goin', they be floppin' and things. It didn't sound like a drum because it was a straightforward beat, but it was gettin' the job done. Some things he cut, Bernie would be in the background and he be poppin' his fingers some kind of way and Johnny would be stompin' and you hear the clickin' from the fingers too, all goin' at the same time. Then the music would come back in . . ."

"Listen," Besman insists, "many times I recorded him for nine hours straight just to get the money back. I'd bring in corned-beef sandwiches, work as long as I had to. He didn't care. It wasn't like a group who'd come in with arrangements, all rehearsed, and every time they play it it'd be the same. With him he didn't know anything, so there was no use preparing anything. Mostly, it was just the subject matter we'd discuss, and the rhythms. I think that I contributed with some of my musicians to the style that the records came out in. But you know what was the worst problem that I had with him? He wanted to sing ballads!" He laughs. "I refused to do it. But there were several that I let him do: one was 'It's My Own Fault,' on which I also played piano. That was the closest I let him do to a ballad, but he begged me. I said no, because if I let him play ballads he wouldn't be John Lee Hooker! That's like 'I'm In The Mood For Love' he wanted to sing that ballad *'I'm in the mood for love/strictly because you're near me,'* but that's what came out. You know why? He can't remember, but he wanted to sing the ballads. I had a battle with him. I said, 'No way,' but that was as close as it came: 'It's My Own Fault.'" I had to change that title, because that came out . . . Chess Records stole that master. I don't know how they got it, but over my piano they overdubbed his voice. I didn't release that record until 1971, and they already had it out in 1955. But the piano is there. That's me playing.[6] Listen, for money they would do anything. Chess wasn't so honest. The experience I've had with these other companies is that they're all crooked."

Let's put it this way: the above speech provides considerable scope for discussion, and it should come as no surprise to hear that Hooker vehemently disputes all of it. First of all, he claims never, ever, to have received any advances or front-money from Besman. "I don't owe him no money, and I never borrowed any money from him, not ever," says Hooker, very firmly indeed. "All I got from him was the money he owed me, and I probably didn't get all of that. He probably gave me what he felt like giving me. He never loaned me no money . . . never. Never. *Never*. I would know if I did. I wouldn't lie, I'd say yes, I had one or two [advances], but I never. I don't dislike the man, I like him, but I don't like what he's saying, and he's not right."

According to documentary evidence cited by Mike Rowe in his liner-note for *Detroit Blues 1950–1952*, a compilation of early non-Besman sides by Hooker and Eddie Burns,[7] Hooker himself had apparently requested a release from the then-current rollover of his annually renewable contract with Besman in order to sign with Gotham Records, to whom Battle had leased four singles—with Hooker billed as "Johnny Williams" or "John Lee"—during 1950 and 1951. "Please send me the contract so I can sign it," ran the text of an undated letter to Gotham written above his signature, and enclosing a copy of his current contract with Besman, which had commenced in March 1951 and was due to expire on February 29, 1952. "I want 2½ cent royalty to start and four hundred dollars

---

6 For what it's worth, Les Fancourt attributes this track—a scary, swirling pre-psychedelic piece drenched in echo and slightly reminiscent of "I'm In The Mood"—to a session cut for Fortune Records soon after Hooker's final session for Besman. It was subsequently acquired by Chess, who released it in 1954. The superb blues piano on this cut is generally credited to Bob Thurman, a Detroit pianist who worked occasionally with Hooker between 1952 and 1954.
7 Released on Collectables COL-CD-516, with a cover photo of Burns rather than Hooker. The British edition of the same collection (Flyright FLY CD 23) features nineteen tracks as opposed to the Collectables edition's sixteen. It includes three additional tracks (one extra by Burns, plus two by Robert "Baby Boy" Warren), but the booklet contains only an abbreviated version of Rowe's liner-note text.

in advance. Send the money along with the contract. I would like it about Wednesday. If I get my release before my contract is expired I will let you know and you can use my name." This particular deal produced no significant fruit—if, indeed, it was ever consummated, which is doubtful—since no further Hooker titles ever appeared on Gotham. The Besman contract must have been renewed, or else there would have been nothing for Besman to release Hooker from. Furthermore, Hooker and Besman cut at least one more recording session before their final falling-out, generating three more Modern singles (and a further pile of sides for Besman's vaults) before they left United Sound together for the last time on May 22, 1952. (On this session, Besman made what was one of his few audible contributions to any Hooker sides of the period: he played rudimentary organ chords on versions of the standards "It Hurts Me Too" and "Key To The Highway," as he had done on a previous session a month or two earlier.)

Besides, Besman had another excellent reason for severing his connection with Hooker; one which had nothing to do with his star's faltering record sales or promiscuous recording habits. "I left Detroit in 1952 because I had six months to live," Besman explains. "I had a very bad sinus condition in Detroit. I'd be sick all the time. When winter came, I was sick. When summer came, I was sick. This doctor said, 'You have a blood infection which will kill you in six months unless we operate on you.' So like any other smart guy I went and got three other opinions, and the other three doctors said that if I left Michigan and went to a warmer climate, with medication I'd survive. So that's why I had to sell my company and stop recording. I went into distribution of an item called Paint-By-Numbers. It was a hobby thing where you had a canvas and pictures divided into numbers. In 1952, my cousin was manufacturing this Paint-By-Numbers, we had this company and I was going to go to L.A. because of the warmer climate, and also because I was stationed in Santa Rosa for a while, which is sixty miles north of San Francisco, and I got to like California, so I'd decided that I was going to come back after the war. This Paint-By-Numbers, I got the franchise for the eleven Western states, and I made more money on Paint-By-Numbers in one year than I would have made [from music] in a lifetime. It was a very, very big product. That's why music didn't interest me. Money is the thing that interested me. I was very successful with that. And then Hooker, at that time, had kinda faded out. He didn't get revitalized until about 1971, when I leased the records to United Artists and he made some sessions with Canned

Heat. That's what revitalized him, Canned Heat. He made 'Boogie Chillen' again with them, called it 'Boogie Chillen No. 2.' All those records he made with Vee Jay and Chess weren't really big numbers, except for one or two, but his records didn't sell in the quantities they sell now."

(Here Besman is being somewhat disingenuous, not to mention just a *leetle* self-serving. It was during those years, when Hooker "had kinda faded out," that he wrote and recorded "Dimples" and "Boom Boom"— two of his biggest, most influential, and most-covered hits; that he made his breakthrough to the young white mass audience, first through the folk scene and later as an icon to successive generations of young blues-rockers, playing to the largest crowds of his career thus far, that he discovered, or was discovered by, a vast new potential audience in Europe; and that he enjoyed his first mainstream album-chart success. But we're getting somewhat ahead of ourselves: all of that lay in an unwritten future impossible for either Besman or Hooker to predict.)

Hooker insists that Besman didn't write "Boogie Chillen": "I had that song and I was playing that around there before I knew him. I met Elmer Barbee and I was playing around and we got it on blank and that went to Bernie, who heard all my stuff I had down on a blank."

But did Hooker talk to Besman about what he was going to do before he did it? "Yeah," he says, "like I do now in the studio." Nevertheless, he insists that he never talked about what a song was going to be about, or what it was going to say. "No. I just do it, like I do now. I don't talk about it. So many people got they name on my records, say they wrote. Jimmy Bracken, his name on, saying he wrote this. Al Smith, Calvin Carter[8]—all them gone now—he wrote this. How can anybody say they wrote John Lee Hooker's songs? I write all my songs. Roy [Rogers] and them will tell you: *nobody* writes songs for John Lee Hooker. Since I left Bernie I've written over a hundred songs. I didn't get 'em off the top of my head; I fix 'em like I want to fix 'em. When I met Bernie I had 'Boogie Chillen'; I got 'In The Mood' from an old big band and put the words to it. It's a completely different song."

Hooker still grumbles about the money that he feels he should have earned back in those days, not because he particularly needs it now, but because he certainly could have used it then, back when he was broke and scuffling. (I once asked Charlie Musselwhite if he was familiar with

---

8 These three gentlemen were associated with Vee Jay Records of Chicago, for whom Hooker recorded between 1955 and 1964. We'll meet them later.

a song, recorded by Hooker in London in the mid-'60s, which begins "*You know that I love you but don't be messing with my bread.*" He laughed heartily and replied, "No, I don't remember that one . . . but I can almost hear it.") Further to this, deponent sayeth not, except to point out two things: first, that as part of his separation from Besman, Hooker did indeed sign the agreement that relinquished his rights and, what's more, that he signed it again almost twenty years later when Besman commenced the first major reissue program of his Hooker material by leasing sides to United Artists and Specialty in the early '70s. And second, that whenever Besman has found it necessary either to assert or to defend the legal validity of that agreement in a court of law, he has won.

But, over and above whatever monies he may or may not have received, what distresses Hooker the most about having to share composing credits with Bernard Besman is the implication that his music isn't really entirely his own. It's one thing to have to give up a piece of your royalties—just about everybody in the blues world has had to do that at some time or another—but it's an entirely different proposition when you have to give up a piece of your soul. "How long since I been without him?" Hooker asks rhetorically. "I've invented plenty stuff, right? I don't like to say it but I'm gonna say it: I'm a *genius* when it come to writin' songs. I *am*. I wrote more blues songs than anybody. I write my own lyrics, my own songs, my own way'a doin' it. I can be in the studio and write songs right in the studio. Right in the studio. 'Boom Boom,' 'Dimples'—all those tunes, all the new tunes."

Left to his own devices, Hooker signed himself direct to Modern. In business terms, this must have been something like jumping from the frying pan straight into the fire. Musically, Hooker was effectively producing himself, with engineer Joe Siracuse still manning the board at United Sound. As he had done on his "outside" sessions, Hooker now alternated between solo recordings—with the occasional participation of Eddie Kirkland—and rough, rocking combo sides featuring an assortment of the local musicians with whom he worked the clubs and bars. While the economics of touring had dictated that he mostly traveled only with the faithful Kirkland, he had worked locally with a band which, at various times, included pianists Bob Thurman, James Woods and Vernon "Boogie Woogie Red" Harrison; saxophonists Otis Finch and Johnny Hooks; and drummers Jimmy Turner and Tom Whitehead.

Whitehead was a stocky Alabama-born drummer, raised by his mother variously in Detroit, Chicago and Cleveland. He'd played drums in school before he quit music to get married, but by the early '50s the lure of the sticks and cymbals had proved too seductive to resist, and he was back behind the kit. "I played with little jazz groups, met John—I hadn't heard nothin' about him—in '53. A piano player—we'd worked together in his band—and me got a job with John. I guess he was havin' a problem, his drummer was ill or something, so this Bob Thurman, he deceased now, he called me up and asked me if I was busy. I said, 'No, not this weekend.' So he said, 'Well, c'mon, I want you to come and play with John Lee Hooker.' I said, 'Who is that?' I had never heard of him. He had made 'Boogie Chillen' already. I wasn't with him then. Fact, he did that by himself, with the box, stompin'. He was playin' at the Club Caribe, down on Jefferson Avenue. I went there and I played with him that night and he asked me, 'What about tomorrow night?' I say, 'Okay, I'll play tomorrow night.' After that he say, 'Hey, I like the way you play. What about playin' with me regular?' I say, 'Okay.' Eddie Kirkland had played with him on and off, and Eddie Burns had played with him on and off. They knew him before I did. Reason I enjoy playin' with him—I'll be frank—is that we could play everything, and then we bring him up. We could play jazz, we could play . . . you know, that's the reason I got attached with him, see. Otherwise I probably wouldn't have, at that time, I bein' younger, you know. He gave the band a lot of freedom. And he was a nice person.

"I found Johnny very nice to work with. Sometimes he would leave to play gigs by himself, and when he come back I might have another job waitin' for him, because he would have me manage the band since he saw that I was very dependable and prompt, you know. No problem, no trouble, you know what I mean. He told me he would like me to manage the band. I would hire horn players sometimes, whatever I thought it needed. He had a group formed already when I came to him which consisted of a trumpet, saxophone—didn't have no bass—piano and drums . . . plus Johnny. I always was bickering all the time because I wanted a bass player. Drummers more comfortable then, more relaxed, to put more into it 'stead of just keepin' just a steady grind. I didn't find it difficult. I enjoyed workin' with him. I like workin' with him, he give the band freedom. That's one thing I have to give him credit for; a lot of musicians don't do that. 'You got to play what I'm playin' and that's it.' But he didn't care what we play when he was off the stand. We play whatever we wanted to play, but then when we call him up we play *him*, and that's that, and you didn't mix that up. That's one of the reasons I really liked playing with him, because he didn't stay on the bandstand all the time, see. We would kinda get things warmed up, you know, and the people really *ready* for him when he come up. We played a little jazz, a little this, a little that, a little everything. And then when he comes, they really ready for the blues, and we just played the blues, see. Say, out of a set, he might do . . . say we were playin' maybe about forty-five minutes, he might do fifteen or twenty minutes, and the band did everything else. They called us The Boogie Ramblers at that time, but we would play some boogies and play some blues too. The saxophone player sing, and the trumpet player sing, so they would sing some blues numbers and things, so it didn't annoy the people, you know. They kinda enjoyed it. We would swing, but we didn't play way *out* there, for dancin' and stuff like that. The people liked us, they liked the band also. He'd never stay up there for the whole set; do maybe four, five songs, and go on a break. Then the band play, you know, and the people be lined up every night at the Club Caribe. I never played with him on Hastings Street; I started with him on Jefferson and we play various places around the city. We played at the Apex Bar on Oakland Avenue and Clay, Latin Casino on Lafayette, Prince Royal on Gratiot and McDougal, Masonic Temple . . ."

"That was the first outstanding band that he had, The Boogie Ramblers," says Burns. "They had horns and everything. Curtis Foster used to play with all of us. I don't know what happened to him. James Watkin also used to play a lot with me, and we all used to play with John. That was before he got The Boogie Ramblers: Bob Thurman, Tom Whitehead, [trumpeter] Jimmy Miller, and Johnny Hooks. It was a long time before he got a bass player, and when he got one, he got one used to be with Paul Williams and The Hucklebucks. One of the things that was clickin' for him was this variety. We had that for a long time in Detroit. As a bluesman you featured, but you got this variety band. That's been goin' on here for years. The band is playin' everything, including your thing. See what I'm sayin'? That way, you gettin' a mixed clientele. You was gettin' a mixed crowd when it was like that. Couldn't nobody say, 'Well, I don't like blues,' because they could say, 'But I like swing music and this rhythm'n'blues.' "

And with The Boogie Ramblers behind him, the Crawling King Snake consolidated his status as king of the Detroit ghetto. No 'bout-a-doubt it: he ruled his den.

... The bulk of black Detroiters, men and women who toiled in hot, dirty factories all week, were not ... "hep cats" ... but folks who wanted a beat to dance away the blues to, and lyrics that talked about the basics of life. In 1953, black Detroit's favorite performer was not jazz giant Charlie Parker, but John Lee Hooker, a foot-stomping, one-beat-boogie bluesman from Clarksdale, Mississippi. Hooker shared the same values and background as the older black masses of Detroit. His songs catalogued his life, especially the transition from rural to urban living, and, in doing so, created a verbal portrait of life as seen by Detroit's black immigrants. And Hooker's metallic guitar strokes were the perfect stimulant for house parties and gin drinking.
—Nelson George in *Where Did Our Love Go*[9]

Though John Lee Hooker was far and away the biggest fish in the Detroit blues pond, the trouble was that it was a very small pond indeed. Detroit and its environs boasted a rich variety of musical traditions during the post-war years, of which the Motown empire is merely the most famous, but if it hadn't been for John Lee Hooker, the city's electric-downhome scene would be merely a footnote. Consider some of the talent either spawned or nurtured in Detroit during Hooker's sojourn: Little Willie John, Jackie Wilson, Johnny Ray and Wilson Pickett, to name but four, all lived and worked there, as did the Reverend C. L. Franklin, African-America's most charismatic churchman. Franklin recorded sermons and services for Chess Records' gospel line, but he was based in Detroit, as was his daughter Aretha, who subsequently did pretty well for herself in the 1960s. There was also a thriving jazz scene and—in the late '60s—a highly distinctive high-energy white rock scene developed around performers like the MC5, The Stooges (starring Iggy Pop), The Amboy Dukes (led by Ted Nugent), Bob Seger and Alice Cooper.[10] Hooker was, and is, the only one of the city's bluesmen to make an equivalent impact on the greater world outside.

---

9 *Where Did Our Love Go: The Rise & Fall Of The Motown Sound*, Omnibus Press, 1986.
10 This isn't the appropriate time or place for a history, however concise, of the indigenous music scene of the Detroit area, but it's worth pointing out that the city can also claim Suzi Quatro and Madonna—though they had to relocate (to London and New York, respectively) to achieve anything—and successful and unique variants of House and Techno music.

There was a heaping handful of talented bluesmen in Detroit, including harpist Aaron "Little Sonny" Willis (who surfaced with a couple of '70s albums for the Memphis-based Stax Records as the company attempted to follow its successes with Albert King and Little Milton) plus guitarists Robert "Baby Boy" Warren and Louis "Mr. Bo" Collins, as well as Hooker's own associates and jamming partners like Eddie Kirkland, Eddie Burns, Andrew Dunham and Sylvester Cotton. However, once we subtract Hooker himself from this line-up, the age-old rivalry between the local blues scenes of Detroit and Chicago begins to look decidedly unequal. For a start, the Chicago scene—with its plentiful recording facilities and massive population of Delta expats—had been established far longer, with pre-war roots stretching back to the heyday of Big Bill Broonzy, Tampa Red and John Lee (the original Sonny Boy) Williamson. An average night out in Chicago could offer the footloose punter Chess Records stalwarts like Muddy Waters, Little Walter, Howlin' Wolf and Sonny Boy Williamson II as well as Elmore James and numerous lesser lights, including veteran pianist Sunnyland Slim and the up-and-coming harpist Junior Wells.

"Unfortunately, Detroit is not the same kind of scene that Chicago was, or is today," says Eddie Burns. "You got a lot of great musicians here, but [Detroit is] a strange scene, has always been, still is. To be successful in Detroit you cannot just become a real successful blues musician only; you have to learn to play something else in Detroit. You don't have to do that in Chicago, but here you do. The biggest, strongest musicians is the ones that has a large variety of what they doing, and the city is still like that today." Tom Whitehead agrees. "The Detroit style is a little different," he says. "See, the Chicago [blues style] is exactly like it was in the Deep South. Detroit doesn't sound direct from Mississippi or Alabama." This is possibly the reason why, ever since Hooker left town, the Detroit blues scene has enjoyed little respect from its more famous cousin across the lake. As Famous Coachman states, more than somewhat resentfully, "Every year we bring Chicago guys in and all through the year we put 'em in places, in the nightclubs here, but Chicago never see fit to book any Detroit acts over to Chicago, not even playin' in a nightclub, or on the festival. Nine years they had a festival; this year is the first they put *one guy* on there; that was Eddie Burns."

"Since I've been travelin' around," Burns concurs, "I find that the Detroit musicians gets less recognition than any of the musicians I know. Now why that is I don't know, but it's true, and if you is not a fighter, you won't make it in Detroit. See what I'm sayin'? You *will not make it* in Detroit, because Chicago has always gotten all of the recognition. You got some super good musicians here, but they trapped. They don't know how to get out. It's politics, you know, just like cattle or sheeps standing in the stall, and they separatin' them, you know. It's not another bluesman here today that's more better known than me. Since Hooker left here, I'm Number One, but I'm not the only one here, and I feel for these other guys, but the connections is so delicate to come by it's pathetic. And that remains today that way. I guess the reason I'm still survivin' is because I *am* a fighter."

Hooker was thus the sole exception to the prevailing Detroit rule. Though Tom Whitehead and The Boogie Ramblers could—and did— perform in a variety of styles during the curtain-raisers they played before Hooker took the stage, he was the only one of the city's bluesmen getting by with nothing but straight, deep blues. His new records for Modern, some of which featured him alone or with Eddie Kirkland but an increasing proportion of which showcased him with piano, drums and saxophone accompaniment, were selling well, even if not as spectacularly as had "Boogie Chillen" or "I'm In The Mood." Nevertheless, he was still broke. "Every time I see him he was out of gas, *heh heh*," says Coachman, laughing. "He had a big engine in the car with a little bitty gas tank, and the small gas tank mean that the car were drinkin' more gas than he could keep in the car. And every time he needed some money he would come by the store: 'H-h-h-h-h-e-e-e-e-e-y-y-y Famous Coachman, I'm outta gas.' He had a TV, and every time it'd break I had to go fix it, and he never had no money to pay me. He had one of them big old pot-bellied stoves right there in the middle of the floor, and they put coal in it to keep them warm. He had a big old TV, had a cabinet that was big, and a seven-inch screen. That's all there was out there then. I used to have to go out there every two, three weeks and put in a brand-new transformer. That was the record: about two, three weeks. Runnin' the whole set with that. When that go out, the sound go out, picture go out. Everything, boy."

By now, the Hookers had moved again: to the house on Jameson and McClellan which would remain as the family home until Hooker finally packed up and quit Detroit for good. There were still bills to pay—a second son, Robert, had been born on July 25, 1953—and there was never quite enough money coming in to take care of everything. Despite Hooker's perennial suspicions that Bernard Besman had been underpaying him, at least Besman had managed to extract *some* money from Modern Records. Hooker himself had rather less luck until, one day, he decided to take matters into his own hands once and for all.

"I never see a true royalty statement. You go over, they be hidin'. Go down to L.A., they say, 'He ain't in.' You call, they say, 'Is that Mr. Hooker there? Just a minute. Oh, he stepped out.' And he sittin' right there, all that kinda crap. I go down there, lay down the law . . . I caught him one day, I went about three times, four times. He didn't know I was comin'. I walked right in, and Jules and Joe were sittin' right there. They eye nearly popped out. I had this guy with me, knew all about publishing, stuff like that. I didn't know about publishing and different stuff, this and that, but he know, and he walked in with me, and they knew him. He said, 'We got to have eight or ten thousand dollars.' And I say, '*What!?*' I ain't never *heard* of that kind of money. I know he was up there, I know I had made way, way, way, way more than that. He took them back in the office, and I sat there for about an hour and a half, and he came out of there with a check for about ten thousand dollars. I don't know what he did to them to get that, but he had all the papers in the world, and he knowed all about the business, and he must've threatened 'em, he must've scared them. His percentage was ten percent, and I had never saw that much money before. Not at once. Barbee would give me money like six, seven, eight hundred, twelve or fifteen hundred when I do those recordings, which was big, big, big money. *I* thought it was. This guy Paul Oscar was the lawyer from L.A., I had been talking to him on the phone, somebody recommended him.

"He had all this stuff set up so I could come down from Detroit to his office. He had made a few phone calls to them, but that day they didn't know he was comin'. He was a big man then. I sat there about an hour and a half, two hours. I sat there by the receptionist, and she said, 'Son, I know you hungry, do you wanna eat something?' I said no. She went next door, got some sandwiches. We done talked and talked. She said, 'Oohh Mr. Hooker, I *love* your music, you is so popular.' They got 'em trained, but she really liked me. After a while, he came out of the office and said, 'I know you hungry, but I got something gonna give you a good appetite, make you eat more.' So we sat in the car, him and his driver. I don't know where his driver had went, because he wasn't in the office. Probably watching the back door, make sure they didn't run out! He said, 'I'm gonna put the biggest check in your hand you ever seen in your life.' I was breathless. I was scared to ask how much. 'Uh-huh.' 'Ain't you gonna ask?' 'Uh-huh.' 'Stop that *uh-huh*! How much you think it is?'

'I dunno, about a thousand?' 'Oh *Lord*. It's ten thousand dollars.' I like to fell out the car. I don't know what he did to get it, but it was the first and last money I got from them."

In April 1954, Hooker signed a standard one-year contract with Specialty Records, another established L.A.-based R&B independent. Characteristically, though, he cut several sessions for Modern[11] before the Bihari connection was finally severed. Specialty's founder Art Rupe had opened for business in 1945, right at the onset of the post-war jump boom, and sophisticated artists like Roy Milton, Percy Mayfield and the brothers Joe and Jimmy Liggins were both to his taste and highly profitable. Furthermore, their well-drilled, highly professional, thoroughly rehearsed approach to recording made for the kind of smooth, organized sessions he preferred to run. Nevertheless, Rupe covered his bets by dabbling in sessions featuring more downhome bluesmen like Frankie Lee Sims or New Orleans' Eddie "Guitar Slim" Jones, whose epochal 1953 hit "Things I Used To Do" gave a blind Georgian pianist named Ray Charles his first break as an arranger and musical director, and a proven hit-maker like Hooker must have seemed like an attractive addition to his roster. So the following month Rupe dispatched Johnny Vincent, one of his staff producers, to Detroit to helm Hooker's inaugural Specialty session. Hooker brought in Tom Whitehead, Boogie Woogie Red and saxophonist Otis Finch, and over two studio days they cut nine sides—some with the full band, some with just Whitehead—under Vincent's supervision, using Esquire Studios rather than Hooker's traditional home-from-home at United Sound. However, once the results were shipped back to L.A., Rupe was unimpressed, and only one Specialty single—the menacing monologue "I'm Mad," backed with "Everybody's Blue," a free-form, one-chord slow blues propelled by Whitehead's bump-and-grind drumming—was issued before the contract was allowed to lapse the following year. Indeed, in 1954 Hooker did more studio work for Modern, to whom he was no longer contracted and whom he heartily distrusted, than he did for Specialty, nominally his current label. Modern released four Hooker singles that year—though some of the tracks had been cut as far back as 1952—to Specialty's one, while "John Lee Booker" had two singles out on Deluxe, and Chess finally got around to releasing "It's My Own Fault," which Hooker had recorded two years earlier for Fortune.

---

11 Not to mention a few sides for Fortune, which subsequently ended up being purchased by Chess.

Meanwhile, the landscape was shifting under Hooker's feet, in more ways than one. In '54 and '55, what Dave Marsh has called "the age of rock and soul" was just beginning. The kind of electric downhome blues championed and epitomized by Hooker in Detroit and Muddy Waters in Chicago was challenged in its listeners' affections by two spectacular new offshoots. Ray Charles, the pianist who'd masterminded Guitar Slim's hit, was cutting for the New York–based Atlantic label, grafting elements of jazz and gospel onto the blues with a series of shattering singles commencing with "I Got A Woman' to lay the foundations of what would soon become soul music; he would soon be joined by a pugnacious Macon-based vocalist named James Brown, whose galvanic "Please Please Please," released by Syd Nathan's King Records out of Cincinnati, even outdid Charles for sheer intensity. Simultaneously, a bunch of greasy-haired white boys, led by Elvis Presley, who'd been hanging around Sam Phillips's Sun studios in Memphis, were sour-mashing up hillbilly music and the blues they'd picked up from the likes of Howlin' Wolf, Ike Turner, Junior Parker and B. B. King into an intoxicating new brew which would eventually become known as rock and roll. Before too long, along came Chuck Berry, a sharp-dressing, duck-walking, motor-mouthed singer/guitarist/songwriter from St. Louis who'd arrived in a very similar place by starting out from the opposite direction, fusing hillbilly rhythms and teen-oriented topics with the blues and jump he and his piano-pumping partner Johnnie Johnson had been playing for years in their hometown clubs. And an ex-boxer and aspiring songwriter named Berry Gordy Jr was about to see his ghetto record store go out of business because he persisted in stocking bebop records rather than the Muddy Waters and John Lee Hooker records his customers actually wanted.

The bluesmen were faced with some uncomfortable choices. They could attempt to adapt and risk alienating their core audience without gaining a new one, or else they could stand their ground and risk atrophying. Hooker chose an each-way bet: in 1955, he shifted his artistic base to Chicago. He signed yet another recording contract, not with the mighty Chess—who already had the cream of the city's downhome bluesmen under contract, as well as Chuck Berry and his foil Bo Diddley—but with Vee Jay Records, a small but ambitious 1953 start-up already challenging Chess's dominance by scoring hit after hit with Jimmy Reed, a sly, laconic, laid-back Mississippi transplant who was to enjoy more chart success in the '50s than either Muddy Waters or Hooker himself.

The decision wasn't taken a moment too soon. In 1955, in order to commence work on what was to become the Chrysler Freeway, the city's bulldozers moved in and began tearing down Hastings Street. The symbolism was inescapable: change was utterly inevitable, and he who was incapable of moving with the times would be lost.

> Everybody consider John Lee Hooker come from Detroit. He put his ties together here and started his family here. I guess he feels that Detroit is his home because he probably had his first gig here, you know. Even though he's not livin' in Detroit, people here still consider him a Detroit artist. A Detroit artist away from home. A Detroit artist out on a gig!
> —Famous Coachman, interview with the author, 1992

John Lee Hooker's Detroit is gone. The Lee Sensation Bar on Oak in the north end of Detroit, not to mention post-war Black Bottom landmarks like the Rainbow Bar and Henry's Swing Club, are ancient history. Only one block of what was once Hastings Street remains, and the Horseshoe Lounge on San Antoine is the last of the old-style black bars, though the Apex Bar still exists, on Oakland Avenue and Clay, as does the New Olympia Bar on Grand River and Grand Boulevarde. The site of Elmer Barbee's store at 609 Lafayette, on the intersection of San Antoine and Lafayette, where Hooker rehearsed for his first recordings, is now a parking lot outside a large, ornate church. The old Black Bottom has been thoroughly yupped out: it's now one of the few enclaves of downtown Detroit where white-flight suburbanites feel safe. Much of the rest of the inner city is now straight-up ghetto: Detroit is an 85 percent black (and hispanic) city. As the businesses on which Detroit's boom years were founded fail, the inner city has been "surrendered" to blacks: in 1992, Detroit had a black mayor (Coleman Young), a black police chief and a black administration thirty years after such changes could have done the city and its people some good. Downtown is one of America's Gotham Cities: a rusted-out hulk of a city where ostentatiously modern buildings and futurist set-pieces like the People Mover elevated train rub shoulders with grandiose, decaying '40s structures that would've made Tim Burton drool. In fact, there was absolutely no need for Warner Bros to construct new Gotham City sets for *Batman Returns*, which was opening the same Independence Day weekend on which Hooker was due to return to the city for a homecoming concert: they could just have taken over downtown

Detroit for a few weeks, taken full advantage of the crumbling splendor of its existing architecture and pumped some much-needed dough into the local economy. Detroit shares an eerie indicator of decay with Mississippi: everything from a hotel room to a packet of cigarettes is seriously cheap; a half or even a third of the prices charged in more prosperous burgs. Unemployment is several points higher than the national average.

Too many of John Lee Hooker's people are gone, too. In July 1992, just two days before he returned to his old stomping grounds for a weekend showcase, his old friend and former pianist Vernon "Boogie Woogie Red" Harrison died of kidney failure, at the age of sixty-six. Red had played with Hooker for eleven years, and had been expected to show up at the concert to meet and greet his old buddy, though the chronic arthritis which had plagued him for the last few years would almost undoubtedly have prevented him from participating in the grand all-star reunion jam planned for the climax of Hooker's set. But Eddie Burns is still around, and on sunny afternoons you can sometimes find him sitting comfortably on the front porch of his roomy, wood-paneled house on Chalmers, off East Jefferson, sipping a beer and contemplating the scenery. Famous Coachman is still here, too, tirelessly promoting the Detroit blues scene— "Hey! Hay! The Blues Is All Right" bumper stickers and all—from his cramped record store on Gratiot, stuffed with gospel and southern-soul records for the older folk (not to mention a small, disconsolate rack of downhome blues) plus a small selection of rap and swingbeat to cater for the local youth, and complete with a chaotic electrical-repair workshop in back. Tom Whitehead, now converted to Judaism and retired from his job driving a truck for the city, still pays his respects to his first love by playing jazz and blues in clubs and bars, in cabarets and at weddings.

Motown, which was founded on the hitherto-untapped talent lurking in the city's housing projects, had packed up and moved to California in 1971, soon after Hooker himself had made the same trek. All they left behind was a tourist-trap museum based in the original offices and studios; they couldn't even be bothered to maintain a regional branch-office, where the successors to the hungry and ambitious young Detroiters upon whose talents the empire was built could audition and train. And admirers of the great country bluesman Son House, at whose feet the likes of Robert Johnson and Muddy Waters had knelt to learn their trade, are still saving up to buy a memorial headstone to mark his grave in the city where he had moved to spend his last years, and where he died.

But nevertheless, John Lee Hooker is coming back to town to grace the Meadow Brook Music Festival—headlined on this particular July 5 by The Robert Cray Band—with his presence. And, for a few spectacular minutes, the glory days of Detroit will be revisited, as the lions of the '50s assemble to roar once more, to sit in with Hooker on the final encore of his set. Boogie Woogie Red has, tragically, been called away to a more pressing engagement, and Eddie Burns is stranded somewhere out on the road, unable to arrange his return to the city in time for the show. Still, Tom Whitehead, Eddie Kirkland, Mr. Bo and Little Sonny are all confirmed, to boogie together with the Hook for what could possibly be the last time. Ever.

The afternoon before the show, Hooker and his party arrive in Auburn Hills on the outskirts of Detroit to check into a suburban hostelry which, though claiming to be a Hilton, more closely resembles a dizzyingly pretentious motel with severe delusions of grandeur. It can't even boast all-day room service, which deficit causes no end of annoyance to the elderly gentleman in the trilby and shades who's registered, under an old Staff and Gotham pseudonym, as "Johnny Williams." Mr. Williams is *tired*. Mr. Williams is *hungry*. Mr. Williams has just flown all the way from San Francisco, and Mr. Williams wants some food. *Now*.

This particular Hilton's policy vis-à-vis guest nourishment outside of designated restaurant hours is to sell microwavable cold snacks from the gift shop. This is *not good enough*. A manager is summoned. He is instructed, not least vehemently by Vala Cupp and Lizz Fischer, whose rooms adjoin that of Mr. Williams and who, in addition to their musical duties, take special responsibility for Mr. Williams's comfort and welfare, that *something is going to have to be done*. Something *is* done. A chef is pressed into emergency service, and soon a reasonably appetizing buffet of cold cuts, dips, corn chips and *crudités* materializes in Mr. Williams's suite. Mr. Williams rumbles his grudging approval, and picks haphazardly at an item or two, leaving the bulk of the buffet untouched. Nevertheless, the point has been made. If John Lee Hooker wants food, he gets food, and nobody—most especially not some perspiring hotel flunkey—is going to tell him he can't have it. The days when John Lee Hooker wanted something and couldn't get it are over. That's all there is to it.

The Coast To Coast Blues Band also check in, but in their own inimitable manner. Lizz Fischer checks out the gym and most of her colleagues investigate the bar. Rich Kirch and Deacon Jones are sharing a nominally non-smoking room but—*hey, fuck that!*—cigarettes are fired up anyway. Jones is, as ever, on the hunt for a card game and, disdaining the house cuisine even once the restaurant has come online, phones out for pizza and ends up in a spirited cussing contest with the sister who eventually delivers it.

Meadow Brook is an open-air auditorium with a capacity of 7,500: the eventual audience ends up numbering a little over 5,000. Members of the Hooker and Cray bands, plus assorted crew members, are soon swarming over and behind the stage, which resounds to the assorted clangs, honks and tweets which inevitably constitute what's generally known in rockbiz parlance as a "sound check." Eddie Kirkland arrives in a black leather waistcoat *sans* shirt and an impressive selection of bandanas, medallions and chains. The Road Warrior wheels in an Acoustic combo amplifier wired up to a battered little practice amp and parts of some ancient hi-fi. He sets up a couple of effects pedals, and then carefully arrays three examples of his awesome collection of junkshop guitars— two Peaveys (including a jagged thing resprayed in an eyeball-torturing gold metal-flake) and a weird no-brand Strat copy—against his jury-rigged amp stack. Standing in the wings, Hooker's manager Mike Kappus watches all this activity in disbelief. Finally, he ambles across the stage and hoists a quizzical eyebrow at Kirkland, still fussing with his gear. "Excuse me," he says eventually, "but you know you're only playing on one song, Eddie." "Looks good, though, don't it," Kirkland replies. It's not a question.

His fellow veterans are also in evidence: Little Sonny, clutching his satchel of harps, turns out in a white safari suit and hat. The towering Mr. Bo, brandishing a cherry-red Gibson 345, is a symphony in pearl gray but, stealing the sartorial show beyond any shadow of a doubt, is Tom Whitehead, immaculate in matching white suit, hat and shoes, and carrying his sticks in a monogrammed leather case. "My daughter say, 'You goin' with John Lee Hooker? Go *sharp!*' " He laughs. " 'There's gonna be a *who-o-o-o-ole* lotta people there. Go 'head, dress up, look good, man.' " And he does. The band barely have time for a sound-check of their own. Kirkland can do little more than test his ramshackle pile of amps and pedals to make sure that everything's wired up and working, while Little Sonny takes a quick honk'n wail on his harp. Whitehead has to content himself with a desultory *whomp* around the tom-toms and a quick *pah-tish-tish-dup* on the hi-hats. Some of the Coast To Coasters enjoy a few discreet jokes at the expense of the senior citizens and their "old-time" sound.

Shortly before 8 P.M., the lanky, bedenimed, baseball-capped Famous

Coachman strides to center-stage, commandeers the microphone and brings on The Coast To Coast Blues Band. Vala Cupp, looking like a Sindy doll and sounding like Etta James, kicks off the proceedings with a scorching take on T-Bone Walker's "Cold Cold Feeling": Mike Osborn's impassioned B. B. King–style solo rates two separate rounds of applause. Deacon Jones—part-preacher, part-rapper—launches into his patented intro from behind the rented Hammond: "In the whole wide world, there's only one man/who can look into muddy water and spot dry land!" he hollers. On cue, John Lee Hooker enters from the wings, resplendent in a pearl-gray suit at least the equal in elegance of Mr. Bo's. Stumping to center-stage, he proclaims, "This is *my* town: Detroit, Michigan! I love you; I love the whole world." Then he goes to work. Planting himself in his chair, he settles his guitar on his lap and unleashes a torrential blizzard of razor-edged notes. "I'm back home again!" he crows. "Boom Boom" careers along like a runaway express train. "I'm gonna get real funky now with 'Crawlin' King Snake,' " he announces, and he is as good as his word.

Garnished with a bravura tenor sax solo by Kenny Baker, "Crawlin' King Snake" positively smolders: an erotic set-piece guaranteed to disturb the nocturnal thoughts of anybody who won't have anybody to sleep with that night. "*Well, well, well . . .*" croons Hooker, as Cupp darts around his chair, leaning so close to him that she's practically inside his guitar. "*Crawl up in your bed, your bed, your bed, wrap around your pretty body, feel good this mornin'* " Hooker incants, their duelling "*mm-humm*'s raising the temperature almost beyond endurance until Hooker cuts the proceedings short with a crisp thank-you. On "Baby Lee," Rich Kirch, who's spent most of the night playing rhythm while Hooker and Osborn take care of the soloing, steps out to play the spiky Strat parts blueprinted by Robert Cray on the *Mr. Lucky* version. Just out of sight of the audience, Little Sonny, Tom Whitehead, Mr. Bo and Eddie Kirkland watch carefully from the wings. The band kick into a slow blues featuring a killer solo by Lizz Fischer. "Play the blues!" commands Hooker. She does. "*Just a lonely man tryin' to find love, in New York City,*" he sings. "Do you dig it?!"

"Serve Me Right To Suffer" is next up, complete with a deep neon-blue solo by Deacon Jones. The Hammond organ is the essential sound of the after-hours ghetto bars of the '50s and '60s, and the oceanic build Jones pumps into his solo makes the Hammond roar like an entire brass section. His ovation is more than earned.

Suddenly it's 8:45. The best part of an hour has passed, though it seems like little more than five or ten minutes. Hooker switches to his open-A-tuned guitar, which means that it's time for the boogie. In MC mode, Deacon Jones launches into one of his signature jivey intros to bring on Tom Whitehead, Mr. Bo, Eddie Kirkland and Little Sonny, who defy expectations by remaining right where they are: in the wings. Hooker dumps his Epiphone, pulls the microphone from its stand, and begins to work the front row. No matter how many times you may have seen him do it, it remains an astonishing *coup de théâtre*, a symbolic magical resurrection, all frailty forgotten, all fatigue transcended, all limitations cast aside under the healing spell of the boogie. Suddenly, a thought occurs: Hooker must have been some kind of a sight to see, way back in the day, as a young man dancing the nights away in the Hastings Street clubs. He and Vala are striking real sparks off each other tonight, rocking and raving, microphone to microphone. Rich Kirch takes his turn for a solo: he's cookin' too, Mike Osborn and Jim Guyett doing soul-revue steps behind him as they play. Lizz Fischer and Kenny Baker turn up the heat still further as they solo over the remorseless, churning groove. "I thought I had enough," roars Hooker, "but I *ain't* had enough!" Deacon Jones rolls a sardonic quote from "When Johnny Comes Marching Home" into his climactic organ break. He's a JAMF of the first water, but he delivers every time.

"The Godfather of Detroit, Michigan, misses his home town!" Deacon declaims as Hooker carefully removes his shades to inspect the front rows before, smiling and waving with grandfatherly benevolence, he ambles off the stage. "Peace, love and blues power!" Jones howls into the utter pandemonium which now ensues. At 9:05 the old guard finally take the stage: first Kirkland, then Mr. Bo, then Little Sonny ("on Mississippi saxophone") and Tom Whitehead. Jim Guyett, Mike Osborn and Deacon Jones return to their stations as Starship Boogie takes off once more, this time with a loose-limbed swingbeat very different from Coast To Coast's smooth, power-driven crank: Little Sonny wailing on his harp, the towering Mr. Bo rippling away on his red 345, Eddie Kirkland grunging like a champ, low and dirty, and Tom Whitehead, his hat set well back on his head, putting a subtly vicious kick behind that time-honored beat. This is Hastings Street's last stand. Chrysler Freeway or no Chrysler Freeway, this night Hastings Street lives again.

After allowing a decent interval to elapse, the Cray band take the stage to close out the night. They're fine, as they always are, but what has preceded them was something more than simply fine. It was unique, irreplaceable, unrepeatable.

Back at the hotel, after the leaders repair to their respective suites for what is no doubt a tranquil and well earned rest, various members of the Cray and Hooker bands assemble in the bar for the traditional post-gig pursuits of drinking beer and talking shit. One notable absentee is the teetotal, vegetarian Lizz Fischer: while her male colleagues chill out in the bar, inflating their waistlines by lifting bottles, she winds down in the hotel gym, inflating her already-impressive biceps by lifting weights. One acquaintance of the musicians comes *this* close to getting himself punched off a barstool by Memphis Horns trumpeter Wayne Jackson, the Stax graduate whose blasting, brassy tone contributes so much soulful authenticity to the Cray Band, for the nigh-capital crime of comparing Hooker's *Mr. Lucky* album to Ice-T's *O. G. Original Gangster*, claiming them both as primo contemporary examples of the African-American genius for story-telling. Like most of the musicians in the Cray and Hooker ensembles, Jackson has zero tolerance for rap, and any notions of a "cultural continuum" are deemed to be little more than trendy, pretentious Brit-crit crap. Fortunately, all is resolved in beery camaraderie by the time the bar finally closes.

Eddie Kirkland isn't around to contribute his thoughts to this informal symposium, however. He's back at the wheel of the Dodge, cigar clamped between his teeth and heading Lord knows where, en route to his next job. And who can honestly say whether, at this particular time, on this particular night, there might just be a few ghostses on the highway after all.

8. Time Is Marchin' On

Sometimes you feel like a club fighter who gets off a bus in
the middle of nowhere, no cheers, no admiration, punches
his way through ten rounds or whatever, always making
someone else look good, vomits up the pain in the back
room, picks up his check and gets back on the bus
heading out for another nowhere. Sometimes like a
troubadour out of the dark ages, singing for your supper
and rambling the land . . .
—Bob Dylan, quoted by Cameron Crowe,
liner notes to *Biography*, 1985

Backbiters mean backstabbers, people double-crossin' you.
"Syndicators" mean they always signifyin'.
—John Lee Hooker, explaining "Backbiters And
Syndicators" to the author, 1992

In 1990s usage, the expression "Vee Jay" generally designates a person
gainfully employed to spout banalities on cable or satellite TV to link
bursts of rock or rap videos. In the world of mid-'50s R&B, by contrast,
"Vee Jay" meant the sparky independent record label which was the only
significant rival to Chess Records' historical domination of Chicago's
black music scene.

Vee Jay Records derived its name from the initials of its founders,
Vivian Carter and James Bracken. Like Bernard Besman, Berry Gordy
and not a few other hopeful music-biz entrepreneurs, Bracken and Carter
started out as proprietors of a record store. However, after five years at
the retail end of the business, they decided to graduate to the more challenging, but potentially more lucrative, realm of primary production.
Their store was located in the ghetto of the blue-collar steel-town of Gary,
Indiana, not too far away from where Delta-born drummer Albert Nelson—soon to change his name and instrument and transform himself into
guitarist Albert King—was playing clubs and bars behind another transplanted Mississippi bluesman, Jimmy Reed; and from where Joe and
Katherine Jackson were beginning to raise the family which Joe, an ex-

boxer and part-time blues guitarist, would eventually mold into a reasonably successful vocal group.

Before too long, Bracken and Carter shifted their base of operations and set up shop in the big city. Their initial productions—singles by Jimmy Reed (signed after Chess, glutted with downhome singers, turned him down), and doo-wop vocal group The Spaniels—were leased to Chance Records. In business since December 1950, Chance was a more established South Side indie with, among other things, a few John Lee Booker releases under its corporate belt, but by mid-'53, Vee Jay was up and running as a label in its own right. Bracken and Carter celebrated by getting married, and—after Chance's collapse in 1954—by inheriting two of Chance's key employees: general manager Ewart Abner and producer Al Smith, the latter a Chicago blues lifer whose career went all the way back to the era of Lester Melrose and Bluebird Records. In tandem with Vivian's brother Calvin Carter, Smith ended up supervising most of Vee Jay's recording sessions.

Vee Jay got off to a pretty healthy start, but they led with pop friendly vocal groups rather than downhome blues. The Spaniels' third release, "Goodnight Sweetheart," and The El-Dorados' "At My Front Door" didn't quite match the achievements of Chess doo-woppers like The Moonglows and The Flamingoes, but they earned the label considerably more chart action than did blues sessions by Reed or Floyd Jones. Nevertheless, no Chicago-based label could afford to ignore the downhome scene completely. Though Vee Jay's first two Jimmy Reed singles had bombed out and the Brackens had just about made up their minds to drop him, his last-chance third release, "You Don't Have To Go," an appositely entitled lazy shuffle left over from his inaugural Vee Jay session, suddenly grew major legs and entered the R&B charts in February 1955. It was the first of a string of fourteen R&B hits and eleven pop-chart entries which made the unassuming Reed the biggest record-seller of all Chicago's downhome bluesmen, easily outgrossing even the mighty Muddy Waters, the magisterial "Godfather Of Chicago Blues" himself.

Some eight years Hooker's junior, Jimmy Reed was an amiable drunk from Dunleith, Mississippi. His sly, relaxed, easy-going music was utterly atypical of the standard Delta-to-Chicago style: there was nothing heavy or dramatic about Jimmy Reed. His records were all peas from the same instantly recognizable pod and they all shared the same characteristics: dryly witty lyrics with an irresistible hook in every song; a lightly loping shuffle or boogie beat; Reed's slurred, nasally drawled vocals (in which he seemed to be laughing quietly to himself at some unstated joke) and his squeaky, tootling mouth-harp, played in a wire rack he wore around his neck and blown in the first position (that is in the same key as the song) rather than in the "crossed-harp" approach (using a harp tuned to the fourth of the song's scale) featured by archetypal post-Delta Chicago stylists like Little Walter. Despite his immense recording success, he influenced few Chicago-based musicians; instead an entire crop of post-Reed bluesmen, including Slim Harpo, Lightnin' Slim and Lazy Lester, sprang up in the bayous of rural Louisiana, where his laid-back, wide-open-spaces approach seemed rather more appropriate to the scenery than the clamorous, gritty sound of the urban tenements and taverns exemplified by the post-Muddy Waters house style of Chess.

In addition to the ingratiating voice and distinctive harp which trademark-stamped each and every one of his records, Reed had two major secret weapons up his sleeve. One was his loyal and long-suffering wife, Mary Lee "Mama" Reed, who not only co-wrote many of his lyrics but served as his prompter in the studio, whispering the words he couldn't read (or was too drunk to remember) into his ear instants before it was time for him to sing them. The other was guitarist Eddie Taylor, an old Delta buddy of Reed's who played the finger-picked signature shuffle-boogie rhythms and bass lines which framed the songs with such seemingly effortless perfection. Taylor—born in Benoit, Mississippi, in 1925—had tutored Reed back down home before they met up again in Chicago and joined forces: in fact, he was the senior partner when they started out together. Like those other two steady Eddies, Burns and Kirkland, Taylor subordinated himself to a charismatic auteur, hiding his light under Reed's bushel, providing the structure and support which enabled the insouciant frontman to shine. And like Burns and Kirkland, he paid a heavy price for his generosity and lack of musical ego: despite a couple of decent-selling singles as an artist in his own right, he remained a footnote to Reed right up until his death on Christmas Day 1985. The Jimmy Reed package all added up to one of the major post-war blues repertoires, contributing songs like "Big Boss Man," "Bright Lights Big City," "Honest I Do," "You Got Me Dizzy" and "Shame Shame Shame" to the blues canon.

Vee Jay's decision to sign up John Lee Hooker was thus a by-product of their success with Jimmy Reed. As the flood of releases with which he'd saturated the market in the years since "Boogie Chillen" had proved, Hooker was by no means a guaranteed hitmaker, and virtually every label in the R&B business had a stash of unreleased Hooker masters in their vaults.[1] In addition, he had a not altogether undeserved reputation for contract-breaking and general unreliability. Nevertheless, he'd also demonstrated that he was capable of whipping out a million-seller every so often, and that was incentive enough for the Brackens and their crew. "Ewart Abner and Calvin Carter, they drove to Detroit and picked me up when I first got on their label," recalled Hooker in an interview with *Living Blues*. "When my [Specialty] contract expired, Abner called me. He said, 'Well, look, we're coming to get you. We ain't gonna depend on you comin' on your own 'cause you may not get here. We're gonna drive there and pick you up.' "

On October 19, 1955, Hooker arrived in Chicago for his first Vee Jay studio date, with the faithful Tom Whitehead at the wheel. Calvin Carter had decided that the company would play safe by fielding their A-team—Jimmy Reed's alter ego Eddie Taylor on second guitar and Reed himself sitting in on harp, with bassist George Washington filling out the sonic picture—for their new client's first session, but since Hooker was recording on unfamiliar turf with unfamiliar sidemen, he wanted at least one musician on board who was already conversant with the intricacies of his personal style. "I was with him when he started with the Vee Jay recording company," remembers Whitehead. "I was with him at United Sound and other places, but I remember distinctly about Vee Jay because we didn't get paid until we got a check, and I was wonderin' about it. But fortunately when I came back to Detroit and took it to one of the record distributors, they cashed it just like that, no problem. Uh-huh. That's where I met all those other guys. Through John Lee Hooker I met Howlin' Wolf, Jimmy Reed—Jimmy Reed was on a few of John Lee Hooker's recordings too, and I met him. I also met B. B. King through John Lee Hooker. I met a lot of the blues fellas after I started playing with him. At that time I got pretty popular around; the guys liked the way I played. Sometime with Vee Jay, other people too. Mostly with Hooker and Jimmy Reed."

Abner described Hooker as "one of the best country blues singers" in a *Cashbox* magazine trade announcement of his signing to the label but, perhaps mindful of the all-too-recent glut of potentially competitive Hooker releases already in the marketplace, Vee Jay cut a mere four sides

---

1 Modern and Chart continued to issue Hooker singles, competing with his new Vee Jay product, well into 1956.

at that particular date. One single was released early in the New Year—
"Mambo Chillen," which reworked Hooker's signature song against a
then-fashionable Latin groove, backed with a deeply cool slow blues,
"Time Is Marching"—but Vee Jay sat on the other two titles and didn't
commission another session until the following March, when the same
musicians, minus Reed, reassembled to cut a further half-dozen tracks.
That first single sold acceptably without achieving palpable hit status, but
it laid the foundations for what was to become the dominant sound of
Hooker's next few years' worth of studio recordings: meatier and more
muscular than Vee Jay's Jimmy Reed recordings, but airier, lighter and
looser than the densely textured, sometimes-lumbering Muddy Waters
and Howlin' Wolf Chess tracks, and cleaner and clearer than the latter-
day Modern combo sides Hooker had been cutting at United Sound in
Detroit. Businesswise, Hooker was a wholly reformed character. According to Les Fancourt's discographical bible, Hooker adhered faithfully to
the terms of his Vee Jay contract, respecting to the letter the "exclusivity"
clause of his deal, and cutting no outside sessions whatsoever for the next
three years. Vee Jay, for their part, made sure that Hooker wasn't over-
recorded: in fact, they only cut ten titles on him in 1956, releasing a mere
two singles that year, but the second of these—"Dimples," coupled with
"Baby Lee"—featured two permanent additions to the upper echelons of
Hooker's repertoire. However, as with many of Hooker's tales, there is
more than one version of the origin story of "Dimples."

*You get these things mostly from women [he told writer Greg
Drust].[2] You see them, the beautiful ladies like that. The way she
walk and the way she talk and she wiggle. And the girl, Mary, you
know, she had beautiful dimples. She was married to a friend of
mine and I told her, "You got beautiful dimples." She said, "Oh,
write a song about me," and that's the way I wrote that. Her husband said, "I can't get along with my wife now—she thinks she's a
big star."*

"I was goin' with this girl called Mattie Lou," Hooker reminisced more
recently, "and she had beautiful dimples. I said, 'I'm gonna write a song
about your beautiful dimples.' She had a nice body, she walk nice, and

---

2   In the booklet to the compilation album *John Lee Hooker: The Ultimate Collection 1948–
1990* (Rhino, 1991).

so I wrote the song *"You got dimples in you jaw."* That come to be a hit." "Dimples" come to be more than just a hit, albeit one which skimmed the lower reaches of the R&B charts and even nudged its way into the pop listings on its original release in August 1956; it was the first authentic masterpiece of Hooker's Vee Jay sojourn. Lyrically, it wasn't that profound—he love the way she walk, he love the way she talk, she got dimples in her jaw, he got his eyes on her, and that's about it—but it's about as close to pop perfection in two minutes and nine seconds as any '50s bluesman ever got, Jimmy Reed not excluded. Launched off a stolidly menacing guitar riff, Hooker's guitar line, like the dub-plate reggae celebrated by The Clash in "White Man In Hammersmith Palais," has bombs in the bass and knives in the treble. Tom Whitehead plays lightly swinging drums dominated by a remorselessly swishing hi-hat, George Washington locks in with a firm but subdued bass-line, and the self-effacing Eddie Taylor provides a rhythm guitar part which glues everything together while staying out of the leader's way. Hooker's guitar remains in the home key of E throughout while the band rock their way around the old twelve-bar corral, but somehow everything hangs together and it all works beautifully. Just *how* sublimely well it worked can be judged by the fact that the first two latter-day attempts to recut the song— once with Eddie Kirkland in 1992 during the *Boom Boom* sessions, and again the following year, this time with an ensemble including Van Morrison and Elvin Bishop on guitar, for the album which eventually became *Chill Out*—have remained in the can, though Hooker finally nailed a happening remake when he teamed up with Los Lobos.

"When he plays with another band," comments Bernie Besman, "then he plays the blues, like twelve-bar, because they don't know any different, and he follows them. That's where Vee Jay made the big mistake, and Chess and all the rest of them, because they sound like Lightnin' Hopkins or anybody else playing the blues. If he'd done ["Dimples" and "Boom Boom"] alone, they would probably have been bigger hits. I recorded him rarely with a group, and that's where it's twelve bars. Because he follows them, and they can't play thirteen, fourteen bars. And so *he* plays with *them*." Unconsciously echoing Besman, Calvin Carter has subsequently recounted his experiences running Hooker's recording sessions thusly: "He was a guy who never rhymed, you know he just didn't have the usual rhyme lines . . . we only ever did one take on everything he did; he'd never do it the same way. Of course you know he didn't read music, but nobody could play with him either." Carter is severely maligning both

Hooker and the hand-picked combination of Chi-town studio musicians and Detroit homeboys who worked on Hooker's Vee Jay sessions: despite the occasional musical hiccup, they not only *could* play with Hooker, but they *did*.

"Most of that band was my band," Hooker explains. "Otis Finch and Evans Johnson, the horn players; Joe Hunter, the piano player; the drummer . . . all them were my original band. Some others fit in, like [Martha and] The Vandellas[3] and some other stuff I had in there with my band, but all that down through there was the guys workin' with me. We was just workin' around town and on the road, and they worked with me regular. That's the reason it sounded so tight. I always lived in Detroit, but Vee Jay was in Chicago, the company was on Michigan Avenue. I would go there with me and my band, so I didn't have to do no lot of rehearsin', because they did know just what I was gonna do. They would rehearse it with the guys they gonna bring in, let them know how I play and show them how it went, and then we'd go into the studio. We didn't stay in there that long; we'd 'bout do a whole session in a day. Two days and we through. I never stay in no studio three and four weeks, *oh* no. I go in there for a half a day and I got an album. I don't know nobody else can do that."

Inevitably, the shifting of Hooker's recording base to Chicago meant that he became an honorary associate member of the South Side blues scene. "I played Chicago a lot, played a lot of blues clubs. The money was a little better than it was in the South, but things was a little more expensive, so it equal out. I had never met Muddy and the Wolf before. You know how it was. You was in Chicago and they was real popular and you had to see 'em. They was playin' all over Chicago in all the bars, and I would go to the bars where they was playin' and meet 'em. I stayed at Muddy's house when I go there. Wolf, I met him and Little Walter, and Jimmy Rogers from the same place I'm from in Mississippi." So was Walter as wild and mean as his reputation might suggest? "Wild? Oh yeah. He carry a gun everywhere. Mean? He didn't take no stuff off of nobody." Then there was another Vance expat, though Andrew Luandrew—pounding his electric piano under his South Side soubriquet of Sunnyland Slim—was an older man who'd left Vance before the Hooker family even moved there. It was on a Sunnyland Slim session that Muddy

---

3 Actually, it wasn't The Vandellas but Motown's in-house backing singers The Andantes, plus Mary Wilson from The Supremes. Still, we'll get to that a little later. Be patient!

Waters received his first recording break. "I didn't know him down there, that's for sure, but I knowed him from Chicago. Old Sunnyland Slim; I admired him so. He was the talk of the town."

Hooker's Chicago sojourn also meant a reunion with a long-lost relative, thirteen years his junior, whom he hadn't seen since Clarksdale days: the slide-guitar virtuoso Earl Hooker. "Earl Hooker, he was in Chicago. He was my dad's brother's son, my first cousin. There was a big gap between me and him: I met him later in Chicago. I knew of him, like I knew of Archie, my nephew. A music-inclined family, but none of 'em keep a career goin' way deep but me or Earl. He never got *real* famous, but he got famous. He was a really good musician, too." Earl Hooker was one of the great lost princes of Chicago blues, an innovator, a musicians' musician par excellence. Unlike the older, more traditional Delta-trained slidemen, he played in standard, rather than open, tuning, and his crisp, melodic, endlessly inventive playing exhausted the superlatives of all who heard him. If his singing had been anywhere near the equal of his guitar work, he would have been a star: he was using a slide and wah-wah pedal in combination even before Jeff Beck. Muddy Waters' "You Need Love"—the blueprint for Led Zeppelin's "Whole Lotta Love"—was simply a Waters vocal overdubbed onto an Earl Hooker instrumental, "Blue Guitar," after Chess acquired the tape and decided to use it as a backing track. "Earl Hooker is the only man I ever saw break a string, hold a note on his guitar while he change the string, keep on playin,' never miss a note," recalled Junior Wells to Andrew M. Robble in *Guitar Player* magazine. "I'll put it this way: Earl Hooker could do more with a guitar than a monkey could do with a coconut." In conversation with Jas Obrecht in the same magazine, Buddy Guy remembered Earl slightly differently, but equally fondly.

"As a blues guitarist," Buddy told Obrecht, "I've never seen anybody could play the way he played it, and especially the slide guitar . . . Earl wouldn't hardly never sing that much, but everything would come out with the slide. He would play the melody and it would sound like someone singing." "He used," says John Lee, "to be kinda wild." That's something of an understatement. According to Buddy, Earl "stole the long cord that I learned from Guitar Slim out of New Orleans. Earl Hooker would steal his tubes [valves] right out of my amplifier. If we'd leave our amplifiers in the clubs 'cause we be back here tomorrow night to jam again, he would go down there again in the mid-day and you'd think he's over there messin' with his guitar, but he would change the speakers out of your amp if you sounded good to him. Then somebody that'd seen him there would say, 'Well Hooker been over there.' And I would just go by his mother's house and say, 'Open the door, man. Give me my speakers and my cord back.' And he would give 'em back. He stammered a lot, kind of like John Lee: 'You-you-you-you sounded so good, I wanted to see what you had that I didn't have' . . . from the first time I met him, I never did see him drink or do nothin'. He had no bad habits other than stealing your stuff." "I don't know," sighs John Lee when Earl's name comes up in conversation. "He was such a gifted musician, but he just wouldn't take it in the right direction. He thought things would improve. I would talk to him, but . . ."

However, one crucial early acquaintance remained elusive. "Tony Hollins went to Chicago; that's where he passed, I guess. He had a barber shop there, but I never did see it. I wanted to go, but I never did get around to it. I never know where he was, but he was there. I know he would'a loved to see me."

The move to Chicago might have worked wonders for Hooker's career and his social life, but as far as any noticeable improvement to his bank balance was concerned, it was just more of the same old same-old. In *Chicago Breakdown*, Mike Rowe quotes a revealing anecdote gleaned from harpist Billy Boy Arnold, who was signed to Vee Jay as a solo artist while recording for Chess as a member of Bo Diddley's original group. "Billy Boy," wrote Rowe, "once heard Jimmy Bracken say, with pride, that he wouldn't pay any artist more than two cents in royalties, but Eddie Taylor did rather better with his forty-three dollars for "Big Town Playboy'!"[4] Hooker may well have expected better treatment from the black-owned Vee Jay than he had received from Besman or the Biharis but, as the saying goes, every brother ain't a brother. "At Vee Jay there was Jimmy Bracken. He was the big boss, and Vivian, his wife. And Al Smith. He was the president of Vee Jay. You go down there to borrow money, you sit there all day just to get . . . they didn't want to give us advances

---

4 Since "Big Town Playboy" sold a more than respectable 37,000 copies, Taylor hadn't done too badly by the admittedly shoddy standards of the time. It's worth remembering that, during the late '50s and early '60s, royalties were less than generous for white artists also. Under the terms of their original British contract with EMI, a highly respectable multinational corporation, The Beatles received one farthing—a quarter of an old penny—for each single sold. Without wishing to delve into the intricacies of Britain's pre-metric currency and the pound-to-dollar exchange rate, it should be sufficient to state that, for every thousand singles sold, each Beatle would have had just about enough money left, before taxes and deductions, to buy one packet of cigarettes.

or nothin'. They did me really in, me and Jimmy Reed," snorts Hooker. "And we made 'em tons of money."

Vee Jay didn't exactly overwork the studio personnel on Hooker's behalf, either. In 1956, they'd cut a mere ten sides on Hooker, in 1957 there were only eight titles recorded, spread over two studio days in March and June. After the first of those sessions, weary of the incessant touring necessitated by Hooker's ever-precarious finances, Tom White-head cashed in his chips. "Well, he started going on the road and I had a day job. I used to take leaves, but he left town for quite some time. Sidemen, well, having kids and things like that you have a lot of respon-sibilities, and drummers are ten cents a dozen."

And so were chauffeurs. Whitehead's "day job" was as a driver, and he'd doubled up as Hooker's chauffeur. When he quit the band, the ami-able Eddie Burns took over behind the wheel. "With the Vee Jay thing, I still was playing with him here and there, but I didn't record anything with him for Vee Jay," Burns remembers. "I was on some of the sessions far as bein' there 'cause, you see, Johnny's not a very good driver. He don't drive very good, and I always was a very good driver. So when he got ready to go [to Chicago] to get money or have a session I used to go with him like that."

There had been no other way out for Whitehead: his family respon-sibilities kept him in Detroit. By the same token, there was no way out for Hooker, either: *his* responsibilities kept him out on the road. And as time marched on, the contradictions implicit in Hooker's situation—being able to keep his family fed and warm only by leaving them behind to work away from home—grew ever more intense. And each time he hit that road, whether it took him to Chicago or way down South, the home fires flickered ever more ominously.

Now Maudie, why did you hurt me?
Oh Maudie, hey,
Why did you hurt me?
You been gone so long,
I miss you so
—John Lee Hooker, "Maudie," 1959

To tear down Hastings Street required a fleet of Detroit city bulldozers, but to subject John Lee and Maude Hooker's marriage to what eventually proved to be unendurable pressure required little more than the stresses and strains of life at the rough end of R&B. The effect of these occupational hazards on their relationship was the initiation of a slow-motion collapse which took until the end of the 1960s to resolve itself. The genial Paul Mathis had served as a buffer between his sister and his brother-in-law, but in January 1955 he quit Detroit for New Mexico to commence what turned out to be a twenty-two-year hitch in the United States air force. However, the danger signs were there early on, even before Paul left town.

"He had a terrible time with her. All through the years, him and Maude had difficulties." From way back in the early '50s, according to Eddie Kirkland, "they was scufflin'. She would show up on jobs and make a scene. One time we did a job in Toledo. I booked it. She found somebody to bring her from Detroit to this club. She walks in, we was up there playin', tooks his *git*-tar and busts it over his head. Yeah! That happened several times. He gave me one of the guitars, was busted in the back where she had took it and hit him 'side the head with it. That was the kind of things was goin' on." Hooker remembers the incident clearly, as well he might. "Oh, she was *terrible*," he groans. "She hit me with the guitar and broke it." His main emotion is sheer relief that he happened, on that particular night, to be playing an acoustic guitar with a pickup attached, rather than his solid-body Gibson Les Paul. If he'd taken a blow from the notoriously dense and heavy Gibson model, Hooker notes ruefully, "I'd'a been crippled the rest of my life."

"My mom wasn't too thrilled about him being a musician," says his daughter Zakiya (or "Vera," as she was still known at that time). "She would have preferred him to go out and get a nine-to-five job, but this was not what he wanted to do, so he wasn't gonna go for that. And there was a lot of pressure there, you know, and there was the pressure of raising the kids. Now that I'm a parent I understand what he was going through, and what it was like having to make sure that we had enough to eat, making sure that we were taken care of even when he wasn't there. Before he had his first big record, he worked at CopCo Steel . . . I don't remember that, but he worked manual labor. I would never ask anybody to go back to that."

"I would go by his house with Maudie his wife, and all the children," says Famous Coachman. "A lot of times his wife would get mad 'cause of me and him stayin' out at night together. He goin',' 'Co-co-co-coachman kep' me out with him all night. I were ready to go but he weren't ready to leave.' They didn't have it that easy when they was raisin' those children. They had a small amount of money and a small amount of everything in the house. We all was makin' it makeshift. He weren't makin' a lot of money, but John would keep him a good car."

"One thing that John did do," Kirkland affirms, "he *loved'ed* his family. He scuffled for his family, and he was concerned about his kids. He was so good to his children: the same now. That was Godlike to see for a man."

"John was really a family man," says Paul Mathis. "The only time he was away from home was when he was takin' care of business, when he was touring. Other'n that, you find him at home." And every time Hooker left Detroit, he felt that he was missing out on another of those precious moments of watching his young family growing up. "They were there, they was at home," he muses. "I just know I had a family and that's about *it*. Come home to 'em, stay a while and get right back out. Wasn't because I wanted to, but because I had to do that. I was young, I could handle it then, you know. I wanted to be home with them; I wished I could've, but I couldn't. Hey, I got to put food on this table, I got to go. So they grew up knowin' when I come through, knowin' that I did the right thing. I'm glad they know that, knowin' that I did that for them, for the kids. They didn't ask to come here. I got 'em here"—he chuckles—"so I got to take care of 'em. So that's what I did."

And just as he valued each moment with his children, they valued each moment with him. One thing Hooker need never fear is that his children might have failed to appreciate him, and what he went through for them. Zakiya realized quite early on that her father was a musician. "I was fairly young. I just considered it to be his job. I didn't look at it as different to other people's jobs, it was just what he did. I thought it was great. He was home with us more than the ones who worked nine to five. I remember he was always a great baseball fan, so we were forced to watch baseball. I *hated* baseball. I mean, to this day I hate baseball. We'd sit there and watch baseball while he smoked a cigarette and drank his coffee. So I never considered it as being different from any other line of work. I loved Detroit, I really loved it. It was nothing like it is now. It's very depressed and . . . dirty and dingy and gray, but when we were coming up . . . I guess maybe we saw it with children's eyes. This was home, and this was where we'd get up and go to the local swimming club or go to parties or visit our friends. This was where our social life was, and it was really, really nice. It wasn't like these children have to grow up today. It wasn't like that. We had a very secure upbringing; my father saw to that. If there was anything that was going on in the undercurrents, we were pretty much shielded from that. We saw some [aspects] of it, but not a whole lot."

So when did her younger brother Robert learn of their father's unusual lifestyle? "Oh man, at a very very young age. He used to go on the road, man, when I was young, and I used to cry. I used to listen to his records, man, and it just did somethin' to me, you know? He's very down-to-earth with you. Some people might get famous and get the big head, look over you and stuff, but he's a down-to-earth person, and he believe in helpin' people. He was a beautiful dad, a compassionate dad. Mama might *pow! pow!*"—he mimes a brace of powerful slaps and laughs heartily—"he might get you, but it wasn't like mama. He was more compassionate. That's how it was. A beautiful man." Nevertheless, coping with John Lee's occasionally lengthy absences wasn't easy for the little boy. "I just had to endure it, had to live with it. He was doin' his thing. That was his way of supportin' his family. It wasn't no job like he was going to Ford or Chrysler or somewhere like that, you know: he was playin' the blues. He was a singer. Sometimes he had to go out of town and play. Well, we just had to live with it."

Nevertheless, when Hooker was there for his kids, he was *there*. "He was fun," laughs Zakiya. "I mean he was *fun*! I can remember him telling us stories, old Southern stories from the Old South. One story stands out to this day . . . about this man—called John—who wanted to go to heaven but he didn't want to die, and when he got there, he wanted his whole body intact. So he was out under a tree, and he was praying one day; he would go out there every day, and he would pray. So this particular day there was a man up in the tree asleep, and he heard John down there praying, and he decided to play a joke on John. He says"—Zakiya deepens her voice into a low, portentous tone—" 'Johnnnn?' John says, 'Is that you, God? Is that you?' 'Yes, John, this is me.' John says, 'I wanna go to heaven whole, soul *and* body. I been good, I tried to be good, whatever.' And so the man tells him, 'Well, John, you come back here tomorrow and you'll go to heaven whole, soul *and* body.' John jumped up and he ran home and he told his wife, and he packed up his clothes, and he was ready to go.

"The next day he went down to the tree, and the man was there and he had a noose, and he hung it out the tree, and he told John, 'Well, John, if you want to go to heaven whole, soul and body, put this noose around your neck, and I'll pull you up.' John says, 'Lord, a noose? That's gon' *hurt*.' The man says, 'John, don't you have faith?' John says, 'Well, yeah, but that's a noose and it's gon' hurt.' 'John, you got to have faith or you can't go.' John said, 'All right,' and he put the noose around his neck, so the man started pullin' the noose and it started to choke John. So John said, 'Waittaminnit, waittaminnit, Lord, you said it wouldn't hurt!' 'John, it'll only hurt for a little while!' 'Lord, I don't think I wanna do this!' 'John, you can't change your mind . . .' and he began to pull on the rope. Now John managed to get the rope off his neck, and he grabbed his suitcase and ran back to the house. He knocked on the door, and his wife let him in, and he said, 'If you see the Lord, tell him I'm not here!' So John ran and hid, and so the man came to the door and knocked on the door, and the lady said, 'Who is it?' He said, 'Is John there?' By then, John had heard the man comin' and he had ran out the back door. All he had on was his clothes, no shoes, no nothin'. He had took off runnin' and so the wife said, 'Well, Lord, John has gone and I don't think you gon' catch him, because he's runnin' without any shoes on, and I *know* you're not gonna catch him.' "

Zakiya sits back in her chair and laughs uproariously. "How's that? At that time it was a funny old story. I remember that. I remember a lot of the other guys would come over, like Eddie Kirkland. He would always tell stories. I can't remember his, but he would always tell ghost stories. It would always be *dark*, and everybody be scared to *death*. They was all bein' really nice people. Dad was always just a really fun person. He is to this day."

"Fun" is also what Maude Hooker chooses to remember from those years. "It was really nice," she says, glowing nostalgically. "We had a lot of fun. We enjoyed each other, raising the kids, and they raising us, yeah. We used to go out and make snowmen, you know, put his little hat on and his little eyes, and the kids just love it, throwin' snowballs at each other. Mm-hm. Yeah! You know what we used to do? Before we'd go in the house, we'd get on the porch and shake it all off off us. Oh, it was so beautiful."

Some of the "fun" was a little less innocuous. "I knew the whole family, used to go over his house quite a bit," says Tom Whitehead. "We would hang out, doin' various things . . . well, I don't like to talk too personal like that, you know. He never had any trouble much outta me. I'd get into it with him sometime, but . . . we used to booze, you know, but I don't approve of it no more. When you get older you have to stop."

"Back in those days," remembers Eddie Burns, "he drinked. And we all used to drink together, and stuff like that, and he was real lively like that. He liked a lot of fun, so you know we used to go to wild parties, and stuff like that."

"I used to love to drink," the now-abstemious Hooker admits cheerfully. "I had this pint of liquor in my car on the way to work one night; I would never go out without a bottle of liquor in my car. Some Courvoisier. I was going to work one night and I was drinkin'. I was high as a Georgia pine. And I got out the car, and I was throwin' up with my finger down my throat, you know how you do it? 'Cause everyone know that the police is around that area. They called me Little John Lee. Little John Lee The Iron Man. They drove by, they said, 'Mr. Hooker, you sick?' I said, 'Yeah, sick to my stummick.' 'Well, can I take you to the doctor, to the hospital? You gonna be all right?' I said, 'I'm gonna be all right, I just eat something didn't agreed with my stomach.' But I was throwin' liquor up. He says, 'You wanna go to the hospital, John Lee, I'll take you.' So I see the doctor at emergence," I say, 'Oh, I'm fine.' I was drunk and he didn't know that. I was throwin' liquor up, and he's sayin,' 'Now you be careful, you hear?' I say, 'Oh yes, officer, I'm gonna be all right . . .' And I went legal out of sight. Soon as he left, I got in the car. Went on to work."

And then there were the notorious "house parties." "You know, these big cities, they got these big bullpens, they call 'em. Not where they keep the heavy crime people, but people they pick up for house parties and drinkin' and stuff like that. Breakin' the law, after-hours places, doin' what they shouldn't be doin'. They busted this place . . . I was walkin' the floor, playin' my guitar. They come up"—Hooker raps his knuckles on the coffee table in his lounge three times: *bap bap bap*—" 'Mr. Hooker? Let me talk to you.' They had the outside staked out, with policemen at the back door and front door. I said, 'Whoah man, stop. You see me playin' this guitar and stop and talk to you?' And there was women goin'—he slips into a coquettish falsetto—" 'Heeeyyyy John! John Lee! John Lee! Play it, baby!' "—*bap bap bap*—" 'Mr. Hooker, you got to let me talk to you.' 'Hey man, I told you, go 'head and leave me alone. I ain't got time to talk to you!' It was the po-lice, and I didn't know it. Plain-clothes. He said, 'I'm the *po*-lice. Put that guitar down.' Everybody say, 'Hooooooaaaaaaald *on*!' Some people started tryin' to get out the back door, and they round 'em up; catch 'em comin' out the back door, run straight into they arms. I put my guitar down, scout around the back door, run right into one of them law. Like that. They go on back in, and they calls a Black Maria. You know that thing they took you down in? Police van. They had about three vanloads with guys, and a vanload of women. Carries us on in—'here you are, man'—throws us in the bullpen, and I had my guitar and amplifier with me. I couldn't leave 'em there, so the police said, 'Bring 'em wit'cha.' He locked us up, my guitar and amplifier with me, somebody was sittin' on the floor, they had they dice in they pocket, shootin' dice in the bullpen, goin' on . . . and I'm sittin' there with my guitar, playin' away.

"The next mornin', we get out. That was Sunday night, and by the time we get out, it's time for people to go to work. If they take 'em in on a Saturday night, they let 'em out on Sunday evenin'. Take 'em in on Friday night, they keep 'em in Friday night, Saturday night, let 'em out on Sunday. Dependin' on when they catch you. They had jobs, they know to turn 'em loose. And they do the same thing next weekend: they catch you, they bust you again, put you back in the bullpen. I was in there playin' . . . they knew who I was in Detroit."

Despite the fact that Hooker was already a popular artist—albeit decades away from his eventual national and international fame—when he was back home he was still emphatically a part of the same blue-collar Delta-expat community that he had joined when he first came to the city. It should therefore come as no surprise that, on nights when he wasn't working, he was still playing local house parties, and happy to be doing so. "He used to like to play parties," confirms Tom Whitehead. "I'd go by with him because he didn't have a drummer, he'd play by just himself. Little after-hours parties, he'd get up on the bar and just sit there and play. I went to a lotta gigs with him like that."

"Oh, I still would do the same," insists Hooker. "I never did change, get no big head, no ego. Do the same things I was doin' when I wasn't famous. Little bars, house parties . . . I *like* that shit. Still do. Once I was at my house. *I* give a house party, right there on Jameson Street in Detroit. There was my wife, Maude, sellin' whiskey, sellin' sandwiches, folks there be playin' blackjack . . . gamblin,' y'know? The house was jumpin'. People would snitch on you, the cops would give 'em a little money to grease they hands. Three dollars, five-dollar, ten-dollar bill to tell 'em where the big thing—the big, big party—goin' on at. They gamblin' there, they shootin' dice, they sellin' bootleg liquor. 'What they doin' over there?' 'Well, they sellin' whiskey over there after hours, gamblin' too.' And they would go there, just like they was goin' to get a drink or a gamble. You would be *po*-lice, but you would act just like you was a citizen, you just one of the crowd who wants to have a good time. He might go in there to watch where the gamblin' at; he may shoot the dice one time; not much, just to make it legal. Then he may buy a drink of liquor, so he can say 'I caught you sell it.' And then they bust you. They go back outside, tell the *po*-lice out there, 'We got 'em.' Then you come back in the house, and the rest of 'em come in and bust you and they got more *po*-lice out there waitin' so you can't get away. They got the house surrounded.

"They got e-e-e-e-e-verybody. They come around with the paddy wagon, got e-e-e-everybody, men and women. But they didn't get me. I hid in the closet. Crawled in with some clothes. They never got the house man! And when they left, they didn't take my wife. When they left, she said, 'Where w'you?' I was in the clothes closet. They got everybody down, they got out, they discovered they didn't have the house man: me! And they come back, come back and got me. Asked my wife, 'Where your husband? Where's Mr. Hooker?' I say, 'Here I am.' They say, 'Let's go.' " Back, presumably, to the bullpen.

Sometimes Hooker would enliven house parties—his own or those of others—by bringing along a famous guest or two. One such was B. B. King though, fortunately, the Big B (rather less big in those days, as it happened) never got dragged off to the hoosegow. "Yeah, B. B. We used to sit up all night long at my house. Diane and my others, they was all little kids. We had a bar in the basement, and an old jukebox. We'd sit down and play guitar and drink 'til the sun come up, me and old B. His music very opposite from me. He always was a nice man, ever since I knowed him. Me and old B went through some things together, boy. Some good ol' times together we went through. We used to put down a lot of liquor and chase women. I don't regret none of it. I have no regrets. We had a really good time together. Some stuff he [might] tell you, you couldn't put in the book. Mostly about women."

And Maude liked to have herself a good time, too. "My mom used to be a party-hearty marty," says Zakiya. Eddie Kirkland concurs: "She's quite a bit younger than Hooker. I knew they had problems. She was quite young at that time, and you know how a young person mind go."

Maude missed the security of regular income, but she also missed the carefree days when she could enjoy herself without the responsibility of looking after a houseful of young children: if anybody was going to be out partying, she wanted it to be her. "She wouldn't tell you 'bout how all she did was run around and drink, stay out all night for two–three

days, leave the kids," Hooker remembers, with no small degree of bitterness. "Mrs. Rivers, the lady next door, used to have to take care of my
kids when I be out of town. She stay out two–three nights runnin' around
with hoodlums. Mrs. Rivers next door took care of my kids, but they
would never tell you that. My kids would never tell you that."

Maude Hooker shared her husband's frustration with his inability to
translate his undoubted popularity and acclaim into hard currency. However, Hooker asserts, she took her anger at the family plight out on him,
playing on his insecurities about the difficulties he faced trying to provide
for his family the way he wanted to. These particular memories seem as
fresh and painful to him as if they'd happened yesterday rather than forty
years ago. "She used to tell me, 'You ain't never gonna get nowhere with
this ol' *git*-tar, ol' starvation box.' She just said it to hurt me, to make
me feel bad. Anything she could say to stab me, she would do it." During
his second British tour in 1964, Hooker revealed to Max Jones of the
British weekly *Melody Maker* that "my happiest time in life is when I'm
on that stage, but anywhere I'm playing is home. I'm happy when I'm
playing that guitar. Take that away, and I feel I'm nothing." And since
Maude took away his guitar both metaphorically (contemptuously calling
it the "starvation box") and literally (beating him over the head with it
in front of an audience), it is hardly surprising either that he did indeed
feel that he was nothing. Or that the consolations provided by the company of the women who made themselves available to him on the road
became ever more appealing.

"Something like that makes an entertainer like him feel like somebody," diagnoses Dr. Eddie Kirkland. "John felt deep inside that the problem he had with his wife, that she probably made him feel like he was
nothing, that he didn't have nobody. That's the most fast thing that'll
turn a man another way. If he don't feel loved, if he feel left out. By him
bein' with another woman, if deep down inside he don't mean anything,
it'll make him feel that he is somebody. If your wife turn away from you,
the first thing you think about is 'All those years that I put in with her,
bein' faithful, and now I don't have nobody.' You feel left out. You feel
left out. You start datin' another woman, keep her ready in case anything
go wrong. It's bad to get in your mind that you're not wanted. That's
why a lot of people commit suicide. You think, 'I don't have nobody in
the world care for me.' That's a bad feelin'. A man reach out sometime
and do things because sometimes he feel that he left out. So that could'a
been John's case through the years. It's hard to be unfaithful to a woman

[when] you know that woman care for you. You can't just walk over there and do it. You got to feel that she don't care."

And sometimes those on-the-road diversions degenerated into outright farce, particularly if that veteran carouser Jimmy Reed was involved. "He had me laughin'," chuckles Buddy Guy, invited to retell his favorite Hooker anecdote, "about how him and Jimmy Reed was in the hotel with these two women and they had a few dollars and they was drinkin' heavy, said he'll make sure that the women don't rip him off. So he take the mattress, and he take the money, and he put it in the center of the bed in between these two mattresses, and he gon' get on it and go to sleep. And 'fore they get the money, they'll wake him up. So when he woke up, the mattress was on top of him, on the floor, and he didn't have nothin' left but his shorts. So he looked around and he didn't see Jimmy Reed, so he say, 'Now I got to go down to the desk and complain to the desk about my pants. I don't have no pants.' So he was trippin', tryin' to get downstairs to complain about how he needed some pants so he can leave the hotel, and Jimmy were already down there—said they had his pants too—and he at the desk raisin' hell, talkin' so loud . . . he looked up, saw John comin', said, 'They got you too, huh, John?' The last time I saw John he told me this. The girls took both of 'em pants, didn't leave 'em nothin' but shorts. He said, 'I was so drunk drinkin' that stuff then, man, d-d-didn't leave me n-n-nothin' but my sh-sh-shorts.' Him and Jimmy was in the lobby with nothin' but shorts on."

The couple's friends were, inevitably, placed in a very difficult position. "Me and Maude was great friends," Kirkland asserts. "Like sister and brother. I used to go out with her older sister quite a few years, and I never had anything to do with their problems. I was her friend, his friend, too. The only thing I can say about Maude: she treated me like a human being. I taught her how to drive a car. Search around, sneak around try to find out what goes on between a man and his wife, none of my business. I could listen to John Lee, what he would say about Maude, but I would never take sides. I'd come over the house, Maude would laugh and talk with me, so I have no jurisdiction to say nothin' about her. I kept my distance. He would tell me, and I would listen, but I would never make no comment, say, 'John, you oughtta leave her.' I have told him, 'Well, John, there's nothin' I can tell you because I'm a friend'a Maude's too, but I hope you can work things out.' Between you and me, there was a lot wrong between them, but it was none of my affair."

Sometimes, according to Zakiya, things got very rough indeed. "If you notice his hands . . . they were having one of their confrontations and she cut his finger, cut the tendon. You'll notice that one of his fingers is always straight, it doesn't bend any more. It was a very rocky relationship. I can remember times when it was really good, but she just was not able to deal with him being a musician, him being gone all the time, and . . . little cheap floozies calling the house." Maude could hardly have been unaware of Hooker's womanizing while out on tour. "She knew this and she was not able to deal with this. I don't know if I could've dealt with it . . . if any woman could."

In January 1959 Hooker kicked off his latest Vee Jay studio date with "Maudie," a song dedicated to, and named after, his wife. The mood of this particular recording session was already a nostalgic one, revisiting as it did early '50s triumphs like "Boogie Chillen," "I'm In The Mood," "Hobo Blues" and "Crawlin' King Snake." "He made one for me, you remember that one?" says "Maudie" herself, laughing. "He got up one morning and said, 'I got to go to Chicago and make a record and I'm gonna make a record about you.' And I didn't think anymore about it, and he really did! He went right over there and that was what he did! When we all heard we was so surprised and laughin' about it. Everybody always teased me about it, about that record. They still do, every now and then: somebody say"—she launches into the song—" '*Ohhh, Maudie . . . why did you do it?*' It was really nice."

"Really nice" is an odd way for its subject to describe "Maudie." Set to a relaxed but swinging Reed-style shuffle beat, it was recorded with only the support of Eddie Taylor and Earl Phillips: Taylor picking out the bass-line on the low strings of his guitar and Phillips slapping gently at his drums. It is indeed a love song, but not by any stretch of the imagination is it one which celebrates love's pleasures and passions. Instead, it's resigned and sorrowful: John declares his love for Maude, but they are apart, divided. He tells her that he misses her, but she—not he—is the one who's "*been gone so long.*" A world of hurt resonates between the lines of its telegrammatic lyric: what we hear in "Maudie" is a man, his voice hollow with regret, singing to a woman whom he loves but whom he knows, in his heart of hearts, that he has already lost.

[The Delta Blues] had gone up the river to Memphis, thence to Chicago, and been urbanized and commercialized. A whole branch of

the recording industry, captained by men who largely looked down on the blues and its Negro composers, grew and prospered by teaching its mild-mannered country protagonists to cheapen themselves with gimmicks, insincere effects, poor arrangements and silly subject matter. Since to the recording directors the blues were both cheap and meaningless, they encouraged the singers to compose blues by the yard, cut ten to twenty sides a session, to pour out bits of rhyme about any and every subject to a blues-hungry public . . . that in spite of all this so much original and superb music [was made] is a testament to the force of the bluesmen who kept coming out of the Yazoo country with their many musical inventions. But what I have heard convinces me that the blues might have flowered so much more fully and richly if these men had not been forced to market themselves.
—Alan Lomax, liner notes to *The Roots Of The Blues*, 1959[5]

Not long after the rock-and-roll craze began to spread, white intellectuals, college students, liberals, cognoscenti, and later the beatnik-folknik crowd rediscovered the blues in their quest for "truth," "vitality" and "authentic ethnicity." Singers who had long been in partial retirement or in total obscurity were unearthed and recorded for posterity. Musicians still active like [Big] Bill Broonzy, Brownie McGhee, and Sonny Terry were quick to adapt their styles to this new audience. Considering the premium placed on authenticity, it is rather ironic that many musicians who had been living in the city since their childhood found it convenient to let themselves be labeled country singers, primitives or folk singers, unhooking their electrical amplification and cleaning up their diction a bit to fit the new roles demanded of them.
—Charles Keil, *Urban Blues*[6]

It wasn't until his third year under the Vee Jay regime that Hooker was able to score his first substantial hit, and it came with an uncharacteristically conventional piece which wasn't even one of his own compositions.

---

5 Available on C D as New World Records 80252-2 and highly recommended, despite the petulance of Lomax's contemptuous dismissal—subsequently recanted, thankfully—of amplified urban blues.
6 This enormously influential book, published by the University of Chicago Press in 1966, was the first major study of the blues to focus on the music as it was then, rather than simply to use the prewar rural blues as a stick with which to beat its vulgar, degenerate urban offspring.

"I Love You Honey," which nosed its way into the lower rungs of the R&B Top 30 toward the end of 1958, had been composed by one Freddy Williams. Hooker's rocking version of "I Love You Honey," recorded the previous June at a session which also gave the song its B-side "You've Taken My Woman," boasted a "direct-time" symmetrical meter, tightly rhymed lyrics, little vocal improvisation and—probably its major selling-point—rollicking boogie-woogie piano breaks provided by Joe Hunter, [7] a stalwart of Detroit's jazz and blues club scene whom Hooker had brought with him to Chicago for the session. His next Vee Jay studio date produced nothing which the company's executives found sufficiently attractive to release, so after the January '59 session at which he cut "Maudie," Hooker took a one-year sabbatical from Vee Jay, and reconsidered his options.

1959 found the denizens of Planet Blues coping with a series of major upheavals. During this pivotal year, a veritable forest of signposts to the future appeared. Right under Hooker's nose, a new musical revolution was brewing in Detroit: Berry Gordy, whose record store had gone under a few years before, had sold a few songs to his cousin, Jackie Wilson. One of them, "Lonely Teardrops," reached Number 7 in *Billboard*'s pop chart; Gordy invested the proceeds—plus everything else he could beg, borrow or otherwise scare up—into independent record production for, among others, United Artists and Chess. In 1959, he moved up a gear, starting up his own record company. He named it Anna, after his wife: the following year, he founded two more labels, which he called "Tamla" and (after the black contraction of Detroit's "Motortown" nickname) "Motown." Gordy's gameplan was the creation of a new kind of rhythm and blues—slick, sweet and tuneful, but still soulful and funky—which would draw its backroom team, including pianist Joe Hunter, from the city's clubs and bars, and its frontline talent from the hungry, ambitious youth of the housing projects. Gordy's intention was to build a new music; one which would profit simultaneously from tapping into black America's need to move on up, and white America's desire to get on down.

In Chicago, Vee Jay was pulling further and further away from South Side blues. Never as thoroughly identified with transplanted Delta music

---

7 Not to be confused either with Ivory Joe Hunter, the silky-smooth West Coast blues-balladeer and composer of "I Almost Lost My Mind," or with his near-homonym "Ivy Jo" Hunter, the Motown producer/songwriter best-known for co-writing Martha & The Vandellas' anthemic hit "Dancing In The Street" with Marvin Gaye and William Stevenson.

as Chess, Vee Jay may not have had big-name rock and roll stars like Chuck Berry and Bo Diddley on its team, but it could certainly punch its weight when it came to the post-gospel sweet soul which was becoming an increasingly important part of the Windy City tradition. Intrigued by a promising young vocal group called The Impressions, Bracken and his team cut the successful "For Your Precious Love," but released it under the name of the band's lead singer, Jerry Butler, whom they signed as a solo artist. This left the rest of the group, including guitarist/songwriter/ auteur Curtis Mayfield, at liberty to take themselves and their music elsewhere. Mayfield continued to write, arrange and produce Butler's records for Vee Jay (generating another major hit, "He Will Break Your Heart," in 1960), but the dazzling string of landmark hits subsequently notched up by the Mayfield-fronted trio version of The Impressions benefited the New York–based major ABC (a subsidiary of the television company) rather than their hometown label.

Meanwhile, as the traditional blues audience continued to shrink, an unexpected new market began to grow: white academics, intellectuals and jazz and folk fans started to take an interest in the music, albeit in its root forms rather than its contemporary extensions. Rinehart published Samuel Charters's *The Country Blues*, unleashing a torrent of scholarly works which focused critical attention onto the hitherto neglected field of rural blues, and giving it, for the first time, the kind of academic respectability which had been lavished on jazz, particularly in Europe, for quite some time. Despite Charters's disdain for contemporary blues—and for contemporary blues singers—Hooker and Muddy Waters were the exceptions singled out as recipients of the author's approval. "From Charley Patton, Son House, Robert Johnson and Bukka White to Muddy Waters and John Lee Hooker," wrote Charters, "there has been an almost unbroken line of great [Delta] singers." The British scholar Paul Oliver's equally influential *Blues Fell This Morning* arrived the following year courtesy of the Cambridge University Press; like Charters, Oliver was an admirer of Hooker's music, and later sought him out in Detroit during a lengthy research trip to the U.S.

In Europe, where early forms of African-American music, notably New Orleans jazz, were the objects of fanatical fundamentalist worship, blues singers had been welcome for years, provided that they were sufficiently "traditional" and "folkloric," and were willing to present themselves as "untainted" by "commercialism." Big Bill Broonzy, Muddy Waters' predecessor as the kingpin of the Chicago blues scene, had been a regular transatlantic visitor from 1951 until his death in August 1958. Broonzy played the "folkloric" role to the hilt, arriving for shows in overalls, carrying on like he'd never before left his Mississippi farm, and assuring his more credulous listeners that he was "the last of the blues singers." That Big Bill's reversion to a style he hadn't touched for decades might have been prompted by purely commercial motives was a possibility that few of his new friends were prepared to entertain. Muddy Waters himself had visited Britain in 1958, where purist critics and audiences were shocked into paroxysms of fear and loathing by his slicing electric guitar and rumbustious performance. (The punchline to *that* particular joke came in 1964, when Muddy returned to the U.K. with an acoustic guitar and a traditional repertoire, only to be confronted by a new generation of blues fans, weaned on The Rolling Stones and The Yardbirds and desperate to have their mojos worked to death.) The impressive share of this European bonanza which was waiting for Hooker had been prefigured by an admiring piece in the French magazine *Jazz-Hot*. Its author, Jacques Lemètre—who, as Oliver would also do a year or so later, had visited Hooker in Detroit during a trip undertaken with his colleague Marcel Chauvard—was the first to describe Hooker as "one of the most primitive (from a musical point of view) and, I would say, one of the most African of blues singers."

In a parallel development, the Newport Jazz Festival, which had been running in Freebody Park, near Newport, Rhode Island, since its establishment in 1954, acquired a sibling event, the Newport Folk Festival. Due to the domination of its rosters by clients of major agents like Albert Grossman and Harold Leventhal, it speedily became known among the more traditional folk musicians as the Newport Folk Agents Festival. The Newport Folk Festival formula involved the juxtaposition of popular whitebread folkies like The Kingston Trio alongside rather more authentic performers like Pete Seeger and The New Lost City Ramblers, while also featuring "world" acts like the Oranim Zabar Israeli Troupe, bluegrass virtuosi Lester Flatt & Earl Scruggs, and—making her major-league debut—the young Joan Baez, as well as those bluesmen who, like the guitar/harp duo Sonny Terry & Brownie McGhee, were already active on the East Coast folk scene.

This new audience developed radically different methods of consumption from the traditional blues constituency, which was strictly a singles market. Hooker was all but unknown to white audiences, though some of the more adventurous white youth across the country had already crossed certain barriers, both visible and invisible, in order to discover him. "Well, on the radio, living in Memphis as a kid," remembers Charlie Musselwhite, "I would hear him on a station from Nashville called WL.A.C, and there was another station from Mexico, XERF, and they would play John Lee Hooker and lots of other blues. Both of these stations were really powerful; XERF I could only get at night, but WL.A.C from Nashville came in a lot clearer. They would play John Lee Hooker and he had this sound which was unlike any other sound. You couldn't hear any influence; this guy sounded only like himself, and it was a real mysterious, sinister sound. I loved it, man, it sounded great. Sounded *tough*. "Hobo Blues," "Crawlin' King Snake." There was a guy that I knew that serviced jukeboxes and he had a garage just piled with thousands and thousands of 45s. I would look through his 45s and anything by John Lee Hooker, all blues records, I would just get 'em. I would go around to junkstores and I'd find 78s of John Lee Hooker. Some had different names on 'em, I remember finding one by a guy named Texas Slim. I never heard of Texas Slim, but as soon as I put the record on . . . that's John Lee Hooker. You can call it Texas Slim, but that's John Lee Hooker. I had John Lee Booker records, I had Johnny Williams records, Birmingham Sam 78s . . . 'Down At The Landing' . . . 'Low Down Midnight Boogie Woogie,' that was the name of that record. I was always fascinated with that sound, especially that drone sound that he would get playing in that open tuning."

In Tulsa, Oklahoma, a kid named Elvin Bishop was also tuning into WL.A.C. Intrigued by a Jimmy Reed record he heard one night, he went out the following morning in search of further enlightenment.

> *I went down to this record store in town that had all the R&B, as it was called then—all I knew was that it was black music—and I stole a bunch of blues records [he told Robert Neff and Anthony Connor].[8] And I started listening to that station every night and gradually got hip to it. Lightnin' Hopkins and John Lee Hooker were the ones I liked the most, especially John Lee—the emotion of it just carried me away.*

Comparatively few white kids, though, had either the good fortune to live somewhere as musically vital as Memphis, or the guts to go prowling

---

8 Quoted in *Blues*, Latimer, 1976.

sticky-fingered through ghetto record stores in search of vintage 78s. The new blues audience favored a new record format: the twelve-inch, 33⅓ rpm microgroove long-player, capable of carrying around twenty minutes of music on each side, enough for a dozen or so tunes in all. Hooker made his first appearance on microgroove in 1959—not to mention his second and third, but we'll get to those in a moment—under fairly inauspicious circumstances. *Highway of Blues*, released by the small Audiolab label, combined a fistful of Hooker's earliest, roughest sides— originally cut in 1949 for King Records—with an equivalent number of tunes by Stick McGhee, Brownie McGhee's less-talented brother who, a decade earlier, had stumbled his way into giving Atlantic Records its first big hit with "Drinkin' Wine Spo-Dee-O-Dee," but never quite managed to follow it up. One copy of that Audiolab album eventually found its way across the Atlantic to Belfast in Northern Ireland, where it fell into the hands of one Ivan Morrison. " 'Baby Please Don't Go' was on it," Van Morrison later told London Weekend Television's *South Bank Show*, "and several other songs like 'Devil's Stomp' and all this slow stuff. 'Baby Please Don't Go' was the only fast number on it. It struck me as being something really unique and really different, with a lot of soul. More soul than I'd heard from any previous records."

Singles appear in the stores and jukeboxes and on the radio; then they suddenly disappear again. By contrast, albums stick around in the racks long enough to have a "shelf-life." Vee Jay's first Hooker album, *I'm John Lee Hooker*, released later in 1959, kept the best of John Lee's late '50s recordings in catalog and in the stores, but the album that did most to redirect his career path hadn't been cut for Vee Jay and did considerably more than simply recycle a stack of old singles. In April of that year, Bill Grauer, boss of the New York–based jazz label Riverside, came to Detroit with a fairly radical idea in mind: he wanted to cut a Hooker session specifically for album release. His intention was to record Hooker solo and *au naturel*; backporch style: with an acoustic guitar and without the thunderous reverb and distortion of the early '50s solo sides. What was more, Grauer wanted Hooker to perform a program of Leadbelly songs, but this overly literal-minded notion of what was and what wasn't "folk" rapidly foundered when it became apparent that Hooker had barely *heard* of Leadbelly. With hindsight, this isn't at all surprising. Huddie Leadbetter was a hero and a cause célèbre among white folklorists who, quite rightly, acclaimed him as a walking library of African-American cultural history, but he meant little or nothing to black record-buyers. By the time he started recording in 1935, his music was a decade out of date, and his attempts at commercial recording—not to be confused with the archival recordings, cut for the Library of Congress under Alan Lomax's supervision, which are his most lasting legacy—sold miserably. Furthermore, despite the "traditional" nature of his work, Leadbelly was a distinct and unique individual, and much of his repertoire was therefore personal to him, rather than simply being a generic representation of a place, time or community. As with Hooker himself, Leadbelly's "authenticity" was inner as much as outer, as intimately bound up with sense of self as with sense of community.

"That [folk blues] was very popular for a while," says Hooker. "[Riverside] approached me. I was between contracts with Vee Jay. My contract was up, and I hadn't re-signed, and I did [the Riverside sessions] between contracts. This is the way to do things. If you free, like a freelance, you can do what you wanna do." And the resulting album, originally released as *The Country Blues Of John Lee Hooker* but subsequently reissued as *The Folk Blues Of John Lee Hooker*, was very much something Hooker wanted to do. "That was good stuff. 'Two White Horses,'⁹ really good stuff." And did it require any radical shift of approach? "Oh, I changed nothing." The session, cut at Hooker's old stamping ground at United Sound but in a distinctly different atmosphere than that which had held sway back in the Bernard Besman era, was something more valuable and important than any contrived recycling of excerpts from the by-then heavily strip-mined Leadbelly repertoire could possibly have been. As Paul Oliver put in his sleeve-note to the British edition of the album, "Perhaps it is well [that Hooker did not know Leadbelly's songs] if only because the present album might not have been made if he had been familiar with them. Instead of singing the blues and songs of another man, which would have been second-hand experience at best, he was encouraged to recall the blues he had heard or sung in his youth."

Hooker may indeed have "changed nothing" for the session, but the circumstances changed him. The unamplified acoustic guitar gave him a smaller, drier, less sustained and reverberant sound than the electric and

---

9   You'll search the Hooker discography in vain for anything entitled "Two White Horses;" that was the original title of the Blind Lemon Jefferson song from which Hooker developed the piece he calls "Church Bell Tone," one of two Jefferson-derived numbers featured on *Country Blues*. The other, "Black Snake Blues," was, along with a similar piece by Victoria Spivey, one of the primary sources for the "Crawlin' King Snake" which Hooker learned from Tony Hollins.

amplified-acoustic guitars featured on his earlier records, and as a result the entire performance is scaled down accordingly: where the '50s sides placed almost equal emphasis on voice and accompaniment, here the vocals are unchallenged for center-stage dominance. Hooker's singing loses the declamatory edge, the dancehall holler, of his previous singles-oriented work; instead there's a quiet, confidential intimacy, an overwhelming sense of eavesdropping on a meditative communication with the singer's own inner being. The longer playing-time offered by microgroove vinyl does away with the constrictive limits of the single's three-minute barrier; the performances become longer and more discursive. The *Country Blues* session was an astonishingly productive one. Grauer left Detroit with enough material for two albums: though the second one, *Burning Hell*, remained in the can until its U.K.-only release in 1964 and took a further three decades to become available in the U.S.A, it was by no means markedly inferior to its more illustrious counterpart. For Hooker's part, the Riverside date gave him the opportunity to try a few things he couldn't possibly have attempted in the rapidly shifting and highly competitive world of the late-'50s R&B singles market: the chain-gang chant of "Water Boy," the sharecropping reminiscences of "Behind The Plow," the nostalgic harking-back to the '20s and '30s hits of Blind Lemon Jefferson and pianist Leroy Carr, the rural ribaldry of the Tommy McClennan-derived "Bundle Up And Go," the primal Delta riffs and lines of Charley Patton's seminal "Pea Vine Special," and—most of all—the debut of what was to become a signature song which remained in the forefront of Hooker's repertoire from that day to this.

"Tupelo" is a one-chord, free-form talking blues which, like Charley Patton's "High Water Everywhere," Bessie Smith's "Backwater Blues" and the "I Rowed A Little Boat" which Hooker developed from them, evokes the terrible flood which devastated the Delta in 1927. The Hooker family were far enough away from the river to escape the direct effects of the flood, but the magnitude of the disaster made it inevitable that tales of the flood entered the folklore of the Delta: everybody in the region, even if they themselves had been lucky enough not to have been forced out of their own homes and farms, had a friend or relation who'd been somehow affected by the calamity. On the face of it, not much happens in "Tupelo." Hooker sets up a rolling, repetitive bass-string riff in the key of E, paced to his slow but remorseless foot-tap, and he talks. In a deliberately casual country-stoic voice, with no shouting or histrionics, he simply tells the tale of something that happened, a long time ago, in a little country town named Tupelo, Mississippi.

"*Did you read about the flood?*" he asks us. "*There was thousands of lives . . . destroyed.*" The guitar riff ominously rolls on, like some force of almost unimaginable power now temporarily quiescent, but capable of erupting, furiously and without warning, at any moment. "*It rained, it rained*—tap, tap goes the foot—"*both night and day. The po' people,*" Hooker continues, his voice still hushed, still matter-of-fact, "*was worried . . . they had no place to go.*" The death-knell guitar continues to toll. "*You hear many people cryin', 'Lord, have mercy. You the only one . . . that we can turn to.'*" Thousands of people, stripped of everything they had or could aspire to, beyond the help of any human agency, calling on the same deity whose power has laid them low. The guitar departs from its basic riff, erupting into brief bass-string flurries. When the riff returns, Hooker hums along in unison with it. "*There was women . . . and there was children,*" Hooker says. "*They was screamin' . . . and cryin'.*" Once again they appeal to the Lord: "*'you the only one now . . . that we can turn to.'*" Once again, he reminds us that it happened a long time ago. "*The mighty flood,*" he says, reverently, "*in Tupelo, Mississippi.*" And then, as if in awestruck obeisance to the sheer enormity of the forces of nature, Hooker at last begins to sing. "*Oh-oh-oh,*" he moans wordlessly. "*Lord have mercy, wasn't that a mighty time.*" And then, almost as an afterthought as the record fades out, "*Tupelo is gone.*"

"John Lee Hooker," wrote Orrin Keepnews in the album's notes, "is a very successful Rhythm and Blues singer of today. But . . . he is also a most authentic singer of the way-back, close-to-the-soil kind of blues." In order to emphasize Hooker's "authenticity," Keepnews presented a somewhat embroidered version of the singer's personal history, quite possibly derived from Hooker himself.

Young John Lee left home to lead an itinerant life that, over a number of years, carried him from the Blue Ridge mountains of Virginia to the Gulf of Mexico, and across Texas from Brownsville to Corpus Christi. He worked at various jobs, but always his first concern was to play and sing blues, with and for whomever he could, and to learn the music that was all around him: in the hills, and on farms, and in the shacks and back room dives and on the streets of towns.

Like many revisionist fables, this one stuck: by 1961, when Pete Welding annotated Vee Jay's *The Folklore of John Lee Hooker*, the timespan covered by John Lee's nonexistent "itinerant" period—his "life of drifting and restless traveling," during which he absorbed the music of "the lumber and turpentine camps, the rough dives, shacks and juke-joints of the rural south"—had expanded to a full sixteen years.

The release of *Country Blues* didn't so much advance John Lee's existing career as give him an entirely new one. The album garnered ecstatic reviews in publications ranging from the *Washington Post* to *downbeat*; folk and jazz critics striving to outdo each other's superlatives in praise of a man whose music they had never previously deigned to acknowledge. Hooker was hailed either as "one of the best examples today of the rural tradition" (his previous history conveniently expunged) or as a prodigal son who had found his way back to the True Path ("a successful rhythm and blues performer . . . returns to the basic blues") after a decade in the wilderness of Philistine commercialism.

> *A singer like Hooker [Orrin Keepnews wrote rather sniffily in the liner-notes to a subsequent Riverside album, That's My Story] can now finally sing the honest blues the way he really feels them. Until very recently, John Lee Hooker had little opportunity to record material of this type. Ever since his recording career got under way in the 1940s, he has functioned largely in the strange, musically hybrid area known as "rhythm-and-blues." But let's face it, in the past decade or so that area has been the only place even faintly like home where a singer of the blues could earn his way. And the fact that Hooker has achieved more than a little success as an R&B performer is probably primarily a tribute to the ability of the real blues spirit to fight its way through souped-up rhythmic monotony and inane lyrics.*

By contrast, to fans of the rough-edged, rocking electric city blues—or, if you prefer, the "souped-up rhythmic monotony and inane lyrics"—which Hooker had created in that "strange, musically hybrid area known as rhythm-and-blues," it was the acoustic folk-blues posture which represented the *real* sell-out. Tony Glover articulates this view in the liner-note to a recent reissue of an early-'60s solo live album, wherein his enthusiasm for Hooker's music in general is tempered only by the faint praise with which he damns the folkie years in particular. "Hooker," he writes, "became a storyteller/showman with a slightly cleaned-up and diluted rep-ertoire . . . it's obvious that he was being careful about his music and the manner in which he presented it—the raunch and fire of his old sides on Modern and Vee Jay is missing." In a similar vein, Colin Escott, writing in *Goldmine* magazine more than thirty years after the release of *Country Blues*, disapprovingly noted that "Hooker's folk blues albums also fea-tured him playing an acoustic guitar. This was the man for whom the electric instrument might almost have been invented, and these stabs at 'authenticity' arguably resulted in some of the least authentic music to bear John Lee Hooker's name." Only Paul Oliver seemed prepared to step outside these contrived barricades and present the case that the artist himself would make: that, essentially, the "folk" and "R&B" records depicted the same man making the same music—"Oh, I changed noth-ing!"—and that only the scenery was different.

> *It would seem hard to reconcile [Hooker's] recent background with the picture of the country singer that has been drawn of him [he pointed out]. But of all city singers who have attained prominence John Lee Hooker has retained the qualities of his rural origins the longest . . . today John Lee Hooker is a city singer and it is artificial and unwise to make a country singer out of him. Nevertheless [Country Blues] is an important record for it shows uniquely the roots of the music that he has shaped into an idiom all his own.[10]*

Vee Jay itself also dabbled a toe in this new market, and their Hooker album provided a musical counterbalance to the revisionist image of John Lee promulgated by *Country Blues*. Hooker's temporary absence from Universal Studios had been effectively disguised by a dribble of singles from the vault—his remakes of "Boogie Chillen" and "Crawlin' King Snake" as well as "Maudie," his only new song released that year—and by the release of *I'm John Lee Hooker*, the first album devoted entirely to his R&B work. Though not billed as such, it was a de facto "greatest hits" collection, gathering together Hooker's most popular Vee Jay tracks thus far, including "Dimples" and "I Love You Honey," alongside the then-current single "Maudie" and his recent remakes of vintage hits like "Boogie Chillen," "I'm In The Mood," "Crawlin' King Snake" and

---

10 From his liner-note to the British version of the *Country Blues*; reprinted, along with a generous helping of Oliver's other sleeve-notes and journalism, in *Blues Off The Record: Thirty Years of Blues Commentary* (The Baton Press, 1984).

"Hobo Blues." The packaging was ostentatiously downhome; the front cover eschewing the uptown imagery associated with the new smooth R&B by depicting a big old coal-fired stove.

Similarly, the folkie-friendly liner-notes emphasized Hooker's rootishness and rurality, as well as continuing that process of self-consciously romanticized mythmaking which has dogged Hooker ever since.

> *He is an itinerant soul [the anonymous author solemnly assured his (surely not "her") readers, recycling Keepnews's potted biography from the Riverside album]. A body who strayed from the Gulf of Mexico, from Corpus Christi to Brownsville to the Blue Ridge Mountains of Virginia—and plenty of area in between. John Lee held many different kinds of jobs. But they only bankrolled him between sessions of pickin' and singin' with anyone who cared to join or listen. He absorbed the authentic folk styles and trends everywhere he travelled . . . but thousands of miles and years of moving intervened before he hit . . . Detroit. [Hooker was, the writer asserted,] first taught by his grandfather to pick out harmony on strips of inner tube nailed in different tensions to the barn door. From this crude and primitive beginning comes the very distinctive and Hooker-styled strumming you'll find herein. [Rather more acutely, the same author pointed out] At times, you'll find the sound hearkening back to the Orient, while often, you'll hear the bagpipe's drone.*

If one middle-class white listener's experience was anything to go by, Vee Jay's policy of shifting their Hooker catalog into the albums market was an unqualified success. Fourteen-year-old John Hammond was the son and namesake of the man who will probably be remembered as the greatest talent scout in all of twentieth-century popular music, with a track record stretching from Bessie Smith's last session to Stevie Ray Vaughan's first, with names like Billie Holiday, Charlie Christian, Bob Dylan, Aretha Franklin and Bruce Springsteen in between. Though his parents had separated when he was a child, young John still had access to his father's extensive record and tape library, and had thus already been exposed to some fairly esoteric country blues, including the works of Robert Johnson, then as yet uncollected on album. Nevertheless, his chance discovery of Hooker's music blew his mind. "The first album that I had of his was called *I'm John Lee Hooker*, and it included 'Maudie' and 'Dimples', all the really heavy-duty ones. And then later on I heard his earlier recordings, and hearing him play all by himself with his foot on a block of wood and him just making the sounds . . . I found it truly amazing and passionate and delightful." Consumed by the urge to perform the blues himself, the younger Hammond proceeded to acquire every Hooker record he could find; only a few years later, he and Hooker would become professional colleagues.

However, it was in the wake of *Country Blues* that John Lee Hooker the acoustic troubadour would be welcomed into places whence John Lee Hooker the raucous city bluesman would have been indignantly turned away. Like, for example, the Newport Folk Festival.

9. Folk Boom . . .

In the thirty years since he learned music . . . from his
stepfather in Clarksdale, Mr. Hooker has embraced several
styles. He has shed none of them, his performances running
the gamut from personal country blues through more
sophisticated, externalized urban blues to heavily rhythmic,
flashy material that borders on rock'n'roll.
—Robert Shelton, *New York Times*, April 7, 1961

The Newport Festival season of 1960 proved to be rather more auspicious
for some than for others. That particular summer, John Lee Hooker
pulled off a memorable double, not only appearing, complete with acoustic guitar, at the Newport Folk Festival on June 25, but returning to
Freebody Park over the Independence Day weekend, one week later, to
perform as a special guest artist with Muddy Waters' band during a special Sunday afternoon blues concert. In folkie mode, he played a set accompanied on stand-up string bass by Brooklyn jazz musician Bill Lee,
the latter a quarter-century or so away from composing the score for his
then-infant son Spike's movie debut *She's Gotta Have It*. The show included impassioned meditations—if that seems like a contradiction in
terms, let it serve as an indication of Hooker's almost supernatural ability
not only to resolve but to embody such contradictions—on "Hobo Blues"
and "Tupelo," alongside a fine, rocking version of "Maudie" flawed only
slightly by the occasional (and wholly understandable) failure of Lee, who
had never played with Hooker before, to second-guess the bluesman's
idiosyncratic method of telegraphing his chord changes.

The Newport Folk Festival provided Hooker with the biggest single
audience he'd ever played to in his life. "I feel like I accomplished some-

thing there," he says. "That was one of the greatest times, Newport. People used to sleep outside, have little tents. You couldn't get a hotel room; it'd be crowded, packed. Joan Baez was one playing there. When I think about that, sometimes I just feel like crying, I'm so happy about the old days. The '60s will never be forgotten, the memory will never die. Great musicians like Brownie McGhee & Sonny Terry, and Joan Baez and myself, and many, many more, blazed a trail at Newport."

The Jazz Festival showcased a different aspect of Hooker's gifts. He appeared, for neither the first nor the last time, with Muddy Waters' band, which at that time featured Otis Spann (piano), James Cotton (harp), Pat Hare (guitar),[1] Andrew Stephenson (bass) and Francis Clay (drums). The conventional critical wisdom on the Waters bands of the '50s tends to favor the line-ups from the earlier half of the decade, particularly the ones which included Jimmy Rogers in the guitar chair and Little Walter on harp, over those from the latter half. However, as Robert Palmer has persuasively argued, the Waters bands of this period more than compensate for their lack of celeb soloists by a greater degree of teamwork and a superior ensemble feel. Certainly Muddy had sufficient confidence in this particular crew's ability to execute his music without instrumental cues from the leader, to lay aside his own guitar and perform strictly as a vocalist for those sections of the set devoted to his more recent material, though his defiantly downhome Delta slide guitar was strongly in evidence on the older songs. The cover photo of the subsequent *Muddy Waters At Newport* album, taken at the foot of the steps leading to the stage, caught the immaculately suited Muddy mere instants before he stepped out before his equally immaculately tuxedoed band, already in full swing with Spann pounding out a rocking boogie shuffle. Ironically enough, the electrified archtop acoustic guitar Muddy is shown clutching so authoritatively was not his. "That was John Lee Hooker's [guitar]," Muddy told Tom Wheeler,[2] "and I just grabbed it for the picture. My own guitar was up onstage, the same red Telecaster I got now." (In fact, the video evidence demonstrates that the instrument in question was a different Fender

---

1 Listed, for some obscure reason, as "Tat Harris" in the credits of the original edition of the *Muddy Waters At Newport* live album, Auburn "Pat" Hare achieved a particular kind of Staggerlee notoriety by recording a song called "I'm Gonna Murder My Baby" for Sun Records in 1954 and doing exactly that, eight years later, after being fired by Waters shortly after Newport for persistent drunkenness. Locked down for a 99-year stretch, he died of cancer in a prison hospital after serving 18 years of his sentence.
2 Quoted in *Guitar Player*, August 1983.

Telecaster altogether: the same early-'50s blond model that he'd taken on his first English tour two years earlier.)

The spur-of-the-moment guitar switch turned out to be fortuitous as well as expedient. Not only did Muddy gain a short-notice photo-prop, but the iconographic significance of clutching a big sunburst archtop acoustic rather than a Fender solid-body was considerably more appropriate, in marketing terms, to the preconceptions of the white folkies and jazzers at whom the bulk of his future work would be aimed.

Much of that Sunday afternoon blues show has been preserved in a series of short films, collectively entitled *Jazz U.S.A*, made under the auspices of the United States Information Agency and introduced by an amiable, bespectacled stiff named Willis Conover, host of a long-running Voice Of America jazz radio show. Unfortunately, the format of the films demanded that the footage be edited into bite-sized chunks, following one piece by each of the artists—Waters, Hooker, cabaret-blues vocalist Betty Jeanette and old-timey guitar/fiddle duo Butch Cage & Willie Johnson, plus piano-instrumental contributions by Spann, and excerpts from evening shows by Dave Brubeck and Ray Charles—with a number by another, thereby destroying the continuity and pacing of each performer's set. By contemporary concert-footage standards, the filming is impossibly sluggish and pedestrian. The camera spends what seems like eternities wandering interminably over the front rows of the audience, catching platoons of middle-aged, middle-class white people in inappropriate clothing clapping spectacularly out of time in the blazing afternoon sun. However, it provides us with unparalleled glimpses of two of the major Delta expats in their performing prime. Most existing film of Muddy Waters was shot in the '70s, after he had lost much of his physical mobility to the after-effects of injuries sustained in a major car crash, but the Waters shown here is a vastly different proposition from the more familiar burly, avuncular figure, perched on a bar stool plucking at his guitar. Here, unencumbered by his instrument, he's rockin.' His knees shimmy, his arms gesticulate, his feet fly and—during Spann's piano solo on the climactic "Got My Mojo Workin' "—Muddy rushes across the stage to James Cotton, gathers the bulky, pompadoured harpist into his arms and sweeps him into a gleefully impromptu lindy-hop. He effortlessly dominates the large open-air stage, whetting the viewer's appetite for a chance to see a performance of similar intensity compressed into the pressure-cooker atmosphere of a South Side tavern.

For his part, Hooker is physically more reticent—gently bouncing to the beat on the balls of his feet, guitar slung across his right shoulder rather than around his neck—but musically he is equally eloquent. Backed by the core of the Waters band—Spann, Hare, Stephenson and Clay—he is depicted on film-clips performing "Maudie," "It's My Own Fault" and a piece introduced by Conover as "Come Back Baby," alternately crooning and snarling his lines through his chipped front teeth while the band, fully accustomed to the vagaries of Delta singers, effortlessly cover his every musical bet. Lean and dapper in his slim-cut Italianate suit, Hooker came across as what he was: a country man utterly at home in city clothes.

Hooker could therefore be said, without significant fear of contradiction, to have had a "good Newport." The festival organizers, on the other hand, had a rotten Newport, and they couldn't even claim that it wasn't their own fault. As Jack Tracy puts it in his *Muddy Waters At Newport* liner-notes,

> Newport Festival, 1960, will go down as the year of the great riot. An estimated 10,000 beer-inflamed youngsters tried to storm the gates of the Saturday night concert and gain entrance. The park already was full. The result? Tear gas, windows broken, heads cracked, and a near-state of martial law declared. The next day, the Newport city council and the heads of the Newport Festival met and decided to call off the remaining two days of concerts. Only the Sunday afternoon program would be allowed to continue. Fittingly, it was an afternoon devoted to the blues. And chosen to wind it up, and thus probably be the last jazz group ever to play the Newport Festival, was the Muddy Waters band.

In a sulphurous essay entitled "Bringing Dignity To Jazz,"[3] the veteran jazz critic Nat Hentoff, then co-editor of the *Jazz Review*, went somewhat further. "Independence Day weekend of 1960 at Newport," Hentoff wrote, "is worth detailing as the most mephitic[4] event yet in the usually inglorious campaign to win wider 'recognition' for jazz." According to Hentoff, the debacle was the logical if not inevitable result of the Festival's own policies:

---

3 Included in *The Jazz Life* (Peter Davies, 1962).
4 Go on, look it up. I had to.

The Newport Jazz Festival has become the bleary symbol of how "success" and "acceptance" can eventually corrode the "image" of jazz more effectively than intermittent Sunday supplement stories about jazz and junk. For several years, the promoters of the Festival had been programming the concerts as if they were vaudeville shows, and had been generally lowering the musical standards of their celebrations of America's "only indigenous art form" until by 1959 the Festival had become the backdrop for a weekend of drinking by as many teenagers as could fit into the town . . . the NJF was ordered to cease all music on Sunday afternoon, July 4. Although the Sunday and Monday night and Monday afternoon concerts were cancelled, the city allowed the Sunday "educational" daylight session to go on in the knowledge that it would attract few people. It was a blues afternoon—one of the best in the Festival's history. There were no big names. The passion of the players and singers reminded one musician, "That's the way this festival started. Music was its reason for being . . ."

The actual climax of the afternoon wasn't included in any of the U.S.IA films: indeed, they contained no allusion whatsoever to the problems which had wrecked the festival. Langston Hughes, the celebrated African-American poet and playwright, had scribbled the lyrics to an impromptu blues (entitled, logically enough, "Goodbye Newport Blues") onto a fistful of Western Union telegram blanks and brought them to the stage, where the song was performed almost immediately. It was sung by Spann, rather than Waters, for one very simple reason. Spann could read, and Waters couldn't.

By the time he played that double-header at Newport, Hooker was back in the Vee Jay fold, but he had put his year-long sabbatical to very good use. On February 9, he had recorded a further acoustic session for Riverside, this time at Reeves Sound Studio in New York City, under the supervision of Orrin Keepnews. Rhythm section support was provided by Sam Jones and Louis Hayes, respectively the bassist and drummer from alto saxophonist Cannonball Adderly's band, then contracted to Riverside. Julian "Cannonball" Adderly was a Floridian who'd played alongside John Coltrane in Miles Davis's legendary *Kind Of Blue* band, and Sam Jones had cut with Davis himself when the trumpeter had made one of his rare guest appearances on Adderly's *Somethin' Else* session for Blue Note the previous year. The resulting album, *That's My Story*, demonstrated that Hooker had absolutely no problem adjusting his music to the light, syncopated swing of a "jazz" rhythm section, though the reverse isn't strictly true: you can virtually hear the sweat dripping from bassist Jones's brow as he continually shifts his chords to stay in sync with Hooker.

That's My Story found Hooker juggling an astonishingly eclectic variety of source musics, considering that he was supposed to be a musical "primitive," miraculously uncontaminated by commercialism and vulgarity. Hooker delved even-handedly into the popular rhythm and blues of his youth, the traditional blues and gospel of his boyhood, his own Modern and post-Modern repertoire, and even the pop hits of the day. The album's curtain-raiser, "I Need Some Money," for example, is a straightforward Hookerization of a contemporary R&B hit, Barrett Strong's "Money (That's What I Want)," one of the earliest Motown classics from the days when the label left some of R&B's rough edges in place. Composed by Janie Bradford and Berry Gordy himself, it later earned the honor of being the only song to be covered by both The Beatles (in late '63 on their second album) and The Rolling Stones (in early '64 on their first EP). Hooker, however, sang it with such laconic, insouciant conviction that many listeners were convinced that his fellow Detroiters had borrowed the song from him, rather than the other way about. (The Doors, who performed the song live but never cut it in a studio, based their version on Hooker's; when two of their in-concert recordings of the songs appeared on CD in 1997, composer credits were awarded to Hooker rather than to Bradford and Gordy.)

In stark contrast, it's followed by "Come On And See About Me": no relation whatsoever to the 1964 Supremes hit of (almost) the same title, but a heart-wrenching adaptation of a traditional gospel tune, performed solo in the meditative mode of "Tupelo," and echoing that song's theme of those abandoned, stripped of all earthly resources and helpless in a hostile and uncaring world, with nothing left to turn to but the mercy of the Lord. However, where "Tupelo" is detached, understated, almost deadpan in its account of catastrophe and horror, "Come On And See About Me" is passionate, fervent, almost unbearably intense: sung in the first person as opposed to "Tupelo"'s third. Set to a slow, quiet foot-tap and the eerie strains of Hooker's open-A-tuned acoustic guitar, it was easily the most gorgeous and affecting vocal performance of his career thus far, a harkening-back to his Baptist childhood. To those "electric purists" who claim to detect nothing of value or merit in Hooker's "contrived" acoustic recordings, this song above all is heartily recommended. Check your ears: better yet, check your soul.

"I'm Wanderin'," a slow blues which begins with a highly entertaining dispute between Hooker and Jones concerning the chord changes, is one of many variations on Charles Brown's perennial "Driftin' Blues"—first recorded by Brown in 1945 when he was a member of Johnny Moore's Three Blazers—which can be found dotted through Hooker's discography. Brown was *"driftin' and driftin' like a ship out on the sea"* whereas Hooker finds himself wandering *"like a ship out on the foam."* (The title assigned, presumably by its producers, to a 1970 version of the same piece over-phoneticizes his pronunciation to create the highly arresting and deeply surreal image of "a sheep out on the foam:" the very stuff of nightmare, to be sure. Another possible interpretation is that Hooker was singing about *"a sheep out on the foal"*—presumably a reference to being out in pasture. Enigmatic or what?)

"Democrat Man" is the album's ringer in more ways than one. For a start, it's the kind of out-front partisan political song which was common in the predominantly left-wing white folk world but—the repertoire of the underrated J. B. Lenoir notwithstanding—such songs were highly unusual in the cagier, more cynical lyrical world of the blues. "You get in places, ooh *whee*, in the *way* backwoods, where they ain't ever come out, and you start that stuff, you act like you wanna be like that, you liable to get torn up," warns Hooker. "You get one of the worst whuppin's you ever seen. Little redneck towns, they ain't never been to a big city. You know"—he laughs, but he isn't smiling. "Rednecks and hillbillies."

For another, it was an adaptation of a recent song by one of the members of Hooker's own local blues community. "I learned that from Bobo Jenkins," says Hooker. "Bobo Jenkins give me that song, he's gone now." The late John Pickens "Bobo" Jenkins, who played simultaneous guitar and racked harp in the manner of Jimmy Reed, was born in 1916 in Forland, Alabama, had reputedly been married nine times, and recorded his "Democrat Blues" for Chess in 1954. " 'Democrat Man,' that was a lovely song," Hooker recalls fondly. It's certainly derived from Jenkins's piece, a mid-slow shuffle with chunky guitar, wheezing mouthharp and keening vocals which shares some audible musical and lyrical ancestry with Jimmy Rogers's "That's All Right" and Eddie Boyd's "Five Long Years." However, Jenkins's punchline—*"The Democrats put us on our feet, baby/you had the nerve to vote them out"*—becomes Hooker's starting point: he puts his own distinct spin onto Jenkins's line and then takes off from there. *"The Democrats put us on our feet,"* sings Hooker, *"and them crazy women vote them out."*

Hooker's political views have never been any great secret. Like many another African-American of his generation from the rural South, he has clear, distinct memories of the Depression, and of the sterling works carried out by the Roosevelt administration, not least among which was the Tennessee Valley Authority scheme which brought electricity to the Delta. Hooker is, by his own cheerful admission, a "yellow dog Democrat": one who wouldn't vote for a Republican even if the Democratic candidate was a yellow dog.[5] (The only Republican for whom Hooker ever had a kindly word was Abraham Lincoln.) "I was speakin' out," he says proudly. "Lettin' people know." *"They told us they'd send your sons home,"* sings Hooker caustically, *"they did just that: sent 'em home to stay without a job."* Foreshadowing a new song which he would record on his return to Vee Jay the following month, he announces, *"I ain't got no shoes, no shoes on my feet"* before continuing *"but I ain't goin' down that welfare sto' no mo'. You know why? Because it won't be long before election time."* And 1960 wasn't a bad year to be putting a marker down for the Democratic Party: the eight-year stretch which the Republicans had commenced in 1952 was about to end. *"I know I'll get shoes, I get clothes . . . when the Democrats get back in again."*

Elsewhere on *That's My Story*, Hooker revisited some of the key items in his core repertoire, like "Wednesday Evening Blues," which he had first recorded at his inaugural session for Bernard Besman, and—under the title of "Gonna Use My Rod"—a truly hardy perennial first recorded for Specialty as "I'm Mad," soon to be revisited for Vee Jay as "I'm Mad Again," and re-recorded several times thereafter as "Bad Like Jesse James"; as well as another old-time R&B hit from the "jump" era, Roscoe Gordon's "No More Doggin'," which he'd first cut for Specialty in 1954.

Come March 1 it was business as usual back at the Vee Jay Chicago corral, with Hooker cutting his first session for them in over a year in the company of guitarist Lefty Bates, bassist Sylvester Hickman, and drummer Jimmy Turner. There was no doubting this particular trio's basic competence, and with a more orthodox bluesman they could probably have delivered a highly satisfactory performance, but they were not ex-

---

5   And let's leave Bill Clinton out of this.

actly the most inspired crew with which Hooker had ever worked. Rather, they were plodders to a man, and—having already recorded three albums' worth of material for Riverside in the previous twelve months—Hooker himself was hardly at his most sparkling. The dozen tunes they cut that day became Hooker's first all-original Vee Jay album *Travelin'*, which came complete with a smudgy, impressionistic cover painting of a generic black man who bore no particular resemblance to Hooker, sitting disconsolately on a beat-up, sticker-bedecked suitcase, and an erudite, sympathetic liner-note from Nat Hentoff, who'd become a fan after hearing "Tupelo" on *Country Blues* and had snared Hooker a spot on a CBS-TV folk-music show earlier in the year. The record company may well still have been aiming Hooker's singles at the jukeboxes of the urban ghettos and the Deep South, but they were simultaneously targeting his albums at the new audience which Hooker had created for himself, without any aid from them, during his year-long sabbatical.

It would be inaccurate, not to mention ungenerous, to deny that the session did indeed provide some notable moments. "Run On" both harked back to "Dimples" and introduced a prototype of the musical setting Hooker would later use in "Boom Boom," which he would write and record the following year; "Solid Sender" was a mesmerically erotic incantation; "Goin' To California" was, as things turned out, eerily prescient, and "I Can't Believe" delved deep into Hooker's own personal domestic sorrows. "It's hard for a man in love," Hentoff wrote perceptively in the liner-note, "to accept the fact that his love, powerful as it is, can't always make another person love him back."

However, it was the very last track they cut that day which brought in the money: it was as if Hooker and his accompanists finally clicked into sync just as the session was drawing to a close. "No Shoes" had its roots in a fragment of lyric which Hooker had created as part of *That's My Story's* "Democrat Man"—"*No food on my table, no shoes on my feet/my children cry for mercy, they got no place to call they own*"—and a musical framework which artfully combined elements of the traditional and the contemporary. A slow, gospelly twelve/eight blues-ballad punctuated by guitar riffs which processed Hooker's guitar with the same shimmering electronic vibrato featured on fellow Vee Jay artists The Staple Singers' successful pop-gospel releases by their leader/patriarch Roebuck "Pop" Staples, it brought Hooker the biggest hit of any of his Vee Jay releases thus far; by late July it had lodged itself just outside the R&B Top 20. As soon as he returned to Detroit, Hooker celebrated by gathering his old pals Eddie Kirkland, Tom Whitehead and Boogie Woogie Red to cut an off-the-books session for Fortune Records.

During his first stint with Vee Jay, Hooker had loyally and conscientiously abided by the terms of his recording contract; but the second time around he did nothing of the sort. Less than two months after the *Travelin'* session, he was in New York City recording a solo studio date, in the Riverside vein but on electric guitar, for the aptly named jazz label Prestige Records. Predictably, Vee Jay weren't about to let a currently hot artist get away with stuff like that. After a brief period of negotiation, the label came to some sort of "agreement" with Prestige and "acquired" the fourteen masters, six of which appeared the following year on Hooker's next Vee Jay album, *The Folklore Of John Lee Hooker*. However; there was nothing they could do about the vast treasure-trove of Hooker sides already residing, quite legally, in the vaults of the labels for which he'd cut so prolifically in the past. Three more Hooker albums appeared in 1960, bringing that year's long-playing Hooker releases to a grand total of five. Crown, the budget-album wing of Modern Records, cashed in with *The Blues*, which recycled ten of its most successful Besman-produced titles including "Boogie Chillen," "I'm In The Mood," "Crawlin' King Snake" and "Hobo Blues," wrapping them up in an arty overhead shot of a male model standing in a ghetto doorway clutching a battered electric guitar and clad in the trademark Hooker outfit of trench-coat, shades, porkpie hat and drooping cigarette. King Records weighed in with *John Lee Hooker Sings Blues*, a selection of titles recorded by Joe Von Battle in August and September of 1948 augmented by a couple of tracks cut by Idessa Malone in March of 1950.

However, the real gem was Chess's *House Of The Blues*, the first album-length harvesting of some of the finest fruits of Hooker's moon-lighting sessions for Joe Von Battle during the Besman years. These sides were as cleanly and cleverly recorded as the best of the Besman sessions: less pop-friendly but considerably more adventurous, they represent one of the creative peaks of the entire Hooker *œuvre*. Even *House Of The Blues's* superb Don Bronstein cover photo is wonderfully appropriate: depicting a tumbledown Delta shack with its occupiers posed warily on the porch, it emphasized Hooker's Deep Southern roots without senti-mentalizing or mythologizing them.

Cats like John Lee Hooker and Lightnin' Hopkins can play them folk clubs with an acoustic guitar and get them off. People look at them and say, "Well, look at that old man. That's all he know." But go down to their own stomping grounds . . . they'll hook up an electric guitar and scare the shit out of you.
—Dr. John, quoted in *Blues*, by Robert Neff and
  Anthony Connor, 1975

By the summer of 1960, Hooker was certainly not short of career options. The success of "No Shoes" had given him his biggest R&B hit for years, while *Country Blues, That's My Story* and his Newport double-header had awakened both folk and jazz audiences to his unique talents. The new "coffee-house" circuit—folk-music cabarets without liquor licenses which served coffee and soft drinks to audiences who were quiet, attentive, respectful and, most important of all, affluent—was his for the taking. Venues like Philadelphia's Second Fret, Boston's Golden Vanity, Cambridge, Massachusetts's Club 47, Chicago's Counterpoint and New York City's Village Vanguard welcomed him, and he them. It was also a lot easier to take his young family to watch him work in this new environment than it was to bring them to the rumbustious taverns. "When we were small," recalls Zakiya, "I remember seeing him perform at either the Apex or the Black And Tan, and he would take us to coffee-houses. I remember the Checkmate, northwest Detroit. I used to love the coffee-houses."

And so did Hooker. Material which was next to impossible for him to perform effectively in the boisterous ghetto bars in which he had worked for the past decade and a half now became central to his act. "I could do ballads," he notes proudly. "From loud music to coffee-houses, that was quite a change, but you got to go with the times. You got to put on the brakes with whatever happens, with the dancin', the youngsters. You got to keep up. Some of the old blues singers couldn't keep up. Some of them couldn't make the switch. I made the switch because I could already do that some. Coffee-houses, I could already do that. I'd played with a little old band in the Apex Bar, the Caribbean, but coffee-houses were so popular, they was everywhere. People would listen to you; the waitresses wouldn't even serve until you finished the song. I could work four, five nights a week in the coffee-houses, get good money. Every city, was coffee-houses."

Or as he put it to Greg Drust, "I wish those days was here again. I really enjoyed just sitting down with my guitar, playing soft, slow blues, quiet, not loud, talking to the people, and they were just right around me in those coffee-houses . . . I know those days are gone, but I still weep and wish they was here again. I wasn't making the money I am now, but it wasn't the money. It was the scene and the people, and what I love to do. I would just really express myself."

For a verbal snapshot of Hooker in the coffee-house years, and an index of how he and his music were perceived by denizens of Planet Folk, we would be hard put to improve on Robert Shelton's report, in the *New York Times* of Friday, April 4, 1961, of Hooker's residency at Greenwich Village's legendary folk room Gerde's Folk City, on West 4th Street. As Shelton described it,

> *Mr. Hooker's voice is immediately arresting, a deep, dark-leather-timbred instrument that turns sullen, nostalgic, brooding or sensuous. He has a rhythmic sense that sets a firm, heart-beat pulse against which he embellishes a smoldering vocal line. He projects his voice in an urgent and intimate fashion that almost makes the listener feel Mr. Hooker's hand is on his shoulder and the song is for him alone. The diversity of Mr. Hooker's material points up the mobility of the simple blues format. "Tupelo" and "Natchez" are bardic recountings of disasters, one telling of a flood, the other of a fire. "Booty Green" is a rollicking dance tune, "Black Snake" is a jealous threat, "Maudie" is a song longing for his wife, "I Want To Walk" is unvarnished sexuality and "That's My Story" is rueful autobiography . . . Mood being as decisive as it is in blues-singing, Mr. Hooker's sets can be erratic, often leaning too easily toward pleasing the crowd with suggestive lyrics or rhythmic excesses. His guitar playing, on an electric instrument, is quirky, sometimes trilling a low bass figure that brings the audience to hushed suspense. At other times, however, he will slap at his instrument crudely, often failing to resolve a chord craving resolution, or traipse off on a run leading nowhere. But his relentless beat and emotional intensity save the day.*

Interestingly enough, neither of the two lyrical extracts quoted by Shelton elsewhere in that piece as indicators of Hooker's emotional and poetic range were original to him: one was from Janie Bradford and Berry Gordy's "Money" and the other from Charles Brown's "Drifting Blues."

And, of course, both were rhythm and blues hits (albeit from different eras), of which folkies were naturally unaware, rather than the "traditional" songs which they seemed to be when Hooker sang them.

Hooker's three-week stint at Folk City has, as it happens, been rather overshadowed by the fact that it represented the first fully professional extended NYC engagement performed by the young singer who was his opening act for the season's final fortnight. Bob Dylan had been bouncing around the Village folk scene for some little while, lionized by some as that scene's rising young prodigy and reviled by others as a bumptious young opportunist. Performing floor spots during the club's Monday-evening "hootenanny" nights, he had made a favorable impression on some of Folk City's habitués, who'd persuaded the club's proprietor, Mike Porco, to give him a shot at opening for Hooker. "He was so excited he was jumping up and down," Porco subsequently told Anthony Scaduto.[6] "His first real job, and working with John Lee Hooker who was liked by everybody, and Bobby probably figured, too, that Hooker would bring a lot of people in." Dylan was most assuredly a fan: even during the first week of Hooker's residency when he wasn't performing himself—nobody, not even Shelton himself, seems to remember who opened for Hooker during that first week—Dylan, according to Scaduto, "spent every night in Gerde's watching [Hooker], talking to him, sponging up his unique urban-country blues guitar."

"I met Bob Dylan in New York at Gerde's Folk City, him and his girlfriend Susie [Rotolo], who I see once in a while," says Hooker. "He were hangin' around me at the old Broadway Central Hotel. I had this suite there, and he had come to Gerde's to hear me and see me and talk to me. I met him there and got acquainted and just got real thick. Every night he'd be right there with me. We'd stay there, we'd party there, drink gin . . . and he got discovered there at Gerde's Folk City. I thought he was a hell of a folk-singer, 'bout one of the best that come along in that field of music. And he was a hell of a songwriter, that was for sure. He fitted right in the pocket, but he don't do that no more. He's with a band and the rock scene.[7] We all had to get away from that, but Bob fitted perfect, because that was how he's known, as a folk-singer. He'd sit around and watch me play; he'd be right there every night, and we'd be playing guitars

---

6 Quoted in Scaduto's *Bob Dylan: An Intimate Biography* (W. H. Allen, 1972).
7 More recently, of course, Dylan has oscillated between high-octane rock-band work and a neo-folk stance which has included an MTV *Unplugged* special and albums of traditional material performed solo. Just as Hooker himself did, we might say.

in the hotel. I don't know what he got from me, but he must've got something. A lot of guitar players have."

According to the account presented by Shelton in his Dylan biography *No Direction Home*,[8] the Hooker gig was not altogether an unmixed blessing for Dylan. "Bob thought only about having his name on a bill with John Lee Hooker, one of the great bluesmen," noted Shelton. "His elation soon soured as he sang for apathetic or noisy drunks and heard the carping of jealous musicians." Dylan was also somewhat pissed off at the lack of attention he received from Shelton himself, who had spent much of Hooker's offstage time attempting to extract biographical information from the taciturn, introverted bluesman, then still unaccustomed to confiding in or relaxing around whites, however seemingly well-intentioned, let alone answering personal questions from them. ("His painfully shy manner and his stammer," Shelton told his *Times* readers, "could give one the impression of inarticulateness. But only until he starts singing the blues.") It wasn't until Dylan was rebooked into Gerde's Folk City the following September, this time as opening act for the old-timey Greenbriar Boys, that Shelton was sufficiently convinced by Dylan to champion him in the famous *New York Times* review which was reprinted on the sleeve of Dylan's first LP.

Hooker's "rabbi" on the folk scene was super-agent Albert Grossman, a legendary entrepreneur with two major qualifications for music-biz management: an economics degree (from the University of Chicago) and an informal grounding in child psychology. Grossman had started out booking the likes of Big Bill Broonzy and the black folk-singer Odetta into Chicago's Gate Of Horn club, branched out into management with Odetta and Peter, Paul & Mary, and subsequently served on the board of governors of the Newport Folk Festival. He blossomed into one of the key rock tycoons of the '60s, his client roster later expanding to include Bob Dylan, Janis Joplin, Paul Butterfield and The Band. Indeed, in *Don't Look Back*, D. A. Pennebaker's justly celebrated documentary film of Bob Dylan's 1965 U.K. tour, the burly, pony-tailed Grossman virtually steals the movie from his client, methodically chewing up TV executives, journalists, hotel staff and anybody else unfortunate enough to get in his or Dylan's way. Hooker describes Grossman as his "manager" at that time, but Grossman seems to have restricted his activities on Hooker's behalf to booking the bluesman onto the folk circuit which he knew so well,

---

8   *No Direction Home: The Life And Music Of Bob Dylan* (Penguin, 1987).

taking no interest in Hooker's recording career or his R&B work. According to Robert Shelton, Grossman was famously vague about the precise nature of his relationships with artists: rather than categorically stating that he was "managing" or "booking" an act, he would simply murmur that he was "working with" or "helping out" or "advising" whichever performer happened to be under discussion.

Let's put it this way: no one who was fully represented by a manager of Albert Grossman's formidable firepower would need to have his contracts read to him by a teenage daughter. Zakiya fondly remembers how much her father loved to have her read to him, but ask her exactly what he liked to have read to him and she replies, "His contracts!"

" 'Read my contract! What's this say? What do I get?' " he would inquire. "In my little mind," Zakiya says, "I didn't realize what it was. I just knew he would say, 'Tell me how much I'm makin',' and I would look it out and say, 'It says you're makin' this and this and this, and then there's a certain percentage that goes to somebody else.' I would get through, and that was my first encounter with music. I was the one whom he would bring them to and say, 'Read this and tell me what it is.' " It may seem surprising that it was his daughter, rather than his wife, to whom Hooker would bring his paperwork, but that is, most emphatically, another story. "If he did [consult Maude], I didn't know," Zakiya flatly insists. "He would bring them to me. I loved him to pieces, and I was glad he'd bring 'em to me to read."

Hooker is, however, adamant that his connection with Grossman helped to kick-start Bob Dylan's career. "He was my manager, Albert was. He did some good things for me, you know. He was there [at Gerde's], he come there every night, just about. 'John,' he said, 'this kid's a hell of a folk-singer. I think I'm going to sign him up.' And I told Bob what he says, and he goes, 'Oh-oh-oh, he ain't going to do that,' and I say, 'He said he will.' Then he took Bob out for lunch or something—I wasn't with them—and they got together and he signed him up . . . I was really happy for him. I still is."

For what it's worth, there are several conflicting accounts of the origins of the Dylan/Grossman liaison. Robert Shelton recalls brokering what he then assumed was their initial contact by effecting an introduction at the Gaslight, where Grossman had dropped in to see Dylan perform during a week-long stint in June of 1961; while Paul Stookey of Peter, Paul & Mary, a Grossman client himself, made a pitch to the big guy on Dylan's behalf at around the same time. Grossman didn't manifest any formal presence as Dylan's manager until after the release of Dylan's eponymous first album—produced by the elder John Hammond, who'd signed him to Columbia Records against massive corporate opposition—in March 1962, but it is widely believed that he was working behind the scenes on Dylan's behalf for quite some time prior to that. Apart from the fact that Hooker is the only person who specifically recalls Grossman hanging out at Gerde's during that April '61 stint, these various accounts are in no way mutually irreconcilable, as Grossman was notorious both for keeping his cards close to his massive chest, and for generally playing a very long game indeed. Plus it goes without saying that an endorsement from John Lee Hooker wouldn't exactly have done Dylan's chances with Grossman any harm. Still, we'll leave the further ramifications of that stuff to the full-time Dylanologists, of whom there is no shortage.

Meanwhile, Vee Jay continued their policy of separate targeting for Hooker's albums and singles. *The Folklore Of John Lee Hooker*, his latest long-playing release, featured a garish oil-painting of a black guitarist, his face and body in shadow but his hands and instrument clearly depicted, performing to a rapt, and almost entirely white, audience. Pete Welding's liner-note reiterated the now-familiar "itinerant" myth, but Welding also proffered a nicely observed first-hand memoir of Hooker's folkie period.

> *When John Lee came to Philadelphia for a week's engagement at the mid-town coffee-house and folk music center The Second Fret [he wrote], I welcomed the opportunity of spending considerable time with him. Watching him perform two sets a night, evening after evening, at after-hours parties, impromptu sessions in his hotel room, etc... I found myself amazed time and time again at the undiluted intensity, power and conviction which he brought to each number, often vesting material which would have seemed vapid or superficial in the hands of lesser artists with real significance, earthy vitality and effusive intension. This ability to create moving and meaningful blues which project his own emotional involvement, utterly absorbing the listener, is a considerable gift, one he has inherited from his Mississippi forebears. Hooker is but the latest spokesman of a strong, continuing and fructifying tradition.*

The album itself was a Frankensteinian patch-job derived from a variety of sources, but it made surprisingly cohesive listening. "Tupelo" and "The Hobo" (aka "Hobo Blues"), licensed from Vanguard Records, who'd recorded Hooker's set from the previous year's Newport Folk Festival, respectively led off the first and second sides; six more solo performances came from the aborted Prestige project; and the package was completed by four newish combo sides recorded in Chicago, reuniting Hooker with Vee Jay studio stalwarts Quinn Wilson (bass) and Earl Phillips (drums) alongside Lefty Bates returning on guitar, plus Jimmy Reed contributing a cameo guest-shot on harp. "I'm Going Upstairs" paid tribute to Howlin' Wolf by emphasizing their common musical heritage; "I'm Mad Again" represented yet another stage in the evolution of the "I'm Mad"/ "Gonna Use My Rod" theme into "Jesse James;" "Wednesday Evening Blues" and "When My First Wife Left Me" replowed familiar ground, and "Five Long Years" was a relatively unadorned performance of a blues standard composed by Chicago pianist Eddie Boyd. "Want Ad Blues," which began extremely promisingly before fizzling out, was the next single (though not, it must be said, a particularly successful one), and only "Take Me As I Am" expanded Hooker's range into new musical or lyrical territory. Performed solo in the key of C and using an entirely different set of chords from Hooker's customary open-A and standard-tuning E settings, it was a plea for love, understanding and companionship from a different kind of woman to the big-legged strutters and mean mistreaters who populate so many of his other songs. Here he sings to a woman who don't need no lipstick and powder, who *can cook and be a good housewife,* and who will, finally, accept him as he is. It should be utterly bathetic, but somehow it isn't.

(The *Folklore* sessions also included a remarkably "straight" and un-Hookerized version of the ancient gospel standard "Will The Circle Be Unbroken," with impeccably cavernous Pop Staples–styled tremoverb guitar performed by Pop Staples himself. Inexplicably, it stayed in the can until 1974, when it was included on the misleadingly-titled compilation *In Person.*)

Hooker's only other album release that year came from Chess, who compiled their remaining early-'50s Joe Von Battle masters as *John Lee Hooker Plays And Sings The Blues,* but whatever his contract may or may not have specified, Vee Jay no longer enjoyed any kind of monopoly on Hooker's recording services. Hooker had most definitely reverted back to his old tricks: wherever he went, he contrived to seize every opportunity to record "outside" sessions. In Miami, he cut a fifteen-song marathon for Henry Stone, already sitting on a pile of "John Lee Booker" sides dating back to 1953, some of which had been released as singles on the

DeLuxe and Rockin' labels. (Stone promptly sold the entire lot to Atlantic Records: the best of the bunch were released as the superb *Don't Turn Me From Your Door* album in 1963, while the remainder surfaced on Stax in 1969 as *That's Where It's At!* Booked for a date at the Auditorium in Newark, New Jersey, Hooker killed two birds with one stone: he recruited Eddie Kirkland to fulfil his traditional dual role as second guitarist and chauffeur, and arranged a session for Savoy Records with producer Fred Mendelsohn. "I went and made that session. Matter of fact, I drove him there," remembers Kirkland. "I brought him [back] to Detroit, turned around and went back to Newark myself to get with Savoy. I wasn't able to get on Savoy, but I got on Prestige."[9] And in California, he even spent a March day in Culver City, recording a solo session for none other than Bernard Besman, who leased some of these fresh "Hooker-Besman compositions" to the Galaxy label. Demonstrating that his hand had lost none of its cunning since his "retirement" from the music business, Besman subsequently assigned alternate titles to several of his new masters and sold them on yet again.

By this time, Hooker was firmly established in his "folk-blues" incarnation. However, his next move not only reunited him—for what proved to be the last time—with the R&B mainstream, but gave him both his first nodding acquaintance with the pop (read young white) audience, and the somewhat belated opportunity to complete his hat-trick of million-selling signature hits. As it happened, he already had a ready-made musical setting: the catchy stop-time call-and-response riff groove he'd used for "Run On" during the previous year's *Travelin'* session. The next ingredient came his way when a bartender at one of his favorite hometown dives unwittingly provided him with the requisite lyrical theme.

" 'Boom Boom,' you heard that?" he asks rhetorically. "Bi-i-i-ig hit. I used to go to this bar—I tell people this, it's true—I played the Apex Bar on Russell and Oak Street in Detroit, on the north side. I played there 'bout a year in that one bar, and it was packed every night I played there. I always would come in there late, y'know. I was drinkin' then, I always had a bottle of Scotch by my seat or in the car. The band would be on the bandstand by the time I'd get there. I run in there, put my coat up, and this young lady behind the bar, name of Willow—like a willow tree— every night she would say, 'Boom-boom, you late again.' Every night, she

---

9 E-mail from Colin Escott to the author, April 2000: "Hooker's Savoy LP with Kirkland was actually done for Freddie Mendelsohn, a one-time Savoy producer who leased it to Savoy but retained ownership. Savoy no longer has rights. I believe it's out on 32/Jazz Records now."

say, 'Boom-boom, y'all is late,' and it came to me: that's a *song*. She kept sayin' that, and I said, 'Willow, you gave me a song.' She said, 'What?' I say, 'Boom Boom.' She say, 'Oh yeah.' And she kept sayin' it. I come in there one night an' I got it together, the lyrics, rehearsed it, and I played it at the place, and people went wild. She gave it to me with the words she was sayin': 'Boom-boom.' "

Then finally—*boom boom*—he lucked into just the right band. Scratch that: the *perfect* band.

The catalyst turned out to be right on Hooker's own Detroit doorstep: his old buddy Joe Hunter, the dazzling pianist who'd worked with him on the city's club and bar circuit, as well as playing on his successful cover of "I Love You Honey" back in 1958. Hunter had gone onto become one of the cornerstones of Berry Gordy's original Motown studio band, but though Motown had enjoyed a few solid hits by late '61—notably Barrett Strong's "Money," Marv Johnson's "Come To Me" and The Miracles' "Shop Around"—the company was still a good many classic smashes away from becoming the "Hitsville U.S.A" pop-soul empire of Gordy's dreams. As a result, the house band, who were making rather less than a living wage from playing what were then comparatively few-and-far-between Motown sessions, were eager to supplement their income with whatever outside work happened to be available. As well as taking on as many non-Motown studio dates as he could arrange, Hunter kidnapped what was virtually Motown's entire A-team and carted them off on tour with Jackie Wilson. This potentially lucrative excursion turned out to be something of a disappointment for the cash-starved musicians: the New York–based Wilson, at that time recovering from a gunshot wound inflicted by an "admirer," was still on the frail side and therefore under doctors' orders not to perform his highly strenuous stage act more than three times a week. This meant that he couldn't afford to pay each member of the band more than seventy-five dollars per week. New York City, then as now, was an expensive place to hang out in on a low wage, and since accommodation and expenses came to around sixty dollars per week, the musicians weren't making enough of a profit to take home any noticeable bacon. The band ended up back in Detroit with their collective tail between their collective legs, so when the opportunity arose to play some Brunswick and Vee Jay sessions in Chicago for higher wages than the still-impoverished Gordy was then able to pay, they naturally jumped at it.

Thus it was that Hooker found himself cutting his next album, *Bur-*

nin', with what turned out to be one of the hottest hit-making studio crews of the '60s. The band Hunter brought with him included the classic Motown rhythm section of James Jamerson and Benny Benjamin, the powerhouse bass-and-drums team behind virtually all of the legendary Motown hits of the next decade. Also along for the ride and the view were guitarist Larry Veeder, baritone saxophonist Mike Terry and, blowing tenor sax, none other than Hank Cosby, later best-known to his bank manager as co-writer and/or producer of several of Stevie Wonder's biggest hits, of which "Uptight (Everything's Alright)," "Fingertips" and "I Was Made To Love Her" are merely the most significant. "Boom Boom," indeed.[10]

While that song failed to hit the R&B charts quite as hard as "Boogie Chillen" and "I'm In The Mood" had done a decade earlier—released at the end of 1961, its stately progress up the charts eventually peaked in mid-June of 1962 at Number 16—it nevertheless turned out to be Hooker's most enduring staple, and deservedly so. "Boom Boom" is, if nothing else, the greatest *pop* tune he ever wrote, not to mention the first to break him into the pop charts: its comparatively modest placing at Number 60 fails to convey the magnitude of his achievement in getting there at all. It was also the most memorable, the most instantly appealing, and the one which has proved the most adaptable to the needs of other performers.

So what's so great about "Boom Boom?" For a start, it has just about the tightest musical structure of any Hooker composition: its verses sedulously adhere to the twelve-bar format over which Hooker generally rides so roughshod, albeit with a neat bar-for-bar call-and-response. *"Boom boom, boom boom,"* sings Hooker; *bam-bam, bam-bam* reply the band. The tension is released in the breaks: "W-o-o-ah!" calls Hooker, and the band rock out for twenty-four boogying bars, swinging irresistibly along until the verse returns.

And then there are those lyrics. As freely unrhymed as the music is tightly disciplined, they represent probably the purest—and least sexist or patronizing—expression of sheer lust in all of popular music. The eroticism of Hooker's music takes many forms: some of his slower, sexier blues, like "Solid Sender," "I'm In The Mood" or the duet version of "Crawlin' King Snake" he performed live with Vala Cupp, literally shiver

---

10 The author learned all this, plus a lot of other fascinating backstage stuff about the classic Motown era, from *Standing In The Shadows Of Motown: The Life And Music Of Legendary Bassist James Jamerson* by Dr. Licks (Dr. Licks Publications, 1989).

with passion; others give free reign to volatile blends of lust and anger, desire and hostility. But "Boom Boom" simply and perfectly encapsulates those moments familiar to anyone with a functioning libido—male or female, straight or gay—who has ever caught sight of a member of which-ever gender they find attractive, and has simply gone, *"Wow."* Or—in Hooker's case—*"How-how-how-how."* When he sings, voice thickened with passion, *"You knocks me out/right offa my feet,"* he evokes the memory of every beautiful stranger any of his listeners has ever seen.

"All the ladies like that," Hooker says of that song, and of "Dimples." "I say things that cater to women and men. Women can think the same ways: shoot those guys down, boom boom, come home with me. So the words make sense. So many songs say the same old things: 'my woman, my baby,' every blues singer says that. I try to say something different. They hit you something like that—like 'Dimples', *'you got dimples in your jaw,'* you know. Women like that, men with dimples, you know. Things like that just catch on."

Which "Boom Boom" certainly did. It was unquestionably the pick of the *Burnin'* litter, but the rest of the session had its moments. Hunter, Cosby, Jamerson, Benjamin and their colleagues are unquestionably best-known for the versatility and virtuosity with which they implemented Gordy's vision of a new black pop which was simultaneously sweet enough for the suburbs and soulful enough for the projects, but they'd learned their stuff in the Detroit bars and they surely had not forgotten how to play the blues, albeit with a sophistication unprecedented in the Hooker *oeuvre*. All that prevents *Burnin'* from being a quintessential "modern" blues recording for the time is the absence of the then-ubiquitous B. B. King–style lead guitar. "Process" was a slow-rocking blues, with darkly riffing horns, in which Hooker inveighs against hair-straightening: not for ideological or aesthetic reasons, but because the fashion induces women to take all their housekeeping money down to the hairdresser's rather than the grocery store. Elsewhere, "Thelma" revisits the musical and lyrical turf of "Maudie," while "What Do You Say" reveals that Hooker was keeping a close ear on his competitors: it opens with a guitar riff similar to some of Bo Diddley's before erupting into a variation on Howlin' Wolf staples like "Howlin' For My Baby" or "Moanin' In The Moonlight."

Most outré, however, is "Keep Your Hands To Yourself," based on the rocking, mock-Latino "Tequila," a huge hit for The Champs back in 1958. The band steam through "Tequila"'s four-bar riff, driven by Benjamin's lashing cymbals and abrupt tom-tom fills while Hooker warns a male interloper of the potentially dire consequences of taking liberties with his woman. What gives the record its tension is that Hooker makes his vocal entry on bar three of the four-bar sequence, half-way through the riff, creating a jarring, disorienting effect which doesn't resolve itself until he realigns with the band.

Not surprisingly, the Motown "experiment" was judged a success— Vee Jay even rushed out a hasty *Best Of John Lee Hooker* in the wake of "Boom Boom"'s success—and Hunter, Cosby and company were re-commissioned in the latter half of 1962 for two more sessions from which Hooker's next Vee Jay album, *The Big Soul Of John Lee Hooker*, released in early '63, was assembled. The first was a "quickie" which produced a mere four sides in the same horn-riffing, piano-tinkling, easy-rocking vein. "Old Time Shimmy" found Hooker announcing for the first, if not the last, time that *"the twist ain't nothin' but the old-time shimmy,"* but "Onions" picked up where "Keep Your Hands To Yourself" left off as a vocal Hookerization of a recent instrumental hit. As the title might suggest, the piece was based on Booker T & The MGs' then-current hit "Green Onions," with its starkly memorable principal riff transferred from slinky Hammond organ to abrasive saxes and the beat stomped rather than shuffled, as Hooker demands that his baby bring him her onions, not to mention black-eyed peas, chicken and other delicacies. "You Know I Love You" and "Send Me Your Pillow" respectively Hook-erized Barbara Lynn's "You'll Lose A Good Thing" (a recent R&B Number 1 which also cracked the pop Top Ten) and the sentimental '40s ballad "Send Me The Pillow You Dream On." Hooker was to repeat the latter trick at his next studio date, when he audaciously Hookerized no less a standard than "I Left My Heart In San Francisco."

"Two of the best-known songs in the *world*—and I reached out and got 'em," he says with some satisfaction. "That's an old song. I sing *"send me the pillow you been cryin' on."* I turned it around, like you miss me, you layin' in bed at night cryin' about me 'cause I ain't around." His Hookerization of "I Left My Heart In San Francisco" as "Frisco Blues" derived from his admiration for Tony Bennett.

I'm not ashamed to say I love his singing and his style, which is not my style, but I love his type of singing [he told Greg Drust]. I love ballads and he's one out of all of them that I picked for my favorite, Tony Bennett. And I used to sit up and play that record and I would hear him sing it and it just go right through me and so I had to do it in my version. And I did it. What gave me the idea for doing it was I met this young lady in San Francisco a long time ago, and we would go out to dinner or she would come to see me play and she liked that song. I went to her house and she would just play that record by Tony Bennett. And she said, "I betcha you could do this." I said, "Yes, but not like him . . . I'd do it in my version."

Hooker's "version" turned out to be a chugging medium shuffle, some-what marred by the spectacularly out-of-tune lead guitar, which rhapso-dizes about foggy mornings and cable-cars in terms which would surely have delighted his future hometown's Chamber of Commerce. The track attained cult status: Leon Russell found its incongruities so delightful that he once cut a rockabilly version of "Misty" as a tribute.

Joe Hunter and his Motown mercenaries were back the next time Hooker went into the studio, and this time they brought company. Hooker has always asserted, and most discographies have supported his claim, that "on my next recording session, I did it with the backing group Martha & The Vandellas. The name don't appear on the record anyplace because at that time they was with Motown Records and I could not use the name." Martha Reeves had started out as a secretary at Motown before parlaying her vocal trio The Del-Phis (herself plus Rosalyn Ashford and Betty Kelley) into regular work as backing singers on Motown sessions. There are two differing accounts of the origin of the "Vandellas" name: the mundane one suggests that it was a simple combination of Detroit's Van Dyke Avenue with the first name of singer Della Reese, but for perverse personal reasons this writer has always preferred the other explanation: that Marvin Gaye bestowed the name on Reeves and her colleagues as a word-play on "vandals" after their high-energy back-up work nearly stole the show on his sessions for "Hitch Hike" and "Stubborn Kind Of Fellow." After paying their session dues, the renamed Del-Phis finally graduated to front-line status as featured artists in their own right, racking up an impressive string of hits commencing with 1963's "Come And Get These Memories."

So Hooker cut with The Vandellas? It's a great story, but external evidence suggests that it's not true. What seems rather more likely is that Hooker simply mistook one Motown back-up vocal team for another. Additional light was cast on this particular Hooker session by Mary Wilson, of the original Supremes, in her autobiography, *Dreamgirl: My Life As A Supreme*.[11]

> *One day [she wrote], Joe Hunter pulled me aside and said, "I can give you a hundred dollars to come with me to Chicago." "Say no more!" Compared to the lousy five or ten bucks we got for every song we recorded, a hundred dollars was a fortune. I went to Chicago with James Jamerson, Hank Crosby [sic], and anyone else Joe wanted to take along. Like many of the other [Motown] bandleaders, Joe was very generous about sharing his freelance work with others. Also with us were The Andantes, Motown's in-house background vocal group—Jackie Hicks, Marlene Barrow, and Louvain Demps . . . this was a session for Jerry Butler that Curtis Mayfield was producing for Vee Jay. We recorded a song called "A Teenie Weenie Bit Of Your Love." I also worked on blues legend John Lee Hooker's "Boom Boom Boom" [sic].*

Pardon? Excuse me? "Boom Boom?" The female backing vocals on "Boom Boom" are about as prominent as the french horns, the string quartet and John Coltrane's five-minute soprano sax solo: in other words, they ain't in there. On the other hand, one of the titles from the session which produced "Frisco Blues" was "She Shot Me Down," a listless, half-assed retread of "Boom Boom" which rewrites the song in the passive voice, enabling Hooker to play a man who is "shot down" and taken home. "She Shot Me Down" does indeed feature female backing singers—presumably Wilson and The Andantes—chanting *"Boom-boom, boom-boom"* in reply to Hooker's lead.[12] Unfortunately, the rest of that particular day's work proved scarcely more productive.

The agenda for the *Big Soul* sessions was obviously to shift Hooker's music about as far away from the world of campuses, coffee-houses and the Newport Folk Festival as it could possibly go. If the object of the exercise was to reposition him squarely at the heart of the R&B market, and reintroduce him to black audiences as a contemporary performer in the tradition of Ray Charles or Bobby Bland, it was an almost unqualified disaster. The earlier, deeply funky, "Onions" session had worked out fine,

---

11 Sidgwick & Jackson, 1987.
12 I am indebted to Norman Darwen for this particular piece of R&B detective work.

but this one ranged from the almost-quite-good—the audacious "Frisco Blues"—to the frankly embarrassing. He doesn't even sing on the title track: "Big Soul" is a chugging, organ-led "Night Train"–style instrumental with the backing singers oo-wahing away for all they're worth and Hooker's guitar rifting darkly away somewhere in the background murk. The session's nadir came with the frankly surreal "No One Told Me," in which Hooker and his accompanists seemingly attempt to improvise a bossanova ballad, supper-club-in-hell style, and succeed only in proving that the style is not one which lends itself gracefully to improvisation.

Still, better was to come. By the time Hooker next recorded for Vee Jay, he had joined the steadily growing number of blues artists who were opening a second front for their music in Europe, thereby establishing the vital new beach-head for the blues which, as things turned out, was to ensure its ultimate survival—not to mention his own.

Europe . . . fills a big gap in the American blues market, and many a bluesman has found to his surprise that his biggest market is in France or England . . . One month Hooker can be found working around joints and bins in Detroit; then he may move to a "folk" nightclub in New York, where he entertains the college set; then on to the Newport Jazz Festival or a European tour; and he occasionally records a tune that becomes a hit rock-and-roll item among teenagers, like his potent "Boom Boom." From one record or personal appearance to the next, Hooker has at least four different audiences to choose from—and choose he does, going around the circle from one group to another, modifying his style and material slightly to suit the tastes of his listeners.
—Charles Keil, *Urban Blues*, 1966

Like not a few other things, the American Folk Blues Festival was the brainchild of Willie Dixon, the gargantuan bassist/songwriter/producer/session fixer who'd served as Chess Records' ramrod and all-around *éminence grise* since 1954. Dixon and the pianist Memphis Slim had toured Israel in 1960 and had a lot of fun, but made so little money that they'd had to gig their way through Europe in order to finance their trip home. Along the way, the German jazz critic Joachim Berendt had put Dixon in touch with Horst Lippmann and Fritz Rau, two German jazz fans turned promoters. Together, they hatched the idea of bringing a package tour of blues artists to Europe under the auspices of Lippmann and Rau's Concert Bureau agency, with Concert Bureau organizing the shows and Dixon co-ordinating the talent. Hooker was hired to participate, alongside his old hero T-Bone Walker, Dixon's sidekick Memphis Slim, folk-blues veterans Sonny Terry & Brownie McGhee, harpist Shakey Jake, and singer Helen Humes, who'd "answered" Hooker's "I'm In The Mood" with her own "I Ain't In The Mood" back in 1951. Bringing up the rear as the house rhythm section were drummer Jump Jackson and, behind his much-traveled bull fiddle, Dixon himself.

Singularly fertile ground awaited the seeds sown by the American Folk Blues Festival. "Authentic" African-American music was highly prized in Europe among a small but influential coterie of buffs and intel-lectuals, and even in generally racist countries, visiting African-American musicians received the kind of treatment appropriate to distinguished foreign artists rather than, say, impoverished students from Senegal or Zaire. The bluesmen played in the most prestigious concert halls, stayed in the best hotels, and were, at least by the standards to which they had become accustomed at home, extremely well paid. By any standards, it was a serious culture shock for all concerned.

"The first time I went to Europe was 1962," says Hooker, "and bo-o-o-oy, it was just like the President or Jesus comin' in. All you could hear was John Lee Hooker. Every night was a sell-out. Standing room only, no matter how big the place was. I stayed over there a long time. I went over there for Horst Lippmann, and then I went back and back and back again. It was just fantastic. I was the biggest thing they ever had over there at that time. I got more bigger over there than I did in the U.S.A, much bigger. My impressions was that it was a lot different [in Europe] in every way. I had to get adjusted to it, gettin' used to the food, adjusted that you couldn't go out any time of night and find somethin' to eat, you couldn't get up in the morning and get yourself a good American breakfast. You couldn't go to restaurants all through the day; they'd eat and close down. A lotta things I couldn't get ad-justed to."

One aspect of the Euro-experience was, however, just like old times: Hooker got himself a hit record from that tour, and he didn't get paid. "You remember a record I did in Europe that was so big, Number One? 'Shake It Baby'? I did that for Horst Lippmann: never got a *dime*." In all fairness to Lippmann, he claims not to have gotten paid either.

No record company wanted to record the blues festival at first [he told Don Snowden].[13] The very first [live album] we produced on our own and it was released on Brunswick, Deutsche Grammophon, Polydor. We paid for all this and actually got nothing for it. We thought it was a good investment because it's part of history to document it on record. Two songs out of this recording got very popular in France—one was John Lee Hooker's "Shake It Baby." Because of the impact of this record, Phonogram came in and for the next years up until 1967, all the festivals have been released by Philips/Mercury in America.

We had a ball, start to finish [reminisced T-Bone Walker to his biographer, Helen Oakley Dance],[14] and couldn't believe the kind of audiences we had. People over there listen. You've got to be a showman back here [in the U.S.]. Over there, the first time I did the splits the fans booed! That was hard to credit, but it was all right with me. They came to hear the music. From there on, I played wherever we were.

During October of 1962, the tour stormed through France, Italy, Germany, Denmark, Sweden and Switzerland: amazingly enough—considering the knock-on impact of the blues on British rock, and post-R&B Brit-rock on multinational pop—no U.K. concerts had been booked. However, thanks to sponsorship from the British jazz weekly *Melody Maker*, a single show at Manchester's Free Trade Hall—billed as "Cavalcade Of Blues"—was added at the next-to-last minute. The souvenir album, however, wasn't recorded at any of the actual concerts, but on October 18 in Deutsche Grammophon's Hamburg studio. Immediately after that night's concert at Hamburg University's Auditorium Maximum, the entire cast shifted lock, stock and the proverbial barrel to the DG studio and, between midnight and 5 A.M., they performed their show all over again, this time for an audience which was not so much an "invited" crowd as one which, according to Dance, "materialized like magic." Nonetheless, they were at least as "live" as any imaginable bunch of paying customers could have been expected to be.

---

13 In *I Am The Blues*, by Willie Dixon and Don Snowden (Quartet, 1989), from which much of this account of the '62 Festival is derived.
14 Quoted in *Stormy Monday: The T-Bone Walker Story*, by Helen Oakley Dance (Da Capo, 1987).

Peter "Memphis Slim" Chatman was one of the greatest blues pianists of a generation wondrously endowed with great blues pianists. It would take a brave man to volunteer to spell Memphis Slim at the 88s, and a doubly brave one to do so if piano was merely his second instrument, and if his primary renown was as a guitarist (not to mention as a vocalist, an acrobat, and a seriously snappy dresser). Several thousand miles away from his Southwestern stomping grounds, T-Bone Walker took the opportunity to let his metaphorical hair down and have some fun as a temporary sideman by unveiling his unexpectedly deft and sparkling piano style. On this European jaunt, he played behind Sonny Terry (though not behind Brownie McGhee) and, more significantly, behind Hooker. Actually, on "Shake It Baby"—the irresistible instant boogie which turned out to be "a big hit all over Europe . . . *the* party record"[15]—*alongside* Hooker would be more accurate. For a whole heap of reasons—the bond of mutual respect between the two men, the joyful explosion of ideas T-Bone unleashes so exuberantly from the piano, the vociferous acclaim of the small but enthusiastic audience—the pair of them simply caught fire.

The song, seemingly conjured from thin air, is little more than a Hookerized extemporization on the same *"shake it one time for me"* monologue which links "Pinetop's Boogie-Woogie" with "Whole Lotta Shakin' Goin' On," with Dixon and Jackson putting some real pump into one of Hooker's favorite backbeats. What makes it happen big-time is the genuine human electricity that crackles back and forth between Walker and Hooker, as pianist and singer/guitarist urge each other on and on in wave upon successive wave of *diminuendo* and *crescendo*. The performance ran a little over four minutes: relatively concise by the standards of the modern single, but decidedly *de trop* for 1962. "Shake It Baby" was therefore split, à la James Brown, into two two-minute chunks, one on each side of a 45. Considering its success as a dance record, partygoers all over Europe were probably injured in the stampedes to flip the record over before the dancers lost the groove.

The other two Hooker selections which made it onto the album were rather less auspicious. "Let's Make It Baby" is an undistinguished "Boom Boom"–alike during which Hooker's idiosyncratic timing consistently wrong-foots his accompanists: as the piece winds down, Hooker can be heard proudly announcing, "My 88 man, T-Bone Walker!"[16] "The Right

---

15 French record producer Philippe Rault, quoted in Dixon and Snowden, *op. cit.*
16 Helen Oakley Dance transcribes this as *"Mighty* 88 man": not accurate, but undoubtedly true.

Time" is a leisurely stroll around the perimeters of an old Nappy Brown hit which had been revived to considerable effect by Ray Charles during his barn-storming show at the 1958 Newport Jazz Festival: Walker, Jackson and Dixon recover with considerable poise from Hooker's decision to start singing the first verse in the tenth bar of a twelve-bar intro.

By November, Hooker had returned to the States, back to the same old grind. Nevertheless, the European tour had proved to be something of an eye-opener: Hooker's horizons, both artistic and financial, had broadened considerably. A bluesman, he now knew, could travel overseas and get the kind of respect—and make the kind of money—which he was denied at home. He could play the finest concert halls, stay in the best hotels, be treated like an artist, and get paid accordingly. Like General MacArthur and Arnold Schwarzenegger, he would be back.

"I remember him doing his first big European tour when I was around twelve, something like that. I remember him getting ready to go to Europe," says Zakiya. "But when he was working around the United States, we still got to see him pretty regular. When he [subsequently] toured Europe we wouldn't see him for maybe six [months] . . . long spans of time. We was always excited when he'd come back because he'd always bring gifts. I look back on it now, and I really admire him because he stuck to what he wanted to do and he didn't let anybody take that dream. He did it. He was just so pleased to be doing his music that he didn't really concern himself a lot with the money. As long as he had enough to take care of his family, and have the things that he needed, he was pretty much satisfied. I'm sure that he knew that *somebody* was cheatin'— you know?—but he just wanted to do his music."

Meanwhile, Hooker was marking time: touring the folk clubs and coffee-houses while preparing for his next Vee Jay session, not to mention enjoying being back in the bosom of his family. "I was playing a gig at a club in Toronto called the Penny Farthing," says John Hammond, recalling his first meeting with Hooker, "and I was on the show with John Lee—I'm sure he doesn't remember it, but I do—and he had just gotten off the bus from Detroit, and he didn't know where he was staying yet. He'd been to Toronto before—this was in the area called Yorkville, which was the Village of Toronto—and this was a coffee-house, and not a great one. I admired him right away. He was just himself, you know, he got himself to his gigs and he played his ass off. I worked on a lot of gigs with him in the early '60s, when I started playing, when he just played acoustic guitar, in Toronto and Detroit and in New York at Gerde's Folk City . . . I've seen him play gigs where he just played electric guitar solo."

A live recording, cut during two successive weekends at San Francisco's Sugar Hill club in early November of 1962, provides some indication of the kind of shows Hooker was performing at that time. Playing solo on electric guitar rather than acoustic—as he preferred to do by this time at all but the most rigidly purist venues—he performed standards associated with other artists, and re-presented or reinvented his older repertoire as well as working up some powerful new material. "I Was Standing By The Wayside" was loosely derived from the same sources as Robert Johnson's celebrated "Crossroads," while "My Babe" (the Little Walter hit which Willie Dixon had created by secularizing the gospel standard "This Train") and "Key To The Highway" (a Big Bill Broonzy composition most frequently associated with Sonny Terry & Brownie McGhee) find Hooker singing the original melodies but junking the chord progressions in favor of his own patented riffs. "Dimples" reappears as "I Like To See You Walkin'," and "Every Night" as "It's You I Love, Baby" alongside an incarnation of "Run On" which bore little resemblance to its original appearance as a precursor to "Boom Boom." An oddly perfunctory "Boogie Chillen" is offset by a moody, deeply-grained "Driftin' Blues" and a bouncy, rocking "I Need Some Money."

Of the two important new songs, "TB Is Killin' Me" borrowed a line or two from St. Louis Jimmy Oden's standard "Goin' Down Slow," but it had an ominous undertow of impending doom which was all its own, while "No Man's Land" was one of his most important songs of the '60s. Essentially an answer to Woody Guthrie's anthem "This Land Is Your Land," it stated precisely the opposite case: that the land belongs to nobody, and that we, as human beings, are doing no more than simply passing through. This was what the Native Americans believed, which was why they were prepared to "sell" the land to European traders for beads and blankets: according to their philosophical lights, anyone who believed that land could be bought, sold or owned was plainly deluded and should therefore simply be humored. Hooker's take on this clash of values is as stark and poetic as anything he ever wrote or sang.

You may have money
Fine clothes and everything
But one day you got to die

And leave it all behind
This land, this land is no man's land
You oughtta be ashamed, you oughtta be ashamed
Fightin' over your buryin' ground

His next Vee Jay studio date, early in 1963, represented a headlong retreat from the botched experiment of the *Big Soul* sessions. This time Hooker performed with only drums for support, though his guitar sound was so full and rich, the (unnamed) drummer so tight and sympathetic, that the absence of a bass or second guitar scarcely proved to be any kind of problem. "My Grindin' Mill" revisited the "Grinder Man" he'd cut for Henry Stone in Miami; the venerable "Bottle Up And Go" harked back to his original Detroit house-party repertoire, and "I Want To Ramble" Hookerized Junior Parker's 1953 Sun recording of "Feelin' Good," which itself had been a reworking of "Boogie Chillen," "Sadie Mae" was a virtual "answer record" to "Process": this time Hooker requests Miss Sadie Mae to *"curl my baby's hair for me"* so that he can see her *"long curly hair hangin' down"*: after all, he tells his listeners, Miss Sadie Mae *"can curl hair better'n anybody else ever hit this town."* Best of all, however, was the exuberantly lascivious "This Is Hip," with its loose-limbed shuffle beat and memorable refrain, *"I messed around an'-uh . . . fell in love."* Inexplicably, the song stayed in the can for almost twenty years, surfacing only in 1981 as the title track of a British compilation, but it proved popular enough to be revived, at a delightfully rowdy and rockin' session with Ry Cooder and the rhythm section from his short-lived "roots supergroup" Little Village, for 1991's *Mr. Lucky*.

Next time around, though, it was back to the big-band format with the Motown moonlighters' last Hooker hoorah. "I Want To Shout" was full-blown jump—deviating only from the archetype with Hooker's resolutely irregular timing and the enthusiastic shooby-doobies (or maybe it's *"Shout, baby, shout"*) from The Andantes (or maybe this time it actually *was* The Vandellas)—as was "I Want To Hug You," the debut of a boogying staple-in-the-making sounding rather less confident than it would do in subsequent incarnations. "Love Is A Burning Thing" borrows its chord changes from Jimmy Reed's "Honest I Do," its lyrical core from Johnny Cash's "Ring Of Fire," and its ambience from the post-gospel big-balladry of Ray Charles, Solomon Burke and Bobby "Blue" Bland. The moving gospelly-ballad "Don't Look Back," later covered by Van Morrison and Them and revived yet again as a Hooker/Morrison duet, had been attempted at an earlier session, but this version was the clincher. The lyrics steadfastly denounce those who are *"living in the past,"* but the weary, regretful tones which cloud Hooker's voice undercut them by saying something rather different. The words tell us that we must be resolute and forward-looking: the voice tells us that things are never quite that simple, and that moving on can be painful even when you know that there is no real alternative.

"Birmingham Blues" paraphrases the classic opening line of Tommy Johnson's 1928 "Big Road Blues" as *"I ain't going down to Birmingham by myself,"* by way of reference to the Civil Rights marches which Dr. Martin Luther King Jr was leading on Birmingham, Alabama, in April and May of 1963, and then follows it with as uncompromising and passionate an expression of pure, cold rage as you'll find in any African-American music of its decade. *"Get me a plane,"* he sings, *"and fly over Birmingham/drop me a bomb, keep on flyin' on."* Soon he's junked the structure (what little there is of it) and begun to preach. He returns to the theme of "No Man's Land"—*"GOD made this land, this land, and he made it for no one man!"* he cries. *"GOD made everybody equal! Equal! EQUAL!"*—but it is now blended with the politics of "Democrat Man," as Hooker begins to praise not Dr. King, but President John F. Kennedy, for his support of the Civil Rights movement. *"One thing I do know,"* he says. *"Our President . . . he are doin' all he can . . . for every man . . . equal rights."* On the fade, he recites a list of the Southern states soon to be visited by those prepared to go down the big road together. Some commentators never tire of pointing out the apparent lack of overt social comment in the blues, but even they would have to concede that "Birmingham Blues" goes an awful long way toward redressing that particular balance.

And "I'm Leaving" simply rocked. There's a certain kind of Hooker song that's really nothing more than a band playing a single riff in a certain groove over and over again while Hooker free-associates on two or three key lines: but when it's the right band playing the right riff in the right groove and Hooker's doing his stuff with the right two or three lines, then the effect is nothing less than magical. "I'm Leaving" is one of those.

The fruits of these sessions were combined on *The Big Soul Of John Lee Hooker's* successor, *John Lee Hooker On Campus*. To a greater extent than anything that had come before, it epitomized the increasing schizophrenia of Hooker's career and of Vee Jay's approach to it. The cover depicted a charcoal drawing of someone clearly intended to represent Hooker, though the white-haired, benevolently smiling, grandfatherly figure shown strumming his acoustic guitar into a pair of microphones bore a rather greater resemblance to Leadbelly in his last years than to Hooker in his mid-forties. Anybody who concluded from the packaging that what they were getting was a live recording of Hooker playing solo to a college audience would have been somewhat nonplussed by the record itself, which juxtaposed selections from both the downhomey drummer-only session and the uptownish big-band date.

On Campus, which turned out to be Hooker's last studio album for Vee Jay, arrived complete with a loftily condescending liner-note finely calculated to appeal to the most patronizing instincts of white readers, and equally likely to offend just about any African-American unfortunate enough to read it, let alone Hooker himself. "John Lee Hooker is one of the few authentic blues artists left in this country today," begins the anonymous author, not unreasonably. However, he (it's bound to be a "he") then goes onto assert:

> *The truth of the matter is that the authentic blues of the John Lee Hooker type was spawned and nurtured in the misery, ignorance and destitution of the Negro in a particular American society. As the plight of the American Negro improved and he became better educated, he developed other methods of expression and sang of his troubles less and less. He became a voter in most states and instead of singing dejectedly about his problems, he went to school and to the polls and learned to do something about them. All the while, the authentic blues was dying out. The American art blues was taking its place. Blues is now sung by artists who enjoy the best of luxurious living. Off-stage, their speech is clipped and articulate. Their wives and children often attend the best colleges and universities . . . only the John Lee Hookers of the profession remain to remind us from whence [sic] all this came—raw, unbridled, painful misery . . .*

In other words: Roll up! Roll up! Getcha "raw, unbridled, painful" "misery, ignorance and destitution" right here! This guy doesn't "enjoy the best of luxurious living!" His family don't "attend the best colleges and universities!" His speech is not "clipped and articulate!" He's still "singing dejectedly about his problems!"

With supporters like this, who needs backbiters and syndicators?

10. ... Blues Boom

Does anybody really think it's weird that all these English "pop" groups are making large doses of loot? It's pretty simple, actually. They take the style (energy construct, general form, etc.) of black blues, country or city, and combine it with the visual image of white American non-conformity, i.e, the beatnik, and score very heavily. Plus the fact that these English boys are literally "hipper" than their white counterparts in the U.S., hipper because as it is readily seen, they have actually made a contemporary form, unlike most white U.S. "folk singers" who are content to imitate "ancient" blues forms and older singers, arriving at a kind of popular song (at its most hideous in groups like Peter, Paul and Mary, etc.), which has little to do with black reality, which would have been its strength, anyway—that reference to a deeper emotional experience. As one young poet said, "At least The Rolling Stones come on like English crooks."
—Leroi Jones (Amiri Baraka as now is), *downbeat*, 1965[1]

You know, the English can say "marvellous" pretty good. They can't say "raunchy" so good, though.
—Bob Dylan, in his celebrated *Playboy* interview with Nat Hentoff, March 1966[2]

And lo, in the third year, the Newport Festivals arose from the dead. In July 1963, after two years in exile by way of penance for the 1960 riots, both the Jazz and Folk festivals returned, suitably chastened, to Freebody Park. Not surprisingly, John Lee Hooker received a return booking to the Folk Festival. Playing in standard tuning on the acoustic guitar in which, by now, he was plainly losing interest, he performed two sets: on July 26 he appeared solo, and on July 28, he was backed by an unnamed acoustic bassist—possibly the unfortunate Bill Lee—with whom he seemed to have little musical rapport. Opening with a Hookerization of Otis Rush's 1956

---

1 As reprinted in Jones's collection *Black Music* (Quill, 1967).
2 As reprinted in *Bob Dylan: A Retrospective*, edited by Craig McGregor (Picador, 1975).

blues hit "I Can't Quit You Baby" (composed by Willie Dixon), he represented "Hobo Blues" (retitled "Freight Train To My Friend") and "Tupelo" (plus its near-identical twin, "Mighty Fire"), reworked Blind Lemon Jefferson's "Matchbox" as "Bus Station Blues," and demonstrated that a single undermiked acoustic guitar couldn't provide enough justice to enable him to do justice to the rocking likes of "Boom Boom" and "Let's Make It." Most memorably, he introduced the feverish "Stop Baby Don't Hold Me," which finds him attempting to fend off a woman who seems to know his desires better than he does, and the affecting "Sometime Baby You Make Me Feel So Bad," some of the lyrics of which seem almost like a personal credo:

> *I still love you*
> *Old time love*
> *I don't have that kind of love, baby*
> *That modern love*
> *I have that love*
> *That old time love*
> *In my heart for you*
> *My love.*

"Me and Brownie and Sonny and all the folk-singers," Hooker tells the audience at one point, "we are here paying our dues to the natural facts. We have come a long way—the entertainers—trying to reach you, to bring you the message of the blues. Sometimes we are traveling late at night, trying to make it to you . . . sometimes you tired when you reach your destination, but you payin' your dues to the facts. We are tryin' to please you the best that we know, and we hope you accept it."

Making his Newport debut that year was young John Hammond. "I first met and played with John Lee in 1963, at the Newport Folk Festival," he says, though—as we've seen—he's placed their first meeting elsewhere and elsewhen in other interviews. "It was one of my first big shows ever, and that was just about at the height of the blues revival of the early '60s. I was on the same stage with John Lee and [Reverend] Gary Davis, Brownie McGhee and Sonny Terry, and Dave Van Ronk, and I was trembling, to say the least. John Lee played acoustic guitar, solo, and mesmerized the whole audience. It was just staggering. He was unbelievable. He did 'Texas Flood' "—Hammond presumably refers to "Tupelo": right natural disaster, wrong song—"and it was just unforgettable. I had been a fan of his since I was about fourteen, and had just about everything that he'd recorded up to that point, so it was beyond my imagination to actually be on the bandstand with him four years later."

The Festival was taped, as were its predecessors in 1959 and 1960, by Vanguard Records. Extracts from Hooker's performance were included on one of the resulting albums, *Blues At Newport '63*, which provided a life-changing experience for at least one listener: a fourteen-year-old girl named Bonnie Raitt, who cited it, some thirty odd years later, as "the record that turned me around."[3]

It still keeps my taste anchored to the more modal and raw Delta blues as opposed to the slicker, urban sound [she continued]. Mississippi John Hurt was singing "Candy Man," John Lee Hooker was on there, and Dave Van Ronk and John Hammond, who were young white blues guys. I'd never imagined that white guys could sing the blues authentically—let alone white women. At fourteen, I sat there trying to figure out all those songs, till my fingers literally bled. There was a mournful quality, a dark of night of the soul, an aching loneliness that, as a teenager, you feel intensely personally—whether you're not getting on with your parents, or feel nobody understands you. There was all that, plus humor and bite and everything else I love about the Delta blues, on that one record.

In a canny example of music-biz horse-trading, Vee Jay licensed two of Hooker's Newport performances to Vanguard Records for inclusion on their album in exchange for the right to release his complete show on their own label as *John Lee Hooker At Newport*, which appeared the following year. However, both Vee and Jay—not to mention Ewart Abner, Calvin Carter, and Al Smith—had rather more on their minds than the vicissitudes of John Lee Hooker's career. At the time, it must have seemed as if Vee Jay was riding high, but with benefit of hindsight, it would be truer to say that the company was riding for a serious fall.

In 1962, Vee Jay had scored a massive pop hit—a chart-topper, no less—with Gene Chandler's surreal post-doowop masterpiece "Duke of Earl." Jerry Butler was doing well, as were Betty Everett, Dee Clark—the latter described by Charlie Gillett as "a singer contracted by the company because of his ability to sound like either Little Richard or Clyde Mc-

---

3 Talking to *Q* Magazine, June 1995.

Phatter"[4]—and Jimmy Reed, then enjoying the tail end of his extraordinary string of a dozen Hot 100 hits. None of this was doing much for Hooker, though. "There were several other big artists that they had at that time, Jimmy Reed, Dee Clark, Jerry Butler. He treated them all better than he did me and Jimmy," he grumbles. "They got some money out of it. [Vee Jay] did me really in, me and Jimmy Reed. You go down there to borrow money, you sit there all day just to get . . . they didn't want to give us advances or nothin'. And we made 'em tons of money. Dee Clark and Jerry Butler, they got clothes, a new car, money—with *my* money and Jimmy Reed's money that we'd been making for them."

The company had also started fooling around with white boys. Thanks to a steer from the ubiquitous Henry Stone, Vee Jay had acquired the services of The Four Seasons, a New Jersey vocal group whose principal assets were the dentist's-drill falsetto of their front man Frankie Valli, and the formidable in-house songwriting machine of independent producer Bob Crewe and former Royal Teen Bob Gaudio, the latter the Seasons' equivalent of The Beach Boys' Brian Wilson. Crewe had cut several tracks on the Seasons at his own expense before schlepping the masters down to a DJs' convention in Miami and playing them to Stone, who—in his own inimitable manner—started a buzz which had label reps swarming like flies.

> *We wound up making a deal with Ewart Abner at Vee Jay [Crewe told Joe Smith].[5] On paper, it was one of the largest deals that had ever been made on a record. Later down the line, I realized that we probably should have made a deal with CBS for five cents a record, because maybe we would have gotten a better count. There were times when Ewart could be found in Las Vegas, blowing a quarter of a million bucks a night at the crap table.*

The Seasons gave Vee Jay three Number One hits in 1963, with "Sherry," "Big Girls Don't Cry" and "Walk Like A Man." According to Frankie Valli,[6] "there was very little money, maybe an accumulation of thirty thousand dollars. Later on, we found out that there was a lot more money, but we never saw any of it." So they quit Vee Jay and signed with Mercury.

---

4 In Gillett's invaluable *The Sound Of The City* (Souvenir Press, 1970 rev. 1983).
5 Quoted in Smith's *On The Record: An Oral History Of Popular Music* (Sidgwick & Jackson, 1988).
6 Smith, *op. cit.*

Vee Jay's other experiment that year was to take on something extremely unlikely: a British rock band. For some years, their British outlet had been via the giant Electrical and Musical Industries combine, better known as EMI, who'd licensed Vee Jay sides for release first on their Top Rank label (originally an offshoot of the Rank Organization cinema chain), and later on Stateside, a catch-all label for product from a variety of smaller U.S. companies, including Imperial, Sue, United Artists, and Berry Gordy's Tamla and Motown labels. EMI's principal transatlantic subsidiary was Capitol Records, which they'd bought out in 1956, and it was Capitol to whom U.S. rights in EMI product were traditionally offered. Despite being owned by EMI, Capitol was fiercely protective of its editorial independence, and the company remained perennially reluctant to take up the option of getting involved with any of EMI's traditionally unsaleable "current English sensations." The parent company was, therefore, often humiliatingly reduced to peddling their wares to the smaller and more adventurous enterprises who were more frequently accustomed to coming, caps—and masters—in hand, to them. Thus it was that Vee Jay acquired, almost by accident, the rights to the first two U.K. chart-toppers by The Beatles.

"The first people I spoke to were Vee Jay," claimed Brian Epstein, The Beatles' manager, in his (ghosted) autobiography *A Cellarful of Noise*,[7] "... because they had done a very good job with Frank Ifield, who was a successful young British star.[8] But of course Ifield had only limited success in America, like every other British artiste since the war." Contrariwise, Beatles biographer Philip Norman states that it was The Beatles' producer George Martin, rather than Epstein, who cut the Vee Jay deal, and that Vee Jay was by no means Martin's first call after receiving the knock-back from Capitol.[9] The Fab Four's in-house blues fans, Ringo Starr[10] and John Lennon, were thrilled to be on the same label as

---

7 *A Cellarful Of Noise* (Four Square, 1964). The ghost was the late and sorely missed veteran PR, sage and *bon viveur* Derek Taylor.
8 Actually, Ifield was a transplanted Australian whose gimmick was yodeling. He peaked with "I Remember You," which reached Number One in 1962; unaccountably, his career went into decline with the arrival of The Beatles and their successors.
9 In *Shout!: The True Story Of The Beatles* (Elm Tree, 1981; rev. Penguin, 1991).
10 Before Starr joined The Beatles, he had made vague plans to emigrate to the States, and had gone so far as to fill out an application form. He had chosen Houston, Texas, as his destination for no other reason than that Lightnin' Hopkins lived there. After The Beatles imploded at the end of the decade, Starr fulfilled at least part of his early ambition by drumming on sessions with both Howlin' Wolf and B. B. King.

cult heroes like John Lee Hooker and Jimmy Reed: The Beatles' first-ever recording session, cut in Germany in the spring of '62, had actually included an attempt at cutting a version of Reed's "Take Out Some Insurance." However, when their delight was scarcely reciprocated. Neither "Please Please Me" nor "From Me To You" made any significant impact on the U.S. charts, and the album *Introducing The Beatles* fared no better. When The Beatles' third British Number One, "She Loves You," also failed to impress the hardnoses at Capitol, it was offered to Vee Jay, who rejected it in their turn. The single ended up with the Philadelphia-based Swan label, a company so tiny that its most notable act was Dickie Doo And The Don'ts.

But Cinderella finally did get to go to the ball: Capitol finally, grudgingly, swung behind The Beatles after "I Want To Hold Your Hand" gave them their fourth U.K. Number One. In January 1964, the record broke out like wildfire when a DJ on a small Washington, DC station began playing it to death—his copy had come not from Capitol, but from his air-stewardess girlfriend who'd picked it up in London—and by the time The Beatles arrived in the U.S. to play *The Ed Sullivan Show* the following month, everything with "Beatles" written on it was sprinting out of the stores like it had stolen something. Vee Jay's licensing deal with EMI had given them a mere one-year lease on their Beatles material, and said lease was about to expire, so they speedily re-released all the Beatles stuff they had before the deal ran out and the rights reverted back to Capitol. Next thing anyone knew, The Beatles were occupying the entire Top 5 with singles on three different labels. Two of them were on Vee Jay.

A steadier and more efficiently run company could have used the income and the prestige garnered by those Four Seasons and Beatles hits to pole-vault itself into the big leagues. (Imagine, if you will, how pop-culture history might have been altered had Epstein and Martin assigned The Beatles' pre-Capitol U.S. rights to Berry Gordy.) Instead, the sudden huge demand for Beatles product actually helped to sink Vee Jay completely. A big hit breaking out suddenly and unexpectedly means that records need to be pressed and distributed *immediately*: like, *yesterday*. Pressing plants demand to be paid in cash on the barrelhead; distributors pay up some time in the future. A company which needs to lay out cash in front to a pressing plant against cash *real soon now* from its distributors needs a strong, steady cash-flow and solid financial reserves, or else a runaway hit can literally destroy it. Steady cash-flow and solid financial reserves were exactly what Vee Jay didn't have.

A variety of factors contributed to the company's ignominious demise. One such was undoubtedly white-owned distributors' resentment of a black label which seemed to be growing too big for the boots assigned to it by the industry, but ultimately the other factors all shared a single common root: the company's deadly combination of financial ineptitude and sheer greed. We've already heard, from Bob Crewe, of Ewart Abner's profligacy at the gaming tables; and as Nelson George dryly points out in *The Death Of Rhythm & Blues*, "Vee Jay is remembered as being extravagant and wasteful even by some black deejays, a group never known to pass up an expensive good time." In his definitive account of the Motown heyday, *Where Did Our Love Go*, George goes into rather more detail:

> One case in point is the free junket to Las Vegas that Vee Jay sponsored for twelve influential R&B deejays in the early sixties. One participant remembers, "They asked us what we wanted. The guys didn't want free poker chips or liquor. They wanted women." So Vee Jay flew in twelve tall blonds from Oslo, Norway, via the North Pole to Los Angeles to Las Vegas, for a Friday, Saturday, and Sunday of fun. The deejays left for work happy on Monday morning. "They could have been bigger than Motown, but," the participant concluded, "they needed a bookkeeper."

Hooker would certainly second that last remark. "The company went under, and I never did see a royalty check. Mm-*mm*! Got *nothin'*. I will never will forget that, either. That will always go with me, what they did."

By the time Vee Jay began proceedings to file for bankruptcy, Hooker wasn't even in the country. He'd cut one last session for them during early 1964, leaving ten tracks for what would have been his next Vee Jay studio album. Surviving session logs don't name the guitarist, bassist and drummer who backed him that time, though the trio in question didn't sound terribly dissimilar to the Lefty Bates/Sylvester Hickman/Jimmy Turner combo which had accompanied him on the *Travelin'* session in 1960. In terms of repertoire, it was definitely a mixed bag. Revisiting "Wednesday Evenin' " and "Sally Mae," Hooker nostalgically returned to the program of his very first session with Bernard Besman almost fifteen years before. The bouncily lascivious "Big Legs, Tight Skirt" and the rather more romantic "Flowers On The Hour" shot for the jukeboxes and the elusive crossover market, while the icily unforgiving "Ain't No Big Thing, Baby"—in which Hooker threatens to send his woman, whom he brought from the Delta and kitted out with nice clothes, back down South if she doesn't mend her ways—showed him in a considerably more ruthless light.

The session's most significant addition to Hooker's permanent repertoire, though, was "It Serves Me Right To Suffer," an agonized slow blues which he has continued to sing ever since. "Some things it do serve you right to suffer," he says, "when you shouldn't have did it, when it hurt someone down the line. Things that you did, when you shouldn't've did it, but you just can't change it." Hooker cites it as the saddest song in his catalogue, and performing it remains a grueling emotional experience. That, he says, is why he took to wearing sunglasses on stage. "To keep from crying, yeah. Blues goes so *deep*. My songs sound so good. I'm not praising myself, not patting myself on the back, but when I hear my own voice, it's so beautiful. The soul sounds so sad, and the words, the lyrics that I'm saying, just hits me. Sad, loving lyrics. I feel teardrops in my eyes, and I put on my sunglasses to keep from people seeing me crying, with tears running down my face.

"But I never know when they're going to hit me. When I'm just singing the tempo stuff, like 'Boom Boom' and the boogie, it don't. But the slow groove—so, so sad, and so deep—I have to cry, and I'm the one singing it."

"It Serves Me Right To Suffer" stretches the concept of Hookerization about as far as it can go. It would be something of an understatement simply to say that the song is "derived from" Percy Mayfield's "Memory Pain": Hooker's "version" of Mayfield's song is not so much a personal adaptation as a straight-up heist. One of the quintessential urbane-blues crooners, a formidable composer and a virtual contemporary of Hooker's (not to mention being no known relation to Curtis), Percy Mayfield was the author of a glittering fistful of classics including "River's Invitation," "Hit The Road, Jack" and "Please Send Me Someone To Love." "Memory Pain" had been recorded at his 1953 comeback session, following a year-long lay-off necessitated by the near-fatal car smash which robbed him of both his matinee-idol good looks and his sense of self-worth. Creatively if not physically, his path had crossed Hooker's before, when both men had been simultaneously contracted to Art Rupe's Specialty label; and when a line from Mayfield's composition "Two Years Of Torture" had provided the stimulus for Hooker's own "Backbiters And Syndicators."

"Memory Pain" is a masterpiece of the blues songsmith's art. The lyrics are simple and laconic, but epigrammatically taut and evocative, with an emotional complexity which lies barely concealed just beneath the surface. Ostensibly penitent and self-exculpatory, the song is in fact loaded with resentment and bitterness toward the departed woman: the more the singer proclaims the justice of his unhappy fate, the more he's actually playing to the gallery and attempting to arouse his listeners' sympathy for himself. No wonder it appealed to Hooker, who must have known the moment he heard it that it was virtually custom-built for him. Mayfield cut the song twice, with the verses sung in different orders, during the first half of 1953, but the version which directly inspired "It Serve Me Right To Suffer"—not to mention a 1969 cover by Johnny Winter—appears to have stayed in the can until it was included on a 1971 Mayfield compilation. Possibly Hooker heard the first version during his year with Specialty, or maybe he heard Mayfield sing it that way live. Smokily crooning over lightly swinging rhythm and a soupy horn section led by tenorist Maxwell Davis, Mayfield sings a total of four verses. Hooker retains the first two virtually intact; drops the third to make room for a dark, clawing guitar solo full of skittering runs, percussive scratching and viciously bent notes; and puckishly replaces the doubled-up first line of Mayfield's final verse—*"I don't see well, I'm absent-minded, I hardly sleep at all/My past put me on a habit of nicotine and alcohol"*—with a personalized full verse of his own: *"My doctor put me on milk, cream and alcohol/He said, 'Johnny, your nerves is so bad, so bad, Johnny, until you just can't sleep at all,'"* thus enabling him to bring the song to a powerful completion with a full restatement of the first verse.

Hooker sings the song much "straighter"—adhering much more closely to orthodox "direct time"—than he does in most of his slow blues performances, hardly ever yielding to the temptation of "gaining" a bar by jumping ahead of the band, as is his customary practice. It is said that mediocre artists borrow and great artists steal—as when Otis Redding acknowledged that Aretha Franklin had "stolen" "Respect" from him;

though she had left him with his composer credit and publishing royalties intact, the song now "belonged" to her—and by this definition, Hooker's annexation of Mayfield's song undoubtedly certifies him as a great artist. His version overpowers Mayfield's; his personalized-lyric change puts the stamp of Hookerization upon it; and ultimately he demonstrates his own-ership by "inhabiting" the song more completely than did its author. Copyright law doesn't work this way—if it did, no songwriter could ever be able to make any kind of a living—but the blues' unique melding of oral tradition and pop process certainly does.

Meanwhile, way over in England, a blues boom was raging. EMI's Stateside label had issued Hooker's eight-year-old "Dimples" as a single, and it was starting to climb the charts. A year and a half after he'd touched down in Manchester with the American Folk Blues Festival, Hooker was flying back to England for his first-ever headlining foreign tour. He was about to reinvade the British Invasion and become a rock and roll star.

It may seem corny to you, but this is true: the groups from England really started the blues rolling and getting bigger among the kids— the white kids. At one time . . . the blues was just among the blacks—the older black people. And this uprise started in England by The Beatles, Animals, Rolling Stones, it started *everybody* to dig-ging the blues. It got real big over there, and then people in the States started to catch on. The last eight or ten years, I really been making it big.
—John Lee Hooker to Robert Neff and Anthony Connor,
  Blues, 1975

"You ever hear'a Newcastle?" demands John Lee Hooker of a British acquaintance. The acquaintance fruitlessly racks his brain, mentally scrolling through a headful of half-forgotten fragments of Delta lore. "Newcastle, Mississippi?" he inquires eventually.

Apparently not. "You ever been to Newcastle?" Hooker asks again, somewhat impatiently this time. "Newcastle in *Britain*. Newcastle . . . boy, that was *rough*. There was a bar I played every night. It was *rough*."

"Was that the Club-A-Go-Go?" the acquaintance asks, recalling a notorious dive founded in that fair city during the early '60s—with decor designed by Eric Burdon, vocalist for the club's original house band, The

Animals—by Mike Jeffery, subsequently manager of The Animals and Jimi Hendrix. Hooker nods: *yes*.

"Fighting outside, *ooohhhh!* And inside. 'Oh,' I said, 'that's *it*. I ain't gonna play here no more.' They were fighting like dogs! Little kids carryin' knives an' all the rest of it . . . *shit*. Oh boy, it was rough. Everybody say, 'Hey man, this ain't nothin', they fight here all the time.' I say, 'Yes, 'n I be in the *middle* of it!' "

To most Brits, weaned on lurid horror stories of American inner-city violence, there is something almost ludicrous in the notion that someone who had survived in the Detroit ghetto, more or less unscathed, for a quarter-century or so, could possibly be taken aback by a bunch of beered-up teenage Geordies. Nevertheless, what's familiar is often reassuring, even if it may seem scary to outsiders. And what's *unfamiliar* is often what catches you unawares.

This is neither the time nor the place for an in-depth account of the birth-pangs of British R&B: the early chapters of any competent biography of Eric Clapton or The Rolling Stones[11] will recount that story in far greater detail than is either necessary or desirable in this particular context. However, in order to understand the peculiar nature of the madhouse in which Hooker was about to find himself—not to mention the differences between the young white blues audiences in the British Isles and the U.S.—we need a word, or a couple of thousand, about the prehistory of the British Blues Boom.

Like—but also *unlike*—other Europeans, Britons had loved African-American music, in both its "traditional" and "commercial" forms, for decades; but it was a rarely consummated love affair, conducted from afar via records and the occasional visit from a genuine American bluesman. "For me," wrote George Melly, the British singer, critic, author and raconteur,[12] describing his emotions *en route* to Big Bill Broonzy's first British concert in 1951, "the idea of hearing an American Negro singing the blues was almost unbearably exciting." Melly had heard his first Bessie Smith record during his childhood in the '30s, and had carried a torch

---

11 I'd recommend Christopher Sandford's *Clapton: Edge Of Darkness* (Gollancz, 1994) and Stanley Booth's *The True Adventures Of The Rolling Stones* (Wm. Heinemann, 1985) respectively, though in neither case is the inquisitive reader spoiled for choice. Despite its clubfooted prose and complete absence of critical judgment, Bob Brunning's *Blues In Britain* (Blandford, 1995), a revision of the same author's *Blues: The British Connection* (Blandford, 1986), is nevertheless both an invaluable reference work and an engaging personal memoir.
12 In *Owning Up*(Weidenfeld & Nicolson, 1965), his autobiographical account of the British "trad" (i.e. New Orleans revivalist) jazz scene of the 1950s.

for "classic" blues and New Orleans jazz for almost twenty years without ever experiencing a performance by a ranking exponent of the art. In the U.S., the carriers of that blues torch were fans and musicians whose primary concern was "folk" music, for the excellent reason that since the blues is a cornerstone of America's folk heritage, no valid exploration of the folk roots of American music could legitimately exclude it. The British folk musicians and collectors, on the other hand, devoted themselves primarily to exploring and renewing their own folk music; songs from the native Anglo-Celtic traditions. Such musicians were encouraged to perform music from their own home communities: Euan McColl, the scene's patriarch, even frowned on the idea of a Londoner performing a Scottish ballad, let alone a Mississippi blues piece, in his Singers' Club. In the United Kingdom, therefore, listeners of Melly's generation primarily collected and appreciated the blues as a member of the musical family ruled by that other great African-American creation: jazz.

The generation fifteen or twenty years younger than Melly and his contemporaries heard the blues in a somewhat different context. Some came to the music via Britain's mid-'50s fascination with "trad": homegrown variations on New Orleans jazz. Both Brian Jones of The Rolling Stones and Pete Townshend of The Who began their performing careers as banjoists in "trad" bands,[13] and *wunderkind* polymath Stevie Winwood was playing piano in a trad band led by his bass-playing elder brother Muff before he was out of short pants. Some arrived via "skiffle," a home-made, lo-budget grab-bag of assorted American folk musics drawing heavily on the Leadbelly repertoire: John Lennon's first instrument was banjo and his first group a skiffle band. Others still had been simultaneously exposed to radio broadcasts by Big Bill Broonzy, Sonny Terry & Brownie McGhee and Josh White—the latter an ersatz bluesman who had, uniquely, started out as a real one—and to the first wave of the rock and roll explosion of the '50s. The likes of Keith Richards and Eric Clapton literally heard Big Bill Broonzy with one ear and Chuck Berry with the other.

"On one hand," affirmed Richards,[14] "I was playing all that folk stuff on the guitar. The other half of me was listenin' to all that rock and roll."

---

13 In Townshend's case, the group in question—The Detours—was primarily a rock band, which also included his future Who colleagues John Entwistle and Roger Daltrey, but their act featured a "trad" section in which Entwistle and Daltrey respectively played trumpet and trombone.

14 In his celebrated 1971 *Rolling Stone* interview with Robert Greenfield, reprinted in *The Rolling Stone Interviews Vol. 2* (Warner Books, 1973).

And it was in the rough, rumbustious energies of Chicago blues that the two streams converged, with the vestiges of the "trad" boom providing the infrastructure. British traditional jazzers had ranged from the most commercial and popsploitative to the most austere and puritanical—in their musical tastes rather than their personal lives, as Melly's *Owning Up* makes hilariously clear. The real ayatollahs, like the legendary Ken Colyer, considered that Louis Armstrong had ruined jazz by introducing the concept of "soloing," and that the music had been in artistic decline ever since 1926. Others, like the enormously influential Chris Barber, had taken a broader view, exploring a variety of opportunities to expand the range and definition of his band. Britain's first skiffle group had been formed within Barber's band and featured Barber's banjoist, Tony Donegan, as its front man: following a surprise hit with a version of Leadbelly's "Rock Island Line," Donegan changed his first name to "Lonnie" (in homage to Lonnie Johnson) and launched his own group.

Barber then repeated the trick with a Chicago blues band-within-the-band, spotlighting the Bessie Smith-styled vocals of his wife, Ottilie Patterson; the guitar of Donegan's replacement, Alexis Korner, and guest harpist Cyril Davies. It was as guest artists with Barber's band that Muddy Waters and his pianist Otis Spann became the first Chicago bluesmen to visit the U.K., creating a major controversy with their rock-scaled levels of amplification. Even without a Donegan-sized hit (or *any* hit, for that matter), Korner and Davies were eventually inspired to leave the Barber band and form their own group. Launched in 1962, Blues Incorporated became the first blues-dedicated electric band in Britain—and, indeed, probably the first white Chicago-style blues band anywhere in the world—and it was Blues Incorporated, and the club which Korner and Davies founded in West London, which provided a focus for the kids who would form the first wave of British R&B bands.[15]

Indeed, it hadn't been until Blues Incorporated arrived to provide a focus that the isolated knots of blues lovers—first in the South of England, and then all over the country—got to meet each other, and realize how numerous and widespread they actually were. Even before 1962, when the major British record companies began to provide U.K. outlets for

---

15 Blues Incorporated eventually schismed: Korner's preference was for a jazzy, urbane-blues approach, while Davies had pledged fealty to explicitly Delta-derived music. After Davies's sudden death, his band, The Cyril Davies All-Stars, was taken over by vocalist Long John Baldry, who renamed it The Hoochie Coochie Men and gave a young singer named Rod Stewart his first job. But that's another story, if not several other stories.

Chicago blues recordings—Vee Jay via EMI's Stateside label, Chess through Pye International's R&B Series—the blues kids collected rare imported records, absorbed whatever scraps of information they could glean from liner-notes, and took their first tentative steps toward teaching themselves to reproduce what they heard on their own guitars, harmonicas and drums.

And they were dedicated. *Boy*, were they dedicated. As well as scouring the specialist record shops, Mick Jagger was sufficiently enterprising to obtain a catalog from Chess Records in Chicago and write away to score his Muddy Waters and Bo Diddley records by direct mail. Brian Jones[16] once came to the verge of a fistfight with another customer— writer Roy Carr, as it happens—over an import store's last copy of a much sought-after Howlin' Wolf album. Guitarist Tom McGuiness, who subsequently enjoyed a string of '60s hits as a member of Manfred Mann but whose first group, The Roosters, had at various times included Brian Jones, Eric Clapton and Manfred Mann singer/harpist Paul Jones, remembers walking three miles just to look at the cover of a John Lee Hooker album. McGuiness didn't actually get to *listen* to the record, but just to see it was enough of a thrill to justify the hike. The likes of Muddy Waters, Howlin' Wolf, Jimmy Reed, Elmore James, Sonny Boy Williamson, Willie Dixon and—of course—John Lee Hooker were literally worshipped as gods.

And so were great rockers like Chuck Berry, Bo Diddley and Little Richard; proto-soulers like Ray Charles and James Brown; and funky jazzers like Jimmy Smith and Mose Allison. The eclecticism of taste which the Brit bands brought to the African-American cultural continuum can best be illustrated by citing the contents of a record collection which Pete Townshend was fortunate enough to "inherit" from an American friend deported from the U.K. for the heinous offense of pot-smoking. According to Richard Barnes, then Townshend's flatmate, this cultural treasure trove included ". . . all of Jimmy Reed's albums, all of Chuck Berry's, all of James Brown's, Bo Diddley, John Lee Hooker, Snooks Eaglin, Mose Allison, all of Jimmy Smith's, Muddy Waters, Lightnin' Hopkins, Howlin' Wolf, Slim Harpo, Buddy Guy, Big Bill Broonzy, Sonny Terry & Brownie McGhee, Joe Turner, Nina Simone, Booker T., Little Richard, Jerry Lee

---

16 Before he teamed up with Mick Jagger and Keith Richards to form The Rolling Stones, Jones had been playing as a soloist, and in a duo with Paul Jones (no relation) under the name of "Elmo Lewis," partly because his full name was Lewis Brian Jones, partly as a tribute to Elmore James, and partly because "Elmo Lewis" was the name of Jerry Lee Lewis's father.

Lewis, Carl Perkins, The Isley Brothers, Fats Domino, The Coasters, Ray Charles, Jimmy McGriff, Brother Jack McDuff, John Patton, Bobby Bland, The Drifters, The Miracles, The Shirelles, The Impressions and many jazz albums including Charlie Parker, Mingus, Coltrane, Miles Davis, Milt Jackson, Wes Montgomery, Jimmy Guiffre [and] Dave Brubeck . . ." Townshend's pal had brilliant taste: as a cross-section of the most important postwar black and black derived American music, this particular selection could scarcely be bettered. Anybody using that stuff as source material would be running on hi-octane fuel; as Hooker himself might put it: pot's on, gas on high.

Viewed with an Africentric perspective and 20/20 hindsight, it's tempting to compare the disproportionate degrees of fame and wealth achieved by the Claptons, Stones or Zeppelins of this world as opposed to the role models from whom they learned their initial stuff, and conclude that the British blues kids were simply thieves: cultural carpetbaggers, neo-colonialist expropriators, and cynical rip-off merchants who sat around telling each other, "Hey, I got a great idea, fellas—let's rob those old niggers blind and make ourselves a fortune!" However, that particular temptation should be firmly resisted. Anyone who'd suggested in those early days—even before The Beatles had busted out of the Liverpool cellars and Hamburg *Bierkellers* to become a national obsession—that there were fortunes to be made, and lifetime careers to be enjoyed, by English kids playing rhythm and blues, would have been mercilessly derided. Many of the musicians were—like Eric Clapton and Jimmy Page—still living with their folks; those who'd left home to play the music and attempted to support themselves by doing so—like Mick Jagger, Keith Richards and Brian Jones—damn near starved to death in the process. Chicago blues was an underground taste, and a self-consciously elitist one at that; a strange fungoid growth which evolved, over several years, in trad's suburban shadow before ultimately conquering its strongholds in London's West End. As George Melly described the process,[17]

It was in a club called The Marquee in Wardour Street, Soho, that British R&B established itself at a time when, in the wider field of pop, The Beatles were carrying all before them . . . the groups at The Marquee varied between the back-porch rural blues and the postwar electric blues . . . on the other side of the road, however, was a

---

17 In *Revolt Into Style: The Pop Arts In Britain* (Penguin, 1970).

club called The Flamingo, and it was here that the third school of R&B evolved: the "soul" blues, Ray Charles–oriented, and much more to the taste of London's growing colored population Georgie Fame was king here. He used organ and saxes, modern jazz musicians; The Flamingo had been a modern jazz club, just as The Marquee had been a traditional jazz club, and, like children who reject their parents and yet betray their origins in everything they do and say, the Marquee blues and the Flamingo soul reflected this. Later a marriage was to be arranged . . .

The spearhead of the R&B breakthrough had been the success of The Rolling Stones. By early 1963, Jagger, Richards and Jones had enlisted journeyman rock bassist Bill Wyman[18] and former Blues Incorporated drummer Charlie Watts to form their classic line-up, and by the time they outgrew the R&B club circuit and graduated to the theaters, cinemas and ballrooms, there was no shortage of other bands waiting in the wings to take over their gigs. In London and the South East, The Who, The Kinks, The Yardbirds (with Clapton on lead guitar), Manfred Mann, The Pretty Things and many others less distinguished were limbering up; The Animals were coming together in Newcastle; The Spencer Davis Group (featuring Stevie Winwood) and The Moody Blues lurked in Birmingham; and in Manchester an eccentric multi-instrumentalist named John Mayall, a contemporary of Korner and Davies rather than Jagger or Clapton, was preparing to relocate to the capital.

The Manchester appearance of the 1962 American Folk Blues Festival had been a significant precursor of what was to come. Jagger, Richards, Jones and their friend Jimmy Page (plus David Housego, the latter's buddy from his skiffling teenage years) were part of the London contingent who'd traveled up to see the show, and the writer/photographer Valerie Wilmer is still vaguely resentful that she had to miss it because her then-boyfriend's motorcycle broke down en route. However, it was the following year's package, featuring Sonny Boy Williamson II, Muddy Waters, Otis Spann, Lonnie Johnson, and Big Joe Williams alongside regulars Willie Dixon and Memphis Slim, which proved to be the watershed.

---

18   Wyman was fundamentally a rocker, but as the late Ian Stewart, the Stones' pianist-turned-road-manager-turned-pianist-again, told Bob Brunning in *Blues In Britain* (Blandford, 1995), "As Bill actually got in the band he went completely overboard on blues, and he really got hung up on the worst blues players, he had to empathize with everything by Lightnin' Hopkins and John Lee Hooker, you know, the kind of stuff that would put you to sleep." There's no accounting for taste, is there?

In sharp contrast with the '62 tour's last-minute one-off performance, the '63 edition enacted a full triumphal march around the nation, delighting the audiences primed for them by the Stones; Sonny Boy Williamson enjoyed himself so much that he decided to stay. In February of 1964, Sonny Boy, backed by The Yardbirds, was the headline attraction at Britain's first R&B festival, held at Birmingham Town Hall. Further down the bill, Steve Winwood and Rod Stewart could be found as respective members of The Spencer Davis Group and Long John Baldry & The Hoochie Coochie Men. Stewart's vocal feature was Jimmy Reed's "Bright Lights, Big City;" Winwood sang "Night Time Is The Right Time" and "Dimples." (And sixteen-year-old Robert Plant, from nearby Kidderminster, was backstage stealing one of Sonny Boy's harps in the hope that some of that magical mojo would rub off. Evidently it did.)

By this time, of course, the Stones were way too big in their own right to serve as anyone's back-up band, but The Yardbirds, The Animals and several others were keen to oblige. The levels of mutual incomprehension thereby reached were staggering, particularly since Sonny Boy was considered a somewhat difficult man even among his peer group back in Helena, Arkansas, but the arrangement ultimately proved mutually beneficial. The expatriate harpist received enthusiastic and committed (if naïve and occasionally hamfisted) back-up, while the groups got a chance to study at the kind of blues university of which they had previously only been able to dream.

For their contemporaries in Chicago, though, "Blues University" was right on the doorstep. Thirty and more years earlier, young white Chicagoans like Gene Krupa, Mezz Mezzrow, Eddie Condon, Davey Tough and Benny Goodman had gone to "class" by soaking up everything they could learn from the greats of the New Orleans jazz diaspora. Their '60s successors—be they locals like Paul Butterfield, Michael Bloomfield and Nick Gravenites or imports like Steve Miller, Elvin Bishop and "Memphis Charlie" Musselwhite—made similar pilgrimages to the bars and taverns of the South and West Sides to learn their stuff first-hand from the real guys. If you wanted to blow harp, you were prepared to buy the drinks and you could convince Little Walter or Junior Wells that you were seriously down with the program, you might learn some stuff, be it licks and techniques or upside-your-head Zen lessons in blues attitude. And if you played guitar, then Muddy Waters, Magic Sam, Earl Hooker, Otis Rush or Elmore James were generally there for the approaching . . . if you dared.

The best of the white Chicagoans learned their lessons very well indeed. They soaked up attitude and ambience as well as licks and riffs, and their "blues" was certainly idiomatically purer and more authentic than anything the Brits were playing. As imitators of the "real guys," they had their transatlantic counterparts beaten all hollow, as any direct comparison of, say, the first Paul Butterfield Blues Band album with the early work of The Yardbirds or the Stones will demonstrate. However, the spiritual and geographical distance which separated the Brit bands from their sources ultimately proved to be their greatest asset. Lacking first-hand knowledge of and access to their role models, they were forced to reinvent the music, to juxtapose styles and idioms which rarely mixed on their native soil, to join up the dots with their own ideas. "If I'm building a solo," Eric Clapton once explained to *Guitar Player*'s Dan Forte, "I'll start with a line that is definitely Freddie King . . . and then I'll go onto a B. B. King line. I'll do something to join them up, so that'll be me—that part . . . Of course, it's not my favorite bit. My favorite bit is still the B. B. or Freddie lines." But out of their creative misunderstandings of the distant worlds of the South Side and the Delta, Clapton and his kind accidentally-on-purpose invented something uniquely their own: a new kind of rock and roll. Indeed, The Rolling Stones, who took the process further than anyone else, ended up virtually reinventing America.

The Brit-blues posse began by identifying with the music because its gritty realism rang truer to their own lives and aspirations than the candy-ass white pop of the time. As Eric Burdon of The Animals explained to a BBC interviewer, "I heard John Lee Hooker singing things like, *'I've been working in a steel mill, trucking steel like a slave/and I woke up this morning and my baby's gone away'*, and I related to that directly, because that was happening to people . . . grown men on my block." (The lyric Burdon is quoting—or rather mis-quoting—comes from Eddie Boyd's "Five Long Years," which Hooker had covered on 1961's *The Folklore Of John Lee Hooker*, but the principle remains the same.) But what began as a process of imitation and emulation, an urge to reproduce the mythic power of the music they heard on their treasured records, ended up as a quest of self-discovery and personal liberation. They set out to unlock the heart of the blues, but instead ended up unlocking themselves. As Roger Daltrey of The Who told Dave Marsh,[19]

---

19 In *The Story Of The Who* (St. Martins Press, 1983).

Because so many of the songs sounded exactly the same, we had to use our imagination to build them up. Blues taught us to use musical freedom. Playing pop before, you just copied a record and that was it. If we got near to the record, we were happy. But blues was a completely different thing altogether. We'd play one verse for twenty minutes and make up half the lyrics.

Pausing only to note the similarity between Hooker's own improvisatory methods and the kind of experimentation described by Daltrey, let us posit that if the Brits had learned to play the blues as "authentically" as Butterfield and his Chicago circle, they might well have rested on those particular laurels, understudying the old masters and refining their craft. Instead, they were impelled to use the blues as a springboard to launch their unlocked selves into work which innovated rather than imitated. If The Kinks or The Moody Blues had been content to remain blues bands, they would have been utterly forgotten by 1966.

Thanks to the good offices of Stateside and Pye International, the R&B kids had enjoyed simultaneous access to two distinct limbs of Hooker's body of work. His early '50s style was well represented by Chess sides originally cut in Detroit for Chance by Joe Von Battle, but his more recent Vee Jay material proved rather more adaptable to the needs of these fledgling bands. By comparison with the more structured repertoires of Jimmy Reed and Muddy Waters—let alone those of Chuck Berry and Bo Diddley, who had one foot in the blues and the other in rock and roll—Hooker's fluid, semi-improvised music was, for British kids, easier to enjoy than to emulate. Nevertheless, quite a few of them tried. According to David Bowie, one of his teenage groups "did a lot of stuff by John Lee Hooker, and we tried to adapt his stuff to the big beat—never terribly successfully. But that was the thing: everybody was picking a blues artist as their own. Somebody had Muddy Waters, somebody had Sonny Boy Williamson. Ours was Hooker."[20]

Unfortunately for Bowie and his chums, they had to "share" Hooker's catalog with others who were rather better known and considerably more adept. Eric Clapton's first-ever studio recording was a version of "Boom Boom" cut at The Yardbirds' first demo session; The Animals also re-

---

20 From an interview by Timothy White in *Rock Lives* (Omnibus Press, 1990). Bowie's kid bands never got around to recording any of Hooker's material for release, but at his fiftieth birthday concert at Madison Square Gardens on January 8, 1997, D B performed a decidedly Hookerized intro to his 1972 hit "Jean Genie."

corded "Boom Boom" for *their* original demos. Unlike The Yardbirds, The Animals reprised the song, albeit augmented with a few choruses of "Shake It Baby,"[21] for their first album—cut in early '64 in the wake of their first smash hit "The House Of The Rising Sun"—and threw in "Dimples" and a bravura version of "I'm Mad Again" for good measure, giving Hooker three of the album's twelve composer credits (Fats Domino and Chuck Berry had to content themselves with two apiece). For their part, The Yardbirds could be heard romping through an uptempo version of "Louise"—a minor Hookerization of a standard theme, most frequently associated with Brownie McGhee, which they'd learned from *House Of The Blues*—on their live-at-The-Marquee debut offering, *Five Live Yardbirds*. The Spencer Davis Group, having gotten their Brummie selves into a studio in April '64 to cut what they fondly hoped was their first hit, essayed a version of "Dimples" which also incorporated large chunks of "Boom Boom," but by the time their single was released that August, somebody else had already had a hit with "Dimples." Against the odds, that somebody was Hooker himself.

It wasn't a particularly big hit: the single peaked at Number 23 or Number 24, depending on which of Britain's competing music-paper charts you checked. Neither was it particularly lucrative: EMI weren't paying fabulous royalties to anyone (even The Beatles) at that time, and the monies they did pay were sent to Chicago to be sucked into the heaving quagmire of Vee Jay's financial implosion, never to be seen again. But it was enough of a hit to make it worthwhile for Don Arden, a former singer, comedian and MC who had turned promoter in order to specialize in importing semi-faded '50s rockers to the U.K., to lure Hooker across the Atlantic for a tour. Hooker's visit was considered a sufficiently momentous event for *Melody Maker* to feature the announcement as a news-page lead in their issue coverdate May 23, 1964. "Blues star John Lee Hooker flies into Britain from America next week for his first nation-wide tour here," the item ran, beneath a 72-point banner headline screaming: "John Lee Hooker—tour all set."

With John Mayall's Bluesbreakers [it continued], Hooker—one of the heroes of British R&B groups—will go around Britain for five weeks. He will televise on Ready Steady Go! *[the hippest British pop*

---

21 The Animals' version of "Boom Boom" was released as a single in the U.S.A—though not into the domestic market—in December 1964; it stalled just outside the Top 40 and was speedily chased by one of their British hits "Don't Let Me Be Misunderstood."

TV show of the era] on May 29, and also broadcast on [BBC Ra-
dio's] Saturday Club . . . John Lee's tour opens on June 1 at Lon-
don's Flamingo, and next day he joins Chuck Berry and Carl Perkins
on a Granada TV blues spectacular recording in Manchester.

There then followed Hooker's itinerary: twenty-five dates spread over just
under five weeks, taking him all over England. The festival package with
which he had toured Europe in 1962 had been first-class all the way: the
troupe had performed in ornate, prestigious concert halls and stayed in
luxury hotels. This was a completely different proposition: a rough-and-
ready club tour with accommodations in the frowsty bed-and-breakfast
boarding-houses which were the British equivalent of the cheap motels to
which Hooker and his peers were accustomed in the States. Furthermore,
the very nature of the all-star package format enabled Hooker to travel
and perform in a hermetically-sealed bubble of peer-group homeys; this
time he was on his own.

John Mayall's Bluesbreakers, appointed by the Arden office as
Hooker's backing group, were no big deal in the summer of '64. To be
precise, they were a hard-working club band then some ten months away
from becoming a big deal; a leap in status directly attributable to Mayall's
recruitment the following April of Eric Clapton, on the rebound from the
increasingly pop-friendly Yardbirds.[22] "John Mayall backed me up when
I was over there," remembers Hooker, though he is characteristically
vague about whether Clapton was on the team at that particular time.
"John Mayall backed me up a long time . . . they were my band. Quite a
few people backed me. Clapton was with 'em at one time then . . . he
didn't remember, but then he remembered that he was with 'em briefly
when I was with 'em. John Mayall livin' in Malibu now. I bump into him
once in a while and we have conversations 'bout the old days, you know."

By the time Arden booked him for the Hooker tour, Mayall had a
major-label album release under his belt, but it had only sold a minuscule
500 copies. While he had already assembled his first great rhythm section
(drummer Hughie Flint and bassist John McVie, subsequently the Flint
of McGuiness Flint and the Mac of Fleetwood Mac), his group was still
not quite ready for prime time. Roger Dean, Clapton's immediate pre-

---

22 The knock-on effects of this particular coup were the establishment of The Yardbirds and
The Bluesbreakers as the hottest guitar chairs in British rock, and the formation of Led Zeppelin
and Fleetwood Mac: Clapton was replaced in The Yardbirds by Jeff Beck and then by Jimmy
Page; and in The Bluesbreakers by Peter Green and then by Mick Taylor.

decessor as the Bluesbreakers' lead guitarist, was a competent but grievously mis-cast player, more comfortable with country-and-western than blues. This was unfortunate, since the Mayall blues aesthetic was purist in the white-Chicagoan mold, prioritizing "authenticity" at all costs and regarding almost all pop with disdain: his masterplan for The Bluesbreakers would only be realized once Dean was replaced by Clapton. Nevertheless, with audience expectations whetted by Hooker's appearance on *Ready Steady Go!*, the first gig of the tour was deemed a roaring success. According to *Melody Maker's* jazz and blues guru Max Jones:

> *After a long damp wait in the tropical heat of a packed Flamingo, Mississippi blues man John Lee Hooker made his London debut on Monday. From where I was jammed it was impossible to see even the top of his head. But what I heard confirmed that Hooker can create the right kind of lowdown blues atmosphere within 20 seconds of hitting his first note. His opening shout "Are you ready?" needed no answer, but got one. Then into the blues—unquestionably the real potent article with his urgent conversational vocal style over his pulsating guitar counterpoint and the throbbing rhythm of John Mayall's Bluesbreakers.*

"That was wonderful," says Valerie Wilmer, "because The Flamingo was *the place* and you had a black-ish audience, plenty of West Indians. It was just this amazing place because it had these reed walls and it had the feeling of being the hippest place in town; sweat running down the walls and this low ceiling over the bandstand which gave you a sort of compressed feeling. I can see Hooker now, standing there and singing. He had a sharkskin suit, silvery sharkskin . . . it just felt very authentic and funky and it was something you didn't often come across."

Others were rather less enthusiastic than Jones and Wilmer. Writing in the mimeographed fanzine *Blues Unlimited*, John J. Broven grumpily pleaded the purist case:

> *In the broiling atmosphere of this one-time modern jazz center, we had a full two hours of synthetic rubbish from The Cheynes[23] and John Mayall's Bluesbreakers. It was then learned that Mayall would*

---

23 A short-lived band formed by organist Pete Bardens, later to join Van Morrison in Them, which included Mick Fleetwood on drums.

back Hooker, and despite protests to John Lee before the show, it was to be. Hooker appeared, and with Mayall's organ and harmonica (yes! He plays both at once!) striving for the limelight, he was content to strum his way through meaningless things like "Dimples," "Boom Boom," "Hi Heel Sneakers" and others. In his whole act he only did two slow blues and of these, only "I'm In The Mood" came off to any degree. But most disappointing was that his guitar work was kept to a minimum . . . what went wrong? Why was one of the greatest living bluesmen transformed into an unexceptional R&B artist? Obviously a lot of blame must go to whoever teamed Hooker with Mayall. If he must have a group, OK, but not an organ! Also John appeared to be under the misconception that he was playing to a "pop" audience . . . blues enthusiasts were definitely to the fore at the Flamingo . . . wasn't this the perfect opportunity to educate the uninitiated. My opinion of Hooker has not fallen . . . He has shown, in odd flashes, what a great bluesman he is. It's just that this tour, for a blues lover, has been so badly presented, if financially a great success.

No less eminent a figure than Pete Townshend lined up alongside Broven in the Disappointed Men league. "I saw John Lee Hooker in London only once in the '60s. It was disappointing. He played with musicians who treated him as if he was another Chuck Berry or Bo Diddley and not—as is the real case—the true 'boss' of '60s electric R&B. His band of British enthusiastic R&B pick-up musicians[24] seemed to feel nothing of his incredible subtlety and elegance. He seemed to serve himself poorly too: we were there to see a great soloist. He was there to make some cash and pull some birds, and he probably succeeded on both counts. He wore a red check suit, and although I felt I was in the presence of a legend, I went straight home and put on some [of Hooker's] solo records to remind myself of the sheer genius of the man."

And Townshend was, no less now than then, firmly convinced of Hooker's genius. "John Lee Hooker stands firmly on one side of a line which, once established, allowed all post-'50s pop to be redefined. Without him there would be no 'power chord.' It is time to give the credit for

---

24 Townshend is unspecific concerning exactly when he saw Hooker play The Flamingo or which band was backing him, but the point he's making remains unaffected.

that little invention to the man who really created it, John Lee Hooker. Take it from me. I know."

"We were the first band to play with John Lee," Mayall recalled in 1991. "That whole thing was something of an experiment. I remember we played the Flamingo, and of course they were more used to things like Georgie Fame all-nighters, so it was a big surprise when people from all over the country turned up and there was a big queue down Wardour Street. Then we toured around the rest of the country . . . and that really paved the way for having British bands play with a lot of other blues artists."

Like many of his fellow Brit blues-boomers, Mayall had completed a rigorous home-study course in the blues, aided immeasurably by access to his father's extensive library of jazz and boogie-woogie 78s, but touring with Hooker—"the first real blues guitarist we backed up"—was his chance to obtain that elusive Blues University degree. "It was a very humbling experience," he told journalist Gregory Isola, "because we all thought we were shit-hot players and knew what it was all about. Then you get Hooker onstage and what you know flies out the window. You feel like rank amateurs. But we picked up a lot. I learned about dynamics from playing with John Lee—the power of not forcing things. You have to be relaxed. John Lee would just sit down in a chair and a deathly hush would come over the whole audience. Such presence . . ."

Mayall backed Hooker again in 1966. Peter Green, freshly recruited as Eric Clapton's replacement, has his own memories of that particular occasion. "I met him when I first joined John Mayall. It was in the very early days, and we had to back him at the Ram Jam Club in Brixton. I was very unsatisfied. I couldn't figure anything out. I tried to back him but I was too loud and I couldn't seem to get the whole thing *down* so I could play ever so quietly and let him go along. I was barely touching the guitar, afraid to do anything because he don't need nobody. Afraid to do anything before he gets used to you and accepts that you're there. I don't think what I did was very good. He was all right, I guess. He's pretty steadfast, for want of a better word, and does his thing. Whatever you're doing, he don't need you particularly. Very delicate, very difficult. It was far too 'experienced' an experience. I couldn't guarantee it would be any different now. What can you play? He doesn't need anyone, does he? Most of his records are him on his own, aren't they?"

Broven was right about one thing: despite Mayall's indubitable enthusiasm and eagerness to please, the Hooker/Bluesbreakers combination

JOHN LEE HOOKER   Exclusive *Modern*
                                            RECORDS
                                            hollywood

John Lee poses for Modern Records with a big ol' box guitar, 1949. Not just his
first publicity shot, but also the earliest known photo of him.
TONY RUSSELL COLLECTION

John Lee hangs out with Detroit harp guy Little Sonny at Joe Von Battle's record store (below) on Hastings Street, 1959. Clearly the Reverend C. L. Franklin, father of Aretha, was a bigger attraction than any bluesman.

The Boogie Ramblers resplendent in '50s Detroit: long-serving drummer Tom Whitehead is on John Lee's left.
PRIVATE COLLECTION

John Lee and Ol' Blondie in the UK, 1964: rocking on *Ready, Steady, Go!*
© VAL WILMER

Took a freight train to be my friend: John Lee and his cousin Earl Hooker, the lost prince of Chicago blues, on the cover shoot for their only recorded collaboration, "If You Miss 'im, . . . I Got 'im."
© MICHAEL OCHS ARCHIVES/REDFERNS

Heal me, Carlos: Hooker and Santana take it to the stage, 1996.
© ROBERT KNIGHT

John Lee rolls with the Stones, 1989, flanked by Woody 'n' Keef. Eric Clapton, out of shot, was also sitting in.
PAUL NATKIN/PHOTO RESERVE

Left: "I'm in the Mood" brings home kudos as well as bacon. Left to right: Grammy, Bonnie Raitt, John Lee, Grammy.
JOFFET/SIPA/REX FEATURES

Below: Blues, the next generation. John Lee at home in Redwood City with his daughter Zakiya.
© ROBERT KNIGHT/
REDFERNS

Left: Me 'n' old B: Hooker and B. B. King celebrate their fifth decade of friendship.
BILL REITZEL

Below: Got my eyes on you: John Lee takes a break to raise the shades, Manchester, 1988.
BRIAN SMITH, COURTESY
JUKE BLUES MAGAZINE

I *am* the Boogie Man.
PAUL NATKIN/PHOTO RESERVE

had failed to gel. Part of the problem was Roger Dean: reliable and musicianly though he was, he not only wasn't much of a bluesman, but he wasn't much of an improviser, either. "Keeping up with the way John Lee played wasn't much of a problem for me, as I was well used to listening to that kind of player," Mayall says, "but for people who were more used to reading music, for instance, it was more of a problem. I think that Roger Dean was confused for a while. We had to tell him, 'Just keep on your toes, and listen to his voice.' We found [Hooker] great to work with; I'd read that he was blunt and not very communicative, but that wasn't the case at all."

One Hooker fan in particular found the recruitment of the Bluesbreakers especially disappointing. Guitarist Tony McPhee was a charter member of an informal clique of blues fans based in Streatham,[25] South London; not only were his group, The Groundhogs, named after Hooker's "Groundhog Blues," but their singer/harpist John Cruikshank actually called himself "John Lee." As soon as the band's manager, Roy Fisher, had spotted the tour announcement in *Melody Maker*, he'd grabbed the phone, called the Arden agency, and offered them "John Lee's Groundhogs" as Hooker's accompanists, only to be told that Mayall's group already had the job. Fisher, McPhee and the Groundhogs duly showed up at The Flamingo for Hooker's opening night, and came away feeling somewhat aggrieved. "They brought Hooker over and put him with John Mayall's band," McPhee griped to Bob Brunning. "I went to see him and I thought, 'This just ain't Hooker, not with keyboards behind. It just ain't working.'"

However, John Lee's Groundhogs—drummer Dave Boorman and bassist Pete Cruikshank completed the quartet—eventually got their chance to work with Hooker. For reasons now obscured by the mists of time, Mayall & Co. were unable to complete the full duration of the tour, and a stand-in ensemble was urgently required. The Arden agency, according to Roy Fisher, "were looking for the cheapest band that would do it, and The Groundhogs were cheap at that particular time." Fisher had a meeting with Hooker at Arden's offices, a deal was cut, and Hooker and the 'Hogs arranged to meet up in Manchester on the afternoon preceding their first gig together. The band arrived at that night's venue, the Twisted Wheel club, in their beat-up van; Hooker, in a car chauffeured

---

25 Though the name is theoretically pronounced "Strettam," glottal-stopped local pronunciation generally renders the "tt" silent.

by Arden employee Patrick Meehan. For all concerned, it turned out to be a serendipitous encounter: the South London boys and the Delta veteran clicked, big time. "He met the band, liked them, got to talking," Fisher recalls. "The rehearsal was thirty minutes on the afternoon of the first gig, a soundcheck-cum-rehearsal. Even John said that McPhee knew some of his old blues songs better than John remembered them, so therefore it wasn't a problem and it just went from there. Because he liked the guys and respected the way they played, he decided the very next day that he didn't want to tour with the chauffeur anymore: he wanted to tour with the band."

It should come as no surprise that Hooker preferred to squeeze into a rundown van already crammed with musicians and amps, rather than travel in the solitary chauffeur-driven grandeur to which his star status entitled him. He was in a foreign country (albeit one from which he was—in the words of Winston Churchill—"divided by a common language"), and he didn't know a soul. He was traveling alone, with no hometown buddy like Eddie Burns, Eddie Kirkland or Tom Whitehead to provide musical, emotional and practical support, and thus he needed companionship. The Groundhogs were not only a nice bunch of kids who idolized and adored him, but a hardworking team led by a guitarist who knew his music—certain areas of it, anyway—back to front. "The Groundhogs were able to follow his changes because they were that much familiar with his records," continues Roy Fisher. "He had forgotten a lot of the early stuff, but those were the things that people wanted to hear, so he had to relearn them, but it was like the group were teaching *him* how they went."

Even *Blues Unlimited* was prepared to grant its approval to the Hooker/'Hogs team. After the "aural torture" of a set by Georgie Fame & The Blue Flames, wrote Graham Ackers of a show at the Savoy Ballroom in Cleveleys, near the northern seaside resort of Blackpool:

> *Hooker came onto a very enthusiastic reception . . . he rolled straight into "Shake It Baby" with great power—perhaps a little too much—as a string broke after two verses! Anyway, true to the maxim of all good showmen, he finished the number to great applause. The next number he played with a Groundhog's Fender—a somewhat unusual sight. The Groundhog repaired his Gibson[26] and*

---

26 An Epiphone, actually, but let's not be too picky.

finished the number with it. Many followed including "Night Time Is The Right Time," "Boom Boom," "Hi Heel Sneakers," "Dimples" (twice) and a blue version of "Tupelo." This last was heavily requested and he was backed only by bass guitar, which heightened the effect. Every number was received with enthusiasm to such a degree that five encores were performed in all. A special mention for The Groundhogs who throughout played admirably. All in direct contrast to the "let's see who can play loudest" approach of John Mayall and crew. In fact everything was just right—atmosphere, backing, amplification and temperature (compared to Tropical Flamingo conditions) and everybody, including Hooker and the 'Hogs, had a ball.

"We went on from there," recalls Fisher, "touring around in a battered old Transit van, which had definitely seen better days, with the band, me, John and all the equipment, but he preferred that to being chauffeured around. He wanted to be with the band, so that's how we toured. This was fine other than the fact that it was a fairly warm time of year, and John suffered with a cold, so there he'd be up in the front seat with his coat, scarf and hat, a blanket over his knees, the heater on, and still complaining about the cold. We'd all be there in T-shirts saying, 'Oh my God,' with sweat pouring off us, and every now and again, when we thought he was dozing off and having a little nap, we'd sneak the window down a little bit and he'd wake up and say, 'Who cracked the glass?' We'd say, 'Oh, sorry, John,' and wind it back up. But it was good that he was traveling with us. The other thing about touring like this would be that also, of course, he decided that he would stay in the same places as the band. Now, bearing in mind that the amount the band were getting for the tour was a pittance—the exact amount I don't remember—we were staying at the most grotty boarding-houses, not hotels. Of course John was staying there as well, so we'd arrive there and usually I'd check out the place beforehand, so by the time John saw the place, it was one o'clock, two o'clock in the morning [before] we'd go back there. It would be freezing cold, of course. His room would have this little gas heater which we had to put on for him, and he would huddle over it. Then in the morning we'd go down to breakfast and this Northern landlady would bustle around saying, 'How'd you want your eggs?' or 'How'd you like your room?' John would go onto complain . . . in a very polite way, but nevertheless complaining, that the room was cold, there was no phone in the room and so on and so forth, because he expected, from the hotels that he'd stayed at on the blues [festival] tour that he'd been on, that he'd have the same situation; not realizing that we were paying the cheapest rate. Lippman and Rau did it well, but unfortunately, the group couldn't afford these places on the pay they were getting, and he wanted to tour with the band. I suggested at the time that maybe we should check him into a better hotel and the band should stay where they were, but he didn't want to do that."

Nevertheless, Hooker hated the food. "In a lot of places, breakfast would be the typical English fry-up: fried egg done not the way you'd want to eat eggs anyway, and bacon that didn't look like American bacon. It was absolutely always a problem. You'd go into a restaurant, and all he'd ever want to eat would be a burger, and they didn't have those here then. They had sandwiches or whatever."

Even in the comparatively sophisticated capital, not everything was to Hooker's liking. "In London I got up in the morning, and in America you get TV all day. I turned my TV on and there was *nothin'*! I said, 'This TV is broken! I can't get nothin'!' and I called downstairs. They said, 'Oh, you don't get nothin' 'til about twelve o'clock, and then you get the BBC, Mr. Hooker.' I said, 'Is that all?' Then you be sittin' there watchin' TV, and at a certain time of night it go *off* early too! And I wouldn't be sleepy! *Click!* Right off and you couldn't get nothin'! And warm beer that make you drunk quick. The pub close up, open up . . . warm beer, the water was warm, the Coke was warm. Warm beer but *strong*. You drink two pitchers of it and you *loaded*."

So there was Hooker, plopped down right smack in the midst of Swinging London. Make that "relatively swinging London": many of the goodies and facilities routinely demanded by Americans—even African-Americans excluded from vast tracts of mainstream American life—were considered luxuries in a Britain still in the process of exorcizing the specter of postwar austerities; a Britain deeply ambivalent both about the loss of its old empire and its fear of becoming part of somebody else's. Hamburgers were difficult to find, and good hamburgers impossible. Restricted pub hours, weird food, part-time television with only two channels, a labyrinthine class system and a set of bewilderingly inconsistent social and cultural codes rendered Britain as "foreign" a country to visiting bluesmen as anywhere else in Europe.

Valerie Wilmer was, at that time, just beginning to make the transition from eager fan to professional photojournalist; and she frequently found herself adopting the role of tour guide and interpreter to visiting African-American jazz and blues musicians. The potential for mutual misunderstanding was massive, and her formidable diplomatic skills were frequently tested to the full. "I used to find myself having to help people out: where to get different kinds of food, where to get drinks after hours, where the off-licenses were . . . There's a story which will illustrate the strange gap between American and British ways: you know that in the States there's nearly always toilets in any kind of restaurant, and it's the law that they have to have them and they have to let you use them? Well, Wimpy Bars had just started here; the first hamburger places in Britain. Curtis Jones, the piano player, was here, and we went out to have a hamburger after a show, and he wanted to use the bathroom. He asked could he use the bathroom and they said no. What they meant was that they don't have one for the public, and you couldn't use theirs. He thought it was racial, and being a deeply sensitive person, he was deeply hurt. He was actually in tears. That would have been in 1963. I had to explain it to him. Things like that were difficult.

"[Pianist] Roosevelt Sykes—who I was also very friendly with; I used to stay with him in New Orleans; a wonderful man, a real philosopher—he and I went out somewhere one day, and he said he wanted chicken and chips and apple pie and ice cream; and he wanted them all on the same plate. This was in some cheapo chicken-and-chips type place, and of course they were . . . you know. And I had my own culture shock when I went to the South and was in people's homes: there was only one plate because they either only had one plate or simply didn't want to bother with it. You *did* have it all on the same plate. Now Roosevelt had been away from that kind of life for years, but it was his sort of thing and I wonder now if he did it just out of devilment, or to say, 'I'm down home.' Another thing about food here was that, among people of my generation, chicken was not very common. You only had chicken at Christmas and Easter, maybe. The Marble Arch barbecue was the first place they had chicken on a spit, that horrible stuff which I [now] refuse to eat, but at the time we thought it was wonderful. It had only just been introduced at the time when those guys came over here, so it was kind of unusual to have chicken and chips. It was not a regular thing to eat here. Those people were really deprived of food. They had the adulation of the fans, and all those people who asked them about records they were on back when God was a boy, and yet they didn't have the food they wanted, and there was always a very ambivalent attitude toward them and their women."

Ah yes, women. Both the African-American musicians and their European female fans were enmeshed in all the complexities of mutual precepts and notions of "otherness' and "exoticism;" each, as far as the other was concerned, had the sweet tang of fruit forbidden in theory but accessible in practice. For many of the bluesmen, born and raised amid the sexual claustrophobia of the South, the readily available company of friendly white girls soon became one of the recognized bonuses of European touring. "When Muddy [Waters] and Otis [Spann] first came here," remembers Wilmer, "it was in '58—that was when I first met them—and then there was the show that Hooker was on that we didn't get to see, and then there was the big blues package show in '63. Memphis Slim was a very intelligent man and very skilled in the ways of the world, and he was actually very nice, but he had a very unfortunate habit of telling tales on everybody. This could be kind of funny, but then you know that he's going to be talking about you when *you* go out the room. He would always tell everybody that when Muddy and Otis first came here, they got a couple of prostitutes and took them back. I know that men always laugh at other men who go with hookers—unfortunate word, that—but the finger was always pointed at them because they were the guys who went with the hookers, rather than the nice girls."

Few, if any, of their peers were to make that mistake again. It was on this and subsequent tours of Britain that Hooker acquired his formidable ladies'-man reputation among white blues-rockers: it is virtually impossible to mention his name to any of the British musicians with whom he worked during the '60s without receiving a metaphorical dig in the ribs and an anecdote beginning with something along the lines of, "I remember John Lee and this girl . . ." For the hardened, dedicated blues buffs Hooker may well have been a legendary hero with fifteen years of classic recordings behind him, but for pop fans he was simply a guy with a danceable record in the charts. And you know what happens to guys with danceable records in the charts.

"He was forty-five at that time,"[27] says Roy Fisher, "and again this was something which was surprising, in a way, because he had the hit record, so therefore when we went to the concerts, he had a mass of young

---

27 Forty-seven, actually.

people, male and female, in adulation, because that's the way they respect someone that's in the charts. This was something he really was not used to, had never really had before, because he wasn't regarded in the same way in America, and even with the blues [festival] concerts you get a very sedate . . . ed elderly audience that would just sit there and politely clap at the end of each number, but not exactly get too aroused, whereas these kids were screaming and yupping and wanted to know about him. As far as the audience were concerned, he was someone that had a single in the charts, therefore they were in awe of him, and he got the adulation that went with that, and all the rest of it. The kids who came to see him after 'Dimples' and 'Boom Boom' were unaware of his status as a blues singer, they didn't know about that. Some of the hard-core blues fans would come along, too, and they were in total disgust of what was going on at that time, from what I know about blues enthusiasts and jazz enthusiasts. He handled it very, very well, but it was something which was obviously totally different for him.

"Undoubtedly he has an interest in ladies, *period*, and at this time, the thought of all these young ladies wishing to know him and wanting to get close to him was very interesting, but that was fine until an occasion which happened soon after we started touring, where I came back into the dressing room at one particular point and he was in a very, very upset state. He was stuttering away and it was obvious that he was upset and I was trying to work out what it was that had upset him, and it was because he had found out that one young lady who had been particularly forceful and had got through to him . . . he had found out about ten minutes later that she was only fifteen." As Hooker must have been keenly aware, back in Mississippi that would have been the cue for a lynching. "He realized very, very fast and got very upset about it. I saw this particular lady, and no way did she look fifteen. She looked eighteen, nineteen because of the make-up and all the rest of it, but she was only fifteen, and that had only come out because he'd asked her how old she was . . . which he did most times. After that he always asked how old they were before he even got involved. He knew the ramifications of America; over here they would have been pretty bad, but not as bad as he thought they would be. She had got very, very upset, because I'd come back as she was leaving, and she was a very pissed young lady because he'd told her to go. He was at least sensible about that, and after that he always made a point of finding out how old they were first."

Quiet, well dressed, polite and unassuming when offstage, and an utterly compelling presence when on, Hooker was as personally attractive to his new-found young fans as any pouting, long-haired teen idol half his age could have been. One such admirer, whom we will call "Sally" because it is not her name, fondly recalls, "I remember going to have a meal with him, and then going back to the hotel and going to bed with him . . . he was quite gentle and everything. He's quite gentlemanly in his way. Even though he was shy, he was very charismatic because he's got this voice, and I thought he was very attractive in that . . . how can I explain it? People like that are often much more attractive than people who are very handsome and sort of putting it about a bit more. He definitely didn't have any trouble with women. He had lots of women, just by being shy. You know how men score in that way."

Under such circumstances, Roy Fisher remembers, Hooker was understandably reticent about discussing his wife and family back in Detroit. "I, because of the nature of the person I am, would tend to ask questions like that when we had quiet moments here and there. He would answer and say, 'Yes, I'm married; yes, I've got some kids,' but he wasn't that outgoing about it, and I kind of think it was a problem to him. I think the family were a problem and he was going through problems with that, so it was something that he didn't really want to get into."

So by the end of his first headlining British tour, Hooker had formed certain lasting impressions about the U.K. He liked the fans (particularly the comelier female ones), the respect, the star status and The Groundhogs; he didn't like the food, the weather and Don Arden. Even today, if you say Don Arden's name to him, he responds as if he'd just been stabbed. "*Oh!* Old Don Arden. Boy, he messed up with me, I'll tell you that. I come home with a check from when I was over there . . . he give me a check for nine thousand dollars. Put it in the bank. It stayed there about a week, and then a woman called me up from the bank, said the check ain't worth the paper it were written on. I was *sick* with hurt. Nine thousand dollars: took me about two, three months to make that money. I was *hurt*."

"The only time that I really saw John get angry during that period," says Roy Fisher, "was when he was referring to Don Arden and the fact that he didn't get his cash on time."

Another difficulty was, according to Fisher, "that there was a lot of people, which he wasn't used to, and he'd get nervous when he had to go on stage if he had to push through a crowd. Sometimes there were minders and people around who would make that easier, but not always.

I don't think Don Arden cared about estimating how popular he would be on that tour, and really he needed a minder: someone bigger than I or Patrick Meehan, if Meehan had continued to chauffeur him around. They weren't really interested; it was just shove 'em out, make the money, and that's it. While I was at the agency working out some dealings with John, I met Little Richard there, and he was due to go out and tour very soon after that, and I'm sure they treated him very much the same way as they treated John. As far as Don Arden was concerned, John was just another artist to make money out of."

In his *Starmakers & Svengalis: The History Of British Pop Management*,[28] Johnny Rogan describes Arden as "the most feared manager in British pop history," an epithet which Arden, who was fond of calling himself "the Al Capone of pop," would undoubtedly consider highly flattering. Instrumental in helping Mike Jeffery break The Animals into the London club scene, he took on the management of The Nashville Teens (who, needless to say, were neither teens nor from Nashville) later in 1964 and the rather more successful Small Faces the following year. Subsequently involved with the likes of Black Sabbath and ELO, his standard managerial tactics combined elaborate legal maneuvers with the threat (and occasionally the use) of extreme violence. Despite his fearsome reputation, it's worth remembering that he has never been convicted of any offense in any court of law. Arden's assistant at that time was a mountainous ex-wrestler named Peter Grant—in fact, it was Grant who had, on Arden's behalf, announced Hooker's tour dates to *Melody Maker*— and it's a safe bet that if Arden had assigned Grant as Hooker's "minder," there would have been zero difficulty escorting the slender bluesman through the throngs blocking his path to the stage. As his subsequent triumph as helmsman for Led Zeppelin's career was to demonstrate, Grant learned several important lessons from his tenure with Arden. Some were based on what Arden did: always get the money, trust in the power of intimidation—what Grant called "verbal violence"—to get results, drive the hardest possible bargain; and some on what Arden didn't do: treat the talent with respect, earn and maintain their loyalty, defend them with your life. Grant would—and, nannying The Yardbirds on their final U.S. tour, actually did—stare into the barrel of a gun while facing down a promoter trying to shark the band out of a one-thousand-dollar gig fee.

Hooker's next British tour was already arranged: he would return in

---

28 Macdonald Queen Anne Press, 1988.

286 / **Boogie Man**

three months' time for more TV and club dates in October and November, and this time The Groundhogs were signed up well in advance. In the meantime, though, he barely had time to drop off his suitcase and electric guitar in Detroit before heading off, acoustic guitar in hand, for his annual slot at the Newport Folk Festival. No more jarring contrast could possibly be imagined. One moment Hooker was in Olde England, slick-suited and rockin', with a record in the charts and hot-to-trot teenage girls screaming over him: the next he was sequestered in New England with the earnest folkies and the antiquarians. Not surprisingly, hardy perennials like Hooker and Sonny Terry & Brownie McGhee found themselves somewhat upstaged that year, because the 1964 festival wasn't just any old Newport show. Instead, it was the year that the ancient gods came back to walk, albeit gingerly, among mortals. For years, Skip James and Son House were merely spectral voices on scratched old records treasured as holy relics by collectors. Now, they emerged from the mists of myth, legends magically made flesh.

Though their paths had never crossed before Newport, Nehemiah "Skip" James and Eddie "Son" House were almost exact contemporaries. They had been born within a few months of each other in 1902, in small Mississippi hamlets within a few miles of each other. They made their classic early recordings a mere year apart (House in 1930, James in 1931) for the same company (Paramount), and in the same location (Grafton, Wisconsin). Both had subsequently abandoned professional music-making, though House had recorded a series of Library of Congress sessions for Alan Lomax in 1941 and '42. Oddly enough, they were "rediscovered" within a few days of each other by two cliques of the same informal network of scholars and aficionados—House working as a school janitor in upstate New York, and James recuperating from surgery in a veterans' hospital in Mississippi—and were reintroduced to live performance at the same Newport festival: House on the main stage, and James at what Samuel Charters has described[29] as a "blues workshop on a cold and damp Saturday afternoon."[30]

Beyond that, they were as different as any two Mississippian singer/guitarists could possibly be. Son House was virtually a founding father of

---

29 In *The Bluesmen* (Oak, 1967).
30 James was rather readier for the world than House, by all accounts: legend has it that after both men had performed, House's rediscoverers approached James's and conceded that "we found the wrong guy."

Delta blues: he had learned from, and traveled with, Charley Patton himself, and had in his turn mentored and tutored both Robert Johnson and Muddy Waters. Hammered out on a steel-bodied National guitar and sung in wracked, grainy chest tones, House's music was muscular and overwhelmingly physical, as solidly rooted in the soil and stone of his home state as a mountain or a tree. James, by contrast, was utterly *sui generis* and represented no significant school, movement or tradition: similar musical devices were indeed used by other bluesmen in and around his native Bentonia, but in terms of artistic achievement or critical acclaim, they hardly represented a peer group. Uniquely unsettling and evocative, he sang in a spooky, brooding falsetto and picked a minor-tuned guitar: his music was as ectoplasmic and eerie as wind through branches. Both men had influenced Robert Johnson—House through direct contact, James through his records—and their twinned legacies embody the mesmerizing conflict at the heart of Johnson's music. With two such men on board, it should have come as no surprise, that year, that Vanguard didn't even bother to record Hooker—or, for that matter, Sonny Terry & Brownie McGhee.

Nevertheless, some of the participants in those two great "rediscoveries" were to play a considerable part in Hooker's future.

The posse which tracked down Skip James included a young Californian guitarist named Henry Vestine; in the same car was John Fahey, a guitarist/musicologist with proven credentials in that area since, in 1963, he'd helped find Booker T. Washington White, another "missing" Delta great of the '30s who just happened to be B. B. King's uncle, and was better known—to his lasting annoyance—as "Bukka" White. Among Fahey's circle was one Alan Wilson, a Boston-born prodigy working simultaneously on a university degree in music and on developing a formidable theoretical and practical mastery of country blues guitar and harmonica. Pudgy, moonfaced and myopic as he was, Al Wilson was certainly no glamor-boy, but he ended up coaching Son House for his return to public performance. Like most elder bluesmen who create—and re-create—their music afresh each and every time they pick up their instruments, House had paid little attention to the precise details of his each and every recorded performance; and since he had not played for decades, he was incredibly rusty. Like most young white blues devotees, Wilson was intimately familiar with each and every nuance of House's classic recordings but, unlike most of his contemporaries, Wilson possessed the musical skills necessary to reproduce those nuances himself. In *The His-*

tory Of The Blues,[31] Francis Davis quotes Dick Waterman's exploration of the resulting paradox:

> *[Wilson] sat down with Son, knee to knee, guitar to guitar, and said, "Okay, this is the figure that, in 1930, you called 'My Black Mama,'" and played it for him. And Son said, "Yeah, yeah, that's me, I played that." And then Al said, "Now about a dozen years later, when Mr. Lomax came around, you changed the name to 'My Black Woman,' and you did it this way." And Son would say, "Yeah, yeah, I got my recollection now, I got my recollection now." And he would start to play, and the two of them played together. Then Al would remind him of how he changed tunings, and played his own "Pony Blues" for him. There would not have been a rediscovery of Son House ... without Al Wilson. Really. Al Wilson taught Son House how to play Son House.*

And when House cut his magnificent *Father Of The Country Blues* comeback album the following year, Wilson was never far from his side in the studio, functioning simultaneously as coach, cheerleader and harp-and-guitar back-up man. Vestine, in the meantime, had returned to California, spending a few grievously miscast months with a prototype lineup of Frank Zappa's Mothers Of Invention. Soon Wilson was to head west to join him in the formation of a band which would—in honor of a 1928 Tommy Johnson song—eventually be known as "Canned Heat."

Meanwhile John Lee Hooker was poised for his second British tour of 1964. If Roy Fisher is correct, Hooker's long-held nervousness concerning Newcastle in general and Mike Jeffery's Club-A-Go-Go in particular may have its roots in one specific occurrence during this jaunt.

"It was without a doubt the best place that John played," says Fisher. "Yes, it did have its rougher element and I think he was kind of nervous about that, but it was really, really good. He was nervous in crowds, and because of the hit record, most places were jam-packed. In Newcastle it was big, and there were about eight hundred people packed into this place, which at that time in a club was a lot of people. The dressing room wasn't at the side of the stage, it was at the back in the managerial offices, so to get him on stage we had to push him through the crowd, so I guess

---

31 *The History Of The Blues: The Roots, The Music, The People From Charley Patton To Robert Cray,* by Francis Davis (Secker & Warburg, 1995).

that's probably what he means. In retrospect, I don't think it was as dramatic as he thought of it at the time. Me, who's not too tall, and John, who's very, very small—five foot seven—it was a problem to get him on stage, because we didn't have any assistance, which at the time pissed me off as well. I had to maneuver him through this crowd. It was the first time in the whole tour that he hadn't been on time to go on stage; most times, unlike many of the other blues singers I can recall, he was always very punctual. The band went on, they played their set, then they would play his intro music and he'd be standing at the side of the stage and then he'd come on. The Geordie reaction was incredible."

> They play the blues there every day and every night
> Everybody monkeys and the beat, all right
> Ask my friend Meyer, he'll tell you so
> There just ain't no place like the Club-A-Go-Go . . .
> The place is full of soul
> Bottled soul, baby
> It's all right there
> John Lee Hooker
> Jerome Green . . . Rolling Stones
> Memphis Slim up there
> Jimmy Reed too, baby
> Sonny Boy Williamson . . .
> —Eric Burdon and Alan Price for The Animals, "Club-A-Go-Go"
>   1965

Elsewhere, though, Hooker was about to discover the downside of Roger Miller's fatuous assertion that "England swings like a pendulum do." Pendulum's do indeed swing, but—almost inevitably—they eventually swing back.

11. Motor City Is Burning

Fri	Oct 30	Jimmy Reed, Sugar Pie De Santo, The Dixie Cups on *Ready Steady Go!*
Sat	Oct 31	Saw Jimmy Reed at Club Noreik. Had to miss John Lee Hooker at Flamingo
Mon	Nov 2	Saw Carl Perkins, Tommy Tucker, The Animals at Gaumont State. Had to miss Jimmy Reed at Flamingo
Wed	Nov 4	Martha & Vandellas on *Top Of The Pops*
Fri	Nov 6	Martha & Vandellas, Kim Weston on *RSG*
Tues	Nov 10	Martha & Vandellas on *Pop Inn*
Fri	Nov 13	Saw The Isley Brothers at East Ham Granada. Had to miss The Soul Sisters at Flamingo
Sat	Nov 14	Perkins, Tucker etc at Finsbury Park Astoria
Wed	Nov 18	Saw Jimmy Reed at Flamingo. Chatted with him for about an hour backstage. Great bloke.
Thurs	Nov 19	Took some records to Jimmy's hotel and had breakfast with him. Geezer called Al Smith from Vee Jay was there. Nice enough bloke but seemed more keen to talk about Betty Everett than Jimmy.
Fri	Nov 20	Jerry Lee [Lewis], Marvin Gaye, The Stones on *RSG*.
Sat	Nov 21	Saw Jerry Lee at Club Noreik
Mon	Nov 23	Saw Jimmy Reed at British Legion Hall, South Harrow. Had to miss Jerry Lee at Eltham Baths
Sat	Nov 28	Saw Howlin' Wolf and Hubert Sumlin at Marquee. —Extract from British soul-rock guru Cliff White's teenage diary for November 1964

After the drought, the deluge. By the winter of 1964, the British Isles were knee-deep in transatlantic musical legends looking to carry the fight back to the home of the British Invasion. For fans endowed with the energy, tenacity, spare cash and geographical opportunity to gorge themselves on this musical feast, it was a dream come true: a veritable embarrassment of riches. This was, according to Cliff White, "a time when American blues, rock and soul originators were coming at us so thick and fast that *we* had to be slick to know which way to jump and *they* had to be bloody marvelous to even so much as justify their reputation, let alone create a lasting impression."[1]

As the battle for the hearts, minds and wallets of British R&B fans intensified, John Lee Hooker defended his market share with admirable tenacity. His second British tour of 1964 commenced with the now-standard rituals of an appearance on *Ready Steady Go!* and a *Melody Maker* interview conducted by Max Jones. On the *RSG!* set, he mimed to his latest EMI/Stateside single "I Love You Honey" and subjected himself to a brief interview with Kenny Lynch,[2] one of the show's hosts. Valerie Wilmer recalls, with laughter, the contrast between Lynch's chirpy black-Cockney questioning—"Woss'yer latest record, man?"—and Hooker's stuttering response—"Uh-whuh-wuh-wuh . . ." "He was sharing a dressing room with a very obnoxious Lulu, who was only sixteen and having her first hit record at the time," says Roy Fisher, "and the other guest was Gene Pitney, who he actually knew, which made John more relaxed, because he was very nervous about doing TV and miming."

Not surprisingly, Hooker was rather more comfortable backstage with the familiar, reassuring figure of Max Jones. Indeed, his mood was effusive-verging-on-gushing and, in marked contrast to the glowering demeanor displayed in the photograph accompanying Jones's story, he seized every opportunity to express his appreciation of his host country.

When I last came over [he told Jones] things were a big surprise to me. Now it's different again. More bluesmen have been over here from the States and gone over real good and . . . more kids are playing the blues and understanding it than even three months ago. It's fantastic. They appreciate blues far more than American kids . . . here, they give the blues artist more respect than American fans do. I find that your younger people know the different songs and dig so deep into them, where the American youngsters want to hear rock-'n'-roll all day. And some of your groups are so good at it. Gosh, I really dig it. That John Mayall group and [The] Groundhogs are definitely my favorites. They're tremendously nice fellows and very

---

1 In his liner-note to the Jimmy Reed Compilation *Upside Your Head* (Charly CRB 1003), whence also cometh the above diary extract.

2 Kenny Lynch was a jack-of-all-trades who darted between singing, song writing, acting and comedy. His peak musical achievement came in 1965, when he and Mort Shuman co-composed "Sha La La La Lee," a Number One hit for Don Arden's protégés The Small Faces. For no apparent reason, he received a knighthood in the early '70s.

good to work with. They try hard to do everything I want. I really
was pleased to see those fellows when I arrived back in England.

The Groundhogs were pleased to see Hooker, too; their experiences with other blues giants had not been nearly as enjoyable as the time they'd spent with John Lee. "He was always a gentleman, always polite," Fisher fondly remembers, "and in that way totally unique, unlike Little Walter or Jimmy Reed, who were totally uncouth. Ignorant, but in the worst possible way. Walter was obnoxious and bad-tempered and got upset very, very quickly. Jimmy Reed was okay on stage when he was playing, but in between times he drank too much and complained about absolutely everything. John said he wasn't happy unless he was bitching about something; John put it down to the hard times that Reed had with his women. You can be illiterate but still be well mannered, which John was but the others were not."

Hooker's lack of formal education was causing him, inadvertently, to commit one serious breach of pop etiquette. "He'd have kids coming around asking for his autograph, and he'd refuse, and this happened a few times, so I took him aside and had a few words with him and said, 'They expect you to sign your autograph, John, because you're famous and this is what they expect you to do.' He was extremely embarrassed and upset about it and the outcome was that he pointed out that he'd never had any schooling so he couldn't sign his name. I got a piece of paper and did a very flourishing "John Lee Hooker" and said, 'Copy this, John, just sign this and they'll be happy.' So he practices it a few times and the next time we went out and played there was this line of kids for autographs, and he was doing it very painstakingly: J-o-h-n-L-e-e-H-o-o-k-e-r. The line was getting longer and longer, and the band were getting ready to go back to the hotel or go to eat, and John would still be there signing his name, and it seemed like it was going to be forever and a day, and I'm thinking to myself, 'Oh my God, what have I started?' But then, realizing that it was taking too much time and he wanted to go and eat the same as everybody else, he started getting blasé and then it would be "J L Hooker" and then "J L H," and the he was quite happy to sign the autographs and carry on, and the kids went away happy."

In his autobiography *All The Rage*,[3] former (Small) Faces keyboard

---

3 Sidgwick & Jackson, 1998.

guy Ian "Mac" McLagan recalls that he and his mates from his pre-Small Faces R&B group The Muleskinners,

> *saw John Lee Hooker put on a great show at The Ricky-Tick [club] in Reading, and afterwards I asked him for his autograph, which he graciously gave me. I handed him the only scrap of paper I had on me, which was a reminder from the finance company that my electric piano payment was overdue. It took him ages to sign it, because his handwriting was so shaky, and I watched fascinated as he drew the "H," formed the two "o"s and then the "k" and the "e." Then he must've had enough, because he didn't bother with the "r." He added his initials underneath and handed it back to me without a word.*

One significant change which occurred between the two 1964 tours was an augmentation of The Groundhogs' line-up. "When he came back the second time we had a pianist, Tom Parker, and his parents came to [a local] gig. At the end they got introduced to John, and asked him whether he would like to come to their house the next day for lunch. And in his charming way he said, 'Oh yes, that would be nice,' so the next day we all went over. So there we are all standing in the living room, chit-chatting away, drinks in hand, and John—who had a habit of clearing his throat and spitting—had the need to do that. So there we are with this fire blazing in the fireplace, and John clears his throat halfway through a conversation with Tom Parker's mother and goes *'ptoo'* into the fireplace, which to him was a perfectly normal thing to do. The unfortunate thing about it was that it was an artificial log fireplace, and the look on Mrs. Parker's face was . . . I wish I'd had a camera at the time. However, with all due respect to the lady, she kept her composure absolutely wonderfully and carried on the conversation as if absolutely nothing had happened. Me and the rest of the group were clenching our teeth rather than laugh in her face. We'd had the experience with John's spitting before, because it was the only time he'd wind the window down in the van, and we'd all duck hoping that it wouldn't blow back in our faces."

Despite the graciousness of his mother, Tom Parker hadn't been the first choice for The Groundhogs' piano seat: Bob Hall, the original in-cumbent, was eventually replaced because of his reluctance to quit his London-based day job. "I toured with Hooker and The Groundhogs for quite a long time," Hall told Norman Darwen, "although I never played on the one record they made together, because that was one of the many occasions I've been told, 'If you don't turn professional with us, you're out of the band.' So I said, 'I'm not going to go professional,' and the week after I left, they had this offer to make a record. The guy they got to play piano was a pub pianist [who] had never played blues before. I had to teach him to play blues, which I did because I wanted to be a help, but he couldn't feel the way Hooker played. I've heard the record, and what Hooker had to do [was to] play his sequence and then . . . wait for the piano player to catch up, because Hooker's things tend to be ten or eleven bars. It was made in IBC Studios. Hooker was great: he had two records in the charts when we were backing him, so we had crowds of people everywhere. It was a tremendous experience."

Hooker had decided to stay on in London past the end of the tour, and brave a few more days of English winter in order to record with The Groundhogs; *Melody Maker*'s Max Jones was once again on hand to act as Hooker's Boswell.

As far as I'm concerned [Hooker told him], this whole tour has been a complete success, and for their part The Groundhogs have been tremendous. I'm bound to say that . . . The Groundhogs are one of the number one best blues groups that you have over here, and it fits in with my type of music perfectly. Because it studies my style anyway, it knows how to work with me. Often the boys know what I'm going to do before I do it. John Mayall has a real good blues band too, but The Groundhogs, they fit better with what I do. Not that I'm taking anything away from Mayall. He has his own style, his own thing going. Oh, he's good.

Anyway, I was so impressed with The Groundhogs on this tour that I contacted Calvin Carter of Vee Jay right away with a view to recording them over here. And I sent a demo disc of two songs by the group for him to hear. He phoned me back and then sent a cable saying he was coming over to London next week and would offer them a contract and record them here. He liked the acetate enough to want to record them with me and on their own. So I'm staying on three or four days to do the recording. The Groundhogs will be backing me, and that's for Vee Jay who will release it in the States, also The Groundhogs' single. What songs will I record here? I know one I'm going to do is "Seven Days And Seven Nights," a new one of mine. I got some more, too, but right now I'm undecided as

to which to do. I want to say this: I'm very pleased that John Lee
& The Groundhogs have been discovered because they're too good
a blues group to remain undiscovered. I tried to do something for
them, and did do something for them, and I'm proud of them. I am
sure they'll become a great favorite of British blues fans, and they'll
be known in America a few months from now . . .

For all Hooker's generosity of intention, his optimism proved to be misplaced. One suspects Calvin Carter of a certain disingenuousness in this instance: after all, even if Hooker hadn't quite realized it yet, Carter was aware that Vee Jay was in full retreat and facing the distinct possibility of complete extinction. It's possible that Carter felt, after Vee Jay had so comprehensively fumbled the Brit ball with The Beatles, that the acquisition of another "English sensation" could conceivably provide the company with last-minute salvation. It is also possible that he already knew full well that the label was ultimately a dead dog, and also that an inside track on a potentially profitable new British band might significantly enhance his chances of finding lucrative employment elsewhere in the record biz. Whatever the explanation—and since Calvin Carter is no longer around, we can't ask him—he evidently considered that the price of a Chicago–London round-trip ticket was well worth the risk. As it happened, the label limped on until early '66—when its final Jerry Butler release entered the charts—before finally closing its doors, but by late '64 they'd effectively withdrawn from the blues arena, leaving the likes of Hooker and Jimmy Reed high and dry. (It is little wonder, therefore, that Al Smith had "seemed more keen to talk about Betty Everett than Jimmy [Reed]" to Cliff White.) Vee Jay continued to release Hooker material right up until the end—his final Vee Jay single, yoking "It Serves Me Right To Suffer" to "Flowers On The Hour," was issued as late as 1966— but they were no longer interested in cutting any fresh sides on him. Which as far as Hooker was concerned, meant that he wasn't making any money.

Nevertheless, when The Groundhogs accompanied Hooker into IBC Studios in mid-November of 1964, they certainly proved their worth. In the rhythm section, drummer Dave Boorman and bassist Pete Cruikshank kept everything nailed down that was supposed to be nailed down, and everything swinging that was supposed to swing. On lead guitar, Tony McPhee presents impressive bluesical credentials. Like those Steady Eddies, Kirkland and Burns, he was able to Hookerize his own individual style to the point where he could create the illusion that John Lee had grown a second pair of hands and was simultaneously playing two guitars: indeed, sometimes the only way to tell which guitarist is playing what, comes when McPhee zooms up to the "dusty end" of the neck, where Hooker was traditionally reluctant to venture. As for the unfortunate Tom Parker, if he had indeed recently acquired all his blues chops in a crash course from Bob Hall, then these rocking, surprisingly assured performances do him considerable honor. His greatest limitation is, as Hall points out, that his inability to adapt to Hooker's idiosyncratic meter straps the band—and John Lee himself—into the straitjacket of the orthodox twelve-bar sequence.

The resulting album was certainly no disgrace, but it remains a decidedly minor part of the Hooker canon. Though the album may not have been an absolute artistic triumph for Hooker, it was a considerable achievement for the fledgling Groundhogs, winning their spurs by keeping musical pace with an acknowledged master. Unsurprisingly, it was solidly located in the tradition of the Vee Jay sides which it was originally intended to complement. Equally unsurprisingly, it slotted straight into what the late Frank Zappa would have dubbed the "conceptual continuity" of Hooker's repertoire by casting light both forward and backward, not merely illuminating aspects of the work he'd already done and previewing songs and themes which would later attain their fullest flowering, but reflecting and transforming recent and current experience. "Seven Days And Seven Nights," the new song which Hooker had mentioned to Max Jones and which ended up as the sort-of-title-track when the album crept into American stores as . . . And Seven Nights on Verve-Folkways Records in 1965, was a haunting free-form slow blues meditation incorporating a few lines of stock lyrics, also included in young Buddy Guy's then-recent "Stone Crazy," which would later serve as the foundation stone of the towering edifice which eventually became "Dark Room." The slow blues variously entitled "It's Raining Here" and "Storming On The Deep Blue Sea" on different editions of the record is a distant cousin of the Charles Brown "Drifting Blues" which had, appropriately enough, "drifted" in and out of Hooker's repertoire for so long. While "Go Back To School, Little Girl," an intriguing variant on the Sonny Boy Williamson staple "Good Morning Little Schoolgirl," may or may not be an explicit allusion to recent encounters with under-aged fanettes, its message is nevertheless quite clear: "*I'll wait on you 'til you get [to be] twenty-one.*" Equally pressing and immediate concerns are expressed in "Don't Be Messing With My Bread": the song isn't dedicated to Don Arden, though it might as well be.

However, the most significant addition to Hooker's repertoire to emerge from these sessions was "I Cover The Waterfront," a radical Hookerization of a Tin Pan Alley ballad already more than three decades old. Composed in 1933 by Johnny Green and Edward Heyman as, according to Donald Clarke,[4] "a promotional song for a film of a novel of the same name,"[5] the song was initially popularized by society orchestras like those led by Joe Haynes and Eddie Duchin. Louis Armstrong recorded it almost immediately, and it was soon taken to the hearts of Broadway and supper-club crooners, later entering the repertoires of Frank Sinatra, Billy Eckstine, Ella Fitzgerald, Mel Torme and Jo Stafford, to name but a few. Like Green and Heyman's other enduring classic "Body And Soul," it subsequently became a standard vehicle for jazz improvisation. "I Cover The Waterfront" was a perennial favorite of Billie Holiday's—Lady Day recorded versions of the song in 1941, '44, '45, '48, '49, '51 and '54— and its plangent melody also endeared it to Charlie Parker, Lionel Hampton, Coleman Hawkins, Django Reinhardt, Art Tatum and the Prez himself, Lester Young. As sung by Holiday, or by Sarah Vaughan, "I Cover The Waterfront" is an archetypal torch song in the grand manner, languorously, sexily melancholic. As played by Parker, it is a ballad both pensive and playful, with the great man simultaneously respectful of the moodiness of Johnny Green's melody, and getting off on the sheer heady delight of the agile, graceful arabesques he spins around it.

By contrast, Hooker dumps not only Green's music but virtually all of Edward Heyman's lyric, retaining only the title and the storyline—that of an abandoned lover waiting patiently by the dockside for the Adored One's vessel to appear on the horizon—incorporating elements of his own Detroit-era "Down At The Landing." Ships arrive, passengers disembark, everyone else's loved one but Hooker's shows up for joyful reunions, he hangs in there, alone and palely loitering. A young girl approaches him, attempts to entice him away, but he opts to remain, steadfastly waiting for his baby. However, Hooker's version has, unlike Heyman's, a happy ending. Long after everybody else has left, he spots a distant ship emerging

---

4 *In wishing On The Moon: The Life And Times Of Billie Holiday* (Viking, 1994).
5 The novel was by Max Miller; the movie, directed by James Cruze and starring Ben Lyon and Claudette Colbert, was—according to Pauline Kael in *5001 Nights At The Movies* (Hamish Hamilton, 1982)—"a commonplace romantic melodrama" which nevertheless included "some strong, memorable scenes."

from the fog, and she's on board: his faith and dedication are rewarded after all. Uncharacteristically, he casts the song in the key of C rather than his preferred E, using "normal" first-position chords of C, F and G7, as a sort-of-slow-blues. The Groundhogs patter along behind him, with Parker sounding exposed and uncomfortable playing organ rather than piano; Hooker's tone is hushed and undemonstrative, apart from the vibrato and growl with which he emphasizes the first person singular.

Artistically, the sessions were a moderate success; as a career move, the project turned out to be a complete bust-out. Calvin Carter did indeed record a Groundhogs single, comprising "Shake It" (a revibe of "Shake It On Down," most frequently associated with "Bukka" White, but which had also been a staple of Tony Hollins's repertoire) and "Rockin," but neither its U.S. release on Vee Jay nor the European issue on Interphon generated any noticeable impact, and the leaders of the British Invasion remained unchallenged. Hooker's album fared little better, not even receiving the courtesy of a U.K. release until 1971, when it snuck out on a budget label. In the States, Verve-Folkways rapidly deleted . . . *And Seven Nights*, and the tapes have been ignominiously bounced around from label to label ever since: sometimes under the near-fraudulent billing of *John Lee Hooker With John Mayall And The Groundhogs*, sometimes—as on the 1969 Wand album *On The Waterfront*—with several tracks retitled and an actually-not-bad horn section overdubbed at some later date by person or persons unknown. In the summer of '65, former Kinks and Who producer Shel Talmy acquired two tracks, "Mai Lee"—Hooker is actually singing *"Mary Lee"* and, to Brit ears at least, pronouncing it "Ma'y Lee"—and "Don't Be Messing With My Bread," for British single release on his short-lived Planet label. However, Planet's star act, The Creation,[6] failed to make a major chart breakthrough, the label went pear-shaped, Talmy released no further Hooker/'Hogs material, and the whole adventure didn't amount to a hill of beans in this particular crazy mixed-up world.

"The British," Joe Gore once wrote in *Guitar Player* magazine, "dis-

---

6 Not that it matters, but The Creation were actually quite an interesting band. Briefly perceived as potentially serious challengers to The Who, they proudly proclaimed, "Our music is red . . . with purple flashes" and mounted a spectacular stage show in which guitarist Eddie Phillips sawed away at his guitar with a violin bow (*way* before Jimmy Page) while singer Kenny Pickett frantically spray-painted giant paper backdrops. Their first single, "Making Time," occupied the no-man's-land between proto-psychedelia and protopunk with crunching surliness, and their second, "Painter Man," was almost as good, but neither reached the U.K. Top 30, and the group broke up. "Painter Man" subsequently resurfaced as a '70s disco hit for producer Frank Farian's protégés Boney M . . . but I digress.

card their heroes as often as they brush their teeth—practically every week." That observation was as true, if not even truer, back in 1965 as it was when Gore wrote it some thirty years later. Many of the bands who'd initially launched themselves on the strength of their affinity for the blues were moving onto pastures new; some drew fresh inspiration from contemporary soul music rather than older blues, and others, in the spirit of furious modernism which became the engine which powered the next wave of British rock, explored the frontier territories of experimental pop opened up by The Beatles. Dispirited, The Groundhogs would attempt to reincarnate themselves as a soul band, and then temporarily dissolve. The Rolling Stones were covering Marvin Gaye and Otis Redding rather than Muddy Waters and Bo Diddley while Mick Jagger and Keith Richards were cutting their song-writing teeth; Eric Burdon and The Animals borrowed from Nina Simone and Ray Charles as opposed to Chuck Berry and John Lee Hooker; The Kinks, never that comfortable as a blues band in the first place, plowed their own unique furrow as Ray Davies settled into his compositional stride. Sensing which way the wind was blowing, The Who—partway through the sessions for their first album—scrapped much of the blues repertoire they'd already recorded and replaced it with more Pete Townshend originals and a James Brown cover. One of the numbers The Who dumped was Howlin' Wolf's "Smokestack Lightnin'," a rave-up version of which had been a highlight of their early stage act. However, the song had by that time already appeared on albums by The Yardbirds, Manfred Mann and The Graham Bond Organisation (featuring Jack Bruce and Ginger Baker in the rhythm section), and was well on its way to becoming a cliché. And for a new group to seem to be selling clichés was instant death: in the excitement of the British Invasion and the pop-art avant-garde, the bluesmen themselves were beginning to seem like clichés. Even the likes of Pete Townshend became increasingly blasé about their former heroes. "The irony was," he once told the present author,[7] "that they all seemed so pathetic, John Lee Hooker in his checkered jacket, doing his cabaret . . . somehow, they weren't able to attend to the quantum jump that we'd made."

The caravan of screamagers and cutting-edge artists thus moved on, but a solid hardcore of blues fans nevertheless remained loyal to the true faith. In a fierce reaction to changing trends, Eric Clapton, the high card in The Yardbirds' musical hand, quit the group as a protest against their

---

7 Quoted in *Crosstown Traffic: Jimi Hendrix And Postwar Pop* (Faber & Faber, 1989).

switch from R&B to Progressive Pop. They replaced him with Telecaster terrorist Jeff Beck, a guitarist much better suited to their new approach, but Clapton's decision to join John Mayall in the summer of '65 effectively sited Mayall's Bluesbreakers at the center of what remained of the blues scene. As far as Hooker was concerned, his enviable Britpop status had evaporated as suddenly as it had originally appeared. Mere months earlier, he'd been riding a small but respectable hit, appearing on the hippest pop TV shows, and receiving respectful notices from the music press. Now he had a brand-new made-in-England album in the can, and couldn't even get it released in the U.K. There would always be work for Hooker in Britain and the rest of Europe—just as there would always be work for him back home in folk clubs, colleges and festivals—but there would be little further glory and even less money.

"I went back and come back," recalls Hooker. "I was [in the U.K.] about a year and a half." During the "year and a half" to which Hooker alludes—the period between the summer of 1964 and the late autumn of 1965—he made four tours, each lasting approximately a month. For his summer '65 tour, there were a few changes made. For one thing, the immediately pre-Clapton edition of John Mayall's Bluesbreakers stepped in as back-up combo in place of the temporarily disbanded Groundhogs. And since Don Arden was now out of the picture, this next tour was booked by another agency, that of the brothers Rik and John Gunnel, who managed Mayall's band and the more soulful and cosmopolitan Georgie Fame & The Blue Flames. (Their roster also included clubland favorite Zoot Money's Big Roll Band, and Geno Washington & The Ram Jam Band, led by an expat American ex-GI whose brassy, all-action soul revue, jam-packed with Stax, Motown and Atlantic cover versions, made him a figurehead for those unreconstructed mods who hadn't switched their loyalties to nouveau pop.) The Gunnels' mini-empire also included The Flamingo and a string of lesser venues like the Bag O'Nails in the West End of London, and a chain of Ricky-Tick clubs throughout the South East.

"Of course they were of the same type as Don Arden," Roy Fisher opines, but Hooker remembers them rather more fondly than that. "They was pretty good by me," he says. "They knowed what I had been through with Don Arden, and they were *straight* with me. They said, 'We know what Don Arden did to you. We not gonna do this to you, we gonna be straight up front with you.' And they were."

The tour itself was certainly no bed of roses. Arriving at London's

Heathrow Airport on Monday, May 10, according to a report by Tony Lennane in *Blues Unlimited*'s July/August issue, Hooker was whisked straight off to Newport. Not his familiar stamping ground of Newport, Rhode Island, but Newport in South Wales: as the car flies, 159 miles due west of Heathrow, in the County of Monmouthshire. With a mere four hours' sleep under his belt, he then found himself onstage at Newport's Majestic Cinema, *sans* rehearsal, banging out the likes of "Boom Boom," "Dimples," "Maudie," "Shake It Baby" and "I'm Leaving" to the extemporized accompaniment of Cops 'N' Robbers, a local combo described by Lennane as "Newport's own brand of codswallop."

"Despite the local 'hood' section jackassing their way through the evening on each other's shoulders," Lennane wrote, "charging through the crowd, gyrating in front of [Hooker], using as much abusive language as their tiny minds allowed and generally disrupting—this was a night I shan't forget." Lennane and Hooker hung out after the show, chatting in the bar. "As we talked some of his records spun and he was anxious all present listened to his *Big Soul* LP, letting us know that The Vandellas backed him. He was full of stories of his later recordings, ignoring the classics on Modern, Sensation and even earlier Vee Jay; ah well." Presumably Hooker didn't repeat to Lennane what he'd said about the *Big Soul* sessions, a few months earlier, to another *Blues Unlimited* contributor, Simon Napier: "I don't particularly like 'em, but . . . say! the bread's good." *BU*'s previous issue had, incidentally, carried a scathing report of a gig which had actually taken place a few days later at the Ricky-Tick club in Guildford, Surrey. The splenetic John J. Broven excelled himself:

John Lee Hooker has embarked upon his third tour (and fourth visit) of England. The very thought of having Hooker here would have aroused frantic, delirious orgasms of rapture as little as two years ago. Now he is taken for granted, to the extent of complete apathy and utter disinterestedness. To all blues observers this must cause alarm, for Hooker is unquestionably a major figure in the postwar blues. On the surface there is an abundance of ammunition for those defeatists who claim that the blues is losing its glamour—I use "glamour" freely, for although the blues is scarcely "glamourized" there can be no disputing that it has been highly, too highly, romanticized but a visit to one of Hooker's performances will reveal the real reason for this apparent negligence. Gone is Hooker, the bluesman of immense stature, whose qualities are known to all; in his place is a pathetically small character, singing a flood of up-tempo numbers whose sole mark of distinction is in the lyrics—which were inaudible anyway; totally devoid of expression or—important—enthusiasm, contenting himself merely to strum a few chords on his guitar in rhythm accompaniment.

On his first tour we were prepared to (and did) make excuses, primarily at the expense of his backing groups; on his second tour one was still surprised that he didn't make more concessions to the blues fan—his show following on the lines of the first, was still aimed at satisfying the fastidious and uninterested teenage audiences. And on this his third tour? I have for one now exhausted all patience. Excuses can still be made—the group, the audience, the promoters—but why should there be? Hooker has had his chance, three times, and each time he has churned out the same, same rubbish. The onus must now fall on his shoulders. He has not only let himself down—he has failed the Blues.[8]

Fairly extravagant language with which to denounce a hard-working man thousands of miles from home attempting to put on a decent show with a borrowed band. Back in London, Hooker had organized himself at least a simulacrum of the comforts of home. "I was living with a girl called Shirley," he says. "She had a nice apartment on Oxford Street. Big *main* street, lotta all kinda clothes shops on that street. I was living over a clothing store." Roy Fisher corroborates: "I remember Shirley. She was just someone whom he tagged onto or tagged onto him. He was quite enamored with Shirley at the time, but then there were many like that." A liaison of a different nature—and of considerably greater long-term significance—commenced on one of his late-night ventures into London's club scene, when he encountered one of his most devoted admirers: Van Morrison, the stocky, belligerent lead vocalist of an Irish band named Them, recently arrived in the Top 10 with an artfully arranged rock rave-up of the staple "Baby Please Don't Go" primarily derived from Hooker's own version. "I know Van [Morrison] about twenty-seven years," he remembered in 1992. "I can't recall when I met Van, but it was in London, I think so. At some club called the Cue Club [a primarily West Indian-

---

8 The archivist who supplied the author with a copy of this particular clipping has appended the scribbled comment: "Blues fans! Dontcha just love 'em?" Say no more.

patronized club in Paddington], and then another place called The Bag O'Nails."

John Broven's purist temper tantrum notwithstanding, Hooker's increasing British familiarity had bred, if not contempt, then at least a degree of indifference. For his second European tour of 1965, he retreated back into the safety-in-numbers of that year's edition of Lippmann & Rau's American Folk Blues Festival revue. By this time, the package's traditions were established solidly enough not to require the personal attendance of its original mastermind, Willie Dixon; and the rhythm section was anchored by a Chess studio stalwart, master drummer Freddie Below. The line-up featured such notables as Mississippi Fred McDowell, Big Mama Thornton, Eddie Boyd, Roosevelt Sykes, J. B. Lenoir, harpmeister Big Walter Horton, and, making his first-ever excursion outside the U.S.A, a wide-eyed young guitarist named Buddy Guy.

"My first trip in Europe in 1965, American Folk Blues Festival," Buddy remembers. "First time I met him, and Big Mama Thornton. I had come over to play the festival with them, and it was at least seven o'clock in the morning. He was drinkin' at that time, Big Mama was drinkin', they had a guy on the show named Doctor Ross, Roosevelt Sykes, Eddie Boyd . . . everybody was drinkin'. Straight whiskey, and hot. I drinks a few drinks, but at that time I didn't. I couldn't keep up with them because I thought you drink sociably, but when I met Little Walter, Muddy Waters and Sonny Boy and them, I didn't know you drink like fish. But anyway, I was upstairs that morning, and all the commotion was downstairs. They had the whole restaurant in this particular hotel in Baden-Baden, Germany. When I walked down, didn't nobody know me, and I didn't know anybody. They was around a table and I heard this guy stutter, 'B-b-b-b-b-b-b-b,' and I thought, 'Well, I know *that's* not John Lee.' So I picked up an acoustic guitar and sat over in a corner and went to playin' 'Boogie Chillen' and somebody came over and grabbed me then. 'T-t-t-t-t-t-uhh . . . who are you?' I said, 'Ohh, I don't bother wit' you.' It was like ten minutes axin' me, 'Who are you?' before he told me who he was, and he didn't say, 'John Lee' then. He said, 'T-t-t-t-I'm Johnny,' and I thought it was somebody else on the show named Johnny—I've got to meet everybody sooner or later, somebody come introduce me to everybody.

"And finally he kept messin' with me so much, in a jokin' manner, and he said, 'T-t-t-t-t-who taught you how to play like J-J-Johnny?' And I'm thinkin,' does John Lee stutter like this? Finally I said something like that, and he just fell out, went to laugh. 'T-t-t-t-you don't know me?' I said, 'No, I don't know you.' 'Th-th-th-th-that's my shit you playin'.' I say, 'You John Lee?' And ever since then we been the best of friends. He kept me laughin' from that day until this one. When I see him now, if I got a concert to do, I try to tell 'em to keep him away from my dressing room, because he keep me laughin'. He got so many stories he can tell about him, Jimmy Reed and Muddy Waters, the times he didn't get paid, and the time they got throwed out of the hotel for tryin' to cook with the electric skillet under the bed . . . ohh, *man!* They got so many stories."

In Willie Dixon's absence, the package's bassist-in-residence was "Lonesome" Jimmy Lee Robinson, a journeyman all-rounder willing and able to move between guitar, bass or drums, depending on what was required on the night. However, such was the warmth of the spontaneous rapport between Hooker and Guy that the latter ended up playing bass for Hooker's portion of the proceedings. The show was recorded in Hamburg on October 8; of the two Hooker numbers, accompanied only by Guy and Below, which surfaced on the resulting album, "Della Mae" was little more than a retread of "Maudie" sailing under marginally different colors. The other, "King Of The World," was rather more intriguing: an idealistic, deeply felt state-of-the-universe meditation in the tradition of "Crazy Mixed-Up World," ornamented by a loping descending Guy bassline which only occasionally collides with Hooker's idiosyncratic meter.

"King Of The World" had been Hookerized from a source incongruous even by Hooker's own catholic standards: it derived from "If I Ruled The World," the Big Number from the stage musical *Pickwick*. Based on Charles Dickens's novel *The Pickwick Papers* and, like most modern Dickens adaptations churned out by the British heritage industry, downplaying the darkness and pain in Dickens's work in favor of warm, twinkly *faux*-Victorian sentimentality, *Pickwick* had been commissioned in 1961 and staged in 1963 as a vehicle for the mountainous Welsh singer/comedian Harry Secombe, co-conspirator with Peter Sellers and Spike Milligan in BBC Radio's groundbreaking *Goon Show*. Composed by Leslie Bricusse and Cyril Ornadel, "If I Ruled The World" had subsequently been revived by Hooker's ballad-singing hero Tony Bennett, and it was Bennett's version which had installed itself in the British Top Ten during Hooker's May '65 tour. "*Eef I-I-I-I-I ruled the wuuuuurld,*" Secombe had shrilled in his manic tenor, "*eff-ree day wood bee tha fi-i-i-i-irst day off spreeeeeeng . . . ,*" but Hooker had a different agenda. If *he* was the king of the world, his initially hushed baritone informs us with gradually intensifying passion, "*there wouldn't be no fightin' . . . wouldn't be no war.*" Furthermore, he tells his beloved, he'd make her his queen and put her on his throne. On Planet Hook, "*there wouldn't be no race riots . . . I'd make everybody equal . . . in the world . . . there wouldn't be no sickness, wouldn't be no death.*"

Hooker, certainly, considers the song to be nothing less than a personal credo. "I wrote one called 'If I Was The King Of The World,' " he says proudly. "Did you ever hear that one? If I was the king of the world, and my woman was the . . . I be the king, she be the queen. Wouldn't be no fightin,' be love and peace everywhere if I were the ruler of the world. That's that song. Roy Rogers heard that and he said, 'That's so true.' " He breaks into song: " '*If I were the king of the world, wouldn't be no fightin', everybody would get along/I'd make my woman queen of the world, and I'd be the king/Wouldn't be no fightin', wouldn't be no racial, if I was the king of the world.*' The king rule everything, and people listen to that, people who fightin' for peace, fightin' for they rights, fightin' to make everybody equal. This land is no man's land. We just passin' through, and that song tell all of that." In the Bricusse and Ornadel "original," Secombe (and Bennett) call for little more than a perpetual Christmas party, where a beaming Mine Host provides perpetual roast beef and mulled wine for suitably grateful poor children. By contrast, Hooker— "*talkin' 'bout a new-born king*"—promises nothing less than heaven on earth and an immediate end to all human suffering.

On a somewhat less exalted level, Hooker's main priority once back home in the U.S.A was to kick-start his stalled recording career. A full year had elapsed since the ill-fated London session with The Groundhogs, Hooker's only studio date since the demise of his relationship with Vee Jay. His next port of call was Impulse Records, the jazz subsidiary of ABC-Paramount Records, itself a division of one of America's three principal television networks, who commissioned a day-long session in New York City on November 23, 1965. A hipper, feistier label than one might have expected considering its heavy-duty corporate origins, ABC had started getting serious about African-American music in 1960, when the company just about broke the Ertegun brothers' collective heart by seducing away Atlantic Records' human crown jewel, Ray Charles. ABC subsequently followed up this coup by picking up The Impressions after Vee Jay fumbled Curtis Mayfield's ball, and signing B. B. King away from Modern. The Impulse success story was founded partly on borrowing Brother Ray from the parent company to cut 1961's epochal *Genius + Soul = Jazz*, and partly on the spoils of another corporate raid on the

Erteguns, in which Impulse practically chased Atlantic out of the modern-jazz business. In 1962, Impulse acquired the services not only of John Coltrane (just as the tenor titan, whose previous important recordings as a leader had been made while still a member of the Miles Davis Quintet, was finally ready to break away from Miles and form his first working band) but also of the "controversial" Ornette Coleman, the walking definition of avant-garde. The proud slogan "The New Wave Of Jazz Is On Impulse!," an integral part of the orange-and-black Mondrian-inspired graphics which adorned the label's sleeves, was therefore no idle boast.

Impulse's A&R chief, the late Bob Thiele, took personal charge of the Hooker project. His production strategy blended the aesthetics of the Vee Jay years and Riverside's *That's My Story* by recording eight sides rather than the usual ten (thereby allowing each performance to determine its own length, thus freeing Hooker from the need to compress the songs to the arbitrary length of a single), featuring Hooker on electric guitar rather than the folkish acoustic instrument, and teaming him up with veteran sidemen from the New York jazz world. Certainly, admirers of Lionel Hampton, Billie Holiday, Gil Evans and Coleman Hawkins would have been rather more familiar with the liner credits of bassist Milt Hinton and drummer David "Panama" Francis than would fans of Muddy Waters, Howlin' Wolf, Jimmy Reed or Sonny Boy Williamson, but the match was nevertheless a good one. Guitarist Barry Galbraith was an electric folkie who'd recorded with Bob Dylan: he, Hinton and Francis may not have been "blues" players in the most literal sense of the term, but they were keenly aware of the common heritage of jazz and blues, plus they had ears and knew how to use them. Furthermore, they were well accustomed to following musicians who were themselves following their noses. The pulsebeat supplied by Hinton and Francis was solid but sensitive: simultaneously firm enough for Hooker to sit on and sufficiently sparse and discreet to allow his improvisational instincts the freedom to wander wherever they might. Galbraith, for his part, provides subtle textures and coloration while adroitly staying out from under Hooker's musical feet: since Hooker juxtaposed the conventional tuning he generally favors for ensemble pieces with the open-A "Spanish" tuning of his early solo work, Galbraith, sensibly enough, sat out the open-tuned songs and performed only on the numbers in "straight" tuning.

The resulting album, *It Serve You Right To Suffer*, broke no significant new ground in terms of Hooker's repertoire, revisiting as it did such staples as "Money," "Bottle Up And Go," "Decoration Day," "Shake It Baby" and the title song, a recasting of Hooker's Percy Mayfield-derived "It Serves Me Right To Suffer." However, whatever the album may have lost in terms of fresh material it gained in increased emotional depth. The longer track-lengths gave Hooker the space to explore the sideroads of the songs rather than simply cruise along their main drags; thus the taut stomping groove customary for Hooker's assorted variations on "Bottle Up And Go" unwinds into an eerily incantatory modal shuffle, and Sonny Boy Williamson I's "Decoration Day"—which Hooker had first assayed back in 1950, during the Besman era—loses its formalized structure to become a free-form slow-blues meditation on the agonies of bereavement. The title song's shift from first to second person represents a change in emphasis as opposed to attitude: rather than moving the song from ostensible self-accusation to vindictive *schadenfreude*, Hooker is talking to, rather than about, himself. Of course, this change plays hell with Mayfield's rhyme-scheme, but Hooker was the last guy in the world to worry his head overmuch about *that*.

It Serve You Right To Suffer was the first blues album to appear in the Impulse catalog, and the last. Despite the record's artistic and critical success, it was decided that Impulse was first and foremost a jazz label, and that nothing should be permitted to blur or dilute that identity. Eventually, *It Serve You Right To Suffer* turned out to be the prologue to a lengthy association between Hooker and the various ABC labels, but in the meantime he was once again "at liberty." In the early summer of the following year, his path led him back to Chicago: this time to Chess Records.

As an eight-year veteran of Vee Jay and an honorary member in excellent standing of the Chicago blues elite, Hooker had no illusions whatsoever concerning the Chess brothers' operation; but he urgently needed to make another record. The terms "Chess Sound" and "Chicago blues" were almost synonymous, but during that uneasy lull between the decline of interest in electric downhome blues among the Delta diaspora and the subsequent arrival of a well-heeled white audience for the music, the label—anxious to diversify into more lucrative sub-genres—was contracting, rather than expanding, its blues roster. Nevertheless, Hooker was no untried newcomer, but a top name in his field whom the company had never before had the opportunity to record for itself, and was therefore a more than worthwhile investment.

In a sense, Hooker had indeed been there before. Some of his most powerful and memorable early '50s sides, cut by Joe Von Battle for local start-ups like Gone and Chance, had ended up being issued on Chess. During his Vee Jay years he'd literally worked opposite Chess: at one time, Vee Jay had based itself at 1449 South Michigan Avenue, just a few blocks up from the famous Chess storefront studio/office building—as immortalized in the title of a Rolling Stones instrumental recorded there in 1964—at 2120 South Michigan Avenue. "They was on the same street," snorts Hooker, "and I never did get no money out of them, neither."

If any individual associated with Chess qualified as the label's in-house auteur, it would probably have to be Willie Dixon, whose contributions as house arranger and producer, songwriter-in-residence, studio bassist and talent scout were the pre-eminent influence which shaped Chess's blues output during the 1950s. However, Dixon wasn't around much anymore by the time Hooker showed up for a marathon day-long session in May 1965. There were a variety of reasons for this. The company was cutting fewer and fewer blues sessions, and the need to move with the sonic times had dictated that Dixon's instrument, the stand-up bass, was replaced on the sessions they *did* cut by electric bass, which he refused to play; plus Dixon's tolerance of Len Chess's smoke-and-mirrors approach to accounting, variable at best, was at one of its lower ebbs.[9] The Hooker session was therefore handled by Ralph Bass, a white guy then in his mid-fifties who'd been picking up Dixon's Chess slack since 1960. Bass had come to Chess via Los Angeles with formidable R&B and jazz credentials: he'd recorded the likes of T-Bone Walker, Lena Horne, Charlie Parker, Charles Mingus, Dizzy Gillespie, Johnny Otis, Billy Ward & The Dominoes, Hank Ballard & The Midnighters, and The Platters for labels including Black And White, and Savoy. However, his greatest claim to influencing the cultural history of twentieth-century America derived from his '50s sojourn with King Records of Cincinnati, where he persuaded the company's irascible boss Syd Nathan into continuing to record James Brown despite a string of flops, thereby enabling the ex-con from Georgia to stay in the game long enough to commence the process of transforming himself into the Godfather Of Soul.

In his liner-note, Bass took pains to make it clear that he understood exactly where this particular client was coming from.

---

9   The reader is once again referred to, Dixon and Snowden's *I Am The Blues* (Quartet, 1989).

The blues ain't nothin' but what you feel [he wrote]. Don't count no bars, don't get "teck," just listen to what the man says. I remember recording a blues singer who had the musicians upset because he couldn't sing in meter.[10] One of the musicians came to the recording date higher than a kite and played from pure instinct, making the fills in the wrong places. Technically, he was correct, but because the blues singer was out of meter, nothing jelled. I finally told him to make the fills only when I pressed his arm. It was important that he had to listen to what the man had to say.

A blues singer has to stretch out. Each time he sings a particular blues, he may change lyrics, or stretch out differently. The important thing is—listen to what the man has to say . . . such a blues singer is John Lee Hooker . . . The modern impressionists, the disciples of the "freedom movement" in jazz, like John Coltrane and Ornette Coleman, have discarded set structural norms and chord progressions—playing out of meter in telling their story. It's not new. John Lee Hooker has been doing it all his life. He will go down in the annals of music as one of the "GIANTS."

Listen to what he has to say.

Suiting the action to the word, Bass booked in some veteran back-up guys of Hooker's own generation: Lafayette Leake was the pianist Chess called whenever Otis Spann was out on the road with Muddy Waters or otherwise unavailable, while drummer Fred Below had put his propulsive sense of swing to work behind Little Walter's dazzling harp on "Juke" back in 1952 and had rarely been out of work since. (The Chess studio was never renowned for keeping the most precise of session logs so, to this day, nobody seems quite sure who played bass on this particular occasion, but the usual suspects for the label's sessions of that era included Leroy Stewart, Jack Meyer and Phil Upchurch.)

Typically, Hooker wasn't prepared to walk alone into this particular lion's den, so he recruited one of his staunchest buddies to watch his musical back, liaise with the locals and—equally typically—handle the driving. "We cut some stuff for Chess in 1966 together," Eddie Burns recalls proudly. " 'Let's Go Out Tonight,' that's me playin' lead on that. I cut with him quite a bit." In this case, "quite a bit" meant a whopping eighteen sides: a highly impressive tally for a single day's work, and

---

10 Bass couldn't be referring to Howlin' Wolf by any chance, could he?

enough material for two albums, though the second album's worth remained in the can, not to see the light of day for another quarter-century. The album which did come out was entitled, more than somewhat misleadingly, *The Real Folk Blues*. As the Bass liner-note implies, this rowdy, rocking, rumbustious date had dropped beats and odd-numbered bars flying all over the place, with all the participants sounding like they were having way too good a time to give a damn. The music was heated to a higher temperature than on the rather more laid-back Vee Jay sides which its style and format superficially resembled, with Hooker, in notably more extrovert vocal form than was his custom, garnishing the more intense and up-tempo performances with throat-ripping growls and screams, and Hooker and Burns striking guitar sparks off each other just the way you'd expect from guys who'd been playing together for years. Throughout, Burns found himself cast in the role of musical mediator, applying his fluent, piercing guitar to the task of bridging the inevitable gaps between Hooker's cavalier approach to meter and a rhythm section audibly accustomed to more orthodox bluesmen.

For a thrown-together, one-day jam-in-all-but-name, *The Real Folk Blues* session covered a remarkably wide swathe of musical and emotional terrain; from rocking, party-down boogies and shuffles to solo meditations; from the broadly comedic showcases for Hooker's raconteurial skills to the rawest, most nakedly self-revelatory confessionals. "Let's Go Out Tonight," to which Burns alludes above, kicked the album off, though the first track actually cut on the day was the lazy, easy-rocking shuffle "Stella Mae." "Let's Go Out Tonight" was the single Chess eventually pulled off the album, albeit in edited form: it Hookerized one of Howlin' Wolf's earliest recordings, "Riding In The Moonlight," with which it shares little more than half a riff (the other half coming from Jimmy Reed's "Big Boss Man" via Tommy Tucker's "High Heel Sneakers"), a theme of sexual cajoling, and the title-rhyming punchline *"while the moon is shining bright."* Storming along for over six minutes in all its full-length glory, it's simultaneously sexy and funny: he's outside her house, she's leaning out of her window, he wants to take her walking in the park, to hug her, kiss her and make love to her, but she's up there, he's down here and by fade-out time, as he and the musicians finally run out of steam, she's *still* up there and he's still down here.

Wasting not and—presumably—wanting not, Hooker seized the opportunity to revisit previously recorded material from which the maximum advantage had possibly not already been squeezed. He had unveiled his own solo acoustic version of Otis Rush's "I Can't Quit You Baby" as "I Can't Quit You Now Blues" during his 1963 Newport set; now he cut it again for Chess, this time with the electric ensemble, under its original title, and with Willie Dixon's composer credit firmly reattached: no way would John Lee be permitted to Hookerize a Dixon song on the big bassman's own home turf. "I Cover The Waterfront," salvaged from the London session of a year and a half before, was performed solo, in a hushed intimate rendition which emphasized, to an almost unbearable extent, the poignancy of its insistence on the triumph of hope over experience, and faith over fear. "This Land is Nobody's Land," premiered during the folk years at the 1962 Sugar Hill club recording as "This World (No Man's Land)," now gained the added dimension of a none-too-veiled commentary on the Vietnam War. Hooker was by no means the only bluesman to bring a politicized edge to his work—both Johnny Shines and J. B. Lenoir had refused to hide that particular ray of their creative light under anybody's studio bushel, and Sonny Terry & Brownie McGhee had stood shoulder-to-shoulder with Leadbelly and Woody Guthrie at any number of barricades—but the forthright political engagement he displayed was certainly unique among blues performers of his rank and peer group. "This Land Is Nobody's Land" was passed over for inclusion on *The Real Folk Blues*—one of several intriguing items jilted, as it happened, in favor of assorted routine shuffles and a pleasant but inconsequential remake of "I'm In The Mood"—and scheduled for that stillborn "second" *Folk Blues album.*

Other gems which didn't make the final cut included "Mustang And GTO" (a Hookerization of fellow Southland-to-Detroit transplant Wilson Pickett's then-recent hit "Mustang Sally;" a Wolfishly swinging up-tempo take on the hoary Delta staple "Catfish Blues"; a rocking update of the 1961 Vee Jay number "Want Ad Blues," where Bass and the band drag Hooker back for a reprise of the song despite his audible attempts to end it, and an intriguing revision of his hardy perennial "House Rent Boogie," a serio-comic, ghetto-realist monologue tour de force worthy of pre-crossover Richard Pryor, based on his earliest Detroit experiences and first recorded in 1950.[11]

In its earlier rocking form of "House Rent Boogie," the overall effect is essentially comedic. Like the master raconteur he is, Hooker shifts his

---

11 Twice, as it happens: once for Bernard Besman and once (as "Johnny Williams") for Idessa Malone's Staff label.

emphasis from line to line according to character and circumstance. As "himself," he wheedles, blusters, cajoles, expostulates; as the landlady, he exudes suspicion and exasperation when the protagonist hits hard times, and cooing, cloying conciliation when she thinks he's back in employment. Reincarnated as "House Rent Blues," however, the mood is modified as profoundly as the pace; the hustling boogie of the original versions displaced by a plangent minor-key slow blues, drenched in pathos and foreboding. This version reminds you that, however clownish and weaselly the protagonist may be, he is nevertheless living on the edge of an abyss.

Hooker's story-telling powers were placed at center-stage once again in the album's most durable new number, "One Bourbon, One Scotch, One Beer." This was a typically audacious Hookerization of an early '50s jump hit, by Amos Milburn, of almost the same title (Milburn preferred to take his Scotch before his Bourbon). Though he'd had hits with "Chicken Shack Boogie" and "Bewildered,"[12] Milburn specialized in drinking songs, notably "Bad Bad Whiskey," "Good Good Whiskey," "Vicious Vicious Vodka," "Juice Juice Juice" and "Rum And Coca-Cola."[13] The alcohol he sang about probably contributed as much to his eventual career decline as the alcohol he consumed: his increasingly specialized target audience were probably too far out of it to locate the nearest record store even if they still had enough cash in their stash to consider buying a record.

"I knowed him, too," claims Hooker. "He was a good man, stayed drunk *a-a-a-l-l* the time. Nice gentleman, though. Very, very, very nice gentleman." What Hooker did with the "nice gentleman's" song was to transform it—literally—into a vehicle for himself; to customize it as ruthlessly as any hot-rodder about to chop a rundown vintage car into a personalized, one-off street machine.[14] He kept Milburn's chorus (altering only the order of the drinks), retained the storyline—guy in bar at closing time trying to get enough booze down his neck to forget that his girlfriend's gone AWOL, harassing a tired, bored bartender who simply wants to close up and go home into serving just one more round—edited the verse down to its essentials, filled in the gaps with narrative and di-

---

12 Scorchingly revived by James Brown in 1961.
13 I am not making this up. Honest.
14 A textbook example of the Hookerization process, this demonstrates as effectively as anything in Hooker's repertoire the manner in which his "organic sampling" approach to composition is a precursor of hip-hop's approach to production. This notion will be explored in greater depth in the next chapter.

alogue, and set the whole thing to a rocking cross between South Side shuffle and signature boogie.[15] The end result is something which, in Hooker's own words, is something "completely different" from Milburn's original blueprint. "I wouldn't do it just like he did it," Hooker maintains, and he didn't. A certain kind of perverse pleasure can be derived from the confusion into which Hooker persists in throwing the band: making vocal entries halfway through four-bar phrases and launching into a chorus, whether the musicians are ready or not, more or less whenever he feels like it. Steady Eddie Burns picks up the cue instantly, responding to Hooker's "*one bourbon*" call with a two-note guitar lick—*rang dang*—leaving the rhythm section to chug away while trying to regain their bearings. Five months later, Hooker would recut the song, in concert in New York City, for a live album on which he was backed by no less eminent an ensemble than the Muddy Waters Band; Muddy's hard-bitten, blues-wise crew didn't fare any better than Bass's Chess sidemen.

With benefit of hindsight, one *Real Folk Blues* track in particular assumes a highly specific significance which could hardly have been apparent at the time. "I Put My Trust In You" is an ominous free-form slow blues—so free-form that the musicians aren't always able to agree about exactly where they are in the chord sequence or, indeed, whether there's a chord sequence at all—which bitterly recounts the final stages in the disintegration of a relationship. "*I just couldn't believe,*" Hooker sings, voice wracked and tremulous, "*that you hurt me the way you did.*" He goes on:

My friends tried to tell me you didn't mean me no good
I didn't believe a word they said
I couldn't believe it
I couldn't believe you would let me down
I done lost everything I had, babe
I can't believe you would let me down
You go downtown to the judge
You tell the judge

---

15   The notion that the guy in "Bourbon" could well be the same protagonist as that of "House Rent" (albeit in its "boogie" rather than "blues" incarnation) was not lost on Hooker's admirer George Thorogood, who incorporated large chunks of the "House Rent" narrative into the splendid version of "One Bourbon, One Scotch, One Beer" which graces his 1977 debut album. "He told me he was gonna do that," says Hooker, "and I said, 'Okay, go ahead.' "

"Everything you got, give it to me"
He looked at me:
"Hit the road, Jack, and don't come back no more" . . .
I'm leavin' now, baby
Done lost my home
'N my brand-new car, baby
I know another man gonna move in
But I can't believe you gonna treat me
The way you did
Now, baby, look-a-here, baby
How could you treat me the way you did?
I couldn't believe you would let me down
Good as I been to you, baby
I'm goin' now, baby
All I got
All I got is on my back . . .

And then he abandons all explicit verbal content, moaning and groaning over his and Burns's eloquent guitar colloquy. Eerily, it seemed as if Hooker had prophetically opened some psychic time-tunnel three years into the future. He'd tried so hard to keep the home fires burning, even though they could only be kept alive through punishingly paradoxical means: the constant roadwork which kept him away from home. Soon those same home fires would rage out of control, devastating the home which they were intended to nurture and warm; but not before a real rather than metaphorical Detroit was engulfed by flames both real and metaphorical.

Well, the Motor City is burning
Ain't a thing in the world that I can do
Because you know the Big D is burnin'
Ain't a thing in the world Johnny can do
My home town is burning down to the ground
Worster than Vietnam

Well, it started on Twelve an' Clairmount that mornin'
I just don't know what it's all about . . .

Fire-wagon tip came in
Snipers just wouldn't let 'em put it out

Firebombs bustin' all around me
And soldiers was everywhere
Well, firebombs fallin' all around me:
And soldiers standin' everywhere
I could hear the people screamin'
Sirens fill the air . . .
—Al Smith (it says here) for John Lee Hooker, "Motor City is
   Burning," 1967

He laughed at accidental sirens
That broke the evening gloom
The police warned of repercussions
They followed none too soon
A trickle of strangers were all that was left alive
Panic in Detroit
—David Bowie, "Panic In Detroit," 1972

On July 23, 1967, smack in the middle of what white West Coast hippies persisted in claiming was the "Summer Of Love," Detroit finally boiled over. Despite the election in 1961 of the young, liberal Mayor Jerome Cavanagh, who had marched with Dr. Martin Luther King Jr. in 1963, and who appointed a crusading, anti-racist police chief named George Edwards, the city's racism remained deeply, endemically institutionalized. Racism in housing, racism in the job market, and—most crucially as far as Detroit's black community was concerned—racism in the day-to-day policing of their neighborhoods.

The city administration's policies, however well intentioned, proved as unable to eradicate these persistent manifestations of prejudice and social inequality as had most of the Civil Rights legislation enacted on a national level by the Kennedy and Johnson governments. Detroit was a tough, militant take-no-shit town—Elijah Mohammad's Nation Of Islam had been founded in the city and still maintained its national base there—and the build-up of black anger and resentment should therefore have surprised no one (even though, the previous year, Berry Gordy was still worrying about the insistence of his former child star, no-longer-so-Little

Stevie Wonder, on recording a pop-soul version of Bob Dylan's anti--war, anti-racist "Blowin' In The Wind" in case it should prove too "controversial" for the delicate sensibilities of Motown fans). Under the circumstances, it wouldn't have taken much to send the city up in flames, and as things turned out, it didn't.

Illegal drinking clubs are, for some reason, known in Detroit as "blind pigs." One such, held at the premises of an organization called the United Civic League For Community Action, had permitted a party which started on the night of Saturday, July 22, to rave on well into the following Sunday morning. In what could conceivably be described as something of an over-reaction to this admittedly shocking breach of laws designed only to maintain the city's legendary peace and tranquillity, the police smashed the doors down with sledgehammers, and hauled eighty-odd customers off to the hoosegow. Someone then chucked a bottle through the back window of a police car, and the Detroit Riot was off and running. Things didn't calm down until the following Thursday, by which time snipers and police had shot it out in running gun battles, the National Guard had been called in, thousands had been rendered homeless after being burned out of their dwellings, and over forty people—including a National Guardsman wasted by so-called "friendly fire" and a shopkeeper battered to death by rioters for attempting to protect his store—were dead.

John Lee Hooker is not, by nature, a street-fighting man, and therefore did not participate in the proceedings. However, he understood its causes full well. It is wholly unsurprising that he felt a great affinity for Dr. King: they did, after all, have in common a Southern upbringing, a Baptist background, and a firm belief in peaceful reconciliation. "This man did a lot of great, great, great things, but now he's gone: Martin Luther King. Boy, he changed the world. Too bad he ain't here now. People like that got so much power to do so much, sometimes they ain't *expectin'* to stay alive. They ain't lookin' to get through this. They say, "I'm gonna *die* tryin'. I'm gonna *fight* this battle. I'm not gonna back up. I'm not gonna let 'em scare me. I'm gonna keep *goin'* with this.' But before he left, he changed things."

Nevertheless, he was also an admirer of Malcolm X. "I know that speech he did. You knew they wasn't going to let him live. He was so *powerful*! That man was the powerfullest man you ever seen. He carried a lot of power. People like that, they don't let 'em live. I guess you noticed that. John F. Kennedy, he was for the right, and they didn't let him live. And his brother Bobby? He was going to be for the right, and he didn't even get to first base. People like [then-President George] Bush, they just do what they want to do."

As it happened, Hooker enjoyed—if that is indeed the appropriate term—a ringside view of the proceedings from his home on Jameson Street.

"I know what they were fightin' for," he says. "Maybe they didn't have to do that, but they hoped to bring out the anger, straighten out a lot of the segregation. I feel bitter about that. A big city like Detroit . . . you know, racial like that. It wasn't like Mississippi, but . . . you know, they hide it under the *cover* there. In Mississippi they didn't hide it, they just come out with it, and that's the only difference. We all could go together in Detroit, everybody the same: white, black, Chinese, everybody go to the same places. It was racial, but they kinda tried to smother it, you know what I mean? It finally got so hot, people got so fed up, that the riot broke out, with all the burnin' and the shootin', the killin', I could just look at the fire from my porch or my window, outside in my yard . . . I could see places goin' up in *flame*, hear guns shootin', robbin' stores, runnin' the business people out of they stores. There was a lotta lootin' goin' on, y'know . . . the po-lice was even lootin'. They was gettin' them some *stuff*. There was an old jewelry store . . . oh, it was big. He run out in the street . . . I felt bad about that, me'n a lotta other people. We felt it was nonsense, that it shouldn't'a happen. We didn't know who started it, but once it started it just kept up. Boy, it burned down. They like to have burned the whole city down. Throwin' bombs, lootin' . . . a kid brought me a brand new *git*-tar, a Gibson twelve-string. Cost about fifteen hundred dollars, boy . . . I got it for five dollars. The kid didn't know what he had!" Hooker laughs in memory of the kid's naïvety. " 'You wanna buy this?' '*Oh yeah!*' 'You got five dollars?' I say, '*Yeah!*' "

"You could see the fire burnin'. You could see the bombs, the smoke goin' up, buildin's goin' up. You see the people runnin' out the stores, the business people leavin' everythin' in there. They was throwin' firebombs in the stores. Run 'em outta there. And they run outta there. A Chinese guy, couldn't speak English . . ." Laughing, he breaks into mock-Chinese babble: " '*Black-man-burn-down! Help! Black-man-burn-down-store!*' " He laughs again, not altogether humorously. "It was layin' in the streets, man. Clothes, brand-new shoes, just layin' there. Couldn't tell no one not to pick it up, and some people did pick it up. Went to jail for stealin' stuff. Two policemen . . . four or five of 'em, they found a *whole* lotta stuff that they done took. They suspended them, and put *them* in jail. Everybody was lootin.' The white, the black . . .

"You know, Detroit never was like down South: you couldn't go here, you couldn't go there. You go anywhere you want to go: some places you could feel it that they didn't want you there, but they couldn't make you leave. Down South, stores you couldn't go in there, or you'd have to come in the back door, stuff like that. You couldn't drink out the same faucet. It wasn't like that there, up North. See, down South they let you *know* how they felt. Here, they shake your hand, stab you in the back. You go any place you wanted to go, and we was all in there together, but it still was there. They'd throw a brick, hide it in they hand. You could feel it in the air. I can't forget how all that started. It was pretty bad. And after that, the whole country went. Watts got burned down. A lotta other places got burned down. Like a *cancer*. You hear everybody say, 'Burn, baby, burn.' That's what they said. 'We gon' *burn, baby, burn.*' They burned down a lotta stuff. Big apartment buildings . . . they run 'em outta there. People be in they shop, and they come outta there in droves, throwin' firebombs, burnin' up the clothes, you know, comin' in there takin' the stuff . . . I was livin' on Jameson, over Charlevoix Avenue. They was burnin' three or four blocks over, but they never come down to where I was.

"And after that I wrote that song called 'Motor City Is Burnin'.' "

That, however, is not what the song's stated composer credit claims. Both Hooker's original 1967 recording of "Motor City Is Burnin'"—cut barely two months after the events it describes—and its 1968 cover by rabble-rousing Detroit anarchopunk pioneers MC5[16] are officially attributed to former Vee Jay executive Al Smith; and thereby hangs a tale, if not several. Smith had landed on his feet following Vee Jay's demise, working with Bob Thiele at ABC on the launch of BluesWay Records, a blues-dedicated sister subsidiary for Impulse. The inauguration of BluesWay was the first acknowledgment by any of the major corporate labels of the existence of a new American phenomenon: a significant white audience for electric blues. This audience was the baby of a new coalition: kids whose interest in the music had been stimulated by the early British

---

16   Marcus Gray posits, in his *Last Gang In Town: The Story And Myth Of The Clash* (Fourth Estate, 1995) that the MC5's version of "Motor City is Burning," included on *Kick Out The Jams* (Elektra, 1968), provided the inspiration for "London's Burning," a key song from The Clash's eponymous 1977 debut album. The Clash song subsequently lent its title to a long-running British TV drama series celebrating the capital's firefighters.

bluesrockers—even though most of those bands, plus the bulk of their domestic clientele, had themselves subsequently moved on to proto-psychedelia, nascent heavy rock, or first-generation Britpop of varying degrees of artiness—and former folkies who had found that the music enabled them to reconcile the conflict between "real" (that is, acoustic rural) blues and danceable, hi-decibel electric sounds. The principal standard-bearers of new-generation, rock-friendly, white-boy blues had been Chicago's Paul Butterfield Blues Band featuring—or, as far as much of their audience was concerned, starring—Mike Bloomfield on lead guitar; and The Blues Project from New York City, whose original ranks included organist Al Kooper and guitarist Steve Katz.

These matters had come to a head at the turbulent Newport Folk Festival of 1965. That particular Newport is best known in rock lore for the stormy encounter between the traditionalist audience and management, and the new-look Bob Dylan, backed for the occasion by an ensemble including Al Kooper and several members of the Butterfield band; Kooper and Mike Bloomfield had played behind Dylan on the historic sessions for "Like A Rolling Stone" and what became the *Highway 61 Revisited* album. Less notorious, but in its way equally significant, was the extraordinary prelude to the Butterfield band's own performance, earlier that same day, at an afternoon blues workshop away from the main stage. The MC for the workshop was Alan Lomax, visibly and audibly miffed to have the purity of his show polluted by young white guys with amplified guitars. Accordingly, he made no attempt to conceal his feelings when it came time for him to introduce the band. In an interview with Tom Yates,[17] Mike Bloomfield described, not without a degree of relish, the resulting melee:

Lomax implied in his introduction that this was how low Newport had sunk, bringing an act like this onto the stage, and our manager, Albert Grossman, said, "How can you give these guys this kind of introduction? This is really out of line. You're a real prick to do this." They got into a fistfight—these two elderly guys—right there in front of the stage, rolling in the dirt while we were playing, and I was screaming, "Kick his ass, Albert! Stomp 'im!" There was bad blood rising, you could tell.

---

17 Subsequently recycled by Ed Ward in *Michael Bloomfield: The Rise And Fall Of An American Guitar Hero* (Cherry Lane, 1983).

In any event, "bad blood" notwithstanding, the electric guys won the argument. Or rather, both camps eventually realized what John Lee Hooker could have told them if anybody had bothered to ask him: that it was *all* blues and it was *all* legit.

BluesWay, however, left the white boys—however funky, street-legal and blues-approved they may have been—to the rock, labels. The new imprint preferred to invest its budget in signing up the Real Guys and marketing them to the new audience. Their flagship act was already in place in the extremely substantial form of B. B. King, who'd been on ABC's books since 1961; the Big B was therefore moved over to BluesWay and given the honor of providing the new label with its inaugural release. BluesWay BLS 6001 was *Blues Is King*, a superb live album easily comparable with, though less celebrated than, B. B.'s earlier classic *Live At The Regal*,[18] but BluesWay BLS 6002 came from Thiele and Smith's first fresh signing: John Lee Hooker. The decision to bring Hooker to BluesWay was highly logical, Captain: Smith knew Hooker from the Vee Jay days, Thiele had worked with him successfully on *It Serves You Right To Suffer* for Impulse, and since the arrangement with Chess for *The Real Folk Blues* had been a one-shot deal, Hooker was then "at liberty" (as opposed to "at Liberty," which would happen later), and eager to sign a new contract with a solid, credible record company. Uncharacteristically, he'd stay (almost) faithful to the ABC group for several years. Equally uncharacteristically—given his legendary reluctance to say anything nice about any record company, *ever*—he appears to have been relatively happy with them, acknowledging that they displayed a greater degree of financial probity than his previous labels.

"They was straighter than a company like Chess or Vee Jay," he allows, albeit a little grudgingly. "They was a lot more legitimate. I made some money with them. I wouldn't say that I got *all* that was comin' to me, but I got treated better."

The first fruits of the BluesWay liaison had sprouted in the form of *Live At Cafe Au Go-Go*, cut in concert on August 30, 1966, at one of Greenwich Village's premier venues: a Delta dream-team collaboration with Hooker's old friend Muddy Waters and his band, including Chicago's master pianist Otis Spann, Muddy himself, and no less than two

---

18 In this writer's admittedly warped perspective, *Blues Is King* is actually superior to *Live At The Regal*: it was recorded in a club rather than a theater, with a correspondingly higher-voltage audience contact, and B. B. had a particularly fabulous guitar sound going that night. This is a minority viewpoint, but please feel free to obtain both albums and compare them at your leisure.

other guitarists. In his liner-note, Stanley Dance beautifully evokes the scene:

> *Backstage, John Lee had sat quietly, strumming on "his wife," as he calls his six-string guitar. The younger men had joined him one by one, first [guitarist] Sammy Lawhorn, then [bassist] Mac Arnold, and then [guitarist Luther] "Georgia Boy" Johnson. "Get it right, get it right!" he muttered—a teacher with pupils—as they played along. After the Muddy Waters band had completed the first part of the set, Muddy introduced him with warm generosity, referring to him as "a killer" and "the champ." John Lee's long, thin foot began to tap out the time, his guitar chords established his characteristic drop beat, and the band swung in behind him . . .*
>
> *John Lee leaned at the mike, solemn, severe and a little stooped. Muddy Waters, Sammy Lawhorn, Luther Johnson and Mac Arnold stood in a row behind him, deadpan, bending with the beat. Otis Spann sat facing him at the piano, his back to the audience. Francis Clay was intent on the rhythmic foundation, and George Smith, who had previously worked with Muddy in 1955, had his mouth-harp ready to add keening cries and wailing embellishments as the opportunity offered. They were as informally dressed as their audience, and although they were "playing for the people," it was without showmanship, almost as though they were playing for themselves . . .*

Beyond pointing out that George Smith's "keening cries and wailing embellishments" are nowhere to be heard on the record as issued, the most salient point to be made about *Live At Cafe Au Go-Go* is that it provides a fascinating glimpse of what might have been if Hooker had invested as much effort into forming and maintaining a first-class full-time band as Waters so evidently had. True, the performance is far from utterly unflawed—the opening seconds of the curtain-raising "I'm Bad Like Jesse James" find drummer Francis Clay anticipating a different song entirely and therefore crashing in with a very different beat; there are sour little pitching discrepancies between the tunings of the four guitarists' instruments (with Hooker himself, unfortunately, the prime culprit); and the rumbustious version of "One Bourbon, One Scotch And One Beer" is, if anything, even more chaotic than the Chess studio cut recorded the previous spring—but the overall tone of the music is dark, slow, swampy-deep, and the degree of emotional rapport between Hooker and the band (particularly the astonishing Spann) nothing less than extraordinary.

The evening's program broke little new ground. "Jesse James" (aka "I'm Mad," "I'm Mad Again" or "Gonna Use My Rod") was a hardy Hooker perennial, premiered in 1954, to which he returned again and again throughout his career. The powerful statement of artistic intent "Heartaches And Misery" reworks 1954's "Everybody's Blues;" "She's Long, She's Tall (She Weeps Just Like A Willow Tree)" dates from the Besman era; while the Tony Hollins–derived "When My First Wife Left Me" goes back further still, to Hooker's earliest demo sessions in Elmer Barbee's back room. Others were of rather more recent vintage: "I Don't Want No Trouble" is simply a retitling of "Peace Loving Man" from *The Real Folk Blues*; and "Seven Days" had enjoyed its first outing during the November '64 London session with The Groundhogs. The occasion did, however, introduce one important new song, "Never Get Out Of These Blues Alive," which would remain in Hooker's repertoire for the remainder of his career. Its theme—"man's inevitable fate," as Dance aptly chooses to phrase it—and title are distantly derived from "I'll Never Get Out Of This World Alive," a doomy, prophetic song by country titan Hank Williams, who died barely two months after its release in November 1952: Hooker's substitution of "these blues" for "this world" speaks volumes about the similarity, and the differences, between the two men's respective outlooks. The Williams record is fiddle-driven, *faux*-jaunty, mock-rueful, tightly-rhymed catch-in-the-throat country with a neat, snappy pedal-steel solo; Hooker's is a deep, meditative free-form blues set to a reflective, slowed-down variation of B. B. King's "Rock Me Baby" riff, with the band telepathically responding to Hooker's cues by shifting back and forth between conventional blues changes and one-chord mode.

On its uppermost surface level, "Never Get Out Of These Blues Alive" is about a man whose woman has left him—what a surprise, a bluesman singing a song about a woman who done left—and as a result he can't sleep, he chain-smokes, he slugs down black coffee, and he can't envisage the day when he will no longer be unhappy. One layer further down, it's one of the purest examples in Hooker's catalog of the archetypal blues response to sorrow and despair: the process of dealing with your situation by first acknowledging it. It represents the exact opposite of the state known in contemporary therapy-speak as "denial." The bluesman but rarely "denies," and even on those occasions when he does, the listener is not intended to be fooled: the "denial" is a bluff which exists solely so that it can be called.

What could emphatically not be denied was the overwhelming need for a massive readjustment of the blues economy: a shift from producing and marketing singles for a black ghetto market to albums designed to appeal to white youth. The denizens of Planet Blues were accordingly divided into those judged to be potentially hippie-friendly, and those who weren't. Blues guys deemed appropriate for the new market received new boots and contracts, while those who weren't were left to wither on the vine and fend for themselves in a rapidly contracting commercial environment. Thus the second half of the '60s saw Vanguard Records add Buddy Guy, Junior Wells, James Cotton and Charlie Musselwhite to the country blues already in their primarily folk-based catalog; Atlantic recording Otis Rush and Freddie King for their Cotillion subsidiary; Chess retaining the services of Muddy Waters and Howlin' Wolf but—at the behest of Leonard Chess's son Marshall, entrusted with the mission of retooling the label's Old Masters for the Next Generation—decking them out in highly unsuitable psychedelic drag. By contrast, Columbia preferred to invest in new-jack blues talent like Johnny Winter and Taj Mahal. For their part, BluesWay expanded their roster by signing up Jimmy Reed—already severely past his sell-by date—and T-Bone Walker. The latter's 1968 BluesWay excursion, *Funky Town*, was a sad affair: the brave new world of post-Stax grooves and *heav-ee* guitar sounds suited T-Bone about as well as a pair of paisley satin bell-bottoms. Writer Ed Ward recalls seeing a late-'60s T-Bone gig where members of his young, aggressively Afro'ed and dashiki'ed band—who'd probably have rather been playing behind James Brown—were mocking the founding father of electric blues guitar behind his back every time he took a solo.

Other veterans developed different strategies for coping with changing times. The more sophisticated Junior Parker, Little Milton and Bobby Bland had already reached an accommodation with the soul era by de-emphasizing the more overtly downhome aspects of their music (Parker had, seemingly, left his harps back in Memphis), and retained the allegiance of the black community by ostentatiously eschewing anything which could possibly be interpreted as pandering to funny-looking white kids. The decidedly downhome Albert King had lucked out by signing in 1966 to Stax Records, the pride of Memphis. The company's stellar studio crew—Booker T & The MGs, Isaac Hayes and The Memphis Horns—

backed Albert's big fat croon and mean, slicing guitar with funky dance grooves easily as hot as those on their massively successful Otis Redding and Sam & Dave hits, which appealed to black and white listeners alike. And B. B. King cruised imperturbably onward, pulling off the improbable stunt of being all things to all men while remaining no one but his own sweet self. He provided BluesWay with its only hit singles, climaxing in 1970 with the Top 20 pop triumph of "The Thrill Is Gone."

Many of the same forces which led young whites to accept and cherish the blues had long since driven their black contemporaries away: classic '50s-style citified Delta blues was about to succumb to the same fate which had once overtaken its direct musical ancestor, the country blues. Part of this can simply be attributed to the cyclical nature of the pop process and its inevitable generational shifts in taste, style and fashion: black youth didn't listen to the same music as their parents (or grandparents) anymore than did the white youth for whom blues was an exciting novelty. But there was much more to it than that: the blues is, essentially, a stoic music which celebrates endurance. For blacks in the '60s, in the era of Black Power, Black Pride, and Black Panthers, stoicism and endurance were no longer enough. It was time to move on up, to say it loud, to demand R-E-S-P-E-C-T, to overcome not in an unspecified future "some day" but *right now*. "*I've been down so long,*" Albert King used to sing, as did J. B. Lenoir before him, and Ishmon Bracey before *him, "that down don't bother me.*" Down definitely did bother African-America's Next Generation, and the blues was *definitely* considered to be all about "down." As B. B. put it in interviews at that time, "A lot of the younger Negroes don't want to be associated with the blues. [They] are trying very hard to raise [their] standards . . . and when they're approached with the blues, [they] figure in a lot of cases, this downs them . . . they don't even know about it, and when they do hear about it they think, 'Well, that's old mom and dad's music.' " For his part, Hooker concurred: "A lot of them don't want to accept [the blues], will not accept it. They think it's a hangover." The emergent new consciousness was thus a mixed blessing for many bluesmen: after decades of being an authentic voice of their communities, they were finding themselves regarded as jokes, Toms or sell-outs by the younger generation within those communities, and increasingly dependent on the whims of whites.

As far as John Lee Hooker was concerned, there was more than an element of unfairness in this new dilemma. "Old-fashioned" and "down-home" his music may have been, but with songs of the caliber and content of "Birmingham Blues," "Democrat Man" and "This Land Is Nobody's Land" in his catalog, he was among the most politically forthright and engaged of the front-rank bluesmen. Nevertheless, he was still vulnerable to both political and generational shifts, and nowhere more so than in his own home town. As Michael Haralambos relates in *Right On: From Blues To Soul In Black America*,[19]

John Lee Hooker, in Detroit for a couple of weeks in the summer of 1968 to appear at a rally in support of Senator Eugene McCarthy's bid for the Presidency, appeared only once at a black venue, the Rapa House, during his stay. Although the Rapa House is hardly a suitable place for a large blues audience—a coffee house run by blacks and patronized mainly by a theatrical and show business crowd—Hooker's appearance, despite advertising in the black press, drew fewer than twenty blacks . . . a young black modern jazz quartet preceded [his] act. As John performs his four numbers, singing intensely and stomping his foot, the young musicians shout mock encouragement and slap their thighs in amusement as they crack jokes about the old blues singer. After the show, John Lee Hooker expresses annoyance . . .

As well he might. "The whites, they really appreciates the blues," he told Haralambos, obviously still simmering from the humiliation received at these young brothers' hands. "They really gets with it, y'know, they really sincere, it's no come-on, it's no gimme, it's no put-on, they for real, y'know, and it can make you feel real good. I can't believe they dig it so deep."

It's not hard to comprehend, nor to empathize with, Hooker's transparent bitterness: his sense of betrayal and resentment. Out on the road, he was a hero or, at the very least, a welcome visitor, but on his own home turf, he was not so much a prophet without honor as a prophet without profit. In the wake of the *Real Folk Blues* sessions, Eddie Burns rejoined Hooker's road band—at least for the kind of work Burns describes as "close around, like Chicago or Cleveland or somewhere like that." However, in Sweet Home Detroit itself the boot was firmly on the other foot. "Over the years I became lead guitar player for him, and then I played with him quite a bit," says Burns. "And then in the '60s, he

---

19 Published in 1974 by Eddison Press as part of their BluesBooks series.

played with *me*, because when the Motown and the Memphis sound came, the blues was takin' a hell of a beatin' back then. So I went to rizzum'n'blues, because you couldn't make no money playin' blues. A lot of blues guys had to hang it up, because they couldn't get no action. He was playing with me, but he was playing the *blues* with me. *I* was playin' the rhythm and blues, because I had that kind of group. I was more or less givin' him work with me. It didn't make no difference whether he was goin' over big and strong or whatever: it was more or less like givin' him some work or whatever. By him bein' John and being with my group and everything . . . see, he played *all* blues at that time, and I didn't. So it was a thing like *we* featured *him*. The blues set, he had it. And I was playin' like *rhythm* and blues: 'Hooky Tonk,' Wilson Pickett and that kind of stuff. That's what *I* was doin'. It worked well: we was workin' something like five nights a week. That was when he was workin' with me, '66, '67, '68, somewhere in there."

Hooker's first BluesWay album, *Urban Blues*, was pretty much a continuation of Vee Jay by other means, albeit with a higher budget and slightly more care. Produced by Al Smith and recorded in Chicago over two days (albeit two days a month apart) in the autumn of 1967, it reunited Hooker with drummer Al Duncan as well as with Eddie Taylor, who played bass on the first session and guitar on the second. In addition to remakes of Vee Jay era chestnuts like "Boom Boom" and "Want Ad Blues," the first session yielded Hooker's recording of the song inspired by the apocalyptic events of the previous summer: "Motor City Is Burning." On (anonymous) lead guitar was a relatively recent acquaintance newly flitted from Chess Records and now "exclusively" signed elsewhere: Buddy Guy.

"I left my day job in August of 1967, my first album with Vanguard," Buddy recalls. "I was playing locally at night in the clubs in Chicago, and goin' to my job every mornin'. The only thing I ever did with John was 'Motor City,' and that was done in late '66 [*sic*]. I axed him about that, you know, I never really heard it. I don't know how did I sound or what. I normally done heard everything I ever helped anybody or was involved with, hear a playback, but I never got that, I never heard that played back." However, he remembers, "I had fun with that."

"Motor City" was by no means the only *Urban Blues* cut attributed to Smith. Out of a dozen tracks, ten were credited or co-credited to Smith; Hooker received solo credit on only two, and those were the remakes of "Boom Boom" and "Want Ad Blues." Hooker and Smith "shared" one of the new songs, "Mr. Lucky." Even "Backbiters And Syndicators," with a complex genealogy dating back as far as the Besman years, had somehow become an Al Smith composition. To add insult to injury, Smith was, in his capacity as Hooker's "manager," quoted more extensively in the liner-notes than was Hooker himself.

"Oh, he had a lotta things that wasn't true," says Hooker; clearly *Urban Blues* was a continuation of Vee Jay by other means in more than simply musical terms. "[Smith] had his name on a lot of 'em, 'Backbiters And Syndicators' and some more of 'em. Jimmy Bracken had his name on a lot of 'em, and he can't write nary a tune."

Nevertheless, by the next time Hooker stepped into the studio for BluesWay, Smith was nowhere to be seen. *Simply The Truth* was cut in New York rather than in Chicago, and it reunited Hooker with Bob Thiele, who took personal charge of the session, rounding up a Big Apple session A-team which included legendary drummer Bernard "Pretty" Purdie. Liner-note writer John F. Szved, a contributing editor to *Jazz* and *Pop* magazine who sat in on the sessions, found Purdie's antics—arraying signs reading DID IT AGAIN! THE LITTLE OLD HIT MAKER "PRETTY PURDIE" AND BING BANG BOOM PRETTY PURDIE AT IT AGAIN: THE HIT MAKER around the studio; sending out for a complete chicken dinner which he set up on his tomtoms while he played—almost as fascinating as Hooker's method of outlining the songs to his accompanists, none of whom (with the exception of harpist Hele Rosenthal) he had ever met before the session. All of the players (apart from Purdie and Rosenthal, the others were guitarist Wally Richardson, bassist William Folwell and keyboard guy Ernie Hayes on rolling piano and simmering Hammond organ) came up trumps here, but it was Rosenthal's salty harp which provided Hooker with this session's primary instrumental foil.

The final release version of *Simply The Truth* demonstrated how far a little care and attention could go when it came to making the difference between a bunch of songs, however cool, and a satisfying album. The eight songs recorded on that particular session were beautifully and sensitively sequenced by Thiele, resulting in inspired juxtapositions of both topic and mood. Hooker's devastating "I Don't Want To Go To Vietnam," a pointed "answer" to the patriotic shibboleths of Junior Wells's then-current "Vietcong Blues," is immediately followed by a paean of praise for "Mini Skirts" and their wearers, particularly those of the "big-legged" persuasion. The joyful boogie vibes of "I Wanna Bugaloo" and "(Twist Ain't Nothin' But) The Old Time Shimmy" alternate with the exquisitely eerie moods of desolation evoked by "Tantalizin' With The Blues" and a Hookerization of Mercy Dee Walton's classic "One Room Country Shack." And there's no nonsense about composer credits going astray here: the sleeve uncompromisingly states "All tracks written by John Lee Hooker."

And the road was good to John Lee Hooker at this time, not just the studio. The era of monster open-air festivals was in full effect by now: only a few months before *Simply The Truth* was recorded, in May of 1968, Hooker had played the Miami Pop Festival—promoter Michael Lang's dress-rehearsal for Woodstock—alongside Jimi Hendrix, Chuck Berry and The Mothers Of Invention. And in October of that year he'd rejoined the American Folk Blues Festival package for another swing through Europe, in the company of—among others—T-Bone Walker, Eddie Taylor and "Big" Walter Horton, though for some reason no album was released even though the now-traditional Cologne recording session did indeed take place as usual. He was making good money, bringing it home, and stashing it away; but as it turned out, that wasn't going to be enough to keep his world intact. The Motor City was still burnin' . . . all the way down.

> Women'll make you drink; women'll make you do all *kind* of things! They're the reason a lot of guys get out and work. They work for women, give them their money; and the women mess over them and don't treat them right and start them to drinking. That's the key to this problem: women is the key. So that's my downfall and just about every blues singer's downfall. The average blues singer, he just can't keep a wife. He ain't *got* no wife, 'cause he's on the road all the time and his home gets tore up . . . so anything he sings is about a woman. If it wasn't for women, there wouldn't be no blues.
> —John Lee Hooker, interviewed in *Blues* by Neff and Connor (Latimer BluesBooks, 1975)

During his Detroit years, John Lee Hooker was, effectively, an absentee father. A loving, loyal father, by all credible accounts, but an absentee father nonetheless. "John was really a family man," says Paul Mathis. "The only time he was away from home was when he was takin' care of business, when he was touring. Other'n that, you find him at home." Undoubtedly true, as far as it goes, but when most of your business is on the road, it is incredibly hard to be "taking care of business" at home as well.

One consequence of Hooker's incessant roadwork was that his sons went virtually unsupervised at times when, at least according to the conventional wisdoms, the presence of a father-figure is at its most vital. Detroit legend depicts John Lee Junior and Robert as a pair of sharp-dressed wild ones, though according to Zakiya Hooker, this is only partially true.

"We always had nice clothes," she concurs. "We did not really want for a lot. Junior was really the person getting in trouble, as opposed to Robert. Robert was kinda almost nondescript. He was just *there*. He was the baby at that time. So Robert was just so"—she makes a disdainful *pfft* sound. "Junior spends a lotta time in [jail]. Drugs seem to be his nemesis. He just can't seem to get past 'em. That was why he couldn't do the music. He and Robert both got involved in drugs, and that and music doesn't mix. They were young, it was an exciting life, they had money, cars, they had anything they felt they wanted. Daddy had made sure of this. I think he can look back now and admit the errors of his ways, but looking back in retrospect doesn't always help. No it doesn't. They say hindsight is 20/20 vision. They could've had anything. Robert plays excellent keyboard. He was on the albums *Never Get Out Of These Blues Alive, Free Beer And Chicken* . . . Robert played very, very, very good keyboard.

"That's another dream I want to follow, learn to play piano . . . I wanted to play keyboards, but when Robert got keyboard lessons, I got a sewing machine [laughs]. I had originally been given the choice, because I was taking sewing in school and I was having such a hard time. I hated the teacher. I hated her; she was just evil, she was the devil. I wouldn't buy my material, I wouldn't do anything, I would just do anything to harass her. So after I'd failed the class three times, I said, 'Okay, it's time to get outta here with this woman,' so I passed the class and I says, 'Well okay, you know you can sew, get a sewing machine.' So then when Robert got the organ it was just *wow*, and I wanted to take piano lessons. And they wouldn't let me take piano lessons! You don't ask why. As a kid you don't ask why. Women were expected to do . . . certain things. Sewing's one of them. My mother taught us to cook, and we're all very good cooks. Junior didn't learn to cook until he was grown. Never had to cook. Robert learned to cook because he loved to eat. He used to be very heavy, had to slim down because of his asthma. Junior was just a spoiled brat."

Was that because he was the oldest boy?

"Sure was. He was just allowed a lot of leeway. From a child, Junior was getting into trouble, in juvenile hall, at maybe thirteen. Junior was strung out. I didn't realize he was strung out until I was grown, because I never really saw it. I don't think [John and Maude] ever found out while he was small, because parents have a tendency to close their eyes to a lot of things, and they probably just attributed it all to him just being a little bad kid."

"We just got to a point where we got wild, man," remembers the Reverend Robert Hooker. "Whew . . . from a long time. My other brother, man, he still is wild. I was in school when I got started, man. I was in Foch Junior High, on Fairway Street in Detroit, Michigan. It was a pretty school. Back then it was bad, but you look up and it's 1994 and it's worse, man."

John Lee Hooker says to this day that it is not strange that his two sons went such different ways. Robert Hooker, decades away from his teens, gives fervent thanks for that.

"Well, when you try and be a good father, man, like any father in his right sense, he want his son, his daughter, he don't want them to live a low-down life. My brother, he let him down, man. He let him down. He was in a different religion to me, but he was in there three-four years, and my daddy was *proud* of him, man. He changed his life, he was workin', got his own business, man, you know? And he just . . . *pssheew*. He let my daddy down, man. Lost his job, his business went under, went back into that old raggedy life . . . and that'll hurt a father, man. I'm glad I'm able to stand, and I'm still standin'. He got one son he can really look to and say I'm proud of, and he can continue sayin' that, because I'm gonna keep on livin' for Jesus, brother, I'm gonna keep on standin'. Man, my brother, he started messin' up probably about the age of fourteen years old. Thirteen, fourteen, somethin' like that. Temptations was there. We just couldn't handle it.

"You ever heard that thing where you be around a person so much their spirit come off on you? You ever heard that? Never heard that, huh? I'm gonna show you an example. Let's say you don't drink no wine. You not no wino. But all the time you hangin' around a wino. You know what's gonna happen? You gonna turn out to be a wino, you keep on bein' around that person. You take a little bit, then *boom!* These demons is real. Dope demons, wine demons, liquor demons . . . you keep on bein' around a person doin' these things, these demons gonna jump off onto

you. That demon gonna get into you, man. They real. You know when I
see it? My brother came to the house in Detroit, Michigan, before I ever
started shootin' any heroin. That boy went in the bathroom, man, he shot
some dope. I said I will *never* shoot no dope. But see, that was just *talk*.
No Holy Ghost power, just *talk*. Next I wind up shootin' dope. Turned
out to be a dope *fiend*. I wasn't no bad boy, man. I was a *good* boy. Just
didn't have no power. *Temptation* around."

It wasn't so much that Junior personally turned Robert onto heroin,
but it was his example which stuck. It was a while before John Lee himself
learned of his younger son's chemical dalliances, but Junior was considerably more blatant. "Man, Junior . . . whoo, *boy*. Junior might have kept
it from him a little while, but if I'm not mistaken he didn't keep it from
my daddy too long before he knew he was doin'. But me, man . . . ooh,
man, my daddy probably didn't know I was into it until I was about
twenty, twenty-one. Gettin' ready to get into church. You know, he probably thought all I was doin' was just smokin' marijuana and drinkin'
liquor."

And if that wasn't enough of a load for any hard-working man to
carry, his marriage was finally beginning to come apart at the seams. And
everybody has a different account of what pulled it apart.

"To be honest with you," says Maude Hooker, over twenty years
later, "I don't know. He was out of town and I was home with the kids.
So one morning, myself, Zakiya and Robert, we was sittin' there in the
living room watchin' TV, and the District Attorney walked in, asked for
me and gave me the papers. I said, 'What is this?' He said, 'Divorce
papers.' I said, 'Di-*vorce* papers?' He actually got the divorce from me.
He told me why, what he wanted to do, but I won't say, because it's so
silly."

She stops talking for a moment, clears her throat. "Well anyway,
that's what happened. He said he wanted to get married to someone else,
period. Bottom *line*. He figured that I would not go through with it, but
I mean if he ask, he gon' get it. That's the way I see it. It took about a
year. I would never have got one myself. It weren't even on my mind.
Whatever we was goin' through, we just go through it and try to patch
it up, but . . . when he really left, we was happy. I didn't have no idea
that that was what was comin' back, when he came back home that was
what he was gonna do. He was on the road, and we was livin' in Detroit
on a street called Jameson. They [the kids] didn't like it. They was wondering why, but I couldn't explain it. How can you explain a divorce?

They was very young at the time, *mm-hm*. This was '69, yeah. It had been twenty-three years."

"Frankly speakin'," says Eddie Burns, "I don't know too much about that divorce. I don't know who did what. I know what he said when he left, but I do not know what went down behind the closed doors."

Others are more forthcoming. According to Eddie Kirkland, "[Maude] should've been a person to help him fight, because she got more education than him. She could'a been a helpful to him by takin' care'a his business, gettin' lawyers and things to help him get his due. That's the same thing what I teach the wife I got now, go back to school, take a course in business administration, help me get what I'm supposed to get. That's what a wife for. 'Stead 'a sittin' around the house bitchin' about the money's not comin' in, you get out help get that money in. The money's already made, get out there and help bring it in. The Lord's very good to John. Things workin' out for him now he's an old man. He ain't got to worry 'bout nothin.' He got just about everything he needs. He got homes, a new car an' shit, money in the bank . . . so, after all, things still workin' out for him. But it could'a been better back then, for her benefit too, if she would'a helped him. You can't just sit down on your butt and look for somethin' to come in if you ain't gonna do nothin' for it. That's wrong. At that time, Hooker didn't know what to tell his wife to do, whether she'd 'a been interested or not. He didn't know no nothin' either.

"I was John's closest friend, so he would tell me things that he wouldn't tell no one else. It was something done that offended John, don't get me wrong. Quite natural, a person's not gonna offend themselves. What I feel about it is this: if she was so much into the Lord, if she would say, 'Hey, I did somethin' wrong, I made a mistake.' But if you deny your wrongness, you can not be too close to God, right? Because if you is, you clean your conscience, say, 'I did some things wrong and I'm sorry that I did. I was young and I made a mistake.' But the average person's not gonna do that. But most of that come from other people talking to your wife, putting wrong ideas in your wife's head. See, when you an entertainer you gotta lotta different things comin' against you, mostly people's jealous. If they find out they can talk to your wife, and your wife'll listen to 'em, that's all they need. Every time you turn around . . . blah blah blah, the wrong thing to "em. See, that's what happened to my wife. John had a lot to be offended about back then, toward his wife. But, as far as I'm concerned, I never got in it. I would always be a friend to her and him both. That's what a friend's supposed to be. Last time I saw Maude was years ago."

For Zakiya, at least, the divorce came as no surprise. "No. I knew that it was coming, because circumstances had just gotten too great for [John] to handle. He just didn't want to deal anymore. That was it. But no, I was not surprised. I think he divorced her . . . no, she divorced him, because—see, I was . . . was I still at home when it happened? I was married in . . . [Zakiya's son] Glenn was born in '69, and I was married in '69, married and out on my own. I lived in Detroit, driving distance, but I can't remember who divorced who. All I remember were the reasons for the divorce, that's why in my mind he divorced her. But she started the divorce. He ended up having to get an attorney and pay for her attorney, the whole ball of wax. He was just tired. He was tired. I love my mom and my dad both, and as an adult looking back, I understand . . . I don't understand, but I can deal with her: what happened with her. And I sympathize with my dad. I see both sides, and I can understand why he left."

And then there's John Lee Hooker's own account. "When I drove from Detroit out here [to California], I was young then, much younger than I am now. When my old lady was divorcing me, she took the house, one of the cars, and she would'a taken all the money in the bank but I beat her to the punch. My booking agent booked me in Vancouver, and that's a *long* way from Detroit. That's a three-day ride. He told her to tell me that the gig was cancelled, and she didn't tell me. She taken me to the train station to get me out of town, sit there with me and have a cup of coffee and some breakfast, make sure she see'd me on the train. I got almost to Vancouver, call my agent to let him know where I were. I say, 'I'm almost to Vancouver.' He say, 'What?' I say, 'I'm almost to Vancouver. You surprised at me?' He say, 'Yes, I am. Didn't Mrs. Hooker tell you, your wife, that the gig was canceled and for you not to go?' I say, 'No.' 'Did she know when you left?' I say, 'Yes, she brought me to the train station, put me on the train.' He say, 'Well, Mr. Hooker, there's something wrong. You better check up. I told her to be sure to tell you not to go to Vancouver.' I was *wa-a-a-yy* almost there, and I had to turn around, come back.

"I stayed all night in that town, couple of nights, I think I did. I was so angry and disgusted with her, I just wanted to be away for a while. I come back in a couple of days and she was shocked. I got me a cab, come to the house, and she wasn't there. The kids were there. They say, 'Daddy, you back already?' 'Yeah, your mama didn't tell me not to go.' 'She said you was going to Vancouver to work.' 'She told you all that?' Diane and Zakiya, they was kids then. When she came back to the house, it was like she seen a *ghost* sittin' there. I said, 'I don't want no trouble.' You know the expression on people's face when they afraid?" He shifts into soft, placatory tones. " 'Hi, how are you?' 'I'm, fine,' I said, 'I didn't play.' She know why, I didn't have to tell her. She had some lady with her. Both of them had been drinkin', loaded. I guessed that she wanted to get me out of town so that they *really* could party, so that really took a lot out of me at the time. Everything run into my mind, wondering why, why did she do it? Why did she send me three thousand miles away knowing there wasn't no gig, knowing I had to get there? At that time I didn't have a *whole* lotta money, but I happened to have money in my pocket. When I called my agent, he said, 'You got money to get back? I can wire you some money to get your ticket.' I had about four, five hundred dollars in my pocket, and I gave him the number where I was at.

"He said, 'If you need me, call me.' If I hadn't had called him, I would've gone all the way to Vancouver. [Maude] used to be *wild*, man. I don't like to say it, but she's a hypocrite, a big hypocrite. She use the church for a shield, but her children know how she is: Zakiya, Diane. They know what she were. Mm-*hm*. You can't hide in the church for what you done did. And I was telling Karen, my youngest daughter—she was over here the other day—I said, 'Honey, you wasn't here, but you was on the way.' Diane had told her, 'Mama was a rollin' stone, used to run around.' I said, 'Yeah, she did, drink . . .' They know she in the church as a shield. They know what she did to me. She wanted the divorce, she told you a lie and said I wanted it. She a *liar*! I never sent her no papers! *She* applied for the divorce, she got the divorce. After she got the divorce, she kicked me out of the house. I *give* her the house. She said, 'It's my house now. You give me the house, so you can't stay here.' I was staying in some little place, a motel or something, while we got the divorce. I got my clothes, put 'em in the motel, got the car and hit the road, all the way along that 61 highway. I drove all the way [to California] by myself. She told me, 'I got the house, and you don't live here no more.' She lyin' through her teeth. If she be a church-woman, why she a liar?

"She the one got the divorce, she the one kicked me out. She was gonna take all the money, but . . . did I tell you about the girl called me to the bank? [Maude] had put in for the stop on the money, but I had a good friend at the bank, she worked there as a teller. Me and her were really good friends; she was a big fan of mine. When she got the stop note, she called me before they processed it, about one o'clock. 'Mr. Hooker? Come down and get your money, because tomorrow it's gonna be tied up.' I said, 'Why?' 'Because there's a note commanding that tomorrow your money be tied up.' I said, 'What about now?' She said, 'No, not now. Get down here.' I got down there, took most of half the money. I left her a little. She got mad, told her lawyer I got the money hid in some other bank. The lawyer said, 'Well, he can't do that.' But I was gone . . . She did some terrible things, things that I wouldn't even *attempt* to tell you. I wouldn't put in the book some of the things she did to me, I wouldn't even *tell* you. She raked me over the coals, but right now now she got a lotta regrets. She never knew I'm 'a get this big."

And, in all fairness, neither did anybody else. After all, there was John Lee Hooker, past fifty years of age, heading west into the unknown with nothing to his name but that name itself. He had a car, a few clothes, two guitars, an amplifier and a little over twelve thousand dollars in cash. He was leaving behind thirty years of personal history in Detroit, twenty-three years of marriage, five children, and a sixth on the way.

If we were doing this as a movie, we could show Hooker, fueled only by coffee, adrenaline and a few "bennies," driving wearily west into the blood-red sunset with all that was left of his life piled into his car. Right then, it would have seemed like the starry-eyed height of optimistic romanticism for anybody to have suggested just how high that California sun might one day rise for him.

Let alone that it could take twenty years.

12. Interlude—Dark Room

And listening to the music was exactly like being back in my
own life, like the blues are supposed to be. The blues don't
make you think—they make you remember. If you've
got no memories, you can't have the blues.
—Andrew Vachss, *Flood* (Pan Books, 1985)

He had this sound which was unlike any other sound. You
couldn't hear any influence; this guy sounded only like
himself . . . You put on a John Lee Hooker record, or you
hear him in person, and it's just like a good movie or a good
book. It keeps lingering, and you can't get it out of your
system. It stays with you. You don't forget about it . . .
After all these years of knowing John, and knowing him as
well as I have, I'm still in awe of him when I'm around him.
I just have so much respect for him. I can never look at him
or think of him as just a buddy. He's just a great human
being, you know, who plays the deepest blues that
ever was. No deeper was ever played.
—Charlie Musselwhite, interview with the author, 1991

The principal difference between artists and everybody else is that civilians
believe that a viable distinction can be made between "art" and "life."[1]
By the same token, the essence of the art of John Lee Hooker is the art
of *being* John Lee Hooker, which in turn means that John Lee Hooker is
not simply, as Pete Welding called him in the liner-notes to a recent reissue
compilation,[2] "everyone's favorite blues singer," but the sole practitioner
of a one-man art form. This book has, thus far, dealt primarily with the
"who," the "when" and the "where" of the career of John Lee Hooker,
and now seems like as good a time as any to take a long look at the
"what," the "how" and maybe even the "why" of "the art of John Lee
Hooker," and why it is so much more than the circumstances of that
career, and the astonishing late-blooming success that climaxed it, which
renders the man and the music unique.

---

1 Not to mention between "form" and "content," but that's another argument.
2 *Alternative Boogie: Early Studio Recordings 1948–1952* (Capitol Blues Collection, 1996).

As an hors d'œuvre: an anecdote, which regrettably requires the author to shift himself out of the protective third person. Once upon a time (to be a little more precise, some time in very early 1980), I ejected a jazz fan from my flat. The guy was then a few-doors-down near-neighbor of mine and, once a few casual conversational encounters on the stairs had established that we both loved music, I invited him around one evening for a few drinks and a few records. During the course of the evening it became apparent that while, in my capacity as an admirer of Miles, Trane, Duke, Mingus and Monk, I was prepared to follow him some considerable distance into his preferred musical territory, he was unwilling to travel even a fraction of a millimeter into mine. Serious ructions commenced when I played him a couple of Clash tunes: he began to foam at the mouth and assert that the only rock musicians whom he considered to be musicians at all were Blood Sweat & Tears (because "they could really play their instruments"). Finally, I kicked something by John Lee Hooker onto the stereo and awaited his reaction.

"Why are you making me listen to this?" he inquired. "This man can barely play the guitar."

It was at this point that I hauled myself to my feet, flung open the door and suggested, in theatrically profane terms, that he depart the premises before I hurt him. This was, in fact, an utterly empty threat—I haven't had a fight since I was thirteen, and I lost that one—but he did indeed take his leave, muttering into his beard. We never spoke again, and shortly he moved out of the block, taking with him two albums (Duke Ellington's *Afro-Bossa* and a rather nice Jimmy Witherspoon compilation) which I had previously been thoughtless enough to loan him. It took a long time to replace those records, but the light was worth the candle simply to be rid of his smugly smirking presence. What I'd found most offensive about his remarks was not so much that he'd dissed *my* taste in *my* home (this is, after all, an occupational hazard when something as important as music is being discussed), but that he had revealed the shallowness of his understanding of the underlying roots, the central core, of his own choice of music. Yes, of course Charlie Parker and John Coltrane were virtuoso players of astonishing fluency, and yes, of course, their music wouldn't have been remotely possible without the ability to apply—virtually instantaneously—an intimidating degree of musical theory, physical dexterity, and instrumental technique. Nevertheless, if that had been all that they were doing, their work would be little more than a historical curio. As it is, the music of Charles Parker and John Coltrane lives and breathes and continues to inspire successive generations of musicians; not simply because of their technical facility or their theoretical grasp, but because of the soulfulness and spiritual content of their music.[3]

And that is *it*. That is the *whole deal*. Music stands or falls by what it makes its listeners feel, and everything else is simply furniture. My unfortunate neighbor had fallen in love with the technical means by which his heroes had chosen to achieve their creative ends, and had completely ignored the ends themselves.

Of course, on one level he was completely right. If—say—you were looking to hire a guitarist to play in the pit band for a Broadway musical, or to sight-read a complex part for a big-band jazz or commercial rock session, and John Lee Hooker had somehow been persuaded to come along and audition, you might well conclude that he could "barely play the guitar." On the other hand, if you were looking for someone to play John Lee Hooker–style guitar and Hooker himself was unavailable or unaffordable, you'd be in deep, deep trouble, since very few people can even pastiche his style convincingly, let alone create freely within it. Hooker's style is one of those which is so utterly deceptive in its apparent simplicity that it seems, to those who worship ostentatious displays of technique and theory, to be almost insultingly easy: literally *artless*. Then you try to do it yourself, or you hear someone else attempting to reproduce it, and then you realize that it's virtually impossible. Reviewing Michael Caine's performance in Lewis Gilbert's movie of Willy Russell's *Educating Rita*, Pauline Kael wrote:

> *Michael Caine is the least pyrotechnic, the least show-offy of actors. He has prodigious ease on the screen; it's only afterward that you realize how difficult what he was doing is . . . The goal of Caine's technique seems to be to dissolve all vestiges of "technique." He lets nothing get between you and the character he plays. You don't observe his acting; you just experience the character's emotions . . .* [4]

---

3 Any Miles Davis fan should be able to tell you that. When Charlie Parker hired a fragile, inexperienced young Miles to replace Dizzy Gillespie—who unlike Miles could boast flawless execution and a terrifying command of the upper register of his instrument—in his quintet, a whole bunch of people, by no means all of them white, thought Parker'd finally flipped. "Miles can hardly play," they said. So much for the experts.

4 *New Yorker*, November 14, 1983; reprinted in Kael's collection *State Of The Art* (Arena, 1987).

The qualities which Kael detects in Caine's acting—transparency, purity, authenticity—are precisely those we find in Hooker's blues. It is the art which conceals itself: it takes you to the heart of the matter almost instantly, placing the minimum of obstacles or filters between the experience of artist and audience.

To play like John Lee Hooker, you have to *be* John Lee Hooker, and this is because the style is the man. The *two* are inseparable and indivisible: one cannot discuss the music without discussing the man, and vice versa. Let us say it once again: John Lee Hooker do not do, he be. His music is the way it is because the man is who he is. What is more, he knows exactly who he is and, over long, hard, painful years, he has refined that knowledge and placed it all at the service of his art. The unique character of the blues depends on one central fact: that the music is impossible to perform convincingly unless the performer knows him- (or her-) self inside out and is prepared to place that self on the line, to occupy the spiritual and emotional center of each and every song. Blues performed without self-knowledge and self-expression is merely a set of gestures and conventions: it can rock your body but it can't roll your soul. As Julio Finn put it in *The Bluesman*:[5]

> *. . . the blues performance is a rite, in which the musician assumes the role of the "elder" and the audience that of the "initiate . . ."the performers' aim is to conjure—in the same sense that the preacher or the Root Doctor conjures—their audience . . . the "true" instrument played in blues cult houses (jook joints) is the audience. The audience, as instrument, produces the spirit which shapes and develops the song. From belonging to the performer it becomes the property of the community; these individual statements are transformed into the testimony of the group . . . the effectiveness of this depends upon how deeply he or she can tap the sleeping roots of the listeners' subconscious. A blues performer can only achieve this when his or her own "soul" is intact.[6]*

This, of course, should not be taken as a suggestion that a blues performer needs to be content, or settled, in order to play the blues. This notion

---

5 *Quartet*, 1989.
6 Emphasis mine.

would turn reality on its head; it would be a complete and utter contradiction of the social, cultural, historical, economic and psychological realities which underpin the music. What Finn is telling us is that in order to fulfil the music's function, the bluesman needs the ability to face, to understand, and—please pardon the *Star Trek* infinitive—to fully accept the emotion of the moment, be it sorrow or anger, joy or regret; and to incorporate that emotion, without let or hindrance or inhibition of any kind, into that performance which is so much more than a performance.

The blues is an art; the blues is an entertainment; the blues is a commodity; the blues is cultural history; the blues is any number of things to any number of people. But, above all, the blues is an eminently practical and functional set of methods and processes for dealing with the most painful aspects of life. Like meditation or yoga in Buddhist or Hindu societies, it is a discipline, a structure, for the focusing of self.

Using the blues as a means of achieving this end is not only the highest priority of Hooker's art: it is almost the *only* priority. In order to do so, he has evolved a style which is unlike any other: it is, simultaneously, utterly unique and personal to him; and a grand archetype which can sound as if it is the fundamental blues on which all other blues, even music recorded before Hooker himself ever even picked up a guitar, let alone walked into a recording studio, is based. Let us therefore look a little more closely at the mechanics of Hooker's music, the materials from which it is constructed, and the processes by which it is made. Hooker himself, as it happens, heartily despises all things theoretical or intellectual . . .

"No matter how much education I didn't have," he will insist, "book education didn't have what was in *here*"—tapping his chest—"and in *here*"—tapping his head. "I could've been a professor, but I repeat myself to you and to whoever read this book after I'm gone: you can*not* get what I got, out of a book. You got to have a talent. There is no one I heard yet can go into a studio like John Lee Hooker and just produce something right on the spot. I can go into a studio with nothin' and come out with one of the beautifullest songs, because I'm very wise up here. People say, 'How can you do that?' I say, 'It's a gif' from God, if there's a God—a Supreme Being.' I have written more songs than any other blues singer—*I* think so—and they wasn't written on a piece of paper. *Here*'s my paper"—and he taps his head once more. "You can't find a feelin' on a piece of paper. I don't believe in no *paper*. Take your paper, stick a match to it. My paper's right in *here*, and in *here*."

... but we're going to need some theory—musical and cultural—even if Hooker doesn't. *Especially* because he doesn't.

If we look at Hooker's first and most prolific years as a recording artist, we find that while he didn't precisely "go into a studio with nothin'," he went in with what may objectively seem like very little. He had mastered two keys, each with its own tuning; a very few basic song structures, and even fewer beats.

Keys first: Hooker's music was—and is—mainly performed in one or other of two basic modes. The first is in the standard "concert" guitar tuning of E-A-D-G-B-E, low to high, and almost invariably in the key of E. The second is in an "open" tuning—that is, one in which strumming the unfretted strings produces a full chord—which mimics the character-istic sound of a first-position chord of A major, in which the second, third and fourth strings are held down at the second fret. Depending on whether those strings are tuned up a full tone or the first, fifth and sixth strings are slackened by the equivalent interval, this tuning (known to traditional guitarists as "Spanish," after the nineteenth-century parlor-guitar standard "Spanish Fandango," which introduced the tuning to the American musical vocabulary) produces either a chord of G (D-G-D-G-B-D) or A (E-A-E-A-C#-E). Most country bluesmen preferred, as do the majority of contemporary musicians who perform in this style, to tune down to G (which placed less strain on precious, hard-to-replace strings), but the higher tension of the A tuning imparts a correspondingly greater sharpness and urgency to the sound. This tuning is also frequently used on the banjo and the Hawaiian guitar: "Once I figured out how to put the banjo G to the guitar," Ry Cooder told *Guitar Player* magazine,[7] "all of a sudden there were all of John Lee Hooker's chords."

"I get the feel that I want," Hooker says of the "Spanish" tuning. "It's a different sound. Different tuning, different sound. Playing open, you're not playing chords. It's picking, it's a different sound altogether, different feelin' from A to E. A-tuning is a real blues funky key. You play

---

7 Interviewed by Jas Obrecht, *Guitar Player*, November 1992. Elaborating on this theme, Cooder explained to the producers of Hooker's *BBC-TV* mini-special that he had enjoyed com-paratively little previous success trying to figure out how to reproduce what Hooker was playing on record. "I never got anywhere until, a couple of years later, I picked up the banjo, began to play it and it was always in G tuning. I began to see these chord progressions and these notes occur in the G tuning, so I started to tune my guitar like that. I went back to the record, pulled the record out and said, 'Ah, *here* it is.' Here's the notes and the chords, and you just had to sit there and figure it out. That led me into the idea of tuning the instrument to chords, which nowadays seems like a simple and obvious enough thing. Back in those days, that was a major discovery for me: in fact, the first major discovery I made on my own without being taught."

slow, not fast—not countin' the boogie, you gotta play that fast. But the slow stuff, you really get the feelin'. It's a deeper feelin' I do in open A than I do in regular tuning. It's a little deeper . . . *real* funky. E is deep but A . . . there's just something about it. It's a really *blues* key."

Then there's picking and strumming: the right-hand stuff. Hooker plays strictly finger-style: striking downwards with the thumb on the bass strings and plucking upwards with his index finger on the trebles. Sometimes, for fast chord strumming, he will use his middle or ring finger, but most of his playing depends on the interaction between that down-stroking thumb and up-swinging index. The first time he saw Hooker live and close up, Pete Townshend was awestruck. "His . . . rhythm playing totally stunned me . . . he appeared to achieve this simply by flailing at the strings aimlessly with his huge hands, but the results were precise . . . Hooker's chord work convinced me that pinning down a precise and solid chordal structure was far more important for me than learning by rote the solos of virtuosos like B. B. King and Buddy Guy."

The bulk of the hundreds of songs Hooker recorded in those early years were constructed around a mere handful of basic templates; a small number of bottles into which to pour an infinite ocean of wine. First and foremost among these was "the boogie," the signature groove he learned from his stepfather Will Moore; but though Moore's is the primary influence most frequently cited by Hooker, his big sister's one-time suitor Tony Hollins, who was the first bluesman Hooker ever heard, comes an extremely close second. And it was Hollins who introduced Hooker to the fundamental themes which were the building blocks, the DNA, of Delta blues.

"[Hollins] used to play, '*I wisht I was a catfish, swimming in the deep blue sea,*' " says Hooker. "That song go way-way-way back, man. Muddy didn't write that song; the first time I heard it was [Hollins]. Tony Hollins would play it when Muddy was a little kid. 'Catfish,' he used to play that all the time, and another song which he give me was maybe a hundred years old. He give me 'Crawlin' King Snake.' I turned that around and made it different, but he give me that song. At that time there wasn't no songwriters, there wasn't no publishers, nothin'. They just made songs up in the cotton fields and stuff like this. It was just a song he made up and passed it onto me, so that made me the writer when I did it my own way. Now the song become so popular, everybody was doin' it, the 'Crawlin' King Snake.' Everybody do's that now."

Among all but the most erudite blues buffs, Tony Hollins's name is not exactly one with which to conjure. He recorded a mere handful of singles during the 1940s, and the two most durable compositions with which he is associated are most commonly attributed to others. "Crosscut Saw," first recorded by Tommy McClennan—of whom more in a moment—was adapted by The Binghampton Blues Boys[8] and credited to "R. G. Ford;" their recording in turn inspired Albert King's, from which all subsequent versions, including those by The Groundhogs and Eric Clapton, were derived. Hollins cut the original "Crawlin' King Snake" in 1941—or rather, he *sort of* did: Big Joe Williams recorded a very similar "King Snake" the same year—but up until very recently the song has generally been credited to Hooker. Listening now to Hollins's slender body of work, and hearing it not only in the context of Hooker's music but of the recorded legacy of the great Delta bluesmen who were Hollins's contemporaries, he sounds a marginal figure indeed: almost all his sides are minor variants of his basic "King Snake" template, his work neither deep nor broad. To Child John, of course, Hollins was a revelation: the man who first opened the door into the realm which Hooker would explore for the rest of his life.

The underlying structures of much of Hooker's early repertoire derive from the work of one of the biggest names in pre-war Chicago blues: Sonny Boy Williamson. Singer/harpist John Lee "Sonny Boy" Williamson should not be confused, though he often is, with another, better-known, harp virtuoso: Alex "Rice" Miller, an older Delta-based performer who took on the "Sonny Boy Williamson" name even before its original bearer was murdered in 1948. Miller, whom we'll call "Sonny Boy Williamson II" for clarity's sake, hosted the *King Biscuit Boy* radio show for the pioneering Memphis station WDIA, cut a series of magnificent sides for Chess in the '50s, toured and briefly resided in the U.K. in the early '60s, and died back home in the Delta in 1965. The original Sonny Boy, for his part, recorded for Bluebird between 1937 and 1948, often in tandem with Big Joe Williams, and early hits of his which found their way into Hooker's bag included "Decoration Day," "Bluebird Blues,"[9] "Bottle Up And Go" and "Sugar Mama." (Sonny Boy's studio partner Big Joe Williams, incidentally, cut variants of "Baby Please Don't Go"—copyrighted in his name, fortunately for him—and "Ground Hog Blues," both of which subsequently became Hooker staples.)

---

8 About whom your humble servant is ashamed to admit he knows *nada*.
9 This pair were also great favorites of the mighty Howlin' Wolf, as it happens.

"Bottle Up And Go" and "Sugar Mama" didn't simply enter Hooker's repertoire under their own colors. They also became templates for many of Hooker's own creations. What's truly fascinating, though, is that they seem to have arrived in Hooker's songbook after a detour via the work of yet another near-forgotten Delta bard: Tommy McClennan.

He sang in a hard, keening high tenor not unlike a Robert Johnson without the shadows or the nuances, but it is his guitar playing which foreshadows Hooker most eerily: in the insistent use of modal fills performed without a slide. Hooker's guitar style is so defiantly personal that it comes as a shock to hear an earlier performer who sounds anything like him, but McClennan's instrumental approach includes passages which suggest Hooker far more strongly than anything—apart from a few obvious "King Snake" licks—in the recordings of Hooker's actual mentor, Tony Hollins. When it is possible to make direct comparisons, as on the material McClennan and Hooker share with Sonny Boy Williamson and Big Joe Williams, the McClennan sides sound almost like vague preliminary sketches for the subsequent Hooker versions. McClennan is more, but only a little more, than a historical curio: one of those likable minor genre artists who enable archivists to join up a few more of the dots linking major figures. He landed up in Chicago at the tail end of the first era of Chicago blues, cutting records for three years before World War II temporarily shut down the American record industry, and by the time the modern era commenced he was out of the game.

Born in 1908 in Yazoo City, Mississippi, McClennan was already performing his own personal variant of "Bottle Up And Go" when he hit Chicago in 1939. The good-natured Big Bill Broonzy took him under his wing, as he was wont to do when promising young singers arrived from Down Home, and advised him that the couplet *"nigger and the white man playin' seven-up/nigger beat the white man, scared to pick it up,"* which McClennan was fond of inserting into "Bottle Up And Go," was unlikely to go down too well with the locals. McClennan sang it anyway at his first big-city house party and ended up leaving via a first-floor window with the remnants of his guitar around his neck. (He nevertheless included this troublesome couplet in his recorded version, which suggests either that folks cut him more slack once he'd made a few records, or else that he'd started employing bodyguards for personal appearances.)

"Bottle Up And Go" came complete with a catchy guitar lick, a stomping danceable groove and a neat structure which divided the twelve-bar (or, in John Lee's case, twelve-bar-*ish*) stanza into verse and chorus:

socking home a different couplet each time and using the title as a punch-line.[10] It became one of the templates on which a significant slice of Hooker's early repertoire is based. Sonny Boy Williamson's "Sugar Mama," especially the way McClennan performed it, was a tautly powerful slow blues whose beat pulsed as remorselessly as your heart. It, too, became a prototype, providing the framework for Hooker's own "Sally Mae." Hooker recorded "Sugar Mama" itself several times throughout his career, most recently on 1995's *Chill Out*, but its echoes still ring whenever Hooker plays an open-tuned slow blues with anything even faintly resembling conventional changes.

Then there were Hooker's home-grown specialties, both essentially deconstructed equivalents of "Bottle" and "Mama." The latter's Hooker-ized twin was an open-ended, free-form slow blues which never (or hardly ever) changed chord: its avatar was "Wednesday Evening," which Hooker recorded for the first of many times at an Elmer Barbee demo session a few months before his first encounter with Bernard Besman. And the former's was, of course, the Boogie.

And those, plus a couple of cousins from the "Catfish Blues" and "Rollin' And Tumblin' " song families, were pretty much all that Hooker brought to the party when he first started recording. Conventional notions of composition would suggest that a man who could play four songs would record four songs, and that would be it. As it was, Hooker recorded well over a hundred sides in the year following the original "Boogie Chillen" session, most of which have been released, and many of which are wonderful. So how did he do it?

John is John, and the way he play is John Lee Hooker, and if you don't study the man's music, you think he's wrong. But as far as I'm concerned he's not wrong, that's John Lee Hooker . . . he's playin' John Lee. I mean: in the beginning of time, who wrote the four bars? If John Lee hadda come along, we probably wouldn't have four bars, we'd'a had just any kind of bar: three-and-a-half bars, five: just as long as it fits. If the shoe fit, it's comfortable. If it don't fit, it's not comfortable. That's the way I think he feel about his music. That's the way I feel about it, you know. I think I got

---

10 Chuck Berry's revved-up, justly celebrated tongue-twister "Too Much Monkey Business" is built on a "Bottle Up And Go" chassis.

advantaged by not takin' my music in school, because I'd'a probably been hung up on this "he changin' too fast" or "he not changin' fast enough" and all that stuff. I don't pay that no mind. As many records as he sold on "Boogie Chillen," I go along with his changes[laughs].
—Buddy Guy, interview with the author, 1993

And one thing[Will Moore] kept pounding into my head: play from the heart and the soul. Don't think about no scales; twelve, sixteen and eight. Play the way you feel. And I did that. But I also learned how to play with good timin', with scales and bars. After I learned the way he taught me to play, it felt so good, people loved it so much that that was the way I did it. I can do it perfect, real perfect, but it wouldn't be me. He said, "Just play until you just feel it in your heart and your head. Forget about the book, the scales" . . . and I did that. And I really loved it. I can turn around and play scales, count it all, 1–2–3–4, 8, 12, 16 . . . I learned all of that, perfectly. I can do it. But when I get to feelin' good, I can jump anywhere and don't think nothin' about it. That's the way I am.
—John Lee Hooker, interview with the author, 1991

From the point of view of an archetypal R & B producer of the '40s or '50s, committed to squeezing the maximum number of usable sides out of the minimum amount of studio time, the ideal performer would be one with a vast repertoire of distinctive original songs and the ability to perform each one consistently from take to take. Hooker was the exact reverse of that ideal: he knew comparatively few songs, and performed them differently each time. For Bernard Besman, this was a nightmare. "Out of the 250 records that I did with him," Besman claims, "there are at least twenty songs using the 'Boogie Chillen' thing. It's the same thing: all he'd do is change the words. If I[had] let him, he'd do 'Boogie Chillen' or 'Sally Mae' over and over again. He has the talent to do that; not many people could do that. But he wouldn't remember what he did on the first song, or the second song. So that was frustrating."

In William Gibson's novel *Idoru*,[11] there is a character whose short attention span makes him the perfect cyberspace researcher: he zaps in-

---

11 Viking, 1996

tuitively from database to database, following connections apparent only to him. Technically, his concentration deficit is a disability; but he has found a context in which what might otherwise be a crippling flaw instead becomes a unique asset. Hooker, by the same token, has built his entire approach to music around the quirk which so infuriated Besman. In *Totemism*,[12] Claude Lévi-Strauss observes that,

> so that pictorial academicism might feel secure, [the painter] El Greco could not be a normal person who was capable of rejecting certain ways of representing the world, but he had to be afflicted by a malformation of the eyeball, and it was this alone that was responsible for his elongated figures ... by regarding the hysteric or the artistic innovator as abnormal, we accorded ourselves the luxury of believing that they did not concern us, and that they did not put in question, by the mere fact of their existence, an accepted social, moral or intellectual order.

Whether Hooker is a compulsive improviser whose vision drives him to reinvent a song every single time he performs it, or a musical *naïf* so scatter-brained and undisciplined that he cannot remember what he's done from one moment to the next, is almost not the point. What matters is that, for Hooker, the feeling of the moment is all; and a song—*any* song—is simply an empty vessel waiting to be filled with that feeling.

And that feeling manifests itself through the body. In most music, the demands of the composition, the piece, assume the highest priority. In order to perform the piece correctly—or, in cases where "correctness" is a less rigid notion, perhaps we should substitute the term "appropriately"—the musician will use his or her body to manipulate the instrument so that it produces the required sounds. The sounds in question are the desired result, the instrument is the medium, and the body—through limb or digit movement, breath or whatever—is therefore the "servant" of the piece or composition. In the case of John Lee Hooker, this process is reversed. The body acts to express the emotion, the "feeling of the moment," and the instrument is there to express and to reflect that feeling. If the feeling dictates that Hooker should, at any given moment, strike a guitar string hard enough to make it ring a microtone sharp of "correct"

---

12 This seminal work was first published by Presses Universitaires de France in 1962; I'm working from the 1969 Pelican edition of the Roger Needham translation first published by Beacon Press in 1963.

pitch—or so that an adjacent string to the one actually struck should sound out alongside it—then he will do so, and never think once about it, let alone twice. Or if he is singing a song, and has not extracted the necessary degree of meaning from a line, he will sing it again . . . and again, and again. Only then will he move onto the next line, and if this plays hell with some pendant's notion of what the song structure *ought* to be—or if the musicians accompanying him start to panic and lose their nerve—then so be it. It's not his problem. The feeling rules the body, the body rules the instrument, and the music is the result. The music is the servant of the feeling, as mediated firstly through the body, and sec-ondly—via the body—through the instrument.

In his 1970 essay "Musica Practica"[13] Roland Barthes creates a dis-tinction between two kinds of music: "the music one listens to, the music one plays." Which is to say: music which is performed in order to be listened to, and music which is listened to only incidentally, because its primary purpose is the function which it fulfils for the performer. Re-garding the latter, he writes:

> *The music one plays comes from an activity that is very little audi-tory, being above all manual (and thus in a way much more sensual) . . . with no other audience but its participants (that is, with all risk of theater, all temptation of hysteria removed); a muscular music in which the part taken by the sense of hearing is one only of ratifi-cation . . .*

In the blues, as in no other music, and the music of John Lee Hooker, as in that of no other bluesman, this distinction collapses. Hooker's work takes a private music—"private" in the sense of "personal" rather than "secret"—into a public sphere while retaining all aspects of the charac-teristic described by Barthes above.

By way of illustration, let's take a detailed look at a specific Hooker performance: "Dark Room," as recorded live in concert at New York's Hunter College in February 1976 and most recently released as part of the Tomato Records double-CD *Alone*. It's neither one of Hooker's most celebrated songs—in fact it is, if the reader will forgive the oxymoron,

---

13 Collected in *Image Music Text* (Fontana, 1977), edited and translated by Stephen Heath.

quite spectacularly obscure—nor does it date from any of his generally acknowledged "classic" periods. Its origins lay in a song called "Seven Days And Seven Nights," which Hooker had recorded twice: first during the November '64 London sessions with The Groundhogs, and again in August '66 while cutting the *Live At Cafe Au Go-Go* album with Muddy Waters and his band. Its next metamorphosis occurred in November of 1970 when it was cut, as "Sittin' In My Dark Room," during the three-day San Francisco session which produced the ABC double-album *Endless Boogie*.

Endless Boogie's version of this ominous, muted free-form slow blues was a team-handed affair. As well as a rhythm section (bassist Gino Skaggs and drummer Billy Ingram), Hooker was backed by two other guitarists (Steve Miller and Mel Brown) plus two pianists (Mark Naftalin and Cliff Coulter, respectively playing acoustic and electric instruments). Their accompaniment is subtle and sensitive—dark, roiling undercurrents of bass and piano, lit and pierced by sharp splinters of guitar—and they *listen*. Hooker sings as a man coming to terms with the departure of his lover; he sits weeping in his bedroom, and even when his friends stop by to visit, his emotions still overwhelm him to the point where he must abandon his guests so that he can grapple with his sorrow in his darkened bedchamber, alone. It is a fine, moody performance, but it somehow doesn't go deep enough: it is not so much that Hooker doesn't have his heart in it, rather that the piece has not yet grown large enough to accommodate that heart.

All of this had changed by the time of the Hunter College show. Hooker was performing solo on electric guitar: without the support of a band, but also without the limitations of one. He opens the show with a brief, hushed version of "Maudie," here retitled "I Miss You So." "Dark Room" itself is preceded here by a letter-perfect performance of "(Bad Like) Jesse James" (aka "I'm Mad" or "I'm Mad Again"), one of those rare Hooker songs which, like "Boom Boom," is graven in marble and almost never changes from one performance to another. In this one, over a single rolling riff which repeats and resolves, repeats and resolves, over and over again, Hooker tells the story of how he was cuckolded by his best friend, and the awful revenge he plans to exact upon that treacherous friend. The torrential litany of threats—casually recited in Hooker's badman voice: hard, dry, uninflected—which climaxes the piece can only be described as "gangsta blues." If Quentin Tarantino teamed up with Ice-T, they could scarcely better it:

I got three boys,
Do my dirty work,
You don't see me,
I'm the big boss,
I do's the payin' off,
After the job is did,
They may cut you,
They may shoot you,
They may drown you,
I don't know,
An' I don't care . . .
'Cause I'm maaad,
An' I'm baaad . . .

Then he goes into detail. Four are going down to the river, but only three are coming back. The victim is going to be gagged, and bound hand and foot, and held underwater—*"just hold the cat there, don't let him up, he been talkin' too much."* Hooker even gives us the bubbles of air—*plu-plupluplupluplup*—which signify his cuckolder's dying breath.

And yet, incomprehensibly, the audience is laughing. The threats are blood-curdling, the vocal delivery is chilling, yet clearly Hooker is visually undercutting the implied violence with body language: gestures and facial expressions apparent only to those in the room with him. The subtext, however, is utterly unambiguous: sometimes a tidal wave of grief can be held back only with a thick wall of anger. On "Dark Room," that wall has crumbled: even the most lurid revenge fantasy must eventually pall, and the sufferer has no remaining option but to confront his pain. All barriers are down: nothing now stands between Hooker and his grief. Or between him and us. There is no irony, no "distance." Nothing is in quotes.

And, as if to emphasize that point, "Dark Room" remains entirely free of any kind of formal structure. It has no pulsebeat, no lyrical organization or rhyme scheme and—with the exception of the single allusion to the chord of B7 with which Hooker prefaces his vocal entry—no chord changes. It is as close as Hooker ever got to presenting the raw, unmediated stuff of his music, its heart, soul and spirit, without furniture or frame.

"Dark Room" begins with a series of exploratory runs—part meditation, part foreplay, part prologue—bristling with pull-offs and hammer-ons and played out of meter primarily on the treble strings. The piece is performed in regular tuning in the key of E, and the ominous, booming plunk of the open bass E string, to which each and every run eventually returns, provides it with its sole anchor. Right from the start, the mood is one of upheaval. The guitar blurts, stutters, interrupts itself. Phrases begin but don't resolve; notes bump into each other, choke each other off. Finally the turmoil quiets. Hooker launches a slower, calmer lick upward from the bass E. A moment of silence, and then—foot quietly tapping in the background—he quietly and reflectively plays a classic bass-string "turnaround" of the kind which normally occurs at the end of a standard I-IV-V twelve-bar chorus, ascending to B7 (the "V" of an E blues) before returning to the root tonality.

Another beat of silence, and then Hooker sets the scene. "*I'm sittin' here,*" he begins, almost to himself, "*in my dark room, dark room*" . . . The guitar stabs twice for emphasis . . . "*In my dark room cryin' 'bout you.*" The voice is low, soft, meditative, burry with suppressed emotion, but the guitar gives the game away. Its roiling blurt permits no ambiguity concerning the nature of that "thinkin'." This man *hurts.* He's not quite ready to admit it to us, but the guitar keeps no secrets. As with all great blues singer/guitarists, from Robert Johnson to B. B. King to Robert Cray, the guitar tells us what the voice will not, or cannot. The voice is the ego, the guitar the conscience, the soul.

Hooker repeats the scene-setting, sitting there in his dark room, adding one more piece of information: "*on my bedside,*" . . . and the guitar underlines it. He starts to repeat: "*on my bed*" . . . and now the guitar will let him go no further, interrupting, blurting out the pain the singer refuses to acknowledge. He's striking the bass strings hard enough to distort both tone and pitch: one could describe it as a self-consciously ugly sound if there was anything whatsoever about this performance which was self-conscious at all. "*I'm sitting on my bedside,*" he continues, undulating the final syllable through eight or nine notes—"*on my bedside cryin' . . . cryin' about you.*" The guitar takes over again, always reaching up-and-out for the treble, always tumbling back down to the bass.

"*You know sometimes,*" Hooker confides . . . one single, jabbing interpolation from the guitar. Then a beat of silence. Then the interpolation, repeated. "*I have friends around me.*" The guitar mutters, skeptically. "*We be sittin' down in the livin' room talkin'*"—the guitar interrupts once again, and the voice breaks in bitter self-mockery—"*me an' my friends.*" *Huh* says the guitar. "*Havin' a little nip together.*" The guitar says *Yeah, sure.* Hooker says, "*I get to thinkin' 'bout how she done treated me so bad*" . . . and then it changes. The guitar stops talking back and just tolls, like a church bell. Once. Twice. An E octave: the open bass E string and the D string at the second fret, the open E thumbed so hard that it rings sharp—*BAAAAAongg*—under the pressure. A quick bass run and then back to the awful, tolling E; the remorseless low E from which there is no escape: not in this piece, anyway.

"*I don't want my friends to see me cryin*"—the word "cry" melismatically stretched across half a dozen notes, the guitar keening into a hurtful trebly blizzard—"*I say, ' 'Scuse me, people' *" . . . —another treble storm, this time ending on an A, the fourth of the E blues scale, implying a continuation—" ' . . . *I got to step into my room.*' " Another treble blurt. "*And then I sit down, sit down, sit down, sit down*"—the guitar tries to get a few notes in edgeways but now Hooker will be interrupted no further. "*I sit down on my bedside*"—and now it is the turn of the voice to interrupt the guitar. "*You know tears come down my face,*" he sings, and the guitar follows. Instrument and voice are no longer in opposition, but in harmony: the public and private faces and voices have now fused. The guitar simply marks time for a beat and then—all anger burned away, leaving nothing behind but a bottomless pit of melancholy, a vale of tears stretching to each and every faraway horizon—it begins to sound the ominous slow bass-string riff from "Tupelo," that tale of an external, rather than internal, flood which subsumes all before it.

"*I don't want the people,*" Hooker murmurs, guitar still restating "Tupelo" beneath his voice, "*to see me cryin' 'bout you.*" Now his voice strengthens, becoming both deeper and sharper as well as richer and louder, anger flooding back: "*you know she did me so bad, so bad*"—that shift from second to third person as "you" becomes "she." He says it again: "*you know she did me so bad, so bad*"—a hit on the bass E-"*you know she did me*"—a giddying swirl of melismas on the last word, and now his rage has become a tidal wave, towering, irresistible, and those savage treble runs return—"*Whoah Lord she did me so bad*"—back to the bass, jabbing down furiously with his thumb until you feel that the string just has to break, or that something must break—"*that every time I think about it*"—voice softening and lowering again, guitar muttering indistinctly—"*you know I can't keep from cryin'.*"

Another moment of silence, and then he starts to hum, *mmmhmmm,* guitar and voice united, blending in seamless union. It almost sounds as if he's "violining"—an electric guitarist's technique in which the volume is turned off as each note is struck and then turned back up as it rings, so that you have a note that fades in from nowhere, with no attack at its leading edge—so soft and sweet is the sound. And then he moans, "*awwwww-hawwwww ohhhhhh-ohhhh.*" It is literally *awwwww*-ful: the pure, unalloyed sound of human grief, not a sound made for an audience, but simply soul and body trying to make itself feel better, to handle the pain any way it can.

And then he sings once more, "*And then the tears come down my face,*" and it is just the most extraordinary moment. You see the tears, you see the face. Hooker's voice is, most frequently, smooth and mellifluous: nothing further from the stereotypical Delta bluesman's rasp—and the ersatz constricted-throat gravel employed by so many white wannabe bluesers—can possibly be imagined. But on the word "tears" a deep, leathery grain colors his voice, supernaturally evocative of the lines on a face no longer young as the tears which can no longer be withheld trickle down, gathering in seams of weathered skin; of the texture and fabric of a life of much pain endured, with no end to that pain in sight.

He moans once again and strikes one sharp chord—*bap!*—on the guitar, and it's over, and we're into something else. But the moment, and the feeling of the moment, remain: the specific moment in a human life which a song evokes, and the moment in which it is performed. No other artist could have delivered that particular performance; Hooker himself could not (would not?) replicate it precisely no matter how much money you offered him to do so. What it is, right there in five minutes (minus applause time): the purest essence of the blues. Not only of John Lee Hooker's blues, but *all* blues. It's what the wood looks like when you learn to stop looking at the trees.

Of course, for some there is no wood: only trees. According to Bernard Besman, what Hooker does isn't the blues at all. As Besman wrote in the liner-note to a compilation of Hooker out-takes:[14]

> *Hooker, though he has since come to be regarded as a blues artist, in my opinion is not. Blues is a form of music characterized by a rigid 12-bar structure, and a repetition of words and themes. John Lee Hooker never followed a set pattern; his songs might have 12*

---

14 From Besman's liner-notes to the three-LP collection *John Lee Hooker's Detroit* (United Artists, 1973); reprinted in the booklet to *Alternative Boogie* (Capitol, 1995).

bars but they'd be just as likely to ramble from 11 in one verse to 18 in the next . . . another thing about John Lee Hooker, he never sings a song the same way twice. There are certain themes that he often returns to, but his music is so spontaneous that each rendition becomes almost a completely new song. So you see, his music is not really "blues," but rather a form of music all his own, which I have chosen to call "early Americana" . . .

By such criteria, whiskey served in a champagne flute rather than a shot glass or highball tumbler would be whiskey no longer. A performance like "Dark Room" is certainly not *a* blues in the purely descriptive sense, that is, form—in other words, it's not a twelve-bar, doesn't have a regular beat or adhere to either a three-chord harmonic structure or an A-A-B lyrical pattern—but in function and content, it is *the* blues.

Reminiscing about his travels during the early part of the twentieth century, "Jelly Roll" Morton told Alan Lomax, "There wasn't any decent music around[Houston, Texas], only jews-harps, harmonicas, mandolins, guitars, and fellows singing the spasmodic blues—sing awhile and pick awhile till they thought of another word to say."[15] In other words, the kind of music Hooker still plays—*the* blues. The original, undiluted, uncut blues.

The deepest blues there is.

The "grain" is the body in the voice as it sings, the hand as it writes, the limb as it performs.
—Roland Barthes, "The Grain Of The Voice," 1972[16]

To say that it is all a matter of feeling is at once to explain everything and nothing. All artists have feelings: hell, everybody has feelings. Even lawyers have feelings. Rather, it is about a particular relationship, or set of relationships, to feeling. And feeling was something of which that young, untried Hooker of the late '40s and early '50s had no shortage. Into that basic gallery of vessels—the traditional slow blues, the free-form slow blues, the boogie, the "Bottle Up And Go," "Rollin' And Tumblin'" and "Catfish" templates—he poured the stuff of his life, his

---

15 Quoted in Loamx's *Mister Jelly Roll* (Grosset & Dunlap, 1950).
16 Collected in *Image Music Text* (Fontana, 1977), edited and translated by Stephen Heath.

observations of his day-to-day world, fragments of things he'd heard on jukeboxes, snatches of blues or gospel songs or romantic ballads he'd heard as a child. And each time the red light went on, these elements would be combined and recombined into something new and unrepeatable.

Sometimes a slow blues would start out with standard changes and then loosen into free-form. Sometimes he'd supercharge a "Bottle Up," "Catfish" or "Rollin' And Tumblin' " sequence with his boogie groove. Sometimes he'd play what was usually a fast song slow, or a slow one fast. Sometimes a piece he normally played solo would be transformed into something different by performing it with drums, sax and piano. And sometimes a song Hookerized, or adapted from another source—Roscoe Gordon's "No More Doggin'," or the celebrated "Driftin' Blues" originated by Charles Brown when he was with Johnny Moore's Three Blazes—would settle into Hooker's repertoire and become an archetype in its own right, capable of being spun off in turn into a galaxy of further variations. "Driftin' Blues," for example, became Hooker's own "Wanderin' Blues," and each time it was performed it drifted—or wandered—further from its original source. Brown had depicted himself driftin' "like a ship out on the sea"; Hooker, by contrast, wandered "like a sheep out on the foal." Sometimes—thanks to various producers' mistranscriptions of Hooker's Mississippi accent—the two images combined to create the surreal vision of "a sheep out on the foam." Brown's song had been thoroughly Hookerized.

The process of Hookerization—a central facet and primary tool of Hooker's creative method, a form of "organic sampling" by which Hooker annexes, adapts, customizes and ultimately transforms devices and motifs derived from traditional and contemporary material from both within and without the blues canon—is simultaneously ancient and modern, African and European. It is as old as the folk process itself: which is to say that it is a fundamental of human communication, older than either language or music. And in contemporary incarnations like sampling or post-modernist intertextuality, that same process is at the very heart of millennial art, wherein the twentieth century is, so to speak, tipped on its side, and all its cultural debris tumbles from its original context to roll up against the millennial barrier in new and startling juxtapositions among which we can wander, scavenge and rearrange.

The folk process, the mechanisms of which are deeply embedded in human consciousness, traditionally worked with the materials in the immediate vicinity of an individual or community: the tales and songs of a specific place and time, cross-fertilized with those introduced by travelers passing through. The mobile arts—first printed, then electric, currently digital—have broadened that catchment area to take in all of known space and time. As a species, we're doing what we've always done, except that—in the late twentieth century—we're doing it with samplers and computers rather than simply with memory and flesh. Learn a song, re-arrange it for your own instrument, write some new words about something that happened around the corner, play it to your friends and neighbors. Download an image or a chunk of text, mess with it, upload it again. It's all the same stuff. It's all "Hookerization."

Bearing Hooker's background in mind, it should therefore not be particularly surprising that first-stage Hookerization would bear as strong a resemblance as it does to the way a preacher works with a biblical text. Leaving aside—for the moment only—the outright plagiarism of Percy Mayfield's "Memory Pain" (the latter aka "It Serves Me Right To Suffer" in the Hooker canon), we find exercises like "I Cover The Waterfront," "Frisco Blues" (derived from "I Left My Heart In San Francisco"), "One Bourbon One Scotch And One Beer" (derived from Amos Milburn's "One Scotch One Bourbon One Beer") or "Messin' With The Hook" (a Hookerization of Junior Wells's "Messin' With The Kid," itself also transformed by the highly unkiddish Muddy Waters into "Messin' With The Man"). In all of these Hooker uses bits of the original piece—a chorus, a lyrical fragment, an opening couplet or even simply a title—as "text" and then moves onto "preach" his own "sermon." And it is his own: Hooker's "One Bourbon" is no more Amos Milburn's than, in a vastly different context, Kathy Acker's *Great Expectations* is Charles Dickens's. No one would call a preacher a plagiarist because the springboard for his sermon is a chunk of the Bible: it is understood both that a preacher is supposed to quote the Bible, and also that the most fundamental essence of the preacherly art lies in the preacher's ability to create an original, affecting and relevant sermon around the theme of the biblical extract he has chosen.

Similarly, if we look at the origins of bebop, we find that the "head" of a tune—its principal melodic motif—also serves as the pegs on which to hang the improvisations which are the real meat in the musical sandwich. Way back at the music's primal roots—the marathon '40s jam sessions at Teddy Minton's club in Harlem during which Charlie Christian, Thelonious Monk, Kenny Clarke and others hewed the basic tenets of the form from the living rockface of earlier musics—the musicians often deliberately chose to deploy quite banal thirty-two-bar pop tunes ("Tea For Two," "I Got Rhythm" and the like) alongside blues themes as springboards for their improvs. Or—to be more precise—as scaffolding for their constructions. The original melody or chord sequence is of little or no intrinsic value or importance: it's simply there to facilitate the creation of the final artefact, and once that "building" has been completed, the scaffolding becomes utterly superfluous. Despite the similarity of method, this is conceptually a very different vessel of seafood from the aural firestorms into which John Coltrane and Jimi Hendrix transformed, respectively, Rodgers & Hammerstein's "My Favorite Things" and Frances Scott Keyes' "Star Spangled Banner," wherein recognition and familiarity with not only the original melody, but the context in which it first appeared and the emotional and cultural luggage it carries, are an intrinsic and essential part of the experience which the performers are attempting to deliver.

While the original tunes unquestionably "belong" to their original composers, the final results are the exclusive property of Coltrane and Hendrix. Nevertheless, while it's certainly possible for a listener unfamiliar with the original melodies to enjoy the performances and even to be "reached" and transported by the sheer emotional power and musical prowess displayed by Jimi and Trane, the full impact and resonance of the finished work are lost on anyone who doesn't know the tune, or who lacks a highly specific awareness both of the significance of the "original" (a cute song about furry animals, snowballs *et al.*, or the American national anthem) and the distance which the improviser has traveled from the tune's point of origin—or, rather, the distance which the improviser has forcibly dragged the tune and, by extension, the listener.

In other words: the listener is required to bring something of his or her own to the party. You're *supposed* to know the tune. If you don't, you're welcome to gatecrash, but please be aware that you weren't actually invited. Most modern listeners, for example, aren't "invited" to Beethoven's *Fifth Symphony*: its ominous four-note intro motif is one of the most famous and instantly recognizable licks in European concert music, but it wasn't original to Beethoven, and would not have been perceived as such by hipper nineteenth-century listeners. The iconic *ta-ta-ta-tummmmm* was one of a group of themes "sampled" by "lovely lovely Ludwig Van" (as Anthony Burgess so affectionately nicknamed him in *A Clockwork Orange*) from the works of a group of revolutionary French composers, including Rouget de Lisle, who wrote "The Marseillaise."

Beethoven's allusions to their work were designed to be decoded by the cognoscenti as specific, but nevertheless ultimately deniable, indications of potentially incriminating revolutionary sympathies.[17]

In the world of hip-hop, so despised by those members of the blues community—including Hooker himself—we once again find the old pressed into service as an essential ingredient in the process of the creation of the new. Sly & The Family Stone's "Everyday People" becomes the core of Arrested Development's "People Everyday." The Detroit Spinners' "It's A Shame" signposts Monie Love's "Mi Sista." The Gap Band's "Ooops Upside Your Head"—the spontaneously adapted source of any number of English football chants—does double duty as the foundation stone of Snoop Doggy Dogg's "Snoop's Upside Your Head." Buffalo Springfield's summer-of-love protest anthem "For What It's Worth" rises from the tomb as Public Enemy's "He's Got Game." It was inevitable that some form of legal framework for dealing with this stuff would ultimately have to be developed, if only to accommodate hip-hoppers' wholesale pillaging of the works of James Brown and George Clinton. Only a Polygram lawyer could tell us how many records have shoplifted Brown's legendary "Funky Drummer" break (played by The Great Clyde Stubblefield), and, during a few lean years in his four-decade career, Clinton's principal income was derived from sampling royalties.

Even in rock and roll, where "originality" is more highly prized and copyrights more valuable, the same pick-it-up-and-kick-it principle applies. The Beach Boys' first big hit, "Surfin' USA" was built on the chassis of Chuck Berry's "Sweet Little Sixteen" (signature guitar licks and all) to the extent that Berry ended up sharing the songwriting credit and royalties with Brian Wilson, "Surfin' USA"'s "actual" composer. The Sex Pistols' "Holidays In The Sun" replays the principal riff of The Jam's "In The City." And Noel Gallagher, mastermind-in-residence of that truly postmodern band Oasis, publicly and repeatedly boasts of the riffs and techniques he's lifted from The Beatles, Bob Dylan, Mott The Hoople, David Bowie and countless others. We are, he tells us, *supposed* to spot them. Our appreciation of *West Side Story* is diminished if we don't know that it's *Romeo And Juliet*; of *Forbidden Planet* if we're unaware that it's *The Tempest*; of Kurosawa's *Ran* if we can't connect it to *King Lear*. By

---

17 This contention was put forward by the distinguished British conductor John Eliot Gardiner in an ITV *South Bank Show* broadcast on May 12, 1996; your correspondent has shamelessly sampled Dan Glaister's preview of the program, published in the *Guardian*, May 11, 1996.

the same token, in Tim Burton's *Batman Returns*, we're *supposed* to notice when he riffs on the celebrated opening shot of Orson Welles's *Citizen Kane*. If we don't, we're excluded from part of the fun. And, if we have no idea of whence the artist started out, how are we supposed to recognize how far (s)he's come?

Quote, sample, allusion, *hommage*. When you get down to it, it's all the same game: that of making art out of other art, and out of whatever we happen to find around us. Thus entire bodies of literature—ranging from Dumas to Conan Doyle to E. L. Doctorow—wherein historical characters mingle freely with the author's own creations; and other bodies still where these "real" but reinvented people meet not only the creations of the presiding author but those of earlier authors. J. G. Ballard's epochal coining of the term "media landscape" provides us with a vital clue: the traditional notion of a landscape is something which is simply *there*, and the artist's job is, equally simply, to depict it. Our contemporary landscape is *constructed*, and any reflection or depiction of it, or even passage through it, thereby forces us to engage with things which have been constructed, previously, by others; and with the notions embedded, overtly or covertly, within those constructions. And thus Andy Warhol's famous Campbell's soup-can—regarded at the time by traditionalist critics and commentators as the absolute epitome of charlatanry—becomes a still life for the industrial era, the age of mass-production. The fact that Warhol mass-produced the work itself is both a logical completion of the process and a simultaneous comment upon it.

In quick succession, then: a brace of caveats, an analogy and a conclusion. Firstly, though it would be tempting to indulge in an act of critical mischief and declare Hooker to be a premature and instinctive (if unwitting) post-modernist, there are more ramifications to post-modernist theory, in its formal academic applications, than the loose, pop-culch journalistic sense in which it is used here.[18] And secondly, Hooker has no more moved into its sphere than he has moved into anything else: rather, it is a matter of the shared influence of common roots between this most complex and arcane body of theory and the instinctive process by which we navigate through our culture.

One small example: when a liner-note writer described Hooker as "a guitarist with fine jazz qualities"[19] and other major jazz critics con-

---

18 Not least among disenchanted *soixante-huitards* lining up to take an Oedipal pop at Daddy Marx.
19 John F. Szved, annotating Hooker's 1968 album *Simply The Truth*.

curred, Bernard Besman was appalled. "Leonard Feather considers him a jazz musician and wrote several articles," he snorted. "I don't know where jazz comes in. People who play bebop are skilled, very good, trained musicians. They have to read the music ... here you take Hooker, who can't read a goddam note, plays 'zap' and doesn't imitate anybody. Sonny Stitt, who I loved, now there was a real schooled musician." As ever, Besman is simultaneously right and wrong: "right" in that Hooker is certainly not a jazz musician in any strict formal sense, but "wrong" in that after the complexities of bebop attained critical mass, many "skilled, very good, trained" jazz musicians, in the wake of Miles Davis's epochal performance of "Walkin'" at the 1955 Newport Jazz Festival, discarded the constrictions imposed by those complexities and set off in search of the free blowing space they found in the simpler and more open structures of blues and gospel themes. These explorations led populists toward "soul jazz," and intellectuals toward what later became known as "free" (unstructured) jazz; both fields capable of learning from what an artist like Hooker had known and practiced all along. Thus the circle closed: the beboppers had to absorb all the theory there was before they could get to that space where they could afford to dump it.

Similarly, post-modernism in its "pop" sense refers primarily to "intertextuality," a term coined by Julia Kristeva to assert that no "text"— be it a song, a movie, a book, a painting, an advertisement, whatever— is a closed universe existing in a vacuum. The way in which it is constructed, perceived and interpreted depends on what is already known. Popular culture in general is instinctively intertextual, and nowhere more so than in popular music; in popular music nowhere more so than in the blues; and in the blues nowhere more so than in the music of John Lee Hooker. The bottom line is this:

Where "intertextuality" and the folk process meet: in the assumption of a mutual familiarity with a shared body of culture and experience which can be freely referred to and drawn upon. Where they part company: with the notion of distance, detachment and irony implicit in all post-modern phenomena. With the folk process in general, and in Hooker's work in particular, nothing is in italics. Neither artist nor audience are insulated or detached, from themselves or each other, by protective layers of quotes. Everything is "meant," and no built-in escape-hatch is provided. You either deal, or you leave.

Q: What comes after "post-modern?"
A: Relief. Clarity. Faith in the future.
—designer Tibor Kalman, interviewed in *Wired*, December 1996

John Lee Hooker's career—all fifty years of it—has been but patchily documented or analyzed. The inquisitive reader will find very little substantial discussion of Hooker's work in the standard classics of blues literature.[20] This is not to suggest that his work has been underrated per se—quite the reverse: his œuvre is universally admired—but rather that the critics and historians of the blues establishment have traditionally preferred a sociologically-based methodology, and therefore concentrated primarily on identifiable schools and groupings of artists, sorting and classifying (analysing and assessing) musicians according to era, style or region. The effect of this particular critical approach on a maverick loner like Hooker has been to drop him into the cracks between categories. Let's take a quick peep at the contents of some of the more prominent boxes into which Hooker doesn't quite fit.

First, let's gracefully acknowledge that he is indeed loosely categorizable as a "traditional" Southern bluesman with a penchant for absolute freedom of musical, lyrical, rhythmic and—most important of all—*structural* improvisation. Contrariwise, most of the front rank of performers in this particular branch of the idiom were (at least) a generation his senior; cut their definitive recordings and earned their reps prior to World War II; lived and worked primarily in the rural South; and fulfilled all the criteria necessary to identify them formally as acoustic "folk" musicians, one and all. If Hooker had been even ten or fifteen years older and had chosen to remain in the South rather than head off to the big city while still in his teens, his links to the likes of Booker T. Washington, "Bukka" White, Robert Pete Williams or Big Joe Williams (and—a trifle more remotely—to his Texan contemporary Lightnin' Hopkins, a fellow compulsive-improviser whose musical and sociological ties to "folk blues" remained far tighter and more consistent than Hooker's despite occasional electric dabbling of his own) would have been more than simply artistic; he might well have had a similar kind of career. Moreover, Hooker would have been relatively easy to classify as "that" sort of bluesman if he hadn't persisted in recording with rock, soul and jazz musicians (as well as fellow

---

20 At least, *this* inquisitive reader did.

blues guys), and performing in a range of contexts reaching from solo acoustic to the soulful side of the uptown street. Not to mention deriving his material from a wide-screen continuum of sources slung between show tunes and Broadway ballads; between contemporary R&B and pop, and folk elements so fundamental that they practically constitute the very DNA of contemporary popular music. Plus every once in a while he racked up a serious hit single: this, Captain, is not logical. So was he then a "Chicago bluesman?" Well, he was . . . and he wasn't.

Which brings us to the second Hooker anomaly: he was sufficiently negligent of the particular requirements of critics and historians to have declined to base himself in Chicago. The postwar electrification of the primal Delta materials is principally associated with Chicago and generically referred to as "Chicago blues," but while the bulk of Hooker's important recordings made during the decade between the mid-'50s and the mid-'60s were indeed cut in Chicago for the city's two leading blues indies, Vee Jay and Chess, his home scene was the Motor City rather than the Windy City, and he thus remained a visiting fireman, albeit a welcome and honored one, in the South Side's retroactively legendary taverns and bars. The near-mythic status afforded to the Chicago scene by outsiders, particularly Europeans, during the '60s didn't just benefit the scene's big fish, but also less exalted players: being a "Chicago bluesman" was by definition a stamp of authority and authenticity. By contrast, the Detroit scene carried with it no such on-board kudos: much to the irritation of hometown cheerleaders like Famous Coachman, local stalwarts Eddie Burns, Eddie Kirkland, Boogie Woogie Red, Baby Boy Warren, Little Sonny and Mr. Bo carried relatively little clout, except among the most erudite blues aficionados, beyond their home territories. As far as the outside world was concerned, Detroit blues had little or no distinctive identity and only one major figurehead; indeed, it seemingly began and ended with Hooker himself. And as far as a strict definition of Chicago blues is concerned, Hooker therefore isn't "that" kind of bluesman, either.

Furthermore, there is a vital musical distinction to be made between Hooker on the one hand and, on the other, Muddy Waters and Howlin' Wolf—the twin Deep-South-to-South-Side titans of the golden decade of Chicago blues, and the artists most directly comparable to Hooker in sociological terms. Chicago blues is, first and foremost, an ensemble music: the talent, personality and charisma of the leader serve to provide focus and purpose, but the art itself is essentially a collective one. Both Muddy and Wolf were bandleaders *par excellence*; forming, leading and nurturing ensembles whose sonic trademark was an inseparable part of (and contribution to) their distinctive musical identities. And while Chess Records wasn't noted for the integrity of its accounting procedures, it was a relatively tight-knit operation which cross-promoted its artists and—primarily through the unique combination of talents stuffed into Willie Dixon's gargantuan frame—supplemented their own creativity with bespoke commercial songs tailored to their talents if they weren't coming up with the goods themselves; and produced their records with one ear on the needs and values of the traditional blues audience, and the other on the wider marketplace outside. Muddy and Wolf thereby worked and created both within the community in which they lived their daily lives; and an artistic community which reinforced and participated in their creativity.

Hooker, on the other hand, has utilized the skills of many superb musicians—from the early days of Kirkland and Burns through the Vee Jay years with Eddie Taylor et al. and the Motown moonlighters via the epochal Canned Heat sessions with Alan Wilson, right up to his '90s collaborations with Carlos Santana, Robert Cray, Van Morrison and others—but at no time was he dependent on any of them for any aspect of his signature sound. There has never been anyone at any stage of his musical life who performed an equivalent function to those fulfilled by Hubert Sumlin or Willie Johnson in the Howlin' Wolf bands, let alone the key-sideman roles played, in various editions of the great Muddy Waters combo, by the likes of Otis Spann, Jimmy Rogers, James Cotton or Little Walter. Muddy and the Wolf were leaders, not loners: Muddy was rather more gracious than the Wolf about utilizing and acknowledging the contributions of others, especially those of Willie Dixon. Hooker, by contrast, never had Willie Dixon, or any real equivalent, in his corner. Bernard Besman goaded him, Burns and Kirkland (literally) accompanied him, and more recently Roy Rogers rode exemplary shotgun, but Hooker has never, even for brief periods, served as anybody else's mouthpiece. Every other bluesman who's gotten even within hollering distance of Hooker's status has done so with way more backup than Hooker has ever enjoyed . . . or sought, or even tolerated. In this respect, as in so many others, Hooker has always been a cat who walked by himself.

Which brings us to the all-important issue of patronage. The ability of any blues or R&B performer to hit that all-important affluent young white market was directly linked in the '60s to the degree of sponsorship and endorsement which that performer received from big-name rock stars. Thus Chuck Berry's career was effectively reignited by The Beatles and

The Rolling Stones, who recorded several of his songs and introduced him and his repertoire to a new generation of listeners. The Beatles' imprimatur also proved invaluable to the launch of the Tamla-Motown acts into the British charts, while the Stones (and their early-'60s understudies like The Yardbirds and The Pretty Things) also performed a similar function for Muddy Waters, Bo Diddley and Jimmy Reed (though Reed had sunk too far into alcoholism to capitalize significantly on this new-found opportunity). Subsequently, the Stones also gave Howlin' Wolf his first domestic mass-audience exposure by insisting that he co-star with them on U.S. TV's top pop program *Shindig*, and by employing Waters, Diddley, B. B. King and Buddy Guy & Junior Wells as on-tour opening acts.[21] The final years of Muddy's career also benefited from the four superb albums, commencing with 1977's *Hard Again*, custom-tailored for him by Johnny Winter, even though Winter was at that time well past his sell-by date as a major arena-rocker.

The 1968 "arrival" of B. B. King as a frontline crossover attraction was heralded by a concert at San Francisco's Fillmore Auditorium where B. B. was introduced to the audience by local hero Mike Bloomfield, receiving a two-minute standing ovation from the hippies before he'd even played a note. Albert King's funky Stax singles enabled him to get over more or less under his own steam, but the enthusiastic endorsements of Eric Clapton (who quoted an A. King solo verbatim on Cream's "Strange Brew" and covered his signature song "Born Under A Bad Sign" on the following year's *Wheels of Fire*) and Jimi Hendrix certainly didn't hurt. Albert's first Fillmore appearance was on a bill with Hendrix, who praised him to *Rolling Stone* and knew the big guy's stuff well enough to sing his solos note-for-note, either by himself or in unison with his pal Buddy Miles. For his part, Clapton also occupied the lead-guitar chair on *The Howlin' Wolf London Sessions*, played on and co-produced an entertaining but patchy album for Guy and Wells, and "adopted" his teenage idol Freddie King, carrying him on several early-'70s tours, scoring him a new record deal and working with him in the studio. And in the 1970s Texas-to-Chicago-to-San Francisco transplant Steve Miller did his level best to transform Muddy Waters' rotund harp alumnus James Cotton into a Beloved Entertainer on the Louis Armstrong model.

---

21 Not to mention Ike & Tina Turner, Stevie Wonder, The Meters, Prince, Black Uhuru and Living Colour, all of whom at various times ran that same gauntlet with varying degrees of success.

So, did Hooker enjoy patronage on the same exalted scale? Not really. Well, "Dimples" and "Boom Boom" were beat-group staples—as acknowledged even by Spinal Tap, whose "Gimme Some Money" (recorded in their early incarnation as The Thamesmen) is a thinly-disguised "Boom Boom" rip—with The Animals, Van Morrison's Them and The Spencer Davis Group in the vanguard. Detroit's MC5 featured "Motor City Is Burning" (not surprisingly), The Doors borrowed "Crawlin' King Snake" (ditto), and the J. Geils Band made a four-course meal out of "It Serves Me Right To Suffer." And then, of course, there was Canned Heat, with whom we'll deal elsewhere, pausing only to point out that during their commercial heyday, they also attempted to do the right thing by the late Texan guitar giant Albert Collins, "The Master Of The Telecaster." However, Collins's flawed Heat-sponsored recordings bombed in the marketplace and failed to ignite his career. As a result Collins "got disgusted" with the music business and spent most of the '70s in semi-retirement.

Raising the "patronage" question inevitably opens yet another can of worms: that of the nature of the relationships between the "original" Delta blues, the postwar Chicago-style electric-band music into which it mutated, and the '60s-and-onward blues-and-beyond rock which Chicago blues helped to inspire. A moderately illuminating parallel can be made by considering this relationship as a johnny-come-lately pop-culch equivalent to the neo-Romantic modernist primitivist movement manifest in the visual arts of the early part of the twentieth century.[22]

In 1984, your correspondent was both sufficiently fortunate to have the opportunity to attend an exhibition entitled " 'Primitivism' In 20th Century Art" at New York City's Museum of Modern Art; and sufficiently prescient to purchase its catalog. It was a wonderful, magical, deeply enlightening exhibition, juxtaposing crucial works by key modernists—Picasso, Matisse, Gauguin, Moore, Klee, Giacometti et al.—with the specific examples of tribal art which inspired them. The exhibition's directors, William Rubin and Kirk Varnedoe, were meticulous in the execution of their intention to avoid patronizing or condescending to the sources of that inspiration, even down to the quotes surrounding the word "primitivism": retaining the essential reference while distancing them-

---

22 Much of the analysis in this paragraph (not to mention portions of the argument which follows) is derived from remarks made by Michael Tucker in his *Dreaming With Open Eyes: The Shamanic Spirit in Twentieth Century Art And Culture* (Aquarian/HarperCollins San Francisco, 1992); Tucker, in turn, refers extensively to Marianna Torgovnick and others.

selves from its more distasteful implications, handling it at arm's length with metaphorical tongs. Nevertheless, the exhibition was still accused, by Marianna Torgovnick, of implicitly suggesting that, "Here is the primitive instance; here is the masterpiece, with the primitive absorbed and transcended."

"In other words," wrote Michael Tucker, paraphrasing Torgovnick's contention, "was not this exhibition simply another version of colonialism, a patronizing acknowledgment of a mythical 'Other' as an essential, yet nevertheless anonymous ingredient of the yeast of modernism?" Those who have followed the blues on its journey into progressive and/or hard rock—or, indeed, African-American music on its broader and more complex route into becoming the mainstream popular music of much of the world—will find this debate a familiar one. Were not '60s white bluesers, still pimply of visage and damp behind their hair-curtained ears, not praised to the skies for executing what were, in many cases, simply clumsy caricatures of the work of African-American masters? Did many of them then not mock or disparage the blues for its intrinsic limitations of form and content—not to mention individual bluesmen for their conservatism or foibles—as they "progressed" into their brave new world of fuzzboxes, flower power and rock operas?

Well, yes and no. Sure enough, Janis Joplin received more plaudits (not to mention more money) for her blunderbuss renditions of "Ball And Chain" and "Piece Of My Heart" than Big Mama Thornton and Erma Franklin ever did for originating the songs in the first place. Eric Clapton was for years routinely voted the world's top blues guitarist. But the key point was that while "real" blues artists progress or mature by going deeper into the music, into its musical and emotional detail, finding more and more nuances in the gaps between the lines and notes, their successors could move only outward, using what they'd learned from the blues to explore other musical realms entirely. To them, the blues was a stepping stone, though an essential one. If a journey of a thousand miles begins with a single step, for many of the rock musicians of the '60s and after, that single step was the one they took into the blues. Their mistake was to assume that there was no more to the blues than that which they themselves were able to draw from it.

They just copy me, and there's nothing I can learn from them.
—Little Walter

However, before we leave the subject of Hooker's pre-breakthrough critical status *too* far behind, it's worth pointing out that he has never been renowned as what journalists consider an "easy interview": a media-wise, self-packaging subject who is both willing and able to serve eager profilers a pre-digested version of his/her life and work. For that matter, neither was Howlin' Wolf, but the grumpy giant was such an outsize personality that he was fun to describe even when he wasn't being notably forthcoming.[23] B. B. King, for his part, has always evinced an intense desire to reach out to others and explain himself, his worldview, his music and its meaning and context to anyone displaying even the faintest signs of empathy and interest; and the fluency, eloquence and personal charm which originally established him as a Memphis radio personality have made it comparatively easy for him to do so.[24] And while Muddy Waters was neither as awe-inspiring a personality as Wolf nor as effusively articulate a spokesman for the blues community as B. B., he nevertheless managed to combine elements of both into a charismatic, dignified and magisterial/ambassadorial persona which rendered him a pleasure, as well as an education, to interview.

While Hooker is celebrated among his intimates as a witty, genial and gregarious man, it's equally undeniable that he is capable of being opaque and uncommunicative in the extreme toward those with whom he does not yet feel sufficiently comfortable to relax, share a joke, and speak his mind. Nowadays, with the mantle of bonafide "stardom" firmly clasped around Hooker's shoulders, misfired interviews still get written up and published, even though in some cases Hooker and his interlocutor barely seem to have been in the same room, let alone the same conversation.[25] However, this is now and that was then: in those early "blues boom" days, a musician's ability to talk (as well as sing and play) himself into the front rank counted for a lot, and Hooker's seemingly taciturn, introverted stance was not exactly a major promotional asset.

The archetypal "lone cat" of the blues was Robert Johnson—the most mythically-correct bluesman who ever lived—but he was in no way

---

23 As beautifully demonstrated by Peter Guralnick in his wonderful pen-portrait "Don't Laugh At Me" (memorably included in *Feel Like Going Home: Portraits in Blues & Rock 'N' Roll* (Omnibus Press, 1971), alongside an equally perceptive and affectionate "snapshot" of Muddy Waters.
24 It must, however, be conceded that no blues performer has ever insisted as vociferously as—we name the guilty men!—Pete Townshend, Frank Zappa and Lou Reed not only on the right to review their own work but to question the ability of anybody else to do so.
25 The authors of such pieces are well aware who they are. Let us refrain from embarrassing them any further.

unique in this respect: most of the pre-war blues guys were itinerant so-loists. The social and demographic shifts of postwar African-America in general, and the mass urban migrations of the Delta diaspora in partic-ular, rooted the bluesmen of the '50s in bands and communities, but Hooker, almost alone among the city bluesmen of his time, traveled solo, and performed with borrowed bands. In a famous and oft-quoted solil-oquy delivered to the cameras of ITV's *South Bank Show* in 1987, Eric Clapton perfectly defined the romantic appeal of the legend of the Lone Bluesman:

> *I felt, through most of my youth, that my back was against the wall and that the only way to survive was with dignity and pride and courage. I heard that . . . most of all in the blues, because it was always an individual. It was one man and his guitar against the world. It wasn't a company, or a band, or a group; when it came down to it, it was one guy who was completely alone and had no options, no alternatives other than to sing and play to ease his pain.[26]*

But few postwar bluesmen still actually lived and worked like that. On the road, they had their bands (albeit often stuffed into cramped, shagged-out vehicles); in the studio, they had producers to shape their work, studio musicians to augment or even replace their regular sidemen, and songwriters waiting in the wings with additional material should their own inspiration not suffice. Only the most successful, like B. B. King with his 300-shows-a-year itinerary, toured so much that they could barely be said to "live" anywhere.

Hooker, of course, could sound "alone" even with a full band pump-ing away behind him. There is more than a little irony in the fact that Hooker's '90s success has been built on collaborations—to the point where some inattentive listeners could have been forgiven for thinking that his full name is "John-Lee-Hooker-and"—because for decades it was an article of faith among many hardcore fans that Hooker sounded best on his own; and among detractors (including Bernard Besman, who of all people should know better) that he was actually incapable of performing effectively with others. But no matter whether he was, on any given oc-casion, accompanied by a dozen musicians or none at all, Hooker's per-

---

26 I cited this same text in *Crosstown Traffic: Jimi Hendrix And Postwar Pop* (Faber & Faber, 1989), and proffer no apologies whatsoever for doing so again here.

formances are invariably one-man shows which take place against the backdrop of his own inner landscape. B. B. King, Muddy Waters and Buddy Guy—to name but three; we could cite dozens should we choose to do so—are essentially extrovert performers. They aim outward; they take a show all the way to the audience. Hooker, by contrast, goes within: to his own still center; in doing so, he takes the audience there with him, and at his center, they find themselves. Hooker is thus not only a human exemplar of the most venerable traditions of the blues, but also of a mystical and spiritual tradition that is older still: far older than the blues, far older even than African-American Christianity.

He is a shaman.

The way he works is just like a preacher. Preachin' the blues . . .
—Charlie Musselwhite, interview with the author, 1991

You know what? If you ever listen to him in that song "Boogie With The Hook" at his closing act, do it to you kinda sound like he's preachin' in there?
—Rev. Robert Hooker, interview with the author, 1994

The only one who could ever move me . . . was the son of a preacher man
—Hurley & Wilkins on behalf of Dusty Springfield and (subsequently) Aretha Franklin, "Son Of A Preacher Man"

Forget your troubles and dance,
Forget your weakness and dance . . .
—Bob Marley, "Them Belly Full (But We Hungry)"

John Lee Hooker was born and raised in the church. Indeed, his earliest and most formative musical, cultural and spiritual experiences came from the church, and from the preaching of his father, the Rev. William Hooker. He is, as it happens, not only the Son Of A Preacher Man, but also the brother of another, and the father of another still.

As John Lee's second son, the Rev. Robert Hooker, and their former flatmate, harp virtuoso Charlie Musselwhite, observe above—and as we've already noted way back at the start of this book—the climax of Hooker's stage act irresistibly evokes the transcendent fervor of charismatic Southern Baptism, wherein preacher and congregation alike are caught up in the ecstatic whirlwind of the descending spirit. In conventional Western religious services, the congregation are there to worship under the direction of their pastor, but the African-American ceremony goes further. It is rooted in the tradition of a fundamental, primal encounter with the powers that drive the universe, in which the participants invite transcendence, offering themselves up to the spirit they invoke in the knowledge that their offer will be, at least for the duration, accepted. It is about more than merely worshiping: it is about *becoming*, and about temporarily ceasing to be. It is the shamanic principle in action.

Who is the shaman? By way of introduction, our old friend *The Concise Oxford Dictionary* gives us "priest or witch-doctor of class claiming to have sole contact with gods etc.," while the *Penguin English Dictionary* offers "priest-magician in primitive cultures." Elsewhere, the shaman is variously described as priest and sorcerer, visionary and healer, and the shaman is indeed all of these; but as far as most anthropological sources are concerned, the shaman's defining attribute is the ability to free his or her (and at the dawn of humanity it was almost always "her") soul from the tethers of mundane existence.

Through study, sacrifice and ordeal, the shaman is one who has earned sufficient strength and wisdom to part the veils separating realities, to travel between this and other planes of existence, to contact the spirits and to return with them—*ay, and what then?* The shaman thus becomes, literally, a human gate or bridge between different realms of consciousness, if not different realms of existence. However, Mircea Eliade, the author of the magisterial *Shamanism And Archaic Techniques Of Ecstasy*, emphasizes that,

> *The specific element of shamanism is not the incorporation of spirits by the shaman, but the ecstasy provoked by the ascension to the sky or by the descent to hell: the incorporation of spirits and possession by them are universally distributed phenomena, but they do not belong necessarily to shamanism in the strict sense.*[27]

"First you lose control," incanted Patti Smith in her visionary "Horses," "then you take control." The art of the shaman is the cultivated

---

27 Your humble servant confesses to not having read Eliade's book; this extract—and the quotation from Shirokogoroff—have been sampled from I. M. Lewis's *Ecstatic Religion* (Penguin, 1971).

development of such virtuosic mastery of both the highest and most fundamental levels of individual consciousness that direct, deliberate control of the surface of consciousness can then be abandoned. The shaman loses one "self" in order to contact and assume another, higher, self. Both possessed and possessing, yielding and summoning: the shaman is thus empowered to transform the experience of others, to transcend and to induce transcendence.

For most Westerners, the primary association evoked by the word "shaman" is of an African or Native American (or Haitian, or Aboriginal) tribal mystic; but contemporary usage (and abuse) of that term actually originated with Russian anthropologists studying the Tungus people of Siberia, in whose language "saman" means "one who knows." It may be instructive at this point to consider, in the light of the extract from Julio Finn's *The Bluesman* quoted earlier in this chapter, as well as my own description of a Hooker concert from the first chapter of this book, S. M. Shirokogoroff's account of a Tungus shaman's seance:

> *The rhythmic music and singing, and later the dancing of the shaman, gradually involve every participant more and more in a collective action . . . the tempo of the actions increases . . . when the shaman feels that the audience is with him and follows him he becomes still more active and this effect is transmitted to his audience. After shamanizing, the audience recollects various moments of the performance, their great psychophysiological emotion and the great hallucinations of sight and hearing they have experienced. They then have a deep satisfaction—much greater than that from emotions produced by theatrical and musical performance, literature and general artistic phenomena of the European complex, because in shamanizing the audience at the same time acts and participates.*

. . . or, indeed, Hooker's own analysis of his performances, drawn from a mid-'70s interview:[28]

> *I watch them. Then I feel their mood with them. I move with them. I get them up and get to rocking with them, and after I get them going, I keep them going—higher and higher; I just don't let them down. I take them in complete command . . . and when one or two*

---

28 From *Blues*, by Robert Neff and Anthony Connor (Latimer Bluesbooks, 1975).

of the crowd start moving, I start moving with them. And when they
see me moving, they start to move. When I get into it, I feel good
all over—higher and higher and higher; there's no limit . . .

Hooker works on precisely these shamanic levels, to precisely these shamanic ends. His music is simultaneously repetitive and unpredictable, his
voice moving freely as his guitar stays where it is. Performing a Delta staple
like "Rollin' And Tumblin'," he starkly illustrates this method by singing a
melody which implies a standard three-chord change while the guitar riff
obstinately remains on the "one" chord. This trance-inducing effect is the
staple resource of modern dance music from James Brown onward: melodic variation atop harmonic and rhythmic repetition. Dance music of this
nature may use Western instruments and vocabulary, but it operates according to an African grammar. African music, from the most traditional
folk forms to the most lushly sophisticated urban pop, will operate like this:
a groove will be set up, either on one chord or on a circular, infinitely re-
peatable riff, and the resources of that riff will be fully explored through
improvisation before another riff is introduced and the musicians then
move on to do the same for another section of the piece.

Such music creates joy and transcendence for some and unparalleled
fear and loathing in others because it's an utter affront to the basic tenets
of Western rationalism: in other words, it disengages the body from the
mind and the intelligence from the intellect. It stops you thinking, and
starts you feeling. It creates an irrational ecstasy.

Hooker has long been acknowledged as the most African of all major
blues singers. Nevertheless, he is unwilling to address or discuss the African aspects of either his music or its purposes: at least, with white boys
he is, and certainly with *this* white boy. Asked if the Rev. William Hooker
and the "respectable" religious members of his community disapproved
of the blues because they may have associated the music with the traditional African spiritual beliefs to which the Christianity of the time was
unequivocally opposed, his response is disdainful. "Africans were a totally
different type of people than the people from around here," he replies.
"African people don't speak good English; I suppose you know that. They
didn't consider theyselves part of us, the black people of Africa, they had
no association with us in that way. Although they was black people, they
was like Jews and Germans: they all white, but they different nationalities.
Part from it come from Africa, but we sung different from them."

If his questioner is sufficiently foolhardy to pursue the point beyond this rejection, he responds with crushing finality. "Well, I think you goin' beyond my recognition. Maybe you read about it, but I can't explain it to you." Quite understandably; though, he is far less inhibited in the company of those he considers part of a more authentic peer group. "He'd talk about it with *me*," harpist/entrepreneur Chicago Beau once told this writer, "he'll sit with me and say, 'Sure, we African men.' " "Quite understandably" because, Marcus Garvey and W. E. B. DuBois notwithstanding, African-Americans of Hooker's generation and background were not encouraged to cherish the "African" in themselves. Indeed, the reverse held true: African culture and history were misrepresented, disdained and denied. In Western popular art from *Tintin* to *Tarzan*, it was the "Dark Continent": depicted as a place of cannibalism, grass skirts, bones-through-noses and living in trees. For African-Americans, it was precisely that "African" which impeded their full participation as "Americans," which held them back, which was cited by white racists as the root of the "inferiority" which justified their unjustifiable treatment. Thus African religious and spiritual values and rituals were mere "primitive superstitions;" light skin was superior to dark; "good" hair was lank, fine, soft, Caucasian, while "bad" hair was rough, coarse, nappy, African. Blond was beautiful, African was ugly. To call someone an African was dangerously close to an insult.

As far as the Malian singer/guitarist Ali Farka Touré, at least, is concerned, the African-ness, the *negritude*, of Hooker's music is so apparent as to be barely worth discussing, as is Hooker's wariness of its discussion. "It's a complex," Touré shrugs. "When I met him in Paris . . . I invited him to come to Mali to see the source of what he does. I'm not running away; I'm in complete agreement that John Lee Hooker was the first. I'm very proud of what I do, but up 'til now I still have a lot to learn. I only know a little bit, but if we are together we are going to discover. He will show me the truth. I invited him to Mali, to come and see his source, which would be good for him. I don't want him to die before he comes to Timbuktu. If he comes, he will find his history and his strength. I told him he must come to Africa. He laughed and waved it off, but then I got quite insistent that it's necessary that he goes, that he *has* to go . . . and then he really started listening. If he went there he would never regret it. I also told him how well-known he is in my village, which really quite surprised him. I told him, "We all listen to your music."

"I thought he was Malian because of what I heard. It was one hundred percent our music. Musically, it's African, but the words are in

American. When you take music such as John Lee Hooker does, you're going to find what we have at home; the greenery, the savannah where you have water. It's poetic, truly poetic, very poetic. All that was missing was for him to speak our language to complete the truth. Everything he does, without exception . . . he can give you the A to Z original resource of the roots of this music."

From such music comes trance. From trance comes ecstasy, and—in the shamanic world—from ecstasy comes healing. In the record which marked his return to the center of the blues stage, and to an honored place in the popular culture of the world, Hooker asserted this truth about as clearly as it is possible to assert anything. *"Blues is the healer,"* he sang over Carlos Santana's hypnotic music, and with that lyric he redefined not only himself and his career, but the hidden history and purpose of the art form to which he had dedicated his life. *Blues is the healer* indeed, but Hooker himself is *The* Healer: with capital letter. That extraordinary cover photo—Hooker's looming figure in silhouette, hands raised and spread—simply sets the visual seal on his assumption of that iconic, shamanic role.

The blues healed me, it can heal you: Hooker acknowledges his own wounds, and his own pain. No one can heal who has not himself been wounded. The Healer is the one who can come with you into your Dark Room. And even if he cannot lead you out, even if his message is that you yourself are the only one who can bring you forth into the light, he can nevertheless be there with you, telling you that the sun *will* rise again, comforting and strengthening you with his presence until the coming of that new dawn.

That's what I been doin'. That's what the Healer do. I take your pain, and I put it on my shoulders, and I carry it along.
—John Lee Hooker, interview with the author, 1994

13. Into the Mythic

A lot of the younger generation didn't *know* about John Lee
Hooker, and they got to know about John Lee Hooker.
—John Lee Hooker, interview with the author, 1989.

An iced-up New York City Wednesday night in December 1989. On 74th
and Broadway, every breath you take freezes your lungs from the inside
out with Gotham fog, but inside the Beacon Theater, Van Morrison has
just spent the best part of an hour and a half inducing a fair facsimile of
total audience meltdown. Backed by '60s Britsoul vets Georgie Fame &
The Blue Flames with Fame himself behind the Hammond organ—plus a
pulse-stopping cameo from Mose Allison, the Mississippi-born senior-
hipster pianist/vocalist/composer who was and remains Fame's prime vocal model—the stumpy Celtic spellbinder entrances and galvanizes the
theater's 2,400 denizens with an extended R&B meditation, waves of
tension contracting and relaxing with a profoundly feral, viscerally erotic
intensity.

Somewhere around the second encore, he begins to pluck at the
maple-necked black Fender Telecaster hanging from his rounded shoulders, grabbing fistfuls of bass runs, scrabbling for clusters of razor-sharp
trebles. "Sometimes I get to thinkin'," he muses, "about Jo-o-o-o-o-
ohhhhhhnn Lee Hooker."

The band settles into a rock-steady boogie groove as Morrison
launches into Hooker's "Dimples"—but the audience isn't watching any-

more. Their eyes are fixed at stage right where, amid a sudden flurry of roadie activity, John Lee Hooker himself ambles into the spotlight in his preacher's hat, arms raised and fingers spread in benediction, light glinting off his bad sunglasses and the diamond motifs on his jacket: the star on his left lapel and the dollar sign on his right.

It is an almost supernatural moment: as if Morrison had, by dint of sheer sorcerous imagination and will, conjured Hooker into existence, materializing him from ectoplasm,[1] summoning his spirit from blues valhalla. At that instant, Hooker seemed as if he had walked straight off the cover of *The Healer*, out of the mists of legend into fleshly reality. In fact, he'd done almost the exact reverse: he had *become* legend, forever left behind the ranks of the half-forgotten bluesmen of the electric-downhome '50s and the blues-boom '60s to assume titanic, iconic stature, like King Arthur emerging from beneath Glastonbury Tor into the harsh light of the dying twentieth century. Not only to fully inhabit his own myth, but to shoulder the entire mythic weight of the blues.

Someone hands Hooker his trusty Gibson 335, and he and Morrison go head-to-head at stage center, song structures and bar lines melting in their collectively generated heat. As ever, Hooker operates in his own time, to the pulse of his own inner clock, refusing to let go of a line or a phrase until he has wrung from it every conceivable emotional nuance. And Morrison—one of Hooker's very few peers in the pantheon of improvising vocalists, alongside Burning Spear and Diamanda Galas—shadows his every step: Belfast echoes Clarksdale as the Fender echoes the Gibson. Hooker and Morrison have their heads together, guitars rumbling and sparking, and they are practically speaking—*singing*—in tongues, messages from an inner blue space, and then suddenly it's over, and he removes his guitar, waves at the audience, and stumps back into the shadows. Even the yuppies are going majorly hogwild: a pink and blue paisley tie—Bill Blass, pure silk—drifts down from the balcony on high and settles lazily into the lap of an acquaintance of Hooker's seated in the stalls.

That's transcendence. And *this* is show business.

A few hours before and a few blocks downtown, a studio audience sits in tiered seats listening to a warm-up man hosing them down in prepa-

---

1   One wit subsequently remarked that it was just as well that Morrison hadn't announced that he'd been thinking about John F. Kennedy.

ration for the taping of yet another edition—the 1232nd, as it happens—of *Late Night With David Letterman.*

Even more so now than he was then, David Letterman is an utterly familiar part of America's cultural furniture; the man who delivered postmodern irony and detachment—*yeah, sure, whatever*—to the hix-from-the-stix via the mundane magic of television. To a British observer, though, he was simply a toothy preppie from Indiana with an unnerving resemblance to the young Teddy Kennedy, whose basic schtick was the shared assumption that he's much too smart to be running a late-nite chat show and that we-the-viewers are much too smart to be watching one, so let's have some *fun*, gang. The show's house band, led by keyboard guy Paul Shaffer, has historically been staffed by A-team En-Why studio heavies: on this particular night the band includes drummer Anton Fig, guitarist Sid McGinniss and bassist Will Lee, the latter a Major Party Animal in cowboy hat and buckskins who racks up his high score on the Wild-And-Crazy-O-Meter by tapdancing on Letterman's desk during the warm-up number.

And it's horrible. This band are horrible in the particular manner in which only highly gifted, expert and experienced musicians can be horrible. Imagine a Holiday Inn lounge band in the late '60s who get terminally pissed off with their gig one night, drop some acid and decide that tonight of all nights they will *play their own music the way they rilly feel it.* So they arrive at the job and open with an instrumental version of Steppenwolf's "Magic Carpet Ride." It's horrible. And these guys are going to back John Lee Hooker? Oh, puh-*leeeeze*!

The show winds its inconsequential way through an urbane gagfest. Actor and comic Harry Shearer—best-known as the alter ego of *Spinal Tap*'s Derek Smalls—holds the congregation enthralled with his account of an argument with an inept TWA ticket deskperson, but the first true highlight of the proceedings arrives off-air during a commercial break, as Letterman tapes a quick promo sting for the night's broadcast. "For comfort you can afford," he deadpans, "watch *Late Night!*" Without missing a beat, someone in a top audience tier shouts, "Take Two!" There's nothing quite like a New York audience.

Behind the row of seats signposted as being reserved for guests of John Lee Hooker, a bespectacled nerd catches the attention of one of the occupiers. "Is that the guy who sings on Pete Townshend's album?" he inquires eagerly. *Yep.* "Is he going to sing 'Iron Man?' " *Nope.* "Ahhhh, *shit*!" No doubt about it, John Lee certainly has a whole new following these days.

Eventually, Letterman announces "one of the world's greatest blues singers," and Hooker himself, guitar at the ready, impassive in hat and shades, ambles out with the funky-hobbit figure of Roy Rogers at his side. The band launches into "Think Twice Before You Go," a track from *The Healer* which had featured Los Lobos backing him up in the studio, but the opening bars are almost obliterated by an eardrum-shredding *SKKRRREEEETCHH* of unwanted feedback. The self-styled "World's Most Dangerous Band" lumber through the song in a welter of missed beats and dropped cues, and the warm-up man milks applause even before the song's trick ending has been delivered.

Finally, Hooker extricates himself from his guitar and slumps into the guest chair for a quick burst of badinage. Such is his degree of composure that for one surreal moment it seems as if he is the host and Letterman the guest. They discuss the then-recent San Francisco earthquake and Hooker allows that it weren't no big deal: when the quake hit he thought his pet cat had just jumped onto his bed. Must be a big cat, says Letterman; yep, says John Lee. Then Letterman asks Hooker to explain the motifs he wears on his lapels. Why the star? "Because I'm the star," Hooker tells him. And why the dollar sign?

"Because," John Lee replies, "I plays for money."

Then Letterman calls another commercial break. Stagehands swarm like ants re-dressing the set for the next guest, a heavily *designed* woman plugging a cookbook. Throughout this frantic buzz of activity, Hooker remains curled up in his chair until someone is sent over to tell him that his segment of the show is complete. It has all been a rush and a mess, two things Hooker simply cannot abide: he may be seriously laid back, but in the end he always gets to where he's going. "When you push people, you make people *nervous*," he states firmly, "and you won't get as good stuff as you would if you just let it flow. You can't be pushing me and gettin' down my throat, 'cause I'm gonna get all nervous then and may get pissed off." On this occasion, backstage, it had fallen to Mike Kappus to soothe his client, who by his own account was indeed "gettin' all nervous and jittery. I had the jitters, and Mike was saying, 'C'mon, c'mon' and I was sayin', 'Hey, hey . . .' "

But none of that was apparent on the set, even when, after the audience has left, quality control prevailed and the song was reshot in the empty theater. Since David Letterman rarely gives interviews, it proved impossible to ask whether John Lee Hooker meant anything more to him than just another guest to fill a five-minute slot on a wintry Wednesday night. For his part, Hooker was standing on the threshold of a moment which would utterly and irrevocably transform not only his own career but the art form to which he had dedicated his life. He was, however, determined not to become overly impressed with the new-found success and eminence accompanying the burgeoning phenomenon of *The Healer*; to remain cautious; to resist any temptation to grow what he calls the Big Head.

"I think John Lee can explain it to you better than I do: he call it 'the big head,' " says Buddy Guy. "Every time I see him, he look at me and say, 'How many your men in the band got the big head?' I say, 'What's that?' He say, 'J-j-j-j-j-you don't know what the big head is?' I say, 'No.' He say, 'That's when they get bigger than you overnight.' I say, 'Naw, you know whenever I'm around you it's time for Buddy to listen.' "

"I am no stranger at all to hit records," Hooker would remind interviewers whom he suspected might possibly be too young to be as aware as he would like of "Boogie Chillen," the original "I'm In The Mood" or even "Boom Boom." "I'm very proud of this album, but I ain't carried away like I ain't never had nothin' before. I'm just real laid-back, y'know. I'm *always* laid-back whatever happen. I've found that the best way to be."

But by the following summer, *The Healer* had gone gold in the U.S. and silver in the U.K., notching up half a million European sales. "I'm In The Mood," his duet with Bonnie Raitt, had earned him his first Grammy. And a man who had long ago learned not to count his chickens before they were hatched would end up with all the golden eggs he could ever have wanted.

I were born a star. Everybody ain't born a star. God didn't make everybody a star. He made some people stars. He made me a legend and a hero and a star. I worked for it, but I had the tools to work with. Some people want to work, some people work, and they ain't got it. But [God] give it to us, and now you got to work to get it up there. "You got it, I give it you, but you got to work for it." I had to get out there and work. Kick doors down, push doors open, get people to help. I got cheated, but I didn't stop. I kept on. I said, "Down the road somewhere is a door waitin' for me, and I'm gonna walk through it." I kept on 'til I got to that door and it come open. I walked in, and I been in there ever since. I ain't been kicked out.

—John Lee Hooker, interview with the author, 1994

Made up my mind to make a new start
Goin' to California with an achin' in my heart
—Jimmy Page & Robert Plant for Led Zeppelin, "Goin' To California," 1971

A legend and a hero and a star. The rules of mythology, as codified by the likes of Joseph Campbell and Robert Bly, are quite clear. Anyone wishing to become a hero and attain legendary status must first embark upon a quest, undertake a journey into hardship, adversity and danger. Sometimes this quest is undertaken knowingly and voluntarily, in order to achieve a specific end. More often it is undertaken simply because there is no other option, and only in retrospect does it become apparent that one is engaged on a quest at all.

Sometimes the hero knows that he is a hero. Sometimes he knows that he is *not* a hero, but wishes to become one. And sometimes he does what he does only to survive and does not realize that he has become a hero, as part of the process of surviving, until much later, much further on down the road.

By definition, the hero's task must seem all but hopeless. The odds must be firmly against him, with utter annihilation rarely more than a hair's-breadth away. Demons, both inner and outer, must be confronted. Obstacles must be surmounted. Battles must be fought. Some will be lost and others won, but lessons must be learned from both. Sometimes the hero has allies and sometimes he is totally alone, but his closest companions are failure and despair, dogging his heels at every step right up until the final conflict.

His ultimate triumph can never be a foregone conclusion: what need is there for heroism if the protagonist is invulnerable and his success is inevitable? At the outset of the quest, the hero—or the protagonist who will become a hero—must appear dwarfed by the immensity of the task ahead. Each small battle won, or lost but learned from, enables the hero to grow in wisdom, strength and determination until he becomes not only equal to his task but superior to it.

And finally, if the hero does not commence his quest in a spirit of humility, then he will certainly be humbled. The lesson of humility will be learned, hard and painfully, along the way.

In the epic landscape of American myth, the quintessential heroic American journey leads literally toward the sun, on the trail heading west. The gold rush, the dustbowl exodus of Steinbeck's Okies, Chuck Berry's "Promised Land," the hippie pilgrimage to San Francisco, the movie-wannabe's Star(dom) Trek to Hollywood. Westward ho: California is where dreams come true,[2] and it therefore exerts its irresistible magnetic pull on a surfeit of dreamers.

"I come out here in 1970," says Hooker. "I drove all the way. I was so mad, I got in my car, throwed all my stuff in the car. Hit Route 66 with my clothes in my car, and a pocketful of bennies. A little money, not much. About twelve thousand dollars. That's no money for California. I had a name—not like I have now—and no connections. I went to San Francisco. I didn't know nobody out here; I stayed with an old friend of mine called Tess Coleman. She's gone now, good friend of mine. I might've lived there a year, I don't know. I left there same year, about the end of that year, went to Oakland. I had an apartment there on 13th Street in Oakland, and Bill Graham started booking me. Different people started booking me in different places. I just started climbing."

Strangely enough, when Hooker moved out to the Bay Area, at least one old friend—his brother-in-law Paul Mathis, in the military since 1955—had arrived at the same destination via a very different route. "Yeah, well, when he came to California I was already here. I came out here in July 1970. I left England and transferred to Travis, which is in Fairfield, California. My sis wrote me, 'You know, John is comin' out there or he's there already.' She gave him my phone number at the base and we got in contact. He was livin' at a small hotel, nothin' expensive."

Hooker's first California album for ABC/BluesWay, cut the previous year, actually turned out to be his last: the parent label folded Bluesway the following year, switching Hooker and B. B. King to the main ABC imprint. *If You Miss 'im . . . I Got 'im* was a promising but ultimately misfired collaboration with his master-guitarist younger cousin Earl Hooker, already wracked with TB and less than a year away from the end of his tragically short life. It was chiefly notable for its fine cover photo of John Lee and Earl, resplendent in cowboy drag, aboard a freight train: "Boom Boom" reappeared as "Bang Bang Bang Bang," and on the

---

2 Allegedly.

slower tunes Earl's wah-wah slide guitar sparred uncomfortably for space with Jeff Carp's amplified harp. Its undeniable highlights were the rocking "Rollin' And Tumblin'" derivative "Baby Be Strong" and two passionate free-form slow blues pieces, "If You Take Care Of Me, I'll Take Care Of You," and "I Wanna Be Your Puppy, Baby."

However, the next Great Leap Forward in Hooker's career involved ABC neither as instigators nor direct beneficiaries.

> I sure like the way you boys boogie.
> —John Lee Hooker to Canned Heat, quoted in liner-notes to
>   *Hooker 'N' Heat*, 1971

> I saw two little white girls in a record shop recently and a John Lee Hooker record comes on. One looks at the other and says, "Listen to that. Somebody's trying to sound like Canned Heat—doing a shitty job of it." I had to laugh but you know, it's not funny.
> —Johnny Otis interviewed in *Rolling Stone* by Pete Welding,
>   December 1971

Five years earlier, two Los Angeles blues buffs had formed a jugband. Both shy, moonfaced, introverted Alan "Blind Owl" Wilson and boisterous, hirsute, sumo-scaled Bob "The Bear" Hite were awesomely erudite country blues record collectors with a yen to perform the music they adored. Wilson was a scholarly multi-instrumentalist adept on guitar, harmonica and piano (he had been an active participant in the relaunch of Son House) and both sang: Hite in a rumbustious, barrel-chested, gravel-throated Charley Pattonesque mode and Wilson with a slithery, eerie falsetto reminiscent of Skip James at his most ectoplasmic. By 1967, the jugband had evolved, as mid-'60s jugbands were wont to do, into a full-on electric blues band. Their project was not so much to approximate the electric-downhome stylings of '50s and '60s Chicago blues as to go back to bedrock country blues sources and rock up their roots from scratch. The name of this band, derived from a 1928 Tommy Johnson record, was Canned Heat. Despite Bob Hite's ludicrous pageboy haircut, they were one of the surprise minor hits of the Summer Of Love's Monterey Pop Festival. Overshadowed they may have been by Jimi Hendrix, Otis Redding, The Who and Janis Joplin's startling debut with Big Brother And The Holding Company, but they nevertheless scored a deal with Liberty Records and had their first album in the stores by the end of the year.

Canned Heat's secret strength was that they were two bands in one. When Bob Hite sang, they were essentially a superior bar band, albeit one with deep blues roots: they were solid and earthy and they rocked. With Wilson up front, they conjured up a hallucinatory, evershifting blues dreamscape where nothing was quite what it seemed and everything flickered at the corner of the mind's eye: they were eclectic and spooky and they insinuated. In the summer of 1968, the Al Wilson edition of Canned Heat enjoyed a massive and unlikely hit with "On The Road Again": simultaneously as "psychedelic" and as "authentic" a whiteboy blues record as anything cut by anybody in the '60s.

But if it was Al Wilson who carried them onto pop radio and into the charts, it was Bob Hite's jovial psychedelic populism—"Hi kids! This is The Bear!"—which defined them onstage. That, and the boogie. Their second album, *Boogie With Canned Heat*, climaxed with "Fried Hockey Boogie," a cut-down studio version of their protracted in-concert finale which took John Lee Hooker's primal "Boogie Chillen" riff, stuffed it full of steroids and hammered it into the ground with extended improv showcases for each member of the band and Hite as MC. The follow-up, *Livin' The Blues*, went further still: the double-album's entire second disc was devoted to a live-in-concert "Refried Boogie" which steamrollered along for a full forty minutes.[3]

Needless to say, the paths of Canned Heat and John Lee Hooker inevitably crossed: even before Hooker relocated to California, students and master had met on the circuit. Hooker and the whimsically nicknamed Heatsters—as well as The Bear and The Blind Owl, there were "Sunflower" (lead guitarist Henry Vestine), "Mole" (bassist Larry Taylor) and "Fito" (drummer Adolfo De La Parra)—became fast friends, but Al Wilson became more than that: an instant soul-mate. "I met him in L.A.," Hooker fondly recalls. "He was livin' out there and they [Canned Heat] was playin' someplace. They had my music *down*. They was playing someplace and I come down, and I met 'em all at the same time, The Bear, and little Wilson. We just hung out together, and I got to know him. We got together, started to get to know each other, and they was into me so, and they really wanted to play with me, they really wanted to do it. My agent and my manager got together and got us together, and we did this album, and it was so *big*."

---

3 Cue Monty Python : do you want the twelve-minute boogie or the full three-quarters of an hour?

In April of 1970, negotiations were complete, and ABC permitted Hooker a one-album holiday from his contract so that he and Canned Heat could team up. "This album" was *Hooker 'N' Heat*, cut at Liberty's L.A. studio over three days the following month with Bob Hite and Canned Heat's manager/producer Skip Taylor in the control room. It turned out to be a major landmark in Hooker's recording career: an artistic and commercial triumph of resounding proportions which not only recaptured and re-created the authentic early Hooker sound of the Bernard Besman era, but managed to hit Number 73 in the pop album charts. There was only one cloud in the sunny skies over this seemingly-blessed project, but it was a massive and lowering one: before the album had even been mixed, Alan Wilson was dead. A devoted ecologist and outdoorsman long before such preoccupations became fashionable, he was found in his sleeping bag, overdosed on barbiturates, in a national park in Torrance, California, surrounded by his beloved redwood trees. He had reportedly become extremely depressed after breaking up with his girlfriend. Hooker and the band were devastated, and the album appeared with a somber cover photograph depicting John Lee and the surviving members slumped in a grungy, dimly lit hotel room. Behind them, a black-framed photograph of Wilson hangs on the wall.

Suggest to Hooker that *Hooker 'N' Heat* was one of the best records he made between the great early ones at the outset of his career and the autumnal renaissance which commenced with *The Healer*, and he will reply that it was absolutely *"the best."* Opine that Al Wilson was the most gifted and creative of the White Blues Guys of the '60s, and his response is equally uncompromising and unambiguous.

"I say that man was a *genius*. You hit it on the button. You hit it just right. Alan Wilson was such a genius. The young man . . . he passed so young. We never know how he passed; some say he O D'ed, some say he committed suicide. I know one thing: he didn't like sleepin' in beds, he would stay out in the jungle outside. Not in the real *heavy* jungle, but in parks. He had a van with a camper on it, you know. He could sleep in there. He liked doin' that. Places like Central Park, but not Central Park, places down L.A. And practice his music, and write. He was a really, really nice person. A little *strange*, but he had things that he wanted to do. If you didn't know him, you couldn't get right into him. You didn't know how to get into that frame he had around him. Inside him, that was beautiful. *Beautiful.* He studied his music so hard all the time that he just kept his mind on this music. He was a nice person, but . . . that's why you thought he was really hard to talk to and get to, but he really wasn't. He was just into his music. When I got with him, he had me down, my music down like you know your ABCs. He could *follow* me. Ain't no way in the world I could lose him when I'm playing. He was just right on me. Alan Wilson you couldn't lose. You know what he did before I knowed him and after I knowed him? He be study my music. Listenin' to it while I'm sleepin', I didn't know where he were. He had me down even before I knowed him. He say, 'I just sit up listen to your music, man, listen to the way you play it. Sometimes you play it with direct changes, sometimes you wouldn't.' He say he just got used to playin' like that. Just listen to the records he playin' with me: you can tell how good he followed me."

He certainly did. The primary reason for the extraordinarily high quality of *Hooker 'N' Heat* is that Taylor and the band, displaying a blend of erudition and self-effacement unsurpassed among the plethora of blues legend/rockstar acolyte collaborations of the time, were determined to cut a John Lee Hooker album featuring Canned Heat rather than a Canned Heat album featuring John Lee Hooker. In deference to the band's chart-riding status, the record was officially credited to "Canned Heat & John Lee Hooker," but there's absolutely no doubt about whose record it really is. Nor, for that matter, whose session it was. There is a highly engaging, involving live-in-the studio semi-documentary vibe to *Hooker 'N' Heat*: the studio chatter, Hooker's warm-up guitar runs and the homiletic preambles which stitch the songs together create a genuine sense of occasion, a real feel of the atmosphere in the room as the record is being made. *Hooker 'N' Heat* sounds as if it took little longer to record than it does to play.

The secondary reason was that Hooker himself was then at the absolute peak of his powers: simultaneously still youthful and energetic enough to pump out the boogie with an awe-inspiringly tireless ferocity; and sufficiently tempered by age and bitter experience to bring to the music a depth and richness to which the comparatively young and callow Hooker of twenty years earlier could never have aspired. At fifty-three years of age and still emotionally raw and spiritually bleeding from the traumatic collapse of his marriage, the disintegration of his family and his enforced exile from the Motor City, Hooker was not only more than ready to boogie, but prepared to bring the full powers of his art to bear on the bluesman's most pressing priority: the healing of the self by the self and, by extension, the healing of others.

The liner-notes—pseudonymously attributed to "Boogie Chillen," but most likely composed by Taylor and Hite—provide an illuminating background to the sessions:

> [Hooker] arrived for the session wearing a plaid cap, leather jacket, black satin shirt and some old dress slacks and carrying the old Epiphone guitar which had been around the world more than once. Once at the studio, we tried out about eight really ancient amps before finding the one that had that real "Hooker" sound—one we hadn't heard on John's records for a long, long time. We built a plywood platform for John to sit on while he played. An old Silvertone amp rested a few feet away. One mike on the amp, one for his voice, and one to pick up John's stompin'—he never quits stompin'! Never far away, a bottle of Chivas Regal and a cup of water to smooth it down.

The format for the album was relatively straightforward. Hooker would kick off the proceedings on his own, harking back to his vintage Detroit years by performing a few solo tunes in his classic style. Then Wilson would join him for a fistful of duets, playing harp, guitar or piano as required. Finally, the rest of the band would pile in for a set of full-tilt ensemble performances climaxing with—what else?—a marathon boogie. Canned Heat's line-up had been going through the early stages of what was to become an almost permanent state of turmoil and upheaval. Henry Vestine was freshly back in the fold after a temporary absence during which his lead-guitar chair had been occupied by Harvey Mandel, a former Chicago running buddy of Charlie Musselwhite's who'd stuck around long enough to appear with the band at Woodstock, participate in a European tour and play on their third hit single, "Let's Work Together." Vestine had quit after a falling-out with Larry Taylor, and the return of "Sunflower" possibly had something to do with Taylor's eventual departure and subsequent replacement by Antonio De La Barreda.

Hite and Taylor's preparations paid off, big time. The elderly pawn-shop amplifier gave Old Blondie, Hooker's trusty six-string companion, that sublime combination of power, sweetness, clank and grime which constitutes blues guitar Tone Heaven. The miked-up foot-stomp—a time-honored Besman trick recycled by many subsequent Hooker producers, including Bob Thiele on *It Serve Me Right To Suffer*—put a solidly percussive four-to-the-bar *thunk* into each and every groove. And Hooker's mature voice was as strong and flexible as even his most demanding admirer could possibly desire: his command of timbral resource and vocal nuance never greater.

"Gotta get myself together here," murmurs Hooker before he kicks into his opening number, but from the first pounding boot and bass-string riff, it was utterly apparent just how "together" he was. He sounded *huge*: the biggest one-man-band in the world. "Messin' With The Hook" drew into Hooker's repertoire one of Chicago harpist Junior Wells's signature songs: a tight, riffy, danceable piece which (unusually in the Chicago blues canon) emphasized the singer's youth in the lyric. Muddy Waters, rarely averse to borrowing songs from juniors and Juniors alike—he'd heisted Bo Diddley's 1955 "I'm A Man" almost immediately on its release—emphasized his own patriarchal status when he reworked it as "Messin' With The Man," but Hooker went further, personalizing it completely. In fact, he Hookerized and deconstructed it so thoroughly that by the time he was done with the song, it bore about as much resemblance to the Wells original as Peking Duck does to a duck.

"The Feelin' Is Gone" borrows its title and its agenda, though not much else, from the same 1951 Roy Hawkins tune upon which B. B. King had based "The Thrill Is Gone," his breakthrough hit of the previous year. Hooker seems tentative at the start of this free-form slow blues: he's so worried, babe, he don't know what to do, babe. But soon, via a lyrical allusion to Howlin' Wolf's "Killing Floor," the ambiguity disappears, swept away by the same tidal waves of grief and anger above which Hooker is struggling to keep his head, and his heart. *"I done got over it, babe,"* he defiantly declaims: like Fox Mulder in *The X-Files*, he wants to believe. And we want to believe him. But he's not quite convinced. And neither are we.

But then he convinces himself, and us. *"The feelin' is gone from me, babe,"* he hollers, over and over again: the process of catharsis enacting itself before our very ears. This achieved, he quietens down, secure in his new-found certainty. *"I done got over it, babe,"* he tells us once more, before—*Whammp!*—one final chord, like a mule-kick to the spine, slams the song to a close.

"[Play something] a little funky," suggests Taylor. "A little boogie?" offers Hooker. "A little funky," repeats the producer. "Okay," says Hooker, and launches into "Send Me Your Pillow," from the 1962 *Big Soul* sessions. By now he's moved up a gear or six into total overdrive: voice, guitar and foot-stomp locked into perfect sync and locomoting with an irresistible surge of pure power. If Hooker's credentials as a grand-master of groove needed any confirmation, this is where you'd go to get it: no solo performer has ever rocked harder. The propulsive force behind this astonishing performance is raw need: loneliness and desire calling out, crying out, reaching out into the void.

By way of decompression, it is succeeded by "Sittin' Here Thinkin'," a meditative slow blues in the "Wednesday Evenin'" mode with Hooker's brooding, abstracted foot-stomp and vocal offset by eloquent, quicksilver guitar flurries, which Hooker had first cut (as "Sittin' And Thinkin'") for Joe Von Battle back at the very dawn of his career. Then it's back to the boogie for "Meet Me In The Bottom," a traditional Delta piece best known via Howlin' Wolf's 1961 interpretation "Down In The Bottom": in characteristic Hooker fashion, the intensity deepens and the pulse accelerates even as the structure unravels.

The next number concerned a topic clearly at the forefront of Hooker's mind, if not exactly close to his heart. Garnished with stormy guitar rumbles and flashes, "Alimonia Blues" looks musically back to the same "Wednesday Evenin'" template he had used a little earlier on "Sittin' Here Thinkin'," and forward lyrically to the epic "Stripped Me Naked" he would record more than twenty years later with Carlos Santana. In terse, sparse, lyrical strokes, Hooker sketches a scenario in which he's hauled before a judge to debate alimony, child support and similar painful stuff. It's the last of the session's solo pieces.

"We're gonna bring Alan out now, John," announces a voice from the control room. "You wanna take a little breather?" But it's straight into "Drifter," a distant scion of the extended slow-blues song family Hooker derived from Charles Brown's "Driftin' Blues" with The Blind Owl's reverb-soaked amplified harmonica illuminating Hooker's desolate blues-scape like neon lights through dockside fog. If Wilson's entry seems tentative, it's because he's *listening*: not just with his ears, but seemingly with his entire nervous system. His acute sensitivity and empathy with Hooker's celebrated idiosyncrasies are nothing short of astounding: it's as if he's extending temporal antennae into the immediate future to predict exactly where Hooker is about to go. Seemingly, he was capable of anticipating not only whether or not Hooker is about to leave a space, but whether that space is one which should be left empty or filled by a harp intervention.

Furthermore, Wilson's harp sound is utterly extraordinary: talky and squawky but never thin or flimsy; huge and rich but never flabby or cloying. Every timbral and stylistic resource in the blues-harp tradition seems to be literally at the tip of his tongue, to be alluded to or utilized at will, and yet he seems free of the need to plagiarize, to ape or mimic the major stylists he has evidently studied so assiduously. Whether delicately simmering like a muted Hammond organ or brassily blasting like a trombone from hell, he is utterly his own man.

When Hooker works with accompaniment from others, a variety of things can happen. If the accompaniment is insensitive and overbearing, it can trample him underfoot like a herd of elephants rampaging through a rose garden. If it's sympathetic and solid and supportive—like The Coast To Coast Blues Band, for example—he'll sit on it as if it was a comfortable, reliable chair. But if it's empathic and inspired, genuine sparks will fly, and he'll respond and engage: "Drifter" ends with an electrifying call-and-response between Hooker's voice and Wilson's harp which creates real anticipation for what is about to follow. They even hit the final chord in perfect unison: Hooker's guitar slams and Wilson's harp sizzles out of the sustain.

Next up: "You Talk Too Much," a boot-stomping up-tempo piece which does little more than enable Hooker and Wilson to refine their partnership by checking out each other's boogie chops. Grouchy, ill-tempered and misogynistic, it counterpoints the bin-done-wrong tenor of much of the session repertoire by suggesting that however flawed his spouse, and their relationship, may or may not have been, Hooker himself was possibly not always the easiest guy to live with.

"You got about ten [songs] now," Hooker informs Hite and Taylor, "I told you, it don't take me no three days to make no album." "It's a triple album," ripostes a voice from the control room. "Well," Hooker replies, "you go for a triple album, you gotta go for triple money." And everybody breaks up laughing, Hooker loudest of all. "Lots of money!" cajoles the producer. "This is a hit album. Don't worry about that money, just keep rollin'." And it was, and they do. "Nothin' but the best," says Hooker, rolling out one of his favorite catchphrases, "and later for the garbage." He then pays tribute to his studious, self-effacing new sidekick. "I dig this kid's harmonica, you know. I don't know how he follow me, but he do." Then, directly to Wilson, "You must've listened to my records all of your life. I just can't lose you."

What follows—after some brief verbal byplay concerning the legendarily awful cooking of The Grateful Dead's Pigpen—is a resounding endorsement of all of the above assertions, Hooker's and the producers' alike: nothing less than the definitive take of one of the key songs in Hooker's repertoire. "Burnin' Hell" was also one of the earliest: Hooker had recorded it as a duet with Eddie Burns at one of his first United Sound sessions with Bernard Besman, and revisited it a decade or so later—at the same studio, as it happened—as an acoustic "folk-blues" exercise for Riverside. The original '49 take is clangy and clamorous; Burns's harp and Hooker's voice and guitar distorted and compressed, high-pitched and urgent, hopped-up and bursting with callow young-blood energy, a torrential outpouring of riffs and images. But there's an aura of real danger to it: in terms of the Baptist codes in which both Hooker and Burns were raised, "Burnin' Hell"'s central assertion—"*Ain't no heaven, ain't no burnin' hell/where you go when you die, nobody can tell*"—is profoundly transgressive and challenging. (Interestingly enough, Son House, from whose epic "My Black Mama" Hooker borrowed the lines, was both a deeply religious and a deeply bitter man who took lengthy sabbaticals from his blues life in order to preach the very gospel which the song claims to disdain.)

The Riverside take, cut ten years later, is more measured, but also more muted: Hooker's acoustic guitar—and Bill Grauer's dry, earnest folkie production—simply lacks the sheer wham of the electric instrument, and Hooker seems inhibited by the absence of an instrumental foil or a partner in crime. However, his voice has grown in richness and weight, the song seems "sorted out" in terms of both its musical structure and lyrical content, and experience has given Hooker audibly increased confidence in both his artistry and his message. Nevertheless, it's the *Hooker 'N' Heat* version which brings the song all the way home. Wilson's performance is simply astonishing. It could be said that, whereas Eddie Burns had to create his original harp part on the fly, Wilson had the advantage of having studied Burns's performance on the '49 take over and over again, not only learning the basics of the part but the ability to improvise and elaborate on it; and thus only seems tall because he was standing on his predecessor's shoulders. Even so, he—you should pardon the expression—*burns* all the way through. If, in movie terms, Hooker's voice is the protagonist and his guitar and foot-stomp the location, then Wilson provides the lighting and the entire supporting cast.

And he drives Hooker into one of the landmark performances of his career. This particular "Burnin' Hell" is a blazing exposition of his core belief: a joyfully seamless reconciliation of religious faith and secular humanism. When he shouts "Ain't *no hell*! Ain't *no hell*!" with guitar and foot pounding remorselessly and tirelessly, and Wilson's harp strutting proudly by his side at the song's raging climax, it is a whoop of celebration, a celebration of our ultimate victory as a species and a culture: our collective liberation from dread.

Plus it rocks. That is to say: it rocks like hell and it feels like heaven. Not surprisingly, Hooker often expressed an interest in rerecording it, and a fresh version, featuring Charlie Musselwhite on harp and postmodern slidemeister Ben Harper, turned up on 1998's *The Best Of Friends*. This is how he himself unpacks the song: "The way I look at it, your heaven is here, and your hell is here. I feel like I'm in heaven. A lotta people love me, I got a few dollars, a place to live . . . that's my heaven. And lovin' people, that's heaven to me. But people that's sufferin', hungry, sleepin' in the streets, don't know where they next meal is comin' from, out in the cold . . . they livin' in hell. For a long time, my parents had me believin' that there was a burnin' hell and there was a heaven, but it has come to me in myself as I grew older and knowledge grew in me that if there is a God then he was an unjust God for burnin' you forever an' ever, stickin' fire to you. If God was a heavenly father, a *good* God, then he wouldn't torture you and burn you. He wouldn't do that. He wouldn't see you burn.

"But, in a way, he tortures you if you got nothin' to eat and hungry, don't know where you gonna get your next meal, don't know where you gonna sleep at, half sick, can't work, driftin' from door to door . . . that's your hell. But you're not bein' tortured with fire, where you get down in this hole being tortured with flames, with fire forever. *No.* So you not gonna fly outta there with wings in the sky like an angel to milk and honey, as I was taught if you go to heaven. You not gonna do that. There's nothin' up there but sky. The only heaven is up there in the big jets and airplanes, with the beautiful ladies walkin' in the aisles. That's your heaven."

Mmmm. Only if you're in first class, John.

Hooker laughs at that. "Yeah, first class. That's your heaven. You'll never get it through to people, because the church has got 'em brainwashed to *death*, the ministers, the preachers. I believe in a Supreme Being, don't get me wrong, but I don't believe that there's a hell that you're gonna be tortured in. I believed in all of that, then I grew up and realized, and I wrote the song: '*Ain't no heaven, ain't no burnin' hell, where you* go *when you die, nobody can tell.'* Nobody knows. Nobody come back and tell you, 'Hey, it's all right, c'mon down.' " He laughs again. "It ain't all right. I could be wrong, but I don't think I'm wrong."

There was no way to top the intensity of "Burnin' Hell," so Hooker and Wilson very sensibly didn't try. Instead, Hooker bounces through a light, playful but majorly groovelicious account of his perennial favorite, "Bottle Up And Go," with Wilson vamping unobtrusively on piano. Then it's back to business: with Wilson staying at the keyboard to sketch a few simple but majestic chords around him, Hooker delivers his 1970 State Of The Nation address, "The World Today," in the hushed but firm tones of a man stating, as clearly and simply as he knows how, his personal credo. Wilson supports Hooker, but stays out of his way. *I hear* you, says his piano, *yes I* know. And that's all he has to say. It's all he *needs* to say.

"Me and Alan gonna do this thing," says Hooker, by way of pre-amble. "It's about what happenin' today, and about what will be happenin' maybe four or five years from today 'til things get down mellow"—guitar lick alert—"all over the world. I want you to listen to this." And the foot starts pounding again, but now it's slow, doomy, ominous. Looking around him, Hooker sees a world, and a nation, riven by ideological and tribal war. In the face of conflict, chaos and despair, with the Kent State shootings still a raw, bleeding wound in the fabric of the American psyche, Hooker reaffirms his faith both in the fundamental decency and goodwill of humanity, and in the ability of the young to learn from their elders' mistakes.

> . . . *I see so many young people*
> *They fightin' in every town . . . on campus*
> *I don't know what they right or wrong*
> *But they tryin' to fight for they rights*
> *The old people*
> *Leave the young kids alone*
> *Let them run they own life . . .*
> *It's a brand new world today*
> *Lookahere now*
> *You find some of the old people*
> *They're not hip to the modern days*
> *They want they kids to live like they live*
> *But no*

Them days are gone
It's a brand new world
One way to solve they problem
It takes time
The old coots die
And leave it to the kids
It'll be a beautiful world
Then there won't be no fightin' on campus anymore
'Cause my kids and your kids
When they grow up
They'll understand
All the old coots are gone in they grave
But as long as they live
There's gonna be fightin' in every town . . . and every campus
The young kids, they walkin' out
The old folks, when they gone
It gonna be a better world to live in
'Cause the young kids
Are the world today.

And he still stands by every word of that.

" 'The World Today,' I was paintin' a picture when I sung that song," Hooker proudly proclaims. "And I had my reasons for doing that. It's true. It's a young folks' world. The old folks should leave the young folks alone. The old coots, they tell they kids what to do, who to talk to, who to be with, who to associate with . . . when the old coots are dead, they can leave it to the young folks and they be able to get along. When the old coots dead and in they grave, then there'll be peace. But [some people] teach they kids to be mean and rude and *racial*. They bring 'em up like that. It's entered a lotta youngsters. They just came out with it: prejudice, hate. That's on both sides, white and black kids. Hate and prejudice, fightin' with each other. 'I'm more than you, you more than me . . .' It's *not*. You take a bunch of cattle, get together two—three hundred cattle, two—three hundred thousand, whatever you want to say. All colors of cattle, they gets along. They don't look at it as white cattle, black cattle, yellow cattle: they all are *cattles*. They flock together. They gets along. When you put a lot of people together, like all nationalities, they don't get along. Pretty soon, they wants to start fighting with each other. Like animals? *Animals* gets along better together than human beings.

"I wrote that tune because of Kent State, and people fightin' all over the world. I can write some of the heavy stuff, the meaningful stuff about what the world need. The world need *peace*. Need *love*." Again not surprisingly, he's considering re-recording this piece, too. "I'm thinkin' about it. I don't want no band. I just want a piano. Just sittin' there, like me and Alan Wilson. The piano's so beautiful."

Again, something completely different: "I Got My Eyes On You," with Wilson switching instrument yet again, this time expertly shadowing Hooker on rhythm guitar, is "Dimples" in all but name. And then the band arrive. With Wilson back on harp, they lollop through the Vee Jay–era "Whisky And Wimmen": Hooker clearly enjoying the opportunity to concentrate his energies on his singing and let the rhythm section take care of all the strenuous work in the engine room. Significantly, it's the first number on the album to require the studio get-out of a fade, as opposed to "live," ending. On the slow blues, "Just Me And You," Henry Vestine's jagged, jittery lead guitar—something like Buddy Guy with a severe migraine—is somewhat at odds with the mellow, seductive mood Hooker seems to be trying to create, and "Let's Make It" is little more than an excuse for all concerned to have themselves some fun cantering around that old "Boom Boom" corral. But—following a quick fade-out and fade-in—it all comes good for "Peavine Special," the ancient Charley Patton tune which was one of the first pieces Will Moore had taught his pre-adolescent stepson so many years before and so many miles away. Here Canned Heat's familiarity and ease with the greater and lesser arcana of Delta blues—and their grasp of how to rock it up Memphis-, as opposed to Chicago-, style—is immaculately showcased: Wilson, back on guitar, playing open-tuned in his unique pianistic style. It sounds exactly the way you'd expect a bunch of guys would feel if they happened to be drinking moonshine in the back of a hay truck, on the most beautiful summer day in history, with all work done and money in their pockets. The greatest compliment we can pay Canned Heat is to say that were it not for the clarity of the track's production values, they'd sound just like the band on a Howlin' Wolf record: one made with Sam Phillips or Ike Turner in Memphis, rather than with Leonard Chess or Willie Dixon in Chicago.

And finally, there's the boogie. Wilson kicks it in on harp: a boogie(-woogie) bugle-call if you ever did hear one. Puckishly enough, the assembled company named this particular episode in the decades-long boogie saga "Boogie Chillen No. 2," but in fact it's "Boogie Chillen Classic" as per Hooker's 1949 hit, Hastings Street, Henry's Swing Club 'n' all. The master is sittin' in with the students, so the groove is a hybrid: more or less Canned Heat's standard take on the boogie as (over)exposed on their "Fried Hockey" and "Refried" excursions, but with little darting jabs from Hooker's guitar to steer them a little further his way, the shepherd keeping his flock to the correct path. But of course "Boogie Chillen" didn't last eleven and a half minutes in 1949, so we get some fairly hefty chunks of soloing in between the verses—Hooker caps Vestine's characteristically angular and abrasive first eruption by asking the listeners, "Do you hear that cat on the harmonica?"—and most of the song's most celebrated constituent parts are out of the way after four-or-so minutes. Which leaves a lot of jamming, honors going inevitably to Wilson's slippery, funky, fat-toned harp, and the reciprocal empathy with which Hooker goads him during the second half of his solo.

"Boogie Chillen No. 2" was the only track on *Hooker 'N' Heat* on which Canned Heat appeared "as themselves"; though their trademarked boogie was essentially Hooker-derived and they were literally licking their chops at the opportunity to "boogie with The Hook," Canned Heat's boogie persona was deeply familiar to, and beloved by, fans of their live shows and albums (though not necessarily those whose acquaintance with the band was limited to their radio hits). The album was a moderate hit, peaking at Number 73 on the album charts in February of 1971. Not a fabulous result in terms of Canned Heat's track record, but a superb score for what was basically a classicist's John Lee Hooker album which made zero concessions to the fashions of the contemporary rock'n'soul mainstream.

One of Al Wilson's final acts before his untimely death had been to contribute an erudite, affectionate liner-note for the first full-scale reissue of the cream of Bernard Besman's Modern and Sensation masters. *Alone*, which brought the original versions of "Boogie Chillen" and "Burnin' Hell," among others, back into the stores for the first time in many years, appeared on Specialty Records, but the real collector's thrill came when Besman cleaned out his vaults and leased a massive pile of out-takes and alternates from those same early years to United Artists. UA were thus able to "follow up" *Hooker 'N' Heat* with *Coast To Coast Blues Band* and, in 1973, a three-album set called *John Lee Hooker's Detroit*.[4] Besman's interpretation of these events is not uncharacteristic.

"Hooker, at that time, had kinda faded out," he claims. "He didn't

---

4 Both packages were subsequently combined in the three-CD collection *Alternative Boogie* (Capitol, 1995).

get revitalized until I leased the records to United Artists and he made some sessions with Canned Heat. That's what revitalized him, Canned Heat. He made 'Boogie Chillen' again with them, called it 'Boogie Chillen No. 2.'" Guitarist Freddie King also had his own take on things. He told Robert Neff and Anthony Connor:

> *Now the average recording company, when they get ready to record a cat like . . . John Lee Hooker, they will get some cat about nineteen or twenty years old to produce it. He don't know what the hell he's doing; he just started playing yesterday. He don't know what the guy wants. Like this Canned Heat produced this thing on John Lee. Good album! Really, I dug it. But it just don't sound like John Lee. Only thing you need with John Lee is give him his guitar, and a piano player, and a drum, and a bass. And mostly just let him have it himself. Not too much psychedelic stuff . . .* [5]

Two things: the first is that ABC didn't consider that Hooker had "kinda faded out." As far as they were concerned, the success of *Hooker 'N' Heat* meant that he was hot—or, at any rate, hottish. And the second is that Skip Taylor, Bob Hite, Alan Wilson and the rest of the Canned Heat posse had worked their collective ass off precisely to give Hooker the kind of sympathetic setting which would allow him to present his music in as pure, uncut and untampered a state as possible. One wonders if you, I, John Lee and Freddie King have all been listening to the same record. Sadly, Freddie isn't around anymore and so we can't ask him, but while his remarks seem inexplicable in the context of *Hooker 'N' Heat*, they ring far truer in the context of the records Hooker made in its wake when he returned to the corporate bosom of ABC.

ABC kept close tabs on the progress of *Hooker 'N' Heat*, and the company learned a lot. The question is whether the lessons they learned were the right ones. It was as if "Boogie Chillen No. 2" was to become the template for Hooker's future recordings. Even before *Hooker 'N' Heat* was in the stores, ABC had him back in the studio with Bill Szymczyk (the most successful record producer with a vowel-free surname in the history of twentieth-century music) and Ed Michel in charge. Their sophisticated soul-rock take on updating the blues had worked wonders for B. B. King, whose career had gone into hyperdrive following the massive

---

5   In Neff and Connor's invaluable *Blues* (Latimer Bluesbooks, 1975).

crossover success of "The Thrill Is Gone," but the formula they devised to sell Hooker to lumpenhippie rock fans was by no means as elegant. What John Lee Hooker's career evidently required in the wake of *Hooker 'N' Heat* was . . . double albums! Long jams! Guest rock stars!

The first fruit of the new phase was the ominously-titled *Endless Boogie*. Recorded over three November days at Wally Heider's studio in San Francisco with big-name rockers like Carl Radle and Jim Gordon (from Eric Clapton's Derek & The Dominos) and Steve Miller in attendance alongside Hooker's regular rhythm section of bassist Gino Skaggs and drummer Ken Swank, the session must have seemed like some blues-rock gangbang. A small army of players trooped in and out of the studio, the only constant factor being multi-instrumentalist Cliff Coulter, wearing keyboard, guitar or bass hats depending on the demands of the track and whoever else happened to be around. The album ended up featuring four drummers (Ken Swank, Billy Ingram, Reno Lanzara, Jim Gordon), three bassists (Skaggs, Radle and Coulter), three keyboard players (Coulter, Mark Naftalin, John Turk), and no less than seven guitarists other than Hooker himself (Steve Miller, Jesse Davis, Dan Alexander, Mel Brown, Jerry Perez, Cliff Coulter and even Mark Naftalin, who found himself in the guitar chair when the producers started rolling tape on a between-numbers jam). (Dave Berger was, however, the only harp player invited.) "Supersession" may well have been the buzzword of the time, but this was ridiculous. In 1977, Miller shared his reminiscences of the occasion with *Guitar Player*'s Dan Forte:

> I got a phone call one day said, "Hey, do you want to come over and play on a John Lee Hooker record?" I said, "Shit yeah, man." Like, "Stop the presses, get my guitar!" I went over there, and the producer's concept of what John Lee Hooker was—they had some dynamite musicians from San Jose there, like Cliff Coulter. Then they had the white boy lead guitar players lined up over here. Literally; I'm not kidding. And John Lee Hooker was sitting in a corner, and he was intimidated by all the guitar players; he wouldn't play any changes. So I watched them doing this, and John Lee would start a groove and then everybody would take it away. By the end of the session I was going, "Hey, John Lee Hooker is a real good guitar player and you're treating him like he was Lonesome Sundown George, and you're just trying to sell records. What's wrong?"
>
> And I talked John into doing a little light acoustic thing. He was

*embarrassed to make a chord change in front of all the studio play-
ers. John Lee has a lot of music in him that hasn't been out. He is
truly a classic, heavy-duty player, but he's been totally abused. He's
one guy I'd like to produce—and when I say produce, basically what
I mean is get him comfortable, get some quality things around him,
and maybe make a suggestion. But not like, "No, no, John Lee;
more like this [snaps fingers], you know." I'd just sit him down and
cut everything. And then add strings [laughs]!*

What Miller was talking about was to record Hooker pretty much the
way Canned Heat had done six months before the *Endless Boogie* sessions, and how Roy Rogers would record him eighteen years later: in
other words, to place Hooker front and center and arrange all the furniture around him. The *Endless Boogie* strategy was almost the exact
opposite: to place Hooker against generic blues-rock backdrops of either
the slow-blues or lumpenboogie variety; dilute or dispense with his
groove; keep his guitar well down in the mix, and effectively render him
little more than a sideman on what were supposed to be his own albums.
In the most extreme cases, it sounded as if Hooker was simply sitting in
on somebody else's jam sessions, contributing the occasional guitar lick
and interrupting the interminable cavalcade of other people's solos to
announce, not altogether convincingly, what a great time he was having.
The boogie "Pots On, Gas On High" and the Chuck Berryish chug of the
title track (the latter aptly subtitled "Parts 27 and 28") add up to almost
twenty minutes of generic riffing that could have been peeled off by the
yard. Similarly, several of the slow-blues entries, including a remake of
"House Rent" (entitled "House Rent Boogie" even though boogie it
don't) and "Sheep Out On The Foam" (yet another "Driftin' Blues" variant), take a very long time to go nowhere in particular.

Endless Boogie does have its moments, though. The free-form slow
blues "We Might As Well Call It Through (I Didn't Get Married To Your
Two-Timing Mother)" showcases both the late Jesse Davis's sublime
slide—he was, after all, the one who devised, on Taj Mahal's revival of
Blind Willie McTell's "Statesboro Blues," the slide-guitar part immortalized by Duane Allman on The Allman Brothers' subsequent and better
known version—and Hooker's aptitude for telling anecdotes of domestic
strife. "Doin' The Shout"—the "little light acoustic thing" alluded to by
Miller—skips along nicely, propelled by Swank's brush-beaten snare. "I
Don't Need No Steam Heat" bumps-and-grinds along with an endear-

ingly raunchy swagger, but this particular lily is somewhat overgilded by the presence of two pianos and three guitars. And then there's the impassioned anti-drug plea "Kick Hit 4 Hit Kix U" (the typographical approach way predates Slade, Prince or 2Pac), subtitled "Blues For Jimi And Janis" and inspired by the deaths, within a month of each other, of two of the icons of the hippie era.

"I think of a lotta stuff like that and try to reach out and get to people," says Hooker, "like that song I wrote when Janis Joplin OD'ed. I'm hopin' that it reached the young people. You know, they took it off the air. They wouldn't play it, why I don't know. They needed to play that." Unwittingly, Hooker did the memory of Jimi Hendrix (to whom he refers throughout as "Jimi Henry") a severe disservice in that song by ascribing his death, like Joplin's, to intravenous heroin abuse. Hendrix died as the result of an accidental overdose of prescription sleeping pills; and post-mortem examination found neither needle marks nor any other physical evidence of hard drug use. Hooker freely acknowledges that, in this respect at least, he was misled by media speculation and loose talk. "When you gone you can't speak for yourself, and he can't speak for himself. Everybody got a different lie. Hendrix did this, Hendrix did that. This killed him, that killed him. Once you gone, they say what they like about you."

Unwittingly, *Endless Boogie* and its successors negatively proved the same point that *Hooker 'N' Heat* had stated positively: that the less musical clutter with which Hooker was surrounded, the better the records sounded. However, the idea that anybody would buy a John Lee Hooker album in order to listen to John Lee Hooker rarely seemed to be uppermost in the producers' minds. *Guitar Player* magazine's February 1972 issue included a sketch by Michael Brooks of Hooker's next ABC studio session, which suggests that the real priority was simple, straight-up market forces. ABC had entrusted Ed Michel with spending their money on recording John Lee Hooker: his task was to generate maximum sales from the minimum investment, and if in the process he could also help to maintain the artist's career longevity, that would be a bonus. "What really concerns Ed as he sits behind the fancifully designed sixteen-track machine," Brooks wrote, "are the 85 percent of recording dates that never get their costs back ... dollars are a serious consideration to any producer."

One man's gangbang is the next guy's supersession. The resulting album, *Never Get Out Of These Blues Alive*, was created at what also turned out to be Hooker's last studio date for ABC, but it was far from being his swansong for the label. (For a start, there was a pair of unremarkable live albums, one cut at San Francisco's Kabuki Theater and the other at Soledad Prison. The latter was chiefly notable for a two-song vocal guest shot by John Lee Hooker Jr, present at the time on what might euphemistically be described as "other business.") Brooks quoted Michel as stating that "from the material done [he] can get enough to do a couple of albums," but as it happened, an intensive two-day blues binge in late September of 1971 ended up providing enough tape for no less than three.

It's faintly surprising that Wally Heider's San Francisco studio hadn't installed a revolving door specifically to cope with the small army of musicians Ed Michel was wheeling in and out for ABC's Hooker dates. Many of them were members in good standing of the formidable bluesdrain diaspora from Chicago to the Bay Area: harpist Charlie Musselwhite, Paul Butterfield Blues Band alumni Mark Naftalin and Elvin Bishop (Butterfield himself and guitar hero Mike Bloomfield, the band's most celebrated grad, were already out there), and one of the two new members of Hooker's road band featured on the album. Though only in his mid-thirties, Memphis-born guitarist Luther Tucker was already a twenty-year blues veteran who'd spent most of the '50s playing behind the volatile harpmeister Little Walter. Plus there was a new keyboard player in the touring posse as well: a teen prodigy taking on his first professional gig. His name was Robert Hooker.

"My daddy had moved to California," the Reverend reminisces, "and I came out to move to California too, and that's when I started playing with him, around about '71, '72, something like that. He sung the song 'I'll Never Get Out Of These Blues Alive.' I started playing with him at the age of . . . what? I might have been sixteen or seventeen years old. I played organ, and I played piano. We went everywhere. We traveled, man, and people *love* John Lee Hooker. I remember we's on a show with Ike and Tina Turner. They were supposed to be the top over him, but the people wanted to hear John Lee Hooker. One of his favorite songs, we used to end it up with 'Boogie With The Hook.' "

Cliff Coulter, Mel Brown, Ken Swank and Gino Skaggs were back: also on board was another bassist (John Kahn), two other drummers (Ron Beck and Chuck Crimelli), keyboard guy Steven Miller (no relation to the guitarist of almost the same name), and no less than three other guitarists, including slide guy Benny Rowe. And therein lay the rub: vast swathes of the album presented a case of too many guitarists spoiling the broth. Too many guitarists overplaying and underlistening. Not enough songs. And too many off-the-peg generic backdrops which could just as well have been slotted into place behind almost any competent Delta-rooted bluesman. Despite the impeccable craftsmanship of the musicians involved, way too much of the music sounds enervated and fussy, deficient in both energy and focus, lackluster, *tired*. But the album nevertheless has its moments. The boisterous "Boogie With The Hook"—"Boogie Chillen" stripped of its narrative structure and reduced to raw groove—which lived on as Hooker's set-closer for the remainder of his performing career, contrives to rock like a beast despite its ponderous load of dueling solos. "TB Sheets" was a dankly haunting free-form slow blues which Hooker had recorded before, notably for Bernard Besman as "No Friend Around" in 1950 and in performance at Sugar Hill as "TB Is Killing Me" in 1962, but this was where the song attained full maturity. Playing Robert Hooker's spooky Hammond off against Michael White's rustily eloquent violin while still leaving enough space for decisive, commanding interventions from Hooker's own guitar, it's a harrowing performance with the emotional power to leave you frozen to the bone.

And then there was Van Morrison.

The one-time Them singer, whom Hooker had first encountered on the London club scene way back in the mid-'60s, had relocated to New York City in 1967 to work with songwriter/producer Bert Berns, who'd co-written Them's second hit, "Here Comes The Night," but their partnership was already proving problematic even before the producer's unexpected death, and Morrison made his escape from New York to settle in Cambridge, Massachusetts. (Peter Wolf, lead singer of the J. Geils Band, was at the time working as a late-night DJ at a Boston radio station, and he remembers an extremely persistent caller with a grating Belfast accent who was always phoning in to request John Lee Hooker records.) There Morrison crafted the distinctive soul/jazz/folk fusion of his groundbreaking *Astral Weeks* and *Moondance* albums. Those records made him a legend, but their hit-bearing follow-ups, *His Band And The Street Choir* and *Tupelo Honey*, made him a star. By 1971 Morrison had once again shifted his base of operations, this time to California, and was thus perfectly placed to show up at Heider's studio to duet with Hooker on the album's title track. Hooker sounds clearly delighted with his famous guest, especially since that guest was an old friend made better than good. "This is *Van Morrison*!" he announces proudly, over the swirl of Naftalin's piano, Robert Hooker's organ, Elvin Bishop's slide, his own and Morrison's guitars and the Skaggs/Swank rhythm section, during Morrison's first vocal chorus. Then he goes to work.

> *Now Van Morrison, he asked me*
> *He said, Johnny*
> *Why-why do you sing the blues?*
> *I said I know I'm doomed*
> *I'm doomed 'cause all I know*
> *Is singin' the blues both night and day*
> *I'll never-never come out alive*

On their first studio encounter, Hooker and Morrison didn't start any fires—not by comparison with subsequent collaborations, anyway—but they sure struck plenty sparks. There was undeniable electricity between them, though Morrison, then a mere stripling of twenty-six, sounds to be a trifle out of his depth. But the bond formed between them back in mid-'60s London was deepened and strengthened, and the relationship proved crucial to both men. To Morrison, an idol with whose music he had grown up turned out to be a staunch and loyal friend. To Hooker, the notoriously touchy and ungregarious Morrison was utterly transparent. Not only did they understand each other, but in the most profound sense of the term, they *recognized* each other.

"Now Van's not a bad person at all," Hooker says fondly. "It's true, he do stick to himself, but he don't dislike people. Van's a *good* person. Van's a beautiful person. He don't like to be around a lot of people he call a bunch of freaks, but he like people. He just want to be to himself. Now he *loves* me. He play with me so much, you know, been around me so much, listened to my records so much that he *know* it. He can just *do* it. I love that man. He's a beautiful, beautiful person, but you got to know Van. *You got to get to know Van.* He's hard to get to know if you don't know him. He ain't the kind of person just to mix with a whole lot of people; he just go shy. If he come here right now, with all these people, he won't say a word, he just sit there. Any way he can get close to me in a room, just him and me, he gon' do it. If he can't get me all to himself, he say"—Hooker lapses into a pretty fair Irish accent—" 'Well, I gotta go, gimme a call.' It ain't a matter that he dislike 'em, that's just the way he are. He like bein' alone, a little shy.

"You might say, 'Well, why is Van shy, famous as he is, as many people as he be around?' That got nothin' to do with it. When you off the bandstand just sittin' around with people, that's when you more shy. When you on that bandstand, once you get goin', all shyness disappear when the people get with you. It's funny, it *do*. But when you come down, there's a few peoples and like you be [too] shy to sit there and talk and mingle with 'em. Van don't sit around and mingle with people. Ain't because he dislike 'em, it's just the way the man is. Before I got to know Van, I thought he was a tough, hard person, but he not tough, he not hard. When you get to know him, he just like a gentle kitten. He *love* John Lee Hooker."

Their title-track duet from *Never Get Out Of These Blues Alive* thus proved to be one of those little acorns from which mighty oaks were *definitely* to grow. By contrast, some fairly strange mutations grew from the marathon session which produced it. Taking the sixteen-track tapes back into the studio and overdubbing horn sections, vocal groups, Sugarcane Harris's fiddle and anything else he could think of, Ed Michel worked his editing and remixing wizardry and squeezed two more albums from the husk and pulp of those two days in San Francisco: 1973's *Born In Mississippi, Raised In Tennessee* and 1974's monumentally bizarre *Free Beer And Chicken*. The latter album boasts extraordinary sleeve art by San Francisco underground cartoonist Dave Sheridan, a contemporary of Gilbert Shelton and creator of The Fabulous Furry Freak Brothers' buddy Dealer McDope: a river of humanity flows uphill toward the peak of a cloud-wreathed mountain of DeMillean proportions. Standing proudly at its summit is a huge red, green and gold neon sign depicting a stylized chicken leg above the legend *John Lee Hooker: Free Beer And Chicken*. On the back cover, ominously bereft of session credits, the sign is replaced by the gates of heaven itself. In lieu of credits or session details, the cover coyly offers, "JOHN LEE HOOKER, The Boogie King, in a recital of traditional and original favorites, accompanied by a goodly number of veritable, variable and venerable rock heavies." As we say in North London: you can't say fairer than that, can you?

Free Beer And Chicken could, with equal plausibility, be described as a cynical, trendhopping exercise in damage limitation; a ghastly travesty of the essence of a great artist; or an eccentric masterpiece of psychedelic-blues kitsch. There's certainly nothing remotely like it anywhere else in Hooker's catalog: whether this is cause for regret or celebration is a matter of personal taste. Much of *Free Beer And Chicken* finds Hooker delving into the funk. The opening "Make It Funky" heists its groove from James Brown and features Hooker exhorting the object of his af-fections to "walk funky;" "713 Blues" and "714 Blues"—a single per-formance inexplicably listed as two titles—is a danceable jam into which Hooker delays his entry for a full three-and-a-half minutes, at which point his unmistakable guitar elbows authoritatively into the mix; and "Home-work," derived lyrically from a '60s Otis Rush tune and groovalistically from The Meters' New Orleans bump 'n' grind and The Pointer Sisters' then-recent polyrhythm orgy "How Long (Bet You Got A Chick On The Side)." Hooker sounds totally at home with the funk, and in many ways it represented a far more constructive contemporary direction for him than the previous ABC albums' hackneyed hard-rock post-blues. One sim-ply wishes that Michel had given these tracks a funk, rather than rock, mix, in other words: more bass and drums, less rhythm guitar.

On the blues side of the fence, there's a stolid, workmanlike "One Bourbon, One Scotch, One Beer," sung dutifully rather than enthusiasti-cally by Hooker and featuring a highly incongruous synthesizer boinging along with the guitars; a fabulous "Bluebird" which is the most commit-ted performance of the entire album, pitting Hooker's impassioned vocal against Robert Hooker's gorgeous electric piano, Luther Tucker's sting-ing, economical B. B.-alike guitar, and a restrained but eloquent horn-section overdub which gives the track the scale and drama of ABC's Bobby Bland records of the same period. And then there's the frankly bizarre stuff: Hooker's highly traditional reading of the Delta staple "Sit-ting On Top Of The World," performed with his guitar in modal tuning, is gradually overlaid with African percussion, kalimba and Sugarcane Harris in an intriguing experiment that gradually gets totally out of hand.

"Five Long Years" features thunderous, rolling Mark Naftalin piano and a guest vocal from Joe Cocker. At least, Hooker is singing "Five Long Years"; Cocker is singing something else entirely. He doesn't so much sound as if he's on a different session as a different planet. When he sings, *"Everything she does is so premeditated/I get down and be sick,"* you believe him. The album winds up with something called "(You'll Never Amount To Anything If You Don't Go To) Collage (A Fortuitous Con-catenation Of Events)," and if you believe that John Lee Hooker would invent a title like that himself, then maybe we'd better have us a talk. Stitched together from three distinct fragments linked by a cappella horns, it's a strange, parallel-(blues-)world equivalent of the "long medley" which climaxed The Beatles' *Abbey Road*. Both works used adroit studio tricknology to rescue from the bin pieces which could never have stood alone; both served as the closing cuts for the albums on which they appeared; and both served as the finales for the respective artists' careers: or, at least, for specific phases of those careers. The Beatles, after all, carried on as four solo artists, and Hooker . . . well, we shall see.

"Collage" begins with "I Know How To Rock," a brief variation on "Rock Me Baby"—prefaced by Hooker accusing Michel of turning him into a rock singer—shifts into "Nothing But The Best," which sounds like the final moments of a "Boogie With The Hook" out-take, and winds up with a lengthy slow blues entitled "The Scratch," sung by and credited to "J. Cocker," who declaims, *"I couldn't care less if it rains in the studio."* At one point you hear him asking Michel, "Who's paying for the [studio] time?": one sympathizes. Then Hooker sings a single, magisterial verse from "Sally Mae," and it's over.

As was Hooker's stint with ABC and, indeed, his relationship with the mainstream of the music industry. Ed Michel did indeed record Hooker again, albeit in the highly uncharacteristic role of back-up guest star, alongside Cliff Coulter, Jesse Ed Davis, Mel Brown and other stalwarts, on a May '72 Lightnin' Hopkins session cut in L.A. for an indie-label start-up which never quite got off the ground. Ominously, the tapes for the resulting album, *It's A Sin To Be Rich,* languished unmixed in the can,[6] which was pretty much par for Hooker's '70s-and-early-'80s course. For the next decade and a half, John Lee Hooker was sighted only slightly more frequently than Bigfoot and the Loch Ness Monster.

CSM: I know you weren't happy in the '70s and the early '80s, because it's like pulling teeth trying to get you to talk about it, man.
JLH: There's a lot of misery, hatred, disappointment . . . all that. I hate to talk about it . . . but it's there. There's a space in there . . . a lot of them were rough years.
—conversation, 1994

On the face of it, things had been looking good. "After [Hooker] moved to California, as far as his career went, that was one of the best things he ever did," says Robert Hooker. "He just got more popular, more pop-

---

6 It finally emerged in 1992 on the Gitanes Jazz label: Hooker appears, with varying degrees of prominence, on five of the eleven selections, including "The Rehearsal" (*sic*) for the title track. The closing "Candy Kitchen" is as close as these two veteran grandmasters of free-form blues get to a full-on duet.

ular, more popular." Paul Mathis agrees: "He was gettin' bigger'n bigger'n bigger. His records was in the shops, records all over the place."

That much is certainly true. By the early '70s, the "John Lee Hooker" racks in the record stores were filled to bursting point. In addition to *Hooker 'N' Heat* and the ABC stuff, there were a whole slew of Besman reissues from a variety of labels, drawing on both the original Modern and Sensation masters and the out-takes and alternates from the sessions which produced them; plus compilations, released by Chess, Atlantic and others, of moonlight sessions from the same era, and various Vee Jay and Riverside albums. Plus Hooker's material remained current in the repertoires of other artists: Jim Morrison performed "Crawlin' King Snake" on The Doors' *L.A. Woman*, and J. Geils Band were making a show-stopper out of "Serve Me Right To Suffer," as documented on their live album *Full House*. However, it was at this point that Hooker opted for life without a recording contract.

"You know you made 'em money, but you didn't get nothin', just little giblets here and there. No statement. They would never send out a record statement so you know like how much you earned and stuff, y'know? And I give it up. I said, 'Heck, I don't want to do this.' That's the way I was then. You wanted to live, to survive, you couldn't depend on no record company. You couldn't depend on record sales. Six months come without proper accounting, you wouldn't get nothin'. They say they hadn't sold this, didn't do that, and you knowed better. That turned you plumb 'gainst all record companies. I just *quit*."

And although Hooker may have learned to love *Free Beer And Chicken* in retrospect, he certainly didn't like it at the time. "ABC and the rest of 'em was trying to turn me into something that I wasn't. I did it, but that wasn't like John Lee Hooker's hard old stuff, you know. You knew it was me, but with all the other stuff built around it: chorus girls, horns . . ."

"Well," says Charlie Musselwhite, "John's attitude was probably 'If they wan' give me some money to make this record, I'm gonna take it.' "

Abandoning his record deal and declining to seek another one left Hooker no option bar earning all his money on the road, which—then as now—is a singularly hard way to live. "There was a gap in there where I wasn't doin' nothin'. I depended on that because I was sick of record companies. I said, 'Hey, I'm just gonna tour.' I got a name, everybody know me, I can make some money, but there's just a certain amount of money I can make, you know? I couldn't make the big, *big* bucks, but everybody know John Lee Hooker. I could go out there and get booked and bring home some bacon that pay bills and a few dollars to put in the bank."

And barring the odd live album, guest appearance and special project—it was this era which created the legend that, as Robert Christgau put it some years later when reviewing *The Healer*, "Hook will . . . walk anybody into the studio for cash up front"—that was how it remained until the dusk of the '80s. And it didn't involve living large. While Led Zeppelin, The Who, The Rolling Stones and other rock superstars of the time were traveling in private jets, throwing TV sets out of the windows of some of the finest hotels in America and snorting cocaine from groupies' navels, John Lee Hooker led a rather more modest working lifestyle. In November 1972, *Melody Maker* published a snapshot, by the Montreal-based journalist Bill Mann, of a somewhat different existence.

> *You really wouldn't expect John Lee Hooker to stay in the best hotels, and he doesn't. He's in Montreal for the second time in as many months, and the 55-year-old blues master is ensconced in a seven-pound-a-night room in a hotel which sits next to several plusher, more expensive inns. Hooker is taking pills for blood pressure. A month ago, he had to cancel the second week of a highly successful engagement here on doctor's orders and fly back to Oakland. "I got the flu now," he says, "I feel just lousy."*
>
> *The hotel has a nice restaurant, but John Lee is eating out of a grocery bag. He opens a briefcase and meticulously pulls some silverware out of it and sets it on a lamp table. Out of the bag comes a half-loaf of bread and some packaged sandwich meat. His son Robert is watching something on TV across the room. "Don't need to eat out on the town," says John Lee. "This here's plenty good enough for dinner" . . .*

Clearly, there was more to the notion of "living the blues" than simply using the phrase as an album title.

As Bill Mann indicates, Hooker had by this point found himself a Bay Area base of operations. "When I first come out [to California] in 1970, I lived on 13th Street about two years, maybe longer, and then from there I bought a house in Oakland, on Buenaventura. Charlie Musselwhite stayed with me while I was there. He lived with me there for a while, and he would go backward and forward. He had this wife and sometimes they didn't get along too good, you know. And he being a really good friend of mine, he would come stay with me whenever they have a falling out. Then he'd go back. I lived there for a few years, might've been five years, I don't know."

Hooker didn't just "live" in Oakland: he was an active member of the community. In 1973, Bobby Seale, co-founder with Huey P. Newton of The Black Panther Party For Self-Defense, ran for Mayor of Oakland, and Hooker played a benefit concert for his campaign, which yielded a highly respectable showing of over 42,000 votes. Elaine Brown, also a former Chair of the Panthers, was running for the city council on the same ticket: she remembers Hooker's "tremendous sense of humor [and] his commitment to our struggle."[7]

On and off, Robert and Junior stayed with their father in Oakland. It is a period which none of the principals are happy to discuss in any significant detail. "I don't wanna talk about it," Hooker says flatly. "It was concerning the drugs, annuhruh . . . no comment. Let's talk about the good stuff."

Charlie Musselwhite is a little more forthcoming, but not much more. "I know Junior pretty well . . . probably I shouldn't get into that," he says. "He's a good guy, though. John used to drink a bit. I don't think he drinks much at all anymore, maybe a little beer. But he *used* to drink"—he laughs—"and I did too, but not anymore. John remembers me when I was drinkin'. In fact, John used to put me up. I didn't have no place to go, I could stay at his house in Oakland. First he had an apartment in Oakland—and I remember that first place he moved to— and then I think the next move was to a home in Oakland, and Robert and Junior were living there too. And I was living there . . . and we were just having a party." He laughs again. "I think he'd been cutting down [on booze] by that point, and I was not showin' any inclination to cut down. I never saw a bad side to John, but I can imagine that if somebody pushed him, he'd push back. He wouldn't take anything from anybody. He always just wanted to enjoy himself. He liked the ladies and . . . I've heard stories, but they're only hearsay, so I won't go into those. And John's seen me in some predicaments he probably wouldn't tell you about."

"Old Charlie Musselwhite!" chuckles Robert Hooker. "He still playin' the blues?" Answered in the affirmative and informed that Mus-

---

7 Fax to the author, July 3, 1998.

selwhite had said the equivalent of "A lotta stuff went down in that house, and I ain't gonna tell you about it," he laughs even harder. "Oh yeah, man. Yeah. *Whoo-oo. Mm-hm.* Yeah, it did, man. Yup. I stayed with my daddy at the house on Buenaventura for maybe about three years. Then I went back to Detroit, Michigan. I wasn't as bad out with my dad as I was later on back in Detroit. Detroit was really, really my downfall. I was *bad* in California, but *Detroit* was . . . that wicked city, Detroit, Michigan."

Like his brother, Robert had gotten strung out on drugs. Ultimately, Robert found his way out through the church. Junior's been through the church, too; as well as the music business and an entrepreneurial stint running Brother John's Tree Service, but he's still searching. "He's in San Quentin. San Quentin jail, man. He still in that wild life, man. He used to play with my daddy. He made an album . . . life is just too much for him. Yeah. Man, I ain't seen him . . . mm, boy, been a long time since I seen him. See, last time I was out here [in California], about two–three years ago, he was suppose to come out and see me, but he never show up. He was probably 'shamed, you know what I mean? Too 'shamed to come out and see me, you know? See, I tell you, he used to be in church, so it was a letdown. That's probably what it was. But it still got a hold on him. He's strong.

"My brother, he let [John Lee Senior] down, man. He let him down. He was in a different religion to me, but he was in [the church] three-four years, and my daddy was *proud* of him, man. He changed his life, he was workin', got his own business, man, you know? And he just . . . *pssheew.* He let my daddy down, man. Lost his job, his business went under, went back into that old raggedy life . . . and that'll hurt a father, man. I'm glad I'm able to stand, and I'm still standin'. He got one son he can really look to and say I'm proud of, and he can continue sayin' that, because I'm gonna keep on livin' for Jesus, brother, I'm gonna keep on standin'. Man, my brother, he started messin' up probably about the age of fourteen years old. Thirteen, fourteen, somethin' like that. Temptations was there. He just couldn't handle it."

Maude Hooker is rather more indulgent toward her errant eldest son. "Both of the boys used to go out with him every once in a while," she says. "Robert's a good piano player, and he can play organ. He used to play in the basement. Bought him an organ, piano, and put it in the basement. He used to play it, and he learned himself. Nobody taught him anything, he just learned. John Junior was a minister also. He was out there in the world and then he came in and he joined church too. He was really good, too. He could play the guitar and the piano, drums, and he could sing. He could do it all. Bless his heart . . ."

As if looking after two wild young sons while making a living on the road wasn't enough, John Lee Hooker had taken on an even more daunting task. Even after all that had happened during his marriage and the rancorous divorce which terminated it, he reassembled his shattered Detroit family out on the West Coast, flying Maude out to join him and the boys in California. "He sent for all of us to come out here, really, truly," says Maude. "He sent for me and the kids and so we came out here and we just packed up and left Detroit, first myself and the three smaller kids, because Robert and Junior, they was already here. He called and asked did we want to come out here. We came out here and stayed for a while, and then we went back home, packed everything and moved on out here. Then Zakiya, then Diane, so we all moved except Robert. He's still back East with his family."

It was an act of emotional—as well as financial—generosity which staggered observers and participants alike. "That just boggled my mind," remembers Zakiya Hooker. "That's how I realized that he is such a good person. I stayed [in Detroit] for a little while, but my marriage got into dire straits because my husband got strung out on drugs and just couldn't handle himself, so my father told me to come out here. Maude was already here. I've never understood why. I think it's because my father just doesn't hold grudges."

Robert Hooker agrees, big time. "Show you how good of a man he is, how many mens is you gonna find—all right?—that the wife and the husband get divorced, and the man still look out for the divorced wife, like she still his wife? Huh? You see what I'm talkin' about? Bought her a car, and he just looks out for her . . . you ain't gonna find too many men like that. I'm tellin' you, man. That's how good of a man he is. Down-to-earth. Good man. Mm-hm. Yeah."

Not everybody thinks that this was ultimately a great idea. Sometimes Hooker himself regrets his decision, but—as with all the decisions he has taken in his life—he nevertheless stands by it. Paul Mathis is, at best, ambivalent. "He's got this firm belief that charity begins at home," says Hooker's former brother-in-law. "I would go so far as to say that he is a bit *too* generous. Like an old friend of mine told me one time, I was the type of guy go buy a case of wine and a couple bottles of whiskey:

'Have a drink, have a drink, have a drink.' This old fella told me, 'One thing about you, Mathis . . .' I said, 'What's that, my man?' He said, 'You too generous to your friends.' And I thought about that. And then the friends come around: 'Hey, you got anything?' 'No, I ain't got nothing, man. Ain't got no more liquor.' And then there were no more friends. No more affection. You cannot buy love. You cannot manufacture it. And that's what bothers me now. Too much love is given out. It's paid for, but it never comes back. But then, you know, that's John Lee for you, you see. Most people are taking John for granted. It happens, and it bothers me."

Mathis freely acknowledges that not many people would split up with their wife, move 3,000 miles away, and then fly her out and get her a house. "Never, but that's what he done. I think he's kinda seein' that that was a mistake. I think he's finally beginning to see that he shouldn't'a done that. Should'a left 'em stay where they were. He's payin' for love he's not gettin', and that is a *fact*."

"They send him on a lot of guilt trips," says Zakiya. "Horrific guilt trips. I always say to him, 'You shouldn't ever be guilty about anything. You've done more than anybody else would have done.' The more he gives, the more they want, and it's not like they're doing something constructive with it. It's just *I-want-I-want-I-want*. He's bought my mom maybe three or four [cars], and Diane I don't know how many. Her first house . . . she lost it; it caught fire and she took the insurance money and didn't do anything with it, and they foreclosed on the house, so he went and bought her another house. When I moved into this house [in Oakland], he had originally bought this house for my mom, and so she decided that she was gonna go back to Detroit and get married. So she moved out of the house and I moved in. At that time I was still looking for a job, I had gotten on welfare. That's when I got the job with the police department, and I was finally able to get off welfare, thank God. There was trouble keeping the house, because it was just me. There was nobody else; but I'm the only one who's managed to keep anything that he's ever given them. My mom, he bought her this house. She didn't want this one, so when she came back he bought her another house."

"Soon she lost the house," says Hooker. "After a couple, two or three years, she lost the house. That be the partyin' goin' on with the money she had. When I left her, you know, she was a partyin' woman. Blew that right away, couldn't keep up the payments. You know when you got money, everybody around you; they knowed she had a little money then. All her so-called-to-be friends; they ain't no friends." He laughs. "They cleaned her out—*voom!*"

It cannot be repeated too often that while these shenanigans were going on, Hooker was spending most of his time on the road, earning the money to finance all this mess the hard way: one piece at a time. To be precise, he was spending most of his time on the blues circuit. In a 1974 interview with Neff and Connor, Howlin' Wolf's former saxophonist Eddie Shaw provided as crisp and evocative a thumbnail sketch of the way things were blueswise at that time as anyone could possibly desire:

> *A club-owner can tell you. It's not that many traveling blues musi-cians to go around. You got fifteen to twenty good blues artists that got groups working on the road. Freddie King. Albert King. B. B. King. Muddy Waters. Howlin' Wolf. Junior Wells and Buddy Guy. James Cotton. Bo Diddley. John Lee Hooker. Hound Dog Taylor. Willie Dixon, who's just started out traveling again. Luther Allison that's doing fair now. Otis Rush. Jimmy Dawkins. Mighty Joe Young that teams up with Koko Taylor. Jimmy Reed, who's in and out. Johnny Littlejohn. This girl from California—Big Mama Thorn-ton got a pretty big band now. Charlie Musselwhite. Paul Butterfield and his blues band. Shakey Horton's getting him a band together and doing a few gigs now. Lowell Fulson is doing a few things. That's about all I can recall. So from a club-owner's point of view, there's not enough good artists to fill fifty-two weeks—to bring in a winner every week. So clubs use the same artists three or four times a year.*

Which, essentially, meant that a blues star with a solid "name" and a capacity for hard work could make some kind of a living without having to cater to fleeting commercial whims or compete with rock superstars to court the mass-market dollar. The blues circuit was there whether or not there was any kind of "blues boom" going on in the mainstream, which was just as well, because in the mid-'70s there definitely wasn't. By the time Muddy Waters left Chess in 1977 to sign with Columbia via its Blue Sky subsidiary—an upheaval equivalent, in blues terms, to the Eiffel Tower deciding that it was bored with Paris and fancied a spell in Rome instead—you didn't even have to be the six-fingered Hound Dog Taylor to count the number of legit blues guys with major-label record deals on one hand. Muddy was with Columbia; B. B. King and Bobby Bland were still with ABC; Albert King was still on Stax (technically an indie rather than a major label, but regarded as a major for its impressive chart performance and impeccable musical cred) and . . . that was it.

The blues circuit was like some kind of weird parallel universe; or one of those dimensions, a heartbeat away from our own, in which Captain Kirk would get trapped on *Star Trek*,[8] leaving him invisible, inaudible and intangible to his colleagues on the *Enterprise*. A whole community of musicians, many of whom were well known—at least by name and *Greatest Hits*—to a large number of rock fans, existing just around a cultural corner which may as well have been a galaxy away.

The *echt* blues-circuit club was and is Antone's, in Austin, Texas. The joint is way better known than its competitors elsewhere in the U.S., though, because in the late '70s it became the hub of a thriving regional blues scene which nurtured the likes of Stevie Ray Vaughan and his elder brother Jimmie, lead guitarist of The Fabulous Thunderbirds, and which enabled the club to draw on a pool of extraordinarily talented local musicians for its house band. Its founder-proprietor, Cliff Antone, recalls, "In 1975, I was downstairs in my club, and someone told me, 'Hey, phone for you,' and I said, 'Who is it?' and they said, 'John Lee Hooker.' Went upstairs and he said, 'Wuh-wuh-wuh-Antone, I heard you have a nice club down there and man, I really want to come play.' I said, 'Well, look, John Lee, you're welcome any time you want. You got a home long as I got one.' So he came down. I had Luther Tucker, one of the few people who really know how to back him up. There's only one person who knew how to better, and that was Eddie Taylor. That's the missing link. Eddie Taylor, man. Vee Jay Records, man. That was the stuff, man. And John Lee'll tell you, Eddie Taylor was the greatest musician who ever lived. Those were the greatest records John Lee ever made, with Eddie Taylor behind him. Anyhow, the first time I had him up we had Luther Tucker playing with him, and Jimmie Vaughan and all those guys . . . the second time I had Big Walter Horton, the harmonica man who had played with John Lee many times before, Eddie Taylor, and Hubert Sumlin, the Howlin' Wolf guitarist. I got 'em all, and I recorded it all on a mobile unit and I still have the tapes. I've never released 'em yet, but John Lee gave me permission to release 'em. That was '75, '76, those years. Then he would call and say, 'I wanna come to Austin, just visit, take a vacation

---

8 Or, when *Star Trek: The Next Generation* reran that particular gimmick, Lt. Geordi LaForge.

here,' because we were that good of friends, you know? He would come and just spend the week with us. He has lots of friends in Austin, lots of people that really like him. To hear him play the lead guitar with one finger like he does is one of the most awesome things I ever heard in my life, man." For the next thirteen years, Hooker was a regular visitor to Antone's.

Economic pressures brought the blues community even closer together. The performers' paths would cross and recross on club, college and festival gigs, and, not surprisingly, they would hang out together off the bandstand. Despite cutting four albums for Blues Way, Jimmy Reed had fumbled his chance for a '60s comeback, but he was still hanging in there. Hooker has fond, if acerbic, memories of the heavy-drinking Reed, who eventually quit the bottle before dying in his sleep, in Oakland, in 1976.

"He was such a gentleman," Hooker recalls affectionately. "He had a drinking problem, like so many people does, musicians 'specially. It wasn't no disgrace and shame, but he did. So many people strung out on alcohol, dope and everything else. I had bought this car, a brand new Buick. We was workin' out of L.A., me and Eddie Taylor, before[Reed] passed in the early '70s. Might have been '72 or '-3. Anyway, we was on the freeway, and it was a long way between bathrooms. Eddie Taylor was driving, and Jimmy said"—Hooker mimics Reed's squawky speaking voice—" 'Pull over, Eddie, pull over! I gotta pee! I gotta pee!' Eddie said, 'Well Jimmy, ain't got no place to pull over. I can't just stop in the middle of the road, I can't do that.' " As Reed: " 'Now J'—he always called me J—'you better tell Eddie to pull over 'cause I got to pee.' I say, 'Jimmy, when he get a chance he gonna pull over. All these cars right behind us, you can't pull over when there's no place to pull over.' " As Reed—'All right y'all.' He was in the back, me and Eddie was in the front. Nice new car. Eddie did found a place to pull over. 'All right, Jimmy, I'm pullin' over.' " As Reed: " 'It too late now, I done peed.' I say, 'What?!' " As Reed: " 'I done peed in the car!' "

Hooker laughs. "I say, 'Oh, *Lord!* In my new car?! You peed all over the back of the car?!' " As Reed: " 'Yeah, I *told* y'all to pull over, and Eddie wouldn't pull over, he *hard* headed. An' you kept on tellin' Eddie to go! I just peed in the car!' He was drunk! Oh, I got mad, and Eddie got mad. Well, we got to the place, and the next day Eddie took the car to the carwash. They washed it and cleaned it in the back . . . he peed in the car!" He laughs again. "He cleaned it up, but that was somethin' else!"

It's funnier now than it was at the time. Hooker's still laughing now. "Yeah, boy . . . that could happen to anybody. You wanna go so bad and you can only hold it so long. He was drinking all the time, he stay drunk and he could only hold it so long. Even me or you or anybody, you drink that much, you gotta go. But Jimmy: 'I done peed in the car, now y'all can keep goin' now.' Oh, I got so mad, I started cussin'. I said, 'God damn this shit.' I said, 'Shit, he done peed in my damn car.' "

As ever, the irrepressible Buddy Guy has a story to cap that one. "He's like that about *his* car, but he was in Junior [Wells]'s car and got a bucket of chicken, and I wish you could'a seen what he did to Junior's car. I told Junior, 'Don't say nothin' because he don't know.' A year later we goes out to Oakland, and he picks us up, and he tells Junior when we gets to the car, 'T-t-t-t-take your shoes off.' Junior says, 'Do you hear that, Buddy?' I said, 'Hold it, be quiet. He don't know that he was puttin' all them chicken bones and grease in your car.' He says, 'Yes I did, too,' and I saw that expression on his face . . ."

But while Hooker might—albeit gently—tease juniors like Junior or Buddy, he would be profoundly supportive of those to whom he, in his turn, looked up. In *Stormy Monday: The T-Bone Walker Story*,[9] Helen Oakley Dance provides an intensely affecting snapshot of Hooker's sensitivity and concern toward his ailing mentor when both men were double-billed at a Pittsburgh gig in the summer of 1974. T-Bone was to die the following year and he was in considerably less than great shape, but Hooker did his best to take the old master under his wing, placing The Coast To Coast Blues Band at Walker's disposal, encouraging, advising. "John Lee lay propped up on pillows," Dance wrote, "watching baseball on TV. 'This is how I take care of things, Bone,' he explained. 'Plenty, plenty rest. Kenny [Swank]'s in charge of my group and knows what to do. They'll help you, man. Everything will be cool.' "

As things turned out, everything was *not* cool: much of Walker's stagecraft and stamina had deserted him, though his fierce pride had not. In defiance of both Lowell Fulson and Helen Oakley Dance advising him to "do like Hooker and use a chair onstage." T-Bone gave the show his best shot . . . and blew it. Dance describes him attempting to placate the

---

9 Da Capo, 1987, *op cit.*

audience by promising to do better next time, despite Hooker standing in the wings muttering, "Don't apologize, man. Don't open your mouth."

Hooker's professional life at this time was quiet but steady: clubs, colleges, festivals, occasional TV gigs and regular swings through Europe. Which was just as well, because he didn't exactly have the smoothest-running machine in the music business behind him, being booked into different parts of the U.S. by different agents, and his drinking didn't help. It was within this context that Hooker launched, somewhat inauspiciously, one of the key professional relationships of his career: with a fledgling agent booking jazz and blues artists into clubs in Milwaukee, Wisconsin. The young agent's name was Mike Kappus, and to suggest that things began poorly between them would be a major understatement.

"My first experience with John Lee was in the early '70s," says Kappus, "booking him in a club in Milwaukee that I brought national talent into, ranging from rock to jazz—John Hiatt, Cheap Trick, Roger McGuinn, to Eddie Harris, George Benson, Les McCann, Mose Allison, Grover Washington, Rahsaan Roland Kirk, Horace Silver and many more, to Muddy Waters, Howlin' Wolf, Willie Dixon, Freddie King, John Hammond, John Lee Hooker, Sonny Terry & Brownie McGhee—basically anyone currently touring in the blues world at the time. I booked John Lee for a date and called up the day beforehand to see about his travel and how he was coming in. John was completely unaware that he was booked here."

"I said," recalls Hooker, shifting into querulous, mock-pathetic tones, " 'Aw Mike, I just been to the *dentist*. I'm *sorry*.' He said, 'Huh?' I said, 'I just been to the dentist. I can't come to Milwaukee.' "

"So that was my first experience of John: him canceling a date on one day's notice," Kappus continues. "But things did improve after that.

"One of the problems he was having at the time was that there was several people doing business with him and sometimes handling different parts of the country, and they would offer him different jobs, sometimes in conflict with each other, and I'm not sure if anybody was really taking care of co-ordinating it, and so there was a problem. When we first started working with John on a more full-time basis, there were people who didn't want to work with him because he had a checkered past with problems with drinking and not showing up for gigs, which was probably just a matter of this lack of co-ordination. But he stopped drinking: there wasn't any of that kind of problem when I started working with him."

Nevertheless, the "problem" had been an acute one while it lasted.

In 1975, various members of Dr. Feelgood—the definitive British R&B band of the era—had been out on the loose in Los Angeles with Nick Lowe (then on a paid vacation as their roadie, but subsequently to become their producer), and had decided to go check out Hooker, a longtime hero whose "Boom Boom" they had cut on their first album, on stage at the Starwood Hotel. As Tony Moon, the band's biographer, described the occasion:[10]

> At the time, Hooker wasn't exactly the revitalized act he was later to become and, having had a few drinks, turned in a desultory show with a third-rate backing band. So bad, in fact, that he sacked two hapless drummers off the stage during the course of the shambolic set . . . the Feelgood entourage left early, feeling disappointed as a much regarded icon bit the dust . . .

Lowe and the Feelgoods subsequently transformed their memories of that night at the Starwood into a British hit single, "Milk And Alcohol," the title of which referred back to the remedy prescribed to Hooker by another doctor entirely in "It Serve You Right To Suffer." Over a pitiless neo-boogie riff, singer Lee Brilleaux gritted out the lyric Lowe had hastily scribbled on the inside of a cigarette packet:

> White boy in town,
> Big black blues sound
> Night club, I paid in,
> Got a stamp on my skin,
> Main attraction was dead on his feet,
> Black man rhythm with a white boy beat,
> They got him on milk and alcohol . . .
>
> Stayed put, I wanna go,
> Hard work, bad show,
> More liquor, don't help.
> He's gonna die, it breaks my heart . . .

As it happened, it was Lee Brilleaux who predeceased Hooker—passing away from lymphoma in April 1994—but not before cutting a hair-raising

---

10 In *Down By The Jetty: The Dr. Feelgood Story* (Northdown, 1987).

version of "Mad Man Blues" which will forever stand in the front rank of whiteboy Hooker covers.

More flattering snapshots of Hooker's in-concert work around this time are provided by a couple of late-'70s live albums released by the since-collapsed Tomato indie. *Alone*,[11] recorded in 1976, presents in their entirety two forty-minute solo sets performed for a New York college audience, while *The Cream*, cut the following year, finds him working out for a California club crowd with that year's edition of The Coast To Coast Blues Band.

Maybe Hooker was tired when he gave the performance preserved on *Alone*. Maybe he was simply in a particularly reflective mood that night. Or maybe his advancing years were beginning to tell on him, draining him of the ferocious energy displayed only a few years before on the *Hooker 'N' Heat* sessions but providing, by way of compensation, a mastery of emotional nuance and detail dwarfing even the startling degree of empathy already displayed in his previous work. Whatever the reasons may or may not have been, the boogies and up-tempo pieces—what Peter Green would call the "rock and roll" numbers—seemed oddly under-cranked and perfunctory, whereas the slower and more meditative end of Hooker's repertoire blossomed as rarely before.

That repertoire was certainly a familiar one: simultaneously as comfortable as a pair of old shoes and as elegant as a vintage Savile Row suit. Relaxed, chatty and discurvive, Hooker opened with an abbreviated "Maudie" (here retitled "I Miss You So"), slipping expertly out of the groove into free-form guitar and back before moving through the exquisite back-to-back renditions of "Jesse James" and "Dark Room" we checked out earlier, to a scarifying intense and heartfelt "Never Get Out Of These Blues Alive": brooding and monumental, the sound of the soul speaking to itself, an internal dialogue rendered audible. The audience applauds, Hooker snaps the guitar into his open-A tuning, and he launches into "a little thing call" 'Boogie Chillen.' "

When Hooker first cut "Boogie Chillen" for Bernard Besman back in late '48, it was an account of what was happening in that particular "now": indeed, the events in the song seemed to be unfolding before him even as he sang. Here at Hunter College, he seems to be singing in sepia, looking back on a very long time ago, into the vanished world of Henry's Swing Club and Hastings Street—"That's in Detroit," he deadpans—with

---

11 Not to be confused with the Specialty reissue album of the same name.

a mellow nostalgia which ripens and diffuses the buzzsaw immediacy of olden days from the harsh, urgent house-rocking of a young hotshot with stuff to prove into the indulgent playfulness of a doting patriarch bouncing grandchildren on his knee.

Still open-tuned, he moves deep—deep, *deep*—into the eerie modalities of "When My First Wife Left Me." "Give some time to change my keys [retune]," he says, "and I'll get 'Boom Boom' for you." It's a populist rather than aesthetic choice for set-closer, since the song doesn't really happen without a band groove no matter how enthusiastically the audience clap time. For similar reasons, the encore of "One Bourbon, One Scotch, One Beer" fares little better.

The proceedings reopen for the second show with "Feel Good," Hooker's variation on Junior Parker's variation on Hooker's "Boogie Chillen," and "Some People," a homiletic monologue in the tradition of "The World Today" or "This Land is Nobody's Land." Next up: a fine, dramatic reading of "TB Blues" and a slow, hushed saunter through a "Wednesday Evenin'" variant (mistitled "Baby Please Don't Go," and duly credited to Big Joe Williams, though it's more an extended meditation on the lyrical themes of Lowell Fulson's "Reconsider Baby"), which is as structurally loose as it is emotionally taut, and vice versa. An engaging canter through "Bottle Up And Go" (which Hooker introduces as "Mama Killed A Chicken") is marred only by the unmistakable sound of a sparse audience clapping resolutely out of time in an echoey room; it briefly lightens the mood before a clenched, intense diptych of "Hobo Blues" and "Ain't Gonna Be Your Doggie," the later incorporating an unscheduled harmonica intervention from the audience. "How deep and how low can you get," says Hooker through the applause. It isn't a question.

"Sometimes I get to singin' these songs," he tells the audience as he tunes up, "and they reaches me so deep . . . because so many people are living in fear, in misery. They *tortured.* You see people on the street: you think they happy, but they not. Deep down inside, behind closed doors, you just don't know what's goin' on. A lotta times, money don't make you happy . . . if you don't have peace of mind, you have *nuthin'.* If you have health and happiness and peace of mind, and a little money to get by—to survive, I should say—it's a beautiful life. You cannot buy love, you cannot buy happiness . . . it's got to flow into you.

"If it ain't down, it just ain't down," he concludes. And he skips into a light, swinging, mellow-down-easy "Boogie Chillen" (this time retitled

"All Night Long") with the audience clapping even further off the beat than before. The Phantom Harp Player returns for the closing, ultra-slow "Crawlin' King Snake." His interventions are not always totally appropriate.

Alone is living room intimate and back-porch meditative, occasionally to excess; by the same token, *The Cream* flows but sluggishly, though undeniably it has its moments. Backed by the September '77 edition of The Coast To Coast Blues Band—John Garcia (lead guitar), Peter Karnes (harmonica), Ron Thompson (guitar),[12] Mike Milwood (bass) and Larry Martin (drums), plus Charlie Musselwhite and Ken Swank sitting in to respectively spell[13] Karnes and Martin on a tune or two—Hooker coast-to-coasts his way through the set, flying by the seat of his chair. The band seem less an integral part of his music (as were the bands of Howlin' Wolf or Muddy Waters, let alone those of Duke Ellington or James Brown), than simply the backdrop against which Hooker's music—wholly contained by and within him, rather than partially invested in his accompanists—exists.

To "a really good friend of mine who have passed on," the then recently-deceased Elvis Presley—"I hope that wherever he restin' at ease"—Hooker dedicates a fine, measured "Tupelo" ("that was his home town") followed, perhaps as a nod to Presley's debut "That's All Right Mama," by the odd-one-out in a night concentrating mainly on slow blues tunes: a peppily up-tempo rockabilly take on Little Walter's "It Ain't Right." Other fare is rather more familiar—"TB Sheets," "Sugar Mama," around up the usual suspects—and, as deep as some of the performances are, it brings little to the party not already present in the songs' previous recorded incarnations. If we'd been at the club the night *The Cream* was cut, we'd almost certainly have thought the show was fabulous. Since we weren't, we're left with the overwhelming impression of a past master marking time.

In fact, the most fascinating—and, with benefit of 20/20 hindsight, the most revealing—aspect of *The Cream* isn't on the record at all: it's on the cover. We see John Lee seated, suited, hatted, in a booth at some classic American retro diner complete with dinky plate-side jukebox terminal; a half-smile on his face, his left eyelid adroop, contemplating

---

12 Thompson went onto form his own band, a reasonably entertaining sub-Thorogood outfit called Ron Thompson & The Resistors.
13 The author humbly requests his Gentle Reader's indulgence for another wholly unprovoked use of the *Star Trek* Infinitive.

what's in front of him: a majorly calorific-looking vanilla ice-cream sundae topped by a cheekily erect cherry. In one hand he holds, not a cigarette, but a pipe: a token of the influence of his fourth wife, a serene young Canadian named Millie Strom, whom he'd met while working in Vancouver. She had encouraged Hooker to cut back on his drinking; and weaned him off cigarettes. Finally, the pipe went also, and Hooker was off tobacco for good.

"I got married then to Millie," Hooker says fondly. "She got me off cigarettes, and the pipe . . . I would say she saved my life. I say I would've been smoking now. She never could stand the smoke, and she used to keep on about the smoke. I was [living] in Gilroy, and she took my pipes and give 'em to the guy next door. She was a big help to me, I admit that. She wasn't a drinking woman and she wasn't a smoking lady, but she helped me get off all this stuff, so I can appreciate what she did."

"She's very quiet and soft-spoken," says Zakiya Hooker, who remains best friends with Millie Strom to this day. "John was playing up in Canada and he met her. She just appeared. She just came. She was just here! She tells you what she's got to tell you, but in such a soft manner that some people may not take her seriously, and think they can just run over her. She was very good for my father, a very calming influence on him. Of course, she had to contend with the crazed family, because they have the tendency to go into his house and treat it like it was their house."

If some others close to Hooker are to be believed, this was something of an understatement: it is alleged that Maude was in the habit of bustling into the kitchen and rearranging things on the grounds that "they weren't the way John likes them," and Hooker seemed unwilling to remonstrate. The marriage didn't last, but in its place emerged a warm, solid friendship which should be a source of inspiration to all divorced couples. Even now, asked by the *Guardian* where and when he was happiest, Hooker cites the years he spent with Millie.

"[Millie] was real nice," says Charlie Musselwhite. "She and John had a good life together while it was happenin'. She really cared about him."

The Hookers had been living "down in Gilroy, which is a pretty good size, a little country town in California," John Lee remembers, though he is spectacularly vague about exactly how long they were there. "Lived there about five or six years, four or five anyway, give or take three or four," he offers, with magnificent disdain. "I sold that house and . . . what did I do then? I sold that house and bought a house in San Carlos, next door to Redwood City."

"John and Millie lived out in San Carlos," recalls Zakiya. "They were together quite a while." However, it was in San Carlos that the marriage broke down. "We parted," says Hooker, "and got a divorce on friendly terms." With that, there is no disagreement. "[John and Millie] did [part friends]," confirms Zakiya. "When he goes up to Vancouver he doesn't get out without seeing Millie. Millie never remarried. The thing with my daddy is that once you're in his life, you're in his life. There's a certain responsibility. We all have to be responsible for helping each other."

And another long loop in Hooker's life was to close during these years, as presidents—Richard Nixon, Jimmy Carter, Ronald Reagan—came and went and Hooker made his living on the road. The church from which Hooker had walked away in his youth reentered his life, through the unlikely agency of his younger son's wife. "It was always on my mind about church," remembers the Rev. Robert Hooker, "but my wife was in church and I was still livin' that wild life, man. And she told me, 'It's either Jesus or leave me alone.' *Whoah!*" he laughs. " 'Either Jesus or leave me alone'! So I chose Jesus.

"You have to realize, see . . . it's deep. It's very deep. Take me, for example. When I was out there, into the drugs and the liquor and all that, it was like that because I didn't have no power. You know why that was? Because Adam, that first man Adam who disobeyed God—see?—God told him and commanded him don't do something and he did it. God told him the day you do it you gon' *die*, you gon' *surely* die, don't even *touch* it. Awright? And Adam disobeyed God, and because he disobeyed God, that's why you got . . . see, a whole lotta people don't understand this. This is why we have all the sin in the world, because of Adam, he disobeyed God. And by him disobeying God, he let the Devil have power. And the Devil is a wicked spirit, and he's living in men. Living in womens, boys, girls, makin' 'em do wrong. This is why Jesus said, in Saint John the third chapter, 'You must be born again.' See, when you repent and be baptizedinthenameJesusChristbefilledwithholyghost . . . you be born again. And then you got power. See, you got power, man, you got power over the Devil. You could be the worst dope fiend in the world, but when you receive the Holy Ghost, man, they can stand right in front of you and just shoot all they want to. Won't make you do it. See, I'm a witness, man. I used to . . . I just couldn't leave that stuff alone, man. Man, I started . . . *whoo*, I started at . . . you know what? I started at the age of fifteen years old. That was my first experience. I was into dope all the way up to the age of twenty-four years old. I mean, I couldn't stop. I tried! Little spells I tried and I stopped, you know, but I had to go right back to it, because I didn't have no Holy Ghost power. See? I went to clinics: that didn't help me. Wasn't until I found the Lord, man, back in 1977. That's what helped me. It wasn't me!" He laughs again. "It's not me doin' it. It's beautiful, man."

And where Robert went, Maude soon followed.

"Well, she was living in California then. I got into the church in Detroit. She was fightin' it a while. One time I came out to California, man, and I was talkin' to my mother and my sister Zakiya and they went to church with me that night, and both of them got baptized, man. Zakiya, she's into the singin' right now, but my mother, she just kept right on. She's a changed lady, man. *Changed* lady. No bad language no more—all right?—she *changed*, man. She can tell you 'bout the church experience, man, how good it make you feel . . . [singing secular] that's her [Zakiya's] thing, if that's what she wanna do, then *amen*. But me in my house, I'm gonna serve the Lord. Like as far as the dope world . . . I'm not gonna go out there and go back to shootin' dope with him [John Junior]. Or drinkin' my Mohawk vodka and JV scotch and my wine, I'm not goin' back to that. It's a different world. I'm in a different place now."

"You know," says Maude, "[Robert] said that one day he was sittin' down and he saw that him and his wife wasn't gettin' along too good, and he figured that something had to be done. So that he went out that Sunday morning, him and his two kids, and he went to one church, and he didn't like that. He said he went to several churches before he really decided which one he wanted to go to, and when he found the right church, then the Lord put it in his mind that [that] was the true church, and that's where he's been ever since. After he got in it, he started on everybody, you know. 'Come go to church,' you know, 'Mother, come go to church.' And truly I didn't get into church until I came here. I wasn't religious and Johnny wasn't. So [Maude's parents] went to church every now and then, Sunday school, we went to church together sometimes. Diane and Vera used to sing in choir, but it was [a] Baptist choir, John used to have a brother, William, who was a preacher. One father taught him to go to church and the next father taught him how to play the blues. He used to sing jubilee, what you call a group. I guess everybody breaks away from something that they do, one way or another. John Junior was a minister also. He was out there in the world and then he came in and he joined church too.'

Zakiya remembers Maude's conversion in slightly less glowing terms. "Life is like a cycle," she says, "and it must have been a weak cycle for her. [Robert] came out one year. He convinced her, found a church, took her to the church, and the next thing we knew she was hellfire and brimstone." But Zakiya was baptized also. "Mm-hm." So clearly it didn't take. "It took. Probably took better with me than it did with them, but in their eyes it certainly didn't take. That's a thing that never ceases to amaze me: how religion can dictate what you should and shouldn't do. I can't imagine God being a vengeful God that's gonna, when you die, burn you forever and ever in some pit fire."

Which is pretty much the way John Lee Hooker sometimes puts it himself. He has his own skeptical takes on Maude's religious fervor. "Now she's a church lady, sanctified and saved. Call herself 'saved' now; she ain't saved. Well, you know, the money I give her, that's devil money. She don't want my records in the house, she shouldn't want the money in her house. That come from bars: people knockin' out windows, kickin' down doors, gettin' drunk. That's where that money come from."

Elsewhere, the big screen was beckoning—well, after a fashion. Comics John Belushi and Dan Aykroyd had been working up their "Blues Brothers" R&B pastiche as part of the top-ranking *Saturday Night Live* TV show and, in cahoots with director John Landis, were in the process of parlaying a series of TV skits into a feature-length movie. They'd already roped in Aretha Franklin, Ray Charles, Cab Calloway and James Brown when John Lee Hooker came on board. "John [Belushi] and his partner Dan Aykroyd was really into the blues," says Hooker. "This woman who was managing me then, Sandy Getz, she contacted them, and I knowed 'em pretty good." According to a story in *Rolling Stone*, they had first met when Hooker was playing at the Lone Star. Belushi, star of *Saturday Night Live*, knew the club's owner, Mort Cooperman, and asked him to arrange a meeting. The story goes that when Hooker was introduced to the extremely famous Belushi, Hooker—not usually to be found in front of a TV screen on Saturday evening—first responded "Who?" when told "John Belushi," as if he hadn't heard correctly. He then lifted his shades to get a better look and said, "You one of them Muppets?"

In the movie, Hooker appears as "Street Slim," immaculate in tan leather jacket and dashingly scarved white safari hat, performing "Boom Boom" on Maxwell Street with various members of Muddy Waters' band as Belushi and Aykroyd track down Matt Murphy at Aretha Franklin's ghetto diner, the Soul Food Cafe. "At that time [being in the movie] helped my career. More people had seen me. They still show that. It sells really well. They got a cassette of that, a video. It was shown all over the world, so that was good, *good* publicity for me. I knowed all those people, too."

Hooker remained in occasional contact with Aykroyd "for a good while" after the movie was made, but he had no idea of just how much dope Belushi was hoovering up behind the scenes. "I really wasn't aware of it until it really happened. He kept it kinda private. He was really gettin' up high, too. His success came so easy and so quick. Mine came hard and it's gonna go hard, 'cause I ain't gonna let go of it."

Scoring Hooker's appearance in the *Blues Brothers* movie was a coup for Sandy Getz, especially since her client is heard again later in the movie: Hooker's Vee Jay remake of "Boogie Chillen" plays in the background as the Blues Brothers Band rolls up for its ill-fated gig at Bob's Country Bunker. However, she missed one important bet: the movie's soundtrack album ended up selling millions, but while most of the movie's major musical set-pieces were featured, both of Hooker's tunes were omitted.[14]

Hooker's next movie experience came five years later, and it was another mixed blessing. This time, he performed with the great harp guy Sonny Terry, plus pianist Bobby Scott and guitarists Roy Gaines and Paul Jackson Jr. on "Don't Make Me No Never Mind (Slow Drag)," a number composed by Gaines, James Ingram and Quincy Jones for the soundtrack of Steven Spielberg's adaptation of Alice Walker's *The Color Purple*, of which Jones was a co-producer. The tune is heard in the scene depicting the Grand Opening of Harpo's jook joint—you know, the bit where Oprah Winfrey punches Rae Dawn Chong practically into the next county—and it's sufficiently compelling for the viewer to end up concentrating more closely on Hooker's magisterial vocal than on the dialogue spouted by the actors in the foreground. However, not only do the musicians remain invisible throughout the scene, but the names of the singers and musicians, including Hooker's, are omitted from the lengthy end credits. That rankled.

"I was heard but I wasn't seen and then they didn't have my name

---

14   In March '91, Hooker received a *Blues Brothers* royalty check for $13.

up," Hooker fumes. "That was *cold*. I felt I was as important as was anybody in the movie. Why couldn't [producer and musical director Quincy Jones] have put my name up there? I thought I was as big a star as any of them in there. People knowed me when they heard my voice. [Steven Spielberg] did a good job. I likeded that movie, but it was kinda sad. That was the first time I knowed Whoopi Goldberg. She's in everything now: *Star Trek*, she's in all sorts of things. *The Blues Brothers*, I'm on the screen, I got credits, that's cool. But this movie, they didn't even have my name up there, nothin'. I was kinda let down. That was kinda disgusting to me."

Between the making of *The Blues Brothers* and *The Color Purple*, your correspondent met Hooker for the first time. The great man was in London during the summer of '82 to play a dream-ticket triple-bill show, with B. B. King and Bobby Bland, at what was then the Hammersmith Odeon. On a dull, overcast Hammersmith noon, Hooker was propped up in a hotel bed wearing a black satin shirt over a sky-blue undershirt. He paid tribute once more to Alan Wilson: "He was *the man*. He was *the person*. He could play *anything*, and after he dropped out that band never was the same. He knowed my music like a book. He were really outstanding."

He talked about his then-current plans and activities: "What I'm doin' now is . . . I haven't been with a record company in a long, long time; but I just recorded a brand-new album. What we goin' to do is find a company to lease the master to. It's a really good album. We planned it really good, all new stuff on there. My partner, he's in Vancouver, Canada—you probably heard'a Vancouver . . . and he sent out a lotta letters to a lotta companies an' he gotta lotta respond. We lookin' to un*load* this album on some company, and it shouldn't be hard to do. Everybody know who John Lee Hooker is: everybody know what I do. It's the same kind of thing, but it's uptempo. It's a modern sound . . ."

He described his musical tastes: "Awwww . . . soul I even hate to talk about, y'know? I don't put it down but it ain't my kind of music, but if kids like it that's okay with me. I listen to mainly blues and I like some of the hard *good* rock. I likes *solid* rock, sump'n with a good beat to it. I like the up-tempo stuff, but it got to have a *feelin'*, ain't got to be just a bunch of noise. And I likes some good jazz . . . but the blues is my bag. That's the only music that I *love*."

And he announced, in plain but eloquent language, his personal credo: "Others have changed. Me, no. I ain't changed. I don't wanna change. I *could* change. I could go into disco . . . I can play it, but I don't wanna play it. I don't *feel* it. I got one cut on the new record where I did it just to try it out, called 'I'm jealous.' It's got a disco beat to it. I did it 'cause we finished recording an' we run out of the things to do on it and so we just jammed it out. Maybe it could be somethin' big, y'know, but I'm so into the blues. I don't care who change, I don't care who go for the big money, I'm gonna do what I like an' what I feel. I *feel* what I do.

"An' I'm doin' really good. I ain't hurtin' for money. I got that. A *lot*. I done invest my money in real estate. I got about five homes in the States. I could retire and never do it no more, but I love it too much. This is my life, y'know . . . Things I like to do when I'm not workin': I love baseball, that's my hobby, and cars are my hobby. I just got me the new Mercedes. You know the 360SL? I got a new one for '82, it's one of the *best* cars made. That's what I like in life: cars, baseball and I like *ladies*"— he chuckled loudly—"but I guess everybody do."

Your correspondent's piece[15] concluded, "The phone rings. Hooker is informed that he is about to be photographed and hops spryly out of bed. He zips up his pants, buttons his shirt, claps his hat onto his head. He says his health is real good these days, it's just that he gets awful tired sometimes."

As it happened, that Vancouver-cut album with the "disco" tune didn't get "a lotta respond" from the major record companies. *Jealous* wasn't released for another four years, and then only by the tiny-verging-on-invisible Pausa label.[16] A richly hued portrait of Hooker, painted by Donna Cline from a photo by Millie Strom, glared from the cover. Inside, Hooker and a Coast To Coast line-up, by then including Mike Osborn and Deacon Jones, worked out on nine tunes, garnished with an extra track, the churchy "We'll Meet Again," recorded near Hooker's new home in Redwood City by a later edition of the band which omitted Osborn but included bassist Jim Guyett and drummer Bowen Brown.

Produced by Hooker himself in a rare foray into the studio control room, *Jealous* was an impressive stab at contemporizing and updating the fundamental Hooker sound without excessive dilution or compromise,

---

15 The article in question appeared in *New Musical Express* for June 5, 1982, and was reprinted in my collection *Shots From The Hip* (Penguin, 1991). This has been a gratuitous and unabashed plug.
16 It reappeared in 1998, reissued by Pointblank and thereby entering the "official" Hooker canon.

backburnering concessions to the hard-rock audience in favor of steeping his signature deep blues and rocking boogies in simmering vats of thick, steamy *funk de luxe*. "Boogie Woman" is one of the grooviest variations extant on the staple Hooker motif, with Deacon Jones and Mike Osborn jamming prototype versions of some of the organ and guitar licks which later became part of the textbook finale to Hooker's live shows. "I Didn't Know," credited to Chester "Howlin' Wolf" Burnett, is primo Vee Jay-style shuffleware played with funk accents. The sensuous simmer of Jones Hammond lends the slow blue items, especially the deeply moody update of "When My First Wife Left Me," a richly satisfying ambience, somewhere between a nightclub and a church. The two versions of "Ninety Days" definitely fall, albeit with catlike agility, into the hard-core boogaloo bag. And that title track turned out to be not so much "disco" as "Got My Mojo Workin'" reincarnated as hustling, hard-charging double-time funk, driven by a steel-thumbed bass riff, supercharged with blasting brass, and generally dead on the double-bump.

Jealous was a very cool record indeed, and its release created few waves whatsoever beyond the precincts of Planet Blues, whose denizens duly acknowledged its merits with a W. C. Handy Award and A Best Traditional Blues Grammy nomination. If it had been distributed, marketed and promoted by a major record company (or even a savvier indie), and if the late-'80s blues-power wave headed by Stevie Ray Vaughan and Robert Cray had already attained critical mass, *Jealous* would have had a more than fair chance of reaching the outside world. Nevertheless, neither of those conditions was in place. However ready the record was, Hooker's business operation, the state of the market and the mind-set of the music business were nowhere near prepared. Nevertheless, the future was just around the bend.

The principal pointers to that future were concealed in the small print on the cover. The "Tour Direction" credit line for The Rosebud Agency was a testament to the steady growth in strength and closeness that had, over the years, taken place in the relationship between Hooker and Mike Kappus.

"When I started The Rosebud Agency," Kappus recalls, "John was one of the first people I called on, or actually, Sandy Getz, acting as his manager at the time. I made a deal to represent John for east of Colorado where she handled west of Colorado directly herself. I'm not sure if it was her or him or whatever, but there were a few problems with John Lee and his manager canceling dates. I turned in my resignation, which evolved into his firing his manager and hiring me exclusively as his agent. I made it very clear that in order to keep his reputation strong, that couldn't happen. Once he made a commitment . . . he could make any number of commitments he wants to, one every five years or two hundred a year, as long as they were kept. While we handled many management tasks for John over the years I didn't [then] see a need for him to hire formal management, and declined a few times when offered. His publishing problems were being looked after by a lawyer he trusted completely, and he had no real active label deal or interest in one."

"Mr. Kappus have did more for me than any agent I ever had, and I had quite a few of 'em," says Hooker. "I never had a lot of managers. I had one, maybe two, but they weren't *strong* as this man. He is a very *strong* young man. He don't back down. Maybe him being that strong, a lot of people don't like him because they can't tear down that fence around him, tear down that fence around his acts. So there's a lot of people don't like Mike. You can understand that, because Mike don't let them intimidate him. They learn that when they come to me, I'll send 'em *to* him 'cause I know that if he say yes, it's gon' be something on my behalf that's going to help me. He not gon' be intimidated by them. A lot of [managers] would intimidate they artist, double-cross they artist, to get something from the artist that he don't know about, to get as few extra bucks in they pocket. He didn't do that. I got full confidence in him. Full, complete confidence. I got everything right in his lap, and I can sleep at night. Me and him have a little disagreement sometimes, but we gets that worked out. He have worked so *hard* for me, more than any other agent or manager have. I took [Rosebud] as family, the whole shootin' match. They takes care of the artist. I was with Mike when I was scufflin': we stuck by each other. He was scufflin', I was scufflin'. We got poor together, now we just about got rich together."

And *Jealous* also carried a warm, eloquent liner-note written by a fellow-resident of the Bay Area and stalwart pillar of the local music scene: a long-term fan turned new personal friend. It read: "John Lee Hooker is a supreme force in American popular music. Listen to Jimi Hendrix's 'Blues Child' [sic],[17] listen to Van Morrison's phrasing, listen to nature's beat: it's keeping time with John's heart, foot and fingers.

---

[17] Presumably a reference to the long "blues" version of "Voodoo Chile" (as opposed to the more familiar acid-funk take) on Hendrix's *Electric Ladyland* (1968).

Boogie within and boogie without, but boogie till you shake off all your worries. John Lee is an ocean of inspiration."

It was signed, "Carlos Santana, March 17, 1986."

Tijuana-born, blues-marinated and Bay Area–based, Carlos Santana had been playing—and, most important, thinking and feeling in terms of—World Music way before the term was codified, let alone banalized. His eponymous groups, showcasing his rich, sweet, sustain-drenched lead guitar, had been fusing urban blues, percussion-heavy *salsa* and transcendently modal jazz since the late '60s, and had gone national—and international—with a bravura performance which had been a major highlight of the *Woodstock* festival and resultant movie. And he was a John Lee Hooker fan, big time: a devout admirer of man and music.

I met [Hooker] a long time ago, in '69 in New Jersey, at the Capitol Theater [Santana recalled in a 1991 interview.][18] I didn't get to meet him again until '84, when he invited me to play with him at the Blues Festival in San Francisco, and we actually jammed together. From then on he started calling a lot, and when he'd be in town I'd go to see him, or he'd come to see me.

I admire him, he's another caliber, another standard. He's one of a kind. He's very original. He doesn't sound like anybody. The only person who sounds like him is Ali Farka Touré, or Jimi Hendrix when he did "Voodoo Chile" . . . John Lee is more earthy. He definitely fits in the category of Supreme Universal Music, 'cause when he moans, everybody understands what he's talking about. You don't have to understand English. A Buddhist monk, or people in Jerusalem or Russia, can understand what he means.

He made me realize I have to feel absolutely and completely what I feel before I play it. Some people, like Ornette Coleman, would say, "If I hear something I won't play that, I'll play anything but." That works for some musicians, but for me I have to feel it completely before I play it. With John Lee you hear the note before he hits it on the guitar. It's like you can hear his hand before it actually hits the note. Jimi Hendrix was like that, but I think it's 'cause he learned it from John Lee. Some people, the emotions are so strong . . . he doesn't play loud, but it's loud when it comes out.

---

18 Said Interview by Paul Trynka: unedited transcripts supplied by, and appearing courtesy of, Mr. Trynka.

*It disarms you, it gives you chills . . . he's a very raw, naked person.
There's no bullshit, nothing fancy, no fancy chords. It's just as raw
as you can be.*

*That's why he always has young girls around, he's got a young
beautiful woman next to him, and they're always grabbing his hands
and rubbing them and feeding him candy . . .*

*He invited me to his house, and I brought him one of my guitars,
and I had this cassette and I said, "John, I have this song . . ."*

Around the time Hooker was releasing *Jealous*, Santana had taken a
movie gig, accepting a commission to compose the incidental music for
La Bamba, film-maker Taylor Hackford's biopic of Ritchie Valens, the
legendary Chicano rocker of the '50s. Not surprisingly, Santana's score
was somewhat overshadowed by the uncanny re-creations of Valens's
classic records, performed by Los Lobos, to which the movie's star, Lou
Diamond Phillips, mimed so energetically; and by the exuberance and
fidelity to detail with which Eddie Cochran, Buddy Holly and Jackie Wilson were impersonated by, respectively, Brian Setzer (formerly of The
Stray Cats), Marshall Crenshaw and Howard Huntsberry. These performances, plus Bo Diddley's thunderous remake of his epochal "Who Do You
Love," produced by Willie Dixon himself, dominated *La Bamba*'s big-
selling soundtrack album, and Santana's original score didn't get a lookin. Nevertheless, there was one piece of music composed for the movie
which was to have a second and far more spectacular lease of life. It came
from a scene in *La Bamba* where Ritchie, played by Phillips, and his
macho blowhard elder brother (Esai Morales) take a trip to Tijuana and
visit a shaman.

> *It was called "Carandero" [continues Carlos Santana]. I sneaked it
> in there when Ritchie Valens goes to Tijuana to see this healer. And
> I played it for [Hooker] and he started singing it right on the spot.
> He said, "Yeah, blues is the healer," and he started singing it as
> soon as I played the tape.*
>
> *And I said, "Man, I think we should record this."*

14. Hey, You Just Gotta Make the Change: Iron John and the Healing Game

Well, the blues is a healer, you know. When you're feeling
down and out and low, when your friends, your woman,
your wife, have kind of leaned from you, put on some
good blues and take that off your mind. Listen to it. It heals.
Blues heals all the world. The music heals the world, and
keeps the world going.
—John Lee Hooker, 1993

"Me and Carlos got together," remembers John Lee Hooker. "He's a man who say, 'You heal a lot of people.' I say, 'What d'you mean?' He say, 'Yeah man, you heal 'em with your voice, and your music, man, is so deep. Well, I got a bunch of music, and it's got no fancy chords, but it's so beautiful.' I say, 'Yeah?' He say, 'We gonna do this thing. What do you think about we name this "The Healer"?' I say, 'What?' He say, 'We name this thing "The Healer."' 'That sound good,' I said, 'but why?' He say, 'Because you do heal a lot of people, all over the world. People sit there, they listen to you, you soothe they mind, you takes they trouble away from 'em. You says things in your lyrics that really heal they problems. We'll name this "The Healer," The blues have healed you, it'll heal me.' I say, 'Yeah, that's a good idea.' We worked on it, me and him and Roy Rogers, my producer . . . I said, 'Carlos?' He said, 'What?' I said, 'Man, I feel a groove. Let's do this.'

"And the first take was it."

The renaissance of John Lee Hooker's career was essentially launched with a single song. "The Healer," Hooker's epochal collaboration with Carlos Santana, begins quietly, almost tentatively. Santana's rhythm guitar sketches in eight bars' worth of a couple of minor chords topped with a decidedly Hookeresque bass-string run. Then the rest of the band enter, like a coooool breeze on a hot night, with a rhapsodic rhumba beguilingly blending organic and synthetic instrumentation: the distinction not so much collapsed as artfully blurred. The effect is not unlike viewing a tropical sunset under the influence of psychedelics, or scanning a panoramic snapshot thereof which has been subtly color-enhanced in PhotoShop. It is a well-nigh perfect fusion of the "real" and the "imagined."

Apart from Hooker and Santana themselves, the musicians who showed up on April 25, 1988 for that date at The Record Plant in Sausalito—the studio walls no doubt still juddering from the psychic aftershock of the sessions for Fleetwood Mac's *Rumours*—included some of Santana's most treasured associates. Armando Peraza, a much-decorated veteran of Latin music not significantly younger than Hooker himself, manned the congas. Ndugu Chancler was behind the drum kit, keeping things anchored but simmering. Chepito Areas played the galvanic, metallic timbales fills which—*rakka-takka-takka-takka*-tang!—slash through the song every time the ambient temperature needs raising a notch, providing "The Healer" with what is effectively—after Hooker's vocal and Carlos Santana's lead guitar—the song's third voice. And the date's secret hero was keyboard guy Chester Thompson: not only responsible for the shimmering, limpid pools of virtual Fender-Rhodes electric piano which define the song's tonal areas but, through the wonders of MIDI synth technology, also supplying the "bass" and the "flute."

The mood builds through three choruses, Santana's guitar probing further and deeper as the tension mounts, Hooker foreshadowing his vocal entry with a subterranean moan which suggests that this tranquil landscape is about to erupt. On the fourth, he delivers the message: *"blues is the healer, all over the world."* In a series of simple, declamatory lines— *"my woman left me, the blues healed me/healed me, it can heal you"*— extended and recombined through his most mesmerizing incantatory repetitions, he lays out the text of his sermon of redemption and forgiveness. Then he commands *"Carlos! Heal me!"* and the firestorm of Santana's guitar, no longer dreamy and euphoric and sultry but volume—cranked and textured with a wah-wah pedal, sizzles across the skies of the soundscape like the most majestic and terrible forces of nature unleashed: awesome and beautiful, searing and cauterizing.

In a voice which rolls and rumbles like thunder, the shaman is calling down the lightning.

As fire from heaven crackles around him, the healer is going to work. His wounds bear witness to his ability to heal ours.

Way back, John, you said "Blues is the healer." The bluesman's job is to take other people's pain on his shoulders and make them feel better.

That's what I been doin'. That's what the Healer do. I take your pain, and I put it on my shoulders, and I carry it along.

Then who heals the Healer, John? Who carries your pain?

Who heal the Healer? God Jehovah. That man heal your faith in him. God.

Extraordinary as it may seem, "The Healer" was cut in one single live take, with nothing overdubbed but Hooker's moan in the third chorus. "When I did 'The Healer,' the first take was *it*," Hooker insists proudly. "Live with the band. We did two, but we decided that the first take was the best one." Santana remembers it slightly differently: they started a second take but partway through someone said something along the lines of, "Nahhhh, why bother?" They figured they already had it nailed. They were right.

Even the video for "The Healer" maintained the same philosophy of combining simplicity, spontaneity, elegance and economy of both expression and expenditure. Shot in ominous sepia, it depicted Hooker and Santana miming the song in a small room draped with hessian backdrops, climaxing in slo-mo footage of Hooker ending a performance with The Coast To Coast Blues Band in his newly-trademarked pose of arms raised in benediction over his wildly applauding audience.

The mighty oak that was *The Healer* sprouted from a very small acorn indeed. Or—to scratch-mix the metaphors—it arose, in a sort of phoenix-ish manner, from the ashes of the debacle that was the launch of *Jealous*: a fine album that, essentially, went nowhere. "*The Healer* project originated with John Lee mentioning to me that Van Morrison was interested in producing a record on him," states Mike Kappus. "I met with Van and I think Van was caught a little offguard about it and at the time just said, 'I don't want to speak about it; I have other people that do my business for me.' He was just very nervous. It was at a show, but he was clearly uncomfortable with talking business at the time. It just didn't work out from a scheduling standpoint, but luckily, it did later on with *Mr. Lucky*. In the meantime, Carlos Santana had been showing up at a lot of John's shows and playing with John and [he] just loved being around John, and he called up and said, 'I just want to tell you that if

John Lee's going to be doing any recording in the near future, I'd really like to be a part of it.'

"And George Thorogood, who'd been a friend of John's for a long time and who was a client of mine at the time, had put a John Lee Hooker song on basically every record, and *he* called up and mentioned also that if there was any project for John Lee, he'd really like to be a part of it. With this in mind, with several of his disciples saying that they'd like to be part of a project, I thought that we should go ahead and make a record, work with these people who'd offered their services, maybe check with a few other likely subjects, people who'd been friends of John's. I'd been around and I'd seen their affection for John, [so] I got the idea for an album consisting of tracks with these and other friends as well as tracks featuring John in a more natural setting than he'd been heard in for many years. I thought, 'Let's not just line up a bunch of stars, but do a record that pays tribute from the people that have been influenced by him and who are good friends. And let's combine that with some of the more acoustic-oriented music that the purists had not heard for years, and produce it in a straightforward manner that wasn't going after any particular trend.' "

Like the guy in the baseball movie said, if you build it they will come. Kappus built it. And they came: a loving pilgrimage wearing down the sidewalk outside the Russian Hill studio in San Francisco. "Everybody wanted to be part of John Lee Hooker. I didn't know that I was that big, or that important. I really didn't. Carlos Santana, Bonnie Raitt, George Thorogood, Keith Richards," Hooker reels off their names with affection and pride, "all the people who loves me. But I was doin' my thing whether they come to my rescue or not. I was still on the move, on the rise, and they wanted to be there, part of me. They wanted to be part of me. Not for the money, but the love they had for me. They knew I was a real person and a real bluesman. They didn't need money, they wanted my *love*. They wanted to work with me, and that's why we teamed up."

Let us take for granted that none of the guests needed any convincing. To a man—and, in one extremely important case—to a woman, they were volunteers all, and all that was required was a compatible itinerary: no posting master-tapes back and forth for these guys. The only person who needed to be talked into anything was Hooker himself. "I said, 'Hey, I'll just hang out, go out and play and come back home, but I won't make no records,' " Hooker says, "so[Mike Kappus] talked me into going into the studio, recording with all these different stars like Carlos and Bonnie Raitt, you know. Mike got these people lined up and we went in the studio, and I had no faith in none of it. I thought [the idea] was a bunch of baloney, but it took off *like wildfire*. I was all over the place, and my price went sky-high. Forty, fifty, a hundred thousand dollars a night. 'The Healer' and 'I'm In The Mood' started that fire. Then I seen the light at the tunnel. And I had [Mike] to thank for it. I was just gonna go round, play . . . I had some money in the bank, I admit, a few houses I could survive on, sell if I wanted to sell, some pretty nice cars . . . but nothin' like I got now. *Nothin'*. But that *Healer* set the world on fire, "In The Mood" come back strong . . . it just go on and on, y'know? So I say, 'Oh gosh, somebody be happy on this, y'know?' And we got some good money."

Mr. Morrison having left the building, Kappus was faced with the task of finding an appropriate substitute producer. Said individual turned out to be just around the metaphorical corner. "Needing a like-minded helper who knew music better, could be trusted by John Lee and who shared my concepts," Kappus recalls succinctly, "I got John Lee's permission to hire Roy Rogers as producer."

Roy Rogers was no stranger: anything but. The hobbitesque Bay Area slidemeister had recently completed a four-year term with The Coast To Coast Blues Band, serving as featured soloist, musical director and general right-hand-man, even collecting the money at the end of the night's work. He also had a debut solo album, *Chops Not Chaps*, under his studded belt, bearing a brief but cordial liner-note above Hooker's shaky signature. It read: "*When he's not working on his own he's in my band. When I hear Roy play his slide guitar—he makes me feel good. He's got it . . . and it's got to come out!*"

"John is not open to drastic change," Kappus observes, "and it is hard for him to trust other people, having been through as many problems as he had. I felt that Roy, even though he had no production experience that I knew of, could be somebody that John could trust, and he understood the concept of the record." As it happened, the guitarist had produced *Chops Not Chaps* himself, cutting it at Russian Hill, and was therefore familiar with the studio and its personnel. But most of all: he knew and loved Hooker, and was known and loved *by* Hooker, and he knew the music inside out, both as a scholar and as a player. "He's a very easygoing person," Hooker says of Rogers, "and he knows how to work with me. He knows I don't wanna be *pushed*. He lays back and lets me do things my way. I'm the kind of person, you start to push and I get kinda *frantic*. You let me do it my way and it come out right every time. Roy know that." The fact that Rogers wasn't an auteurist superstar producer with an attitude problem was another bonus: he was under no illusions about whose session it was, or who the star was. He knew that he was there to make a John Lee Hooker record, not a Roy Rogers record with John Lee Hooker on vocals. Bottom line: he was a *fan*.

Guess who controls your destiny? *Fans*.
—Ice-T wising up sucker MCs, "You Played Yourself"

Ultimately, what paid off for Hooker was precisely that: his destiny was controlled by fans. However, in this context, that meant fans of the caliber of Rogers and Kappus. They both shared one central premise: that Hooker was not simply a musical ingredient to be tossed into somebody else's pot as part of somebody else's dish; but that Hooker's music, served up *au naturel*, was a more than adequate main course in its own right. To this end, the triumvirate of Hooker, Kappus and Rogers formed Blue Rose, an independent production company. Kappus brought the business experience, the overall vision, the muscle and the hustle: Rogers the hands-on musical expertise. And Hooker, quite simply, brought Hooker. From now on, Hooker would no longer be at the mercy of the whims and vagaries of record companies. Blue Rose would make Hooker's records and sell them onto the labels as completed packages.

The strategy was straightforward, purposeful and impeccably laid back. Every few months, whenever any of the bonded collaborators swung within grabbing distance of San Francisco, Blue Rose would book an afternoon at Russian Hill. Guests were canvassed as to what song(s) they would like to cut with Hooker. Each session would concentrate on just a few songs, occasionally freshly written but mostly culled from Hooker's capacious back catalog; the backup musicians would be hand-picked to suit the guest, and the songs. And no session would run over three hours. Drummer Scott Mathews, who played several sessions for *The Healer* and its immediate successors, summarized Hooker's recording method as going into the studio, asking, "Where the food?," eating, announcing, "I'm tired, let's do this quick and get out," doing three takes, and going home. Hooker doesn't dispute this.

"Yeah, I'm nervous," he admits. "I ain't just sayin' that. The studio make me nervous. I go in there an' do what I'm gon' do an' get out. I don't wanna sit around there goin' over an' over this an' over an' over that. I have my boys down, I go in there, get me a little sandwich, eat it and say, 'Let's go to it.' The more you do it, the weaker your voice will get, you know. I do it when my voice is *strong*. I get in there, get the guys together and say, '*Hey*, y'all, let's do it.' Two takes and I got it. I do two, maybe three songs, that's the most. Pack up and get outta there."

Roy Rogers didn't have a problem with any of that. "It seemed like a natural thing," he says. "I didn't have any trepidation about doing it. I was so close to John and always kept a very close friendship with John, so it really was the three of us that put our heads together: Mike Kappus as executive producer and me being producer in the studio with the music. It was a question of putting together the right song and the appropriate person, and that decision was never made from a commercial standpoint. It was always: what's gonna work? What's gonna be fun? Who is John comfortable with?

"My work is in setting it up: the pre-production is really the thing. You don't want to work too hard when you're in there, not with John Lee; otherwise you might as well shoot yourself in the foot. You want to make it as comfortable [as possible], then either the magic happens, or it doesn't. We go for that magic, you know. All along I said, 'Boss, if you're happy, I'm happy.' " Clearly, the days of locking Hooker into a studio with a bunch of musicians for hours or days on end, and not letting him out before there was a double-album's worth of material in the can, were long gone. This was record-making at a pace which suited Hooker. And, bit by bit, the reels of tape mounted up on Kappus's shelf.

The process began, unassumingly enough, as soon as the debris of New Year's Day 1987 had been cleared away from the streets of San Francisco. On January 2, Hooker and Rogers, plus Hooker's longtime friend Charlie Musselwhite and his bag of harps, checked into Russian Hill to cut with Canned Heat. Their personnel had been unstable since the death of Bob "The Bear" Hite some years before, and sometimes they'd resembled a drummer with a revolving door more than a band, but the trio who made the date were authentic enough: the Canned Heat credentials of guitarist Henry Vestine, bassist Larry Taylor and drummer Fito De La Parra—all of whom had been on the team for the epochal *Boogie With Canned Heat* album back in 1968—were second to none.

They cut four tracks that day: three for the shelf and one for *The Healer*. The track that mattered was "Cuttin' Out" which, as "I'm

Leavin'," dated back to the Vee Jay days. With Hooker, Vestine and Rogers all rocking on guitars and Musselwhite blowing his brains out on harp, it ought to have been cookin', and it was. Five weeks later Hooker and Rogers were back for a solo acoustic session which yielded no less than eight tracks. Two of these, "No Substitute" and "Rockin' Chair," ended up on *The Healer*; two more, "Deep Blue Sea" and a severely Hookerized country song, "Hittin' The Bottle," the latter uncharacteristically performed in the key of C, remained in storage, until they were included on *Chill Out*. In April, they cut again: this time with Charlie Musselwhite and a rhythm section including Scott Mathews on drums. This session generated four tracks: "That's Alright" appeared on *The Healer*, another, the slow blues "Thought I Heard" was slipped into *Boom Boom*. But the track which actually sparked the session—a remake of "Burnin' Hell," previously cut in the early Detroit days with Eddie Burns and on the *Hooker 'N' Heat* session with Alan Wilson, remains unissued to this day.

So how was it for Musselwhite to cut with Hooker? "Well, I'd get a call, and it would be like no rehearsal. Just into the studio and 'What key is this?' and then John would just start everybody off. Listen and follow. For *The Healer*, which Roy Rogers was producing, he said, 'Listen, we're gonna do "Burnin' Hell," ' and he sent me a copy of the original version that John did, and we get in the studio and I remember thinkin', 'John's really gonna do this tune, huh? Just like this? On the record?' " He laughs. "So I listened to the original recording with Eddie Burns playin' and we cut it, but it weren't no relation to the original at all." Not surprising: it was actually a different tune, "Heaven And Hell," which, according to Mike Kappus, "has the same groove as 'Burnin' Hell' but with different lyrics." "There was another tune that John and I did together," continues Musselwhite, "just the two of us, that was really deep, but according to Roy it was just too heavy, so they didn't want to put it on the record, but it might get released some other time. After all these years of knowing John, and knowing him as well as I have, I'm still in awe of him when I'm around him. I just have so much respect for him. I can never look at him or think of him as just a *buddy*. He's just a great human being, you know, who plays the deepest blues that ever was. No deeper was ever played."

And so it went, through the rest of 1987 and into 1988. Rosebud's star client Robert Cray came in bringing his bass player Richard Cousins—with Mathews back behind the drum kit—to recut "Baby Lee," with its tricky-funky stop-start backbeat. " 'Baby Lee'? I told Robert I wanted to do it just like the old one," says Hooker. "He listened to the record, the old one, before we did it. And we went in and what a job he did on it." A richly soulful singer and a sparkling guitarist, Cray was an army brat, born in Georgia but raised on the move in various bits of Europe and the U.S., who'd cut his musical teeth on a classic '60s mix of Beatles, Hendrix and soul, leavened by the fertile loam of blues-rich family record collections. He'd launched the first baby-band edition of The Robert Cray Band in the Pacific Northwest during the '70s, working his butt off around the club and college circuit, and by the second half of the '80s he'd even become a pop star, scaling the upper reaches of the album charts with *Strong Persuader* and getting his handsome mug onto the cover of *Rolling Stone.*

"The first time I heard John Lee Hooker must have been in the mid-'60s," says Cray. "My aunt was a big blues fan: she had Jimmy Reed and John Lee Hooker . . . what really amazed me was the deepness of his voice and his style. It wasn't until later on that I really started to understand and listen properly, 'cause that first time I was around twelve years old. Then later on when I was seventeen I started listening some more, and the thing I really liked about John Lee Hooker was how many bars he played—like 13, 14, 15 bars! It was a type of music where there aren't any rules—the man is saying what he wants to say, and I enjoy that to this day. When he's playing with other musicians he always tries never to do the same thing twice, so you got to stay on your toes. You got to be listening to him all the time. He'll change the words, he'll change the bars: he'll play 13, 14, 15 bars! So when he makes a change you really got to be on your toes, otherwise you'll be left behind.

"The first time I worked with John was probably in the late '70s [with] a younger version of The Robert Cray Band that was playing at the University of Montana. We'd never met John Lee before, but we were booked together and we had to be his backing band on the spur of the moment. He joined us on the bandstand and sat on a chair and he just started playing. We didn't know what songs he was gonna play, and we didn't know what key anything was in, we didn't know what or where the changes were, so it was quite a challenge. The whole band was just thoroughly confused and disappointed and were going, 'Who the hell is this guy and what is he doing?' I just laughed and said, 'This is one of the greats, the original guys.' And he was so friendly, so nice afterwards. We said, 'John, how many bars are there in your songs?' And he said, 'Hey, you just gotta make the change . . .'

"When you record with John, the thing that I notice the most is that you won't spend a lot of time in the studio. You follow John in what he does. And you're gonna get it in one or two takes and that's about it. John's gonna get up, put his hat on, and go, 'Thank you, fellas.' "

Like Cray, George Thorogood was a circuit veteran who'd taken his bare-knuckle boogie and bullyboy slide—a four-alarm chili concocted from freshly minced chunks of Hound Dog Taylor, Elmore James, Chuck Berry, Bo Diddley, and not a little John Lee Hooker—from Delaware bars to the satellite stage of Live Aid, where he brought on Albert Collins to play to half of the planet as *his* guest. Thorogood's first, eponymous album, released by Rounder Records in 1977, carried an amusing period-piece liner-note in which the label formally apologizes for sullying its folkie purity with such a vulgar release, and featured a masterstroke conflation of Hooker's "House Rent Boogie" and "One Bourbon, One Scotch, One Beer" into a single narrative. "He told me he was gonna do that," recalls Hooker, "and I said, 'Okay, go ahead.' " Thorogood's commercial breakthrough album, 1982's *Bad To The Bone*, had included an insanely speeded-up "New Boogie Chillen"; a copy of the gold-album award hangs on Hooker's wall. Factor in his band's agency deal with Rosebud, and it should therefore come as no great surprise that Thorogood contributed to *The Healer*, weighing in for a duo session remaking the venerable "Sally Mae," the B-side of "Boogie Chillen," originally cut for Hooker's very first session with Bernard Besman in Detroit at the dawn of Hooker's recording career, from before Thorogood was born.

Most of the guest participants in *The Healer* were friends of Hooker's before the sessions. After the sessions, they all were. "I've known Carlos Santana a long time, Bonnie Raitt a *real* long time," Hooker mused, "I didn't know Los Lobos,[1] but they sure know my music." That they did. Having led a double life as a traditional acoustic band playing Mexican folk music in restaurants and at parties—if you got married in East L.A. between the mid-'70s and the early '80, Los Lobos probably played your wedding—and taking their hard-edged, lyrical electric roots-rock into Hollywood's post-punk club scene, they found themselves as incongruous chart-toppers with the uncanny re-creations of Ritchie Valens's music which they cut for Taylor Hackford's Valens biopic *La Bamba*—the movie for which Carlos Santana had created the score which generated

1 As a matter of fact, he had met the band—albeit briefly—when they found they were both gigging in Florida.

the musical background for "The Healer"; wheels within wheels, synchronicity-a-go-go. Their showcase was "Think Twice Before You Go," still unfortunately credited to Al Smith, which had originally seen the light of day on Hooker's debut ABC release, 1967's *Urban Blues*. Hooker sang live with the guitars and rhythm section; Rogers overdubbing Steve Berlin's rumbling baritone sax and David Hidalgo's exuberant accordion immediately afterward.

And then, of course, there was Bonnie Raitt: "My baby!" as Hooker affectionately dubs her. In a lengthy career more fraught with ups and downs than most, the former Boston folkie, Delta blues maven, Mellow Mafia singer-songwriter and virtuoso slide-slinger has been platinum and she's been nowhere, and along the way she's been everywhere in between. When she and Hooker cut "I'm In The Mood," she was definitely "in between." She was in between record deals: dumped by Warner Bros, who'd been her home base since 1971, but not yet picked up by Capitol, with whom she confounded the conventional wisdom of the music business by scoring the biggest successes of her career.

"Bonnie had been doin' it herself on her shows, which I didn't know until she told me, and she had it down so *pat*. She said, 'I'm gonna do that'n with you, "I'm In The Mood." If I ain't gonna do "I'm In The Mood" I ain't gonna do nothin'.' I said, 'Okay, Bonnie, you do it.' She said, 'Yeah, I do it all the time.' So we didn't change anything. We just sat down. It was just tremendous, is all I can tell you. She's such a beautiful person, and I love her like I don't know what."

"It was love at first sight," says Raitt of her first encounter with Hooker, back in the early '70s. "I never really played with him until we did the duet, because we weren't really in a situation where it was possible. There wasn't a lot of jamming at blues festivals, and I always admired him so much it would have been intimidating." This time, she wasn't intimidated at all. The basic quartet—Hooker, Raitt, Rogers and Mathews, no bass player—didn't quite get it in one take, but, as Raitt says, it was "pretty close. We just went over the structure of the song, and we really didn't know what it was going to come out like.

"It was really one of the most erotically charged afternoons of my life. He just wore me out. The lights were low and we were just *looking* at each other and neither of us knew how to end it. We just got into it. He had his sunglasses on and I was just staring at him, head to head, sitting on chairs. At the end of it I just said, 'I need a towel!'

"It was incredible. If I was still smoking I would have had a cigarette afterwards."

In the song's video, Raitt makes an entry worthy of Clint Eastwood. The first you see of her is a pair of cowboy-booted, bejeaned legs striding purposefully through the dust: a Blueswoman With No Name toting a Stratocaster, rather than a Winchester, swinging at her side. The way the album is sequenced, "I'm In The Mood" segues in straight from Santana's tranced-out dreamscape: the second half of a classic one-two punch. Hooker's guitar sets the tone: grinding, strident, jagged, almost deliberately jarring the listener out of the memory of Santana's rhapsodic groove. Then Mathews's drums kick in, Rogers's guitar starts to chugging and Hooker begins to sing, paced at every line by Raitt's lean, mean slide. By the end of the track, with Hooker and Raitt calling each other's love down across that steady groove, we just about *all* need a towel. It's not surprising that the pair of them won a "Best Blues Recording" Grammy for that one.

April '88 was *hot*. Just three weeks after the session with Raitt, Hooker went to Sausalito to meet up with Santana and cut "The Healer" itself, the song after which the entire project would be titled. With that in the can, the album was done. And then the fun began.

I have no idea where my life began,
But I am a mighty Iron Man
—John Lee Hooker in the title role of Pete Townshend's *Iron Man*

"I can remember when I heard ['The Healer']," says Taj Mahal. "That blew my *mind*! Santana brought that Latin thing to it, and it didn't take everybody away from the feel. I thought it was just *tremendous*. I read this article where Carlos was talkin' about how he was tryin' to approach the music, and then he saw [the great bluesmen] and they played their inside out, as opposed to their outside in. He watched B. B. King, Albert King, Albert Collins, Freddy King and John Lee Hooker . . . the great musicians played this emotional stuff that he wanted to commit to his music, and when you hear Carlos you know that he's a totally emotional player. That record was one of the most beautiful things that ever happened. I couldn't hear nothin' for *weeks* because of that record . . ."

Ludicrous as it may seem in retrospect, launching *The Healer* turned out to be a hard sell. Mike Kappus had to pull out all the stops to cut a halfway decent deal and get the album into the stores. "I wanted to finish the album first and then sell it to a company," he says, "because John Lee didn't really have a high profile at all with record companies. He'd sold very small numbers here and there [and] there wasn't a market for John Lee Hooker. I wanted to make a package that represented something special first, because if I went in [cold] with John Lee Hooker, there wouldn't be anything there for him. There was such a prejudice about how many records John Lee Hooker could sell, or how many records a seventy-year-old man singing the blues could sell, regardless of who the guests were.

"At the time there were [specialist] blues labels that would have been interested in signing John, but the money would be small and the pro-motional budget wouldn't be there, and I really had a belief that this record could make a major impact. As it turned out, even with Robert Cray, Carlos Santana, Bonnie Raitt and Los Lobos, record companies were still reluctant to part with any real monies for this, and it took a year to get anybody to sign a deal for a reasonable fee."

It's an attitude with which Taj Mahal, for one, is rather too familiar. "It's like managers in the music business who get this idea that there's only so many people who're gonna buy the records based on their ina-bility to make sure that everybody gets to hear it, right? They go, 'Blues equals 25,000 copies.' No, no, no. There's a bigger audience than that in the world. I know this myself 'cause I seen 'em. There's a *huge* audience, but they won't do anything 'cause it's gonna cost 'em something. How can you have a music that comes from the results of people dealing with coming to the West and trying to make this thing work, and it's all over the place, but you want to limit it to 25,000 people? Yet you'll spend a whole lotta money on some people playing an odd and weird and crazy version of that stuff that doesn't make any sense, that doesn't pull any energy, that doesn't complete any circles, that doesn't make people's lives better, that doesn't give them any kind of high-level connection to the universe as it exists? To me, it's crazy. Given an opportunity, given tools . . . *you have to use them.*"

In the case of *The Healer*, synchronicity once again ended up playing a part. A small label named Chameleon Records had recently acquired the wandering Vee Jay catalog and already had a full-scale reissue pro-gram of all of Hooker's Vee Jay albums—plus a best-of compilation drawn therefrom—in the works. The acquisition of the U.S. rights for

Hooker's all-star new album—for what Kappus describes as "still a very, very low fee"—therefore seemed like a fairly sensible investment, though the label passed on the deal the first time Kappus approached them. At a time when the financial break-even threshold for a conventional blues album was deemed to be approximately 10,000 copies, a deal like the one with Chameleon—predicated on potential sales of 50,000—was indeed a pretty good one by Planet Blues standards. Outside the U.S., the brass ring was grabbed by Silvertone, a feisty start-up masterminded by Andrew Lauder, a visionary A&R guy previously associated with the U.K. wing of United Artists in their '70s heyday, and subsequently with the ranking U.K. indie Demon Records, though they didn't release the album in the U.S.

"The record took off and started doing very well in England," says Kappus. VH-1, MTV's "adult" subsidiary, was playing the hell out of Hooker and Santana's video for "The Healer" single, but Chameleon were still not working the record to Kappus's satisfaction. "We ended up doing a great deal of the work out of [Rosebud's] offices, contacting the major record stores and seeing if they had the product, if they knew about the product, and so on. They didn't realize that Carlos Santana and Los Lobos and Bonnie Raitt and Robert Cray were on it, and when they did and they started playing the record in the stores, it became one of the top records for in-store play. More and more people started picking up on this, and we'd stay on top of the record stores and found out that they were running out of stock, remind the record company that they were running out of stock and getting them reorders. Otherwise it could have been completely forgotten. It could have been passed over.

"But we stayed on the case, and we got over 50,000 record sales in America, and once again we were contacting all the record stores and finding out that they were selling out. We contacted the record company, and they were wary of printing anymore records, because by that point they had recouped their investment. They were wary of printing up a bunch of records that wouldn't sell."

So, in his own unique manner, Kappus started leaning on Chameleon. "He *did!*" says Hooker, laughing, "Yeah! He had to *force* 'em! They weren't goin' to reorder because they was too tight with money! The record was like a house afire, was *burnin'*, and he had to force 'em, [or] else they wouldn't'a did that. People came by, couldn't get it. He forced 'em to do that. He is a good businessman."

Kappus himself puts it rather more prosaically. "I *convinced*[2] them that if they don't sell this month, they will sell next month, or the month after. Get 'em out there and they will sell. It sold well over 500,000 sales in America, but all the way down the line, even as the label were selling the records, they still didn't have faith that this was a valuable, viable project."

"I knew that someday, the public . . . the blues is gonna wake them up," says Hooker. "They gonna *have* to put the blues on TV and pop stations, because the people is *hungry* for the blues, all over the world. They want to see it on TV, they want to hear it on radio, but they haven't been doin' it. I'm *kinda* surprised, but I'm *not* surprised. I figured it was comin', but I figured I'd never be here to see it, but now it's happenin'. The time was right. The public was ready. I opened the door for a lot of blues singers. I brought the blues back. I really jumped it up sky high. I broke the barrier. Buddy Guy's career took off right after that. I opened the door for a lot of blues singers . . . or so they tell me. I didn't say that."

Well, yes, he did, but Hooker can be forgiven a little *faux*-modest coyness. After all, as Kappus points out, "*The Healer* was a great success, and of course after the first album many companies were not only open to the prospect of signing John Lee, but to the prospect of signing other blues artists. *The Healer* had a major impact on the entire genre of roots music. The door had been cracking open for years for roots music with George Thorogood and Stevie Ray Vaughan and Robert Cray, but here was an older artist, one of the originators, actually having success on the level of a contemporary rock star."

The lesson was not lost on the music industry. Silvertone signed up Buddy Guy, who'd been kicking around the business without a decent record deal for almost as long as Hooker had, and *Damn Right I Got The Blues*, the first album under the new deal, complete with guest appearances by the likes of Jeff Beck, Eric Clapton and Mark Knopfler, became a palpable hit. Virgin Records snapped up the U.S. rights to Hooker's next album (though European rights remained with Silvertone for one more album before the Virgin deal went worldwide) and inaugurated a dedicated blues-'n'-roots label called pointblank, the roster of which included Albert Collins, John Hammond, Pop Staples and—by the time of 1992's *Boom Boom*—Hooker himself.

---

2 Italics mine.

And lo, he looked about him and saw that it was good. Hooker will still deliver, at the drop of a decorated Homburg, his standard diatribes concerning record companies and the terrible things they do to artists in general and John Lee Hooker in particular, but at least now he has something to cite as a contrast. "Record companies do [cheat]. They'll do that. They're crooked, record companies. Virgin don't do that. [pointblank boss] John Wooler ain't got his name on nothin', but he don't need to. I ain't sayin' they ain't crooked, but they pretty good with me. They very honest with me. I gets *lots* and *lots* of money from Virgin Records. I got good management, [and] good people work for Virgin. They do's it legal, that's what I like about 'em. They ain't got a bad reputation as a cutthroat. Most record companies now have just about *got* to go straight now, because the artists have got wise and smart. They don't deal with that stuff anymore. They used to do the blues singers in really bad when they first started up, but now? It's pretty well hip now. Pretty well straight. You don't get as much of that now as you did back then in the '50s and '60s. There's still some of that goin' on, don't get me wrong, but they were more *out* with it then. Now everybody wised up and smarter. We got lawyers, we got managers, which we didn't have then, accountants, we got good *everything*. We got all of this which I didn't have when I was young and didn't know how to do all of this. It's good for them too, so the record companies won't get a bad reputation, you know?"

The prelude to the success of *The Healer* had included a couple more fortuitous concatenations of events.[3] One was a guest appearance with The Rolling Stones at the Atlantic City show on the 1989 tour: Hooker took stage front—standing up for once—for a furious, storming assault on "Boogie Chillen," while Keith Richards, Ron Wood, Bill Wyman and fellow-guest Eric Clapton lurked back by the amps with their guitars and let him get on with it. The other was rather more elaborate, somewhat more significant, and set another jewel into the crown of Hooker's hat: slotting into place one more jigsaw-piece of the modern-day Hooker mythology.

During the mid-'80s, Pete Townshend had opted, as part of his post-Who therapy and general redefinition of self, to serve a spell as an editor at Faber & Faber, one of London's oldest and most prestigious publishing houses. As well as publishing *Horse's Neck*, his own first book of short

---

3 I am, of course, indebted to Ed Michel for the coining of this felicitous phrase.

stories, and commissioning a series of extremely fine volumes,[4] he conceived the idea of a musical adaptation of one of the company's bread-and-butter properties, *The Iron Man*, an ecological fable by Poet Laureate Ted Hughes. The title character is, as Townshend puts it in his notes, "a large self-maintaining robot programd to destroy any machinery or system that threatens man": simultaneously a symbol of earth—if soil is the planet's flesh, then iron ore is its bones—and, as a "made" thing, of man's interaction with his world. As far as Townshend was concerned, there was only one choice of "actor" for a character so heavily weighted with symbolism: John Lee Hooker.

"I wanted a primordial voice," writes Townshend.[5] "The voice from R&B that I remember first being disturbed by was Howlin' Wolf, but JLH's voice is less that of a macho monster, more of a dark, frail masculine soul. He evokes something whale-like in a way, a spirit that is thrashing powerfully beneath the surface, but in grave danger from the world and his own restrained anger and vengefulness. Ted Hughes's Iron Giant in the story has no history; we must project it onto the story for ourselves. Hughes invites us to ponder with him: 'Where had he come from, nobody knows.' The first time I heard the blues by JLH that's how I felt—where does this come from? It was so familiar to me, so resonant, and yet so obviously not of my experience or society. Could I have been *remembering*?"

"The Iron Man" had been one of Hooker's nicknames back in Detroit: the honorific bestowed on him by his friends to acknowledge his powers of stamina and endurance during those long years of working in steel mills by day and playing in bars by night. Now he was The Iron Man once more: not just to his friends, but to the world.

The character has two songs to sing in Townshend's musical: "Over The Top," in which the Iron Man, smashed to pieces in a fall from a clifftop, faces the task of rebuilding and reconstructing himself; and "I Eat Heavy Metal" wherein, restored to full metal health and prowling the countryside for sustenance, he takes on all the military equipment deployed against him. A demo tape arrived on Hooker's doorstep in late '88; listening to it, he found himself initially nonplussed. Naturally, he recalled Townshend and The Who from '60s days in London—"Yeah! They was *loud!* He's deaf, y' know!"—but this kind of music was a very

---

4 Including one by the present author.
5 In a fax to the author, December 1997.

different proposition from his memories of the brash young bashers of yore.

"When Pete Townshend asked me to do it I laughed at him," Hooker confesses " 'Iron Man? Gargling gasoline? What do you mean by this? That ain't me. That ain't the blues.' But he just said to me, 'If anyone can do it, you can.' "

Pete Townshend has fond memories of the session. "It was completely natural. It was tricky to get used to the fact that his young blond girlfriend was younger and prettier than any I had known, but despite his crisp suit, elegant hat and sharp demeanor, there was humility. He couldn't read music or text, and learned each line parrot-fashion. He said it wasn't blues, but he could feel it nonetheless. It was an affirmation for me to sense that he felt at home with what I was doing because I know how deeply everything I do is rooted in his own work."

Eventually released a month or two in advance of *The Healer, The Iron Man* served notice that, no matter how familiar the world might feel it was with John Lee Hooker, the old master was still capable of coming up with a surprise or two. The songs, and the title, soon attached themselves to Hooker, so it was just as well that he liked the songs—"['Over The Top'] is such a pretty song, and that 'I Eat Heavy Metal' sounds good"—even though recording them was extraordinarily difficult for him. "This was a very rough day in the studio," remembers Mike Kappus. "The words and phrases were completely out of John Lee's vocabulary and even with on-the-spot coaching, Pete ended up just having John speak most of the words, later using a synclavier to make them sound sung."

Needless to say, *The Healer* received *major* good press. Two exceptions stand out, for vastly different reasons. The first has all the tragi-slapstick appeal of full-tilt farce: a review of the album by Bay Area rare record dealer Frank Scott, in his Downhome Music Catalogue, fumed, "what a bunch of self-indulgent crap by producer Roy Rogers . . . this record says nothing about John Lee Hooker's music but a whole lot about the producer's fantasies. Coupled with a cover that looks like something from a *Nightmare On Elm Street*, we have a record that is an insult to a great artist."

Anything which elicits that kind of chicken-brained response from a blues purist just *has* to be wonderful (he shouldn't have joined if he can't take a joke). The second was rather less easily dismissed. Robert Christgau, the "Dean Of American Rock Critics," unchallenged master of the single-para album review and possessor of a wit sufficiently arid to turn the Atlantic Ocean into the Gobi Desert, drastically misread the situation as he dryly opined in his syndicated column,

> *Pushing one hundred thirty now, Hook will still walk anybody into the studio for cash up front. Though the pickings have been getting leaner, here anybody includes Carlos Santana, George Thorogood, Bonnie Raitt, Robert Cray, Canned Heat and Los Lobos, most of whom commit crimes against his ageless essence which tone up the proceedings considerably. And for the purist market, the product concludes with four solo stomps. B+*

There were inevitable down-sides to *The Healer*'s success, and to Hooker's newly elevated status. One was a flooding of the album market by cheapjack reissues and compilation albums issued by record companies who weren't overly conscientious about royalty payments. The other is a feeling among some of the old Planet Blues posse, that John Lee Hooker had somehow passed beyond their reach and left them down in the bottom.

In the back room of his club in Austin, Texas, one night in 1992, Cliff Antone is thumping a table and working himself up into a rage. "Nowadays [Hooker's] management has come between people like me and him, and that is something I hate very much. His management is under the philosophy that they need to make him the most money possible, and they have no regard for friendships like mine and his. It's not John Lee; it's his management and booking agent that are *so hard-core* that they're only concerned with *how much money* they can make. Now maybe that's the way to be, but if that was the case then I wouldn't be here, and he wouldn't be there either. You're takin' him away from the club atmosphere. This is family. They're going to book him here this month at a rock club, a reggae club, a punk club because we can't pay ten thousand dollars for one night."

Yeah, but Cliff, if John's regular price is fifteen thousand dollars, then you're getting a third off . . .

"That's only because no one else would pay that much down here. He knows it's wrong. There's no way around it. This is serious bullshit, man. I stood by him when no one wanted him. So if those people that can draw don't play at the club anymore, then it makes it that much harder to keep the club going. They have to give back . . . there's no other clubs like this, maybe one or two out in the country, but not many. He's got to help me keep this going. It's not like I'm making a big piece of money doing this. We're strugglin' to keep the doors open. We're doin' a benefit just to pay our taxes. It's a serious problem. It always happens, too. They did this with Robert Cray. The people that made him, as soon as he was big, they took him away, you see? They don't give nothin' back. Their only concern is money. Well, is that what it's all about? How much money can he have? How much money can he use? Is that all there is to life? Should I turn this into a college disco and make ten times more money? I worked with him for seventeen years and now, because of The Rosebud Agency and their philosophy, it's either pay ten thousand dollars or you can't have him. That's what success has done, and it needs to be noted—in my opinion. It shouldn't be overlooked if the truth is to be known about this. Success isn't all it's made out to be, if you turn your back on the people that helped you. Didn't he call me? Didn't I stand by him all these years?"

This argument cuts way little ice with Mike Kappus. Still behind his desk at Rosebud long after his employees have gone home for the evening, Kappus sighs deeply. "Oh. That's a unique case. There's a circuit of bars [that JLH used to play] but everybody else understands and appreciates the fact that John has had success and they know perfectly well . . . actually, most clubs don't call for John anymore, because they understand that he's not going to be playing clubs, but those that do will say, 'I gotta ask, I'm sure I can't afford it, but how much is John Lee getting these days?' We tell 'em, and they say, 'It's a shame, we'd love to have him back, but I understand that it can't work.' The fact is that maybe it's harder for people that deal strictly with blues to understand something like that, because they're not used to quick changes in an artist's popularity in the blues world, and the same goes for the jazz world. Generally, there's a gradual change over a long period of time.

"We actually did run through this with a major blues festival, too, where they were contacting us and not making a very quick decision about whether they wanted to spend the money for John Lee, but they started contacting us as *The Healer* was at maybe 100,000 sales, and John Lee's price was above what it had been prior, but the next time they called it was at 200,000 sales, so in the time between the two calls it had already sold more than any other blues artist in America had sold in any given year for the last ten years, so obviously there's going to be a slight price increase. By the time they finally decided they definitely wanted to move, every time they would call back, they left such a large space in their pondering whether or not to pay the new high price for John Lee Hooker, it did go up. The price doesn't stay the same when, since the last conversation, you've sold more records than you have in the preceding ten years. The price does tend to change, and that caught at least this one place by surprise. Most people understood this. They look at the charts; they turn on VH-1 and they saw John Lee on there all the time; they saw John Lee on an awful lot of magazines . . . they realized that this wasn't just an interesting coincidence, and now for [the extra] five thousand dollars he'll draw so many more people.

"Well, there's business people around who know that if you draw a lot more people, you're worth a little bit more money. We're primarily reacting to price, and the highest prices that we get for John generally are those that are offered to us by people trying to convince us to take a date, or percentages that are earned by the actual sales on the door: we've actually made a guarantee of a lower amount. Frequently, the new ground is set by the commercial performance, or by somebody trying to convince us to take a date. In the blues world or the jazz world, career movements upward are generally much more gradual, and those that aren't thinking in terms of what happens in the world of rock, in that kind of realm that John is in—his pop sales, he's in the pop charts and everything—those people understand that if you sell ten times as many records as you've ever sold before—John's probably sold ten times as many records on *The Healer* as he'd sold in the preceding ten years all combined—that's certainly going to have an effect."

Furthermore, Kappus points out, Hooker has played the tiny Sweetwater Club in Mill Valley (capacity 125, jam packed) more times than any other venue during their entire association: it's simply that he likes the vibe there and gets on well with the owner. "This is only one clear example among many," Kappus asserts, "which would counter Antone's claims, including an endless list of benefits and other events in which John Lee gives back to friends and the less fortunate at little or no compensation to himself . . . or his representatives."

Meanwhile, as *The Healer* went through the roof—or what passes for the roof on Planet Blues—Hooker was continuing his version of Bob Dylan's "Never Ending Tour": the Never Ending Recording Session. Hooker is never per se working on an album: by the same token, he is never *not* working on an album. Sessions went down whenever they needed to go down: some toward Hooker's own albums, and some toward the outside projects for which Hooker was increasingly in demand.

One such was Roy Rogers's lovely take on Robert Johnson's "Terraplane Blues"—a Rogers/Hooker duet with the former playing exquisite Johnson-style guitar and the latter supplying equally immaculate Hooker-style vocals—which appeared on *Slidewinder*, Rogers's second solo album. Another was a rather more ambitious project: Hooker's first full-scale movie soundtrack. No *Blues Brothers* or *Color Purple*–style cameo appearances, but the full-on real deal.

In movie-crit terms, *The Hot Spot* was a chunk of botched Texas noir, in which some promising ingredients—Dennis Hopper as director, legendary pulpmeister Charles Williams's novel *Hell Hath No Fury* as source material—were counterweighted by a poor script and a charisma-bypassed leading-man performance by *Miami Vice* alumnus Don Johnson. The score, on the other hand, was an absolute gem, which is cast-iron guaranteed to outlast the film. The man in charge was Jack Nitzsche[6] (co-composer of "Needles And Pins," former cohort of Phil Spector, The Rolling Stones, Neil Young and collaborator with Ry Cooder on the stunning blues-noir scores for *Performance* and *Blue Collar*) who opted for a semi-improvised blues soundtrack, and assembled a dream-team to perform it. On drums was legendary studio musician Earl Palmer, who'd played Little Richard's New Orleans sessions in the '50s and been on Phil Spector's Wrecking Crew team in the '60s. (More controversially, Palmer had—by his own account, anyway—worked key Motown sessions in the '60s, with himself and Carole Kaye, on drums and bass, creating and performing parts generally ascribed to the famed Detroit rhythm section of Benny Benjamin and James Jamerson. However, *that* particular can of worms is best not opened here.)

On bass was Tim Drummond, another known associate of Neil Young and a hardened studio veteran; but the most startling item on his CV was a tour of duty with James Brown, which included playing to black GIs in Vietnam: about as funky a credit as any groove-crazed white boy could desire. On acoustic guitar and vocals was Taj Mahal. John Lee Hooker and Roy Rogers appeared as themselves. But Nitzsche's master-stroke was drafting Miles Davis as featured soloist, taking what would essentially have been, in any conventional blues ensemble, the harmonica player's role. And, no matter who the harp player might have been—Charlie Musselwhite, Junior Wells, the resurrected ghosts of Little Walter or Sonny Boy Williamson, *anybody*—it would still have been a deluxe,

---

6 No relation to the philosopher of almost the same name.

all-star version of the standard blues jam. With Miles on board instead, it became something else entirely: a haunting collection of ominous moans, bump-'n'-grind boogies and slow shuffles which enabled Hooker to prove that he didn't need words—apart from disconnected phrases like "*so sad*" and "*it ain't right*"—to sing the deepest and most emotionally complex blues; Miles to demonstrate that he was as much at home in Hooker's menacing dreamscape as in any of the myriad territories he explored during his long and extraordinary career; and Taj to recycle his beloved "Wild Ox Moan." Plus the rocking "Bank Robbery" was utterly unique in the annals of contemporary music. After all, where the hell else can you hear Miles Davis do the boogie?

Amazingly enough, this startlingly sensuous and intimate music wasn't *quite* as live as it sounds. During the three-day session, Hooker, Rogers, Taj and the rhythm section cut for two days, and on the third day Miles came in and overdubbed his stuff.

"For all the raw and rudimentary type of sound that he has, John is a consummate professional," says Taj Mahal. The pleasure with which he recalls the *Hot Spot* date is utterly self-evident. "He is himself and he plays it the way he plays it. The guys that played on *The Hot Spot* . . . all of us love John Lee. The day that Miles came in to play—*Miles*, who never deals with anybody on any other level than, 'I'm Miles, I'm here, and this is how it goes,' to watch Miles really completely give the generational credit, not in any words that he said, but his personal admiration for John Lee Hooker was . . . it wasn't about the notes. It wasn't about, 'How much jazz do you play?' He knew who John Lee Hooker was, and what it was all about. The reason that Miles was as hip as he was, is that he was always paying attention to what was goin' on . . . always *playin'* attention." As far as Miles overdubbing on the third day rather than performing live with the rest of the band goes, Taj is equally emphatic. "Miles wanted to be there. If it was a session he didn't like, he would've *sounded* like he didn't want to be there. Plus he's dealt with all the technology that was around, and he knew how to handle it. I love all that stuff that happened there. And Tim Drummond! And Roy Rogers! And Earl Palmer! We had *Earl Palmer* playing with us! All of us loved Earl. It was like a bunch of musicians that Jack Nitzsche got together. All these guys wanted to play together and had respect for each other . . . so it was *not a problem.*"

For Hooker, sharing a project with Miles Davis was both a professional honor and a personal pleasure: a professional honor because . . .

hell, because Miles was *Miles*, just as Hooker was *John Lee Hooker*; and a personal pleasure because the session provided the opportunity for a reunion. "When I was living in Detroit in the '50s, he used to come in the bar, slip in the bar where I were. I been knowin' Miles a long time. He was wild. He was a very young man then. Miles was a very good person; he just had his way of livin'. He didn't do nobody no harm, he just didn't like to have a lot of people hangin' around him all the time. A man just like to keep to himself. Wasn't nothin' wrong, just Miles bein' Miles. He wasn't a mean man, he just didn't like bein' around a lot of people."

Ever the diplomat, Hooker didn't mention just why Miles had chosen to come hang out in Detroit for the six months which spanned autumn '53 and early 1954. Never the diplomat, Miles did.[7]

> *As soon as I kicked my habit I went to Detroit. I didn't trust myself being in New York where everything was available. I figured that even if I did backslide a little, then the heroin that I would get in Detroit wasn't going to be as pure as what I would get in New York. I figured that this could help me and I needed all the help I could get.*

The day he recorded his contribution to *The Hot Spot*'s soundtrack, Miles paid Hooker one of the most treasured compliments of his entire career. "That is a very big thing coming from a person like Miles Davis, because he is one of the greatest men that ever lived in jazz. The guy liked me a lot; and when he got through playing, he looked at me, he give me a big hug, and he say, 'You the funkiest man alive.'

"I said, 'What you say?' He say, 'You the funkiest man alive. You in that mud right up to your neck.' That mean the deep, *deep* blues, you know, and I think that was a great compliment coming from him, from a jazz man especially: I mean, jazz and blues, they practically the same thing. It's great to hear it coming from a great jazz man, talking about a great blues man."

In his liner-note to the soundtrack CD, Dennis Hopper paid handsome and eloquent respects to both of these venerable titans while pumping up each of their respective personal myths:

---

7 In *Miles: The Autobiography* (Simon & Schuster, 1989) by Miles Davis with Quincy Troupe.

Miles Davis . . . who I have known since I was seventeen . . . punched out the heroin dealer and said he would kill me if I ever did it again. I've wanted him to score every movie I've ever made and we finally got it together, man. John Lee Hooker . . . proves you can make a steady diet of fried chicken well into your seventies and still try to get all of those pretty young things into a hot tub.

And the sessions just kept on coming. The Salkind movie production dynasty who made the *Superman* and *Three Musketeers* movies had discovered the merits of shooting two movies back-to-back on the same sets and with the same cast, and Blue Rose had cottoned on to the same trick. What was to become 1991's *Mr. Lucky* formally kicked off on April 9, 1990, with—*miracolo!*—Van Morrison finally showing up to cut a simmering "I Cover The Waterfront" for *Mr. Lucky* and a stirring medley of "Serve Me Right To Suffer" and "Backbiters And Syndicators," which stayed on Mike Kappus's shelf until 1995's *Chill Out.* (Booker T. Jones, the Stax mainstay whose Booker T & The MGs hit "Green Onions" had served as the basis for Hooker's own Vee Jay-era "Onions," overdubbed his Hammond organ parts in Hollywood the following February.)

The Texan titan Albert Collins, the Master Of The Telecaster, for whose astonishing guitar sound the word "searing" was specifically invented, was the next to weigh in. For the first time, Hooker and Rogers brought in members of The Coast To Coast Blues Band for an album session, and so Ken Baker (sax), Deacon Jones (organ), Jim Guyett (bass) and Bowen Brown (drums) did the honors for *Lucky*'s "Backbiters And Syndicators," with Mike Osborn and Rich Kirch plugging in their guitars to join in on "Boogie At Russian Hill," a storming jam on Hooker's patented set-closer which Kappus and Rogers sat on until they assembled *Boom Boom* in 1992. When BBC2 staged their Hooker tribute concert a year or two later, Collins paid fulsome tribute to Hooker. "He been my idol all these years," he told the show's producer, Mark Cooper, "and I'm so glad that he still here to carry me along with him. He extraordinary because he got young kids playin' with him, and he playin' the same thing he did forty years ago. That's my man. I love him. He's a beautiful man."[8]

Then came Johnny Winter, checking in at Russian Hill to cut "Susie" with his regular rhythm section of bassist Jeff Ganz and drummer Tom

---

8 So was Collins, but sadly he's here no more: the biggest guitar tone in the business was stilled when he died in 1993.

Compton. "Working with John Lee was real quick, man. We just went in the studio, set up the equipment and played. It took us longer to set up than it did to record the tracks! We recorded ['Susie'] twice: once with an acoustic bass and once with an electric bass. We did one other track [the still unissued 'Face To Face'], then that was it! Three takes and finished!

"John didn't even show me the chords before we started recording, but I know pretty much how John works. He changes whenever he wants to so I knew [we] were gonna have to really watch him. I wish he could have stayed longer and done a few more things, but he had a real bad cold and wasn't feeling that great—he had to get a bunch of stuff from the drugstore. I'd like to have done four or five tracks and done a few runs through; as it turned out, we didn't even get to do two takes of each of the songs we recorded. I didn't sing on the tracks, just played guitar, changing whenever he changed. In the past when I was doing sessions with Muddy Waters or playing live with him, Muddy would pretty much change on time, but when John has finished whatever he's singing, he just changes regardless of whether it's the "right" time or not—you don't know when the change is gonna come but you know it's not gonna be normal.

"It was a lot of fun!"

Next up was Robert Cray and his team, cutting *Mr. Lucky*'s title track and *Boom Boom*'s "Same Old Blues Again." John Hammond rounded out the 1990 studio dates with an absolute peach of a session, which yielded three songs, two of which made the cut for *Mr. Lucky* and the third, a joyful canter through Hooker's perennial "Bottle Up And Go," waiting in the wings for *Boom Boom*. "Highway 13" was an astonishing atmosphere piece: Hooker driving through the pouring rain with Hammond's plunking National guitar and eerie mouth-harp by his side, Scott Mathews's brushed drums wiping his windshield. "Father Was A Jockey" was rocking jump-up braggadocio—hey, it's a guy thing; I've never heard a woman boasting in song that she learned her sexual prowess from her mother.[9]

Unlike either its predecessor or its successors, the final sequenced configuration of *Mr. Lucky* featured no solo performances by Hooker. As Kappus explains, "The reason why there are two tracks with John Ham-

---

9 Compare and contrast: Annette Peacock's "My Mama Never Taught Me How To Cook" (punchline: *"but my brother taught me how to suck . . . seed"*), from *X-Dreams* (Aura, 1978).

mond [was] to try to offer that acoustic sound in the absence of solo tracks. We had a glut of . . . by the time we'd finished everything off, we'd put out the word to various people and we'd worked on the project and as we neared the end, several of the people we'd talked to suddenly came in and said that they were ready to do something. We found ourselves with more guests than we could squeeze in on the record and still have separate solo tracks. And we hadn't recorded any solo tracks yet, so John Hammond was the only one with two tracks on the record, to offer a little taste of the acoustic side."

To speak of "a glut" may seem ungracious, but there was certainly no famine. The album was completed in four more sessions between January and May of 1991. The first brought in Johnnie Johnson, Chuck Berry's piano-playing *alter* ego from St. Louis, alongside Ehrman, Mathews, and Mike Osborn, for a romp through "I Want To Hug You," and a still-unissued "Up And Down."

"I first met John Lee Hooker in New Orleans, when NRBQ called me to come do some work on the piano," Johnson recalled. "It was a great thrill to be with him, you know, because for years I've always heard of John Lee Hooker and his music, and to find out that I was going to play with him . . . hey, this is awesome. I couldn't wait until I met the man, and then when we finally did meet, face to face, we hit it off. That was when he asked me would I be interested in making a recording with him. I told him never to make a record or nothin' less he call on me to be his piano man. So far, so good! So I made the recording with him. He is the *easiest* man I worked with yet to record or play with. He's very cooperative in everything, so I wouldn't say he's hard to work with. If you're a musician, you can shift, too. You can't just go up there with one thing and think you can blend in with what he's doin,' so you got people prepared to do what he do. You can feel it comin' on, if you a musician. I been playin' blues for quite a while, and it was when I was with Albert King that I learned all these different keys which came in handy when I played with artists like John Lee Hooker. So I had no problem with him, and his character is beautiful. He has his own style of playin', his own style of singin', and the songs that he sings hold everybody's attention."

And then in April came Keith Richards, The Human Riff, the heart and soul of The Rolling Stones. "The first John Lee Hooker record I heard was 'Crawlin' King Snake,' funnily enough. Maybe that's why I said, 'That's the one I want to do for the album.' I just thought 'Crawlin' King Snake' was so mysterious and so individual. You're not going to mistake

John Lee Hooker for anybody else, and it was just such a fascinating sound, and so different to other stuff I'd heard; in a way more archaic. It felt so electric, and sounded as if he'd jumped a generation. It was so dark and swampy. I learned those John Lee Hooker chords, which are very strange shapes, and it immediately affected everything I did since.

"At the Stones' gig in Atlantic City, John came on, and Eric [Clapton] was there, too. John came by and I'd heard [*The Healer*] and said, 'Nice job, John.' Then at the beginning of this year [1991], John calls up and says, 'I'd really like you to do a track on this album.' He asked me what song I'd like to do. I said, 'I wanna do a song about a subject you're really interested in, John. Let's do "Crawlin' King Snake." ' "

"We just went in the studio and did three takes, and I think it was the first take we used on the record. It was all over in an hour and I said, 'John, that's too short,' and he said, 'Yeah, I'm too tired.' He's a sweet guy. I had a great time with him. I think *I'm* getting on, but this guy's nearly twice as old as I am,[10] and he's still playing. It kind of gives you hope!"

The evening after the session, Rich Kirch discovered that you don't have to die to go to heaven. It was his birthday, and there he was, having dinner and a postprandial jam with his two all-time musical heroes, John Lee Hooker and Keith Richards. He and Keith even wrote a song together.

The version of "Crawlin' King Snake" which John Lee and Keith cut on April 11, 1991—with the omnipresent Scott Mathews on drums and Canned Heat's Larry Taylor anchoring the bassline—is one of the stellar items on an album already embarrassingly overstuffed with gems. Both men are past-masters of the greater and lesser arcana of "Spanish" tuning; and both men are renowned for the idiosyncracy of their phrasing. The meshing of Keith's weird way with a groove and Hooker's weird way with a groove creates an agonizingly beautiful rhythmic tension behind Hooker's menacingly reverbed vocal.

"John Lee is definitely a man," says Richards. "He's no spring chicken, but I went over to his house for a barbecue just after the session and he had a whole school of young ladies with him, all of them guitar players, so you end up in John Lee's front room with everybody plugged in hammering away, and John just sits in the back there eating, going, 'Yeah, yeah, that's pretty good.' "

---

10 This is a slight exaggeration.

Less than a fortnight later, Hooker was back in Sausalito, cutting once more with Santana. Apart from Chester Thompson and Carlos Santana himself, it was an all-new band, including the young Hawaiian bassist Benny Reitveld, soon to jump ship to work with Miles Davis during the master trumpeter's final years. If the intent was to re-create the magical moment which produced "The Healer," then it failed; after all, how often can you catch the lightning in a bottle? "Chill Out" was, indeed, a post-"Healer" attempt to juxtapose Santana's music with Hooker's philosophy, and while it was cool, funky and felt—as the world heard when it was exhumed to serve as the title track of Hooker's 1995 album—it was no "Healer." However, "Stripped Me Naked," the cut that ended up on *Mr. Lucky*, was a very different beast indeed.

For subject matter, Hooker strip-mined the residual trauma of his divorce from Maude, two decades past and half a continent away. Where "The Healer"'s music was warm and tranquil, the angular jazz-funk of "Stripped Me Naked" generates a palpable sense of unease. This time, the sonic world Santana constructs for Hooker to inhabit is a treacherous and inhospitable cityscape, delineated by an undulating chord sequence of serpentine menace, stalked by Reitveld's spiky bass and chilled by Thompson's icy synth, using a vocal sample sounding like eerily calm robot voices going "ahhh." The contrast with the human voice of Hooker—the most *human* voice ever recorded—could scarcely be greater.

Hooker's downtown, back in the divorce court from hell. His wife is looking to take everything he's got—his money, his house, his car, everything—to strip him naked. And the judge is on her side. "That was a mean old judge," he muses, half-admiringly. And this time, Santana's guitar isn't healing him, but mocking him.

By May 11, when Hooker and Ry Cooder had finished cutting "This Is Hip"—a Vee Jay out-take which had become a Hooker connoisseurs' favorite as the title track of a 1980 U.K. compilation—at a Hollywood studio, Blue Rose pretty much had the new Hooker album in the bag, not to mention much of the next one. Cooder brought along drummer Jim Keltner and bassist Nick Lowe, the rhythm section of Little Village, his short-lived "roots-rock supergroup"[11]: presumably Lowe didn't invite Hooker to join him in a quick chorus of "Milk And Alcohol." With Johnnie Johnson on piano and Cooder's trusty back-up singers Terry

---

11 Named after a fairly obscure Sonny Boy Williamson track.

Evans, Bobby King and Willie Green supercharging the choruses, the track boasted a swing, solidity and swagger which were utterly impeccable.

Mr. Lucky's front cover showed a seraphically smiling Hooker, wearing a beautiful suit, reclining against a beautiful old Buick with a beautiful old cherry-red Epiphone Sheraton guitar in his lap. The back cover triumphantly emblazoned its roll call of celebrity drop-ins in strict, egalitarian alphabetical order. There they were: Albert Collins, Ry Cooder, Robert Cray, John Hammond, Johnnie Johnson, Booker T. Jones, Van Morrison, Keith Richards, Carlos Santana ... "and many more." *Mr. Lucky* took *The Healer*'s Guest Star Syndrome about as far as it could go. With Hooker's next pair of albums, Kappus and Rogers resisted the temptation to play "Can you top this?"

Boom Boom and Chill Out reflected the shift in Hooker's own concerns: as he wound down his touring schedule yet further and concentrated his attention nearer home, he would start to carry The Coast To Coast Blues Band, plus other—non-famous—friends from the Bay Area blues scene with him into the studio. There would be more solo sessions, or duets with Rogers. Less and less emphasis would be placed on the participation of big-name colleagues. Boom Boom would feature performances by Albert Collins, Robert Cray, Charlie Musselwhite and John Hammond, as well as, on the thunderous remake of the title track, a stunning cameo by Jimmie Vaughan, former guitar enforcer of The Fabulous Thunderbirds and big brother to the late Stevie Ray Vaughan. And *Chill Out* included on its rosters Carlos Santana, Van Morrison, Booker T. Jones and the veteran Charles Brown, composer of the perennial "Merry Christmas Baby" and Hooker's own lifetime favorite "Driftin' Blues," complete with his regular band. Nevertheless, all these names were buried in the credits for their individual tracks rather than emblazoned on the sleeves.

The spotlight was now firmly on John Lee Hooker; not on his famous friends, but on the man himself, and his music, and his own unique gifts. He was also mastering the art of Zen Stardom, the mystical process by which an artist does less and less work while their media presence becomes progressively more and more ubiquitous. If, to mangle a cliché in a phildickian manner, nothing ubiks like ubiquity, then Hooker in near-retirement loomed larger over the media landscape than most bluesmen at their active peak. The paradigm indicator of Hooker's iconic status was, of all things, a TV commercial. Lee Jeans, conscious of ranking a distant third to Levi's and Wrangler in the Great American Legwear League (Mythic Division), launched a campaign around the slogan "The Jeans That Built America," centering around Great Americans Called Lee, including Jerry Lee Lewis, Robert E. Lee, Gypsy Rose Lee, Marvel Comics figurehead Stan Lee, and guess who. In a truly giddy piece of myth-making, Hooker—or, to be more precise, a stunt double shown in long-shot silhouette—is seen clambering from a railroad boxcar in a haze of mist to the strains of "Boom Boom." Then cut to the great man himself, performing the song on stage with The Coast To Coast Blues Band.

In Britain, where folks care about such things, the song promptly zoomed into the Top 20. A clip from the vid was even shown on *Top Of The Pops*, and the revisionist take of "Boom Boom" thereby became a bigger hit than the original had been almost thirty years earlier. The commercial spawned a legion of imitators, wherein blues became a signifier of authenticity, and all manner of African-American senior citizens in Big Suits and jaunty hats certified all manner of products as The Real Thang. Nothing and no one, it seemed, could be more "real" than John Lee Hooker—or someone like him. It didn't even have to be the real John Lee Hooker.

Meanwhile, the real John Lee Hooker stayed home, and took life easy. Even when *Boom Boom* was nominated for a Grammy, he spared himself the hassle of making a trip to New York to attend the awards ceremony. Instead, he stuck to his sofa, and watched the proceedings on television. After firing off a few cursory comments about performers like Whitney Houston ("Oohh, I could just kiss her all over") and a certain crew of veteran hard-rockers ("They ain't *shit*"), he tipped his hat over his eyes, folded his hands across his paunch, and went to sleep.

He looked after his health and watched what he ate, though the exercise bike his daughter Zakiya bought for him gathered dust despite her thoughtfully taking the precaution of setting it up in front of the TV set, and his resolute aversion to most kinds of physical activity generated some cause for concern among friends, family and colleagues. He saw a star with his name installed on the sidewalk of Hollywood Boulevard. Like Buddy Guy in Chicago and B. B. King in Memphis, he even lent his name to a club: John Lee Hooker's Boom Boom Room, opposite the old Fillmore West site in San Francisco. And back in the music, he lent his colossal presence to the endeavors of others: when, in the spring of 1993, B. B. took a leaf out of Hooker's book to record *Blues Summit*, an album of duets,[12] Hooker was there, with Roy Rogers and most of Robert Cray's band, including Cray himself, to cut a version of Willie Dixon's "You Shook Me" which saw King venturing onto Hooker's musical turf, rather than the reverse. The highlight of an album by no means deficient in great moments—other featured guests included Buddy Guy, Albert Collins, Etta James and Cray—the track was a testament to the generosity of spirit of both men, and to the strength and durability of a friendship which had lasted almost forty years.

Others who benefited from Hooker's benign intervention included Van Morrison and President Bill Clinton: he guested at a San Francisco concert by one, which was subsequently issued as a live album, and played an election rally on behalf of the other. And over a decade after the project was first mooted, the full-scale John Lee Hooker/Van Morrison collaboration finally took place. Though its lead track was a storming version of "Dimples" performed with, and produced by, Los Lobos, Van The Man's participation in 1997's *Don't Look Back* was literally hands-on; he produced and played guitar on ten of the eleven tracks, and sang on four. The title track was a vintage Hooker blues-ballad Morrison had recorded with Them back in 1964. Apart from "Dimples," the album's wildest card was a radically Hookerized and thoroughly deconstructed version of Jimi Hendrix's "Red House;" Hooker had recorded the song once before, for a limited-edition CD release which juxtaposed several *very* different takes on the piece by Hendrix himself with a 1989 Hollywood-cut reading of the song by Hooker and, among others, Booker T. Jones. Then he'd sung it more or less straight, faithfully following "the great Jimmy Henry's original blue(s) print and personalizing it only with his patented one-bar anticipation of each chord change. This time, under Morrison's production aegis, he took Hendrix's signature slow blues all the way back down the line to Hooker Central Station.

Yet the album's centerpiece was a song called "The Healing Game." It clearly meant a lot to Morrison, who by now had taken to sporting a full-scale John Lee Hooker look, complete with trademark Hooker-style suit, hat and shades, because he not only included the song on an album of his own which he was recording more or less back-to-back with the Hooker sessions, but he made it his record's title track. Due to the tightness of Morrison's own schedule, the album provided an unwelcome flashback to the bad old recording ways of the pre-*Healer* era: too many

---

12 B did it again four years later, with 1997's *Deuces Wild*.

songs cut at too few sessions; too much haste, not enough speed. Once again, many sparks are struck—with Hooker and Morrison together, how could it be otherwise?—but, once again, too few tracks catch fire. Nevertheless, on "The Healing Game" itself, they catch the lightning. Morrison's own subsequent version seems flat by comparison.

These days, Hooker does what he wants, how he wants. He listens to advice from those he the considers qualified to give it, and then he does what he wanted, anyhow—*boogie, chillen!* Those whose advice he doesn't take generally appreciate why he doesn't take it. Unless, that is, that person is Bernard Besman. "I saw him play a concert at the Palace," recalls the venerable entrepreneur, "and I told him at that time . . . as a matter of fact, he's had a lot of bad reviews when he plays with his group. *Terrible.* Because people want to hear him play how he plays. I talked to him some time ago and I said, 'John, do some numbers yourself and then have them come in at the end, because people don't come to hear the band, they come to hear you.' But he doesn't follow that advice. He still plays with the band."

Hooker knows full well that people still love to hear him play solo, but he has his reasons. "Oh, I know that. Yeah, I know. I been told that a lot of times, but I don't like playing by myself anymore. I play by myself some once in a while, but not all the time. I wouldn't want to do that all the time. With the band, a small trio, something like that . . . but people do want to hear me by myself a lot, they want to hear some of my records of me playing by myself. I give 'em some of that. Whenever I cut an album I try to do a little solo stuff on it, but I don't want to do it all the time. Things change, but I'm still playing the same thing I played then. I ain't playin' no different. I just ain't playin' as much. I just go with the band, sit on top of the groove, just sit there and enjoy it. I might do a solo album sometime. Oh boy, I can play by myself.

"I can play the *hell* out of it by myself."

So, these days, who are Hooker's true peers? No one in the blues, that's for sure. There's B. B., of course, and B. B. is fabulous indeed, but he's a different kind of creature and a different kind of artist, and he has walked a very different kind of path. We not only need to look beyond the blues, but beyond music itself, to two of Hooker's most distinguished contemporaries: to Nelson Mandela and William S. Burroughs.

After decades of imprisonment, Mandela only assumed his rightful place on the world stage at an age when most politicians are retiring. However, when he was finally able to do so, he became the best-loved statesman not only in Africa, but in the entire world. He was admired for what he stood for; for what he'd been through, and—ultimately—for what and who he was. Simultaneously Burroughs—another guy, incidentally, who knew how to wear the hell out of a snappy suit and hat—had spent decades defining an art incomprehensible to most and derided by many; gaining the approbation of a (comparatively) small but highly discriminating audience; enjoying an ineradicable effect on world literature but receiving comparatively petty rewards for doing so. His career then came under the direction of a young, tenacious, loyal and hardworking acolyte named James Grauerholz—Burroughs's equivalent to Mike Kappus, if you like—who got his tangled business affairs under control and negotiated the contracts that enabled him to produce one final burst of great work: the trilogy comprising *Cities Of the Red Night, The Place Of Dead Roads* and *The Western Lands*. Burroughs died in 1997 at the age of eighty-three, lionized, wealthy, dripping with awards, and waited on hand and foot: his place in world literature, and in the art and culture of the twentieth century, finally acknowledged and utterly beyond dispute. It was a long time coming, but it came.

Say something once: why say it again? Because some things need to be said more than once. Like this: John Lee Hooker takes it easy. But he takes it.

By way of illustration: while John Lee and Van Morrison were working on *Don't Look Back* at The Plant in Sausalito, something else was going on down the hall. Hard-working roots-rockers Big Head Todd & The Monsters, fronted by singer/guitarist Todd Park Mohr, were hard at work on their latest album, *Beautiful World*, under the production guidance of former Talking Heads keyboards and guitar guy Jerry Harrison. And then synchronicity kicked in, yet again.

As Mohr explains it, "Jerry Harrison had asked us to cut 'Boom Boom' after seeing us perform it prior to making *Beautiful World*. It was one of the first songs we had played as a band, and became an audience favorite when we revived it at the request of our road crew. The band was very reluctant to cut it, and it wasn't considered in the running to appear on *Beautiful World*.

"John Lee had been working at The Plant, down the hall from us, when the idea occurred to us to try to get him to sit in on 'Boom Boom.' I remember challenging Jerry on this point, telling him that that was the only way we were going to use the track. To me, covering the song without Hooker would just be covering a song, and something outside the spirit of what we wanted for the record. Involving John Lee makes the song a tribute, and it is one of our most relished experiences to have been able to honor him with his own music. At any rate, Jerry brought John Lee in. We were reluctant to believe it was really going to happen.

"When John Lee entered the studio, even Jerry, our unemotional music highbrow, was ecstatic and a little fearful. John has an overwhelming presence, and when you see him, you want to be a fly on the wall. He was exactly as I'd always imagined him, decked in a pinstripe suit with suspenders. He seemed ageless and still driven to life. He sat down and boomed his 'Boogie Chillen' bit for about nineteen minutes, as we tried to coax a few lines of 'Boom Boom' out of him. 'That's another song, you understand,' he protested, because we only paid him for one. As soon as he heard the guitar break he couldn't resist.

" 'Who's the guitar player?' he asked. Brian [Nevin, (drums)] pointed at me. He looked at me and said, 'You bad.' Hearing him say that to me was like getting my driver's license. I had been legitimized. When he finished, he muttered jokingly, 'Where's the beer? Where's the keg? Where's the pot?' "

And life went on. The 1998 Grammy Awards doubled Hooker's Grammy stock virtually overnight with a Best Traditional Blues Album award for *Don't Look Back* and a Best Pop Collaboration With Vocals award (shared with Van Morrison) for the title track; neatly bookending his Best Traditional Blues Album award for *Chill Out*, and Best Blues Recording for his "I'm In The Mood" duet with Bonnie Raitt.

Plus he found the time to cut a brand-new lead-off track for *The Best Of Friends*, the best-of round-up from the post-*Healer* era which certified the arrival of his career at the half-century mark. Not surprisingly, he recut "Boogie Chillen," this time in a scorching full-band incarnation complete with guitar by Eric Clapton—though the impossibility of reconciling the two men's schedules meant that they couldn't be in the studio simultaneously and therefore "met" only on tape—riding out on a passionate incantation of self-assertion and self-definition.

"I am," he sings, *"the Boogie Man."*

All in a day's work. Yeah? Right. All in a *life*'s work.

Let me tell you somethin'
'Bout my life

At night I lay down
To sleep at night
Lovin' people
Keep me happy
Down through the years
I don't care who you are
Or where you come from
I love you
I love you
Do you understand?
—John Lee Hooker, on "Loving People," by Ollan Christopher,
    Zakiya Hooker and Chris Patton; from Zakiya Hooker's *Another*
    Generation Of The Blues

The highest purpose of the universe is to develop and grow and, as it does so, to heal itself, and everything within it, from the necessary wounds of development and growth. This is no dichotomy: no either/or, but a single continuous process, and the cycle cannot be broken. Without change and the possibility of change, there is only stasis and entropy. But change and growth create conflict; conflicts create wounds; wounds create pain. From these there can be no exemption, and no protection. Instead of protection, there can be—must be—healing. For without healing and the possibility of healing, there is only death. Thus the universe is forever wounded, and forever healing.

To be a healer is to serve, very directly, the purpose of the universe. If we, or the world as we perceive it, seem to be damaging ourselves faster than we can heal, then we are in danger; and it is only healers who stand between ourselves and extinction. Because if we cannot be healed, or learn how to heal ourselves, we shall die.

The universe will go on without us. If we inflict more damage upon this planet than it can sustain, the planet will protect itself by wiping us out. Then it will heal itself; and, as part of that healing it may or may not develop anything which we could recognize as "intelligent life." Or, more to the point, anything which could recognize *us* as "intelligent life."

Damage comes in many forms, and so does healing. We can be damaged in body, and damaged in spirit. And we can respond to such damage in a variety of ways. We can refuse to recover, and simply die in our footsteps. We can drag ourselves around the world as walking wounded.

We can seek revenge, hunt down those who have tormented or injured us, and seek to torment and injure them in our turn. Or we can heal, and we can forgive.

It is not enough simply to say that healing implies forgiveness: the two are inseparable. Each is a way of "making right." Neither can retroactively undo or unmake the original injury—*make it not so, Number One!*—but damage can indeed be repaired. Once healed, or once forgiven, we can be "as good as new." And the ultimate triumph of the healer's art can be to make ourselves or others better than new, because simply to be "new" is to be untried, untested, untouched, unexposed to the dangers posed us by our world and by ourselves—and to those which we, in our turn, pose ourselves, and our world.

To have been damaged by those dangers, or to have become a manifestation of those dangers and thereby to have, knowingly or unknowingly, damaged others—and to heal or be healed, to forgive or be forgiven—is to have become part of the essential process of the universe: to have learned, and to have grown; and to have participated in, and aided, the processes of learning and growth in others. Most of all, it is to demonstrate, to ourselves and to others, the eternal truth of that most ancient of blues adages, that "trouble don't last always."

We must needs make peace with very many angry ghosts, and in order to do that we need all the healers we can get. John Lee Hooker is such a man. He is a healer by both instinct and philosophy and each beyond doubt enriches and deepens the other; but the instinct comes first, and the philosophy after the fact. While he is here, we must treasure him. When he is gone, we must treasure his memory, his legacy, his work.

And we have to understand precisely what the nature of that work is. John Lee Hooker's gift is not specifically located in his ability to sing, or to play guitar, or to write songs, or to boogie-rock an audience cold. His gift is that he has been blessed with the power to reach way deep down into himself, into parts of himself that most people don't even know exist, and to bring up from there the deepest truths about himself. And, having done so, to present those truths to us—through his words or his guitar licks or simply the physical sound of his voice—in such a way as to put us in touch with the hidden truths of how *we* feel, to connect us with parts of ourselves that we, maybe, didn't even know existed. To connect us with the most fundamental essence of our own humanity: that which we share, not through choice or ethics or ideology or through any kind of decision but as a basic fact of our existence—as basic as the need for oxygen or water—with every other member of our species on this planet.

In *Iron John*—a title so resonant in this context that to even attempt (if you will indulge the author by pardoning yet another use of the *Star Trek* infinitive) the process of deconstruction would be to debase it— Robert Bly writes eloquently of the need to grieve, and of the dire consequences of denying that need. To heal the grief you got to feel the grief. John Lee Hooker's music does just that: it helps you to feel it, and feeling it heals it. He gives you permission to grieve in a culture which otherwise denies that permission.

And that will last forever. Long after John Lee Hooker—the body, the physical entity, the old geezer with the deep voice and the suit and the hat and the shades—is long gone, John Lee Hooker—the artist, the healer, the boogie man—will be here, for as long as recorded music exists, or—if the folk process holds up—maybe even longer. For all of us, and for generations yet unborn, John Lee Hooker will always be there for us: a spirit guide pacing the pathways of the heart and the backstreets of the soul, reporting back what he has seen and heard and felt. And, by doing so, giving us something warm and solid to hold onto during those long wracking nights in the dark room; helping us to map our own way out of the traps we have built for ourselves; letting us know that others have been where we are now, and that they got out, and that in the end, despite everything, they found their own happiness, and their own peace of mind.

Healing us. Forgiving us. Teaching us to heal ourselves, and to forgive ourselves. Letting us start fresh, and whole, and clean: the way we thought, back when we were hopelessly mired in the bad craziness, that we could never possibly be, ever again.

Because blues *is* the healer. Really, truly. And John Lee Hooker is the greatest healer the blues has ever known.

In the words of Ice-T: I'm outta here like I stole sump'n. Right now, I'm going to leave you one-on-one with Mr. Hooker. Evoke that voice: impossibly deep and rich and slow and dark, with infinite gradations of emphasis and a slight stutter; confidential, intimate. *Listen*

"I been out here a long time, about forty-five or fifty years. I got enough money. I need never work anymore: just sit back and let Mike do the dirty work and bring the checks in. I may go in the studio once in a while . . . I feel that now, at this stage, anything I make gonna sell so much now 'cause it's from John Lee Hooker. Even if it ain't the number-one best, it's gonna sell so much because of my name. Whatever

I do, they're gonna buy it whenever I come up with something. I always try to make the best, so I'm gonna kick back and try to enjoy what life I got left . . . and love people, which I do, and that's about it.

"I can't run these roads anymore. I ain't twenty-one anymore. There come a time in a man's life—a man or woman—that there's an end out there somewhere ahead of you. And my end's ahead of me. Years go by; you gets older. Nobody stays young. I ain't young, I ain't no spring chicken, but at times I feel pretty good, so I just want to sit around and enjoy what I done made over the years. Enjoy my family and my friends, and I just want to go out there once in a while and help people—the poor people, the homeless people—do benefits, help raise a little money for them. That's what I want to do.

"I put everybody in the same basket: I don't love *this* person, hate *that* person. I love *all* people. Some things that comes out of them I don't like, you know? That body stuff—you know, flesh and blood? I *love* that. But what comes out of it—your mouth, what you stand for—I don't like that. I don't dislike you as a human being—what God made. No, no. I feel good when I help somebody, and that's what I'm gonna do now.

"It's hard to retire. One way you can do this: you get sick and you *cain't*. You go as long as you can, until you *cain't* go. As long as you on your feet, you can walk around, can *breathe*, you go out there once in a while. But when you *cain't*, it's a different story. I know where you comin' from; you understand where I'm comin' from, too, but I will never completely retire. I will go out there once in a while . . . and do it. To keep on doin' it.

"You have it in your mind that you want to do that, but when the day come and you say, 'Well, this is it . . .' you cain't. You stay out a little while, maybe a month or two . . . and then you come back out. The Stones retired, they come back . . . The Who done at least two farewell tours . . . *Oh* yeah. I know what you're sayin'. Tiner [Turner], she done some farewell tours, too! When I say that, Mike kinda laugh. I can see that in his face: he don't believe I'm gonna retire.

"I may lay out for a long time. I'm thinkin' on it. 'Well, this is it. There ain't no more.' And then we say, 'Well, John Lee Hooker come back out of retirement."

"It's hell on this planet, and your hell is here while you alive. Your heaven and hell is what you make it, but it is someplace God Jehovah will let you go, but there ain't such a thing as you gonna burn in fire and you gonna go to hell. Right now, I think I'm in heaven, what you call heaven. I think I'm living good and enjoying people, I'm very successful, I got people around me who love me—so that's my heaven and my paradise. Lovin' people, people lovin' me. I repeat myself again: the most important things in life [are] your health, friendship, and people. Give love, you get love back. No matter how much money you got, I got, anybody: you got no health, money don't mean nothin'. You can't enjoy it, you miserable. If you got health and a little money to survive, you's okay.

"And *peace* . . . *of* . . . *mind*. Peace of mind takes people around you who love you; health; a little money for good living, and good people. They give you peace of mind. If you ain't got that, you ain't got peace of mind. If you ain't got that, you got problems. You tormented, people always buggin' ya, making your nerves bad, things on your mind . . . you can't have peace of mind. If you got people who love you and you know they do, and your health . . . you got *peace* . . . *of* . . . *mind*.

"I'm goin' to say this, and it's true: the blues was here the day that the world was born. Sadness, loneliness; it come from man and woman. A woman gets sad 'bout her man done left her, man gets sad 'bout his woman done left *him* . . . started hummin' sad songs. Somethin' 'bout a woman. You can't say nothin' . . . a man can't say nothin' that ain't about a woman. A woman can't say nothin' without sayin' somethin' about a man. That's what it come from, now, 'cause even Adam was in the garden. It's no sin. Do you see in the Bible anywhere where singin' is a sin? This leads into what I'm going to say. God, if there is such a thing as God, because we all believe in a Supreme Being: he wants you to do right, love people all over the world, and that's what I'm doing. I'm serving people all over. I'm *serving* people, I'm reachin' out, gettin' people, helpin' people. I do benefits, I gives 'em. That's treatin' 'em as God want. And all the people that I don't see, *my song* reaches them all over the world. I never see 'em, I never *will* see 'em. But my *voice* is all over the world: John Lee Hooker on a record. I'll be here for *ever*, but my body won't. Accordin' to the Bible, you doin' what God want you to do: help people. People that need help: the sick, the needy, crippled kids. I do's all of that. I study givin'. I'm a Christian, but I just don't run to church. I don't believe in runnin' to church. I don't believe in gettin' on my knees prayin'. I don't believe in that.

"I can sit right in my house and do good. You notice me: you see how I love people, you see how I welcome *all kinds of people* into my house, all nationalities. To me, I sees no color: I see people. I see a human being that God planted here on this earth. He made one race, that's the human race. He made all different flowers, different colors, nationalities, but he made one race, the human race. But our people don't see that. They fight among each other, then they run to church: segregated churches. I look at 'em, and talk about this, and people say, 'You should have been a minister, you says things that's so true.' No, God—if it is a God, ain't none of us ever seen him, but we do know there's a Supreme Being run this earth, all the stuff on this earth. Who put it there? Who created it? We never seen God, but there is a Supreme Being, and he made one race, and that's the human race. Two arms, two legs . . .

"One race! You see flowers in your yard: you got all colors of flowers: red flowers, blue, yellow, but they all flowers. You know what I mean? It's all flowers, but it's all one race. That's the truth! If the whole world see'd and felt that way . . . it's all one race, the human race. We all breathe alike. We own nothin' on this earth, we don't own *nothin'*. We don't even own the clothes we got on our back; we just wears them, and use them. When we leaves here, we takes away nothin'. Nothin' you brought into this world, nothin' you gonna take away. You say, 'I own this land.' You don't own land, just the land you gonna be buried in. *You owns nothin'*. I don't own this house, I'm just usin' this house. The money I spend is paper; that paper's gone. You only own enough spot to be buried in and you don't own that. When they put you in there someone might plant stuff over on top of that. It's a hole in the ground, that's all you have. If you don't do that, they put you in a incinerator and cremate you. Material things, fine cars, fine houses . . . yes, it's nice to have this, it's nice to be using that. It's nice to enjoy things like that while you here on this planet which you know you just passing through, but why can't we let *everybody* enjoy something, saying, 'I want all of this'? Why can't we share this like we ain't gonna stay here always? Why can't we share the wealth and what we claim is ours, what we accumulate and say is ours? Why can't *everybody* get together and share that with the human race, which is one race?

"The ones that got all the power and money, they look down on the poor. They see you layin' there on the ground, they see you scufflin', they never gonna reach out and give you a helpin' hand, say, 'C'mon, I wanna help you.' No, they ridin' high. They leavin' all of that *here*. They got *nothin'*. It go from generation to generation. I could go on and on, speak the rights and the wrongs, but I know 'bout life, what life is all about, how people should live . . . *enjoy* while you here, you passin' through. I know we gonna have sickness, pain. We not gonna be happy all our lives. We not gonna be smilin' all the time. On this earth you gonna have trials and tribulations, sad days, sick days . . . but that's life. But try to enjoy while you here . . . and enjoy *people*, not thinkin' that I'm more than you or you more'n me, I'm the big star and I'm more'n you . . . *no*. I'm just a creature of the human race God give a talent to, said, 'John, you use this. I'm blessin' you with this, now you go out and bless someone else. Go and share your wealth, help the poor.' That's the way I look at life. There's an old saying that what goes around comes around. You know, I don't know nobody I dislike or I hate. There's some people I don't approve of they lifestyle; I don't associate with them because they are not in my category, the life I want to live, and that direction. But I look upon them as a human being; we the same. God made us all, we the same.

"Every word I said is true! I'm not God, but I do know that I'm a very smart person. I don't act like just this old shoe in the corner don't known nothin'. That's the way I am I think [things] are gonna get better, but you know for the human race it's gonna maybe get down to be the end of their time, but the world ain't gonna never end. Somewhere, maybe in a hundred years from now, everybody's gonna realize they just one race, the human race, but right now it's a long way from that. It's got way, way, *way*, better than it was fifty years ago, you know? Fifty years ago, I'm *here* and you *there*. You couldn't sit in my house. Now, as the years go by, that's gonna get better, better and better. We won't be here to see it. Men gonna have to come together, lock hands. Not because of the color of your skin, [but] because you's a *man*. We just human beings, flesh and blood. We all bleed alike. Your clothes, or what you look like, don't make you no more.

"I don't know nothin' that'll stop me from playin' the blues. I'll never retire. I'll be doing this until God Jehovah call me to the next world, and I'm hopin' I can play there. Once you a blues singer in your blood, you can retire from the public, but in your heart and in your blood you never retire 'til you *gone*. You know I wrote that song—me and Van Morrison did it—called 'Never Get Out of These Blues Alive?' I'll never—I'll *never*—get out of these blues alive. I'll be dealing with the blues 'til the day I done gone. *Never* get out of these blues alive. Yeah."

I never build myself up. I let the people do that. I'm the most laid-back person, and I let them build me up. If you ask me, I say, "I'm just a guy playin' some blues."

Afterword: Saharan Boogie

Not surprisingly, John Lee Hooker hasn't yet gotten around to accepting Ali Farka Touré's invitation to visit his home village of Niafunké in the Timbuktu province of northern Mali. Thanks to the good offices of World Circuit Records and the *Daily Telegraph*, however, I was able to do so on his behalf in the summer of 1999, in conjunction with the release of *Niafunké*, an album Ali recorded in situ with the aid of a mobile digital recording studio.

The overland journey to Niafunké from Bamako, Mali's capital, is not an easy one. The first stage is relatively uncomplicated—drive approximately 250 miles down long straight roads to Mopti via Segou, following the heat-shimmer to the horizon—but once you've crossed the Niger, just outside Mopti, things change. There are no more road signs. There is no more road. There is only the desert, a hard-baked golden plain marked only by a maze of dirt tracks and scrawny, scrubby bushes and shrubs. To reach Niafunké, you need to traverse more than another 160 miles of desert and cross the Niger once more.

Ali is driving at the head of a convoy of four-wheel-drive jeeps traversing the edge of Dogon country. He is in the lead because Niafunké is impossible to find unless you already know exactly where it is. However, we've gotten too far ahead of the rest of the vehicles, so we pull into a tiny village to take a break and give the others time to catch up. As is Ali's wont whenever arriving in a new village, he slams a fresh tape into the deck and cranks the volume. This time it's a tape by John Lee Hooker: to be precise, it's *Hooker 'N' Heat*.

The effect is galvanic. From toddlers to elders, a crowd has already gathered around the jeep, and as the music hits, everybody starts to dance. Ali and I leap out to join them. All 111 degrees of the noonday Sahara sun seem to be pounding down on us—an epithet which only seems like a cliché when you're not actually undergoing the experience—as the music explodes into the superheated air and we dance around the jeep to the tireless, hammering boogie of Hooker's "Burnin' Hell." One young guy literally pleads to be given the tape. I have to explain to him that it's not my cassette but Ali's, and that it's one of his favorites.

"They don't understand the words," Ali explains later, "but they recognize the music as theirs. The roots"—he emphasizes the words: *les racines*—"are the same." In fact, he laughs, "At first they think it is my music and they ask 'Ali, where's your guitar?' "

As well they might. All of Ali Farka Touré's music derives from the various tribes and ethnic groupings of the Timbuktu province, and those aspects of his music which sound, to Western-oriented ears, most like the blues are specifically those drawn from the Moorish Tuareg nomads of northern Mali and sung in their language, Tamacheq; and the Gambari groove of the Moorish Peul peoples from the Mopti area, which bear an unmistakable family resemblance to John Lee's boogie and slow blues. But those musical connections which first led European critics to dub Ali "the John Lee Hooker of Africa" are deep ones indeed. That John Lee Hooker is "the most African of blues singers" (just as Bo Diddley—Mississippi-born and Chicago-raised, but with family roots of his own in Louisiana—is the most African of rock 'n' rollers) has been a critical truism since the point was first made in the late '50s, but it is more than simply a musicological issue. Appropriately enough, the first writers to notice were French.

In Mali, the leather-thonged amulets which some folks wear around neck, thigh or bicep are called *gris-gris*, a term generally applied to the paraphernalia of the animist spiritual traditions often lumped together into the admittedly imprecise category of "voodoo;" and one instantly familiar to those with even the most superficial acquaintance with the culture of Louisiana, even if it's only via a copy of Dr. John's classic first album, *Gris-Gris*. Similarly, a canoe is known as a *pirogue* both in the bayous of Louisiana and on the banks of the Niger: two examples among many from what we might call the French Connection. During the days of slavery, it made a certain grisly economic sense for French slavers to have shipped Africans kidnapped from those parts of Africa which they controlled to their own areas of hegemony in the Americas. What is now the Republic of Mali was part of what was then French West Africa, just as Louisiana was once a French colony in the U.S.

John Lee Hooker tells us that he learned his unmistakable guitar groove from his stepfather, Will Moore. Though Hooker was born and raised in the Mississippi Delta, Will Moore was from Louisiana. And it was Louisiana which nurtured the spores of Tuareg and Peul music and culture until, in new settings and new forms, they were able to flower once more. So it should therefore come as no surprise that when Hooker's music is heard by the denizens of a Saharan village so small that its name, and its very existence, are known only to locals, they should greet it like a message from a long-lost relative. As Ali says, they recognize his music as theirs.

John Lee Hooker will probably never go to Timbuktu. But then he doesn't need to. He's been there all along.

Acknowledgments: Thank You, Fellas

It's in him, and it got to come out. This book wouldn't have come out at all if it wasn't for the efforts of a virtual regiment of people, all of whom are owed a Big Drink. Some of them may even get one.

First and foremost, total love and respect to the man himself, John Lee Hooker, for inviting me into his life; and, through the many hours of interviews which provided the narrative spine of this book, rigorously turning over the topsoil of that life, including a few areas which I'm sure he would have preferred not to discuss. In the same breath, I thank the Hooker extended family, most prominently Archie Hooker, Zakiya Hooker, Robert Hooker and Paul Mathis; plus John Lee's many friends and associates, notably Martin Thompson; and the then personnel of The Coast To Coast Blues Band: Kenny "Dr. Funkenstein" Baker, Brother Bowen Brown, Vala Cupp, Lizz Fischer, Jim Guyett, Deacon Jones, Rich Kirch and Mike Osborn. None of these folks had actually chosen to invite some English guy to come hang out with them for weeks on end, but they nevertheless made me feel utterly welcome. And Archie's cooking is wonderful. Where's that cornbread recipe then, Arch?

Next up, I want to thank Mike Kappus, John Lee's manager, for selecting me to be the author of this book, and for sticking with me through what turned out to be a decidedly bumpy ride. By the same token, big props go out to the past and present staff of The Rosebud Agency, most notably Steve Lee and Tom "Agent Cooper" Chauncey, for facilitating arrangements and generally doing the biz. Richard Wootton, John Lee's U.K. PR guy, recommended me to Mike Kappus in the first place. And none of this would have happened without the inspired intervention of Pete Townshend, who in his own inimitable manner talked—on second thoughts, let's make that "arm-twisted"—me into taking up Mike's offer when I wavered in the face of what seemed an impossibly daunting task.

Major shout-outs are also due to my agent, Antony Harwood of Gillon Aitken Associates, and my publisher, Tony Lacey at Viking Penguin U.K., who turned out to be true twin towers of strength when the going got seriously rough. It's a privilege to have guys like these on your side.

Guides, philosophers and friends who helped map out the terrain and who raided their vaults included these stalwarts of the BritBlues Posse: Roy Carr, Mike Rowe, Tony Russell, Neil Slaven, Mike Vernon and Cliff White: couldn't'a done it without y'all. Nuff respeck.

During the process of creating *Boogie Man*, I was fortunate to be granted interviews and/or correspondence by many individuals, not all of whom are directly quoted in the text but all of whom helped immeasurably. In alphabetical order, let's have some of that o-o-o-o-o-old soul clappin' for Clifford Antone, Bernard Besman, Elaine Brown, Eddie Burns, Chicago Beau, Famous Coachman, Roy Fisher, Billy Gibbons, Peter Green, Buddy Guy, John Hammond, Archie Hooker, Maude Hooker, Robert Hooker, Zakiya Hooker, Mike Kappus, B. B. King, Rich Kirch, Eddie Kirkland, Taj Mahal, Paul Mathis, Charlie Musselwhite, Mike Osborn, Rick Parsons, the late Jimmy Rogers, Roy Rogers (no relation), "Sally," Sid Seidenberg, the late Robert Shelton, Ali Farka Touré, Pete Townshend, Wade Walton, Tom Whitehead and Valerie Wilmer. My blues brother Joel Rosen rode shotgun for the interviews with Clifford Antone and Jimmy Rogers; Nick Gold of World Circuit set up the interview with Ali Farka Touré and also served as interpreter, and the late Kathy Acker co-conducted the interview with Taj Mahal.

This material has been supplemented by interviews conducted by others: Tony Knox, producer of London Weekend Television's South Bank Show documentary about Hooker's life and times, generously supplied full transcripts of his team's own interviews with many of the above and others, including Bernethia Bullock, Van Morrison and Jim O'Neal. Equally generously, Mark Cooper provided unedited video of his interviews, derived from a special edition of BBC2's much-missed *Late Show*, with Ry Cooder, the late Albert Collins, Peter Coyote, Robert Cray, John Hammond, Johnnie Johnson, Charlie Musselwhite and Bonnie Raitt. And Paul Trynka, currently of *Mojo* and formerly of *The Guitar Magazine*, gave me access to transcripts of his Hooker-related interviews with Ry Cooder, S. P. Leary, John Mayall, Keith Richards, Carlos Santana and Johnny Winter. Mark Bliesener supplied the testimony of Todd Park Mohr.

When additional quotations have been derived from previously published material, the original sources are cited in the footnotes. In some instances, I have blended material from a variety of sources in order to achieve the most complete and coherent narrative possible: for example, the interviews with Mike Kappus featured in Chapters 13 and 14 fuse extracts from my own interview with Mike, from the *South Bank Show* interview, and from our correspondence.

Others also went out of their way to help on the road. In the Bay Area, there were the various constituents of the Hooker Community cited above. In Austin, Texas, the good guys included Clifford Antone, Ed Ward and all involved with South By Southwest. In Detroit my rabbis were Famous Coachman, Thom Jurek and all at *Metro*, Ben Edmonds, Robert Jr Whitall and Susan Whitall. In Mississippi, Joel Rosen dropped everything for a week to drive me around the Delta and plug me in to the *zeitgeist*, not to mention opening up the archives at Ole Miss in Oxford, Mississippi, and introducing me to Dick Waterman. In Clarksdale, Mississippi, I was indebted to Mrs. Jessie Hooker, Euliss Broom, Clarence Dixon, Early Wright at WROX, Jim O'Neal, Dr. Patty Johnson, Robert Birdsong, Wade Walton, and Sid Graves at the Delta Blues Museum; and in Vance, Mississippi: James Thomas, Florence Jenkins (daughter of Marih) Walker, and Mr. & Mrs. Rick Parsons at the Fewell Plantation.

Small portions of this book previously appeared, in radically different form, in *Q*, *MoJo*, the *Daily Telegraph* and *New Musical Express*; I have also sampled bits of my own text from *Blues On CD: The Essential Guide* (Kyle Cathie). And many of the ideas discussed in Chapter 12, notably the relationships between post-modernism and the folk process, and various aspects of shamanism, were honed during hours of conversation with Kathy Acker.

This book was originally intended to run to 100,000 words, and to take approximately eighteen months to write. Instead, the original manuscript came in at over 275,000 words and took over eight years to produce. As ruefully stated earlier, it was a bumpy ride. The Roll Of Honour of those who worked on the author, as opposed to the book, during this time, includes Jon & Jackie Atwood, Sean Blanchard, Felicity Brooks, Deborah Crippen, Johnny Guitar Crippen aka Tha Dook, Bill & Kathy Dulborough, Paul Du Noyer, Neil Gaiman, Igor Goldkind aka The Big Ig, Vivien Goldman, Caroline Grimshaw aka Grimbo The Great, Peter Hogan, Dik Jude aka Lee Van Spleef, Roz Kaveney, Gary Lammin, Spike Liseiko, Ian MacDonald aka I. Mac (as opposed to "iMac;" sue 'em, Ian), Bernard MacMahon, Peter Mannheim aka Data Sheriff, Dave Marsh, Polly Marshall aka Pirate Pol, Alan Mitchell aka Jah Worf, Lucy O'Brien, Tom Paley aka Honest Tom, Patti Palladin aka Pal Pat, Tony Parsons, Joel Rosen, Tim Rostron, Stephen Russell aka Barefoot Doctor, Jon Savage, Silvie Simmons, Su Small, Mat Snow, Neil Spencer, Tony & Kate Tyler, Del LaGrace Volcano, Ed Ward, Neil & Kathy Waterman, Alison West, Jack Womack and Elizabeth Young, who through the vagaries of alphabetical ordering always comes last in lists like this when she invariably deserves to be placed much higher.

As ever, Harold Waterman, my guardian angel in accountant's clothing, successfully prevented the author and the Inland Revenue from killing each other. (So far, anyway.)

Vital words of support and encouragement also came from Jeff Beck, Robert Christgau, David Fricke, Robert Gordon, Vernon Reid, Ice-T and Ernie C from Body Count, David Evans, William R. Ferris and Dick Waterman. And extra texture goes out to David Hilliard, formerly Chief Of Staff of The Black Panther Party and now of the Dr. Huey P. Newton Foundation, for all the conversation during the week of Marxism 98 in London.

Above and beyond the call of duty, friendship or anything else: the aforementioned Ian MacDonald sold me an Apple Macintosh 8200/120 when my old IIcx died on me in the summer of 1997, and willingly deferred payment until I could afford it, thereby enabling me to keep on working when all about me was collapsing.

Kathy Acker saved my life. I wish I'd been able to return the compliment.

And then there's Anna Chen, my cherished comrade, who said *come with me if you want to live*, and made me realize that, despite everything . . . I did. With her.

Peace—I'm outta here.

CSM

Appendix: Nuthin' But the Best 'n' Later for the Garbage (A Necessarily Selective Discography)

Meanwhile, in another part of the forest . . . let us attempt to distinguish the wood from the trees. The collected works of John Lee Hooker represent a discographer's nightmare as well as a listener's dream: hundreds of tracks cut for dozens of labels over five decades' worth of recording. Moreover, record company catalogs have a habit of changing hands from one owner to another or getting themselves assigned to different distributors in different territories, with the same "families" of tracks made available in different combinations on different compilations.

Then we have to factor-in Hooker's penchant for perpetually returning to and reinterpreting his core repertoire for each phase of his career, generating a number of performances of key songs (often radically diverse) under a variety of different titles. Simply knowing the title of the particular Hooker song you want doesn't necessarily mean that you're going to walk home with the specific performance which enchanted you when you heard it on the radio or around someone else's house.

As a result, the task of answering the ostensibly simple question "Which John Lee Hooker tracks do I need and where do I go to get them?" isn't quite as straightforward as it might seem or, indeed, as it ought to be. It therefore makes sense to divide Hooker's gargantuan output into specific periods and cherry-pick each one for the best representations of its finest moments.

Before doing so, let's consider the absolute bottom-line solution to the problem of assembling a basic John Lee Hooker collection. The 1998 pointblank compilation *The Best Of Friends* rounds up highspots from the *Healer*-and-after modern era—as opposed to the "Modern era"— along with three toothsome nuggets not included on any previous releases. And Rhino Records' beautifully-packaged and conscientiously-annotated two-CD set *John Lee Hooker: The Ultimate Collection 1948–1990* does a better job of providing a one-stop-shop encapsulation of the Hooker oeuvre than any casual consumer could reasonably expect, climaxing with the added bonus of a 1990 live duet version of "I'm In The Mood" featuring Hooker and Bonnie Raitt backed up by Roy Rogers. If you don't have any Hooker records and you want an affordable, comprehensible map of the territory which can be purchased for a moderate outlay and auditioned in a single evening, these two items are just what Doctor Blues ordered.

Of course, they're likely to prove to be merely tantalizing tasters for the greater riches which lie beyond. In which case: read on, y'all.

Phase One: The Detroit Years, 1948–1956

At the dawn of his career, Hooker was recording "officially" under the aegis of Bernard Besman for Modern and Sensation; and unofficially for anyone prepared to slip him a few bucks to cut a pseudonymous single or two. Your first port of call for the juiciest fruits of the Besman sessions—and the earliest recordings of hardy Hooker perennials like "Boogie Chillen," "I'm In The Mood" or "Crawlin' King Snake"—should be *The Legendary Modern Recordings 1948–1954* (Ace, Europe; Flair/Virgin, U.S.A), supplemented by other Ace compilations like *Blues Brother, Graveyard Blues* and *Everybody's Blues* (Specialty in U.S.A); the last of which incorporates material Hooker cut for Modern after his split from Besman. (Besman subsequently opened his Hooker vaults to release a veritable tidal wave of out-takes, now formally collected on the Capitol Blues Collection three-CD set *Alternative Boogie: Early Studio Recordings 1948–1952*.)

This is where it gets interesting: those "official" recordings are shadowed by the subsidiary bodies of work cut for Joe Von Battle and others in those backroom moonlight sessions, many of which are easily a match for the contemporary Besman sides. An excellent two-CD collection, *The Complete '50s Chess Recordings* (Chess/Universal), assembles one such; and *Don't Turn Me From Your Door* (Atlantic) another.

Phase Two: The Vee Jay Years, 1956–1964

Signing to Vee Jay in 1956 gave Hooker his first stable recording deal. Unfortunately, this vital part of Hooker's recording career is largely represented in record stores by illicit material. The various bootleggers who have put out material over the years have never paid a cent to the artist. As this book goes to press, Vee Jay's owners are believed to be taking steps to end this practice and perhaps we can look forward to authorized issues from the crucial Vee Jay years.

Interregnum 1: The Acoustic Year 1959–60

Midway through his Vee Jay stint, Hooker took a one-year sabbatical to record three acoustic folk-blues albums for Riverside, though only two were released at the time. Hooker has very fond memories of playing the folk clubs and "coffee-houses," and true enough, those acoustic settings gave him the opportunity to prioritize backporch intimacy as opposed to barroom hollering, performing solo on *The Country Blues Of John Lee Hooker* and backed by a sensitive jazz rhythm section on *That's My Story* (both currently on Ace). His performance at the 1960 Newport Folk Festival, *Concert At Newport*, was issued on Vee Jay but spiritually belongs with the Riverside albums.

Interregnum 2: The Vee Jay/ABC cusp, 1966

Hooker went a-wanderin' (like a sheep out on the foam?) before settling down to his next major record deal. Stylistically speaking *It Serves Me Right To Suffer* was essentially an update of *That's My Story*, teaming Hooker up with jazz musicians in a chamber-blues setting. Recorded for ABC's jazz subsidiary Impulse, it was most recently available in the U.S. on MCA and in Europe on BGO. The riproaring *The Real Folk Blues* was also cut as a one-off, this time for Chess, and is available via Universal (formerly MCA) in the U.S. and Europe, alongside *The Missing Album*, which collects the tracks recorded at the same sessions but reserved for a follow-up album which remained unissued until Hooker's post-*Healer* success in the '90s. A European MCA compilation, *The Complete Chess Folk Blues Sessions*, which compiled all the fruits of that day's labors onto a single CD, was available for a while but has subsequently been deleted.

Phase Three: The ABC/Blues Way Years, 1967–1974

Hooker's stint with the Big Label commenced with three strong (and strongly recommended) albums—*Live At Cafe Au Go-Go* (on which he was backed by Muddy Waters and his band), *Urban Blues* and *Simply The Truth*—before the energy began to dissipate. *Endless Boogie* and *Never Get Out Of These Blues Alive* undeniably have their moments, but *caveat emptor*: they also have their *longueurs*. Available in the U.S. via MCA/Universal and in Europe via BGO Records or See For Miles, this particular section of the Hooker catalog was filleted on two MCA compilations, *Tantalizin' With The Blues* and *The Best of John Lee Hooker*, which latter also incorporates a few early-50s Chess sides for good measure. Hooker's most powerful album from the latter part of this period wasn't even cut for ABC/BluesWay, but for Liberty: *Hooker 'N' Heat*, the epic double-album team-up with Canned Heat, is available as a double-CD in the U.S. via Rhino and, minus two tracks, as the unwieldily titled single European CD *The Best Of Hooker 'N' Heat . . . Plus* from See For Miles.

Phase Four: The Wilderness, 1974–1989

The ABC experience soured Hooker on dealing with record companies, and his recordings during this time were few, far between, and mostly undistinguished. The exceptions include Tomato's solo live double-CD *Alone* (1976), which contains some astonishing performances, first and foremost of which is the extraordinary "Dark Room"; and *Jealous* (1986), produced by Hooker himself for the tiny Pausa label, and subsequently reissued by pointblank.

Phase Five: *The Healer* and After, 1989–present

In 1989, the release of *The Healer*—on Chameleon Records in the U.S. and Silvertone in Europe—kicked off Hooker's golden decade, and in 1991, the goodie-packed, radio-friendly *Mr. Lucky* (apart from anything else, a masterpiece of sequencing) cemented his newly-earned status. The subsequent albums—*Boom Boom, Chill Out* and the mainly Van Morrison-produced *Don't Look Back* (all on pointblank)—were deeper, darker, less immediately approachable but ultimately equally satisfying. Hooker also appeared, in a radically different context, performing two songs on Pete Townshend's musical adaptation of the late Ted Hughes's *The Iron Man* (Virgin), as well as guesting on albums by B. B. King, John Hammond, Charlie Musselwhite, Zakiya Hooker, Van Morrison, Roy Rogers and Big Head Todd & The Monsters. And, on pain of major cultural deprivation, don't you dare leave the store without a copy of *The Hot Spot* (Antilles), the magnificent movie soundtrack on which Hooker collaborated, albeit via overdubbing, with Miles Davis.

To summarize: your basic Hooker library goes something like the following. I have included only those records that are in print as we go to press:

Fundamentals

John Lee Hooker: The Ultimate Collection 1948–1990 (Rhino); *The Best Of Friends* (pointblank)

The Detroit Years, 1948–1956

The Legendary Modern Recordings 1948–1954 (Ace, Europe; Flair/Virgin, U.S.); *The Complete '50s Chess Recordings* (Chess/Universal); *Don't Turn Me From Your Door* (Atlantic)

The Acoustic Year, 1959–60

The Country Blues Of John Lee Hooker (Ace); *That's My Story* (Ace)

486 / Boogie Man

The Vee Jay/ABC cusp, 1966

The Real Folk Blues (Chess/Universal)

The ABC/BluesWay Years, 1967–1974

Live At Cafe Au Go-Go (BGO, Europe; Universal, U.S.); *Urban Blues* (BGO, Europe; Universal, U.S.); *Simply The Truth* (BGO, Europe; Universal, U.S.); *Hooker 'N' Heat* (Rhino, U.S.) or *Hooker 'N' Heat: the Best Of . . . Plus* (See For Miles, Europe); *Never Get Out Of These Blues Alive* (Universal, U.S.; See For Miles, Europe)

The Wilderness, 1974–1989

Alone (Tomato); *Jealous* (pointblank)

The Healer And After, 1989–present

The Healer (pointblank); *Mr. Lucky* (pointblank, U.S.; Silvertone, Europe); *Boom Boom* (pointblank); *Chill Out* (pointblank); *Don't Look Back* (pointblank)

Plus

Original Soundtrack: The Hot Spot (with Miles Davis and Taj Mahal) (Antilles; Europe; PGD/Verve, U.S.); *The Iron Man* (Pete Townshend, plus Nina Simone, The Who et al.) (Virgin, Europe; Atlantic, U.S.)

Index

208, 217–20, 223, 231, 240, 301, 304, 349, 418
Mayall, John, 11, 268, 272–77, 279, 291–92, 294, 298, 300
"Maybellene," 164
Mayfield, Curtis, 87, 209, 243, 260, 305
Mayfield, Percy, 178, 260–62, 307, 356
MC5, 174, 318, 365
Meadow Brook Music Festival, 182–86
"Mean Old World," 104–5
Meehan, Patrick, 278, 285
"Meet Me In The Bottom," 388
Melly, George, 263–65, 267–68
Melody Maker, 14, 204, 246, 272, 274, 277, 285, 291, 294, 407
Melrose, Lester, 94, 188
"Memory Pain," 260–62, 356
Memphis Horns, The, 186, 323–24
Memphis Slim (Peter Chatman), 94, 244–45, 247, 268, 282, 289
Mendelsohn, Fred, 237
"Messin' With The Hook," 356, 387
Michael Bloomfield, 319n
Michel, Ed, 396, 399–400, 403–5, 447n
"Mighty Fire," 254
Milburn, Amos, 110, 312–13, 356
"Milk And Alcohol," 417, 460–61
Miller, Roger, 289
Miller, Steve, 269, 349, 364, 397–98
Mills, Irving, 165–66
Mingus, Charles, 267, 308, 337
"Mini Skirts," 327
Miracles, The, 238, 267
"Mi Sista," 358
"Miss Eloise," 141
Missing Album, The, 484
Mississippi Goddam, 14
"Misty," 242
Modern Jazz Quartet (MJQ), The, 117
Modern Records, 114n, 132–33, 135, 137–39, 141, 143–46, 150, 163–64, 171, 176–78, 190n,

217, 225, 229, 301, 305, 395, 406, 482
Mohr, Todd Park, 465
"Money (That's What I Want)," 225, 231–32, 238, 307
Monk, Thelonious, 337, 356–57
Moody Blues, The, 268, 271
Moon, Tony, 417
Moonglows, The, 188
Moore, Minnie Ramsey Hooker (mother), 23, 32–33, 35–36, 39, 41, 43, 127–29, 131
Moore, Will (stepfather), 32–40, 42–44, 60–61, 71, 111–12, 127–28, 130–31, 342, 346, 394, 476
Johnny Moore & His Three Blazers, 109–10, 132, 226, 355
Morrison, Jim, 406
Morrison, Van, 3, 57, 192, 212, 250–51, 274n, 302, 363, 365, 375–76, 401–3, 429, 434, 436, 456, 461, 463–66, 473, 485
Morton, Jelly Roll, 354
Mothers of Invention, The, 10–11, 288, 328
"Motor City Is Burning," 315, 318, 326, 365
Motown, 181, 193n, 208, 225, 234–35, 241–43, 250, 257, 259, 300, 316, 326, 363–64, 453
Mr. Bo (Louis Collins), 147–48, 175, 182–85, 362
Mr. Lucky (album), 3, 7, 80–81, 184, 186, 250, 434, 456–58, 460–61, 485–86
"Mr. Lucky" (song), 327
Muddy Waters (McKinley Morganfield), 10–11, 17–18, 27, 34, 48–52, 57–58, 60, 94, 111, 118, 120, 123n, 128, 136, 139, 144, 157–58, 175, 179, 181, 188–89, 191, 193–94, 209–10, 220–24, 265–69, 271, 282, 287, 299, 303–4, 306, 309, 313, 320–21, 323, 342, 349, 356, 362–64, 367, 369, 387, 412–13, 416, 420, 425, 457, 484

Muddy Waters At Newport, 221, 223
Muddy Waters Band, The, 26–27, 81, 157, 313
Muleskinners, The, 293
Mullican, Moon, 126
Musselwhite, Charlie, 93, 170–71, 211, 269, 323, 336, 369–70, 386, 391, 400, 406–9, 412, 420–21, 438–39, 453–54, 461, 485
"Mustang And GTO," 311
"My Babe," 249
"My Black Mama (Part 1)," 38, 288, 390
"My Black Woman," 288
"My Grindin' Mill," 250
"My Sweet Lord," 58

Naftalin, Mark, 349, 397, 400–402, 404
Napier, Simon, 301
Nashville Teens, The, 285
"Natchez," 231
Nathan, Syd, 179, 308
Nation Of Islam, 315–16
Natural Four, The, 87
Neff, Robert, 211, 230, 262, 328, 371n, 396, 412
Never Get Out Of These Blues Alive (album), 329, 399–403, 484, 486
"Never Get Out Of These Blues Alive" (song), 81, 322–23, 400, 403, 418, 473
Nevin, Brian, 466
"New Boogie Chillen," 441
Newport Festivals, 10–12, 51–52, 81, 210, 219–24, 230, 233, 236, 243–44, 248, 253–55, 286–87, 311, 319, 360, 483
New York Times, 220, 231, 233
Niafunké, 474
"Night Time Is The Right Time," 269, 279
"Ninety Days," 428
Nitzsche, Jack, 453–54
Nobles, Gene, 132
"No Friend Around," 401
Nolan, Tom, 61
"No Man's Land," 249–51
"No More Doggin'," 227, 355
"No One Told Me," 244
Norman, Philip, 257
"No Shoes," 228, 230